Bakery Technology and Engineering

Second Edition

some other AVI books

Food Engineering
    Fundamentals of Food Engineering, Second Edition *Charm*
    Encyclopedia of Food Engineering *Hall, Farrall and Rippen*
    Food Processing Operations, Vols. 1, 2, and 3 *Joslyn and Heid*
    Food Dehydration, Vols. 1 and 2 *Van Arsdel and Copley*
    Handbook of Refrigerating Engineering, Fourth Edition, Vols. 1 and 2 *Woolrich*

Food Technology
    The Technology of Food Preservation, Third Edition *Desrosier*
    Economics of New Food Product Development *Desrosier and Desrosier*
    Economics of Food Processing *Greig*
    Quality Control for the Food Industry, Third Edition, Vol. 1 *Kramer and Twigg*
    Cereal Technology *Matz*
    Bread Science and Technology *Pomeranz and Shellenberger*
    Food Science *Potter*
    Freezing Preservation of Foods, Fourth Edition, Vols. 1, 2, 3, and 4 *Tressler, Van Arsdel and Copley*
    Food Oils and Their Uses *Weiss*

Food Chemistry and Microbiology
    Phosphates in Food Processing *deMan*
    Microbiology of Food Fermentations *Pederson*
    Food Analysis: Theory and Practice *Pomeranz and Meloan*
    Food Enzymes *Schultz*
    Proteins and Their Reactions *Schultz and Anglemier*
    Carbohydrates and Their Roles *Schultz, Cain and Wrolstad*
    Chemistry and Physiology of Flavors *Schultz, Day and Libbey*
    Lipids and Their Oxidation, Second Printing *Schultz, Day and Sinnhuber*
    Soybean Chemistry and Technology, Vol. 1, Proteins *Smith and Circle*
    Practical Food Microbiology and Technology, Second Edition *Weiser Mountney and Gould*

Nutrition
    Milestones in Nutrition *Goldblith and Joslyn*
    Nutritional Evaluation of Food Processing, Second Edition *Harris and Von Loesecke*
    Proteins As Human Food *Lawrie*
    Progress In Human Nutrition *Margen*

Food and Field Crops Technology
    Cereal Science *Matz*
    Poultry: Feeds and Nutrition *Schaible*
    Potatoes: Production, Storing, Processing *Smith*
    Tree Fruit Production, Second Edition *Teskey and Shoemaker*
    Peanuts: Production, Processing, Products *Woodroof*
    Coconuts: Production, Processing, Products *Woodroof*
    Tree Nuts: Production, Processing, Products, Vols. 1 and 2 *Woodroof*

Milk and Milk Products Technology
    Ice Cream, Second Edition *Arbuckle*
    Dairy Lipids and Lipid Metabolism *Brink and Kritchevsky*
    Drying of Milk and Milk Products, Second Edition *Hall and Hedrick*
    Fundamentals of Dairy Chemistry *Webb and Johnson*
    Byproducts From Milk, Second Edition *Webb and Whittier*

Bakery Technology and Engineering

Second Edition

SAMUEL A. MATZ, Ph.D.
Vice President
Research and Development
Ovaltine Products/Division of Sandoz—Wander
Villa Park, Illinois

WESTPORT, CONNECTICUT
THE AVI PUBLISHING COMPANY, INC.
1972

© Copyright 1972 by
THE AVI PUBLISHING COMPANY, INC.
Westport, Connecticut

All rights reserved

Library of Congress Catalog Card Number 75-179038
ISBN-0-87055-109-4

Printed in the United States of America

Preface to the First Edition

There are a number of good texts on bakery technology which either deal principally with small bake-shop practices or concentrate on fundamental scientific principles to the exclusion of the engineering aspects of the subject. It is not the purpose of the present volume to compete with these works. Instead, we have attempted to provide those interested in bakery science with a discussion of the scientific principles of modern large-scale processing methods and to give them an introduction to the application of automation in the bakery. In order to provide a complete one-volume treatment, rather extensive descriptions of the chemistry and technology of the most important raw materials are included, as well as discussions of the fundamental processing techniques which can be applied to doughs and batters. We believe that our approach is new and that the book fills an important need in the literature of food technology.

This book is a collaborative effort of more than twenty different authors. By using a battery of experts, we hoped to avoid the excessive reliance upon the literature which sometimes results in the perpetuation of errors, and to bring new ideas into print. Authors were selected from among those scientists and engineers who have a close and continuing acquaintance with modern commercial practices in their specialized areas. Attempts were made to obtain authors who had fresh and non-derivative views of their fields.

Bibliographies of considerable length have been appended to most of the chapters. Where the bibliographies are reduced in size, the cause is a dearth of pertinent literature rather than a lack of diligence on the part of the authors.

This book is not directed to cereal chemists and bakery engineers alone, although its most obvious appeal is to these groups. Food technologists connected with industries which supply raw materials for bakery products should find the book helpful in directing new product development and product improvement studies. Marketing and sales personnel should find the material presented to be of value in orienting themselves with respect to factors affecting product quality and the economics of production. Administrators who are not technically trained will find in this one volume a unified treatment of the technology and engineering of their business which can make more meaningful the reports of their research, development, and quality control personnel.

Space limitations preclude the listing of all of the persons who supplied advice, information, reviews, illustrative material, and encouragement during the preparation of the book. Acknowledgments are incomplete for this reason, but the following list includes persons other than authors who reviewed chapters or made other substantial and time-consuming contributions to the book.

    Mr. Welker Bechtel, American Institute of Baking, Chicago.
    Mr. Howard Clark, Standard Brands, Inc., New York City.
    Mr. Rowland J. Clark, The W. E. Long Co., Chicago.
    Mr. W. W. Clark, Baker Perkins, Inc., Saginaw, Mich.
    Mr. Harry Feige, Saginaw, Mich.
    Dr. C. G. Ferrari, J. R. Short Milling Co., Chicago.
    Mr. W. W. Hartman, Maine Machinery Works, Los Angeles.
    Mr. Nison T. Hellman, Froedtert Malting Co., Milwaukee, Wisc.
    Mr. Jason Miller, E. F. Drew Co., Boonton, New Jersey.
    Mr. Marshall W. Neale, American Spice Trade Association, New York City.
    Mr. Kenneth R. Rand, Quality Bakers of America, New York City.
    Mr. Keith H. Redner, Battle Creek Packaging Machines Co., Battle Creek, Mich.
    Dr. Gerald Reed, Red Star Yeast and Products Co., Milwaukee, Wisc.
    Mr. Haryl C. Simmons, Gopher Grinders, Inc., Anoka, Minn.
    Mr. P. H. Valentyne, Baker Perkins, Inc., Saginaw, Mich.
    Mr. L. P. Weiner, Pabst Brewing Co., Chicago.

In addition, much gratitude is due to Dr. Martin Peterson of the Quartermaster Food and Container Institute for the Armed Forces who generously gave valuable counsel during the initial stages of planning of the book.

The preparation of the volume would probably have been impossible had it not been for the repeated assistance of Mr. Victor Marx and Mr. Bernard Bergholz, Jr. of the American Society of Bakery Engineers. These gentlemen suggested the names of most of the authors and assisted the editor in many other ways.

We are not sanguine enough to expect that the book will be without errors. The editor would appreciate having his attention called to any mistakes which the reader may detect. Suggestions for improvement in organization, style, or content will be carefully considered in the preparation of subsequent editions of the volume.

SAMUEL A. MATZ

April 1, 1960

Preface to the Second Edition

The First Edition of this book was well-accepted, and a rather large printing was ultimately sold out. When I started drawing up plans for the Second Edition, it became clear that the collaborative method used in assembling the manuscript for the earlier volume had led to a somewhat uneven presentation. To correct this situation, I decided to write a completely new manuscript which would follow the general plan and have the same objectives as the First Edition, but would have a more uniform style and level of presentation. This book is the result of that approach.

By far the greater part of the text is new. In a very few instances, brief sections from the First Edition were included when I thought the discussion was still up-to-date. When the retained sections are by other authors, the source is clearly identified.

Although the format of the First Edition was generally followed, I considered it necessary to broaden the scope of the book, covering certain subjects which previously had not been discussed in detail. This decision led to the inclusion of new chapters and rearrangement of the old topics. Some of the original chapters were made shorter, for example, by deleting lengthy discussions of the processing methods used to make some of the ingredients, since I thought such details would be of minor interest to most readers. If all of the original material had been retained, the additions would have caused the book to be excessively long and its cost would have been prohibitive for many persons.

The purpose of the book remained the same—I attempted to provide those persons interested in bakery science with the principles of modern large-scale processing techniques. Since the properties of ingredients are inextricably linked with the processing response of doughs and batters, and with the quality of the finished products, characteristics of the most important raw materials have been discussed at length.

The plan of the book is to discuss the ingredients, formulas and procedures, equipment, and the management of technical services in separate sections, each containing several chapters. In the section dealing with ingredients, characteristics of the various materials and the quality control tests applied to them will be discussed, as well as the effects they have on the finished products. Representative formulas and procedures for all major kinds of bakery foods are included in Section II, along with suggestions for variations. The third series of chapters describes the equipment used in bakeries, its control, maintenance, and interaction with doughs and batters. The fourth and final section comprises chapters dealing with product development, quality control, and nutritional supplements.

Bibliographies are appended to all of the chapters, and the reader will find that the dates of most of the references are later than 1960, the year in which the First Edition was published. The bibliographies include general references as well as sources of specific citations in the text, and thereby provide a starting point for extended studies of collateral subjects.

This book is not directed to cereal chemists and bakery engineers alone, although its most obvious appeal is to these groups. Food technologists connected with industries which supply ingredients and packaging materials for bakery products should find the book helpful in directing new product development and product improvement studies. Marketing and sales personnel should find the material to be of value in orienting themselves with respect to factors affecting product quality and the economics of production. Administrators who are not technically trained will find in this one volume a unified treatment of bakery technology and engineering which can make reports of their research, development, and quality control personnel more meaningful.

Suggestions, illustrations, data, and other valuable contributions were received from sources too numerous to list in the preface. Special thanks are due to the following, who reviewed chapters or otherwise gave substantial assistance:

Mr. Jack Butler, Packaging Technical Service, American Can Company, Neenah, Wisconsin.

Dr. Donald E. Westcott, Chief, Plant Products Division, Food Laboratory, U.S. Army Natick Laboratories, Natick, Massachusetts.

November 18, 1971   Samuel A. Matz

Contents

CHAPTER   PAGE

Section 1. The Materials of Baking

1. FLOUR 1
2. WATER 24
3. LEAVENING AGENTS 35
4. SWEETENERS 49
5. SHORTENINGS, EMULSIFIERS, AND ANTIOXIDANTS 61
6. MILK PRODUCTS 82
7. EGGS 108
8. FRUITS AND NUTS 118
9. FLAVORS AND COLORS 135
10. MINOR INGREDIENTS 149

Section 2. Formulations and Procedures

11. FORMULATIONS AND PROCEDURES FOR AIR-LEAVENED, STEAM-LEAVENED, AND UNLEAVENED PRODUCTS 165
12. FORMULATIONS AND PROCEDURES FOR CHEMICALLY-LEAVENED BAKERY PRODUCTS ... 189
13. FORMULATIONS AND PROCEDURES FOR YEAST-LEAVENED BAKERY FOODS 207
14. FORMULAS AND PROCEDURES FOR MAKING ADJUNCTS 237
15. BULK HANDLING OF INGREDIENTS 259

Section 3. Engineering

16. WEIGHING AND MEASURING EQUIPMENT 277
17. MIXERS AND MIXING 307
18. MAKEUP EQUIPMENT 328
19. CONTINUOUS PROCESSING OF BAKERY PRODUCTS 361
20. FERMENTATION AND PROOFING ENCLOSURES 387
21. OVENS AND ASSOCIATED EQUIPMENT 410
22. SLICERS 438
23. PACKAGING EQUIPMENT AND MATERIALS 460
24. AUXILIARY EQUIPMENT 483
25. FREEZING AND OTHER SPECIAL PRESERVATION METHODS 496

Section 4. Technical Functions in Bakery Operations

26. RESEARCH AND DEVELOPMENT 537
27. QUALITY CONTROL 560
28. NUTRITIONAL CONSIDERATIONS IN FORMULATING BAKERY PRODUCTS 574
INDEX 588

SECTION 1

The Materials of Baking

CHAPTER 1

FLOUR

Flour is the ingredient which distinguishes "bakery products" such as bread and rolls from "baked confections" such as macaroons or meringues. Wheat flour can give unique textural and appearance characteristics to many of the items in which it is used, while other cereal flours from rye, corn, oats, and sorghum, and soy flour may also be used to contribute special texture, flavor, appearance, economic, and nutritional qualities to bakery foods.

Wheat flour is unique among cereal products in that it can be made into cohesive elastic doughs when it is mixed with water under appropriate conditions. Because of their physical characteristics, these doughs will retain leavening gases throughout the various handling procedures necessary for making bread and rolls, and they can be made to yield finished products of low density with fine, uniform cell structure and a soft resilient response to chewing. Flours and meals made from rye, barley, oats, and sorghum give doughs which are much less elastic and extensible; they do not retain leavening gases well; and they tend to yield finished products which are coarser and denser.

Both the inherent quality of the wheat and the milling conditions to which it is subjected can lead to differences in the suitability of the flour for a given purpose. Since different bakery products may require different characteristics, a wheat which is entirely satisfactory for making bread flour may be totally unsuited for making pastry flour. The limits within which the milling quality of wheat can vary are genetically determined, while the level achieved by any particular sample of wheat is affected by growing conditions, cultural practices, and the treatment of the wheat during and after harvest.

WHEAT VARIETIES

The only wheat species of importance for milling into bakery flour is *Triticum vulgare*. The following discussion concerns varieties of this species.

For commercial purposes, wheat intended for flour milling is divided into the following types:

(1) Hard red spring wheat—grown primarily in the Northern Great Plains states. The flours are usually high in protein and have strong gluten. They are especially suitable for hearth and pan breads, rolls, and specialty breads. These wheats may be blended with weaker wheat to improve the baking quality of flour.

(2) Hard red winter wheat—produced in largest quantity in the Southern Great Plains states. Most of the wheat grown in the United States is of this type. The flours are intermediate in protein percentage and strength. Most white pan bread is made with these flours and they have a general usefulness for bakery goods.

(3) Soft red winter wheat—grown in many regions of the country, but the region of greatest production is east of the Missouri and Mississippi rivers and below the Great Lakes. Flours from these wheats are used mostly for cakes, cookies, and pastries since their protein content is low and the gluten relatively weak.

(4) White wheat—grown in rather small quantities in many sections of the country. This grain is even lower in protein content than the soft red wheats and yields flour which may be suitable for cakes, pies, cookies, and other pastry products.

Each type includes many varieties, of which several may be of commercial importance at any time. New varieties of supposedly superior characteristics (yield, disease resistance, or baking quality, etc.) are introduced each year, and some achieve widespread acceptance by farmers, displacing older varieties. The quality of the varieties falling into any of the above categories can vary greatly. The mere fact that a wheat variety is classified as hard red spring, for example, is no assurance that it can be milled into a satisfactory bread flour although the odds are good that it can be. Wheat stocks used for milling may include combinations of several varieties, mixed so as to give flour of predictable quality. Adjustments of the milling conditions are made to optimize the quality of the flour obtained from a given mill stock.

MILLING

The modern flour milling process as applied to wheat can be divided into six main parts: (1) Reception and storage of wheat. (2) Cleaning the grain. (3) Tempering or conditioning. (4) Separation of the wheat kernels into flour and by-products. (5) Treatment of the flour with additives. (6) Packaging and storage of the products.

Reception, storage, and cleaning are aspects of milling which need not concern us here but tempering or conditioning is a vital part of the milling process. It involves dampening and, perhaps, heating the grain to make the outer bran layers flexible and less apt to break up during the grinding stages. Time, temperature, grain characteristics, and moisture are all critical factors in tempering and must be adjusted to obtain the desired results under the milling conditions which will be used.

The aim of the milling process is to separate the endosperm from the bran and germ and grind it into a fine powder. The more efficient the process, the less bran and germ is mixed with the finished flour. A very small amount of flour for specialty purposes is still produced on stone buhr mills, but the rest is made by grinding wheat between steel cylinders. All modern mills are based on combinations of roller mills, sieves, and air separators (see Fig. 1.1).

The first sets of rolls encountered by the wheat kernel have corrugations or ridges running lengthwise on the cylinder. One of each pair of these rolls will be running faster than the other. The purpose of these "break" rolls is to shear open the kernel, leaving the bran layers as nearly in one piece as possible. As the cut and crushed pieces pass between pairs of rollers set increasingly closer together, the endosperm is scraped off with minimal fragmentation of the bran layers. The germ generally separates as a single piece during these steps. The endosperm pieces, varying in size from an impalpable powder to small chunks, are separated from the bran and germ by plansifters and purifiers. The former are stacks of sieves of varying fineness, while purifiers combine sieves and controlled air currents to remove small pieces of bran from the larger chunks of endosperm (middlings).

After the endosperm has been separated from most of the bran and germ, it passes between pairs of smooth rollers having the function of reducing the particle size. After each "reduction," the material flows to sifters where it is classified by particle size. Flour is removed and oversized material is sent back to the reduction rolls for further processing.

The bran, the germ, and that part of the endosperm which is too contaminated with bran to be sent to the flour stream form the millfeed fractions which are sold for cattle feed. The theoretical yield of flour is about 85%, but only 70–72% is achieved in practice.

The amount of flour removed, or the extraction, is a determinant of the strength of the flour. The way in which the different flour constituents are assembled in the finished product also affects flour quality. The extent of starch damage is another way in which milling conditions are reflected in bakery performance.

The much-reproduced diagram (Fig. 1.2) by Dr. Swanson (1938) illustrates very well the relationship of the different products which result from the milling of wheat. The milling process is such that a vast number of combinations of the different mill streams is theoretically possible, but the usual goals are to produce bran as clean as possible of endosperm material, flour as free as possible of bran, and the minimum amount of shorts consistent with the achievement of the other two goals.

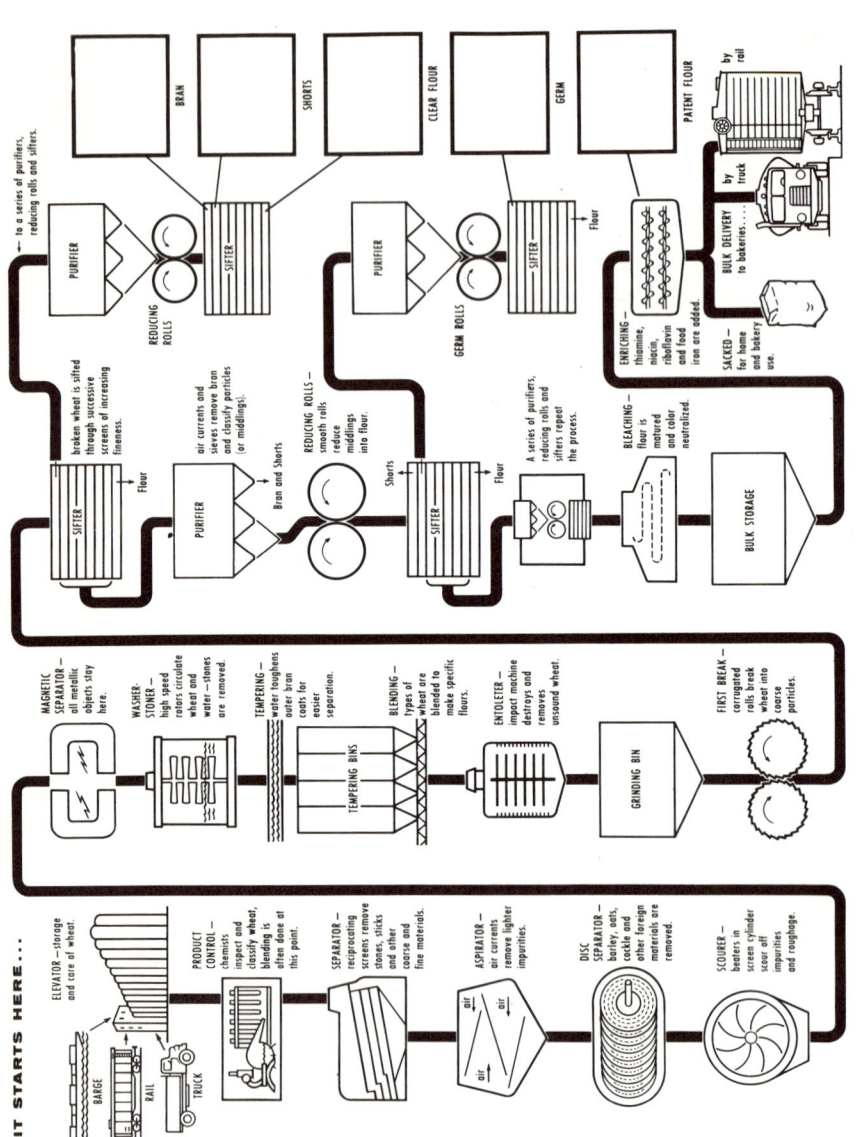

Fig. 1.1. A Simplified Diagram Showing How Flour Is Milled.

FLOUR

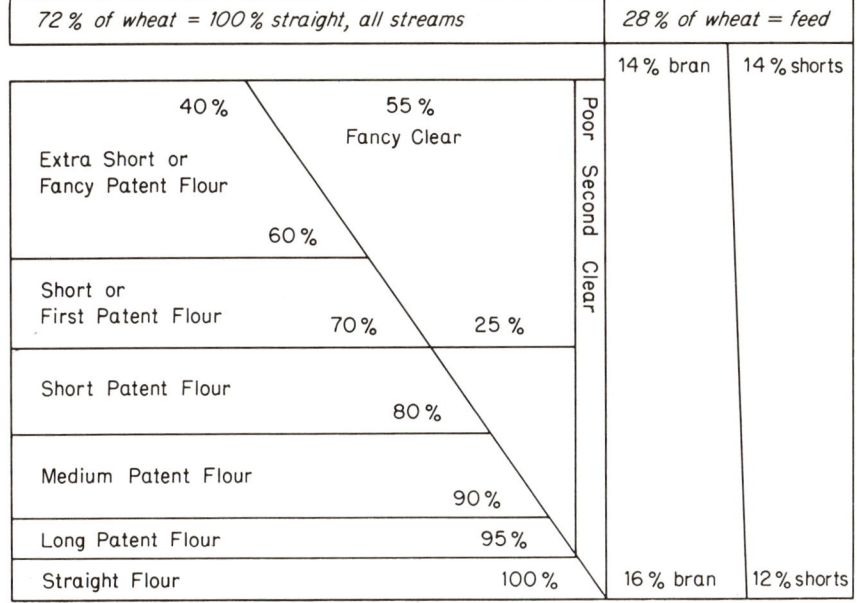

Fig. 1.2. Chart Showing Relationships of Flour Grades.

Graham flour or whole wheat flour is made by combining all, or most of the mill streams to give a product containing substantially all of the constituents of wheat as they exist in the intact berry. It is not made, as a general rule, by simply grinding the berry to a powder in one step. This flour is extremely subject to the development of rancidity and seems, also, to be very susceptible to insect infestation.

Flour is often treated with additives. These may be bleaches such as benzoyl peroxide, maturing agents such as chlorine dioxide, enzyme sources such as malted wheat flour, and enrichments such as vitamins and minerals. These additives and their effects will be discussed in the chapter "Minor Ingredients."

In the last couple of decades, air separation techniques and impact milling—to a lesser extent—have been commercially introduced (Fig. 1.3). Air classifiers separate flour particles on the basis of their size and density, and they are effective in the subsieve range, i.e., with particles less than about 60 μ in diameter. It is necessary to further grind normal roller mill flour by impact mills or other systems (e.g., turbo-mills) in order to obtain a stock of particles this small. The advantage of air classification is that particles of different sizes in the subsieve range tend to have different contents of protein and starch so that it is possible to obtain a starch-rich

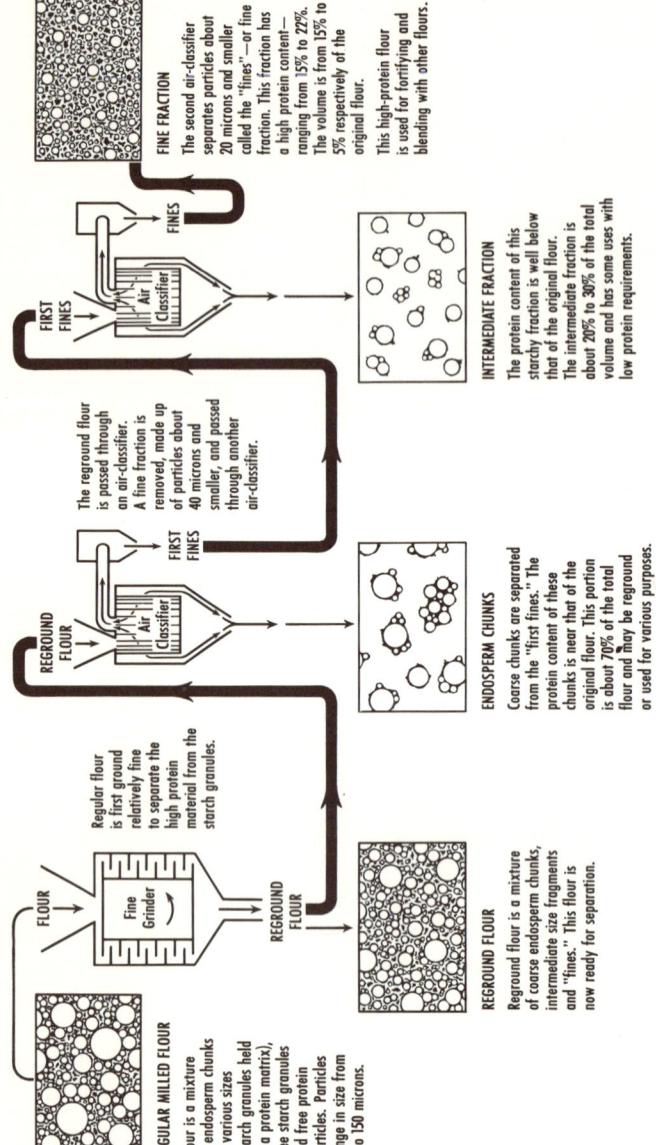

FIG. 1.3. How Flour is Fractionated.

This schematic is a generalization of the fractionation process. The number and sequences of operations vary with different types of flour made from various types of wheat and for the specific uses of the flour. Particles of flour shown are approximately 100 times actual size. White areas in circles indicate starch granules and black portions indicate protein. Flour particles are measured in microns: 1 micron = 1/25,000 in.

and a protein-rich fraction. The high-protein fraction from a hard red winter wheat flour might function well in hearth bread, for instance, while the low-protein material would be particularly suitable for angel food cakes, etc.

Classes of wheat, and even varieties within classes, vary in their response to air-classification or turbo-milling. The protein content of the high-nitrogen fraction is generally greater for hard wheats than for soft wheats. Fractions of very low protein content, suitable for use as industrial or food starch, can be obtained from the soft and club wheat classes. Hard wheat endosperm tends to break along the cell walls, while soft wheat endosperm divides in a more random fashion, with actual cell disruption (Bode *et al.* 1964).

Grades of Flour

It is important to understand the specialized nomenclature applied to commercial flour grades. The principal grades are:

(1) Straight flour—the total amount of flour milled from the wheat; all of the flour streams combined; 100% of the extraction or about 72% of the wheat.

(2) Patent flour—flour made from purified endosperm middlings. It is lighter in color and lower in ash than straight flour. A fancy patent represents about 40–60%, and a short patent about 70–80% of the total extraction.

(3) Clear flour—the flour remaining after the patent flour streams have been diverted, i.e., the straight flour minus the patent flour. It is stronger, darker, and speckier than patent flour from the same wheat. A fancy clear is the portion remaining after separation of the fancy patent, and a first clear flour remains after separation of short patent.

(4) Stuffed straight flour—a straight flour to which some clear flour has been added.

(5) Cut straight flour—a straight flour from which only part of the middlings have been removed.

WHEAT AND FLOUR CONSTITUENTS

The range of composition which can be expected to occur in the United States in a crop year is shown in Table 1.1. The average compositions of wheat and various flour grades are shown in Table 1.2.

Carbohydrates

Starch is the principal carbohydrate of wheat and flour, comprising in excess of 70% of the weight of straight flours. It is present as granules of 2 distinct size ranges, small spherical granules of about 5–15 μ in diameter and lenticular particles from about 20–39 μ in diameter. The

TABLE 1.1
APPROXIMATE COMPOSITION OF WHEAT

Determination	Range of Analyses Low	High
Protein (Nx5.7)	7.0	18.0
Mineral substances (ash)	1.5	2.0
Lipids (fats)	1.5	2.0
Starch	60.0	68.0
Cellulose (fiber)	2.0	2.5
Moisture	8.0	18.0

Source: Shellenberger (1959).

TABLE 1.2
COMPARATIVE COMPOSITION OF WHEAT AND FLOUR GRADES

Type of Wheat	Protein Content of Wheat at 14% Moisture (%)	Grade of Flour	Extraction of Flour Based on Wheat (%)	Ash in Flour at 14% Moisture (%)	Protein in Flour at 14% Moisture (%)
Soft red	9.80	Straight	72	0.38	8.20
		Short patent	35	0.30	7.50
		Baker's patent	65	0.34	7.90
		Clear	10	0.68	9.90
Hard spring	13.50	Straight	72	0.47	12.90
		Short patent	35	0.39	12.00
		Medium patent	60	0.41	12.20
		Long patent	65	0.43	12.50
		First clear	10	0.70	15.50
		Second clear	4	1.20	16.50
Hard winter	12.90	Straight	72	0.47	12.10
		Medium patent	60	0.41	11.70
		Long patent	68	0.45	12.00
		Second clear	4	1.20	16.00

Source: Schopmeyer (1960).

amylose content is 19–26%, with an average of about 25%, the remainder being amylopectin. Gelatinization temperature is dependent on concentration, pH, and other factors but generally falls in the range of 133°–140°F.

Starch is not usually considered as a major factor influencing flour quality, but there are some indications that starch may influence mixing time and dough handling characteristics (Table 1.3). Some of the starch granules are broken during any milling operation, but especially rigorous treatment such as fine-grinding may rupture a fairly large number of particles so that susceptibility to amylase action and the absorption are increased.

Flour contains small amounts of sugar. According to Koch et al. (1951), aqueous extracts of baker's patent flour contain 0.01% glucose, 0.02% fructose, 0.10% sucrose, 0.08% maltose, 0.18% melibiose, and 0.07% raffinose. Dextrins, cellulose, and gums are also present.

Lipids

Wheat lipids are located largely in the germ and consist of fatty oils, phosphatides such as lecithin, and unsaponifiable material known as sitosterol. The unsaponifiable fraction of wheat germ oil is particularly high in the tocopherols which possess vitamin E activity. The fatty oils consist mostly of glycerides of oleic and linoleic acids. The total ether extractable materials in the wheat kernel amount to about 1.5–2.0%. Fancy patent flour ordinarily contains about 1% of these substances while higher extraction grades have slightly more. Sullivan and Howe (1938) computed the percentages of fatty acids present in the lipids extracted from patent flour by petroleum ether and reported the following results:

	%
Total saturated acids (83% palmitic)	15.6
α-linolenic acid	0.84
β-linolenic acid	2.96
α-linoleic acid	25.49
β-linoleic acid	20.51
Oleic acid, by difference	34.60

It is generally conceded that the lipids of wheat do have a definite effect on the baking quality of flour. The exact mechanism by which this influence is exerted is not known, in spite of numerous studies made on the subject; but it is thought that both surfactant effects and reactions with proteins are involved.

TABLE 1.3
PROPERTIES OF VARIOUS WHEAT STARCHES

Starch Source	Amylose (%)	Intrinsic Viscosity (1 N KOH)	Amylograph Peak Height[1] (BU)[2]
Hard red spring wheats			
Selkirk	23.5	2.01	760
Justin	25.1	1.73	550
Crim	26.9	2.45	610
Thatcher	24.7	2.13	630
Durum wheats			
Mindum	27.5	2.06	600
Lakota	26.4	1.94	645
Wells	26.4	1.86	615
Hard red winter wheats			
Super Triumph	25.9	1.88	620
Comanche	23.4	1.55	710
Soft wheats			
Monon	24.3	1.49	675
Seneca	23.9	1.83	650

Source: Medcalf (1968).
[1] Amylograph data obtained using the carboxymethylcellulose technique.
[2] Brabender units

TABLE 1.4
MINERAL CONTENT OF WHEAT AND MILL PRODUCTS CALCULATED AS THE ELEMENTS FROM ANALYSIS OF THE ASH

In Parts per Million of Product, on Dry Basis

Element	Wheat	Patent Flour	Clear Flour	Low-grade Flour	Total Mill-run Middlings	Bran	Germ
Total ash	20,500	4,820	8,040	14,620	47,620	67,480	50,410
Magnesium	1,898	308	624	1,327	4,546	7,166	3,801
Calcium	452	180	227	376	1,115	1,158	692
Phosphorus	4,440	1,162	1,910	3,511	10,446	15,208	12,533
Potassium	2,370	552	875	1,553	5,633	7,098	5,542
Zinc	100	40	48	129	319	562	420
Iron	31	8	11	22	71	95	68
Manganese	24	2	5	12	48	112	67
Copper	6	2	2	4	13	14	9
Aluminum	3	0.6	2	7	8	27	25

Source: Sullivan and Near (1927).

Mineral Content

Most of the inorganic substances of wheat is contained in the bran and the aleurone cells. A flour showing a relatively high ash content will probably have more bran particles in it. Ash content is, therefore, an indication of extraction, since higher extraction flours will contain more bran and aleurone. Wheat varieties vary in ash content, so flours of the same extraction from two different varieties of wheat may have different percentages of inorganic substances. Soft wheats yield flours of lower ash content than do hard wheats. The ash content of wheat and flour also varies with crop year. Taking all of these variables into consideration, flours with ash contents of 0.3–1% can be obtained.

The metallic elements present in typical wheat and mill products are shown in Table 1.4. Other elements present in the ash in other than trace amounts include sodium, aluminum, chlorine, and silicon.

Vitamins

Wheat, like the other cereal grains, contains appreciable amounts of vitamins of the B group, but it is almost completely lacking in vitamin C, unless the grain is sprouted. Vitamin D is also absent. Although wheat does contain carotenoids, they consist entirely of xanthophyll which cannot act as a precursor of vitamin A. The oils of the embryo of wheat are rich sources of vitamin E.

It has been estimated that the endosperm of wheat contains 24% of the total thiamine, the germ 15%, and the outer layers 61%. Riboflavin is similarly distributed but a somewhat higher proportion of the total is found in the endosperm. The germ has the richest concentration of riboflavin, but it is relatively low in nicotinic acid.

Because of their location in the kernel, most of the thiamine, riboflavin, and niacin are removed by milling. As shown in Table 1.5, most

TABLE 1.5
VITAMINS[1] CONTAINED IN WHEAT AND MILL PRODUCTS

Vitamins	Wheat	Bran	Shorts	Red Dog	Germ	Low Grade Flour	First Clear Flour	Patent Flour
Thiamine	0.393	0.629	1.34	2.80	1.35	1.08	0.245	0.076
Riboflavin	0.107	0.334	0.347	0.322	0.487	0.124	0.048	0.032
Niacin	5.45	26.6	16.0	8.01	4.53	3.86	2.09	1.01
Pantothenic acid	1.09	3.91	2.66	1.82	1.04	0.915	0.675	0.483
Folic acid	0.050	0.088	0.135	0.120	0.205	0.042	0.018	0.011
Biotin	0.0114	0.0440	0.0350	0.0250	0.0174	0.0108	0.0042	0.0014
p-Aminobenzoic acid	0.383	1.48	1.26	0.781	0.370	0.295	0.126	0.033
Choline	163.0	154.0	176.0	174.0	265.0	148.0	151.0	161.0
Inositol	315.0	1340.0	1080.0	808.0	852.0	341.0	113.0	0.33

Source: Calhoun et al. (1960).
[1] In milligrams per 100 gm of 14% moisture product.

TABLE 1.6
CONCENTRATION OF AMINO ACIDS[1] IN WHEAT AND MILL PRODUCTS

	Patent Flour	First Clear Flour	Low-grade Flour	Red Dog	Shorts	Bran	Germ	Whole Wheat
Arginine	3.73	3.87	4.68	6.84	6.85	6.60	6.88	4.71
Histidine	1.92	2.06	2.14	2.22	2.20	2.22	2.26	2.12
Isoleucine	3.91	4.02	3.72	3.42	3.31	3.29	3.48	3.78
Leucine	6.63	6.59	6.33	5.77	5.64	5.51	5.75	6.52
Lysine	1.97	1.94	2.54	4.13	4.18	3.77	5.28	2.67
Methionine	1.73	1.71	1.67	1.70	1.62	1.48	1.91	1.74
Cystine	1.76	1.85	1.67	1.40	1.44	1.45	1.19	1.66
Phenylalanine	4.77	5.04	4.64	3.55	3.44	3.58	3.38	4.43
Tyrosine	3.27	3.35	3.20	2.85	2.85	2.82	2.84	3.25
Threonine	2.64	2.73	2.76	3.11	3.03	2.86	3.42	2.76
Tryptophan	0.92	1.01	1.01	1.25	1.29	1.58	0.98	1.13
Valine	4.32	4.44	4.45	4.91	4.84	4.69	4.90	4.69

Source: Hepburn et al. (1960).
[1] As grams of amino acid per 16 gm nitrogen.

of the water-soluble vitamins of the wheat end up in the millfeed fractions, i.e., bran, shorts, and red dog. Although the germ is relatively rich in certain vitamins, it constitutes only 1–2% of the kernel, so its contribution to the whole is minor.

Protein

Protein content of wheat samples, as usually reported, refers to the total nitrogen content, as determined by the Kjeldahl procedure, multiplied by the factor 5.7. The total protein content of wheat samples may vary from a low of about 7% to a high of almost 18%. These extreme values apply to only a very small percentage of all wheat, and the usual range is about 8–10% for soft red or white wheats and 12–14% for hard wheat. Approximately 80% of this protein constitutes the gluten fraction, the water-insoluble protein complex which makes up the structural framework of low-density bakery foods. Gluten is located exclusively in the endosperm and so a large percentage of it is recovered in the flour.

Gluten, when extracted from the flour by washing, can be separated into two fractions—glutenin (soluble in dilute acids or alkalies) and gliadin (soluble in 70% ethanol). It was the early idea that these fractions were homogeneous proteins, but subsequent research established that each one consists of several components.

It has been pointed out that the outstanding feature of gluten composition is the very high content of glutamic acid, which, in the gliadin fraction, constitutes nearly half of the entire protein substance. There is also a large percentage of proline but relatively small amounts of basic amino acids and of tryptophan. The relative proportions of the amino acids vary between samples. Table 1.6 lists the amounts of certain amino acids of particular nutritional importance found in wheat and several mill products. In spite of several studies, it has not been possible to correlate gluten strength with variations in amounts of any of the amino acids.

TESTING WHEAT AND FLOUR FOR BAKING QUALITY

The initial evaluations applied to wheat as it enters the channels of commerce are certain physical and organoleptic tests intended to indicate in a very general way its suitability for milling. The wheat is also identified by type which provides further information as to its milling and baking potential. The United States Official Grain Standards specify limits on test weight, damaged kernels, foreign materials, wheat of other classes, moisture, and odor (as well as some specifically named contaminants) for seven categories of wheat: Hard Red Spring, Durum, Red Durum, Hard Red Winter, Soft Red Winter, White, and Mixed Wheat.

Wheat samples can be of the same type and grade and yet be milled into flours having very different baking qualities. Some tests for the inherent baking quality of wheat can be applied directly to the grain or to products obtained from the grain by fairly simple laboratory milling operations (Miller and Johnson 1954). Since variations in the milling process itself can have a pronounced effect on the quality of flour obtained from a given lot of wheat, the bakery technologist is more interested in tests that can be applied directly to the flour he receives from the mill. A tremendous amount of effort has been devoted over the last 100 yr or so to the development of more or less objective methods which can give ratings of a flour's suitability for its intended use.

Part of the problem in developing evaluation methods for flour is the insistence of some individuals on having a single-figure score which will indicate to them the suitability of the raw material for their specific products. Complicating the picture is the unwillingness of suppliers, chemists, and their own quality control people to explain the situation adequately and forcefully to bakery production managers and purchasing agents. In order to establish a framework for the following discussion it should be understood that there is not now and there will not be in the future any single-figure score which will sum up the quality of a flour for every use to which it may be put.

The reasons for this situation are obvious enough. The responses of a flour to processing conditions (its machinability), and its contribution to the organoleptic properties (the eating quality of the piece made from it) depend upon different fundamental qualities. The most that can be reasonably expected is a "go—no go" type of answer which will indicate suitability or unsuitability of the sample for use in a given process for a given product.

Most of the tests applied to flour (and other bakery ingredients) are included in the latest edition of the *Approved Methods of the American*

Association of Cereal Chemists (Anon. 1970). These procedures can be categorized as (1) performance or baking tests, (2) physical tests, (3) organoleptic evaluations, and (4) chemical analyses. Each of these techniques has certain special advantages, but performance tests have the particular advantage that their results can be immediately related to the value of a flour for a specific purpose.

Performance Tests

The most meaningful performance tests are baking tests which yield a sample similar in most respects to the finished bakery product. The formula, conditions, and manipulations used to prepare the sample should reproduce as nearly as possible their counterparts in the plant. When these requirements are met, results can be obtained from performance tests which are very helpful in evaluating the suitability of a flour for its intended use, i.e., its quality.

The difficulties with most performance tests are that they are wasteful of labor, their reliability depends upon the skill and conscientiousness of the operator, and the results cannot be reported as a single figure score. There are scoring schemes which purport to summarize in a single figure much of the information which it is possible to derive from such procedures, but all of them have obvious deficiencies in general use.

The term "strength," when used to denote the suitability of flour for making pan bread, encompasses the sum of such factors as absorption, mixing tolerance, dough handling properties, gas retention, and loaf volume which are expressed in the final product as conformance to consumer desires and adaptability to the usual processing techniques. When its limitations of precision are fully understood, it is a useful term. To expect to have a single figure score for strength is, however, to be overly optimistic.

Strength is related to protein quality and quantity. Generally speaking, the more protein a flour has, the stronger it is. The unexpressed assumption in this rule is that a fixed proportion of the total protein makes up the gluten or structure-forming proteins. Not all glutens have the same extensibility and cohesiveness. These, among other properties, determine the quality of the protein. The quality and the quantity of the gluten as they interact in dough, are the determinants of flour strength. Other factors, such as the amount of reducing substances present, may effect the strength, but the top limit is determined by the quality and quantity of gluten present in the flour.

The best way of obtaining an overall pass-or-fail evaluation of a flour is to use it under conditions which will prevail in the particular production setup and then determine the compliance of the finished product to a set of standards. Because a production run for test purposes is inordinately expensive and time-consuming, methods have been developed which are supposed to duplicate on a small laboratory scale the conditions encountered in plant runs of bread, cakes, cookies, etc. Since complete duplication of conditions is manifestly impossible, and since the correlation between laboratory variables and plant variables is seldom linear or even predictable, some difficulty in interpreting the results of these bake tests has been encountered.

Physical Dough Testing

Elaborate mechanical and electromechanical devices have been designed for evaluating the baking quality of flour. Some of these have achieved considerable popularity. The usual principle underlying the design of physical dough testers is the measurement of resistance to mixing or to extension of a dough of standard composition under carefully controlled conditions. As long as the results obtained by using such devices are kept in proper perspective, they can be useful as rough indicators of the strength of the sample. Their greatest value in quality control is, perhaps, in verifying the uniformity of different lots of flour. It has been pointed out, however, that dough properties change continuously as the dough is carried through the various steps leading to the production of bread or other bakery items and that these changes are related only rather loosely to preceding states. Consequently, testing

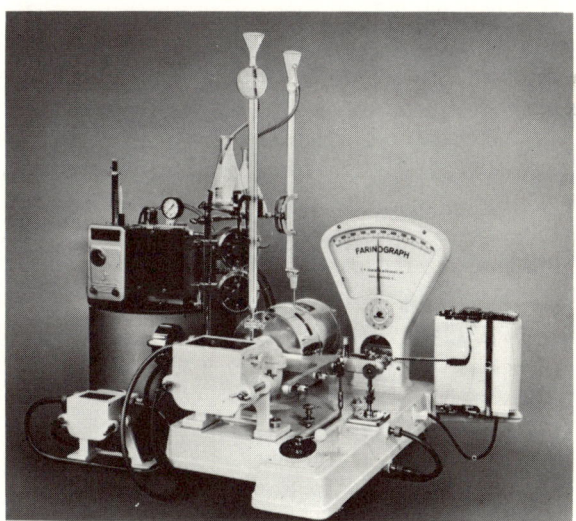

Courtesy of C. W. Brabender Instruments Co.

FIG. 1.4. THE FARINOGRAPH WHICH EVALUATES DOUGH DEVELOPMENT TIME, RESISTANCE TO DOUGH BREAKDOWN, AND MECHANICAL TOLERANCE OF DOUGHS.

of the dough at some selected time can give only a rough measurement, at best, of the overall quality of flour.

The Farinograph is a well-known and widely-used apparatus which measures the resistance to mixing stress of a standard dough (Fig. 1.4). Curves are generated by a recording mechanism. These graphs are evaluated by measuring, for example, dough development time, resistance to breakdown (stability), and mechanical tolerance index. The general practice has been to bring all flours to a consistency of 500 Brabender units (the middle line on the chart) by first running a titration curve with a dough to which increments of water are added from a buret as the dough is being mixed. A subsequent test with the exact amount of water added at the start generates the curves used for evaluation. Farinograms are helpful as guides to comparative strength and mixing tolerance. Spring wheat flours usually give stronger farinograms than hard winter wheat flours of approximately equal protein content. Hard winter wheat harvested in the northwest spring wheat area, however, yields farinograms equally as strong as those given by the spring wheat flours.

The mixograph is an earlier, simpler, and cheaper device for measuring resistance of doughs to mixing. In essence it is a miniature high speed dough mixer with four vertical planetary pins revolving about three pins fixed vertically in the bottom of a small cylindrical bowl. The bowl is placed in the center of a lever system, one end of which is restrained by a spring-loaded device while the other end carries a pen that records the lever movements on a chart. The height, width, weakening angle, and area of the curves are supposed to be correlated with protein content and loaf volume.

The extensograph measures the resistance to stretching offered by a cylinder of dough (Fig. 1.5). The force required to stretch the dough is automatically plotted against the distance it stretches to give the extensograph curve. Doughs are mixed under standard conditions, as in the farinograph, and may be measured at intervals to show changes in extensibility with time. The height and shape of the curve are supposed to give important information regarding the changes in dough behavior with time. It has been reported to be especially useful for studying the effects of oxidants on doughs. Neither the farinograph nor the extensograph can be applied successfully to fermenting doughs.

The Chopin alveograph is not much used in this country but it has achieved considerable popularity in Europe (Scott-Blair and Porel 1937). In this method, a bubble is blown in a thin disc of dough by means of air pressure. As the pressure is gradually increased, it is automatically recorded on graph paper. The time versus pressure curve so produced can be interpreted as indicating the characteristics of the flour or the dough made from it. The curves generally show a peak from which the graph line descends until the bubble finally bursts and the graph line immediately drops to zero pressure.

The time taken to produce the Chopin graph, as measured along the horizontal axis, is an indication of the elasticity (stretchability, distensibility) of the dough. The area encompassed by the curve and the X axis is considered to be roughly proportional to strength of the flour, and it is referred to as "W" or the Chopin energy factor in the jargon of this test.

There are many other physical dough-testing devices discussed in the literature of cereal chemistry. One of the best reviews is that of Miller and Johnson (1954).

Chemical Tests

The chemical tests most frequently applied to flour are analyses for moisture, ash, protein, fat, and pH. The gluten washing test, in which the cohesive proteins of flour are separated by washing a dough in repeated changes of water, is also more properly regarded as a chemical test although frequently described as a physical test.

The moisture test is usually conducted by drying the sample in atmospheric or vacuum ovens. Results are helpful in fixing the absorption to be used in the doughs and permit reporting of other data on a uniform moisture basis, usually 14%.

The ash content is useful in determining flour grade. Since the mineral content of the bran is about 20 times that of the endosperm, lower

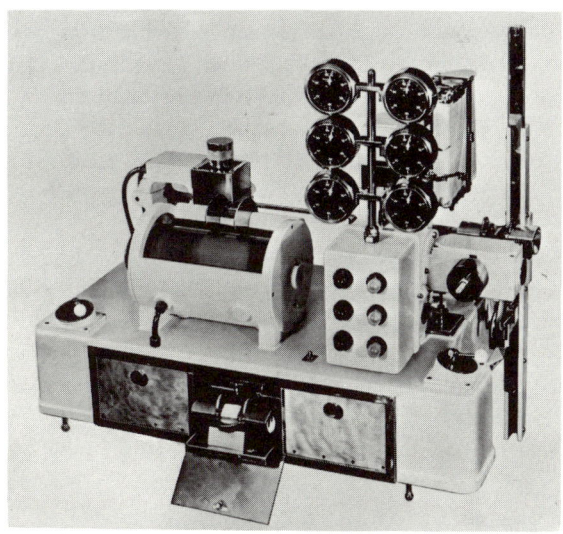

Courtesy of C. W. Brabender Instruments Co.

FIG. 1.5. THE EXTENSOGRAPH WHICH MEASURES DOUGH'S RESISTANCE TO STRETCHING.

grade flours having greater amounts of bran will exhibit a higher ash content. High ash of flour of comparable grades is, however, highly correlated with the ash content of the wheats from which the flour was made. Flour which contains mineral enrichment gives anomalous results in these tests.

The color of flour as affected by flavone pigments is also related to flour grade and ash, and methods have been developed for measuring the pigments in acetone extracts of flour or measuring the reflectance of flour at certain wavelengths. The Pekar test, a simple visual comparison of side-by-side patches of a standard and a test flour which have been pressed down (and sometimes wetted) to give a smooth surface, was an earlier practical way of estimating flour grade.

The protein content of flour is a very important parameter in estimating the baking quality of flour by chemical means. The Kjeldahl test, based on the titration of ammonia released by an acid digest of the flour when excess alkali is added, is the favorite test. It actually measures the total organic nitrogen, which the analyst converts to protein by multiplying by a factor of 5.7 in the case of flour. Other factors apply to other materials. The quantity of protein determined in this way is closely related to the baking quality of the flour.

Since the Kjeldahl test has a number of disadvantages, such as the necessity for handling quantities of corrosive reagents, the acrid fumes evolved from the digests, and the time required, many other methods for estimating the protein content have been recommended. Among these tests are the biuret reaction which measures the peptide linkages present in the sample. The protein is peptized with potassium hydroxide, and treated with copper sulfate, after which the color intensity is measured spectrophotometrically. Another method relies upon the binding capacity of protein for some dyes. Complete equipment systems for the routine measurement of protein by dye-binding are commercially available.

Procedures which allow an estimate of the baking quality of flour by measuring the rate at which the flour particles sediment in acid solutions have attained considerable popularity. These tests are based on the amount of water taken up by the flour and so measure a combination of protein quality and quantity. The Zeleny sedimentation test, probably the most widely known of these procedures, is much more rapid and almost as accurate as some of the protein measuring tests.

RYE FLOUR

Rye is a cereal grain closely related to wheat. Because it yielded more than wheat in cold climates and poor soils, it became the most common bread grain in Northern Europe. The tastes acquired because of necessity became the basis for traditional preferences which carried through generations far removed from their ancestral origin, as in many other examples. The physical properties of doughs made from rye flour are definitely inferior to those made from wheat flour because the proteins of rye will not form an extensible, elastic gluten with good gas-retaining properties. A loaf made with rye flour as the only cereal ingredient is far too coarse and dense for the average American taste, and so mixtures of wheat flour (usually a high protein spring clear flour) and rye products are used for commercial "rye" breads. True pumpernickel is an exception; it is made with a very coarse rye meal. Some Scandinavian flat breads, in which very little leavening effect is wanted, are made with flaked rye kernels.

Milling

Rye milling is somewhat similar to the milling of wheat in that a gradual reduction system of roller mills and sieving devices are used. Purifiers are not oridinarily used, however, because the soft rye endosperm does not break out in chunks. Both the break and reduction rolls are corrugated, the latter to forestall the flaking tendency of rye particles. Most of the flour is released by the break rolls. Cleaning can be performed on the same kind of equipment used in flour mills but requires closer control because of the greater variation in kernel dimensions between the rye grades. The grain is washed and tempered to about 14.5–15.5% moisture before milling.

About 80% extraction is obtained in milling rye. Color increases and quality diminishes as the extraction rate is raised, given uniform mill stocks and milling conditions. Since color is an important quality factor, low extraction flours are sometimes bleached with chlorine, nitrogen peroxide, or benzol peroxide. Maturing agents are not effective as enhancers of the baking quality.

Rye flour can be separated by air-classification into two or more fractions having different protein and starch contents. Such a separation does not have the economic and practical value it has when applied to wheat flour.

Composition and Quality Factors

In this country, at least, the principal criterion of the quality of rye flour is color. Dress (granulation) and flavor are also important quality factors. Protein content and ash are associated with color (Table 1.7) but are only secondary indicators of quality. The protein content has very little to do with the baking properties of the flour or meal.

A finely ground low extraction flour can approach a patent wheat flour in appearance. Since rye flours are cheaper than wheat flours, the light ryes have occasionally been used for replacing some of the wheat

TABLE 1.7
ANALYSES OF VARIOUS RYE FLOURS

Rye Flour	Protein Range (%)	Protein Avg (%)	Ash Range (%)	Ash Avg (%)	Fiber Range (%)	Fiber Avg (%)	Fat Range (%)	Fat Avg (%)
White	9.1–9.7	9.4	0.62–0.81	0.71	0.4–0.5	0.44	0.9–1.1	1.0
Light	9.3–10.9	10.3	0.66–0.92	0.81	0.4–0.6	0.55	0.9–1.2	1.1
Medium	10.9–14.7	12.0	1.01–1.53	1.23	1.0–1.4	1.14	1.4–2.0	1.6
Dark	11.8–17.1	16.5	2.07–3.16	2.42	1.9–4.5	2.98	2.6–3.0	2.8

Source: Schopmeyer (1962).

TABLE 1.8
SIZE CLASSIFICATION FOR COARSE AND FINE RYE MEAL

	Pumpernickel (%)	Fine (%)
Over 8 wire	30	10
Over 20 wire	46	40
Over 40 wire	14	20
Over 60 wire	5	5
Thru 60 wire	5	25

Source: Schopmeyer (1962).

flour in cookies and other applications where gluten is of little importance and the slightly different flavor can be covered up with other ingredients.

Excessive amylolytic and proteolytic activity in the flour can cause trouble in handling and defective loaves. High enzyme levels are due to the inclusion of sprouted rye kernels in the mill stocks and, in normal years, will not be a problem.

The carbohydrates of rye include sugars, pentosans, dextrins, hemicelluloses, and a mucilaginous or gummy material thought to be a pentosan polymer. It is the latter substance which causes the stickiness of rye doughs and it probably contributes to the poor gas-retention properties by limiting the hydration or cross-linking of rye proteins. Rye starch is similar to wheat starch in many respects, but it gelatinizes at a lower temperature.

CORN MEAL AND FLOUR

Relatively small quantities of milled corn products are used in the bakery industry as ingredients in specialty breads, corn muffins, and the like. They may also be used to dust the oven and peel when making hearth breads.

Corn flour is produced by dry milling of corn, as opposed to the wet-milling process which is used to make corn starch products from the grain. Some small country millers still grind whole corn for the local trade or for health food stores, but these meals develop rancidity in a few days, so it is the universal practice in large mills to remove the germ in order to improve storage stability. Dry corn milling consists of the basic steps of cleaning the corn, tempering, degerming, grinding, and separating. Tempering is often accomplished by washing the corn, removing excess water, and allowing the wet grain to rest in tempering bins until it reaches a uniform moisture content of 19–23%. The tempered corn is passed through a degerminator to crack the kernels and remove the germ. The degermed stocks are dried to about 15% moisture and then ground to the desired size in a mill consisting of rolls, sifters, and aspirators. The particle size groups of the commercial endosperm products are grits, cones, meal, and flour, in order of increasing fineness. The yield of endosperm products is between 65 and 70% of the whole kernel. Other milling processes, such as that of Anderson and Trommer (1968), have been devised to increase the yield of endosperm or to improve the purity of the meal. The Anderson and Trommer milling procedure involves a two-step tempering of the grain followed by an abrasive removal of bran by wire brushes before grinding and sieving.

Corn flour contributes water absorption capacity but not strength to doughs. Assuming that the flavor is satisfactory, the chief quality factors of corn flour or meal are moisture, color, fat content, and particle size. Free fatty acid content and peroxide value of the extracted oil are sometimes determined as indicators of fat deterioration and, indirectly, of the remaining storage life. Table 1.9 gives specifications for corn meal (Larsen 1959).

SOY FLOUR

Soy flour has been used as an ingredient in order to raise the protein quantity and quality of bread. Soy flour is high in lysine, an essential amino acid which is present in wheat at levels insufficient to allow complete utilization of the wheat protein. Use of milk in the bread accomplishes the same effect, but protein concentrates from soy are cheaper than milk protein.

Solvent-defatted soy meal is the usual base for the concentrates. The meal must be treated to remove solvent and toasted to destroy enzyme

TABLE 1.9
SPECIFICATIONS FOR CORN MEAL

Type of Measurement	Test Used	Values	Units of Measurement
Moisture	Air oven	14.5 Maximum	Percent
Particle size	Screens	16 to 40	USBS[1] Sieves
Fat content	Ether extract	1.5 Maximum	Percent
Appearance	Visual	Normal	...

Source: Larsen (1959).
[1] U.S. Bureau of Standards.

activity before it is suitable for food use. Particle size, color, flavor, and water-absorption capacity are quality factors. The full-fat meal is more expensive and is also likely to contribute off-flavors although recently developed methods have apparently overcome these deficiencies. There are several kinds of purified proteins which are obtained by extracting the meals with aqueous solvents and then precipitating the nitrogenous substances. The purified proteins can be quite expensive.

Several workers have showed that up to 8% of soy flour can be added to pan bread with only slight changes in appearance, flavor, and texture. It appears that additional oxidizers may be required in some cases. Defatted flour has good water-absorption potential but does not, of course, contribute to the elasticity or cohesiveness of doughs.

Enzyme active soy flours have been recommended for bleaching bread doughs, in a patented process.

BIBLIOGRAPHY

ANDERSON, H., and TROMMER, D. W. 1968. Dry milling corn process. U.S. Pat. 3,399,839. Sept. 3.

ANON. 1970. Approved Methods of the AACC. American Association of Cereal Chemists, St. Paul.

BARRETT, R. 1964. Microtest to evaluate wheats for cookie quality. Cereal Sci. Today 9, 97, 100–101, 150.

BODE, C. E. 1954. Research at the soft wheat quality laboratory. Part I. Trans. Am. Assoc. Cereal Chemists 12, 108–112.

BODE, C. E. 1959. The soft wheat quality laboratory. Cereal Sci. Today 4, 259–263, 280.

BODE, C. E., KISSELL, L. T., HEIZER, H. K., and MARSHALL, B. D. 1964. Air-classification of a soft and a hard wheat flour. Cereal Sci. Today 9, 432–435.

BLACK, H. P. 1969. A laboratory air-classifier. Cereal Sci. Today 14, 358–360, 362–365.

BRENNEIS, L. 1965. Flour granulation versus cookie spread. Biscuit Bakers' Inst. 40th Annual Training Conf. Apr. 7.

CALHOUN, W. K., HEPBURN, F. N., and BRADLEY, W. B. 1960. The distribution of the vitamins of wheat in commercial mill products. Cereal Chem. 37, 755–761.

DONELSON, J. R., and YAMAZAKI, W. T. 1962. Note on a rapid method for the estimation of damaged starch in soft wheat flours. Cereal Chem. 39, 460–462.

FINNEY, K. F., MORRIS, V. H., and YAMAZAKI, W. T. 1950. Micro versus macro cookie baking procedures for evaluating the cookie quality of wheat varieties. Cereal Chem. 27, 42–49.

FUHR, F. R. 1962. Cookie spread—its effects on production and quality. Bakers Dig. 36, No. 4, 56–58, 78.

GRAY, J. S. 1960. Quality control of raw materials. Biscuit Cracker Baker 49, No. 1, 18–20.

HANKS, W. T. 1957. Quality control in the biscuit plant. Biscuit Cracker Baker 46, No. 4, 41–44.

HEPBURN, F. N., CALHOUN, W. K., and BRADLEY, W. B. 1960. The distribution of the amino acids of wheat in commercial mill products. Cereal Chem. 37, 749–755.

HOLLINGSHEAD, T. E. 1948. Cracker manufacture. Trans. Am. Assoc. Cereal Chemists 6, 148–150.

IRANI, R. R. 1961. Particle size distribution data. Cereal Sci. Today 6, 35–39.

JOHNSON, D. H. 1965. Correlating laboratory tests to production. Biscuit Bakers' Inst. 40th Annual Training Conf. Apr. 7.

Koch, R. B., Geddes, W. F., and Smith, F. 1951. The carbohydrates of Gramineae. I. The sugars of the flour of wheat. Cereal Chem. 28, 424–430.

Larsen, R. A. 1959. Milling. *In* The Chemistry and Technology of Cereals as Food and Feed, S. A. Matz (Editor). Avi Publishing Co., Westport, Conn. (Out of print.)

Larsen, R. A. 1970. Milling. *In* Cereal Technology, S. A. Matz (Editor). Avi Publishing Co., Westport, Conn.

Matz, S. A. 1959. The Chemistry and Technology of Cereals as Food and Feed. Avi Publishing Co., Westport, Conn. (Out of print.)

Medcalf, D. G. 1968. Wheat starch properties and their effect on bread baking quality. Bakers Dig. 42, No. 4, 48–50, 52, 65.

Micka, J. 1958. The effect of flour aging on the quality of soda crackers. Cereal Sci. Today 3, 216–218.

Miller, B. S., and Johnson, J. A. 1954. A review of methods for determining the quality of wheat and flour for breadmaking. Kansas Agr. Expt. Sta. Tech. Bull. 76.

Nelson, C. A., and Loving, H. J. 1963. Mill-stream analysis—its importance in milling special flours. Cereal Sci. Today 8, 301–302, 304, 326.

Niernberger, F. F., and Johnson, J. A. 1970. A computer approach to wheat quality analysis. Cereal Sci. Today 15, 117–119, 128.

Pence, J. W., Hanamoto, M. M., Pinney, C. F., and Bean, M. M. 1968. Baking performance of air-classified fractions from selected Pacific Northwest Wheats. Cereal Sci. Today 13, 304–342, 344, 358.

Pomeranz, Y., Finney, K. F., and Hoseney, R. C. 1970. Molecular approach to breadmaking. Bakers Dig. 44, No. 3, 22–26.

Schopmeyer, H. H. 1960. Flour. *In* Bakery Technology and Engineering, S. A. Matz (Editor). Avi Publishing Co., Westport, Conn.

Schopmeyer, H. H. 1962. Rye and rye milling. Cereal Sci. Today 7, 138, 140–143.

Scott-Blair, G. W., and Porel, R. 1937. Extensimeter for testing flour doughs. Cereal Chem. 14, 257–262.

Shellenberger, J. A. 1941. Flour and cookie quality. Bakers Dig. 15, 206–208.

Shellenberger, J. A. 1959. Wheat. *In* Chemistry and Technology of Cereals as Food and Feed, S. A. Matz (Editor). Avi Publishing Co., Westport, Conn.

Sollars, W. F. 1956. Evaluation of flour fractions for their importance to cookie quality. Cereal Chem. 33, 121–128.

Sollars, W. F. 1959. Effects of the water-soluble constituents of wheat flour on cookie diameter. Cereal Chem. 36, 498–513.

Sullivan, B., and Howe, M. 1938. Lipids of wheat flour. Cereal Chem. 15, 716–720.

Sullivan, B., and Near, C. 1927. The ash of hard spring wheat and its products. Ind. Eng. Chem. 19, 498–501.

Swanson, C. O. 1938. Wheat and Flour Quality. Burgess Publishing Co., Minneapolis.

Vidal, F. D., Flanders, T. E., and Joiner, R. R. 1965. Baking characteristics versus physical tests with matured flours. Cereal Sci. Today 10, 32–40.

Ward, A. B. 1967. Recent manufacturing techniques and applications of wheat flour. Proc. 8th Annual Symp. Central States Sect., Am. Assoc. Cereal Chemists.

Whitby, K. T. 1961. Particle sizing in the milling industry. Cereal Sci. Today 6, 49–56.

Wichser, F. W. 1958. Air-classified flour fractions. Cereal Sci. Today 3, 123–126.

Yamazaki, W. T. 1953. An alkaline water retention capacity test for the evaluation of cookie baking potentialities of soft winter wheat flours. Cereal Chem. 30, 242–246.

Yamazaki, W. T. 1954. Research at the soft wheat quality laboratory. Part II. Trans. Am. Assoc. Cereal Chemists 12, 113–120.

Yamakazi, W. T. 1959A. Flour granularity and cookie quality. I. Effect of wheat variety on sieve fraction properties. Cereal Chem. 36, 42–51.

Yamazaki, W. T. 1959B. Flour granularity and cookie quality. II. Effects of changes in granularity on cookie characteristics. Cereal Chem. 36, 52–59.

CHAPTER 2

WATER

INTRODUCTION

The quality of water used as an ingredient can have greater effects on bakery products than is generally recognized. The amount and types of dissolved minerals and organic substances present in the water can affect the flavor, color, and physical attributes of the finished baked goods as well as the machining of doughs, marshmallows, icings, etc. The average temperature of the water and the fluctuations around the average can be important factors in performance of a given formula. The differences in bacterial flora and other suspended contaminants are of obvious interest to any food producer.

The quality of ingredient water is established by the initial status of the water, the treatments applied to it, and the conditions of storage and transport subsequent to treatment. Most bakeries probably use either municipal supplies or water from deep wells. In either case, the water will undoubtedly be potable. However, water which is perfectly acceptable for drinking and suitable for most food processing applications may have to be further treated before it will be adequate for certain specialized food and beverage uses. Doughs are probably less sensitive to minor differences in ingredient water than are some other foods. Marshmallow, jellies, and similar adjuncts may be more sensitive. The initial requirement for any water used in food processing is that it comply to legal standards for drinking water. These standards have been clearly set forth by federal agencies.

Congress has passed (in 1967) a Water Quality Act requiring each state to establish water quality criteria for all interstate waters and to develop a plan for the implementation and enforcement of the criteria. In general, the standards must be such as to enhance the quality of natural waters for their "...use and value for public water supplies, propagation of fish and wildlife, recreational purposes, agricultural, industrial, and other legitimate uses. Numerical values should be stated for quality characteristics where available and applicable. Biological or bioassay parameters may be used, where appropriate." Until these laws are promulgated, other guidelines must be used and, of these, the U.S. Public Health Service Drinking Water Standards are most familiar.

PUBLIC HEALTH SERVICE DRINKING WATER STANDARDS

The current standards for drinking water to be used on common carriers engaged in interstate commerce were prepared by the U.S. Public Health Service in 1946 and issued in revised form in 1962 by the U.S. Department of Health, Education, and Welfare. These Federal Standards are used as guidelines by many states and municipalities in setting up limits for potable water. The American Water Works Association regards the standards as being minimum requirements for the protection and well-being of individuals and communities, and advocates the establishment of the standards as the criteria of quality for all public water supplies in the United States. Water which does not conform to the standards should not be used as an ingredient in foods regardless of the legal status of the standards in the locality of the plant.

The standards specify that the water supply shall be obtained from the most desirable source which is feasible, and efforts should be made to prevent or control pollution at the source. If the source is not protected by natural means, the supply shall be adequately protected by treatment. Adequate protection by natural means is defined as involving one or more of the following processes of nature that produces water consistently meeting the requirements of the standards: dilution, storage, sedimentation, sunlight, aeration, and the associated physical and biological processes which tend to accomplish natural purification of water by infiltration through soil and percolation through underlying material and storage below the ground water table. Adequate protection by treatment is defined as meaning any one or combination of the controlled processes of coagulation, sedimentation, absorption, filtration, disinfection, or other processes which will produce a water consistently meeting the requirements of the standards. This protection also includes: processes which are appropriate to the sources of supply; works which are of adequate capacity to meet maximum demands without creating health hazards, and which are located, designed, and constructed to eliminate or prevent pollution; and conscientious operation by well-trained and competent personnel whose qualifications are commensurate with the position and acceptable to the reporting agency (the official State health agency or its designated representative) and the certifying authority (the Surgeon General of the U.S. Public Health Service or his duly authorized representative).

The standards direct that frequent sanitary surveys be made of the water supply system in order to locate and identify health hazards which might exist in the system. According to definition, the water supply system includes the works and auxiliaries for collection, treatment, storage, and distribution of water from the sources of supply to the free-flowing outlet of the ultimate consumer.

Approval of water supplies is to be dependent in part upon: (1) enforcement of rules and regulations to prevent development of health hazards; (2) adequate protection of water quality throughout all parts of the system, as demonstrated by frequent surveys; (3) proper operation of the water supply system under the responsible charge of personnel whose qualifications are acceptable to the reporting agency and the certifying authority; (4) adequate capacity to meet peak demands without development of low pressures or other health hazards; and (5) records of laboratory examinations showing consistent compliance with water quality requirements of these standards.

Responsibility for conditions existing in a water supply system is held by (1) the water purveyor from the source of supply to the connection to the customer's service piping, and (2) the owner of the property served, and the municipal, county, or other authority having legal jurisdiction from the point of connection in the customer's service piping to the free-flowing outlet of the ultimate consumer. As can be seen from the preceding requirements, the food manufacturer would be considered responsible for the condition and quality of the water in his service piping before and after any treatment in his plant.

Tables 2.1 and 2.2 list desirable and essential limits for chemical substances in water supplies. Semiannual analyses for these substances are usually considered adequate. Furthermore, drinking water should contain no impurities which would cause offence to the senses of sight, taste, or smell. Turbidity should not exceed 5 units, color should not exceed

TABLE 2.1
DESIRABLE LIMITS FOR CHEMICAL SUBSTANCES IN POTABLE WATER

Substance	Maximum Concentration,[1] Mg/Liter
Alkylbenzene sulfonate (ABS)	0.5
Arsenic (As)	0.01
Chloride (Cl)	250
Copper (Cu)	1
Carbon chloroform extract (CCE)	0.2
Cyanide (CN)	0.01
Iron (Fe)	0.3
Manganese (Mn)	0.05
Nitrate (NO_3^-)[2]	45
Phenols	0.001
Sulfate $(SO_4^=)$	250
Total dissolved solids	500
Sinc (Zn)	5

Source: Anon. (1962).

[1] These concentrations should not be exceeded if, in the judgment of the reporting agency and Certifying Authority, other more suitable supplies are or can be made available.

[2] In areas in which the nitrate content of water is known to be in excess of the listed concentration, the public should be warned of the potential dangers of using the water for infant feeding.

TABLE 2.2
ESSENTIAL LIMITS FOR CHEMICAL SUBSTANCES IN WATER SUPPLIES

Substance	Maximum Concentration,[1] Mg/Liter
Arsenic (As)	0.05
Barium (Ba)	1.0
Cadmium (Cd)	0.01
Chromium, hexavalent (Cr^{+6})	0.05
Cyanide (CN$^-$)	0.2
Lead (Pb)	0.05
Selenium (Se)	0.01
Silver (Ag)	0.05

Source: Anon. (1962).
[1] Presence of a substance in excess of the maximum concentration constitutes grounds for rejection of the supply.

15 units, and the threshold odor number should be 3 or less for general use water (see references for definition).

ANALYSES OF WATER

Standardized techniques are available for determining nearly all of the water quality factors thought to be important. Some of the procedures have attained official, or quasi-official, status through inclusion in *Standard Methods for the Examination of Water and Waste-water* (Anon. 1970). Nearly all of these tests referred to in *Drinking Water Standards* (Anon. 1962) are included in that book.

Some of the analyses which have been standardized are: acidity, alkalinity, aluminum, arsenic, boron, calcium, carbon dioxide, chloride, chlorine (residual chlorine), chlorine demand, chromium, color, specific conductance, copper, cyanide, fluoride, grease, hardness, iodide, iron, lead, lignin, magnesium, manganese, albuminoid nitrogen, ammonia nitrogen, nitrate nitrogen, nitrite nitrogen, oxygen, oxygen consumed, pH, phenol, phosphate, potassium, residue, selenium, silica, sodium, sulfate, sulfite, tannin, taste and odor, temperature, turbidity, and zinc. There are alternate or tentative methods for some of these factors. Since the standard methods are readily available, there is no point in reproducing them here.

There are three more or less traditional bacteriological tests applied to water: (1) counts of growth on gelatin plates incubated at 68°F; (2) counts on agar plates incubated at 99°F for 24 hr; and (3) the coliform count. The latter criterion has been superseded as a standard by the "Most Probable Number (MPN) of *E. coli*," which has been defined as "the bacterial density, which, if it had actually been present in the sample under observation, would more frequently than any other have given the observed analytical results."

Plate counts at 68° or 99°F are not particularly important as indicators of water safety, but they are useful as routine quality control tests in the various water treatment procedures and as means for determining the sanitary conditions of basins, filters, etc. The coliform test is the ultimate measure of bacteriological safety of water supplies.

It is sometimes necessary to make an estimate of the planktonic organisms (e.g., algae, diatoms) in a reservoir or other water source. This is usually done by direct microscopic count on a sample concentrated by filtration or other means.

Determination of biological oxygen demand (BOD) is important as an indicator of the extent of pollution of water sources and the potential for spontaneous recovery of these supplies. BOD is the total amount of oxygen taken up by those microorganisms which are present and which act on the available nonliving organic matter. The BOD has been defined by the American Public Health Association as "the oxygen in parts per million required during stabilization of the organic matter by aerobic bacterial action." It has also been stated that "Complete stabilization requires more than 100 days at 68°F but such long periods of incubation are impractical in any but research investigations, consequently a much shorter period of incubation is used."

The bacterial consumption of oxygen may be partially offset by the photosynthetic processes of microscopic plant life which produce oxygen and consume carbon dioxide.

Turbidity, color, and odor are routinely determined when a complete water analysis is performed. Turbidity is a measure of the extent to which light passing through the water is reduced in intensity by suspended material such as clay, organic debris, or certain industrial wastes. It can be determined by a Jackson candle turbidimeter or by continuously measuring and recording devices. For some food uses, a rather high level of turbidity can be tolerated, but for many beverages, jellies, and other transparent products, the highest attainable degree of clarity is preferred.

Color of water is defined as that difference in hue caused only by those substances actually in solution. It can be the result of mineral or vegetable pigments of natural origin or it can be caused by soluble organic or inorganic materials from sewage or industrial effluents. To obtain a quantitative estimation of "color" the analyst visually compares a sample with standard platinum-cobalt solutions or with colored glass tubes or discs under standard conditions.

WATER TREATMENT

Nearly all water obtained from surface sources (rivers, lakes, impounding reservoirs) must be treated to remove suspended material, dissolved color and flavor vectors, and microbiological contaminants. The details of these treatments are too complex to be set forth here, and the reader who is interested in such information as it applies to food is referred to *Water in Foods* (Matz 1965) and similar texts. In general, sedimentation with or without added coagulants, filtration, and chlorination is needed for most water supplies.

A thorough course of treatment for making potable a raw water of low quality might involve: (1) sedimentation in a large impounding reservoir; (2) coagulation (the formation of a voluminous flocculent precipitate by adding iron or aluminum salts under the proper conditions); (3) allowing the bulk of the precipitate to settle out in a reservoir or tank; (4) filtering the decantate from the preceding step through specially prepared beds of sand or gravel to remove residual precipitate and other impurities; (5) filtering through activated charcoal which will adsorb many dissolved substances affecting the color, odor, and taste; and (6) chlorination (see Fig. 2.1).

It is often desirable to further treat municipal or well water in the plant to eliminate off-flavors or other undesirable characteristics. Some firms offer modular systems which can be used in any required combination to furnish ingredient water of the needed purity. The available operations include: (1) prefiltration using filter media which eliminates the necessity for expensive, space-consuming flocculation and settling, and which can be cleaned by either automatic or manual back-flushing; (2) organic compound adsorption by activated charcoal or by special weak-base organic scavenger resin which can be automatically regenerated in place; (3) reverse osmosis pretreatment to reduce the salt content of saline water; (4) cation or anion exchange for removal of specific ions in waste treatment; and (5) ultrafiltration for final particulate removal. Several manufacturers offer combinations of equipment or "package plants" for treatment of raw well or surface water or further treatment of municipal water by food manufacturers (Fig. 2.2).

EFFECT OF WATER IMPURITIES ON BAKERY FOODS QUALITY

The dissolved mineral substances in absorption (ingredient) water consititute but a very small fraction of the soluble material in bakery products. Except for certain dietary products, bakery foods will contain from about 0.3–0.8% of "ash." Some mineral constituents also come into the dough with the milk, yeast food, dough improvers, chemical leavening agents, and other ingredients. In spite of the presence of these competing ions, the salts found in water will sometimes have a significant effect on the machinability of the dough as well as on the appearance and texture of the finished products. These effects are more evident in high absorption goods such as soda crackers or bread than they are in sweet goods. The interrelationship of water quality and characteristics of such

FIG. 2.1.

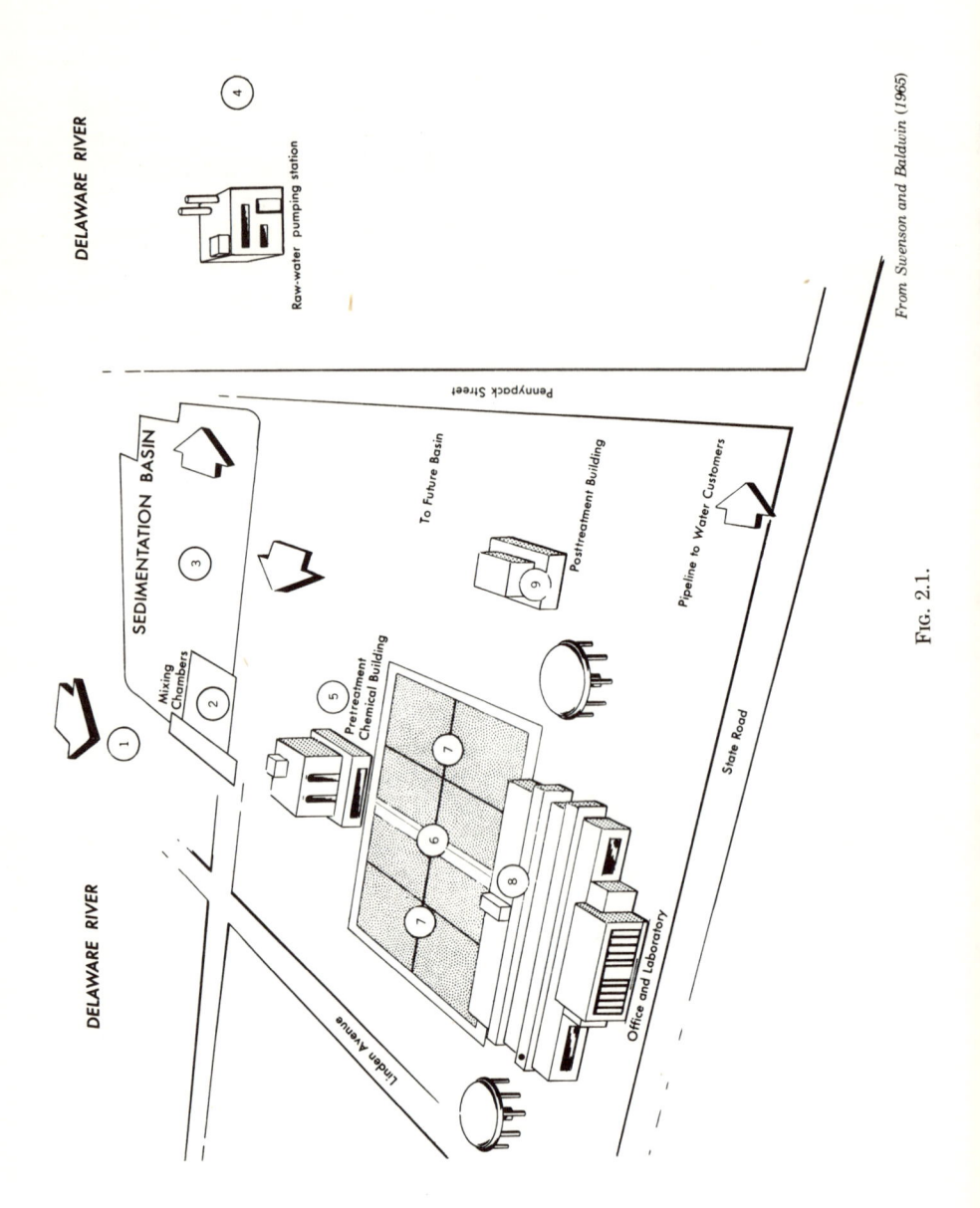

specialty goods as cookies has seldom been commented upon in the literature.

Most of the work which has been reported deals with effect of water impurities on fermentation rates. Although the investigations were originally done with bread formulations, many of the conclusions are also applicable to cracker doughs and sponges. Brooke (1939) reported that copper salts, iron salts, aluminum salts, tannins, silicates, and phosphates, in the forms and quantities found in natural water supplies, do not ordinarily affect fermentation. Evidence was found for an effect on fermentation of the following salts: calcium oxide, calcium carbonate, calcium sulfate, magnesium chloride, magnesium oxide, and sodium bicarbonate.

Soft waters may result in sticky doughs which require less than the normal amount of ingredient water, but this may be overcome by increases in the use of the proper type of dough improvers or of more salt. Monocalcium phosphate has wide use as a water corrective in bakeries and is also found in many yeast foods.

A systematic study of the effect on fermentation and dough quality of calcium carbonate, calcium sulfate, calcium oxide, magnesium chloride, and magnesium oxide was made by Brown (1939). Addition of magnesium and calcium salts led to increased dough stiffness. The phenomenon, which has been observed by many others, has been attributed to the reaction of gluten proteins with the cations in question, especially in cross-linking types of interactions. Brown found that sodium bicarbonate did not affect dough fermentation or loaf volumes when added at levels up to 1000 ppm. Magnesium oxide was also ineffective up to 500 ppm, but led to decreased loaf volumes when larger amounts were added. Beneficial effects on fermentation and loaf volume were observed when 50–500 ppm of magnesium chloride, 100–1000 ppm of calcium carbonate, and 50–300 ppm calcium sulfate were used. Because of its alkalinity, calcium hydroxide had increasingly deleterious effects on the fermenta-

---

FIG. 2.1. A TYPICAL WATER TREATMENT SEQUENCE

Water treatment steps: 1—River water enters here. 2—Water chlorinated. 3—Water settles. Heavy particles sink. 4—Water pumped to pretreatment building. 5—Various chemicals (chlorine, alum, lime carbon) are added. Chemicals and water are stirred in rapid mixing basins. 6—Slow mixing to form "floc" (see alum below). 7—Water settles for 2½ hr as floc carries impurities to bottom. 8—Water filtered through 94 rapid sand beds. 9—Final chemical treatment (chlorine, lime, fluoride, phosphate).

Purpose of Chemicals: Chlorine—destroys organic materials. Phosphate—lessens pipe corrosion. Fluoride—lessens tooth decay. Carbon—controls taste and odor. Alum—forms "floc" (snowflakes) to trap impurities. Lime—helps floc formation; lessens pipe corrosion.

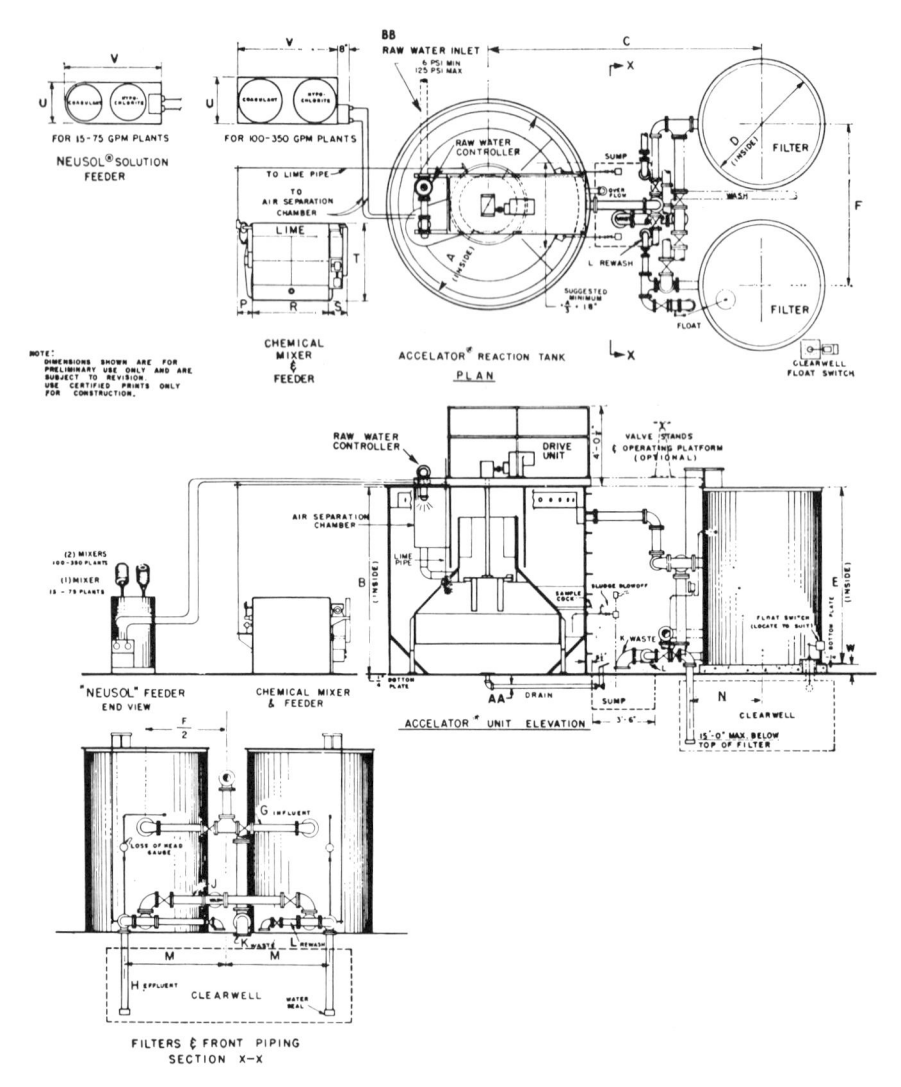

FIG. 2.2. A PACKAGED TREATMENT PLANT USING GRAVITY FILTERS

tion rate and loaf volume when absorption water containing 100, 500, or 1000 ppm was used to disperse the yeast, as is normally the practice in dough preparation. When the yeast was mixed with the dry ingredients before the calcium hydroxide solution was metered into the mixer, the adverse effect of the alkali was not observed. Evidently the buffering effect of flour, which is considerable, was sufficient to bring even the 1000 ppm solution down to a pH that was not inhibitory to the yeast. Results obtained with magnesium oxide solutions were not as extreme as when calcium oxide was used.

Haas (1927) believed that few salts normally occur in water in sufficient concentrations to exert an important effect on dough fermentation. He recognized, however, that the alkali chlorides and sulfates, and particularly calcium sulfate, were beneficial to doughs because of their gluten strengthening function.

Swanson (1966) reported a case in which water treated with copper sulfate for algaecidal reasons resulted in the production of unmarketable bread. Further investigation revealed that as little as 3 ppm of this chemical has a profound effect on fermentation.

Chlorides and fluorides from the absorption water are thought to have little effect in bread doughs (Kirk 1951; Dunn 1941). Others have stated that chlorinated water shortens fermentation time, at least to a slight extent, and improves bread quality, especially if lower grade or weaker flours were used. The effect of chlorine may vary according to whether the combined or residual disinfectant is present.

In many instances, the adverse results of using water of poor quality may be offset by adding appropriate amounts of certain types of dough improvers (Kirk 1951).

It is difficult to understand why waters differing by 100–200 ppm can have detectable effects on dough properties when the ionic contribution by other ingredients far outweighs the contribution of the water minerals. Skovholt (1948) suggested that the trace elements found in water might play a more important role than ordinarily believed. It is known that less than 1 ppm of vanadium will substantially modify dough characteristics. Cadmium is also very effective, the amount of this element entering a dough from plated mixer arms being sufficient to retard fermentation. Both of these substances apparently act by suppressing yeast metabolism.

The general effect of divalent ions on polymers bearing carboxyl groups is to cause more or less transient bonds between molecules with a resulting toughening or strengthening of gels and an increased viscosity of solutions. A hardening is apparent when traces of calcium ions are added to many kinds of fruits and vegetables due to the interaction of this cation with pectic substances. Less pronounced results are observed with gluten, gelatin, etc. Stronger concentrations of sodium or potassium (or other monovalent ions) are necessary to cause a reversal of this phenomenon, assuming constant pH.

Iron and manganese, present in many water supplies, can cause discoloration which becomes particularly evident in such things as marshmallow and icings. They are not generally found in concentrations sufficient to affect the texture of doughs or finished products.

BIBLIOGRAPHY

ANON. 1970. Standard Methods for the Examination of Water and Waste-water, 13th Edition. American Water Works Assoc., New York.

ANON. 1962. Drinking Water Standards. U.S. Public Health Serv. Publ. 956.

ANON. 1963. Water Analysis Procedures. Hack Chemical Co., Ames, Iowa.

BETZ, W. H., and BETZ, L. D. Betz Handbook of Industrial Water Conditioning, 3rd Edition. W. H. and L. D. Betz, Philadelphia.

BROOKE, M. M. 1939. Survey of basic work on the effects of various minerals on fermentation. Proc. Am. Soc. Bakery Engrs. *1939*, 84–86.

BROWN, E. B. 1939. The effect of minerals on baking, using sponge and straight doughs. Proc. Am. Soc. Bakery Engrs. *1939*, 88–91.

DUNN, J. A. 1941. Salt and water. Proc. Am. Soc. Bakery Engrs. *1941*, 70–71.

HAAS, L. W. 1927. Water in baking. Proc. Am. Soc. Bakery Engrs. *1927*, 80–81.

JAMES, G. V. 1965. Water Treatment, 3rd Edition. Chemical Rubber Co., Cleveland

KIRK, D. J. 1951. Effects of hardness and acidity of water on fermentation. Bakers Dig. 25, No. 6, 28–30, 34.

MATZ, S. A. 1965. Water in Foods. Avi Publishing Co., Westport, Conn.

PICKERING, C. S. 1936. The interpretation of a water analysis, and the effect of water on dough fermentation. Am. Soc. Bakery Engrs. Bull. *104*.

SKOVHOLT, O. 1948. Water in baking. Bakers Dig. 22, No. 4, 65–66, 81.

SWANSON, A. T. 1966. The effect of water on the fermentation process. Proc. Am. Soc. Bakery Engrs. *1966*, 48–57.

SWENSON, H. A. and BALDWIN, H. L. 1965. A Primer on Water Quality. U.S. Govt. Printing Office, Washington, D. C.

CHAPTER 3

LEAVENING AGENTS

INTRODUCTION

There are several materials and agents which provide the leavening or "raising" effect in bakery foods. Carbon dioxide from added chemical reagents or from yeast fermentation is the principal leavening gas. Water vapor also makes a considerable contribution to the volume increase in many cases. Air incorporated during whipping and expanded by the heat of the oven is a very effective leavener of products based on egg white foams. Ethanol may play a role in expanding the vesicles in fermented goods. When ammonium bicarbonate is used in cookie formulations, the release of ammonia during baking can add to the volume increase. Oxygen derived from added hydrogen peroxide has been patented as a leavening process, but is not currently being used. In this chapter, the characteristics and functions of bakers' yeast and leavening systems based on the release of carbon dioxide by chemical reagents will be examined.

CHEMICAL LEAVENERS

Gas Sources

In chemically-leavened foods, the source of carbon dioxide is either sodium bicarbonate or ammonium bicarbonate, although acetone dicarboxylic acid has been suggested and perhaps used experimentally to yield that leavening gas. Ammonium bicarbonate is useful only in products that are to be baked to a low moisture content, since there is retention of the ammoniacal odor if the water percentage remains high in the finished food. Potassium bicarbonate has been employed as a component of leavening mixtures for baked products intended to be consumed in sodium-free diets, but it is very hygroscopic and tends to impart a bitter flavor to the foods in which it is used.

The popularity of sodium bicarbonate as a gas source is based on its low cost, lack of toxicity, ease of handling, relatively tasteless end products, and high degree of purity of the commercial product. An additional advantage of this bicarbonate is that its solutions tend to be less alkaline than, for example, the carbonates so that localized regions of very high alkalinity are less apt to be formed as the granules dissolve in the dough.

When such regions are present, reactions leading to undesirably colored and flavored spots may occur.

Soda has some disadvantages. Among them is its rather rapid rate of solution at room temperature, a feature which reduces the amount of control which can be exercised over its leavening action.

Typical samples of sodium bicarbonate, USP, will have the chemical analysis shown below:

	%
Carbonic acid gas	52.32
Total alkali	36.88
Sodium bicarbonate	99.840
Sodium carbonate	0.057
Sodium chloride	0.007
Other substances	0.096

Specifications for baking soda should include a purity requirement and particle size limitations. The latter will be determined by the use for which the soda is intended. A powdered sodium bicarbonate, 65–75% of which will pass through a 200-mesh screen, is suitable for most doughs and batters. Granular soda is satisfactory for batters with a high percentage of water. Particles which are too large or which remain undissolved for other reasons may cause erratic bakeout and lead to brown or black spots on the crust and yellow spots in the interior. Common size requirements for granular soda are that 100% shall pass through an 80-mesh sieve, and 75% or less shall pass through a 200-mesh sieve. A complete particle size analysis of these and four other kinds of soda is given in Table 3.1.

When sodium bicarbonate is dissolved in water, there results a mixture of sodium ions, carbonate ions, bicarbonate ions, undissociated carbonic acid, and dissolved carbon dioxide. The proportions of the last four components are determined by the temperature of the water, the concentration of hydrogen ions (which is, of course, related to the amount of added soda), and the partial pressure of carbon dioxide over the solution. When other substances are added to the water, the situation becomes much more complex, and the calculations of theoretical yields from doughs give values which differ by unpredictable amounts from the observed volumes. Predictions of the direction of the changes resulting from most variations can be made, however.

Considerable amounts of carbon dioxide can exist in aqueous solution above pH 8. Below the point of neutrality, very little of the compound will exist in dissolved form, and below pH 6 the amount present can be considered negligible for most purposes. In more complex systems, especially those involving colloidal components, much carbon dioxide

TABLE 3.1
PHYSICAL CHARACTERISTICS OF COMMERCIAL SODIUM BICARBONATE

Cumulative Percentage Retained by:	Powdered No. 1 (%)	Fine Powdered No. 3 (%)	Fine Powdered No. 3DF (%)	Granular No. 4 (%)	Granular No. 5 (%)	Extra Coarse Granular No. 6 (%)
29 mesh[1]	—	—	—	—	—	—
42 mesh	Trace	—	—	—	Trace	13.00
65 mesh	NA[2]	—	—	—	27.00	91.00
100 mesh	0.50	0.01	—	1.50	92.50	99.32
170 mesh	17.50	3.50	Trace	80.50	99.00	99.60
200 mesh	30.00	9.00	0.5	91.00	99.70	99.65
325 mesh	63.00	30.00	15.0	97.50	99.80	99.76
400 mesh	76.00	36.00	45.00	98.50	99.90	99.86
Apparent density, Lb per cu ft	55.6	47.	52.5	56.25	45.2	42.8

Source: Anon. (1959).
[1] The various screens are given by mesh number. In cases where mesh does not correspond with screen number, the comparison is as follows: 29 mesh is equal to U.S. Standard No. 30; 42 is equal to U.S. No. 45; and 65 to U.S. No. 70. In all others the mesh designation and the U.S. Standard numbers are identical.
[2] Not available.

(in one or the other of its states) can exist in a bound form. Evidently the ions are held by loose bonds to the electrophilic sites on proteins and other compounds. These bonds are weak and readily broken at higher temperatures, or by competition for the carbon dioxide-containing sites by increased concentrations of hydrogen ions.

Evolution of carbon dioxide from pure solutions of sodium bicarbonate is slow, especially near room temperature. When soda is added to dough, gas evolves at an appreciable rate, at least initially, because doughs usually have a pH between 5 and 6. In the absence of added acids, the dough pH quickly becomes alkaline and gas production decreases. To obtain the maximum yield of gas, and to control the rate of evolution, acids are added to the dough along with the sodium bicarbonate. Soda crackers are a special case in which the neutralizing acid is formed as a result of the activity of yeast and other microorganisms.

Ammonium bicarbonate is used rather extensively in cookies and in a few other products that are baked almost to dryness. It volatilizes completely to ammonia and carbon dioxide under the influence of heat. The extreme solubility of ammonia in water leads to slow evolution of this material until most of the moisture has been removed, leading to the possibility of off-flavors remaining in the baked product. Commercial ammonium bicarbonate is a mixture of substances, mostly bicarbonate, carbonate, and carbamate.

Leavening Acids

The function of a leavening acid is to promote a controlled and nearly complete evolution of carbon dioxide gas from a dough in which the latter compound exists in its dissolved or bound forms. Obviously, the acid must be edible and yield edible and nearly tasteless end products. It should exist in the solid form at normal storage temperatures; it should be economical and easy to handle; and it should not have any weakening effect on gluten. Several acids meeting these requirements and having the capability of releasing gas from doughs at desirable rates have been developed. Some of these are listed in Table 3.2. The neutralizing values given in the Table are helpful as starting points in formulating leavening systems, but it should be emphasized that the amounts of acid required to give neutrality (or any desired pH) in a baked product may be quite different from the amounts calculated on the basis of the neutralizing value.

The compounds listed in Table 3.2 are not acids in the usual chemical sense of the word. The phosphates and cream of tartar are actually metal salts of partly neutralized acids, while others such as sodium aluminum sulfate react with water to liberate acids. The initial pH of water solutions or suspensions of these chemicals is often in the range of 4–5, and this is only slightly below the level of some unleavened doughs.

The chemical formulas of these compounds do not adequately define their function in doughs. Small amounts of additives included during manufacture can have important modifying actions. For example,

TABLE 3.2
SOME COMMON LEAVENING ACIDS

Chemical Name	Chemical Formula	Common Name or Abbreviation	Speed at Room Temperature	Neutralizing Value[1]
Monocalcium phosphate monohydrate	$CaH_4(PO_4)_2 \cdot H_2O$	$MCP \cdot H_2O$	Very fast	80
Monocalcium phosphate anhydrous	$CaH_4(PO_4)_2$	MCP	Slow	83
Dicalcium phosphate dihydrate	$CaHPO_4 \cdot 2H_2O$	DCP	None	33
Sodium acid pyrophosphate	$Na_2H_2P_2O_7$	SAPP	Slow to fast	72
Sodium aluminum sulfate	$Na_2SO_4 \cdot Al_2(SO_4)_3$	SAS	Slow	100
Sodium aluminum phosphate hydrate	$NaH_{14}Al_3(PO_4)_8 \cdot 4H_2O$	SALP	Slow	100
Sodium aluminum phosphate anhydrous	$NaH_{14}Al_3(PO_4)_8$	SALP	Medium	110
Potassium acid tartrate	$KHC_4H_4O_6$	Cream of Tartar	Medium fast	50
Glucono-delta-lactone	$C_6H_{10}O_6$	GDL	Slow	55

[1] Parts by weight of sodium bicarbonate which will be neutralized by 100 parts of the baking acid under standardized conditions. Neutralizing values may vary greatly as dough composition is changed.

companies specializing in leavening acids usually offer several different types of sodium acid pyrophosphate. Although the chemical formulas of the main constituent are the same and analysis reveals variations only in the trace elements, the slowest reacting member of the series will cause an initial rate of gas evolution considerably slower than the rate given by the fastest reacting member.

According to Tucker (1959), there is some evidence that the activity of enzymes in flour can change the reactivity of sodium acid pyrophosphate, especially the slow-reacting type. He has evaluated certain flours which speeded up the reaction of slow-type sodium acid pyrophosphate to 3 or 4 times the normal rate. Freshly milled flours from new-crop wheat were particularly potent in this respect.

Monocalcium phosphate monohydrate was the first of the phosphate leavening agents and has been used commercially for about a century. When used alone, it reacts very rapidly with bicarbonate to release 60% or more of the available carbon dioxide from batters during a 2-min mixing period at 80°F. It becomes virtually dormant at room temperature during the bench period, possibly due to the generation during the initial mixing period of an intermediate form of dicalcium phosphate containing only one hydrogen ion. The heat of baking renews the reaction and causes the release of the remaining carbon dioxide. The reaction characteristics limit application of the compound to doughs and batters in which early fast release and a dormant period are appropriate. Some examples of such products are pancake mixes, cookie mixes, angel food cakes, and pizza doughs. In combination with slower acting phosphates, monocalcium phosphate monohydrate can be used to expedite the initial gas release without impairment of bench and oven reactions. It has a particular value in forming gas cells and increasing their number during mixing of batters and doughs.

Anhydrous monocalcium phosphates are very fast acting but can be coated with a slowly soluble layer of potassium and aluminum phosphates. A delayed leavening reaction is the result of the outer layer's resistance to penetration by water. Only about 20% of the available carbon dioxide is released during mixing, while 40–50% additional will be released during a 10–15 min bench period. Anhydrous MCP is used in combination with MCP monohydrate in pancake mixes to improve texture and tenderness, and also in cake mixes, self-rising flour, and baking powder.

Dicalcium phosphate is never used alone as a leavening acid but it can be used in a combination system to provide some acid release very late in the baking cycle. It does not function during the bench period, but only when the temperature has reached 135°–140°F, usually after 20–30 min baking time. Its chief function is to adjust the pH level.

Sodium aluminum phosphates have high neutralizing values and so are economical to use. Several grades differing in rate of acid release are available from some manufacturers. They usually react relatively slowly. For example, one grade will release about 22% of its gas during mixing and 8% during 10–15 min on the bench, with the remainder being released after the batter reaches 120°F. Advantages are apparent improving effects on bread structure in some cases (perhaps due to the aluminum ions) and the bland flavor of the end products of the reaction. These compounds have good buffering action leading to pH levels near 7 in many cases. They are best used in combination with other leavening acids in cakes and hot breads.

All ingredients with an acid reaction will also participate in neutralizing sodium bicarbonate. These include not only such obvious acids as fruit juices, buttermilk, and the like, but molasses, honey, corn syrup, and many other fairly common ingredients.

Baking Powder

According to the definition issued by the federal government, "Baking powder is the leavening agent produced by the mixing of an acid reacting material and sodium bicarbonate, with or without starch or flour. It yields not less than 12% of available carbon dioxide. The acid reacting materials in baking powders are: (1) tartaric acid or its acid salts; (2) acid salts of phosphoric acid; (3) compounds of aluminum; or (4) any combination in substantial proportion of the foregoing."

The requirement for 12% of available carbon dioxide could theoretically be satisfied by including about 23% sodium bicarbonate. However, the necessity for a margin of safety to compensate for loss of gas in storage and by other conditions operating to reduce yield in any given sample dictates the use of a greater amount. Most manufacturers have formulas calling for about 26–30% of soda. The remainder of the baking powder consists of leavening acids, fillers, and diluents such as calcium lactate which have a modifying effect on the evolution of carbon dioxide from the system. There is ample evidence that the diluents are not entirely inert, but serve to inhibit premature reaction of the leavening components due to moisture pickup during storage and to modify to some extent the reaction rates during the first stages of mixing.

Table 3.3 gives suggested compositions for some typical baking powders. Most commercial (manufacturing) baking powders are based on sodium acid pyrophosphate because of its good stability under bakeshop conditions. The typical off-flavor is not as objectionable under these conditions because most of the baked products contain large percentages of sugar which tend to mask the flavor.

LEAVENING AGENTS

TABLE 3.3
BAKING POWDER COMPOSITIONS (BY PERCENTAGE OF WEIGHT)

		Phosphate-Sodium Aluminum Sulfate (Double-acting Types)					
Constituents	Straight Phosphate	Household Types			Commercial Types		
		1 (%)	2 (%)	3 (%)	1 (%)	2 (%)	3 (%)
Sodium bicarbonate granular	28.0	30.0	30.0	30.0	30.0	30.0	30.0
Monocalcium phosphate, monohydrate		8.7	12.0	5.0	5.0		5.0
Monocalcium phosphate, anhydrous (coated)	34.0						
Corn starch, redried	38.0	26.6	37.0	19.0	24.5	26.0	27.0
Sodium aluminum sulfate		21.0	21.0	26.0			
Sodium acid pyrophosphate					38.0	44.0	38.0
Calcium sulfate		13.7					
Calcium carbonate				20.0			
Calcium lactate					2.5		

Source: Anon. (1958).

YEAST

Large quantities of bakers' yeast are used in the production of bread, rolls, sweet doughs, pretzels, and crackers. The advantages of yeast leavening, as opposed to chemical leavening, are that it can contribute a characteristic taste and aroma and the evolution of gas can continue over a much longer period of time. The principal disadvantage is that it is somewhat more difficult to control. In some items, the fermentation flavors can be undesirable. The yeast leavening process is also more expensive than chemical aeration.

Gas is generated by fermentation, part of the metabolic activity of yeast. Many microorganisms can ferment sugars with the production of carbon dioxide, but the one best adapted for leavening bakery doughs is *Saccharomyces cerevisiae*, or bakers' yeast. This organism is a fungus of the type which does not form mycelia. Special strains particularly suitable for leavening have been developed over the years by commercial producers.

Each yeast cell can perform very many different chemical reactions, but those of most concern to the baker are in the group making up fermentation. The most obvious manifestations of these changes are the production of carbon dioxide and ethyl alcohol. Sugars such as glucose and fructose are the substrates which are transformed by fermentation. A simplified equation describing the sum total of the fermentation reactions is:

$$C_6H_{12}O_6 \rightarrow 2\ C_2H_5OH + 2\ CO_2$$

The carbon dioxide is responsible for raising the dough while ethanol contributes to the aroma of baked products.

The sugars which are consumed in fermentation are usually the simple sugars glucose or fructose which result from the action of enzymes on the more complex molecules of sucrose, maltose, starch, or similar relatively complex carbohydrates. Sucrose and maltose can be broken down to simple sugars (hexoses) by enzymes present in the yeast cell, but starch and dextrins cannot be attacked by *Saccharomyces cerevisiae*. Enzymes present in flour, or in diastatic malt, are responsible for the production of sugars (dextrose or maltose) from the starches present in doughs. When glucose or fructose are present, they are fermented in preference to maltose and when these hexoses and sucrose are completely used up, there is a lag period of much reduced gas production before the yeast cells become adapted to the fermentation of maltose.

The side reactions accompanying alcoholic fermentation provide relatively small amounts of flavoring substances. Not all of these have been identified, but they include acids, such as acetic, aldehydes, and esters. Compounds which are not in themselves desirable from a flavor standpoint may react during baking with other substances to give essential components of baked bread flavor. The question of the composition of flavor of yeast-leavened baked products, such as bread and crackers, is a complex one which is gradually being resolved through the use of modern instrumental methods of analysis (e.g., gas chromatography).

Yeast, as received by the baker, is either in the compressed or the dried state. The former product contains about 70% moisture, while the latter will contain approximately 92% solids. In either case, the product is entirely composed of yeast cells except for minor quantities of additives included to promote dispersability or for other reasons. A cell of commercially grown bakers' yeast will average from 4–6 μ in width and 5–7 μ in length. They grow as single cells or pairs and reproduce asexually by forming buds or daughter cells which separate and continue the life cycle. There is also a reproductive form termed an ascus which contains resistant units, the ascopores, but these are never seen in commercial yeast preparations.

Lactic acid-producing cocci are always present in compressed and dry yeast, in numbers which vary from perhaps 10,000 to several million per gram. Their contribution to dough fermentation is negligible because compressed yeast contains about 30 billion yeast cells per gram and the yeast cell weighs about 50 times more than 1 of the lactic acid-producing organisms so that the total active material in the form of yeast cells is about 500,000 times the amount present as bacterial cells.

Compressed yeast is sold in wax-wrapped blocks of 1- or 5-lb weights. Unwrapped yeast in 50-lb cases is also available. Crumbled compressed yeast in plastic lined bags or boxes is being offered by some suppliers. Fresh yeast is delivered to most accessible locations on a regular schedule by refrigerated trucks operated by the major manufacturers.

Although compressed yeast is quite suitable as an ingredient for any yeast-leavened dough and is used by the majority of bakers, other operators have found that active dried yeast has some advantages for their situation. Among these benefits are stability at room temperature, ease of measuring, and better dispersibility. A disadvantage is the necessity for mixing the dried granules with water in a narrow temperature range before they can be added to the other ingredients.

Active dry yeast is manufactured from a different strain than compressed yeast and it has a slightly longer lag period before starting maltose fermentation. It can tolerate drying, high sugar concentrations, and some inhibitors such as propionates better than can the compressed yeast strains. It also supplies more reducing substances such as reduced glutathione and so may lead to slacker doughs unless more oxidants are used in the formula. One hundred pounds of compressed yeast has about the same activity as 45 lb of active dry yeast in straight and sponge doughs.

A major advantage of active dry yeast is its resistance to deterioration when stored at room temperature. Compressed yeast loses about 6.5% of its activity during 2 weeks storage at 40°F, while at $-10°F$ it loses about the same amount in the first 2 weeks but remains fairly stable thereafter. Although active dry yeast will lose about 73% of its activity in 4 weeks at 70°F when stored in air, it will deteriorate only about 1% per month when packed under nitrogen.

Active dry yeast is sold in 10-lb bags and 300-lb drums. For situations requiring a shelf-life of several months, active dry yeast can be packed in hermetically sealed containers in an atmosphere of nitrogen or in vacuum.

It is essential that dried yeast be rehydrated with water between 105° and 110°F if maximum activity is to be achieved. Rehydration is almost instantaneous, so far as individual yeast cells are concerned, but it may take a few minutes for water to penetrate to the center of the granules. After rehydration has been accomplished, the yeast may be chilled, or even heated to temperatures slightly above this range without damage to its fermentation ability. The heat damage to membranes and enzymes explains the loss in activity when dry yeast is rehydrated with hot water, but the reason for the almost complete loss of fermentation power which results when the rehydration water is at low temperatures is less obvious.

When compressed yeast is mixed with water at temperatures in the range of about 32°–120°F, it remains essentially quiescent, no appreciable quantities of gas being evolved. The rehydration of dried yeast with water at a temperature which permits it to retain viability is followed by a significant evolution of carbon dioxide. As shown by Matz (1957), this is due to fermentation of the endogenous reserves of carbohydrates, principally the disaccharide trehalose. This sugar is a storage carbohydrate which is accumulated by the yeast cell under the conditions of aerobic growth it encounters in the tanks of the manufacturer. Trehalose is apparently separated from the enzymes which could integrate it into the fermentative cycle by cell membranes or other partitioning means which prevent it from being used during the normal hydrated phases of the cell's life cycle. When the cell is dried, however, these membranes become porous and part or all of the trehalose can be eluted from the cell by the rehydration water. Once the disaccharide is outside the cell, it becomes available for fermentation. Many other cell constituents are also removed from the cell by the rehydration water if the temperature is low enough. This may be the cause of loss of viability in cells rehydrated with ice water, since much of the soluble cofactors, nitrogenous substances including nucleotides, and other essential metabolites are transported outside the cell where they cannot be used. The failure to retain the soluble materials under conditions of cold rehydration seems to be due to actual "holes" in the partitions or membranes and not to any failure of a selective permeability mechanism. These holes are repaired very rapidly at room temperature and above so that most of the constituents are retained within the cell. Some of the more soluble materials, such as trehalose, are partially eluted. There is a fairly rapid closing of the discontinuities even with moderately cold water (but not with ice water), although the interval between contact with water and closure is long enough to allow much of the soluble material to be leached out (Fig. 3.1). At high temperatures, above about 130°F, the semipermeable membranes may be wholly or partly denatured with the copious effusion of solubles from within the cell to the external medium.

Yeast cells which are rehydrated to about 25% moisture by water in the vapor phase can be mixed with ice water and very little leaching of solubles is observed (Fig. 3.2). This vapor rehydration can take place at any temperature, including ice water temperatures. Such experiments indicate that the discontinuities in the membranes are repaired by moisture alone and do not require the presence of liquid water. Rela-

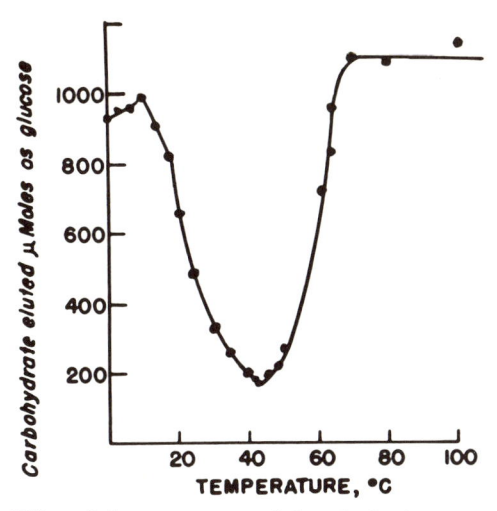

FIG. 3.1 Effect of the temperature of the rehydration water on the carbohydrate eluted from one gram (dwb) of active dry yeast.

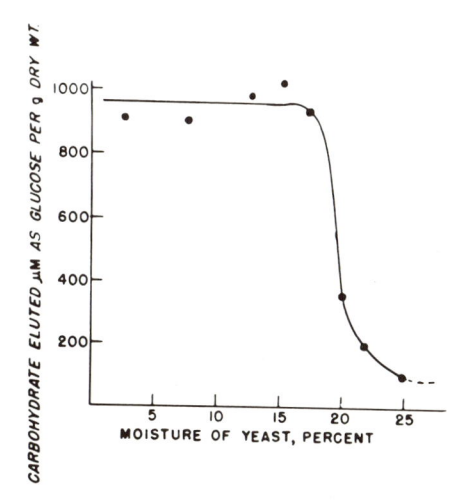

FIG. 3.2 Elution by ice water of carbohydrates from active dry yeast which was rehydrated to various moisture contents by water vapor.

tively few water molecules must be required to satisfy the moisture requirement for membrane rehydration since the bulk of the repair phenomenon occurs in the narrow range of 18–20%, or 2% of the cell's weight. This result would be expected if the partitioning structure represented only a small proportion of the total mass of the cell.

When the pH of the eluting medium is varied, it is found that a maximum elution of carbohydrate by low temperature solution occurs near

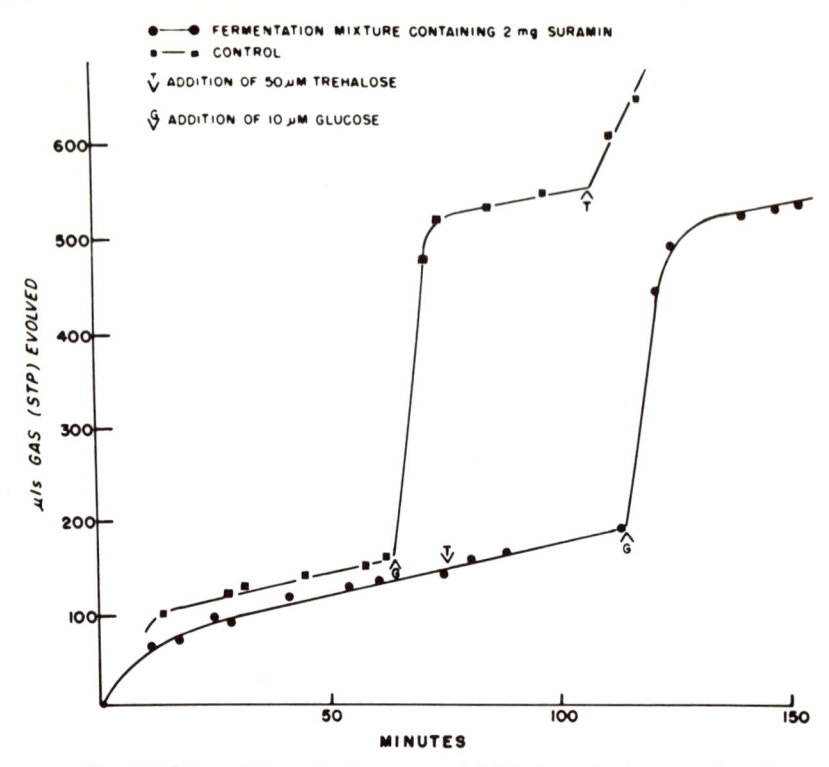

FIG. 3.3 Effect of Suramin (an enzyme inhibitor) on the fermentation of glucose and trehalose by rehydrated active dry yeast.

pH 3.0. Low concentrations of KCl cause an increase, and high concentrations a decrease, in the amount of solubles washed from the cell. These observations, along with some other evidence, point to protein as the material which must be rehydrated in order to close off the passageway through which solutes are lost.

The trehalose which is retained within the cell is fermented much more slowly, if at all. The pH of the intercellular solution has a marked effect on trehalose utilization, indicating an external locus for the initial attack on the disaccharide. Glucose and fructose utilization are affected very little by the pH of the medium. Addition of Suramin, an enzyme inhibitor which does not penetrate the cell wall, almost completely abolishes the fermentation of external trehalose, but has little or no effect on glucose fermentation (Fig. 3.3). The initial step in the anaerobic utilization of glucose is reduced about 90% by addition of uranyl ion, and fermenation of added trehalose is reduced as much or more by the reagent (Fig. 3.4). All of these data demonstrate that an essential catalytic step in the utilization of trehalose occurs outside the semipermeable membrane. Other

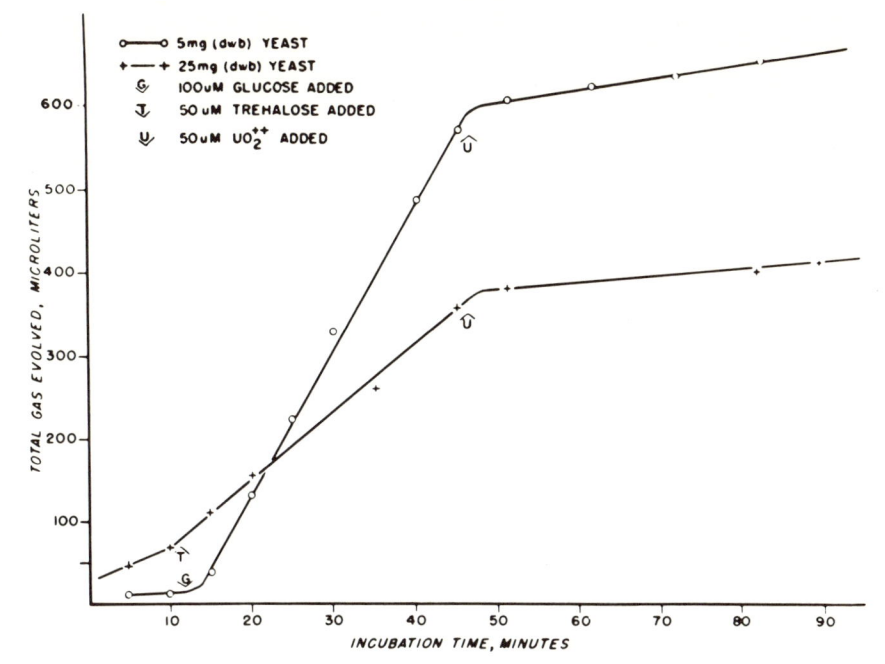

FIG. 3.4 Effects of uranyl ion on the fermentation of glucose and trehalose by rehydrated active dry yeast.

data, such as the ineffectiveness of sodium fluoride in reducing the rate at which reducing substances, probably glucose, are accumulated in digests of yeast and trehalose, indicate that the initial step in the fermentation of trehalose outside the cell is probably the splitting of the disaccharide into two glucose molecules. Following this lead, Matz (1957) obtained a trehalase from autolysates of bakers' yeast and partially purified it. The enzyme appeared to be identical in many respects to invertase, but was not identical to it.

BIBLIOGRAPHY

Amsz, J., Dale, R. F., and Peppler, H. J. 1956. Carbon dioxide sorption by yeast. Science *123*, 463.

Anon. 1957. Yeast—its characteristics, growth, and function in baked products. Nat. Acad. Sci., Nat. Res. Council Publ.

Anon. 1958. Monsanto Phosphate Leavening Agents. Monsanto Chemical Co., St. Louis.

Anon. 1959. Church & Dwight Sodium Bicarbonate. Church & Dwight Co., New York.

Anon. 1966. Modern Leavening with Sodium Aluminum Phosphate. Stauffer Chemical Co., New York.

Bailey, L. H. 1930. Development and use of baking powder and baking chemicals. U.S. Dept. Agr. Circ. *138*.

Baker, J. C. 1957. The effect of yeast on bread flavor. Bakers Dig. *31*, No. 5, 64–68, 79.

BARACKMAN, R. A. 1931. Chemical leavening agents and their characteristic action on doughs. Cereal Chem. 8, 423–433.

BARACKMAN, R. A. 1954. Chemical leavening agents. Trans. Am. Assoc. Cereal Chemists 12, 43–55.

BURROWS, S., and HARRISON, J. S. 1959. Routine method for determination of the activity of bakers' yeast. J. Inst. Brewing 65, 39–45.

CONWAY, E. J. 1958. Recent Studies in Yeast and Their Significance in Industry. Macmillan Co., New York.

DEMIS, D. J., ROTHSTEIN, A., and MEIER, R. 1954. The relationship of the cell surface to metabolism. X. The location and function of invertase in the yeast cell. Arch. Biochem. Biophys. 48, 55–62.

FELDBERG, C. 1959. Glucono-delta-lactone. Cereal Sci. Today 4, 96–99.

FELSHER, A. R., KOCH, R. B., and LARSEN, R. A. 1955. The storage stability of vacuum-packed active dry yeast. Cereal Chem. 32, 117–124.

FINNEY, K. F., McCAMMON, J. F., and SCHRENK, W. G. 1949. Effect of varying concentrations of certain metals and their salts on gas production and loaf volume. Cereal Chem. 26, 140–148.

FREUND, O. 1961. Yeast production and practices. Cereal Sci. Today 6, 320–322, 324, 329.

FREY, C. N. 1957. Yeast—its Characteristics, Growth and Function in Baked Goods. Proc. Symp. Q. M. Food Container Inst., Chicago.

HETZEL, E. N., and TAYLER, G. E. 1946. Stabilized sodium pyrophosphate and process of making it. U.S. Pat. 2,408,258. Sept. 24.

KRAMER, L. A., and NETHERTON, L. E. 1958. Stabilized low reaction rate sodium acid pyrophosphate. U.S. Pat. 2,844,437. July 22.

MATZ, S. A. 1957. Studies on Metabolism of Active Dried Bakers' Yeast upon Rehydration. Ph.D. Thesis, Univ. Calif.

MITCHELL, J. H., JR., and ENRIGHT, J. J. 1957. Effect of low-moisture levels on the thermostability of active dry yeast. Food Technol. 11, 359–362.

PEPPLER, H. J., and RUDERT, F. J. 1953. Comparative evaluation of some methods for estimation of the quality of active dry yeast. Cereal Chem. 30, 146–152.

THORN, J. A., and REED, F. 1959. Production and baking techniques for active dry yeast. Cereal Sci. Today 4, 198–200, 213.

TUCKER, J. 1959. Present and prospective applications of phosphates in foods. Cereal Sci. Today 4, 91–92.

VAN WAZER, J. R., and ARVAN, P. G. 1954. Chemistry of leavening. Milling Production 23, No. 2, 3–7.

ZIEGLER, H., JR. 1956. Effect of inactive dry yeast on doughs. Bakers Dig. 180, No. 6, 80–81.

CHAPTER 4

SWEETENERS

INTRODUCTION

Very few bakery products are made without some added sweetener. The types of sweeteners most commonly used are sucrose (either cane or beet sugar) and various hydrolysates of corn starch. Depending upon the quantity used, these sweeteners can affect not only the taste but also the texture and appearance of the baked product. In the subsequent discussion, sweeteners are classified as: (1) sucrose and invert sugar, (2) sweeteners derived from corn starch, and (3) other sweeteners.

SUCROSE

Commercial sucrose—refined cane or beet sugar—is one of the purest ingredients available to the food manufacturer. The composition of the fractional percentage of nonsucrose material in beet sugar differs slightly from that in cane sugar, but in practice the two sugars can be used interchangeably.

Sugars from various manufacturers do not differ significantly in composition, although syrups are not always as consistent. Nearly all commercially available sugar contains in excess of 99.8% sucrose, with less than 0.05% moisture, about 0.05% invert sugar and other carbohydrates besides sucrose, and a trace of ash. Different granulations of sucrose are offered for sale, and products having similar names may vary in particle size distribution between manufacturers.

Table 4.1 gives a typical sieve analysis of the granulations of sugar commercially available (Bohn and Junk 1960). The common varieties of powdered sugars are ultrafine (Confectioners' 10X), very fine (Confectioners' 6X), fine (Confectioners' 4X), medium, and coarse. They are used for icings, frostings, uncooked candies, and for dusting on finished products. The 6X sugar is suitable for cream fillings and icings.

Sugars of the fine particle sizes tend to cake badly if stored for long periods of time. This problem can be alleviated by adding about 3% of corn starch or, less often, 1% tricalcium phosphate during grinding.

TABLE 4.1
TYPICAL SCREEN ANALYSIS OF GRANULATED SUCROSE

Sieve Analysis		Confectioners AA or Medium Granulated	Sanding	Bottlers, Manufacturers or Fine Granulated	Standard Granulated or Extrafine Granulated	Bakers' Special or Fruit Granulated	Standard Powdered or 6X	Extrafine Powdered or 10X	Fondant and Icing	Dehydrated Fondant, Drivert or Dri-fond
Tyler Screen, Percent on	U.S. Screen Percent on									
8 mesh	8 mesh	...	...	...	...	...	...	...	...	...
10 mesh	10 mesh	5.6	...	...	...	...	...	...	...	...
14 mesh	16 mesh	59.0	...	...	...	...	...	...	...	...
20 mesh	20 mesh	27.4	9.3	...	...	...	...	...	...	...
28 mesh	30 mesh	7.4	49.2	4.3	0.1	...	...	...	...	...
35 mesh	40 mesh	0.4	37.6	74.5	13.8	0.4	...	...	...	...
48 mesh	50 mesh		3.3	18.6	40.2	1.7	...	...	...	...
80 mesh	80 mesh		0.3	2.3	40.6	24.8	...	...	...	...
100 mesh	100 mesh					32.3	0.3	0.1	...	...
150 mesh	140 mesh					31.6	1.8	1.4	...	...
200 mesh	200 mesh						6.6	2.4	...	...
270 mesh	270 mesh						8.2	3.0	...	...
325 mesh	325 mesh						10.8	7.0	...	...
Through last sieve		0.2	0.3	0.3	5.0	9.2	72.3	86.1	99.0[1]	99.0[1]

[a] The extremely fine grain size of fondant and icing sugar makes the regular screen analysis impractical. However, practically all particles will pass through a 325 mesh standard sieve having .0017 in. openings. The average particle size of fondant and icing sugar is about 20 μ, i.e., .0008 in.

Some bakeries make their own powdered sugar by pulverizing granulated sucrose in a Schultz-O'Neill or Mikro Pulverizer mill. Automated grinding systems can be set up to provide a constant supply of powdered sugar as it is required with minimal attention from plant personnel. Some of the newer designs of pulverizing systems deliver cooled sugar and operate substantially dust-free. Corn starch can be automatically added at about the 3% level if the sugar is customarily held for more than 24 hr before use.

Sugar should be stored under dry conditions (less than 60% RH) and variations in humidity should be avoided. When the sugar is exposed to atmospheres of high water activity, moisture is absorbed on the surface of the particles and a thin layer of concentrated syrup forms bridges between the granules. When the humidity decreases, the water may evaporate leaving the crystals cemented together in large lumps. Since relative humidity or water activity is directly related to air temperature, sugar should not be stored where a wide variation in temperature is apt to occur.

The obvious advantages, in many applications, of handling sugar in dissolved form, have led to the extensive distribution of sucrose as syrups. Sucrose syrup is available at 66.5–68% solids content, or at the limits of solubility of sucrose at ordinary temperatures. Refinery syrups or liquid brown sugars are also available in some localities. Two or three grades, varying in color and composition, are usually offered. For example, water white grade is a sparkling clear syrup with very low impurities while light straw can be used whenever a small amount of color and a slightly higher percentage of nonsugars will not adversely affect the final product.

Refiners' syrups are obtained by special processing of material drawn off from the intermediate steps in the manufacture of cane sugar. They have a relatively strong flavor and a dark color which can be advantageous in certain bakery uses and tolerated in some others. Since they are usually priced lower than pure granulated sugar, substitution is desirable wherever it is feasible. These syrups contain a total of 50–75% sucrose and invert solids combined, and other substances making up 70–80% solids.

Liquid sugars are usually cheaper, on a solids basis, than bagged sugar, if they can be received in bulk. In comparison with bulk dry sugar, the situation is not as clear, and may vary with the date and the location of the consumer. If they must be received and handled in drums, the syrups are more expensive. Suppliers of liquid sugar will finance receiving and bulk storage installations and amortize them with a surcharge on each pound of syrup purchased.

INVERT SYRUPS

When a sucrose solution is heated in the presence of an acid or certain enzymes, each carbohydrate molecule reacts with water to give a molecule of D-glucose and a molecule of D-fructose, often called dextrose and levulose, respectively. This mixture of dextrose and levulose in equal weights is known as invert sugar. Because of the chemical combination with a water molecule, there is a net gain of over 5 lb of sugar for each 100 lb of the original sucrose. In addition, the sweetness of the solution increases considerably, and more of the solids will dissolve in any given amount of water. These obvious advantages have resulted in a considerable market developing in invert syrups and in syrups containing invert combined with sugar.

Sucrose syrup is available at 66.5–68% solids content, this being the limit of solubility of sucrose at ordinary temperatures. If part of the sugar is inverted, the resulting syrup will retain higher concentrations of solids in solution. Common types of these mixed syrups contain 73–76% solids with 30–60% invert. "Totally" inverted syrups contain 72–73% solids with perhaps 5% of this being sucrose.

All of these products are reasonably resistant to microbiological spoilage during storage, but the invert syrups are somewhat superior in this regard due to their higher osmotic pressure. There has been some controversy about the relative sweetness of sucrose and invert sugar in foods and beverages, but, when solutions are compared directly, it is generally agreed that invert sugar is definitely sweeter on a pound-for-pound basis (Table 4.2). For each individual application, a separate evaluation should be made.

MOLASSES

The juices extracted from sugar-bearing plants and concentrated by boiling are called molasses. These thick syrups contain other sub-

TABLE 4.2
RELATIVE SWEETNESS OF SUGARS AND SUGAR ALCOHOLS

Sucrose	100
Erythritol	200+
Fructose	173
Invert sugar	130
Mannitol	100
Glucose	74
Sorbitol	54
Xylose	40
Maltose	32
Rhamnose	32
Galactose	32
Raffinose	23
Lactose	16

Source: Biester *et al.* (1935); Cameron (1947).

stances besides sugar that are present in the plant juice, and the ash content is often quite high. Sulfur dioxide is sometimes added as a preservative. Open-kettle molasses is produced in the West Indies by boiling cane juice until most of the water has been evaporated, and is an edible grade as opposed to some industrial grades used mainly for the production of alcohol, as feed ingredients, etc. (Table 4.3).

Blackstrap molasses is the final molasses removed in the sugar manufacturing process. It has an exceedingly high color and a flavor with a very bitter character.

BROWN SUGAR

Brown sugar is made in two different ways. Brown sugar from cane syrups results from stopping the purification process short of the final steps so that some of the molasses flavoring ingredients are retained in the finished product. Such a procedure does not yield an acceptable-flavored product when applied to beet sugars, so in this case brown sugar is made by adding cane molasses to fully refined sugar crystals. Total sugar content ranges from 90 to 95%, and moisture from about 2–4%. Brown sugars are composed of very small crystals covered with a film of highly-refined, dark-colored, cane-flavored syrup. On a solids basis, these sugars are always slightly more expensive than ordinary granulated sugar. The syrup contributes a characteristic color and flavor which is considered desirable in graham crackers and many kinds of cookies.

At one time, refiners produced 15 grades of brown or "soft" sugars, ranging from No. 1, with a slight creamy tint, to the very dark brown No. 15. Because of the limited demand for the finer gradations of color, most refiners now produce only 4 grades, No. 6, 8, 10, and 13. The retail varieties are light brown (No. 8), dark brown (No. 13), and medium brown (No. 10).

Moisture content ranges from about 2% in the lightest type to about 4% in the darkest type. If most of this moisture is lost through exposure to atmospheres of low relative humidity, the sugar crystals will be cemented into a solid block. It is this familiar change which cre-

TABLE 4.3
CHARACTERISTICS OF DIFFERENT TYPES OF MOLASSES

Type	Total sugars (%)	Sucrose (%)	Invert Sugar (%)	Ash (%)	Color
Open-kettle	68–70	43–45	24–26	1–2	Reddish yellow
First centrifugal	60–66	48–50	13–15	13–15	Light yellow
Second centrifugal	56–60	36–38	20–22	20–22	Reddish
Blackstrap	52–55	25–27	27–29	27–29	Dark brown

ates numerous difficulties in commercial use of brown sugar and which has led many cookie and cracker bakers to turn to various syrups, or even to flavor concentrates to be used in combination with granulated sugar. At relative humidities of 65–70% brown sugars will retain their moisture and remain soft.

The total sugar content varies from about 95% in No. 6 to 91% in No. 13. From 1 to 5% of the sugar is present as invert.

SWEETENERS DERIVED FROM CORN STARCH

Vast quantities of liquid and dried corn syrups are consumed by the baking industry. These products, which consist of corn starch hydrolyzed to varying degrees, have the outstanding advantage of being cheaper, on a solids basis, than refined cane or beet sugar. These sugars are not interchangeable on an ad lib basis, but substitution of the cheaper material is often successful if minor adjustments are made in formulas and slight differences accepted in the finished product. Too, there are instances in which a corn syrup has functional advantages over sugar.

The two specifications of prime importance in corn syrup procurement are the dextrose equivalent (DE) and the degrees Baumé. The former figure indicates the extent of conversion, and thus the sweetness, viscosity, and preservative quality of the material, while the latter datum is related to the solids content. For some special syrups, additional information is required, since the distribution of molecular species is not always the same for syrups having similar DE.

Corn starch may be hydrolyzed by acids, by enzymes, or by a sequence of acid hydrolysis followed by enzyme conversion. The normal end product of acid hydrolysis is dextrose while the acid-enzyme process leads to a syrup of relatively high maltose content. The dextrose-maltose ratio can be varied as desired, within limits. The ratio is influenced both by the type of enzyme employed and by the extent of the preliminary acid conversion. See Table 4.4 and Fig. 4.1.

TABLE 4.4
CARBOHYDRATE COMPOSITION OF FIVE COMMERCIAL CORN SYRUPS

Types of Conversion	DE	Mono-	Di-	Tri-	Tetra-	Penta-	Hexa-	Hepta-	Higher
Acid	30	10.4	9.3	8.6	8.2	7.2	6.0	5.2	45.1
Acid	42	18.5	13.9	11.6	9.9	8.4	6.6	5.7	25.2
Acid	54	29.7	17.8	13.2	9.6	7.3	5.3	4.3	12.3
Acid	60	36.2	19.5	13.2	8.7	6.3	4.4	3.2	8.5
Acid-enzyme	63	38.8	28.1	13.7	4.1	4.5	2.6	—	8.2[1]

Source: Anon. (1965).
[1] Includes heptasaccharides.

SWEETENERS

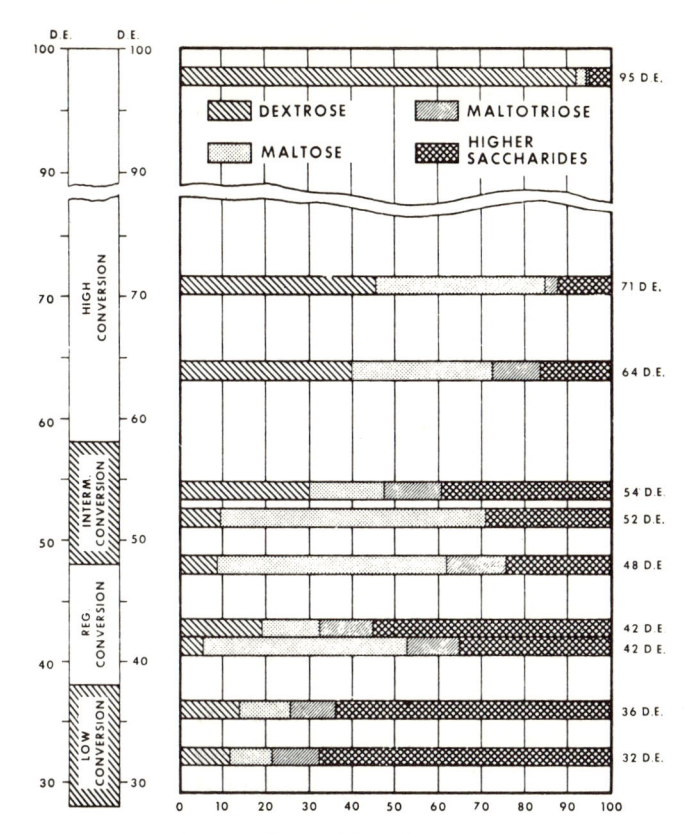

Fig. 4.1 Composition of corn syrups

Dextrose equivalent (DE) is based on an analysis for total reducing sugars, the results of which are expressed as glucose calculated as a percentage of the total dry substance. That is, it is the percentage of pure glucose which would give the same analytical effect as is given by the total of all the different reducing sugars actually present. Commercially available corn syrups and sugars fall into the following classes (Hoover 1964):

Low conversion corn syrup: at least 28 but less than 38 DE.
Regular conversion corn syrup: at least 38 but less than 48 DE.
Intermediate conversion corn syrup: at least 48 but less than 58 DE.
High conversion corn syrup: at least 58 but less than 68 DE.
"Extra" high conversion corn syrup: DE of 68 or higher.
Crude corn sugar "70": DE of 80–89.
Crude corn sugar "80": DE of 90–94.
Dextrose: DE of 100.

DE can vary over a wide range. The "regular" corn syrup of most manufacturers is a 42 DE product. Lower conversion syrups are available for users desiring less sweetness, greater viscosity, or other special qualities. Most biscuit and cracker bakers prefer the high conversion syrups, available up to 71 DE or even higher, because of the added sweetness, greater fermentability, and enhanced browning effects. The lower viscosities facilitate transfer (flow and pumping) of the material. The hydrolysis reaction can be continued to give almost 100% conversion to dextrose, but crystallization of glucose from the reaction mixture makes impractical the commercial handling of syrups higher than about 71 DE.

Corn syrups may be specially treated. For example, ion exchange techniques are sometimes applied to reduce the mineral content of the material. The low ash content contributes to the clarity of hard candy since salts do not precipitate out as the candy batch moisture is reduced. Removal of the ash (mostly sodium chloride) also improves the flavor of the syrup.

Special high maltose syrups are available. To make these products, the hydrolysis is "guided" by special techniques so as to yield a larger percentage of disaccharides (maltose) and less monosaccharides (glucose) than normal.

As rapid control tests, determination of either refractive index or density will serve as indications of solids content. Manufacturers' specifications usually quote degrees Baumé. The latter figure is an indication of the specific gravity and can be determined by special hydrometers. It is impractical to take hydrometer readings at room temperature because of the very high viscosity of corn syrup under these conditions. It is customary, therefore, to make the determination at 140°F and add an arbitrary correction of 1.00° Baumé to the reading. The resultant figure is called "commercial Baumé" and is approximately equal to the value that would have been obtained at 100°F, the Baumé basis on which the syrup is sold.

When the degrees Baumé and the dextrose equivalent of a syrup are known, the dry-substance concentration can be determined by reference to published tables. A 43° Baumé high conversion corn syrup has about 2% more solids per unit volume than does the 43° Baumé regular conversion corn syrup.

Degrees Baumé of commercially available syrups vary from 41 to 46. In a regular 42 DE syrup these figures are roughly equivalent to a range of 76–84% solids. Most corn syrups are now being distributed at 43° Baumé, equivalent to a specific gravity of 1.42 or a weight per gallon of 11.82 lb. Higher concentrations lead to exceedingly viscous syrups which are difficult or impossible to handle with ordinary equipment, especially if the syrup has a low DE.

All corn syrup manufacturers offer low conversion (in the range of 28–38 DE), regular conversion (38–48 DE), intermediate conversion (48–58 DE), and high conversion (58–68 DE) products. Additional varieties are frequently available.

Corn syrup solids and dextrose are available for those users who desire a higher concentration of solids or who do not want to handle the liquid form. As the name suggests, corn syrup solids (as well as dextrose) are prepared by drying corn syrups. The normal moisture content of these products lies between 3 and 3.5%. Corn syrup solids are offered at several dextrose equivalents, but the common type is 42 DE. The usual dextrose is a monohydrate of glucose.

Complete hydrolysis of the starch is required to produce dextrose. The conditions for hydrolysis, therefore, are adjusted so as to give a maximum dextrose content in the hydrolyzate. After purification and concentration, as in the manufacture of corn syrup, the highly refined dextrose liquor is seeded with dextrose crystals from a previous batch. Crystallization is then carried under carefully controlled rates of cooling in large crystallizers equipped with spiral agitators.

After approximately 100 hr in the crystallizers the crystalline dextrose monohydrate (one molecule of water held in the crystal with each molecule of dextrose) is separated from the "mother liquor" in centrifuges, washed, dried, and packed in 100-lb paper bags. The mother liquor separated from the crystals by the centrifuges is reconverted, clarified, concentrated and then passed through another crystallization cycle. As before, the dextrose crystals which form during this second cycle are removed by centrifuges. The dextrose so obtained is redissolved in water, added to new starch hydrolyzate and recrystallized to yield dextrose monohydrate. The mother liquor from the second crystallization, dark brown in color, is called "hydrol" or "feeding corn-sugar molasses" and is widely used in animal feeding and in industrial processes.

The production of anhydrous dextrose (containing no combined water) involves still further processing. Anhydrous dextrose belongs to a different crystal system from that of dextrose monohydrate. Crystalline dextrose monohydrate from the centrifuges is redissolved in water to form a solution containing about 55% dry substance. Activated carbon is added to this solution and the mixture is heated to about 160°F for 30 min. The solution is then filtered until perfectly clear after which it is run into an evaporator called a "strike pan" for crystallization. Seeding with crystals from a previous batch is not required since graining conditions are effected through evaporation. Evaporation is continued until crystallization has reached the desired stage. Centrifuging separates the crystals from the remaining liquid; then the crystals are washed with a hot-water spray. Finally, the anhydrous dextrose is removed from the centrifuges, dried, pulverized, and packed.

Recent advances in corn hydrolysate treatment have made it possible to prepare syrups having a substantial amount of D-fructose (Table 4.5). The advantages of these syrups to the baker are the higher solids content which can be obtained, the greater sweetness, and the lower viscosity as compared to conventional corn syrups. It is possible to get sweetness equal to sucrose syrups at a substantially lower cost (Piekarz 1968).

OTHER SWEETENERS

Nutritive Sweeteners

Honey.—The composition of honey varies depending upon the source and other factors, but a typical analysis would be: water 17.2%, protein 0.3%, ash 0.2%, carbohydrates 82.3%, and no fat. The sugars are mostly D-glucose and D-fructose, with substantial percentages of sucrose and traces of several other sugars.

Honey is classified on the basis of the flower from which the nectar was obtained. There are probably more than a hundred honey types sold to consumers throughout the world, but only a few are of importance to bakers. The lighter colored and milder flavored honeys of commercial importance are clover and alfalfa, while sage and buckwheat are darker and more strongly flavored. An imported honey of considerable importance because of its low price but relatively strong pleasant flavor is Yucatan honey.

Maple Syrup.—This material is a very expensive source of sweetening and characteristic flavoring. It is made by boiling down the sap obtained from the sugar maple tree. The typical flavor is not present in the sap and develops only during processing. Maple syrup contains about 66% solids and the solid sugar cake about 93%. Most of the solids consist of sucrose but several percentages of invert sugar are also present, and there is around 1% of ash.

Lactose.—Lactose is derived from the fractionation of milk or some

TABLE 4.5
EXAMPLES OF CARBOHYDRATE COMPOSITION OF FRUCTOSE-CONTAINING CORN SYRUPS

Syrup Identification	D-glucose	D-fructose	Maltose	Higher Saccharides
A	43	14	31	12
B	50	30	10	10
C	50	42	3	5
D	70	20	3	7

Courtesy of Corn Industries Research Foundation

of its by-products such as whey. It is nearly always more expensive than sucrose and is much less sweet (about 0.16 compared to sucrose as 1.00). For applications where a bland solid material is needed to fill out a formula, as in cases where it is desired to reduce the sweetness of a cookie filling but starch or corn syrup solids are found to be unsatisfactory diluents, lactose may be of special value. This sugar is offered in crude, edible, and pharmaceutical grades, in several particle sizes, and in at least two crystal forms. It has been stated in the literature that rotary cookie doughs containing 3–4% lactose (flour basis) release more readily from the dies and cause the cookies to maintain their shape better during baking (Reger 1958).

Nonnutritive Sweeteners

Although several new artificial sweeteners are under investigation by government and private research groups, this category is presently limited to saccharin for all practical purposes. This compound is 2,3-dihydro-3-oxobenzisosulfonazole. Because of its greater solubility, the sodium salt is used more frequently than the free acid form. Authors differ on the sweetness of saccharin relative to sugar. In dilute aqueous solution the acid form is about 300–500 times sweeter than sugar, but in specific bakery applications these ratios may not be applicable. Furthermore, an exact match to the flavor contributed by sucrose may sometimes be unobtainable with saccharin. Many people find that saccharin has a bitter taste, especially at higher concentrations. Saccharin can only be used in those foods and at those concentrations permitted by the U.S. Food and Drug Administration, and special labeling regulations must be followed.

In many bakery products, such as cookies and crackers, use of saccharin to replace sugar in dietetic formulations leads to difficulties in providing adequate bulk and maintaining desired texture in the finished product. Microcrystalline cellulose has been used in certain products to achieve bulk and influence textural qualities. This nonnutritive substance is quite expensive. Sorbitol or mannitol may be suitable for these purposes in products such as syrup, but they do provide calories. In gel-type foods, additional gelling agents can be used to replace the texturizing effects of sugar in some instances, but not in pectin-based jellies.

BIBLIOGRAPHY

Anon. 1952. Sugar—Its Types and Uses, Competitive Products. Sugar Information, New York.
Anon. 1965. Corn Syrups and Sugars, 3rd Edition. Corn Industries Research Foundation, Washington, D.C.

BARHAM, H. N., JR., and JOHNSON, J. A. 1951. The influence of various sugars on dough and bread properties. Cereal Chem. *28*, 463-473.
BAXTER, E. J., and HESTER, E. E. 1958. The effect of sucrose on gluten development and the solubility of proteins of a soft wheat flour. Cereal Chem. *35*, 366-374.
BECK, K., and ZIEMBA, J. V. 1966. Are you using sweeteners correctly? Food Eng. *38*, No. 12, 71-73.
BIESTER, A., WOOD, M. W., and WOHLIN, C. S. 1935. Relative sweetness of sugars. Am. J. Physiol. *73*, 387-400.
BOHN, R. T., and JUNK, W. R. 1960. Sugars. *In* Bakery Technology and Engineering. S. A. Matz (Editor). Avi Publishing Co., Westport, Conn. (Out of print.)
CAMERON, A. T. 1947. The taste sense and the relative sweetness of sugars and other sweet substances. Sugar Res. Found. Sci. Rept. Serv. *9*.
DAHLBERG, A. C., and PENCZEK, E. S. 1941. The relative sweetness of sugars as affected by concentration. N.Y. State Agr. Expt. Sta. Bull. *258*.
DEPPERMAN, L. O., and WITTENBERG, W. R. 1966. Sugar granulation as related to product uniformity. Biscuit Cracker Baker *55*, No. 11, 30-33.
FLICK, H. 1964. Fundamentals of cookie production, including soft type cookies. Proc. Am. Soc. Bakery Engrs. *1964*, 286-293.
HOOVER, W. J. 1964. Corn sweeteners. *In* Food Processing Operations, Vol. 3, M. A. Joslyn and J. L. Heid (Editors). Avi Publishing Co., Westport, Conn.
JOHNSON, J. A. 1952. Dextrose as a sugar agent in bread. Bakers Dig. *26*, 71-74.
JOHNSON, J. A., MILLER, D., and WHITE, J. A., JR. 1959. Honey in your baking. Kansas State Univ. Extension Serv. Circ. *281*.
KELLY, N. 1964. Sugar. *In* Food Processing Operations, Vol. 3, M. A. Joslyn and J. L. Heid (Editors). Avi Publishing Co., Westport, Conn.
MATZ, S. A. 1965. Water in Foods. Avi Publishing Co., Westport, Conn.
MONEY, R. W., and BORN, R. 1951. Equilibrium humidity of sugar solutions. J. Sci. Food Agr. *2*, 180-185.
PIEKARZ, E. R. 1968. Levulose-containing corn syrup. Bakers Dig. *42*, No. 5, 67-69.
REGER, J. V. 1958. New aspects of an old sugar—lactose. Cereal Sci. Today *3*, 270-272.
WATT, B. K., and MERRILL, A. L. 1963. Composition of Foods. U.S. Dept. Agr. Handbook *8*.

CHAPTER 5

SHORTENINGS, EMULSIFIERS, AND ANTIOXIDANTS

INTRODUCTION

This chapter will be devoted primarily to a description of the functional properties of fats, oils, emulsifiers, and antioxidants in bakery products. Details of manufacturing processes for these substances will be limited to those necessary for an understanding of the properties (Fig. 5.1). Readers interested in further information on the production techniques used to make shortenings for the baking industry should consult Woerfel (1960).

Shortenings are essential components of most bakery products. The kind and amount of shortenings and emulsifiers in the formula affect both the machining response of the doughs and the quality of the finished products. Coatings and fillings are dependent upon the fats and oils for the structural properties of the composition.

Fats and oils are triglycerides of fatty acids, that is, 3 fatty acid molecules combined chemically by ester bonds with 1 glycerol molecule to yield a molecule of fat or oil. The fatty acids are straight chain compounds bearing a single carboxyl group. Naturally occurring fatty acids almost always have an even number of carbon atoms between 4 and 26. Melting point increases with chain length, and fatty acids with 12 or more carbon atoms are solid at room temperature.

If the fatty acid contains double-bond linkages, it is classified as unsaturated. Such compounds tend to be considerably more reactive than saturated fatty acids and they melt at lower temperatures than their saturated counterparts.

So far as melting points and reactivity to a number of reagents are concerned, fats reflect in a general and approximate way the properties of the uncombined fatty acids which have gone into their makeup. Table 5.1 gives the fatty acid composition of a number of food fats.

Shortenings may be classified either on the basis of their chemical or physical characteristics, the raw materials from which they are made, or the application for which they are intended.

NATURAL FATS AND OILS

Butter

Butter contains over 80% butterfat, about 16% water, 0.5% lactose, and 0.1–3.0% ash (mostly from added salt). The structure of butter consists

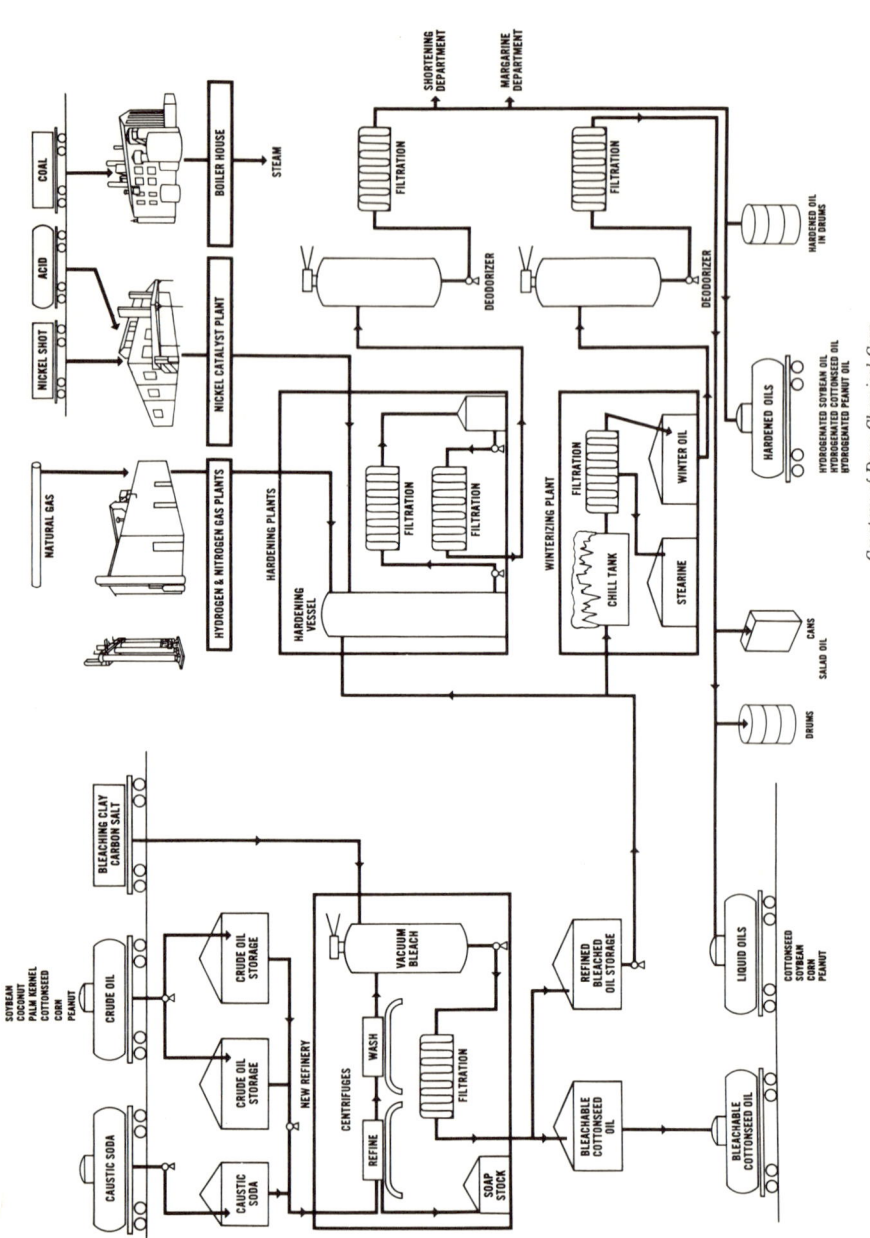

Fig. 5.1 Flow chart of edible oil processing. *Courtesy of Drew Chemical Corp.*

TABLE 5.1
FATTY ACID COMPOSITION OF COMMON FATS AND OILS[1]

Name	Chain Length	Unsaturated Bonds	Babassu	Butter fat	Cocoa Butter	Coconut	Corn	Cottonseed	Lard	Olive	Palm	Palm Kernel	Peanut	Rapeseed	Rice Bran	Safflower	High Oleic Safflower	Sesame (USA)	Sorghum	Soybean	Sunflower	Beef Tallow	Mutton Tallow
Caprylic	8	0	7	1.5	—	8	—	—	—	—	—	4	—	—	—	—	—	—	—	—	—	—	—
Capric	10	0	5	3	—	7	—	—	—	—	—	4	—	—	—	—	—	—	—	—	—	—	—
Lauric	12	0	45	4	—	48	—	—	—	—	—	50	—	—	—	—	—	—	—	—	—	—	—
Myristic	14	0	15	12	0.5	18	0.2	0.9	1	—	1	16	0.1	—	0.5	—	—	—	—	—	—	2	1
Palmitic	16	0	9	25	25	8.5	12	23.5	23	14	46	8	11	3	17	8	5	9	12	11	8	35	21
Stearic	18	0	3	9	35	2.3	2.2	2.5	9	2.5	4	2.5	3	1.5	2.5	3	1.2	5	1	4	3	16	30
Oleic	18	1	13	—	37.5	6	27	18	46	68	37	12	46	32	46	13	84	42	31	25	20	44	43
Linoleic	18	2	2	1	2	2	57	54	14	15	10	3	31	19	32	75	10	43	53	50	67.8	2	5
Arachidic	20	0	0.1	1	—	—	0.3	0.3	0.2	0.4	0.4	0.1	1.5	—	0.5	tr[2]	tr	tr	0.1	0.4	0.5	—	—
Linolenic	18	3	—	—	—	—	1	0.3	1	0.7	0.3	0.1	1.5	10	1	1	tr	0.5	2	8	0.5	0.4	—
Gadoleic	20	1	—	—	—	—	—	—	—	—	—	—	—	10	—	—	—	—	—	—	—	—	—
Behenic	22	0	—	—	—	—	—	—	—	0.2	—	—	3.3	0.5	—	—	—	—	—	0.3	0.2	—	—
Lignoceric	24	0	—	—	—	—	—	—	—	—	—	—	1.3	—	—	—	—	—	—	—	—	—	—
Others:	4	0	—	3	—	—	—	—	—	—	—	—	—	—	—	—	—	—	—	—	—	—	—
	6	0	—	1	—	—	—	—	—	—	—	—	—	—	—	—	—	—	—	—	—	—	—
	12	1	—	0.4	—	—	—	—	—	—	—	—	—	—	—	—	—	—	—	—	—	—	—
	14	1	—	1.5	—	—	—	—	—	—	—	—	—	—	—	—	—	—	—	—	—	—	—
	16	1	—	4	—	—	—	—	—	2	—	—	—	23.5	—	—	—	—	tr	—	—	—	—
	22	1	—	—	—	—	—	—	—	—	—	—	—	—	—	—	—	—	—	—	—	—	—

Source: Adapted from a Table by Drew Chemical Co.
[1] As percentage of total fatty acids.
[2] Trace.

of a continuous phase of solid butterfat enclosing globules of liquid fatty material and drops of aqueous solution. Crystals or agglomerates of solid fatty substances may also be present in forms sufficiently large to be detected microscopically. Some authorities claim that a second continuous phase composed of aqueous solution exists in butter.

Butterfat is a mixture of many different glycerides. The relative proportions of these compounds are controlled by the breed of cattle, the season of the year, and particularly, the type of feed. The aqueous phase contains milk proteins, native minerals plus any added salt, lactose, and other skim milk and wash water components. It is the aqueous phase which is the principal source of flavor in butter.

Since butter is quite expensive relative to most other fats, its use is restricted to those products in which its flavor makes a significant contribution to the acceptability or in which its use permits advertising claims of marketing value. Low-score butter is often preferred to the blander high-score products. Specially "ripened" butter of extremely high flavor is in wide use for cookies. Butter is classified in the following grades according to its flavor, color, etc.:

U.S. Grade AA or U.S. 93 Score
U.S. Grade A or U.S. 92 Score
U.S. Grade B or U.S. 90 Score
U.S. Grade C or U.S. 89 Score

The relatively low-melting point of butterfat leads to the occurrence of greasiness in products containing moderate to high levels of this ingredient. Although this greasiness causes annoyance when the product is handled and tends to smear packaging material and to be related to early development of rancidity, there are indications that it has certain organoleptic attractions for the consumer.

Lard

Lard is used in vast quantities in bakery products. It has a distinctive natural flavor which is thought to be desirable in crackers.

Lard is classified on the basis of the rendering method used as either prime steam, dry rendered, open-kettle rendered, or continuous process lard. Lard sold commercially to bakers and other food processors is called refined pure lard and may be made by any of the preceding methods. The characteristics of lard are governed by the composition of the hog fat from which it is made, by the method of rendering, and by the refining processes applied to the extracted fat.

Variations in hardness of the lard depend upon the body location of the fats rendered. For example, internal fats, such as leaf fats, are always higher in melting point than fat from the external portion of the carcass.

The refiner controls and standardizes his product by selecting and blending different fats. Special grades are produced by segregating certain fats and by special rendering methods. Pure leaf lard, which has the highest melting point, is made only from leaf fat. If a still firmer shortening is required, hydrogenated lard flakes can be added to the natural fats. By varying the amount of hydrogenated material, any reasonable melting point can be obtained.

Large amounts of straight refined lard with added antioxidant are used in bread, rolls, pie crusts, and crackers. Characteristics of this and other types of lard are given in Table 5.2.

Beef Fats

Beef tallow is made from edible fatty tissues of cattle. As with lard, its physical properties vary considerably depending upon the history of the cattle from which the fat is taken. It is normally a hard plastic fat having a melting point of about 110° to 120° F. Because of its hardness, it is subjected to further processing rather than used as a basic shortening in the baking industries.

Beef fats rendered by special methods are separated by fractional crystallization into oleo oil (low melting fraction) and oleostearin (high melting fraction). Oleo oil is used in cookie doughs and sandwich fillings. In dough, it has excellent stability due to inherent antioxidant substances and its shortening effect is good. It also has better creaming ability than lard, making it adaptable to products where the cream-

TABLE 5.2
CHARACTERISTICS OF TYPICAL GRADES OF LARD

	Pure Refined Lard Prime Steam	Open-kettle 100 % Leaf	Rendered Pork Fat	Hardened Lard
Maximum free fatty acid (%)	.50	.25	.60	.50
Maximum moisture (%)	.10	.10	.10	.10
Maximum color	10 Y 1.5R	10Y 1.5R	35Y 3.5R	10Y 1.5R
Congeal point (°F)	79 to 86	88 to 91	75 to 82	95 to 100[1]
Wiley melting point (°F)	96 to 103	109 to 113	91 to 102	115 to 118[1]
O.T. melting point (°F)	89 to 96	107 to 110	86 to 97	. . .
Capillary melting point (°F)	98 to 105	113 to 117	93 to 104	118 to 122[1]
Stability (no antioxidant) (hr)	4	7	6	4

Source: Woerfel (1960).
[1] Variable depending upon the amount of flakes added.

ing stage is essential to the development of dough or batter properties, as in vanilla wafers. The short plastic range (from about 70° to 80°F) and relatively low melting point make it a fair substitute for coconut oil in some applications.

Vegetable Oils

Soybean and cottonseed oil are the principal raw materials for hydrogenated vegetable oil shortenings. Where bland flavors, good creaming properties, or vegetable origin are important, hydrogenated fats prepared from soybean or cottonseed oil are the shortenings of choice and they are used in breads, rolls, pastries, icings, etc. Coconut oil is widely used in the cracker and cookie industry as a spray fat, and in fillings and coatings. Cocoa butter is an essential part of pure chocolate coatings and is used in a few other special formulas. Peanut, corn, and palm oils are less frequently utilized.

Vegetable oils as pressed or extracted from the seed contain many nonglyceride components (impurities). Among these may be found free fatty acids, amino acid polymers, phospholipids, resins, pigments, mucilaginous substances, and carbohydrates. Crude oils are not usable directly in bakery products because of these impurities and must be processed to remove the more objectionable compounds. The refining process involves mixing the oil with alkali and then washing it. Deodorizing by steam or vacuum stripping may follow this treatment.

All vegetable oils offered to bakers have been refined and deodorized. They are usually bleached. Cottonseed oil may also be treated to remove the higher melting fraction to give a "winterized" or salad oil. Although for many purposes soybean oil and cottonseed oil may be used interchangeably, the latter has the reputation of being more resistant to oxidation or flavor reversion.

Refined soy and cottonseed oils, as such, have limited application in bakery goods formulation. They are usually further treated by blending, hydrogenation, addition of emulsifiers and antioxidants, and other processes.

MODIFIED SHORTENINGS

Hydrogenation

Hydrogenation is the process by which hydrogen is added directly to points of unsaturation in the fatty acids. Hydrogenation of fats has developed as a result of the need to convert oils to solid fats and to increase the stability of the fat or oil to oxidative rancidity.

Hydrogenation of oils is a technique permitting the manufacture of plastic shortenings which have many uses in bakery foods. Virtually all of the vegetable shortenings used in this branch of food industry have undergone hydrogenation. The process permits shortenings of almost any desired melting point to be made with little difficulty.

Interesterification

Molecular rearrangement or interesterification is another method for changing the chemical and physical structure of fats. This process causes the reshuffling of the fatty acid moieties between the glycerol residues so that a more random distribution exists. It is accomplished by catalytic techniques at relatively low temperatures. The net effect is usually to increase the plastic range. Lard so treated has many of the desirable textural characteristics of vegetable oil shortenings. It will cream satisfactorily and contributes less of a greasy sensation when used at high levels. Molecular rearrangement is not commercially applied to fats other than lard.

Margarines

Although retail margarine is designed to resemble butter as closely as possible, bakers' margarines have a considerably wider range of properties. The consistency of the fat portion may be adjusted to minimize the greasiness normally found in baked goods containing butter, or it may be blended with softer fats to insure ease of incorporation into Danish doughs. The margarine may or may not be colored and it can be flavored to varying intensities. Baker's margarines are generally packed in 50-lb cubes but some are also available in 2½-lb sheets and 5-lb or 10-lb blocks to facilitate preparation of Danish.

The special shortenings developed for puff pastries are somewhat similar to margarines in composition. They contain meat fats, vegetable oils, water, and salt. The water content contributes to the "lift" and layering of the pastry. Lecithin and monoglycerides may be included. Sometimes the water is replaced by skim milk or cultured milk for added flavor. The fat component should be waxy and somewhat elastic to insure maintenance of coherent layers as the shortening thins out under repeated sheeting.

Liquid Shortenings

A type of shortening called fluid or liquid shortening has achieved some popularity in the baking industry. These materials are composed of an oil such as soybean oil with dispersed particles of emulsifier and hard fat and are liquid at temperatures above 50°F. Because they can be transferred and stored as liquids at room temperature, they are more convenient than plastic shortenings. Although stability varies depending upon the constituents, a maximum storage life of about 3 to 6 weeks without nitrogen blanketing has been quoted.

A number of advantages have been claimed for liquid shortening, in addition to the convenience of transferring and storage. These include: (1) a reduction of 10–20% of the total shortening is possible in bread and rolls, (2) better crust color and bloom, (3) texture of the bread is not as gummy, and (4) whiter crumb. The same authority said that the formula and procedural changes which may be required are: (1) 1–2 % more absorption, (2) mix time 10% longer, and (3) greater sponge expansion (Tubb 1966).

ANALYTICAL TESTS APPLIED TO SHORTENINGS

As with most ingredients, the most nearly definitive test for shortening is a performance test under actual conditions of use and consumption. Since tests of this sort are often impractical and are too expensive and time-consuming for routine use, other procedures have been developed to evaluate certain characteristics of shortening likely to affect the quality of the finished product. Some of the most useful of the present-day analyses are described briefly in the following section. A detailed description of all common tests applied to fats and oils can be found in *Official and Tentative Methods* published by American Oil Chemists' Society (Anon. 1958).

Melting Point

Fats, being mixtures, do not have the sharp melting points of pure compounds. Any natural fat will contain some liquid and some solid material over a wide range of temperatures. Increases in the proportion of liquid component as the temperature is raised causes a gradual softening and liquefaction. Conversely, on cooling the fluid, clouding is first noticed followed by a pasty condition and, finally, by development of a hard solid. "Plastic range" is a term used to describe the range of temperature in which the fat appears to be solid but can still be readily deformed. Because of these considerations, establishment of the melting point is rather inexact in most cases. There are several methods in use to establish this datum and they differ primarily in definition of the end point.

The capillary melting point is the temperature at which a sample of the fat contained in a small glass tube becomes completely clear. The open tube melting point slip point, or softening point, is the temperature at which a solidified sample in an open tube immersed in water will soften sufficiently to rise under the buoyant effect of the water.

In the Wiley melting point test, a molded tablet of the fat is allowed to float at the interface of a water and alcohol bath. The temperature of the bath is gradually raised and the end point is taken to be the temperature at which the tablet assumes a spherical form.

Ordinarily each of these "melting points" will be different for a given fat. The closed tube melting point will be the highest of the three temperatures while the open tube will be the lowest, in most cases. The congealing point, determined by cooling liquid fat until it becomes cloudy, then transferring it to a 68°F air bath and observing the highest temperature reached as the fat congeals, will be different from any of the melting points.

Stability Tests

The degree of resistance to rancidity development is an extremely important characteristic of fats and oils. The fresh product can be tested for free fatty acids or peroxides to get a general, rough idea of the extent to which deterioration has already occurred. Tests based on bringing the sample to a stage of detectable rancidity by controlled heating are perhaps more meaningful from a practical point of view.

The active oxygen method or AOM test is widely used for determining stability to oxidative deterioration. In this procedure, air is bubbled through fat held at 208°F. The end point is the time at which a peroxide value of 100 meq per kg is reached. Other peroxide value end points may be specified for certain fats to give a better correlation with sensory perception of rancidity. A modification of the AOM test using a temperature of 230°F is widely used because deterioration occurs more than twice as fast at the higher temperature, so that results are available much sooner than they would be using the lower temperature.

The Schaal test consists of holding a sample of the fat, or a product containing it, in an oven maintained at 145°F. The sample is examined daily, or more frequently, and the time required to reach a condition of detectable rancidity is recorded. Cookie or cracker crumbs made with the fat in question can be tested in this manner and the results are directly applicable to distribution problems. The interaction of product and packaging can also be estimated by placing strips of the packaging material in contact with crumbs of the product.

Peroxide value is determined by reacting a sample of the fat with potassium iodide and titrating the excess iodide with potassium thiosulfate. It is expressed as milliequivalents of oxygen per kilogram of fat. Peroxide value is an indication of the extent to which the fat has already reacted with oxygen and thus indicates approximately how much storage life remains. The deodorization process applied to shortenings reduces the peroxide value to zero.

The free fatty acid content of a fat or oil is essentially a measure of the amount of hydrolysis which has occurred. Since hydrolysis and oxidation are the reactions leading to rancidity, the peroxide value and free fatty acid content together give a reasonably good picture of current status and future prospects of a shortening. Free fatty acid is determined by titration with a standard solution of alkali.

Solids Fraction Index (SFI)

The proportion of solid to liquid fat in a shortening at a given temperature has an important relationship to the performance of the shortening at that temperature. This proportion cannot be deduced from the melting point of the fat or from the consistency of the shortening at the given temperature. However, it can be accurately determined by a technique called dilatometry. The principle of the test is measurement of the change in volume of samples of constant mass held at a series of temperatures. Density of a liquid glyceride will differ from that of the solid form, so, as the temperature of a fat is progressively raised, additional molecular species will liquefy and lead to changes in volume of the total sample. The situation is complicated somewhat by the mutual solubility of the various glycerides which also varies with temperature.

An apparatus of the type shown in Fig. 5.2 (Pontius 1965) is used in conjunction with a series of water baths to determine the solids fraction index (SFI; also called the solids factor index). The sample of melted fat is placed in a chamber attached to a calibrated and graduated capillary tube, then solidified. The instrument containing the solidified fat is allowed to stand (temper) at certain standard temperatures, then heated gradually to melt the sample. The increase in volume is read by observing the movement of an indicator fluid in the capillary tube. Examples of the per cent solids found in different shortenings by this method are shown in Table 5.3 (Stingley *et al.* 1961). These figures can be converted into chart form. Fats with a wide plastic range will produce a flatter curve with small differences in the SFI at each temperature. Fats having a shorter plastic range will have a steep curve, generally being high at the low temperatures and low at the high temperatures.

Plasticity

The apparent viscosity or plasticity of shortenings affects both the way the shortening combines with other ingredients during dough mixing and the final consistency of the dough. The plasticity changes with temperature, of course, but it also changes with "working" independently of any significant change in temperature of the mass. There is no direct or obvious relation of this property with any of the test results previously described. A number of viscometers have been devised to give measures of plasticity. Since the system is a complex one, the rheology is not entirely clear, and the tests have been empirical.

SHORTENINGS, EMULSIFIERS, AND ANTIOXIDANTS 71

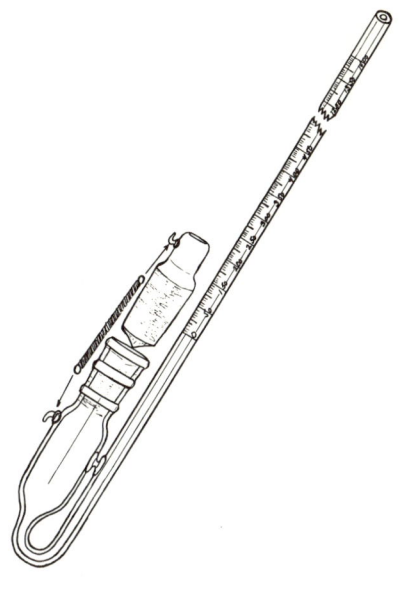

Courtesy of W. I. Pontius
FIG. 5.2 APPARATUS FOR DETERMINING SOLIDS FRACTION INDEX.

TABLE 5.3
PERCENTAGE OF SOLIDS IN SHORTENINGS AT VARIOUS TEMPERATURES (SFI)

	50°F	70°F	92°F	104°F
Coconut oil	51.5	24.0	Nil	Nil
Oleo oil	28.0	13.5	1.8	Nil
High stability hydrogenated vegetable oil	40.5	27.0	7.5	1.0
Lard	27.0	21.0	4.7	2.3
Hydrogenated vegetable shortening	29.0	21.0	15.0	8.5
Meat fat shortening	29.5	22.0	17.5	10.5
Tallow	42.0	29.9	21.8	14.4
Puff paste shortening	31.0	28.0	25.0	19.0

Source: Stingley *et al.* (1961).

Generally, they are based on measurements of the force required either to move a perforated disc through a mass of the shortening or to extrude the shortening through an orifice. The change in the measurement, as the operation is repeated on the same sample, gives an indication of the plasticity of the shortening. In other tests, a cone of specified dimensions and weight is placed on the surface of the fat and allowed to sink in for a given time. Various modifications of these basic techniques designed to give closer control of conditions or to make continous recordings of the change in consistency as the sample is worked have been described by Loska and Jaska (1957).

Flavor and Odor

Except for butter and lard, it is generally desired that shortenings have a bland flavor, although, as Thomas (1968) points out, all shortenings do have a characteristic flavor even though it is usually faint. Taste panels consisting of 2 to 10 experienced members can be used to verify the absence of off-flavors in samples of shortening received for use as ingredients. Evans (1955) describes procedures for setting up, conducting, and evaluating panel tests. Experience has shown that good agreement and reproducibility can be obtained in these tests.

Other Tests

Iodine value is a measure of the number of double bonds present in the fatty acids. It indicates the degree of unsaturation of the fat or oil, and is a rough measure of the storage stability. If the material is unhydrogenated, the iodine value is evidence of the type of oil. Hydrogenation decreases the iodine value, as does oxidation of the double bonds (Table 5.4).

Smoke point, flash point, and fire point are valuable tests for frying fats. They involve gradual heating of the fat in standard equipment under rigidly specified conditions and noting the temperature at which the material emits smoke or catches fire.

PERFORMANCE TESTS

Since most of the analytical tests do not give results which correlate directly with the behavior of the shortening in a bakery product, it is very useful to test the sample by using it as an ingredient in a small batch of the product prepared under standardized conditions.

Since one of the more important functions of the shortening is its role in creaming and in leavening cakes, many shortening manufacturers test each lot of shortening for this factor. It is customary to select formulas in which the function of the shortening is critical. For all-purpose shortenings, a lean pound cake formula which contains no chemical leavening is commonly used. With high absorption shortenings, a 140% sugar white cake may be chosen. Conditions of the test are kept constant so that the only variable is the shortening under test. Mixing is carried out in a room controlled at a constant temperature and the degree and techniques of mixing are standardized. Ingredients are carefully weighed as is the final batter. Various means may be used to insure the uniformity of other ingredients from test to test.

Specific gravity measurements may be made on the batter during mixing. In the case of a pound cake, these measurements relate very

TABLE 5.4
ANALYTICAL CHARACTERISTICS OF SELECTED NATURAL FATS AND OILS

	Butter fat	Cocoa	Coconut	Corn	Cotton seed	Lard	Palm	Palm kernel	Peanut	Rape- seed	Rice Bran	Saf- flower	Sesame (U.S.A.)	Sor- ghum	Soy- bean	Sun- flower	Beef Tallow
Typical iodine no.	30	40	9	125	110	73	50	17	98	101	110	132	110	115	130	130	40
Range of iodine nos.	25–35	35–43	8–12	120–128	105–116	65–80	45–55	16–20	90–110	95–108	100–120	127–140	100–120	105–120	125–140	120–140	35–50
Range of saponifi- cation values	216–240	190–200	254–262	189–193	189–198	190–198	196–200	244–255	180–195	183–194	188–192	190–194	188–195	188–195	188–194	188–195	193–195
Wiley melting point (°F)	82–95	79–99	76	—	—	88–110	104–110	80	—	—	—	—	—	—	—	—	100–110

Source: Drew Chemical Co.

closely to the actual cake volume on the finished baked cake, since the leavening is largely due to the aeration of the batter.

After baking, the cakes are measured for volume and scored for other characteristics. Various methods of volume measurement of cakes have been used including seed displacement and measurement of the height of the cake at various points. The total volume of cake may be reported or the cake may be weighed and its specific volume calculated in terms of milliliters per 100 gm or milliliters per pound used.

Shortenings intended for use in icings may be tested for icing volume. This consists of creaming the shortening with powdered sugar and water and other appropriate ingredients under controlled conditions. At specified intervals during the mixing, specific volume is determined by filling a container of known volume with the icing and weighing it. The shortening is considered satisfactory if the volume of the icing exceeds a certain minimum value and is satisfactory in other respects. In testing certain icing formulas, particularly those containing high percentages of moisture, the icing may be held and observed over a period of time for the separation of free water.

It might be here observed that it is desirable to test a shortening intended for dual use in cakes and icings for both properties since performance in a cake does not insure good performance in an icing or vice versa.

The absorption test does not exactly simulate any particular operation. It consists of placing a weighed quantity of shortening in a mixing bowl and slowly adding water to it at a constant rate. The end point is observed when free water that cannot be incorporated into the shortening is observed in the bowl. The results of this test are usually expressed in the amount of water incorporated as a percentage of the shortening used. All-purpose shortenings will normally show less than 200% water incorporation while good quality emulsified shortenings will generally absorb in excess of 500% and up to 800% of water. This test does not correlate directly with either icing volumes or cake volumes, since it is possible to have products with a low water absorption which perform well in both of the other functions. There does appear to be some relationship to icing volumes, however, and extra high water absorption values will usually be reflected in high icing volumes.

The creaming quality of a fat may be tested by somewhat simplified procedures rather than a complete cake test. A dry creaming volume determination in which only sugar and fat are creamed together may be run. Fats which cream equally well at this stage may behave differently after the addition of liquids; therefore, a wet creaming volume including water is somewhat more meaningful (Woerfel 1960).

FRYING FATS

Fats used for frying doughnuts, turnovers, and similar products must have different properties from the fats intended for use as shortenings or as coatings. A high smoke point and excellent stability to hydrolysis and oxidation at elevated temperatures are essential characteristics. In most markets, the frying fat is expected to contribute little flavor of its own to the finished product, while other regions are accustomed to the flavor of lard. Hydrogenated cottonseed oil is the most common frying fat and it is bland.

A suggested specification for frying fat and an indication of the changes which occur after a short period in the kettle are given in Table 5.5. The fresh fat, as it is received, will not be completely satisfactory for frying doughnuts, because the heat transfer characteristics—partly a function of the viscosity—are not optimal. If the kettle is replenished from time to time with small additions of fresh fat, an equilibrium state can be maintained in which the finished product always has satisfactory properties. When the frying equipment contains all fresh fat, it must be "broken in" by heating the fat at frying temperatures in contact with product until a free fatty acid content of about 0.4% is reached, or until the product is being cooked as desired.

Fat is broken down to free fatty acids, glycerine, etc., by steam from the product, by oxygen from the air, and by heat. Excessive deterioration is evidenced by smoking, darkening, and foaming. Methyl silicone is often effective in reducing foaming. Filtration is effective in removing particles which can char and discolor product but it does not retard oxidation and it does not effect the free fatty acid composition or the viscosity of shortening (Moyer 1965).

TABLE 5.5
SPECIFICATION FOR A FRYING FAT

	Solid Fat Index	
Temperature (°F)	Fresh Fat	"Broken-in" Fat
50	40 ± 3.0	37 ± 2.0
70	27 ± 2.0	24 ± 2.0
80	22 ± 1.5	19 ± 2.0
92	16 ± 1.0	14 ± 1.0
100	11 ± 1.0	9 ± 1.0
	Other Analytical Characteristics	
Titratable acid as oleic (%)	<0.05	0.35–0.80
Smoke point (°F)	>420	—
AOM Stability (hr)	>50	—
Peroxide value (meq per kg)	<0.5	—
Viscosity at 212°F (centistokes)	8.25 ± 0.25	8.35–9.50

Source: Adapted from Moyer (1965).

EMULSIFIERS

Emulsifiers are surface-active agents which are mainly noted for their ability to promote the formation and improve the stability of emulsions. In bakery foods they may have desirable functions apparently unrelated to their emulsifying action. There are some very potent emulsifiers which cannot be used in foodstuffs because of legal restrictions. A few are acceptable in most standardized foods, however, and several more are permitted for nonstandardized foods.

The unifying characteristic of emulsifiers is the presence of a hydrophilic group (dissolving in aqueous solutions) and a lipophilic group (dissolving in lipids) on the same molecule, but not all such molecules have practical effects as surface-active agents. It is not necessary that the hydrophilic and lipophilic groups have equal effectiveness, and, as a matter of fact, it is usual to find that one or the other dominates the actions of the emulsifier. The variability in performance of different emulsifiers is due to the relative potency of the two kinds of regions, their spatial relationship, the size of the entire molecule, and certain other factors.

Without some kind of screening system, the time required to select an emulsifier of optimum function for a given application might prove to be prohibitive. A prescreening system or emulsifier rating scale which is rather widely used is the HLB system (Anon. 1963A). In brief, this method provides rules for assigning an HLB (hydrophile-lipophile balance) number to the combination of ingredients which is to be emulsified, and then directs the selection of an emulsifier or blend of emulsifiers having the same number. The HLB numbers of all common emulsifiers can be found in the literature. Unfortunately, it is not as easy to secure the HLB numbers of many of the ingredients in doughs and batters. Apparently, the HLB numbers are of little or no value for predicting the starch-complexing ability of surfactants.

Some emulsifiers form complexes with starch, and particularly amylose. It appears that the starch must be gelatinized before the full effect of the complexing action is observed. The exact form of the reaction is a subject of continuing debate, but the most recent opinions seem to favor the view that a kind of clathrate is formed, with the long amylose molecule wrapping around an extended molecule of, e.g., monoglyceride.

Lecithin

Lecithin, a mixture of phospholipids, is found widely distributed in nature, but is commercially prepared almost exclusively from soybean oil at the present time. It exists preformed as a contaminant in crude soybean oil, and the commercial method of preparation involves precipitation from the oil and subsequent purification. It may be further processed by bleaching, etc. Lecithin is the least expensive of the emulsifiers and is relatively potent. It does contribute a flavor which may be objectionable in some products.

Commercial grades of lecithin are classed according to total phosphatides, color, and fluidity. The amount of phosphatides in commercial lecithin ranges between 54 and 72%. The product specifications usually report the concentration of phosphatides as "per cent acetone insolubles." Color is stated as unbleached, single bleached, and double bleached. The bleaching process tends to reduce the effectiveness of lecithin as a surface-active material. The consistency will be "plastic" or "fluid."

Flavor is an important consideration since the off-flavors due to the lecithin itself or to the carriers mixed with it often are apparent in the finished product.

Lecithin can be dispersed in water to form hydrates; similar responses occur with propylene glycol, glycerine, etc. It will dissolve in mineral oils, animal and vegetable fats and oils, ethers, and most hydrocarbons. It is easily mixed into doughs and batters.

Lecithin is not used to any great extent in bread and roll doughs, even though it does improve texture and softness retention, perhaps because it does have a fairly obtrusive flavor and color which may become objectionable in these bland products. It has been used in cracker and cookie doughs, where it modifies the consistency, frequently making machining easier by reducing stickiness. In some cases, the shortening content can be reduced as compared to formulations without lecithin. In the finished baked product, the effect on flakiness, tenderness, and other shortening-related factors is not as pronounced as that observed in the dough. Greasiness of cookies with high shortening content is often reduced by the addition of a small amount of lecithin to the dough.

Large amounts of lecithin are used by the cacao products industries. Addition of a fraction of a percentage of lecithin to melted chocolate results in a dramatic drop in the viscosity. As a result, the chocolate is easier to handle, molds sharper, and releases entrapped air quicker. In this application, it is probably more accurate to refer to lecithin as a surfactant rather than as an emulsifier.

Mono- and Diglycerides

These emulsifiers consist of fatty acids chemically combined either 1 or 2 on a glycerol residue. The uncombined -OH groups on the glycerol moiety provide the hydrophilic portion of the molecules. It has been shown that monoglycerides are far more effective than diglycerides in reducing surface tension, but the nature of the manufacturing process is such that some diglycerides (and, for that matter, some triglycerides, or fats, plus free glycerol) are inevitably included in the reaction mixture. Molecular distillation can be resorted to as a means of separating the monoglycerides from other components of the mixture. Diglycerides are said to be helpful in dispersing the monoglycerides throughout doughs and the like.

The common basic raw materials for monoglyceride manufacture are lard and vegetable oils such as cottonseed oil (usually hydrogenated). This results in a mixture of fatty acid moieties combined in random fashion with glycerol. Special mixtures and more or less purified fatty acids can be used to give monoglycerides of specific composition.

Monoglycerides, but not diglycerides, exhibit a starch-complexing reaction. In bread and rolls, an important manifestation of this reaction is a retardation of the rate at which the interior of the loaf, or crumb, becomes firm. In other words, monoglycerides slow down the texture-staling phenomenon, and the bread stays soft longer. Hard rolls show a better retention of the crispness of the crust, and there may be other effects. Experiments have shown that about 0.5% monoglyceride, based on flour weight, gives nearly optimal results in retarding staling (MacDonald 1968). The commercial preparations most frequently used as bread ingredients are the so-called "high mono" products, which have about 65–70% monoester content, and a mixture of distilled monoglycerides (high purity) with about 30% fat. The Standards of Identity restrict the amount and kind of monoglycerides which can be used in bread and rolls.

Emulsifying shortenings for cakes were first offered in the 1930's. These materials contain added glyceryl monostearate. They permitted the baker to make cakes with higher percentages of sugar, water, and fat, i.e., the flour could be decreased relative to these ingredients. The surface-active agent functions as an emulsifier and whipping agent making the batter easier to prepare by dispersing the ingredients and facilitating the incorporation of air bubbles. In the 1940's emulsifiers such as sorbitan monostearate and polyoxyethylene sorbitan monostearate became available as separate ingredients (Johnson 1965).

Since cookies and crackers do not undergo the texture staling typical of bread, because of their low moisture content, monoglycerides are not commonly added to these doughs and batters. Hot doughs such as graham cracker doughs and hard sweets might possibly have improved machining properties if a percentage or so of monoglycerides were incorporated into the dough.

Other Surfactants

Important surfactants analogous to monoglycerides have been prepared using propylene glycol, polyethylene glycol, and sorbitol as the polyhydric component in place of glycerol.

Polymers of glycerol and esters of polyglycerol have had limited usage in bakery products and in adjuncts such as icings and coatings (Babayan 1968).

Among the surfactants which have been applied to nonstandardized doughs and batters are sorbitan monostearate, polyoxyethylene sorbitan monostearate, propylene glycol monostearate, glycerolactopalmitate, and sucrose esters of fatty acids.

Calcium stearoyl lactylate has achieved some popularity as a conditioner for bread doughs and the like. The exact mechanism of its action is not known, but when added to the sponge it improves mixing tolerance, extensibility, and stability of the dough. In many cases, it also increases volume and produces a finer and more uniform cell structure. The dosage level is 0.5% or less based on the flour.

Sodium stearoyl fumarate, which is permitted by the Standards of Identity up to 0.5% of the flour weight, appears to react with the gluten, improving the gas retention properties. It also complexes with the amylose during baking to delay retrogradation, in a manner similar to monoglycerides. Grain and volume of the finished product are often improved.

ANTIOXIDANTS

Antitoxidants are materials which can retard the development of certain off-odors during storage of fat-containing foods. Natural antioxidants are found in many "nonpurified" fats, such as cocoa butter, and certain chemical compounds can be added to fats to accomplish this purpose.

Although antioxidants are of little importance for preserving high moisture bakery products such as bread and cakes, they may be needed in crackers, cookies, and snack products which are expected to remain edible for several months. In addition, antioxidants are usually added to bulk shortenings since the conditions of storage and length of storage create the danger of rancidity development.

From a chemical standpoint, rancidity is of two types: (1) hydrolytic rancidity, which can lead to the occurrence of soapy flavors, and (2) oxidative rancidity which causes the pungent or acrid odor characteristic of badly deteriorated fat. When hydrolytic rancidity occurs, oxidative deterioration is facilitated. Oxidative rancidity is unquestionably the most important of these two mechanisms so far as effects on food acceptability are concerned. The susceptibility of a fat to oxidation depends to a considerable extent upon the number of unsaturated bonds in the fatty acid moiety. Polyunsaturated fats are very prone to the development of oxidation while fully saturated fats and oils are much more resistant.

A great deal of research activity has been directed toward finding substances which will retard the development of oxidative rancidity in foods and at the same time be acceptable to federal regulatory agencies as a food additive. At the present time, only three chemical compounds are commercially important as antioxidants for foods. They are butylated hydroxyanisole (BHA), butylated hydroxytoluene (BHT), and propyl gallate. Citric acid or phosphoric acid may be added to improve the effectiveness of the antioxidants but they do not themselves function directly to prevent fat oxidation.

Companies such as Eastman Chemical Products offer mixtures of anti-oxidants in convenient diluted forms. They can also provide advice as to the legality of proposed uses of the materials.

BIBLIOGRAPHY

ANON. 1958. Official and Tentative Methods of Analysis, 2nd Edition. Am. Oil Chemists' Soc., Chicago.
ANON. 1963A. The Atlas HLB System, 3rd Edition. Atlas Chemical Industries, Wilmington, Del.
ANON. 1963B. Food Fats and Oils. Inst. Shortening Edible Oils, Washington, D.C.
BABAYAN, V. K. 1968. The polyfunctional polyglycerols. Food Prod. Develop. 2, No. 3, 58, 60–62.
COCKS, L. V., and VAN REDE, C. 1966. Laboratory Handbook for Oil and Fat Analysts. Academic Press, New York.
ELLING, J. W. 1952. Types of crust. Proc. Am. Soc. Bakery Engrs. *1952*, 275–280.
EVANS, C. D. 1955. Flavor evaluation of fats and oils. J. Am. Oil Chemists' Soc. *32*, 596–604.
FERGUSON, R. 1967. Dough conditioning. Proc. Am. Soc. Bakery Engrs. *1967*, 72–79.
JOHNSON, R. H. 1965. Emulsifiers made understandable to the baker. Proc. Am. Soc. Bakery Engrs. *1965*, 206–210.
KNIGHTLY, W. H. 1969. Use of emulsifiers in bakery foods. Proc. Am. Soc. Bakery Engrs. *1969*, 128–138.
LEDUC, R. 1968. Shortening: A bakery chemists' panoramic view. Snack Food *57*, No. 9, 29–33.
LOSKA, S. J., JR., and JASKA, E. 1957. A disk rheometer applicable to measuring shortening flow properties. J. Am. Oil Chemists' Soc. *34*, 495–500.
MACDONALD, I. A. 1968. The functional properties of various surface active agents. Bakers Dig. *42*, No. 2, 24–26, 28–29.
MOCK, J. P. 1964. Shortenings—their processing for specialized uses. Bakers Dig. *38*, No. 8, 53–57.
MOYER, J. 1965. Selection, maintentance, and protection of frying fats. Proc. Am. Soc. Bakery Engrs. *1965*, 273–278.
PONTIUS, W. I. 1965. The meaning of solids factor index. Armour & Co., Chicago.
RICH, A. D. 1942. Methods employed in expressing the consistency of plasticized shortenings. J. Am. Oil Chemists' Soc. *19*, 54–57.
RICHARD, W. D. 1968. Fluid shortening. Proc. Am. Soc. Bakery Engrs. *1968*, 99–105.

STINGLEY, D. V., VANDER WAL, R. J., and WHEELER, F. E. 1961. The solids content of shortening and its significance to the baker. Bakers Dig. *35*, No. 8, 16–19.

STINGLEY, D. V., and WHEELER, F. G. 1956. The meaning of commonly quoted analytical values of shortenings as related to shortening performance. Cereal Sci. Today *1*, 39–42.

THOMAS, B. L. 1968. Specifications: what do they really mean? Snack Food *57*, No. 12, 30–32.

TUBB, G. O. 1966. The use of liquid shortening in bread. Proc. Am. Soc. Bakery Engrs. *1966*, 102–106.

WOERFEL, J. B. 1960. Shortenings. *In* Bakery Technology and Engineering, S. A. Matz (Editor). Avi Publishing Co., Westport, Conn. (Out of print)

CHAPTER 6

MILK PRODUCTS

INTRODUCTION

Milk has been defined as the whole, fresh, lacteal secretion obtained by the complete milking of one or more healthy cows. It must contain not less than 8.25% milk solids not fat, and not less than 3.25% milkfat (Table 6.1). As is clear from this definition, the unmodified term milk means cows' milk.

Milk is a biological commodity and, like all such, varies in its properties according to the breed of cow, geographical location of the herd, climatic conditions, type of feed, and other factors. The principal constituents of milk are butterfat, milk protein, lactose, minerals, and water. A minimum standard varying from 3.0 to 3.8% fat content is specified by the laws of each state. Most states also establish a minimum either for total solids (from 11.2 to 12.25%), or for milk-solids-not-fat (from 8.0 to 8.5%). In some states it is permissible to adjust the fat content of bottled milk by adding or removing cream or skim milk while other states prohibit these adjustments. Other dairy products are also subject to regulation of fat and solids in most states. If the food is introduced into interstate commerce, it must meet federal standards as well.

Milk and milk derivatives have several effects on bakery foods and the result is, generally, improvement of the flavor and physical characteristics as well as the nutritive value. In bread, addition of properly heat-treated nonfat dry milk to the dough will generally improve the crust color, increase water absorption, and modify dough handling properties. The added water tends to be retained in the finished loaf with the result that the bread is somewhat softer. The lactose, being retained throughout processing, causes toast made from the bread to color more readily and more uniformly.

Whole milk is used mostly in premium goods where the flavor contribution of butterfat can be worthwhile. Butterfat also has a pronounced shortening effect exhibited primarily as a weakening or breaking down of any gluten structure which may be present. So far as its shortening action is concerned, properly selected cheaper fats can usually be substituted for butterfat with equivalent results.

In addition to the fresh fluid products, milk and its fractions are concentrated, dried, and mixed with other substances to improve their utility for baking purposes (see Table 6.2).

FLUID MILK PRODUCTS

The fluid milk products of commerce include whole milk, skim milk, buttermilk, and whey. They are characterized by containing relatively large percentages of water and so they are bulky and more expensive to

TABLE 6.1
TYPICAL ANALYSIS OF FLUID WHOLE MILK

Milk Constituent	%
Milkfat	3.5
Protein	3.5
Lactose	4.9
Ash	0.7
Water	87.4

TABLE 6.2
COMPOSITION OF MILK AND MILK DERIVATIVES

Product	Water	Fat	Protein	Carbohydrate	Ash
Fluid whole milk	87.4	3.5	3.5	4.9	0.7
Fluid skim	90.5	0.1	3.6	5.1	0.7
Cream 20% butterfat	72.5	20.0	2.9	4.0	0.6
Cream 30% butterfat	63.4	30.0	2.5	3.6	0.5
Cream 40% butterfat	54.3	40.0	2.1	3.1	0.5
Plastic cream, 80% butterfat	18.1	80.0	0.7	1.0	0.2
Milkfat (butteroil)	0.1	99.9	—	—	—
Butter (unsalted)	17.5	81.0	0.6	0.4	0.5
Butter (salted)	15.5	81.0	0.6	0.4	2.5
Buttermilk	90.5	0.1	3.5	5.1	0.8
Cheddar cheese	37.0	32.2	25.0	2.1	3.7
Cheese whey	93.2	0.3	0.9	5.1	0.5
Process American cheese	40.0	29.9	23.2	2.0	4.9
Dry whole milk solids	2.0	27.5	26.4	38.2	5.9
Milk-solids-not-fat (MSNF)	3.5	1.0	35.6	52.0	7.9
Dry buttermilk solids	3.5	5.0	34.7	49.0	7.8
High acid buttermilk solids (5.0% lactic acid)	4.0	5.0	34.5	43.7	7.8
Dried whey	6.2	1.2	12.5	72.4	7.7
Plain condensed whole milk	70.0	8.5	7.8	11.9	1.8
Plain condensed skim milk	70.0	0.2	11.1	16.2	2.5
Plain condensed whey	32.0	0.6	10.1	51.3	6.0
Evaporated milk	73.7	7.9	7.0	9.9	1.5
Sweetened condensed whole milk (42.0% sucrose)	27.9	8.6	7.7	12.2	1.6
Sweetened condensed skim milk (42.0% sucrose)	28.0	0.2	11.1	16.2	2.5
Sweetened condensed whey (38.0% sucrose)	24.0	0.3	5.6	28.7	3.4
Malted milk	2.6	8.3	14.7	70.8	3.6
Lactose	0.15	—	—	99.85	—
Sodium caseinate	3.5	1.5	90.0	1.0	3.5

Source: Anon. (1963).

store and ship than are the dried equivalents. In addition, they are quite perishable and must be kept under refrigeration and used within a short time of collection. Because of these disadvantages, they are relatively high cost ingredients, except in areas where local supplies are plentiful and of good quality.

CONCENTRATED MILK PRODUCTS

This class of ingredients includes whole milk, skim milk, buttermilk, and whey from which a major portion of the water has been removed. These products are referred to as condensed if only water has been removed, sweetened condensed if sucrose has been added and water removed, and evaporated if water has been removed and the end product canned and sterilized. In concentrated milk products the increased solids content, plus the added sugar in the sweetened versions, results in finished products which have useful storage lives varying from weeks to months. Being concentrated they also occupy considerably less storage space, weigh less per unit of active ingredients and can be economically transported relatively great distances. Generally, however, refrigeration and rather reliable supply arrangements and inventory control are needed if concentrated milk products are to be integrated into a production program. Concentrated milk products are viscous fluids which are adaptable to bulk handling and liquid metering operations.

DRIED MILK SOLIDS PRODUCTS

Dried milk solids products are based on the raw materials discussed under fluids, but they have had nearly all of their moisture removed and are available in powdered or granular form. These ingredients far exceed the fluids and concentrates in commercial significance to the baker. They occupy a minimum of storage space, and have very good stability at ordinary temperatures. These advantages lead to dependability and uniformity of supply, ease of inventory control, uniformity of quality, and relatively stable pricing.

Dried Milk-Solids-not-fat (MSNF)

The three principal stages in converting fluid skim milk into MSNF are (1) preheating of the fluid milk, (2) condensing, and (3) drying. Variations of conditions existing in any of these treatments can change the characteristics of the finished material. Adjustment of the time and temperature in the preheating step is the most common technique for modifying the qualities of the dried milk in a desired direction. The primary effect of these changes in processing is a modification of the status of the protein molecules.

Preheating includes pasteurization which requires raising the temperature of the milk to at least 145°F and maintaining it for not less than 30 min, or to 161°F for at least 15 sec. Other temperature-time combinations giving equivalent results may be used. Minimal heat treatments of this type are used for dried milks, designated low-heat, and are intended for making into cottage cheese and other uses requiring the lowest possible degree of protein denaturation.

The changes occurring as a result of preheating, the extent of which depend on the intensity of the process, are (1) enzyme inactivation, (2) protein denaturation, (3) destruction of microorganisms, (4) nonenzymatic browning, and (5) other poorly defined chemical and physical changes. The denaturation of whey proteins has been found to be a good indicator of the degree of preheat treatment the milk has undergone.

If the MSNF is intended to be used for bread or other yeast-leavened products much more rigorous preheating is required. Omission of this step leads to a product which can seriously weaken the gluten structure of dough. The necessity for high-heat treatment of milk to be used as a cookie ingredient has not been clearly shown. In addition to the high-heat milk solids and the low-heat product described previously, there are milks made by heat treatment of intermediate intensity and used for special purposes not usually connected with baking.

After the preheating phase, the milk is condensed or partially dried under vacuum. Evaporation may take place at temperatures ranging from 80°F to 185°F. Solids concentration is brought up to about 35–45%. The combined effects of preheating and condensing give bakery type MSNF a relatively high water absorption capacity. Absorption can be still further increased by an additional heat treatment (frequently by steam injection) of the condensed milk—superheating. High water absorption is merely one aspect of the baking quality of MSNF and other characteristics must be considered in evaluating the overall quality.

The concentrated milk is reduced to powder by roller- or spray-drying equipment. Roller dryers can be of atmospheric or vacuum types. Milk solids produced by roller drying undergo considerably more heat changes than does spray-dried milk. In specific cases, the highly cooked, sometimes almost caramelized flavor of roller-dried powder is desirable, but its reduced solubility and darker color are generally regarded as defects. Perhaps 90–95% of the milk solids produced in this country is dried on spray equipment.

In roller drying, the condensed milk is fed into a trough formed by two large metal drums rotating in opposite directions. These drums are heated internally by steam under pressure so that the surface temperature can rise considerably above 212°F. A film of milk is picked up by the drum as the surface moves through the trough area. As this film emerges from the pool of liquid, the water begins to evaporate rapidly. The layer of dried-milk formed by this process is removed by a doctor blade. Vacuum-drying equipment is based on similar principles except that the drums are enclosed in a chamber which can be partially evacuated.

In spray drying (see Figs. 6.1 and 6.2), the milk is forewarmed to about 160°F by a heat-exchange apparatus and then atomized into a stream of air heated to temperatures of about 200°–500°F. The atomizing means is designed to yield very small and uniform droplets from which the water is rapidly evaporated by the heated air. The powder falls to the bottom of the chamber and is removed. Loss of the latent heat of evaporation operates to maintain the droplets at below the boiling point of water—temperatures of not much more than 150°F being the highest reached by the milk in well-adjusted apparatus. In order to minimize the heat damage, the temperatures of milk and air, and the rates of introduction of air and milk into the apparatus, are regulated so as to assure passage of the particle out the the heated zone before the moisture is completely lost. When made under optimum conditions, the milk will receive very little additional heat damage during the spray drying process. Milk powder prepared under these conditions is virtually completely soluble and has a mild flavor and light color.

Dried Whole Milk

Dried whole milk contains not less than 26% milkfat and not more than 4% moisture. Both spray- and roller-dried types are available. As with most other dried milk products, food grade dried whole milk is available in Standard Grade, and Extra Grade (indicating the highest quality). Dried whole milk is subject to rancidity development and stocks should be controlled very closely. In most cases, crackers and cookies can be formulated with butter and MSNF instead of dry whole milk to avoid this problem.

Modified Dried Whole Milk

Whole milk can be modified by certain enzymes to increase the intensity of the fat flavor. The composition of the product is the same as that of regular dried whole milk for all practical purposes. The changes occur principally in the lipids, and a similar process can be applied to butter. These flavor concentrates are used to a great extent in chocolate candy. They have a place in filling formulations as well. They have not been successful in chocolate enrobed goods because of the difficulties ensuing from the incorporation of butterfat in these coatings. They can be used in cocoa-flavored confectioners' coatings.

MILK PRODUCTS

```
                    Receive Milk
                         ↓
                       Cool
                      (40°F)
          ┌─────────────┴─────────────┐
          ↓                           ↓
       Preheat              Standardize fat to SNF
       (95°F)                      1:2.769
          ↓                           ↓
      Separate                     Preheat
          ↓                        (160°F)
      Pasteurize                      ↓
          ↓                    Filter (or clarify)
    ┌─────┴─────┐                     ↓
    ↓           ↓                 Homogenize
Low-heat MSNF  High-heat MSNF     (3000 psi)
(161°F for     (161°F for            ↓
  15 sec)       15 sec)             Heat
    │            ↓              (200°F for 3 min)
    │         Preheat                 ↓
    │      (185°F for 20 min)      Condense
    │            ↓                    ↓
    ↓         Condense              Preheat
 Condense        ↓                  (160°F)
    ↓          Reheat                 ↓
  Reheat       (165°F)                Pump
  (145°F)        ↓                 (2500 psi)
    ↓          Filter                 ↓
  Filter         ↓                 Spray dry
    ↓           Pump            (180°F outlet air)
   Pump       (3000 psi)              ↓
(3000 psi)       ↓                   Cool
    ↓         Spray dry              (90°F)
 Spray dry  (185°F outlet air)        ↓
(185°F outlet    ↓                   Sift ──────┐
   air)         Cool                  ↓         │
    ↓          (100°F)            vacuum treat  │
   Cool          ↓                plus nitrogen │
  (90°F)        Sift                  ↓         │
    ↓            ↓                 Package ←────┘
   Sift       Package
    ↓            ↓
 Package       Store
    ↓        (room temp)
  Store
(room temp)
```

Courtesy of Hall and Hedrick (1966)

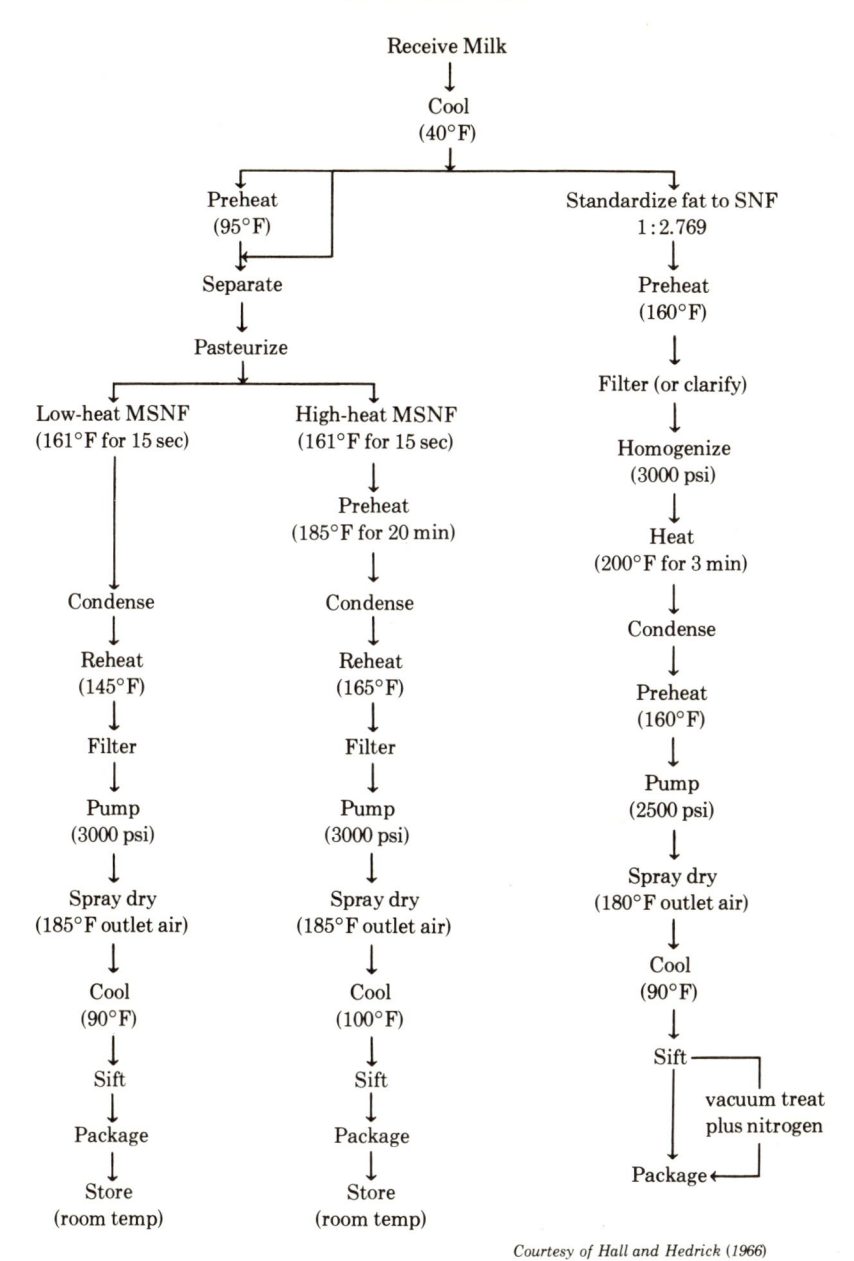

FIG. 6.1. FLOW DIAGRAM FOR MANUFACTURE OF SPRAY PROCESS NONFAT DRY MILK (MSNF) AND DRY WHOLE MILK.

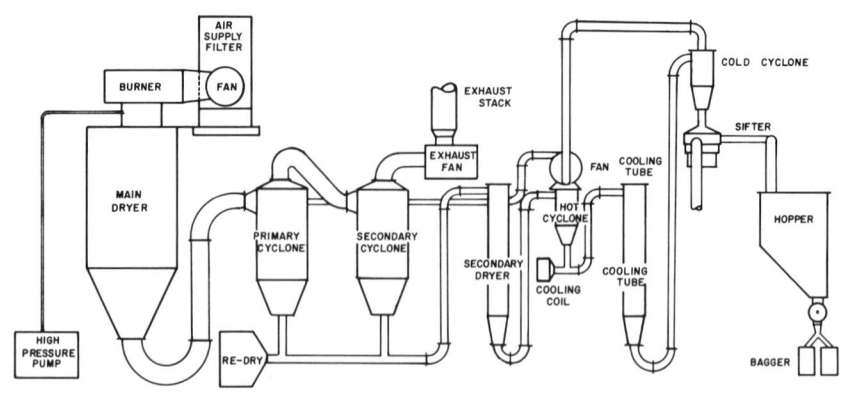

Courtesy of Hall and Hedrick (1966)
FIG. 6.2. SPRAY DRYING SYSTEM WITH TWO DRYING CHAMBERS.

TABLE 6.3
EXTRA GRADE REQUIREMENTS OF MSNF

	Spray Process (Not Greater Than)	Roller Process (Not Greater Than)
Milkfat (%)	1.25	1.25
Moisture (%)	4.0	4.0
Titratable acidity[1] (%)	0.15	0.15
Scorched particles (mg)	15.0	22.5
Solubility index[1] (ml)	1.25	15.0
Bacterial estimate (per gm)	50,000	50,000

[1] Determination made upon reliquified sample.

TABLE 6.4
EXTRA GRADE REQUIREMENTS OF DRY WHOLE MILK

	Spray Process	Roller Process
Milkfat (not less than) (%)	26.00	26.00
Moisture (not more than) (%)	2.50	3.0
Titratable acidity[1] (not more than) (%)	0.15	0.15
Bacterial estimate (not more than) (per gm)	50,000	50,000
Solubility index[1] (not more than) (ml)	0.50	15.00
Scorched particle (not more than) (mg)	15.0	22.5
Copper (ppm)	1.5	1.5
Iron (ppm)	10.0	—
Flavor-odor	Normal	Normal
Color	Normal	Normal

[1] Determination on reliquified sample.

Buttermilk

There are two kinds of dried buttermilk, regular and high acid. Both types should contain at least 4.5% butterfat and not more than 5.0% water. Commercially available products are usually spray dried although some roller-dried material is occasionally offered. The nonfat solids fraction is essentially the same as in skim milk solids (MSNF). The best grades of dried buttermilk are suitable as replacements for MSNF in most cookies and will provide additional richness in flavor and shortness in texture due to the small amount of butterfat which they contain. There is also an emulsifying action attributable to the presence of a small amount of phospholipids. High acid buttermilk has a distinctive flavor which may or may not be desirable depending upon the product. The lactic acid it contains (about 5.0%) will react with sodium bicarbonate causing loss of leavening power unless the quantity of soda is adjusted to compensate for this factor. Dried buttermilk is generally cheaper than MSNF although the difference in price has narrowed considerably in recent years.

Dried Whey Products

Whey is a by-product of cheese manufacture, being the liquid which is drained off the curd. For many years, attempts were made to utilize whey (primarily in the dried form) as a raw material in bread since it has good nutritional properties and is very inexpensive. Variable flavor quality, mostly from poor to terrible, and bad effects on the physical properties of dough have prevented its widespread use. Recent improvements in storage and handling of the raw material and in processing techniques have greatly improved the potential of dried whey as a bakery ingredient.

TABLE 6.5
EXTRA GRADE REQUIREMENTS OF DRY BUTTERMILK SOLIDS

	Spray Process	Roller Process
Milkfat (not less than) (%)	4.50	4.50
Titrable acidity[1] (not less than) (%)	0.10	0.10
(not more than) (%)	0.18	0.18
Bacterial estimate (not more than) (per gm)	50,000	50,000
Scorched particles[1] (mg)	15.0	22.5
Alkalinity of ash[2] (per ml)	125	125
Moisture (not more than) (%)	4.00	4.00
Solubility index[1] (ml)	1.25	15.0

[1] Determination made on reliquified sample.
[2] Ml of 0.1 N HCl per 100 gm.

TABLE 6.6
EXTRA GRADE REQUIREMENTS OF HIGH ACID BUTTERMILK

	%
Butterfat (not less than)	4.50
Titratable acidity[1] (not less than)	0.50
Moisture (not more than)	5.00

[1] Determination on reliquified sample.

Whey from Swiss cheese and Cheddar cheese operations are the usual raw materials for drying. These give "regular" or "sweet" dried whey. Acid wheys are obtained from the processing of cottage cheese and cream cheese, in which a high level (up to 10%) of lactic acid is generated (Table 6.7). Formerly suitable only for animal feeds, acid wheys are now being introduced into certain foods where the lactic acid favorably affects the flavor or function of the product. Fortified whey contains added proteins from materials such as casein, MSNF, and soy extracts. Its principal advantage is the increased water absorption, which is helpful in bread and roll manufacture, etc.

Liquid whey was formerly dried by drum dryers or by conventional one-stage spray drying with the result that scorched and hygroscopic products were obtained. Spray drying is complicated by the approximately 73% lactose contained in whey. Lactose can solidify as anhydrous alpha- or beta-lactose, as the hydrates of alpha- or beta-lactose, or in an amorphous form. Only alpha-lactose hydrate is stable at normal storage temperatures and humidities, and the other four types will eventually change to the most stable form, causing caking and other problems. At the present time, the liquid is dried by a 3-stage process combining evaporating to a 50% solids slurry, spray drying to about 10% moisture, and then tumble drying the powder to less than 5% moisture. This rather complicated procedure yields a stable, relatively nonhygroscopic product with minimal heat damage. The lack of hygroscopicity is due to the formation of the stable form of lactose crystals by drying conditions (Singleton *et al.* 1965).

As shown in the Table 6.7, dried whey has about 12% protein, and this is good quality protein. The remainder is mostly lactose which can improve crust color and add slightly to the sweetness of the finished product. There is a considerable amount of ash which may be detected as a salty or

TABLE 6.7
COMPOSITION AND pH OF DRIED WHEY PRODUCTS

Component	Regular Whey (%)	Fortified Whey (%)	Acid Whey (%)
Protein	12.0	17.5	12.5
Fat	0.9	1.0	0.5
Fiber	0	0	0
Ash	8.0	10.5	11.5
Moisture	4.5	4.5	1.5
Calcium	0.6	1.6	0.6
Phosphorus	0.6	1.8	0.6
Sodium	0.7	0.9	0.7
Lactose	73.0	67.0	64.0
Lactic acid	—	—	4.5
pH of 50% slurry	6.95	7.8	4.5

Source: Adapted from Singleton *et al.* (1965).

metallic flavor. Whey proteins have very adverse effects on bread doughs and other developed doughs, leading to stickiness and loss of strength. These effects can be overcome, or substantially so, by adequate heat treatment of the liquid before it is dried. Singleton *et al.* (1965) claim that the flavor and color are improved when acid whey is added to chocolate bakery products and fermented doughs.

The chief advantage of dried whey over MSNF is, however, the economic advantage. The flavor contributions of skim milk and whey are different, and this can be either advantageous or disadvantageous.

Dried whey which has been modified by partially deionizing it or by removing some of the lactose has recently become available. These materials are relatively high priced and for this reason will be used mostly as nutritional supplements when a very high level of protein is desired.

Other Dried Products

Other dried dairy products which are used to a limited extent in the baking industry are:

Malted Milk Powder.—A mash composed of wheat flour and malted barley is mixed with whole milk or partially skimmed milk and dried, first in a vacuum pan and then in a special vacuum chamber having strong agitators. It is used as a flavor, primarily in icings.

Chocolate Crumb.—A mixture of sucrose, whole milk, and chocolate liquor which is processed in various ways before spray drying or drum drying. It has a flavor different from a simple mixture of the ingredients and is used mostly in ice cream or confections although a small amount goes into bakery goods.

Dried Cream.—Designates dried milk products having 40–70% milk fat, usually 50–60%. It can be spray dried either by regular methods or by foam techniques. The latter are said to give products with less heat damage, a "drier" (i.e., less greasy) body and texture, and superior flowability. Dried creams provide a simple means for introducing butterfat into doughs and batters, and may be useful in icings and frostings.

Dried Sour Cream.—Foam spray drying is also recommended for sour cream to avoid the discoloration which often occurs during regular spray drying. It can be used in doughs, batters, and frostings although, as a rule, the "fresh" (undried) material is preferable if a good source is handy.

CHEESE

Cheese is used in the bakery as an essential ingredient in cheese cake and cheese Danish. In some areas, cheddar-flavored bread attracts a limited but devoted clientele. Possibly cheese could be used more widely than it presently is as a flavor for different kinds of bakery foods.

The wide choice of varieties gives the culinary experimenter many opportunities for new product development.

Cheese begins as the casein curd precipitated from whole or skim milk. A few unusual types are made from whey. In the United States, cow's milk is used almost exclusively, but goat's milk and ewe's milk are processed in other countries.

The curd is precipitated by rennin (an enzyme preparation) or by acid which is either developed in the cheese by lactic acid bacteria or added directly to the milk as a chemical. Combinations of these methods are used. Baker's cheese is an example of an unripened cheese made from skim milk by lactic acid precipitation. It is important that baker's cheese has a soft, dry, pliable curd which can be kneaded or worked almost like a dough, but which is not sticky. The flavor should be mellow and characteristic, definitely not harsh, aromatic, or metallic. The flavor and texture are controlled, as much as they can be controlled, by the adjustment of processing conditions. The cheese generally contains about 74% moisture.

Baker's cheese is often delivered in 30-lb tins or polyethylene-lined 50-lb cartons and can be frozen in these containers and kept for a year or more without appreciable deterioration. It can be dried but seems to lose some of its desirable characteristics as a result, though powders are satisfactory for many purposes and are more uniform than different lots of the fresh material.

Cottage cheese is a soft, unripened white cheese made from skim milk. Curd size, amount of cream added, lactic acid and diacetyl content, and texture vary among manufacturers and among lots. It is usually made by rennet coagulation although there are kinds which are set by lactic fermentation and have a more pronounced flavor. In recent years, coagulation by the direct addition of acid to the milk has been developed. Cottage cheese must contain at least 4% butterfat and not more than 80% moisture, the balance being mostly protein. Although it does not have the textural and handling properties of baker's cheese, cottage cheese has been at times substituted for baker's cheese or used in specialty items.

Ricotta cheese, much used in Italian specialties, is made today from cooked whole milk which has been slightly acidified with acetic acid or lactic acid starter. It has a soft and creamy texture with a pleasant, slightly caramelized flavor. An earlier variety was made by high temperature heating of acidified cheese whey. Fat content may vary from 5 to 13% and moisture from 72 to 78%, while the protein will average about 12%. Importata, which is also familiar to many bakers of Italian type foods, is somewhat similar to ricotta except that it is drier and firmer in texture.

Of all the hundreds of varieties of ripened cheeses, only cheddar is of much importance to bakers. The precipitated curd is pressed into "wheels" or other shapes and allowed to age for weeks or months until bacterial and other changes give it the typical odor and texture. Due to the extreme variability of commercial material, many bakers prefer to buy dehydrated cheese which has been standardized for flavor and color. It is also easier to mix into doughs.

CONSTITUENTS OF MILK

Proteins

The principal proteins of milk are casein, lactalbumin, and lactoglobulin. These probably should be regarded as classes of proteins rather than as single compounds. Casein is the structure-forming, water-binding protein. When coagulated by acids or enzymes it forms the basis for virtually all cheeses. When casein is removed from skim milk, it leaves behind the whey proteins. In bakery products, casein assists in forming the porous structure and is regarded as a toughener. All the proteins of milk appear to be effective as flavor mellowers or blenders. They also participate in the browning reaction of crusts in combination with reducing sugars.

The milk proteins have a high protein efficiency ratio. Because they are relatively high in lysine, they are excellent supplements for cereal proteins (Table 6.8).

Carbohydrates

Evidently the only sugar present in milk is lactose. This is a reducing sugar, a disaccharide containing glucose and galactose moieties. Lactose is considerably less soluble than either sucrose or glucose. It is also much less sweet, being rated by some investigators as only about 16% as sweet as sucrose. In baked goods, it functions as a tenderizer. Since it is a reducing sugar, lactose participates in nonenzymic browning and improves coloration in the oven.

Lipids

As shown in Table 6.9, virtually all of the lipid materials in whole milk are triglycerides of fatty acids. It is this class of compounds which is separated in the butter-making process although a certain proportion does go into buttermilk. Carotenoids, the yellow coloring materials in butterfat, are made up of roughly 90% carotene and 10% xanthophyll. The phospholipids apparently tend to stabilize the milkfat suspension, and have a small emulsifying effect on doughs. The sterols are high molecular weight alcohols, primarily cholesterol, which are soluble in fats.

Vitamins and Minerals

On a wet weight basis or on a caloric content basis, milk is not a particularly good source of vitamins, as shown in Table 6.10. It is common practice to add vitamin D to milk at a level of 400 USP units per quart, to benefit infants.

Milk is an excellent source of calcium and phosphorus, which are especially important in the nutrition of babies (Table 6.11). It is low in iron, averaging about 3.0 ppm. Other elements present but not shown in the Table are copper 0.3 ppm, zinc 3.0 ppm, silicon, 2.0 ppm, and fluorine 0.15 ppm.

The mineral constituents of milk play important roles in the coagulation of proteins during heat processing. Calcium and magnesium facilitate the precipitation of proteins while phosphates and citrates tend to protect them or keep them in suspension during sterilization procedures or other heat treatments. It is common practice to stabilize milk which is going to be canned or otherwise heat shocked by adding, for example, disodium phosphate or citric acid.

TABLE 6.8
AMINO ACID COMPOSITION OF CASEIN AND LACTALBUMIN

Amino Acids	Ranges of Values[1] Casein	Lactalbumin
Glycine	0 – 0.4	0.4
Alanine	1.5 – 1.8	2.4
Valine	7.2 – 7.9	1.0 – 3.3
Leucine	9.3 – 10.5	14 – 19
Phenylalanine	3.2 – 3.9	1.2 – 2.4
Tyrosine	4.5 – 6.5	0.9 – 1.9
Serine	0.4 – 0.5	1.8
Threonine	3.9	5.3
Isoleucine	6.5	0
Cystine	0.25	1.7 – 4.0
Proline	7.6 – 8.7	3.8 – 4.0
Hydroxyproline	0.2	?
Glutamic acid	20.0 – 21.8	10.1 – 12.9
Hydroxyglutamic acid	10.5	10.0
Aspartic acid	1.4 – 4.1	1.0 – 9.3
Tryptophan	1.5 – 2.2	2.7
Arginine	3.8 – 5.2	3.0 – 3.5
Histidine	2.5 – 3.4	1.5 – 2.6
Lysine	6.0 – 7.6	8.4 – 9.9
Methionine	0.4	?
Dodecanoamino acid	0.75	?

Source: Davies (1936).
[1] As percentage of the total amount of each of the protein types.

TABLE 6.9
COMPOSITION OF MILK LIPIDS

Class of Lipid	Range of Occurrence (%)
Triglycerides of fatty acids	97 – 98
Diglycerides	0.25 – 0.48
Monoglycerides	0.016 – 0.038
Keto acid glycerides	0.85 – 1.28
Aldehydogenic glycerides	0.011 – 0.015
Glyceryl ethers	0.011 – 0.023
Free fatty acids	0.10 – 0.44
Phospholipids	0.2 – 1.0
Cerebrosides	0.013 – 0.066
Sterols	0.22 – 0.41
Free neutral carbonyls	0.00001 – 0.00008
Squalene (a triterpene)	0.007
Carotenoids	0.0007 – 0.0009
Vitamin A	0.0006 – 0.0009
Vitamin D	0.00000085 – 0.0000021
Vitamine E	0.0024
Vitamine K	0.0001

Source: Kurtz (1965). See this reference for molecular weight bases, etc.

GENERAL QUALITY TESTS FOR MILK AND MILK PRODUCTS[1]

Each type of milk has its own peculiar, yet important specifications. There are certain of these that are common to all types of milk and are indicative of the overall quality, the quality of the processing, or the quality of the original raw material used. References are cited for each of these methods for specific details of methodology (Anon. 1949).

Butterfat

Commercially, the butterfat content of most liquid dairy products is determined by the Babcock Test. This test involves a volumetric measurement of the fat present in a previously weighed or measured portion of fluid after the digestion of milk proteins by sulfuric acid.

The somewhat more precise technique for butterfat determination involves the ether extraction of the fat with evaporation of the extracting solvent, and drying of the extracted fat in a vacuum oven, with final gravimetric determination of dry fat from a given weight of sample.

Since milkfat or butterfat is the most costly milk constituent, the pricing of any milk product is necessarily based,to a large degree, on its fat content.

---

[1] Mykleby (1960).

TABLE 6.10
VITAMINS IN FRESH MILK [1]

Vitamin	Concentration [2]
Vitamin A	0.34
Carotenoids	0.38
Vitamin D [3]	23.6
Vitamin E	0.6
Vitamin K [4]	1000.0
Ascorbic acid	16.0
Biotin, total	0.035
Choline	130.0
Choline, free	40.0
Folic acid	0.0023
Inositol, total	130.0
Inositol, free	60.0
Nicotinic acid	0.85
Pantothenic acid	3.5
Pyridoxine	0.48
Riboflavin, total	1.57
Thiamine, total	0.42
Thiamine, free	0.23
Vitamin B_{12}	0.0056

[1] See Corbin and Whittier (1965) for the original references.
[2] In milligrams per liter except where noted; midpoint of reported ranges.
[3] USP units per liter.
[4] Dam-Glavind units per liter.

TABLE 6.11
AVERAGE VALUES FOR MILK SALT CONSTITUENTS

Constituent	Content [1]	No. of Samples
Calcium	1.23	824
Magnesium	0.12	759
Phosphorus	0.95	829
Sodium	0.58	491
Potassium	1.41	472
Chlorine	1.19	1579
Sulfur	0.30	80
Citric acid	1.60	307

Source: Compiled by Corbin and Whittier (1965). See their article for original sources.
[1] In grams per liter of whole milk.

Moisture

While vacuum oven techniques, with drying to constant weight, are the most widely accepted techniques for determining moisture content, there are other more rapid methods that may be used under varying conditions, and where official accuracy is not required.

Lactometer.—The lactometer is a hydrometer calibrated to read in terms of the specific gravity of fluid milk products (Anon. 1949). Under constant temperature conditions fluid milk products of known fat content will vary in specific gravity depending on their solids-not-fat and (by difference) their moisture content.

This method is commonly used for production control purposes in fluid and concentrated milk products.

Toluol Distillation.—This method for moisture determination is based on the evaporation of water from a known weight of dried milk product (Anon. 1948). This moisture is, in turn, condensed and measured volumetrically. Toluol having a boiling point forms an azeotrope of about 185°F, and can be used as the heat transfer media for this purpose. This is the commercial test commonly used for moisture determination in dried milks. High moisture content (above 4%) in dried milk products will cause rapid flavor deterioration, possible browning of product, and lumping. Low moisture content (below 4%) of dried milks is, in fact, fundamental to their overall utility value.

Infrared Moisture Meters.—This moisture test depends on heat from an infrared source to rapidly dry materials (usually powders) to constant weight. This technique is widely used in production control because of its rapidity (5–10 min).

Acidity

Essentially all fresh milk products are slightly acidic. This acidity is measured by determining the quantity of standard alkali required to neutralize the acidity in a given quantity of milk sample (Anon. 1949). The value is expressed as percentage of titratable acidity calculated as lactic acid. Acidities above those known to be normal for any specific milk product are indicative of bacterial decomposition of the product; those below normal indicate neutralization.

Bacteria

The bacteriological quality of milk products can be estimated by one or more of three general techniques (Anon. 1948, 1949):

Reduction Tests.—These are tests for bacterial activity which can be applied to raw fluid milks. Results are expressed as hours "reduction time" required for methylene blue or resazurin dyes to be reduced to colorless or varying hues of color. These are tests for bacterial activity rather than bacteria numbers, and are usually used in grading of raw milk supplies.

Microscopic Clump Counts.—This technique involves the staining and actual counting of numbers of bacteria in a certain quantity of milk. These counts are usually expressed as clumps per milliliter (in the case of fluids) or per gram (in the case of powders). This type of analysis will generally give an estimate of total numbers of bacteria in a material, some of which may be live cells and others dead. The microscopic clump count is widely used for appraising the bacterial quality of raw fluid milk and more recently has been applied as a test for determining the processing history of MSNF. High microscopic clump counts of MSNF are generally indicative of poor quality raw milk and/or poor manufacturing practice in processing.

Standard Plate Counts.—The standard plate count is the almost universal industry technique for estimating the living bacterial organisms in raw or pasteurized fluid, concentrated, or dried milk products. Specifically, it estimates the number of organisms that will grow in the standard plate count media at 92°F.

These counts are expressed as organisms per milliliter for fluids or per gram for powders. Since a "plate count" is a measure of viable organisms, it is a quality criterion of particular concern in products and processes where certain types of fermentations, storage conditions, or lengthy shelf-life are involved.

There are numerous other tests for bacterial quality where specific organisms are involved. The coliform test, thermophilic spore counts, and blood agar counts are examples of these. Specifications involving such characteristics are often worked out between the supplier and purchaser of milk products.

Flavor and Odor

The flavor and odor of all sweet milk products should be bland, slightly sweet, and free from acid, feed, and other foreign flavors (Anon. 1948, 1949). Flavor and odor of dried milk products are usually determined on a reconstituted basis. With certain types of highly heated milk powders, cooked flavors of varying degrees are to be expected and may even be desirable.

Scorched Particles

The scorched particle test, formerly referred to as a sediment test, involves the reconstitution of specific quantities of milk powders with filtration through a 1¼-in. diameter cotton pad to determine the presence of burned milk particles or any other extraneous material (Anon. 1948). Modern drying techniques should produce powders with a minimum of scorched particles.

Solubility Index

The solubility index test is performed by reconstituting known quantities of powders under carefully controlled conditions and, after centrifuging to accentuate separation of insoluble material, measuring the quantity of material gathering in the bottom of a centrifuge tube (Anon. 1948).

The solubility index measures the relative quantity of destabilized milk protein (particularly casein) in dried milk powders. A high solubility index can be caused by excessive heat in drying, developed acidity in a raw milk supply, or physiologically unstable milk. Roller process powders are characterized by high solubility indices while spray process powders characteristically have low solubility indices.

SPECIAL TESTS FOR BAKING PERFORMANCE

It has been discussed earlier that dried milk powders used for baking purposes must possess certain qualities beyond the general quality required for Extra Grade Powder. Whey protein denaturation and its associated chemistry, water absorption, and, of course, final baking performance are the special qualities required in powders for bakery use.

HARLAND-ASHWORTH WHEY PROTEIN TEST
(KURAMOTO ET AL. 1959)

Apparatus and Reagents

Test Tubes.—25 by 150 mm lipless, Pyrex or soft glass.

Funnels.—Diameter, 50 mm, stem length, 65 mm; diameter 90 mm, stem length, 65 mm.

Filter Paper.—S&S No. 602, 9 cm, S&S No. 605, 15 cm pleated filter paper.

Cuvettes.—Optically matched.

Pipettes.—Ostwald-Folin type 1, 2, 3, 4, and 5 ml; volumetric 5, 10, 20, and 100 ml.

Balances.—(1) Analytical balance for weighing the 2-gm sample of MSNF (2) torsion balance (± 0.1 gm) to weigh the salt and the 20-gm samples of MSNF.

Water Bath.—Thermostatically controlled to 98.6°F ($\pm 1°$).

Spectrophotometer or Colorimeter.—The spectrophotometer or colorimeter being used by the individual laboratory.

Saturated Sodium Chloride.—Add 1 kg of cheese or butter salt to 2 liters of distilled water and heat the mixture to near boiling, with frequent stirring to insure complete saturation. After cooling to room temperature, filter the solution through S & S 605 pleated filter paper. Do not use sodium chloride containing anticaking agents for the preparation of this reagent or for saturation of the sample.

HCL Solution (10 gm/100 ml).—23 conc HCl, CP reagent, plus 77 ml of distilled water.

Standard Reference Powders.—Low-heat MSNF and high-heat MSNF.[2]

Nephelometer Standard.—N equals 78 (Coleman Instruments, Chicago).

Procedure

Reconstitute 2 gm of MSNF in 20 ml of distilled water in a 25 by 150 mm test tube. Add 8 gm of NaCl, stopper, and place in a water bath at 98.6°F for 30 min. Shake the contents of the tube from 8 to 10 times during the first 15 min of the incubation period, to ensure complete saturation of the sample with NaCl.

Without cooling, shake mixture to facilitate pouring, and filter through S&S No. 602, 9 cm filter paper. Refilter through the same filter paper if the first portion of the filtrate is cloudy. Collect approximately 5 ml of filtrate.

Pipette a 1 ml aliquot of the filtrate into a cuvette. Dilute the filtrate with 10 ml of saturated NaCl solution. Stopper the cuvette with a rubber stopper and mix by slowly inverting once.

Add 2 drops (delivered from a 5 ml volumetric pipette) of the HCl solution, to develop the turbidity. Stopper the cuvette and mix the acid with the diluted filtrate by slowly inverting twice. Care should be taken to prevent the formation of foam.

Within 5–10 min after adding the acid, invert the cuvette once again and

---

[2] Available, together with their respective serum protein nitrogen values (Kjeldahl), from American Dry Milk Institute, Chicago.

measure the turbidity in the instrument used in the particular laboratory, with the wavelength set at 420 mμ. Adjust the instrument to 100% transmittance with a diluted casein-free filtrate made by diluting 1 ml of the original filtrate with 10 ml of saturated NaCl solution.

Make duplicate determinations on each filtrate and, for each transmittance reading, obtain a value for serum protein nitrogen from the standard curve. Take an average of the duplicates and report as milligrams serum protein nitrogen per gram MSNF.

Duplicates should agree within 2% transmittance. If they do not, another pair should be analyzed and the average of the four determinations used for the final value.

Preparation of Standard Curve.—Reconstitute 20 gm (-0.1 gm) each of the standard low-heat MSNF and the standard high-heat MSNF with exactly 200 ml of distilled water in 500 ml Erlenmeyer flasks.

Saturate each reconstituted milk with 80 gm of NaCl, stopper the flasks, shake for 1 min, and incubate at 98.6°F for 30 min. Shake the mixtures from 8 to 10 times during the first 15 min to insure complete saturation, allowing them to remain undisturbed for the remainder of the incubation period.

Without cooling or further agitation, except that necessary to permit pouring, filter the mixture through S&S 605, 15 cm pleated filter paper. In cases where the first portion of the filtrate comes through cloudy, refilter through the same filter. Continue filtration until approximately 100 ml of filtrate have been collected. Cover the filters with a watch glass during the filtration, to prevent excessive evaporation.

Pipette proportions of low-heat and high-heat filtrates into 25 by 150 mm test tubes as follows:

Tube No.	Low-heat Filtrate, Ml	High-heat Filtrate, Ml
1	10	0
2	8	2
3	6	4
4	4	6
5	2	8
6	0	10

Stopper the tubes containing the combined filtrates and mix by slowly inverting the tubes twice.

Pipette 1 ml aliquots of the mixed filtrates into cuvettes, dilute with 10 ml of saturated NaCl, and develop the turbidity as described previously.

Plot the standard curve, using serum protein nitrogen (SPN) values (Kjeldahl) per gram of powder for the horizontal axis and percent transmittance as the vertical axis on 8.5 by 11 in. graph paper (1 mg SPN equals 1 in., 10% transmittance equals 1 in.). It is essential that the difference in transmittance readings between the low-heat and high-heat filtrates be as large as possible, preferably at least 35%.

Day to day reproducibility of the instrument may be checked by use of a nephelometer standard (N equals 78, Coleman Instruments).

Interpretation of Results

MSNF for which the Harland-Ashworth Whey Protein Nitrogen test is specific, will contain on the average 9.12 mg of serum protein per gram of solids. The serum protein content of raw skim milk in different sections of the country can vary between 8.52 and 9.96 mg per gram solids. Since denaturation of this whey protein fraction is associated with good baking quality, a high degree of denaturation and low level of undenatured serum protein is desirable for a yeast raised dough type of product. Opinions among technologists vary as to specific undenatured whey protein values required in the baking industry. From experience, it is apparent that undenatured whey protein values of 1.0 mg/gm or lower are generally very adequate. Some data (Ashworth and Krueger 1951) would indicate that values of 2.0 mg/gm or below are satisfactory for most bread making purposes. It should be stated, however, that as whey protein denaturation values drop from 2.0 mg to 1.0 mg there is a definite tendency for higher absorption values in the MSNF. Tentative standards for "high heat" or bakery grade MSNF have been established by the American Dry Milk Institute as 1.5 mg or less.

In lieu of the laboratory bake test, the Harland Ashworth Whey Protein Nitrogen test is, perhaps, the most widely used technique for evaluating baking quality of MSNF. It is used as a control testing procedure by most large producers of MSNF, as well as by technologists in the baking industry. It is natural, therefore, that it has become a basis for bakery grade specifications in many segments of both industries.

MSNF processed with low temperature treatments will show undenatured whey protein nitrogen values in the order of 6.0–8.0 mg/gm, indicating the rather substantial difference existing between high-heat and low-heat MSNF by this analysis.

The Harland-Ashworth Whey Protein Nitrogen test is applicable to both spray and roller process MSNF. It is also being used to some degree on dried buttermilk solids for evaluating baking quality though no data have been published supporting this application as of this date.

HOFFMAN-DALBY FARINOGRAPH TEST

Equipment

Brabender Farinograph. Laboratory scale or balance.

Method

The absorption of a spring wheat flour is determined by titrating a 300-gm sample ("as is" basis) with water until a maximum dough development of 500 Brabender units is obtained (Hoffman *et al.* 1948). Place 150 gm of flour, 150 gm of the MSNF in the farinograph mixer, and add the amount of water computed as follows:

Let F be the absorption of the flour in percentage based on the original titration of the flour.

Courtesy of Land O' Lakes Creameries

FIG. 6.3. A LABORATORY FOR ROUTINE ANALYSIS OF MILK POWDERS

Then the percentage of water to be added to the mixture will be:

$$\frac{F + 65}{2}$$

(Thus an absorption of 65% is arbitrarily assigned to the milk.)

An average sample of MSNF when mixed with flour will reach the 500 line immediately, but within 30 sec or so the mixture will soften. After 10–14 min mixing, the pointer will again reach the 500 line. Then add more water in 1.5 ml portions, to hold the pointer on the 500 line during further mixing until maximum absorption is measured. Let X be the final absorption of the mixture; the absorption of the MSNF is:

$$2\left(X - \frac{F}{2}\right)$$

Record two factors: (1) development period (the time required in minutes for mixture to reach a consistency of 500 with the original addition of water); and (2) final absorption of milk.

Spray Powder

The same basic procedure is used for spray as for roller MSNF except that an original 40% absorption is substituted for the 65% absorption for roller powder.

Interpretation of Results

Roller Process Powder.—Hoffman *et al.* (1948) reported the following tentative baking quality ratings of MSNF from results of farinograph tests:

Development Period	Percent Absorption	Rating
Under 10 min	Over 70	Excellent
10–12 min	Over 70	Good
12–16 min	Over 70	Fairly good
12–16 min	67 to 70	Fair
Over 16 min	Under 67	Poor

These general standards have been used by certain segments of the baking industry as purchase specifications for roller process MSNF. However, little substantiating evidence has been published supporting this classification.

Spray Process Powder.—Specific farinograph absorption values for spray process MSNF have not been published. It is known, however, that low-heat MSNF will exhibit absorptions well below 40%. High-heat powders will vary from about 40% to as high as 60%. Values of 45–50% are common for high-heat powders. Values of 50–55% represent spray process powders of relatively high absorption. When absorption values of over 55% are reached, this represents spray powders of exceedingly high absorption. These high absorptions are often, though not always, reflected in somewhat high solubility index readings. It is felt by many that this high solubility index is not of great significance in bakery type powder.

BROOKFIELD VISCOSITY TEST (NAIR 1959)

Apparatus Required

(1) Gram scale; (2) Waring blendor; (3) graduated cylinder (500 ml); (4) spatula; (5) suction flasks (1000 ml); (6) vacuum pump and trap setup; (7) 400 ml Berzelius beakers; (8) Brookfield Viscosimeter Model LVF; (9) beakers (1000 ml); and (10) watch glasses for 1000 ml beakers.

Reagents Required

(1) Distilled water; and (2) defoaming agent (diglycol laurate).

Method

(1) Weigh 143 gm of powder; (2) measure 333 ml of distilled water at 77°F and add water to Waring blendor; (3) add milk powder; (4) mix for 10 sec; (5) stop mixer and scrape down adhering powder from the sides of the tumbler with a spatula; (6) mix for 2 more minutes; (7) pour mixture into a 1-liter beaker and cover with a watch glass; (8) place in a water bath at 77°F for 2 hr; (9) just before 2-hr period ends, remove foam with tablespoon; (10) pour remaining liquid carefully into the liter suction flask and add 2 drops of diglycol laurate; (11) place flask under full vacuum for a few minutes; hold vacuum treatment to a minimum to avoid moisture loss; about 10 min is usually sufficient; (12) transfer sufficient liquid to the 400 ml beaker to reach notch on No. 1 spindle; (13) place beaker in 77°F water bath while taking readings; (14) level viscosimeter and allow to warm

up before taking readings; (15) when changing speeds have motor running and hold clutch lever down; and (16) readings to be taken at all speeds, but reported at 60 rpm speed only.

Calculations

(1) Readings made on 100 scale with No. 1 spindle. (2) Multiply reading at 12 rpm by 5; 30 rpm by 2; 60 rpm by 1.

Interpretation

This viscosity test measures the viscosity of 30% solids reconstituted spray process MSNF. Its application for baking purposes depends upon the significance of higher viscosities in a final prepared dry mix, or other bakery product. The viscosity of low-heat MSNF will fall in the range of 12 centipoises or below; high-heat MSNF will usually vary between 15 and 25 centipoises. High absorption high-heat MSNF may go up to 30 centipoises or higher by this test.

There is no universal agreement among bakery technologists regarding the significance of absorption values except possibly that relatively high absorption values are good. Of greater significance in many larger bakery operations is uniformity of absorption so as to have reasonable assurance of consistent shop performance from batch to batch and from one lot of dry milk to another.

The Laboratory Bakery Test

Since it is impractical to evaluate MSNF in a baking test under commercial conditions, a laboratory scale baking test possibly comes the closest to approaching this goal. Commercial baking procedures vary in different plants because of differences in methods, equipment, and customer preference in different areas of the country. For this reason it is felt the ideal laboratory baking test is one that will accentuate the weakness in milk which is of greatest concern to any specific type of end use.

As a general guide for an experimental baking test, the American Dry Milk Institute (Anon. 1961) has suggested the following for the straight dough or sponge dough method.

The only equipment needed for making such experimental baking tests is the small (C-10) Hobart mixer equipped with a dough hook, a small gram scale, and two or more gallon jars or cans. The gram scale is recommended due to the fact that small amounts of some supplemental ingredients must be weighed. The experimental formula can easily be translated into the commercial size formula by substituting pounds for grams.

In making the test, it is customary to make two separate doughs as nearly alike as possible. In the experimental doughs more yeast and yeast food are used, and the doughs are usually made about one degree warmer than would be the case in commercial procedures. The following formulas and methods have been successfully employed by many bakers.

MILK PRODUCTS

Straight Dough Formula

	Grams
Flour	600
Water (variable)	406
Yeast	15
Yeast food	3
Sugar	30
Salt	12
Shortening	24
MSNF	36

If malt is being used, use same percentage as currently used in regular commercial-size doughs.

Method.–Mix the same as regular doughs, except about one degree warmer. Place the mixed dough in a tall type, one gallon jar or can in fermentation room. When the dough recedes upon pressing with the fingers (about 2½ hr), scale into 2 pieces to make 1-lb loaves. Allow about 20 min recovery time and then mold into loaves. Give regular proof.

Some bakers scale the loaves and pass them through the rounding machines, mark them properly and send them over the overhead proofer and through the molding machine. They are properly labeled, placed in the proof box, and baked in the oven with regular run of bread.

Sponge Dough Formula

Sponge:	Grams
Flour	390
Water	230
Yeast	12
Yeast food	3

Mix at about 78°–80°F and allow to ferment for 5 hr.

Dough:	Grams
Flour	210
Water (variable)	175
Sugar	30
Salt	12
Shortening	24
MSNF	36

If malt is being used, use the same percentage as currently used in regular commercial-size doughs.

Place sponge in mixer bowl and add the water. Put about half the dough flour on top of the water and then add all the other ingredients, except the shortening. Mix into a smooth batter and then add the remainder of the flour and the shortening. Mix until smooth and dry.

Mix the dough at about 80°F. Allow to rest 15–20 min. Scale into loaves. Follow the same procedure as indicated with straight doughs. Loaves may either be hand molded or passed through the rounder and overhead proofer.

In performing the bake test any number of adjustments may be necessary to adapt conditions to any particular shop practice. Bromate levels for example, should be adjusted and the correct quantity of water for any specific powder must be used. A good quality milk powder will produce a dough which remains easy to handle throughout the baking process, and which produces a good loaf volume and quality score. For comparative purposes a known poor and good quality dry milk powder should be included in each day's test.

If these tests are done carefully, a very good indication of the baking performance of the milk powder will be provided.

BIBLIOGRAPHY

ANON. 1948. The grading of nonfat dry milk solids. Am. Dry Milk Inst. Bull. *911*.
ANON. 1949. Laboratory Manual. Methods of Analysis of Milk and Its Products. Milk Industry Foundation.
ANON. 1960. Standard methods for the examination of dairy products. Am. Public Health Assoc., New York.
ANON. 1961. Breads made with nonfat dry milk solids. Am. Dry Milk Inst. Bull. *107*.
ANON. 1963. Composition of foods. U.S. Dept. Agr. Handbook *8*.
ANON. 1965. Standards for grades for the dry milk industry. Am. Dry Milk Inst. Bull. *916*.
ANON. 1971. Standards for grades of dry milks including methods of analysis. Am. Dry Milk Institute, Chicago,
ASHWORTH, U. S., and KRUEGER, G. J. 1951. Chemical factors affecting the baking quality of nonfat milk solids. IV. Minimum heat treatment for maximum loaf volume. Cereal Chem. *28*, 145-152.
CHOI, R. P. 1959. Dry milk—processing for specific uses. Cereal Sci. Today *4*, 39-42.
CORBIN, E. A., and WHITTIER, E. O. 1965. The composition of milk. *In* Fundamentals of Dairy Chemistry, B. H. Webb and A. H. Johnson (Editors). Avi Publishing Co., Westport, Conn.
DAVIES, W. L. 1936. The Chemistry of Milk. Van Nostrand Reinhold Co., New York. (Out of print.)
GREENBANK, G. R., STEINBARGER, M. C., DEYSHER, E. F., and HOLM, G. E. 1927. The effect of heat treatment of skim milk upon the baking quality of the evaporated and dried products. J. Dairy Sci. *10*, 335-342.
HALL, C. W., and HEDRICK, T. I. 1966. Drying Milk and Milk Products. Avi Publishing Co., Westport, Conn.
HEINEMANN, B. 1963. Manufacturing standards of the dry milk industry. Cereal Sci. Today *8*, 7-8.
HOFFMAN, C., SCHWEITZER, T. R., SPOTTS, E. D., and DALBY, G. 1948. Evaluation of the baking properties of roller process nonfat dry milk solids by a farinograph procedure. Cereal Chem. *25*, 385-390.
KURAMOTO, A., JENNESS, R., COULTER, S. T., and CHOI, R. P. 1959. Standardization of the Harland-Ashworth test for whey protein nitrogen. J. Dairy Sci. *42*, 28-38.
KURTZ, F. E. 1965. The lipids of milk: composition and properties. *In* Fundamentals of Dairy Chemistry, B. H. Webb and A. H. Johnson (Editors). Avi Publishing Co., Westport, Conn.
LAUCK, R. M., and TUCKER, J. W. 1962. Functional properties of calcium and protein in nonfat dry milk used in food products. Cereal Sci. Today *7*, 314, 316, 322.
LIPKA, D. H. 1963. Dried milk products in prepared mixes. Cereal Sci. Today *8*, 10, 12.
MYKLEBY, R. W. 1960. Milk and milk derivatives. *In* Bakery Technology and Engineering, S. A. Matz (Editor). Avi Publishing Co., Westport, Conn.

SINGLETON, A. D., HANEY, H. N., and HABIGHURST, A. B. 1965. Adapting dried whey products to present-day bakery operations. Cereal Sci. Today *10*, 53-55, 62.

SKOVHOLT, O., and BAILEY, C. H. 1932. The effect of temperature and of the inclusion of dry skimmilk upon the properties of doughs as measured with the farinograph. Cereal Chem. *9*, 523-530.

SWORTFIGUER, M. F. 1963. Nonfat dry milk in dough systems. Cereal Sci. Today *8*, 15-16.

WEBB, B. H. 1963. Use of dairy products in bakery goods. Cereal Sci. Today *8*, 6-7.

WEBB, B. H., and JOHNSON, A. H. 1965. Fundamentals of Dairy Chemistry. Avi Publishing Co., Westport, Conn.

WEBB, B. H., and WHITTIER, E. O. 1970. Byproducts from Milk, 2nd Edition. Avi Publishing Co., Westport, Conn.

CHAPTER 7

EGGS

INTRODUCTION

Eggs affect the texture of bakery products as a result of their emulsifying, leavening, tenderizing, and binding actions. They add color and nutritional value and, in many cases, desirable flavor. They are essential for obtaining the characteristic organoleptic qualities of most cakes, and are traditional in many types of rich yeast-raised goods.

There is no Federal definition or Standard of Identity for shell eggs, but Title 7 CFR part 56 of the Agricultural Marketing Act controls interstate distribution of this commodity. *U.S. Standard Grades and Weight Classes for Shell Eggs* as well as *Regulations Governing the Grading and Inspection of Egg Products* are quality guides in the absence of a Standard of Identity for shell eggs.

The U.S. Food and Drug Administration has issued *Definitions and Standards of Identity for Eggs and Egg Products* (Anon. 1966) which defines: (1) Liquid eggs, mixed eggs, liquid whole eggs, mixed whole eggs. (2) Frozen eggs, frozen whole eggs, frozen mixed eggs. (3) Dried eggs, dried whole eggs. (4) Egg yolks, liquid egg yolks, yolks, liquid yolks. (5) Frozen yolks, frozen egg yolks. (6) Dried egg yolks, dried yolks. (7) Egg whites, liquid egg whites, liquid egg albumen. (8) Frozen egg whites, frozen egg albumen. (9) Dried egg whites, egg white solids, dried egg albumen, egg albumen solids.

The different terms used in each of the above categories are synonyms, as far as the Standards are concerned. These egg products must be prepared from the egg of the domestic hen, i.e., duck eggs and the like cannot be used as they have been in the past. Small amounts of certain additives such as monosodium phosphate and sodium silicoaluminate are permitted by the Standards if they are declared on the label. In addition, there are various nonstandard combinations of eggs with other ingredients usually intended to improve the functional characteristics.

In Table 7.1 are listed most of the egg products offered to the bakery trade. Individual suppliers may offer combination products other than those listed, however, and may tailor a product to individual requirements if the order is large enough. The conversion factors are approximate, of necessity, since the raw material itself is variable in solids con-

EGGS

TABLE 7.1
TYPES OF EGG PRODUCTS AVAILABLE TO BAKERS

Type	Container	Conversion Factor[1]
Shell eggs, fresh or storage	30-doz case	0.84
Bulk liquid eggs	Tank truck	
Whites		1.00
Yolks		1.00
Whole Eggs		1.00
Frozen egg products	Friction-lid metal cans	
Whites		1.00
Whole eggs		1.00
Whole eggs plus extra yolk		1.00
Yolks		1.00
Whole eggs plus corn syrup[3]		1.11
Egg yolks plus sugar[3]		1.11
Egg yolks plus salt[3]		1.11
Whole eggs plus salt[3]		1.11
Dried egg products[2]	Bags, boxes, and drums	
Whites, spray dried		7.24
Whites, pan dried (flake albumen)		7.00
Whole eggs, standard		3.70
Whole eggs, glucose-free		3.70
Yolk solids, standard		2.72
Yolk solids, glucose-free		2.72
Whole egg solids, plus sugar[4]		2.33
Whole egg solids plus corn syrup solids[4]		2.33
Yolks plus sugar[4]		1.49
Yolks plus corn syrup[4]		1.49

[1] Multiply pounds of product by this factor to obtain equivalent pounds of bulk liquid egg, white, or yolk.
[2] In addition, dried whole eggs and dried yolks (any style) can be procured in free-flowing form.
[3] Based on frozen product containing 10% (dried weight) of carbohydrate, this will vary depending on supplier.
[4] Based on dried products containing 33% carbohydrate. May vary among different suppliers.

tent. The factors are suitable for converting to equivalent amounts of egg, yolk, or white solids and are not intended to have any relationship to functional efficiency of the materials, since this is dependent upon the method of preparation, storage conditions, and other factors which are not predictable.

COMPOSITION

Liquid whole eggs and the frozen and dried products derived from them vary in composition depending upon the characteristics of the shell eggs used in the breaking operation. Some of this variation is the result of differing proportions of white and yolk in the eggs, and may be affected by the strain of chicken and its nutritional history. Small eggs from pullets tend to have a lower proportion of yolk, while the small eggs laid by old hens have a greater proportion of yolk to white, as compared to larger eggs. The typical composition of liquid or frozen whole egg and dried whole egg is given in Table 7.2. Many specifications for frozen

TABLE 7.2
COMPOSITION OF EGG PRODUCTS

	Liquid Whole Egg (%)	Dried Whole Egg (%)	Liquid Egg White (%)	Dried Egg White (%)	Liquid Egg Yolk (%)	Dried Egg Yolk (%)
Solids	27	96	14	95	51	96
Protein	13.3	47.2	11.6	78.6	16.7	31.4
Fat	11.5	40.8	—	—	31.6	59.4
Nitrogen-free extract	1.10	3.90	0.80	5.42	1.2	2.25
Glucose	0.32	1.07	0.40	2.71	0.21	0.40
Ash	1.00	3.55	0.80	5.42	1.50	2.82
Lecithin	1.52	5.41	—	—	4.18	7.84

whole egg require a minimum solids content of 26%, and some years ago this was valid. Recent changes in handling practices, including more rapid transfer of eggs to breaking stations with resultant decrease in water loss by evaporation, and breeding for larger eggs (which results in a greater proportion of white to yolk) has led to a decrease in the solids content. Forsythe (1963) recommended lowering of solids requirements in whole eggs to 25%.

When egg white and yolk are carefully separated in the laboratory under ideal conditions, about 65% of the total can be recovered as egg white. In commercial breaking and separating operations, however, the albumen is found to comprise about 55% of the total edible portion. The lower commercial yield is almost entirely due to the adherence of some white to the yolks in the high speed operation. Thus the 45% solids egg yolk commonly used by bakeries contains approximately 14.5% white, and the 43% solids yolk contains almost 20% white.

Accidental contamination of white with yolk during the breaking operation results in decreased whipping response in albumen when used in meringues and marshmallow. It is also possible that some yolk lipid migrates into the albumen during storage of intact eggs. There are other changes during storage which effect the proteins, and, consequently, the foaming ability of the egg white. In spray-dried albumen, the intense shearing forces to which the fibrils of protein are subjected may also affect whipping quality.

The individual protein constituents of egg white, as reported by three different groups of investigators, are listed in Table 7.3.

The lipids of egg, all of which are present in the yolk are composed of glycerides and phospholipids in the approximate ratio of 2:1. About 30% of the fatty acids in the glycerides are saturated. The phospholipids, which are responsible for the emulsifying properties of yolk, are made up of about 60% lecithin, 25% cephalin, and 15% "others." There is also a significant amount of cholesterol in egg yolk.

TABLE 7.3
PROTEIN COMPOSITION OF EGG WHITE

	Percentage of Egg White Solids
Ovalbumin	54.0
Conalbumin	13.0
Ovomucoid	11.0
Lysozyme	3.5
Ovomucin	1.5
Flavoprotein (apoprotein)	0.8
Ovoinhibitor	0.1
Avidin	0.05
Unidentified proteins, mainly globulins	8.0

Source: Feeney (1964).

The color of whole eggs and egg yolks depends to a very great extent upon the plant pigments which are in the feed the chickens consume. Therefore, color may vary with the season, source, method of processing, and other factors. If the premium for dark yellow yolks is sufficiently high to justify the added cost, the egg producer may add supplements high in xanthophylls to the feed mixture.

The glucose in egg white leads to the development of off-flavors and darkening during storage as a result of the nonenzymatic browning, or Maillard reactions which occur between this reducing sugar and the amino groups of the proteins. In the manufacture of dried albumen or dried whole egg, glucose is removed by fermentation (using yeast or bacteria) or

TABLE 7.4
AMINO ACIDS IN EGG PROTEINS

	Percentage of Total Protein		
	Whole Egg	Egg White	Egg Yolk
Arginine	6.7	6.3	7.2
Aspartic acid	5.8	6.0	5.5
Cystine	2.2	2.5	1.7
Glutamic acid	12.3	12.4	12.1
Glycine	3.7	4.0	3.5
Histidine	2.7	2.7	2.9
Isoleucine	7.0	7.2	6.9
Leucine	8.5	8.5	8.5
Lysine	6.8	6.6	7.2
Methionine	3.3	4.1	2.4
Phenylalanine	5.4	6.1	4.6
Serine	7.7	6.9	8.9
Threonine	5.5	5.2	6.1
Tryptophan	1.9	2.0	1.8
Tyrosine	4.6	4.6	4.6
Valine	8.2	8.8	7.3

Source: Adapted from a compilation by Everson and Souders (1957). See their article for original sources.

by enzymatic oxidation using a commercial preparation of enzymes. Albumen treated by these techniques is called stabilized.

The percentage of glucose in yolk is about half that in white and is less of a storage problem, perhaps because staling or spoilage usually occurs as a result of reactions other than nonenzymatic browning, and the odors, tastes, and colors, resulting from these other reactions obscure changes involving glucose. Stabilized yolks can, however, be prepared by procedures similar to those used for stabilizing whites.

Although egg white is low in vitamin content, the yolk is a good source of many of these nutrient factors, particularly A, D, E, folic acid, biotin, and choline.

BACTERIOLOGY OF EGG PRODUCTS

Egg products are very susceptible to contamination by microorganisms, including pathogenic species. These organisms can originate from the egg itself, especially the shell exterior, from egg handlers, from equipment, from containers, and from the air. If the liquid products are held at room temperature, proliferation can occur very rapidly. Because of the health hazards involved, it is important to establish and enforce bacteriological standards for the eggs used in bakery products. Reasonable standards include maximums of 10,000 viable bacteria per gram in all frozen and dried egg products except for frozen whites where a limit of 50,000 per gram is more realistic. Yeasts, molds, and coliforms should be restricted to less than 10 per gram.

In the last few years, there has been much concern about contamination of egg products with Salmonella. This is a microorganism which can cause food poisoning (rarely fatal). According to regulations effective June 1, 1966 all egg products must be free of viable Salmonellae organisms when tested by a specified procedure. Although the motivation for this regulation is certainly highly commendable, its implementation has caused certain practical difficulties to users of frozen and dried egg products. Whole egg and egg yolk can be pasteurized in high temperature-short time equipment with little loss of functionality, but treatment of albumen in a similar manner leads to deleterious changes in whipping properties. In the last few years, modification in heat-treating methods and the use of additives has greatly reduced the loss of foam-forming abilities due to pasteurizing, but it is generally conceded that egg whites treated so as to be Salmonella-free lose some of their capacity for being whipped.

Banwart and Ayres (1956) first showed that it was possible to significantly reduce numbers of Salmonella by holding albumen of less than 6% moisture at 122°F. The beating properties actually improved somewhat. The present goal is to completely eliminate these microorganisms from the eggs.

Atkin (1966) discussed at some length the effect of pasteurizing egg products on their baking response. He pointed out that pasteurization is not new as applied to whole eggs or fortified whole eggs, but not until recently were practical methods developed for treating egg whites.

There are three general methods of pasteurizing egg products:

(1) One method is particularly applicable to whole eggs. It is based on application of carefully controlled heat for a given time (140° to 143°F for 3.6 min). A slight reduction in viscosity of thawed product is frequently observed.

(2) The hydrogen peroxide-catalase method is more suitable for egg whites. The hydrogen peroxide is added to the egg white, and the mixture is heated in the range of 125°-130°F for 3½ min, then cooled. When the mixture is cool, catalase is added. A slight reduction in viscosity and some white clumps result.

(3) There is another method which is applicable to egg whites. Aluminum sulfate and lactic acid are added, the eggs are heated to 140°-143°F for 3.5-4 min and cooled. There is a reduction in viscosity, some white clumps appear, and turbidity develops in the liquid phase.

Atkin concludes that performance of treated whites in finished products is similar to that of untreated whites, though adjustments in processing conditions may be necessary, especially in products whose structure is based primarily on an egg white foam.

The rapidity with which egg white can be whipped, the maximum specific volume of the foam, and the stability of the foam can be altered for the better by certain additives. It has been known for a long time that lowered pH improves these functional properties of egg albumen. The type of acid used to accomplish this effect is a factor in the degree of improvement, that is, the anionic portion of the additive as well as the hydrogen ion determines its effectiveness. Citric acid and lactic acid seem to be preferred additives. When dry mixes are made up, phosphoric acid salts or tartaric acid salts can be used.

Surface-active agents also influence whipping properties. Triethyl citrate and various anionic surface-active agents (as some common detergents) are effective. Apparently, these additives act to partially overcome the effect of adventitious yolk fat as well as to increase the ease of surface denaturation, permitting the more rapid formation of a stiff foam.

FREEZING AND DRYING OF EGGS

Frozen Eggs

At one time, it was necessary for bakers to break their own eggs, but this time-consuming and often unsanitary practice is now very rare, and bakeries of all sizes and degrees of complexity buy eggs in frozen or dried form. At least one very large bakery uses a bulk handling system with chilled liquid egg products delivered daily from the supplier. Egg whites, egg yolks, whole eggs, and whole eggs fortified with yolks are available in either dried or frozen forms. There are also many combination products consisting of one or more of the raw materials combined with additives such as salt, sugar, corn syrup, or cereal or leguminous materials (such as defatted soy flour).

The usual container for frozen eggs is a 30-lb friction-lid tin. Eggs to be frozen are broken and separated in the usual manner, the chalazae and other fibrous and shell material are separated by sieves or strainers of various types, additives such as sugar or salt are mixed into the mass, the mixture is cooled to about 40°F by plate heat exchangers, and the final product is filled into tins which are quickly transferred to a blast freezer.

Recent announcements by leading purveyors of frozen egg products have informed users of the availability of these ingredients in small, easily disposable packages. These containers, usually either the plastic-coated milk carton type or plastic bags, should also be easier to thaw than the 30-lb tins and are certainly easier to handle and dispense from. It is to be expected that the new containers will ultimately displace cylindrical cans even though their cost may be slightly higher.

Drying Methods

There are four main types of drying procedures which have been used for preparing dried egg albumen:

(1) Spray drying is by far the most common method of dehydrating egg whites in this country, and it yields a product which is entirely satisfactory for most purposes if the raw material is of good quality and the drying conditions are closely controlled.

In the past, there has been some controversy over the relative merits of spray-dried and pan-dried albumen for meringues and other foam-based products. It was observed that the early spray-dried egg white sometimes had whipping properties very inferior to those of the pan-dried product. Improvements in dehydration technology (relating particularly to atomization techniques), acidification, and use of surface-active additives now make it possible to produce a spray-dried albumen that is superior in performance to fresh egg white.

(2) Foam drying is similar to pan drying, but the layer of wet material is thicker and the albumen is foamed by whipping before it is placed in the drier.

(3) Pan drying is the original process and was used for many years in the Orient before being practiced here. In this procedure, a thin layer of egg white placed in a shallow pan or tray is warmed and exposed to a current of warm air. The crystals which result may be ground to a pow-

der before being packaged. The product is used mostly in the confectionery industry but is suitable for some bakery products.

(4) Freeze drying: the egg white is first frozen and then subjected to vacuum to remove the water vapor. This technique can be made to yield a very high quality product with virtually no detectable heat damage, but it is relatively expensive.

For structure-forming functions in doughs, as in cookies and cakes not based on a meringue, retention of whipping quality is of minor consequence.

So far as the relative quality of frozen and dried eggs is concerned, there is no simple answer. Both frozen and dried eggs deteriorate in storage at a rate dependent upon the conditions. Initial quality (before freezing or drying) is very important. Generally, frozen eggs retain more of the original properties. Powdered eggs are unquestionably more convenient to use and to store. The thawing and dispensing of frozen eggs can lead to sanitation problems. Reconstitution and sequence of addition are critical factors in use of dried eggs.

There are many combination products available in the frozen egg and dried egg categories. These may contain corn syrup or syrup solids or cereal adjuncts such as soy flour. These added ingredients are supposed to improve handling properties, functionality, or other features of the base egg. In low-moisture cookie doughs, it is difficult to obtain uniform dispersion of dry yolks (they tend to ball up), and the yolk and soy flour blends are of value here. Each user must decide whether or not these combinations of ingredients offer any advantages under the conditions existing in his plant. Generally speaking, the undiluted products are to be preferred for the simple reason that, dollar for dollar, more units of active ingredient can be obtained in this form.

Agglomerated egg albumen has become available in the last few years. This material has substantially the same properties as other dried albumen except that it can be dispersed more readily in water. One brand contains about 10% lactose, used as the agglomerating agent, and 0.1% sodium lauryl sulfate, a surfactant added to improve the wettability. If dispersability is a problem in your processing method, agglomerated albumen could be the answer and the slight added cost per unit of active ingredient might be offset by the more nearly complete functioning of the albumen.

Although it is possible to reconstitute dried egg products to the basis of the original moisture content, it is more convenient (and for most purposes just as acceptable) to use standard ratios.

Three pounds of water added to 1 lb of whole egg solids is the recommended ratio to yield the equivalent of 4 lb of liquid whole eggs. One part of dried yolk plus 1.25 parts water is the approximate equivalent of

2.25 parts of fresh or frozen yolk. Addition of 7 parts water to 1 part spray-dried albumen yields 8 parts of liquid white.

Tests for protein, fat, total solids, and inorganic matter are common tests applied to egg products. Obviously, odor, taste, and color must be representative of a typical fresh egg. For the baker who does not have facilities to make elaborate tests of the functional properties of each batch of egg products he receives, a sensitive performance test based upon the most critical piece in his formula book must be devised. The next best solution is to buy from a reliable supplier and trust in his quality control. Egg products packed in continuously inspected plants are identified by the U.S. Dept. of Agri. emblem on the package. This is an indication of excellent initial sanitary quality and the absence of inferior materials. It is not, of course, any protection against storage deterioration. Eggs are standard items of commerce and any material offered substantially below published market prices is undoubtedly inferior in some manner. Some bargain frozen eggs offered to bakers in the past contained a large proportion of nonfertile hatchery rejects.

In bakery products, egg yolks contribute color, flavor, shortness due to the fatty materials, and an emulsifying action. Egg whites contribute principally structural qualities which are expressed as appearance or texture characteristics. If of good quality, egg whites should cause little change in flavor although they apparently can act to blend off or ameliorate harsh odors and tastes. Whole eggs, and blends of whites and yolks in other than normal proportions, will have properties intermediate between those of the separated components, except that any amount of yolk will prevent formation of meringue-type foams from albumen.

A booklet describing all of the common test methods for egg products has been compiled by the Institute of American Poultry Industries (Anon. 1968). Included are details of sampling methods, test for total solids, fat by acid hydrolysis, NEPA yolk color, AOAC yolk color, salt content, sugar content, whip test for liquid egg white, whipping test for dried albumen, surface film method for percentage of yolk in whites, Stuart solubility index, percentage of insolubles of dried albumen in aqueous solution, palatability, acidity of ether extract, bacterial plate count, coliform count, *Escherichia coli*, yeast and mold count, *Staphylococcus* count, direct microscopic count, and *Salmonella*.

BIBLIOGRAPHY

ANON. 1966. Definitions and Standards of Identity for Eggs and Egg Products. U.S. Food, Drug, and Cosmetic Act Regulations, Part 42. U.S. FDA, Washington, D.C.

ANON. 1968. Chemical and bacteriological methods for the examination of egg products. Inst. Am. Poultry Ind., Chicago.

ANON. 1969. Egg pasteurization manual. U.S. Dept. Agr., Agr. Res. Serv. *ARS 74-78*.

ANON. 1971. The egg products industry. U.S. Dept. Agr. Econ. Res. Serv., Marketing Res. Rept. *917.*
ATKIN, L. 1966. Egg products and how to use them. Proc. Am. Soc. Bakery Engrs. *1966*, 248–256.
BANWART, G. J., and AYRES, J. C. 1956. The effect of high temperature storage on the content of *Salmonella* and on the functional properties of dried egg white. J. Food Technol. *10*, 68–73.
CSONKA, F. A., and JONES, M. A. 1952. Factors affecting the percentage of certain proteins in egg white. J. Nutr. *46*, 531–537.
EVERSON, G. J., and SOUDERS, H. J. 1957. Composition and nutritive importance of eggs. J. Am. Dietetic Assoc. *33*, 1244–1254.
FEENEY, R. E. 1964. Egg proteins. *In* Proteins and Their Reactions, H. W. Schultz and A. F. Anglemier (Editors). Avi Publishing Co., Westport, Conn.
FORSYTHE, R. H. 1963. Chemical and physical properties of egg products. Cereal Sci. Today *8*, 309–310.
FORSYTHE, R. H. 1970. Eggs and egg products as functional ingredients. Bakers Dig. *44*, No. 5, 40–46.
FORSYTHE, R. H., and FOSTER, J. F. 1950. Egg white proteins. I. Electrophoretic studies on whole whites. J. Biol. Chem. *184*, 377–383.
LONGSWORTH, L. G., CANNAN, R. K., and MACINNES, D. A. 1940. An electrophoretic study of the proteins of egg white. J. Am. Chem. Soc. *62*, 2580–2590.
MACDONNELL, L. R., *et al.* 1955. The functional properties of the egg white proteins. Food Technol. *9*, 49–53.
PARKINSON, T. L. 1966. The chemical composition of eggs. J. Sci. Food Agr. *17*, 101–111.
ROMANOFF, A. L. 1943. Morphological and physicochemical differentiation in various layers of avian albumen. Food Res. *8*, 286–291.
SMITH, C. F. 1959. Shell egg deterioration: Diffusion of yolk lipids into albumen as the natural cause of failures in performance. Poultry Sci. *38*, 181–192.

CHAPTER 8

FRUITS AND NUTS

Fruits and nuts are used in large quantities in bakery products. The heavy consumption of fruit in pie fillings and of nuts in sweet goods such as coffee cake is readily apparent. Smaller but significant amounts are used in Danish pastry, doughnuts, cakes, icings, etc. The presence of fruits or nuts is clearly correlated in consumers' minds with high quality and they tend to evaluate the bakery product not only in terms of the color and flavor contributed by the fruits or nuts but also by the characteristic shape and texture of individual pieces as indicative of the quantity and quality of the ingredient.

Since these materials are agricultural commodities they not only have an inherent variability related to the different varieties of plant from which they are harvested, but are also subject to the vagaries of climate, water supply, disease, infestation, harvest damage, storage deterioration, and other influences good and bad which affect the quality of all natural products. As a result, the job of quality control is made more difficult. Uniformity is not always attainable and specifications must take the natural variability into account.

FRUITS

Some of the fruits used in large quantities by the baking industry are apple, strawberry, cherry, blueberry, and peach. The most important dried fruits are raisins, currants, figs, and dates. Probably very few bakers buy the whole fresh fruit for further processing in their plant. It is much simpler from a scheduling standpoint to buy frozen or canned bulk fruit even when the fresh fruit is in season; labor costs are much less and the resultant baked goods are perfectly satisfactory if due care has been exercised in selection of the ingredient.

Apples

Canned apple slices of the following varieties are on the market at most times: York Imperial, Baldwin, Stayman, Jonathan, Golden Delicious, Greening, Rome Beauty, Gravenstein, Pippin, and Wealthy. Suppliers will frequently be able to supply either firm, medium, or soft textured slices on demand. Firm textured slices may be York Imperial, while medium Golden Delicious may be supplied to those bakers wanting a more tender slice. Many bakers prefer Stayman Winesaps or Jonathans for flavor.

Frozen apple slices are offered in 30-lb tins while hot-pack slices are sold in No. 10 cans. Evaporated apples (about 24% moisture) and dehydrofrozen pieces are also available. Solid pack No. 10 cans of nominal 7-lb contents will yield drained fruit weighing at least 108 oz, while light weight packs will yield 96 oz.

Raisins and Currants

The raisins of commerce are dried grapes of the Muscat or Thompson seedless varieties. Table 8.1 gives the average composition of raisins. Natural Thompson raisins (the dark kind) are dried untreated grapes while the golden Thompsons have been subjected to a sulfur dioxide treatment which bleaches out the natural pigments.

In high moisture bakery products, raisins are often soaked before they are mixed into the dough. Such a treatment is often desirable if it brings the fruit to a moisture content in equilibrium with that of the dough. However, excessive water in the raisins will lead to effusion of acid and sugar into the dough with consequent deleterious effects. Too much softening of the fruit makes it more susceptible to breakage during mixing. Raisins in normal condition, exhibiting a moderately flexible structure, will have a moisture content of 15–17% and will be in equilibrium with a relative humidity of about 50% at room temperature. Adding 6 lb of hot water to 100 lb of fruit and allowing the mixture to stand 3–4 hr is sufficient to soften the raisins enough to permit their use in soft cookies (Bergholz 1957).

The currant is a very small, dark, round, grape that yields, when dried, a small raisin of excellent quality for baked goods. The California prod-

TABLE 8.1
ANALYSIS OF COMMERCIAL RAISINS

	%
Moisture	16.1
Total sugars	71.0
Total reducing	70.7
Fructose	39.3
Glucose[1]	31.4
Sucrose[1]	0.3
Crude fiber	0.9
Nitrogen	0.5
Ash	1.8
Acidity (as malic)	1.6

Source: Bolin and Affleck (1966).
[1] By difference.

uct is generally referred to as the Zante currant. There are imported dried fruits of similar types under different names. Zante currants are not closely related to the true or bush currant which is not dried, but used in jams, jellies, and preserves.

Figs

The sole use of figs in cookies is as an ingredient for the jam in fig bars. Fig paste is generally ground on order from whole figs. It is commonly shipped in 80-lb cases with polyethylene liners. The moisture content will be about 23%.

The chief domestic varieties of figs are Calimyrna, White Adriatic, Kadota, and Black Mission. The Calimyrna is a large, onion-shaped, tender, green-skinned fig with an excellent flavor. This variety has been highly recommended as a fig jam ingredient for bakery use. It is the domestic version of the Smyrna, which is probably the best fig for jam use.

The White Adriatic has a bright green skin which turns bright amber as it is dried. Ordinarily, Adriatic figs do not make a good jam alone because they lack natural sugars and flavor, and contain a slight excess of crude fiber. When blended with other figs of high sugars and more pronounced flavor, a very satisfactory jam can be produced.

The Kadota fig has no seeds. The meat has a light color and a pleasing taste. The thickness of the skin causes the figs to be very hard to dry out, so that they must be ground into paste near where they are grown. Due to its lack of seed and the toughness of its skin, the Kadota is not recommended as a sole fig ingredient for jam. It can be used as part of a blend depending on individual preference for jam characteristics.

Black Mission figs have excellent flavor and texture, but when dried turn very dark, becoming almost black in many cases. Dark fig jam is associated in the consumers' minds with poor flavor, low grade raw materials, and poor manufacturing practices. If used in the proper blend it can enhance the flavor and texture of jams based on other varieties.

In order to produce an ideal jam it is necessary to combine a fig with high color and flavor with one of good texture and seed quality. For this ideal jam, use of an imported Smyrna fig for color and flavor and a White Adriatic for texture has been suggested.

Ripe figs on the tree will analyze approximately as follows:

	%		%
Moisture	78.0	Fiber	1.7
Protein	1.4	Sugars	16.0
Fat	0.4	Acids	0.1
Ash	2.4		

After drying, the average fig will have the following analysis:

	%		%
Moisture	24.0	Fiber	5.8
Protein	4.0	Sugars	62.0
Fat	1.2	Acid	0.6
Ash	2.4		

Figs for jam should preferably not be treated with sulfur dioxide. The fruit is sized into the following categories: Fancy, Choice, and Standard, with a range of 28/32 in. diameter (for Standards) to 42/32 in. diameter (for Fancy).

Fig paste will darken with time. Storage at 45°F or lower will retard this undesirable change. Figs should be stored in a conditioned room of approximately 50°F with minimum 40°F and maximum 60°F. A relative humidity between 50 and 60% is preferred. Too low a humidity will tend to dry out and harden the figs. High humidity will cause loss of sugars due to condensation of water on the fig and subsequent leakage of syrup and may also lead to mold growth.

Figs seem to be unusually susceptible to insect infestation. Fumigation at appropriate intervals and careful protection between times is the only sure way to prevent loss. Figs should be stacked in such a manner as to afford maximum air circulation around packages.

Before grinding the figs into jam, the blocks should be broken up and inspected for foreign matter. The broken pieces are usually washed by being conveyed through a water spray. Soaking is to be avoided. Figs are often ground directly after washing.

Jam can be made according to the following formula:

	%
Figs	50
Granulated sugar or a combination of sucrose and dextrose (corn sugar)	30
Corn syrup[1]	12
Invert syrup[1]	7.8
Salt	0.1
Acid	0.1

[1] Or 19.8% high conversion corn syrup may be used instead of the corn and invert syrups.

Water is varied to give a moisture content between 20 and 25% which results in a suitable consistency. Flavorings, scrap such as bar ends, and other materials may be added. Starch thickeners such as confectioners' corn flakes are sometimes used to adjust the texture. Wheat bran at about the 5% level is said to reduce shrinkage. Citrus oils, and especially lemon oil, or vanillin may be added, but many producers do not use supplemental flavors. The fig is unusually low in acid for a fruit, and this deficiency can be alleviated by including a small amount of citric acid in the jam.

Both horizontal and vertical mixers can be used for mixing fig jam. The following procedure is for mixing jam using a horizontal double arm mixer:

Creaming Step.—Add thickeners, granulated sugar, flavors, salt, acid and fig paste. Cream for 15 min at 20 rpm. Great caution must be taken not to cream at too fast a speed to prevent whipping air into the jam. Presence of too much air could cause trouble during baking through expansion of air pockets in the jam. Air pockets between the jam and the jacket leaves the bar vulnerable to damage and is unsightly in appearance.

Second Stage.—Add invert syrup, corn syrup, water (variable). Mix for 10 min at 20 rpm with periodic checks to insure desired moisture from 20 to 25% (Webb 1965).

Cherries

Cherries are available in frozen, canned, and candied forms. Canned cherries include the two general types red sour pitted (RSP) and sweet. The predominant RSP variety is Montmorency. Napoleon (Royal Ann) is the important light-colored sweet variety while Bing and Lambert are popular dark-colored sweet cherries. Flavor, firmness, and appearance are affected by the variety, stage of maturity at harvest, processing conditions, and storage conditions. Size is established by grading. Number of blemishes is related to the original condition of the cherries, effectiveness of sorting on the inspection belt, and processing. Most sweet cherries are packed in syrup, and RSP in water. A No. 10 can of RSP packed in water should provide a minimum drained weight of 74 oz of fruit.

Designation of grade and standards for grades of canned cherries are administered by the Agricultural Marketing Service of the U.S. Dept. of Agr. Canned RSP cherries are classified as Grade A—Fancy, Grade C—Standard, or Grade D—Substandard. Canned sweet cherries are classified as Grade A or Fancy, Grade B or Choice, Grade C or Standard, and Substandard.

Marshall (1954) quoted the following reasons for user preference of frozen cherries as compared to canned cherries: (1) more attractive, natural appearance; (2) superior flavor; (3) firmer texture; (4) economy and convenience in handling; and (5) greater immunity from loss of flavor, color, and appearance. On the other hand, some bakers prefer the flavor of the canned product.

The pack of frozen sweet cherries for institutional or manufacturing use is small. Large quantities of RSP cherries are frozen for these applications, however. Montmorency and English Morello are the principal varieties. The most common container is the 30-lb round tin. Drums are also used (about 450 lb of fruit plus sugar).

Sugar syrup or dry sugar is added to cherries being prepared for freezing. When dry sugar is used, as it generally is if the 30-lb containers are being packed, it is added in an amount which will give either 1 part of sugar to 5 parts (by weight) of fruit or 1 part of sugar to 4 parts of cherries. These packs are designated 5 + 1 or 4 + 1 respectively.

The recommended temperature range for permanent storage of frozen cherries or other frozen fruits is 0°–5°F. At these temperatures minimal changes should occur in a closed container. Exposure of any surface to the atmosphere will result in color changes and drying.

Maraschino cherries and other candied forms are manufactured from brined cherry stock. This material is substantially devoid of the original flavor and color of the fruit. To the brined cherry, which provides the base shape and texture, are added the desired colors and flavors. Soaking in gradually increasing concentrations of sugar syrup (after removal of the brine by leaching) results in saturating the plant tissue with the syrup.

Strawberries

Although the flavor of strawberries is compatible with many kinds of baked foods, the structural collapse which occurs on cooking and leads to loss of attractive appearance and texture limits their use in pies and the like. Strawberry jams, jellies, and their imitations are desirable adjuncts for Danish pastries, cookies, etc.

A typical analysis of fresh strawberries is shown below (Watt and Merrill 1963):

	%
Moisture	89.9
Protein	0.7
Fat	0.5
Total carbohydrate	8.4
Fiber	1.3
Ash	0.5

Because the texture losss and flavor changes during freezing and thawing are somewhat less drastic than those resulting from heat processing, the frozen fruit is greatly preferred to the canned when piece appearance and fresh flavor are important (as in pies), and not much of the canned fruit is sold to bakers. Concentrated purées or juices are available, usually with the volatile materials recovered and added back or packed separately, for use in jellies and fillings. Jams and other cooked fruit-and-sugar combinations are hot-packed.

Frozen strawberries for bakery use are packed in drums, 30-lb tins, No. 10 cans (about 6½ lbs net) and 10-lb tins. Most of these are sugared at the 4 + 1 level by alternately filling fruit and sugar into the container. Sugared berries may be half-sliced or cut into discs of ¼-7/16 in. thickness. Individually quick frozen (IQF) berries are packed without sugar in enameled slipcover cans or plastic-lined fiberboard boxes.

Varieties considered suitable for freezing are Marshall, Northwest, Shasta, Dixieland, Klondike, Midland, Dorsett, Sparkle, Pocahontas, Joe, Tennessee Shipper, Siletz, Tennessee Beauty, Catskill, and Blakemore.

Standards for frozen strawberries have been issued by the U.S. Dept. of Agr. and some of the states. More than 80% of the frozen strawberries packed in this country are grown on the west coast. The Pacific Northwest produces most of these. Large quantities of frozen strawberries are imported from Mexico. They can be of very good quality but tend to rather nonuniform, and stringent quality control measures are indicated to police procurements.

NUTS

Nuts are used as garnishes and texturizing and flavoring ingredients for sweet dough products, cakes, doughnuts, etc. Peanuts are probably the most common nut used in bakery products, followed by coconut, pecans, almonds, walnuts, cashews, and filberts. Small amounts of macadamia nuts, pistachios, and other expensive varieties are used in luxury goods. There is also a considerable consumption of almond paste and kernel paste in fillings, etc.

Much care should go into the selection and storage of nutmeats since they are very susceptible to the development of off-flavors. Rancidity is the main problem but shelled nuts also tend to absorb off-odors such as tobacco and paint from their environment.

Nuts should be stored in the shell and at low temperatures whenever possible, since these conditions will minimize staling. Bakers should insist on delivery of freshly shelled nuts from the latest crop year. Most large nut processors will keep their stocks in the shell and break out the nutmeats only on the receipt of orders. Some brokers and distributors, however, may retain boxed nutmeats for excessive times under unsuitable conditions. Although it is certainly easy to identify rancid nuts, the detection of advanced storage deterioration which has brought the material to the brink of detectable rancidity is not so easy. Although tests for peroxides and free fat acidity are helpful, but they do not always give a clear indication of the remaining storage life.

The presence of aflatoxin in nuts (particularly peanuts) has received considerable governmental attention in the last few years and doubtless will attract increased regulatory action as detection and enforcement methods are perfected. Aflatoxin refers to a series of compounds some or all of which are carcinogens. They are produced by certain fungi which are widely distributed in nature. Contamination by the substances can be found in lots of nuts which are not obviously moldy. The U.S. Food and Drug Administration has been increasing its surveillance of commercial shipments of peanuts and lots are occasionally condemmed because of the presence of excessive amounts of aflatoxin. All reliable suppliers will have had their stocks analyzed for the contaminant, but it is advisable for purchasers to specify that shipments must conform to U.S. FDA standards in this as in all other respects.

Various kinds of simulated nuts have been offered as replacements for the more costly natural products. These may be simply nut-flavored "crunches" similar to streusels, expanded cereal products, processed soybean meats, or more elaborate compositions designed to duplicate the appearance, texture, and flavor of some specific nutmeat.

Peanuts and Peanut Butter

According to Woodroof (1966), the classification of types and varieties of peanuts is loose and many intermediate forms are found. The relatively small, somewhat spherical Spanish type is grown mainly in South Africa and in the Southwestern and Southeastern United States. The Virginia type is considerably larger and the kernel is longer or football-shaped. The runner type is approximately intermediate in shape and size. There are also Valencia and Tennessee red or white types, but they are currently of relatively minor economic importance.

The number of kernels per pound of Spanish peanuts will vary from about 1100 to 2000, of runners from 900 to 1100 and of Virginia from 176 to 864.

Peanuts when freshly dug have a moisture content of 30–39%. Upon air-drying in the shell, this drops to 5–10%. Roasted peanuts will have a moisture content of about 0.5–1.5%, the same as peanut butter. The average composition of peanut kernels is shown in Table 8.2.

Dried shell peanuts retain good organoleptic properties for a year or more if kept free from infestation and protected from foreign odors which they might absorb. When shelled, the storage life is reduced by about ⅔; if blanched and split, another ⅔ of the potential stability is lost. Chopping and roasting can further reduce shelf-life.

TABLE 8.2
COMPOSITION OF PEANUT KERNELS

Constituent	Range (%)	Average (%)
Moisture	3.9–13.2	5.0
Protein	21.0–36.4	28.5
Lipids	35.8–54.2	47.5
Crude fiber	1.2– 4.3	2.8
Nitrogen-free extract	6.0–24.9	13.3
Ash	1.8– 3.1	2.9
Reducing sugars	0.1– 0.3	0.2
Disaccharide sugar	1.9– 5.2	4.5
Starch	1.0– 5.3	4.0
Pentosans	2.2– 2.7	2.5

Source: Freeman et al. (1954).

Spoilage is the result of development of oxidative rancidity, absorption of foreign odors, and color changes. Woodroof (1966) states that these changes occur 3 times faster in shelled peanuts and 9 times faster in hulled and blanched nuts than in raw peanuts in the shell. Roasted nuts have a short storage life due to the acceleration of the reactions leading to oxidative rancidity. Chopping the nuts further speeds the development of off-flavors because of the greater surface area exposed to oxygen. Thus, cured peanuts in the shell might have a useful storage life of nine months or more if held under cool and dry conditions, while chopped and roasted peanuts can be expected to exhibit off-flavors in a couple of weeks.

Various methods have been suggested to improve stability of roasted nuts in or on cookies and candies. Among these are patented procedures involving adding of antioxidants or coating the nuts with a mixture of zein and acetylated monoglycerides. These methods are useful in extending the life of the nuts.

Peanut butter is an important constituent of certain cookie doughs and is sometimes used in fillings. A proposed standard of identity has been issued by the federal government. This would allow as much as 10% of certain seasoning and stabilizing ingredients including up to 3% of hydrogenated vegetable oils. Salt, dextrose, and emulsifiers are other ingredients commonly used in peanut butter. Either blanched or unblanched kernels may be used, but in the latter case, a label declaration of unblanched peanuts must be made. Extent of roast is classified from USDA No. 1 (lightest) to USDA No. 4 (dark).

Peanut butter is sold in bulk in steel drums, in fiber drums with plastic liners, and in fiber boxes with liners. There are three basic grinds: (1) smooth, in which the particle size has been reduced below the perceptible limit; (2) regular, having a definite grainy texture; and (3) chunky, similar to regular with the addition of a substantial amount of large particles (about $\frac{1}{16}$ in. in the greatest dimension).

Peanut butter to be used as an ingredient in cookies should be of a special high-roast type to yield the most flavoring power per dollar of cost. The peanuts should be roasted to a point just short of the development of bitterness or scorched flavor. Blanched peanuts are highly desirable as the raw material. Specification of the variety of peanut is generally not feasible. The question of whether or not to use additives depends to some extent on the method of dispensing the material. If it is to be scooped from partially filled barrels, the presence of some stabilizer is essential to prevent stratification in the drum, i.e., oil separation. When fiber boxes with plastic liners are used, stabilizers are also desirable in order to prevent leakage, and other handling problems.

There are three grades of peanut butter: (1) U.S. Grade A is practically free from defects and has good color, flavor, texture, and aroma; (2) U.S. Standard Grade is fairly free of defects and has fairly good flavor, aroma, color, and consistency; and (3) Substandard includes products failing to meet the requirements of the other two grades.

Peanut butter is fairly resistant to the development of rancidity if stored in light-proof containers and protected from oxygen. Temperatures in the 50°F range are preferred. If the oils are allowed to soak into fiberboard, rancidity occurs quickly. Stability of the butter depends to a considerable extent on the conditions to which the peanuts were subjected before being ground.

Peanut meal, similar to butter from which most of the oil has been removed, is useful as a flavoring material for fillings. Much of the peanut flavor is lost with the oil, however. The advantage over peanut butter is that the low-melting oils, which tend to leak into base cakes and chocolate coatings, have been mostly removed.

Almonds

There are two species of almonds, the bitter and the sweet or edible almond. Of the latter, there are two classes, the hard shell and the soft shell. The almonds of commerce are principally soft-shelled.

In world trade, the major producers of almonds are Spain, Italy, Portugal, Morocco, Iran, and the United States. Some almonds are imported into the United States, mostly from Spain, but most of the almonds consumed here are domestically grown.

California is the only important almond-growing state in this country. Seven varieties that dominate the U.S. market are Nonpareil, IXL, Ne Plus, Peerless, Drake, Mission, and Jordanolo. These varieties have the following characteristics (Woodroof 1967):

Nonpareil

Papershell. Accounts for approximately 50% of total California production. Shelled for grocers and confectioners. Natural or blanched kernels favored by salters and bakers. Basic raw material for Sliced Natural.

IXL

Softshell. Generally sold in shell due to its attractive appearance. Also shelled for the confectionery trade.

Ne Plus

Softshell. Popular with the grocery trade for sale in shell. Shelled Ne Plus are extensively used for sugar panning (Jordan Almonds) by confectioners.

Peerless

Semihardshell. Attractive, plump appearance. Sold almost entirely in shell. Widely used in nut mixtures.

Drake

Semihardshell. Has steady demand in shelled form from confectioners and almond paste manufacturers.

Mission

Semihardshell. Shelled and sold as meats. Favored by confectioners (pronounced almond flavor blends well with chocolate) and is basic raw material for cocktail almonds.

Jordanolo

Softshell. A superb almond of outstanding flavor and appearance. Largest kernels are blanched for nut salters. Smaller kernels used in sugar panning.

The U.S. Dept. of Agr. has established Standards for Grades of Shelled almonds including U.S. Fancy, U.S. Extra No. 1, U.S. No. 1, U. S. Select Sheller Run, U.S. Standard Sheller Run, U.S. No. 1 Whole and Broken, and U. S. No. 1 Pieces for almonds of similar varietal characteristics, as well as Mixed Varieties, and Unclassified. There are also Standards for grades of almonds in the shell, which are not of much significance to the baking industry.

Standard Sheller Run, the lowest quality class, consists of kernels just as they come from the cracking machines, of mixed sizes, free of dust and shell but containing some broken pieces. Select Sheller Run, contains few broken pieces and is offered in different sizes. Fancy consists of almonds closely sized and without defects, as regular in shape, size and color as is practicable. They are free of double-nuts, dust, shell, and broken pieces.

Standard Sheller Run is statisfactory for making almond paste, chopped or sliced nuts, and the like. For garnishing, where appearance is of primary importance, Fancy should be specified. The size, which should also be specified, is defined as the number of almonds to the ounce.

In the U.S. market, most almonds are marketed through growers' federations, such as the California Almond Growers Exchange, which enforces quality standards and markets cooperatively. This organization classifies its output of shelled nuts as follows:

Shelled Almonds

The variety, grade, and size are specified. Piece sizes for whole nuts of the different varieties range from 18–20 kernels per ounce to 40–50 kernels per ounce.

Almond Pieces

There are 12 recognized sizes and shapes of pieces (Woodroof 1967): (1) Sliced natural, unblanched. (2) Sliced, blanched. (3) Slivered, blanched. (4) Broken, blanched. (5) Splits, Nonpareil, blanched. (6) Halves, Nonpareil, unblanched, cut lengthwise. (7) Cubed, unblanched, cut crosswise. (8) Steel cut, medium, unblanched. (9) Steel cut, small unblanched. (10) Steel cut, fine, unblanched. (11) Meal, unblanched. (12) Diced, roasted buttered, unblanched.

For most applications, it is desirable that the kernels be blanched, i.e., the brown skin removed. A typical treatment involves contacting the almonds with 180°F water for 3 min, and then skinning by hand or by special machines. If they are to be kept any length of time, the excess moisture must be removed. California almonds can be obtained already blanched and with the moisture content brought back to safe levels. Nuts should always be stored in air-tight containers to prevent moisture pickup.

Almonds are relatively resistant to rancidity development as compared to pecans or peanuts, but they will deteriorate with time, and the decrease in acceptability is accelerated by blanching or roasting. It is desirable to store the nuts at freezing temperatures if they are to be held for several months. Moistureproof and insect-resistant packaging should be used for room temperature storage, of course. If the nuts must be roasted and held for several days or weeks, it is helpful to apply the antioxidants BHA and BHT in spray form or in the roasting oil.

Almond paste is prepared from finely ground almonds with or without sugar and other additives. Kernel paste is a less expensive replacement made mostly from apricot kernels.

A formula for almond filling which may be suitable for some bakery foods is made of the following ingredients mixed to a smooth paste:

	Parts
Kernel paste	15
Almond paste	7.5
Granulated sugar	12
Flour, bread	4
Eggs	2
Water	2

Cashews

Cashew nuts are produced in India and East Africa. Virtually all of the U.S. consumption amounting to about 70–80 million pounds annually is imported from India but may include some East African nuts processed there. There is no commercial production of cashew nuts in the United States.

Composition of cashew nuts on an "as is" basis has been given as (Watt and Merrill 1963):

	%
Moisture	5.2
Calories	5.6 (per gm)
Protein	17.2
Fat	45.7
Total carbohydrates	29.3
Fiber	1.4
Ash	2.6

The United States has not established standards for cashew nuts, but the Cashew Export Promotion Council of India has established grading and marketing rules which apply to cashews exported from that country. These rules define grades for whole cashews, scorched wholes, dessert wholes, white pieces, scorched pieces, and dessert pieces.

Whole cashew kernels are classified according to size:

Identification Symbol	Size Range, Kernels per Pound
W210	200–210
W240	220–240
W280	260–280
W320	300–320
W400	350–400
W450	400–450
W500	450–500

Cashews are packed in square metal tins which are hermetically sealed. Generally, a few inches of vacuum is drawn before sealing. The tins of approximately 4-gal. capacity contain 28 lb of Baby Bits and 25 lb of other sizes. The nuts are comparatively stable when stored in the unopened tin at room temperature. A year of useful shelf life can be expected when they are refrigerated.

Pecans

Pecans are highly regarded as decorative and flavorful additions to bakery foods. Because of their higher cost relative to most other nuts, and the fluctuations in supply, they are usually reserved for premium goods.

The pecan is a native American tree. It will not survive severe winters and so is restricted to the milder climatic areas. Nuts are harvested from both wild and cultivated trees. There is more variability in the pecan crop than that of most other nuts. Because of the fairly recent trend toward cold or frozen storage, the fluctuations in supply and prices have been somewhat reduced.

After harvesting, pecans are put in dry storage to undergo curing. During this period of about 3 weeks at room temperature, the moisture of the entire nut decreases to about 8.5–9.0% and that of the meat to about 4.5%. Free fatty acids and peroxide value of the lipids increase, and the tannins of the seed coat oxidize with a resultant color change from pale to medium brown. The overall effect of these changes is to develop in the kernel the characteristic pecan appearance, aroma, flavor, and texture. The nuts will gradually develop staleness and rancidity at a rate dependent upon the temperature as storage continues. Conditions of 40°F with 70–80% RH are necessary if the fresh flavor is to be retained more than 3 months. At 0°F the in-shell kernels will retain good quality for more than 5 yr.

Heating pecan meats to an internal temperature of 176°F in dry air or oil doubles the shelf-life by inactivating oxidative enzymes. Higher temperatures produce a partially cooked flavor, while roasting to 365°F for 15 min by dry roasting or infrared rays destroys natural antioxidants (accelerates rancidity development) but increases the aroma and flavor many times. This is a favorable situation for baked goods which are to be consumed soon after preparation but has unfavorable implications for cookies, frozen baked foods, and similar items entering a rather long distribution system. Antioxidants such as BHA or BHT can be added to increase shelf-life.

If pecan meats are dried below about 3.5–4.0% moisture content, they become too brittle and suffer excessive breakage during handling.

U.S. Standards for shelled pecans were promulgated in 1956. The four grades for shelled pecans are U.S. No. 1 Halves, U.S. Commercial Halves, U.S. No. 1 Pieces, and U.S. Commercial Pieces. There is also an "Unclassified" category which is not regarded as a grade. The size of halves are specified according to the number of halves per pound while pieces are classified in accordance with a sieve test. The halves grading system is:

	Halves per Lb
Mammoth	200–250
Junior Mammoth	251–300
Jumbo	301–350
Extra Large	351–450
Large	451–550
Medium	551–650
Topper	651–750
Large Amber	400 or less
Regular Amber	more than 400

Development of the so-called amber color is a kind of storage deterioration probably related to relatively high temperatures and high moisture content.

Coconut

Most of the coconut preparations available as cookie ingredients are based on the dried meat of the ripe coconut. This may be further processed by cooking the coconut with sugar and glycerol or by toasting. Principal countries of origin are the Philippines and Ceylon.

In unsweetened coconut, the only variables available to the purchaser are particle size and particle shape. This material will consist of about 65% fat, 2–3% moisture, fiber, carbohydrate, protein, etc. The fat is comparatively stable.

The cuts offered by one manufacturer are:

Extra fine—a very fine ground coconut, about the same in texture as granulated sugar, particularly suitable for wire-cut coconut cookies.

Macaroon—about 95% of this material will pass through a 40 mesh screen, making it somewhat finer in size than coarse ground corn meal. This cut is used primarily in macaroons and other applications where a definitely chewy texture is desired.

Medium—this cut is about $1/16$–$1/4$ in. in length and will pass through a 16 mesh screen. It can be compared in particle size to topping salt and is used as a topping on open-faced marshmallow cookies.

Coarse—an irregular cut of 1/8–1/4 in. in length and up to 1/8 in. in thickness.

Rice—a uniform cut averaging 1/8–1/4 in. in length and similar to rice in appearance. Recommended by the manufacturer for use on marshmallow cookies.

Short shred—approximately 75% of this cut will be between 1/4 and 3/4 in. in length.

Fancy shred—these shreds vary from 1/2 to 2 in. in length, but most of the particles will be in the shorter lengths. The length of the pieces make this cut unsuitable for cookies.

Chip or slice—large flat pieces are called chips or slices and find little use in cookies.

Flake—a very thin flake having an average length of 1 1/2 in. It is sometimes used in cookies when a rough texture effect is desired.

When included in the cookie dough, coconut will usually increase spread. Shredded particles will increase spread more than will an extra fine grind.

Sweetened coconut shreds contain approximately 39% fat, 53% carbohydrate, and 3% water. It is considerably more expensive than the unsweetened product. Plastic coconut is the finely ground dried meat. Liberation of the oil through rupture of the cell walls causes the product to feel softer than the granular dried material. Mixed products such as coconut syrup and coconut honey are sometimes offered. They generally consist of some form of sugar ingredient cooked with the freshly ground coconut meat. Colored coconut shreds are available from a few manufacturers.

Toasted coconut can be added to cookie doughs to give a nut-like flavor and crisp texture. Other ingredients are added before the coconut particles are oven toasted. The range of piece sizes offered by one dealer are described as thin flake, extra fine, macaroon, medium, rice cut, nuggets, shred, and chip.

Specifications for coconut products should include a limitation on moisture of about 3%, a fat minimum of not less than 60%, and a description of the particle size and shape. Flavor and appearance specifications, always difficult to quantitate, should include at least a requirement that the product be free of visible foreign material and discolored particles, and have a typical taste and aroma. Specifications for yeast and mold count, lipase activity, and *Salmonella* are desirable if they can be enforced.

Walnuts

The American black walnut (*Juglans nigra*) is used in relatively small amounts in baked foods where its distinctive flavor can make a positive contribution to acceptability. It is more common to use English walnuts (*J. regia*) which are milder in flavor and lower in cost.

The English walnut is widely cultivated today, with centers of production in middle and southern Europe, as well as in California and some other parts of the southern United States. Some of the popular varieties in the United States are Payne, Eureka, Hartley, and Franquettes. These all yield nuts satisfactory for the baking trade, with the Franquettes being somewhat lighter in color than the others.

When harvested, the kernel moisture content may be as high as 35%. This is reduced by mechanical drying, and the in-shell nuts are stored at about 4.0% kernel moisture until needed for shelling.

Shelled walnuts quickly darken and develop rancidity under unfavorable exposure to moisture, heat, light, and air. Maximum stability is at about 3.1% moisture. There is an almost linear increase in stability with decreasing temperature of storage. Antioxidants can be applied to the kernels to retard rancidity development.

U.S. Standards for grades of shelled walnuts were issued in 1959. The grades consist of U.S. No. 1, and Commercial. There is also an "Unclassified" category for portions of walnut kernels which have not been classified in accordance with either of the foregoing grades.

BIBLIOGRAPHY

BERGHOLZ, B., JR. 1957. Elements of raisin bread production. Trans. Am. Soc. Bakery Engrs. *1957*, 77–82.

FREEMAN, A. F., MORRIS, N. J., and WILLICH, R. K. 1954. Peanut butter. U.S. Dept. Agr. *A1C-370*.

HOWES, F. N. 1953. Nuts—Their Production and Everyday Uses, 2nd Edition. Faber and Faber, London.

MARSHALL, R. E. 1954. Cherries and Cherry Products. Interscience Publishers Div., John Wiley & Sons, New York.

WATT, BERNICE K., and MERRILL, ANNABEL L. 1963. Composition of Foods. U.S. Dept. Agr., Agr. Res. Serv. Handbook *8*.

WEBB, W. E. 1965. Fig bar production. Biscuit Production Club Res. Rept.

WHITELEY, P. R. 1965. Ingredient proportions of jams, jellies, and cream fillings. Biscuit Maker Plant Baker *16*, 390, 393–394.

WOODROOF, J. G. 1966. Peanuts: Production, Processing, Products. Avi Publishing Co., Westport, Conn.

WOODROOF, J. G. 1967. Tree Nuts: Production, Processing, Products, Vol. 1 and 2. Avi Publishing Co., Westport, Conn.

WOODROOF, J. G. 1970. Coconuts: Production, Processing, Products. Avi Publishing Co., Westport, Conn.

CHAPTER 9

FLAVORS AND COLORS

INTRODUCTION

In a sense, nearly all of the ingredients used in bakery products could be considered as flavors since they contribute something to the odor or taste of the finished product. Sugar and salt, as well as the compounds resulting from yeast fermentation, can have major effects on these properties, but they are also textural modifiers and have other functions unrelated to flavor. The fruit fillings in pies and other pastries dominate the character of the product. The discussion in this chapter is restricted, however, to those substances which are added in relatively small amounts primarily for their flavor modifying function. A section on natural and artificial coloring agents is also included.

SPICES AND OTHER FLAVORING MATERIALS[1]

Spices are defined as dried products of plant origin which are used primarily for seasoning food. Fresh, high quality spices offer innumerable ways for a baker to introduce variety to his line. Each type is imported from several different sources and the quality will vary accordingly. The most sensible buying procedure is to make sure that the supplier is reputable and to take the attitude that quality is more important than minor price differentials. The few pennies difference between grades is not worth the chance of failure in flavoring, especially as the quantities usually employed in commercial baking operations are small. All spices should be stored in a cool, airy, and dry room. Limits of storage life are not clearly defined, but it is certain that is is never wise for a baker to speculate with these aromatic ingredients. Buy only according to current needs and make sure the containers are tightly covered when not in use, since volatile oils will excape on lengthy exposure to the air.

For those buyers wishing to check the quality of their spice purchases, the American Spice Trade Association, 82 Wall Street, New York, makes available a series of methods for spice analysis. Included are procedures for testing volatile and nonvolatile oils, total ash, starch, crude fiber, etc.

---

[1] Material for this section on spices was supplied by Marshall W. Neale of the American Spice Trade-Association. Analytical values were adapted from those in the Chemists Yearbook.

The entire set of eleven methods is priced at $1.24 per single order or $1.00 per set plus postage on orders of more than one.

Cinnamon

Cinnamon, our most important baking spice, comes from the bark of an evergreen tree. The member of the cinnamon family most used in the United States is *Cinnamomum cassia*, which in spice trade vernacular is usually shortened to cassia. This plant is native to China, Indochina, and Indonesia. There is another spice of similar properties that goes under the term cinnamon also. This is *Cinnamomum zeylanicum*, or Ceylon cinnamon. It is quite different in color, texture, and flavor strength from cassia and very little is used here, but it is popular in Mexico and in Europe. There are three varieties of cassia in commerce today—Saigon cassia, Batavia cassia, and Korintje cassia. Saigon is a product of Indochina while Batavia and Korintje are both Indonesian cassias. Imports from China have been nonexistent since the United States embargo on communist goods.

Saigon Cassia.—This is considered to be the finest cassia a baker can use. It comes from a bark that is grayish brown on the outside and reddish brown underneath. As a result, ground Saigon is slightly lighter in color (sometimes even grayish brown) than either Batavia or Korintje cassias, which have an even reddish brown color throughout.

Cassia bark is slit and stripped off young trees and rolled into quills (commonly called cinnamon sticks). As they arrive in the United States these quills are from 2 to 3 ft long. Saigon quills are graded according to thickness of bark: thin, medium, and thick. A certain proportion of Saigon also comes in as broken stick, graded No. 1 and No. 2. Thin quill Saigon is recognized as the prime quality because the thin bark from the small twigs of the tree has a higher volatile oil content and finer quality of flavor. Buyers should understand that the term thin quill is not merely descriptive of good cassia, but is a specific grade. Saigon cassia has become very scarce and expensive the last few years. It is possible that much of the cinnamon being sold as "Saigon" is, in fact, some other kind.

Korintje Cassia.—This product comes from Sumatra and adjacent islands, including one by the name of Korintje. The bark is thick, in general, and dark reddish brown in color. There are two grades, "A" and "C", the "A" being the thinner and more highly flavored of the two. Though it is not as aromatic or as intensely flavored as the Saigons, Korintje is considered a good cassia.

Batavia Cassia.—This is from the same general area as Korintje, but is characteristically a product of the lowlands whereas Korintje comes mostly from the uplands. It is sometimes known as Padang cassia. The bark is usually thinner than Korintje and it has a somewhat lighter color. The flavor is not as strong as either the Korintjes or the Saigons and as a result, Batavia is normally the lowest priced. If Batavia cassia is mixed with water before it is added to the flour, there is danger that it will form a mucilaginous mass which can prevent a smooth blending of the other ingredients.

Cassia yields from 0.5 to 5% volatile oil.

Cinnamon is compatible with the flavors of sugar, chocolate, coffee, apple, peach, and pear.

Nutmeg

This spice is the seed of a peach-like fruit of a tropical evergreen tree. The seed is oval in shape and ranges in size up to 1¼ in. in length. Although it is native to the Molucca Islands, it is imported mostly from Indonesia and the West Indies today. The two principal grades are East Indies and West Indies. They are graded large, medium, and small according to the number per pound. Large average 60–75 per lb; medium, 90; small, 100–110. East Indian nutmegs usually have a slightly higher oil content and thus command a higher price.

Nutmeg yields from 7 to 15% of volatile oil. One part of the oil is soluble in three parts of 90% alcohol.

This spice is compatible with sugar, apple, cherry, peach, pear, and coffee flavors. When in the common granulation, 12¾ tsp of the spice equal 1 oz.

Mace

The fleshy arillode or skin which surrounds the nutmeg (seed) inside the nutmeg fruit is also a spice. The entire fruit looks something like a small peach. The outer layer, however, is a thick husk inside of which is the lacy mace layer surrounding the seed. Major sources are, of course, the same as for nutmeg, i.e., Indonesia and the West Indies. When harvested the mace is vivid red, but this changes to a light orange after drying. It is sold as East or West Indies, No. 1 or No. 2, according to color and quality.

Mace yields 7–14% volatile oil. One part of the oil is soluble in 3 parts of 90% alcohol.

The spice is compatible with sugar, custard, and cherry flavors, among others.

Cloves

This spice is the dried, unopened bud of an evergreen tree native to the Molucca Islands, now a part of Indonesia. Today, we import most of our cloves from Zanzibar and Madagascar. Either of these sources can produce excellent cloves so that grades are not so much a matter of origin as of individual quality.

Cloves contain a high percentage of nonvolatile penetrating oil and so should not be stored for long in fiber or paper containers lest the oil soak through. The oil is present in amounts of 14–21% of the spice. Clove is compatible with sugar, most stewed or preserved fruits, and pumpkin.

Ginger

Ginger is the root, or rhizome, of a tuberous perennial plant of the tropics. It is native to southern Asia but today is imported from Jamaica, India, and Africa. After harvesting, the roots are separated into small pieces that in the trade are called hands of ginger. Jamaican ginger is traditionally rated as top grade, primarily because of its appearance. In Jamaica the ginger is peeled after harvesting and the resultant product is lighter in color and considered to be smoother in flavor. However, Cochin ginger, the product of the State of Cochin in India, is an excellent grade for baking. African ginger, the lowest priced of the three has a harsher flavor, but would be suitable for something like gingersnaps where strength is considered a virtue.

Ginger yields from 1 to 3% of volatile oils. One part of the oil is soluble in 3 parts of 70% alcohol.

Bakers use the spice in gingerbread and doughs for cakes, cookies, wafers, and pies. The flavor is compatible with sugar, orange, pear, and pumpkin.

Allspice

This substance is the dried, nearly ripe, pea-sized fruit of an evergreen tree. It is native to the Western hemisphere and today is imported from Jamaica, Mexico, Guatemala, and other parts of Central and South America. It takes its name from the resemblance of its flavor to a blend of cloves, cinnamon, and nutmeg. However, the predominant flavor is that of cloves. Jamaican allspice is considered the best quality. The products of the other sources are rated more or less equal to each other at a level below the Jamaican variety. The buyer should make sure that the source is specified.

Allspice contains 3–4.5% of volatile oil. One part of the oil is soluble in 2 parts of 70% ethyl alcohol.

Its baking uses are in doughs for spice cakes and cookies, in pies and tarts, and in fruitcake. The flavor can be used in conjunction with sugar, blueberry, pineapple, pear, and apple flavors.

Cardamom Seed

Cardamom seed is the dried fruit of a plant from the ginger family. It is native to India, and today we import it mostly from India, Guatemala, and Ceylon. The reddish brown seeds are contained in a fibrous capsule (from 8 to 16 seeds per capsule) which may be either greenish-brown in color or a creamy white if it has been bleached. For pickling and similar uses the whole pods are available, but if the seeds are to be ground as for use in baking, decorticated cardamom (seeds removed from the pods) is specified. Guatemalan and Indian cardomom rank about equal in quality.

The oil in cardamom represents about 3.5-8% of the seed weight, and has the following properties:

Specific gravity at 59°F: 0.922-0.950
Optical rotation at 68°F: $+22°-+40°$
Refractive index at 68°F: 1.460-1.470

Cardamom is suitable for flavoring Danish pastry, fillings for eclairs and cream puffs, and pies. It is compatible with sugar, blueberry, grape, apple, and pumpkin flavors.

Poppy Seed

These are the tiny seeds of an annual of the poppy family. The plants are native to Asia but today we import most of our supply from the Netherlands, Poland, Argentina, and Iran. Blue poppy seed, a type made famous by the Dutch, is considered the highest quality because it can be used for garnish as well as for flavor. Blue poppy seed is actually a slate blue color. For fillings where a smooth texture and the rich, nutty flavor of the seed is desired, it is possible to buy ground poppy seed that has been mixed with honey or sugar. While these seeds do come from the poppy plant, they have no narcotic properties.

Poppy seeds do not contain essential oils. They do contain a fixed oil in amounts of from 50 to 60%.

The seeds are used as toppings for breads, rolls, and crackers, fillings for coffee cakes, strudels, and other pastries, and sometimes in cakes.

Caraway Seed

This spice is the fruit of a biennial of the parsely family, native to Europe. It is imported mostly from the Netherlands and Poland. Netherlands caraway is recognized as top grade. For the bakery trade, caraway is available ground as well as whole. This true caraway has no relationship to the charcoal caraway or black caraway, a small black seed that is used mainly for toppings on breads of central European and Russian origin.

Caraway yields from 3 to 7% of volatile oil. One part of the oil will dissolve in 10 parts of 80% alcohol.

Caraway is almost indispensible in the making of rye bread, and it is also good in corn muffins, cheese rolls, and certain kinds of cakes and cookies. It is compatible with the flavors of sugar, apple, peach, apricot, and rye.

Anise Seed

The fruit of a small annual plant of the parsley family, when dried, becomes the spice anise. It is oval in shape, somewhat like caraway, but is greenish-brown in color. It is native to Egypt, but most of our present supply comes from Spain, Mexico, and Turkey. Quality of the spice from each source is about the same. The flavor is recognized by most people as licorice. Very similar in flavor, but botanically unrelated, is star anise, a small star-shaped cluster of seeds. Star anise was formerly imported from China and has not been available since the embargo on communist goods.

The essential oil in anise seed is present in amount of 2 to 3%.

In baking, anise seed is used in icings and fillings for cakes and cookies, and toppings for coffee cakes and sweet rolls. It is compatible with sugar and most stewed fruits.

PURE AND ARTIFICAL VANILLA

Vanilla is certainly the most common flavoring added to bakery foods. It is not only a very desirable flavor by itself but also is an essential note in chocolate goods and many other compound flavors. Vanilla is the fruit of an orchid cultivated in tropical and semitropical countries. The pods, much like long string beans in appearance, are cured in special ways to bring out the characteristic aroma and taste of vanilla.

Although the ground pod can be added to foods as an ingredient, it is more common to use alcoholic extracts, which incorporate nearly all of the desirable flavor notes. These extracts are aged in glass or stainless steel containers until the reactions which lead to improved aroma have occurred.

The vanilla beans of commerce are described by type or region of origin, such as Mexican, Bourbon, Tahitian, etc. It is of little value for the baker to prescribe the bean blend for the extracts he purchases, since there is no reliable way to police the deliveries.

Pure vanilla extract is defined under U.S. FDA Standards in part as follows, "Pure vanilla extract is the solution in aqueous ethyl alcohol of the sapid odorous principles extractable from vanilla beans. In pure vanilla extract the content of ethyl alcohol is not less that 35% by volume and the content of vanilla constituents is not less than one unit weight of vanilla beans per gallon." The term "unit weight of vanilla beans per gallon" is defined as 13.35 oz of beans having a moisture content of 25% or less. Ingredients such as glycerine, propylene glycol, sucrose, dextrose, and invert sugar are listed as optional ingredients.

Since all manufacturers make vanilla extracts by very similar processes, and with concentrations of flavorants limited by the Standards, the flavor quality of different extracts will depend upon the types of vanilla beans used.

It is unfortunate that vanilla extracts sold to manufacturers have the reputation of being the most frequently adulterated of all food ingredients. The baker will find it advisable to buy only from reliable suppliers and to be prepared to pay more than the lowest quoted price. Careful evaluation of incoming shipments is important for keeping the supplier honest. Chemical analyses alone cannot determine the quality of the extract or its purity, but the lead number, the ash content, and the vanillin content are helpful in establishing a baseline.

Powdered vanilla or vanilla sugar is made by mixing ground beans with sugar or by coating sugar granules with an extract.

Oleoresin of vanilla is prepared by evaporating under vacuum the filtered extract of comminuted vanilla beans. It consists mostly of the resinous substances of the vanilla beans with very little of the balsamic flavor of the original extract. Oleoresin can be diluted with solvents to give the 10-fold extracts sometimes sold. No more than 4-fold concentration is possible by extraction methods.

It can be shown by panel tests that consumers prefer bakery products which are made with pure vanilla extracts as opposed to artificial flavors when two products are compared side by side (Bowden 1968). The difference in acceptability ratings is usually slight, on the average, and tends to disappear when there is not a comparison sample immediately available. Many very successful food products such as the most popular chocolate bar rely entirely on artificial vanilla flavor.

Although it is apparent that artificial flavors cannot approach the fine aroma and delicate taste contributed by good quality vanilla extracts, most consumers find vanillin or mixtures of vanillin and ethyl vanillin to be perfectly acceptable substitutes for the natural product. In very delicately flavored pastry creams and fillings, the differences between vanilla and vanillin are fairly obvious, but it is considerably harder to distinguish between chocolate products, for example, which are flavored with the two substances. Since the synthetic materials are so much cheaper, on an equivalent strength basis, than the vanilla extract, most bakers are willing to forego the fine nuances of flavor, which usually are not appreciated by their customers, in favor of a more competitive ingredient cost.

The aromatic components of both artificial and natural vanilla extracts tend to be lost in the baking process. The minor constituents of vanilla distill off quicker than vanillin or ethyl vanillin, so the change during baking is more apparent in products containing true vanilla extracts. The loss is greatest at elevated oven temperatures and in products baked almost to dryness, such as cookies.

Ethyl vanillin is considerably more expensive than vanillin but it does have a stronger flavor. The flavor quality of the two compounds is different, however, so a meaningful comparison of ingredient cost is difficult. Frequently the best results are obtained by using mixtures of the two compounds.

CACAO PRODUCTS

Chocolate is prepared from the seeds of an evergreen tree of the genus *Theobroma*. Several of these seeds are borne in a pod resembling somewhat a large acorn squash. After removing the seeds from the pod and fermenting them to facilitate the removal of the surrounding pulp (and to cause certain desirable flavor changes), they are dried or "cured." Next follows a roasting step which further develops the flavor and loosens the outer covering of the seeds. After the hull and the germ are removed by milling, the remainder of the seed, called the nib, is ready for processing into chocolate. The nibs are subjected to grinding and milling procedures which reduce the nonfatty substances to colloidal size and develop the texture which is characteristic of chocolate liquor, bitter chocolate, and bakers' chocolate (these are synonyms).

Addition of milk solids and/or sugar together with other flavoring materials such as vanilla, and sometimes emulsifiers, to chocolate liquor produces the "eating" chocolate varieties milk chocolate, sweet chocolate, and bittersweet chocolate. These products contain a minimum of 10, 15, and 35% chocolate liquor, respectively. In Table 9.1 the composition of several cacao products is compared.

Cocoa is chocolate from which a substantial proportion of the fatty material has been removed. This is usually accomplished by pressing, but sometimes solvent extraction is used to remove a very large percentage of the cocoa butter. It is usually agreed that the best chocolate quality and flavor are contained in the liquor, especially when it has been produced from good quality Accra, Bahia, or Arriba beans. Off-grade and poorer beans such as Sanchez mid-crop, Lagos, and mid-crop Accra are frequently used to prepare the low priced cocoas of commerce. Cocoa from superior beans can be obtained readily, but it sells for a premium.

FLAVORS AND COLORS

TABLE 9.1
COMPOSITION AND pH OF PRODUCTS DERIVED FROM CACAO

	Nibs, Roasted (%)	Chocolate Liquor (%)	Breakfast Cocoa (%)	Cocoa, Medium Fat (%)	Dutched Breakfast Cocoa (%)	Sweet Chocolate (%)	Milk Chocolate (%)	Chocolate Syrup (%)
Moisture	3.0	2.3	3.9	4.0	5.0	1.4	1.1	31.0
Ash	2.8	3.2	5.0	5.5	8.0	1.4	1.7	1.9
Protein	10.5	8.0	8.0	8.7	7.7	4.0	6.0	3.5
Fat	55.0	55.0	23.8	16.0	21.5	33.0	33.5	1.1
Fiber	2.6	2.6	4.6	5.0	4.3	1.4	0.5	0.6
Alkaloids	1.45	1.4	1.9	2.1	2.0	0.4	0.4	—
Carbohydrate[1]	25.2	26.6	44.3	48.7	40.2	61.3	55.2	56.0
pH	4.9	5.2–6.0	5.2–6.0	5.2–6.0	6.1–8.8	5.2–6.0	5.2–6.0	—

Source: Watt and Merrill (1963).
[1] Other than fiber.

Even though chocolate liquor undoubtedly has a superior taste and aroma, cocoa performs quite adequately in most bakery foods. The advantages of chocolate liquor are much less evident here than in eating chocolate, and the price differential is such as to convince most bakers, even those who deal in top quality goods, that a good grade of cocoa is entirely adequate for their purposes.

As stated above, the flavor quality of chocolate liquor is related to the type and origin of the bean, and the desirability of cocoas is related to the type of chocolate from which they were produced and to the percentage of fat which they contain. By U.S. FDA Standards (Anon. 1958), breakfast cocoa must contain a minimum of 22% cocoa butter. Bakers frequently use a less expensive grade which contains from about 8 to about 15% cocoa butter. The Standards identify cocoa having less than 10% fat as "low-fat cocoa." In unpublished experiments by the author, it has been shown that consumer panels cannot differentiate significantly between cocoas of 14 and 18.5% fat when they used as the flavoring ingredient in devil's food cakes. This finding applies only to cocoas made from the same lots of nibs, of course.

Treatment of cocoa nibs with alkalies (such as potassium carbonate) at some stage during the roasting process profoundly changes their characteristics and gives the "Dutched" chocolates and cocoas of commerce. Some of the changes observed are: the color of the cocoa becomes darker; the flavor changes and becomes stronger; some of the cocoa butter is saponified; the starch is partially gelatinized; cellulose materials swell; the natural cocoa acids are neutralized and the slightly acidic pH changes to a nearly neutral or slightly alkaline pH; and, some of the tissues are disintegrated. The net changes of importance to the baking industry are the changes to color and flavor, which sometimes make it possible to use less of the flavoring material, and an increase in the solution stability of the product. The pH change can also create problems with the leavening system, since a decrease in soda or an increase in the acidic components of the batter or dough is necessary in order to maintain the hydrogen ion concentration at the desired level in the finished product.

Bakers using natural cocoa sometimes achieve a result similar to Dutching by increasing the final pH of devil's food cakes to rather high levels. The cocoa pigments assume a different color and the flavor changes under these conditions. The so-called mahogany color of a true devil's food cake is due to these reactions.

Federal specifications are frequently useful guides for establishing commercial requirements. The U.S. Dept. of Agr. specification for cocoa (Anon, 1952) stipulates that breakfast type cocoa must contain at least 22% cacao fat and medium-fat cocoa must contain from 10 to 22% of cacao fat. Dutch process cocoas, according to this specification, shall have added alkaline materials (selected from among those permitted to be used for this purpose by the FDA) equivalent in neutralizing power to not more than 3 parts of anhydrous potassium carbonate per 100 parts of cocoa (sic) nibs from which the cocoa was made. All cocoas shall have a particle size such that 99% of the cocoa shall pass through a No. 140 U.S. Standard Sieve after it (the cocoa) has been disintegrated and washed with petroleum benzine.

The U.S. Dept. of Agr. specification for chocolate and sweet chocolate (Anon. 1949) requires that bitter chocolate contain not less than 50 and not more than 58% of cacao fat. Vanilla flavored sweet chocolate shall contain not less than 25% of chocolate liquor together with the addition of such amounts of cacao butter as may be needed to give a smooth consistency with the amount of sugar used, the total fat being not less than 30%. The total sucrose content shall not exceed 57% and the product shall be flavored with vanilla, vanillin, or ethyl vanillin, and it may contain lecithin, phosphatides, and other stabilizers.

Many writers have published tables of correction factors to apply to the shortening percentage when cocoas of varying fat contents are used in the formula. Actually, cocoa butter is not a particularly good shortening agent and probably does not function in this capacity to any great extent in the usual formula. At any rate, the use of a universal correction factor for all types of bakery products is certain to lead to trouble. When a product containing cocoa is to be formulated, it should be developed in the usual thorough manner and not by calculations involving published correction factors.

Tests applied to cacao products to determine their quality include: (1) fat content, (2) particle size, (3) color—both intrinsic and potential, (4) pH, (5) moisture content, (6) flavor, and (7) microbiological contamination.

The color and flavor are best evaluated in the food in which the ingredient will be used, since both of these characteristics can change markedly depending upon the processing conditions and associated materials. Color, especially, is much affected by the pH of the finished product.

Because of the method of manufacture, it is difficult for the cocoa processor to hold the fat content closer than within 1% of the specification figure. For this reason, it is customary to specify at least a 2% range, such at 10–12% fat. There are significant differences between fat content determined by the Soxhlet extraction technique and the acid hydrolysis method, the former giving considerably lower values, so it is necessary to state in the specification the analytical procedure by which the fat will be determined. In this country, the Soxhlet extraction technique is the preferred method.

The pH of a water slurry of natural (nonalkalized) cocoas will vary depending on many factors in the history of the material, and some of these factors are not controllable by the manufacturer. Alkalized cocoa can generally be held within a range of ±0.2 units by controlling the processing conditions.

Particle size is not quite as critical for bakery use as for some other applications (chocolate milk, etc.). It is more important to get fine-ground cocoas for use in icings and fillings than for doughs and batters. A cocoa of very fine particle size might be described as 0.5% maximum on a 325-mesh screen. A reasonably satisfactory fineness for cocoa to be used in batters would be 0.5% maximum on a 200-mesh screen. Although there are several procedures being used for wet-screening cocoas, a method developed by technologists at the Robert A. Johnston Co. seems to have several advantages over all others. It avoids the usual rubbing and spraying techniques needed to disperse agglomerates and facilitate the passing of fine particles through the sieve. This method involves suspending a wire mesh, which has been fitted with sidewalls more than an inch high, in a bath of solvent that can be ultrasonically vibrated. The solvent enters through the screen and fills the sieve about halfway, so that there are two "chambers," the ultrasonic bath and the sieve compartment, communicating with each other through the screen. The rapid and continuous agitation afforded by the ultrasonic vibration keeps the particles suspended in a continually renewed bath of solvent. A few seconds usually suffices to wash out all of the soluble fat.

COLORS

Color additives in the baking trade are substantially restricted to decorative adjuncts such as icings and ornaments for cakes, but there are some minor applications for coloring doughs yellow, etc. Those colors which are used are frequently purchased as compounded mixtures in liquid or gel form designed for easy measuring and incorporation. All food colors, however, must be selected from series approved by government agencies. There are two categories of acceptable color additives, the certified list and the uncertified group. The certified colors include the chemically synthesized dyes and their lakes. Lakes are water soluble dyes adsorbed or chemically bound to insoluble substrates. Uncertified colors are principally derived from plant materials by various processing techniques and, in many cases, have been approved for food applications because of a long history of prior usage. At the present time, the lists shown in Tables 9.2 and 9.3 are in a state of flux. For example, FD & C Red No. 2, which has been used in large quantities for many years, has come under suspicion and may be delisted or at least limited in usage. Substitutes might be Red No. 3 or the new Red No. 40.

CARAMEL COLOR

Caramel color is an important ingredient for the baking trade because it is widely used to darken rye breads. The light rye flours are desired for their superior flavor, but they are totally inadequate to give the dark brown color expected by the consumer. Caramel gives the baker flexibility in adjusting color without affecting the flavor.

TABLE 9.2
UNCERTIFIED COLOR ADDITIVES FOR FOOD [1]

Color Additive	Restrictions on Use
Annatto extract	—
Beta-carotene	—
Beet powder	—
β-apo-8'-carotenal	15 mg per lb or pt
Canthaxanthin	30 mg per lb or pt
Caramel	—
Carmine	—
Carrot oil	—
Cochineal extract	—
Cottonseed flour, toasted partially defatted cooked	—
Ferrous gluconate	Black olives only
Fruit and vegetable juices	—
Grape skin extract (enocianina)	Beverages
Paprika and paprika oleoresin	—
Riboflavin	—
Saffron	—
Titanium dioxide	1% or less
Turmeric and turmeric oleoresin	—
Ultramarine blue	Salt only
Carbon black (Impingement) [2]	—

[1] Feed (animal) additives not included.
[2] Provisionally listed.

TABLE 9.3
CERTIFIED COLOR ADDITIVES

Color additive	Restrictions
Permanently listed	
FD&C Blue No. 1	—
FD&C Red No. 3	—
FD&C Yellow No. 5	—
Orange B	Sausage casings only
Citrus Red No. 2	Orange skins only
Provisionally listed	
Blue No. 1 Lake	—
Red No. 3 Lake	—
Yellow No. 5 Lake	—
FD&C Red No. 2[1]	—
FD&C Blue No. 2[1]	—
FD&C Green No. 3[1]	—
FD&C Red No. 4[1]	Maraschino cherries only
FD&C Violet No. 1[1]	—
FD&C Yellow No. 6[1]	—

[1] Lakes of these colors are also provisionally listed.

Caramel coloring has no relationship to caramel candy. The baker's variety is manufactured by heat treating high DE corn syrups in the presence of reactants such as certain alkalies. It is a very dark, almost black syrup of about 11 lb per gallon density. The pH will be near 4.0–4.2, the solids content will be near 65%, and it will be fairly low in viscosity. The flavor will be mild.

Although the hues or spectral distributions of colors from the different kinds and brands of caramel are similar, this ingredient imparts varying shades to bakery products depending upon the amounts used and the background colors. The color of the finished product may range from a light tannish yellow to a very dark brown, as in some "pumpernickels." Usually between 1 and 5% of the flour weight is used in diet, wheat, and rye breads.

The common containers for caramel color are 5-gal. steel pails, 30-gal. steel drums, and 56-gal steel drums. Bulk deliveries in rail tankers and tank trucks are available. Color changes continue in storage, but even so, high quality caramel colors can be stored a year or longer at room temperature. Under certain adverse conditions, caramel can polymerize into an amorphous irreversible gel.

Dry, powdered forms are sold by some manufacturers, but they are usually considerably more expensive then the syrups.

BIBLIOGRAPHY

ANON. 1949. Chocolate and Sweet Chocolate. U.S. Dept. Agr. Specification *JJJ-C-271a*, Febr. 7.

ANON. 1952. Cocoa. U.S. Dept. Agr. Specification *JJJ-C-501b*, Oct. 7.

ANON. 1958. Definitions and Standards for Chocolate and Cocoa Products. Food, Drug and Cosmetic Act No. 2, Par 14. U.S. Food and Drug Administration, Washington, D.C.

BATES, G. C. 1967. Use less—get more. Food Eng. *38*, No. 10, 26–28.

BOWDEN, G. L. 1968. Judicious use of vanilla. Proc. Am. Soc. Bakery Engrs. *1968*, 299–304.

DOWNEY, W. J. and EISERLE, R. J. 1966. Cereal Sci. Today *11*, No. 11.

GUENTHER, E. 1966. Spices. *In* Encyclopedia of Chemical Technology, 2nd Edition, Vol. 10, R. E. Kirk and D. F. Othmer (Editors). John Wiley & Sons, New York.

LINNER R. T. 1965. Caramel coloring. Bakers Dig. *39*, No. 2, 16–17, 19.

PARRY J. W. 1962. Spices: Their Morphology, Histology and Chemistry. Chemical Publishing Co., New York.

PECK, F. W. 1955. Caramel color. Food Eng. *26*, No. 3, 20–24.

WATT, BERNICE K., and MERRILL, ANNABEL L. 1963. Composition of Foods. U.S. Dept. Agr., Agr. Res. Serv. Handbook *8*.

CHAPTER 10

MINOR INGREDIENTS

In this chapter, the ingredients which are used in relatively small quantities in bakery foods will be discussed. It is only in the sense of quantity that they are "minor" components. In terms of their effects on the sensory qualities and physical characteristics of the product, they are frequently very important ingredients—even indispensable.

To some extent this chapter serves as a catch-all to include those ingredients which could not be fitted into the categories described in the preceding chapters. The decision as to where an ingredient belonged was a difficult one in many cases. For example, malt products are described in this chapter even though the nondiastatic versions would have fitted very well into "Flavors and Colors." Salt is also described here because of its pronounced effects on fermentation and other dough properties which are separate from its flavor enhancing effect.

MALT PRODUCTS

Malt is prepared from a cereal grain, usually barley, by moistening it with water, allowing it to sprout under controlled conditions, and then drying it at elevated temperatures. Witt (1970) has given a detailed account of its manufacture. The natural processes accompanying sprouting create or release in active form large quantities of enzymes and change the constituents of the grain in many ways. The greatest consumption of malt is by the alcoholic beverage industries, but considerable quantities are used in milling and baking.

Malt products available to the baker may conveniently be classified as malt flour, malt syrup, or dried malt syrup. Each of these categories may be further subdivided into diastatic and nondiastatic products. Malt flour is the ground grain itself, malt syrups are concentrated water extracts of the grain, and dried malt syrups are derived from their liquid counterparts by removing most of the moisture at elevated temperatures.

Malt is fairly high in vitamins and essential amino acids and so is a nutritionally valuable additive. Table 10.1 gives a complete breakdown of the nutritive properties of malt flour. Malt syrup contains 60–65% carbohydrate, 5.5–6% protein, 1.5% ash and 20–25% moisture.

TABLE 10.1
THE COMPOSITION OF BARLEY MALT FLOUR[1]

General Analysis (%)	
Protein	11.5–14.5
Fat	1.5–2.5
Ash	2.0–3.0
Fiber	2.0–6.0
Nitrogen free extract	68.0–74.0
Composition of Fat (% of Total Fat)	
Stearic acid	5.10
Oleic Acid	16.40
Palmitic	8.20
Linoleic	49.40
Linolenic	0.82
Vitamin Content (Mg/Lb)	
Biotin	0.1
Niacin	41.0–68.0
Pantothenic acid	2.0–7.8
Pyridoxine	2.7–3.6
Riboflavin	0.9–1.8
Thiamine	1.3–1.6
Choline	Trace
Inositol	Trace
Essential Amino Acid Content (% of Malt)	
Arginine	0.65
Histidine	0.29
Isoleucine	0.52
Leucine	0.81
Lysine	0.49
Methionine	0.18
Phenylalanine	0.62
Threonine	0.43
Tryptophan	0.22
Valine	0.70
Mineral Content	
Aluminum (ppm)	2–9
Calcium (%)	0.08–0.13
Copper (ppm)	4–12
Fluorine (ppm)	9–12
Iodine (ppm)	0.07
Iron (ppm)	20–50
Magnesium (%)	0.10–0.19
Manganese (ppm)	10–18
Nickel (ppm)	0.34
Phosphorus (%)	0.30–0.50
Potassium (%)	0.30
Silicon (%)	0.20–0.90
Sodium (ppm)	0.30
Sulfur (%)	0.13–0.22
Zinc (ppm)	16–20

[1] Courtesy Froedtert Malting Co.

The minerals and low molecular weight nitrogenous compounds present in malt are said to be useful as yeast "nutrients."

Diastatic Malt

Diastatic malt products differ from their nondiastatic counterparts in having considerable enzymatic activity. The malted grain from which these products are derived is a veritable storehouse of enzymes, most of which have never been adequately investigated, but the only two types which are of importance to the baker are the proteolytic enzymes and the amylolytic enzymes. The latter group, comprising the "diastase" of the older writers, contains at least two different enzymes, commonly designated alpha-amylase or the dextrinizing enzyme, and beta-amylase or the saccharifying enzymes. Alpha-amylase splits the starch molecule at random points, forming smaller molecules of widely varying size. The net effect of this enzyme is to reduce the viscosity of susceptible starch suspensions with the production of relatively small amounts of fermentable sugars. End products of the reaction are chiefly dextrins (compounds containing several glucose residues) which cannot be used by bakers' yeast. There is some doubt that the amounts of alpha-amylase normally encountered in sound flour have any significant effect on its baking properties in the absence of native or added beta-amylase.

The action of beta-amylase on starch results in the production of maltose by the progressive release of terminal sugar residues from the starch molecule. This enzyme cannot attack the starch molecule inside the points at which it is branched, and so a residue of limit dextrin of high molecular weight remains. These limit dextrins cannot be fermented, but they are customarily produced in smaller amounts than the dextrins resulting from the action of alpha-amylase.

When the two types of amylases act in conjunction, a much greater conversion of starch into fermentable sugars results than when either of them acts alone. Alpha-amylase can act between the branch points which halt hydrolysis by beta-amylase. The new end groups exposed by this action are then subject to attack by beta-amylase. As a result, the amount of limit dextrin is decreased and the effective concentration of molecules capable of being hydrolyzed by beta-amylase is increased so that both the rate and the final yield are considerably increased in starch suspensions containing mixtures of the two enzymes. For example, the rapid and relatively complete conversion of starch to fermentable sugars, typical of the action of malt, is a consequence of the combined action of alpha-and beta-amylase. Conversely, the slow rate of sugar development in unsupplemented flour suspensions or doughs results from a deficiency of these enzymes and particularly of beta-amylase.

The action of beta-amylase on undamaged starch granules is very slow. Alpha-amylase does attack the undamaged (no visible damage) starch granules at an appreciable rate. Both enzymes attack gelatinized starch very rapidly, but this reaction cannot be of much importance in the bread-making process because the starch in dough does not become gelatinized until virtually all of the enzyme activity has been destroyed by heat. Starch granules which have been mechanically damaged during milling are also broken down by both alpha-and beta-amylase. Perhaps 3–4% of the starch granules in a hard wheat flour sample are visibly damaged. This mechanical damage is due to shearing forces and pressures exerted during the milling of the grain on the granules and on the endosperm matrix containing the granules. Consequently, the proportion of damaged granules is a function of the milling conditions, and may vary not only from mill to mill, but also between flours of different extractions. However, flours of similar extraction made from the same types of wheat and made at the same mill should have a rather constant proportion of damaged granules.

The capacity of malt to convert starch to reducing substances (maltose) can be expressed as the Lintner value, °L, or as maltose equivalent. When tested by the standard procedure (Anon. 1957), degrees Lintner equal about ¼ of the maltose value. In each case, the rating of nondiastatic malt is theoretically zero, although in practice malts of 10°L or less are classified as nondiastatic malt. A good barley malt flour might rate as high as 124°L. Diastatic malt syrups commercially available have ratings of 20, 40, or 60°L, and are described as low, medium, or high diastatic products, respectively.

The federal Standards of Identity for bread (1952) permit the use of nondiastatic malt syrup and dried malt syrup, and/or diastatic malt syrup, dried malt syrup, malted barley flour, and malted wheat flour in all varieties of bread and rolls covered by the standards. Maximum and minimum quantities of these ingredients are not specified.

Diastatic malt syrups are frequently recommended for use in bread formulas at the rate of 1–1¼ lb of syrup per hundredweight of flour. An excessive amount may darken the crumb, favor overfermentation, and promote the tendency of the dough to become sticky.

Nondiastatic Malt

Nondiastatic malt products have been subjected to temperatures high enough to inactivate substantially all of the amylolytic or starch-digesting enzymes present in the sprouted grain. These malts are used principally to impart flavor and color to baked products. They also have some effect on texture and supply fermentable carbohydrates and other nutrients to the yeast.

Nondiastatic malt products are high in sugars and low molecular weight dextrins which have been more or less caramelized by the high temperature processing which they have received. Consequently they can contribute a detectable amount of sweetness to products in which they are used. In addition, there is a peculiar and characteristic flavor to malt products which many people find very desirable. The use of malt in malted milk is a clear indication that there is a true liking for malt flavor in a large segment of the population. The color changes accompanying the caramelization and other nonenzymatic browning reactions which result from the high temperature processing make the product valuable as a coloring agent. It is frequently used to add color to dark rye breads and whole wheat breads. Special dietary breads may also make use of this property. On the other hand, use of high roasted malts in white bread is definitely limited by the darkening which is observed with moderate additions.

Both diastatic and nondiastatic malt contain considerable quantities of sugars including maltose, a disaccharide which is fermented by bakers' yeast late in the bread making process when glucose and fructose are absent, and glucose, a monosaccharide which is used very rapidly by fermenting yeast. If a dough does not contain maltose, the other fermentable sugars may be exhausted before the period of pan proof, a critical time when sustained gassing power is necessary in order to produce loaves having good volume. If maltose is present in the dough, either initially or through the action of amylolytic enzymes, the monosaccharides glucose and fructose (or sucrose, which is rapidly split into these monosaccharides by an enzyme present on the cell wall of yeast) are used first, then a lag period ensues, and finally the maltose is attacked leading to a final relatively rapid stage of gas production. This means that there is an inherent mechanism for assuring adequate gassing during pan proof if the doughs contain adequate maltose and the fermentation conditions are properly adjusted.

There are two ways of getting maltose into doughs. One method is to add the sugar to the dough in the form of malt, and the other is to rely on the production of maltose from the flour starch by diastatic enzymes. The latter approach is discussed in the next section.

ENZYME PREPARATIONS

Fungal Proteases

Fungal protease acts on dough by breaking down the flour proteins. A mellowing effect on the dough results. Mixing requirements of strong flours used in sponges can be considerably reduced when proteases are used. These enzymes also increase the extensibility of doughs and thus are of value in controlling the pliability, eliminating buckiness, and insuring proper machinability. In many cases, it is possible to eliminate these difficulties without resort to added enzymes through changes in processing conditions, absorption, etc.

The fungus *Aspergillus oryzae* is usually employed for production of proteases for the baking industry. The mold is grown in a liquid medium which contains the necessary nutrients. As it grows, the mold excretes into the medium many enzymes, among them the desired protein digesting catalysts. After a time, the solid material is removed by filtration or centrifugation, and a mixture of organic compounds including the proteases is precipitated from the liquid as a result of the addition of some solvent such as ethyl alcohol or of inorganic salts. Usually, no further purification of the precipitate is attempted, and drying, and sometimes standardization by adding inert fillers, are the only remaining steps before the enzyme preparation is packaged.

For retail sale, the proteases are frequently made into tablets of standardized activity. The strength of the preparation is commonly expressed in terms of hemoglobin units. These indicate the rate of hydrolysis (or solubilization) of hemoglobin, which is a convenient standard substrate. A potent precipitate may exhibit an activity of 100,000 or more hemoglobin units (HU) per gram. Dilutions offered to the bakery trade often have an activity of about 300 HU per gram with a suggested rate of usage of 4 oz per 100 lb of flour.

Salt inhibits the action of fungal proteolytic enzymes on gluten, so that their effect on straight doughs containing about 2% salt is negligible. When active dry yeast is used as the leavening agent, proteases are not normally employed since the yeast itself has a mellowing effect on the dough (Reed and Thorn 1957).

Fungal Amylases

These enzymes are distributed as replacements for the amylolytic enzymes of diastatic malt. They provide a means of adding necessary starch digesting properties to a dough without also adding the flavor and color of malt. In general, the fungal preparations are also cheaper per unit of activity than malt. On the other hand, they do not have the nutritive quality of grain preparations, and in many cases the flavor of malt is needed. The general discussion of the net effect of malt diastase on dough properties is also applicable to fungal amylases.

Enzymatically Active Soy Flour Derivatives

Enzymatically active soy flour is used extensively in the commercial preparation of white bread. The enzymes chiefly concerned are the lipoxidases, although proteinases and beta-amylase play a minor role. Alpha-amylase is absent.

Lipoxidases in bread dough have three functions:

(1) Bleaching of the carotenoid pigments with the result that whiter bread may be obtained with both unbleached and bleached flours (bleached flour usually contains a substantial amount of carotenoid pigments).

(2) Influencing dough properties; frequently this is the most important

function. Doughs containing lipoxidases possess what bakers term greater "mixing tolerance" and dough extensibility, which means that they can be mixed longer and machined without damaging the rheological properties required to make good bread. The improvement in mixing tolerance can be demonstrated by the farinograph, and improvement in dough extensibility may be observed readily by the experienced baker during various stages of bread making.

(3) Contributing bread flavor. The soybean contains at least two lipoxidases, one active chiefly on triglycerides and the other on fatty acids (Koch et al. 1958). Research in recent years has shown that the lipoxidases promote the oxidation of gluten, strengthening and improving dough properties. The effect on dough properties is thought to be the result of lipoxidase action on the lipo-protein complexes of flour. The latter apparently are connected with bread volume, crumb firmness, grain, and texture. Because dough properties are improved by soy enzymes, bread quality is also enhanced. Among the improvements obtained are finer grain, softer texture, and retardation of staling.

The beta-amylase of soy flour is unique in that it has greater heat stability than the beta-amylase of wheat and barley. Thus, sugars are produced from starch by soy beta-amylase for a considerable time after wheat and barley beta-amylase are heat inactivated. For baking procedures which exhaust sugars during fermentation, this action will contribute to a better crust color and to a more vigorous fermentation at the end of the baking process.

Two types of product containing enzymatically active soy flour are available to the commercial baker. One type consists of soy flour with partially dextrinized corn flour or other cereal flours or starches. A second type contains, in addition to soy flour, calcium peroxide and sometimes phosphates. The latter type of product is used principally for the well-known calcium peroxide effect, which is to increase water absorption and to form drier, less extensible doughs. The effect of lipoxidase here is superimposed on the calcium peroxide effect and desirable dough extensibility is restored without imparing water absorption.

The product called Wytase contains full-fat, enzymatically active soy flour and dextrinized corn flour. Enzyme activity is standardized at a level which requires optimum usage at the rate of 1% based on the flour. The corn flour fraction is prepared from purified corn grits, heat dextrinized under controlled conditions to provide uniform water absorption, which is a satisfactory measure of the degree of conversion of the starch. The corn flour fraction thus modified contributes to water absorption and bread yield. It also provides a more readily available substrate for amylase activity than unmodified starches do. Doughs made with 1% Wytase will normally require 1% additional water.

Depending somewhat on the quantity of enzymatically active soy flour used in the bread formula and also on the quality of some of the other ingredients, especially shortening and milk solids, bread will have a pleasing flavor regarded by many to be the most important reason for using a product of this type. Recent work on bread flavor suggests that the lipoxidases initiate mild reactions of the fatty components of a bread dough, and these are sufficient to produce minute quantities of cleavage products of the aldehyde type which contribute pleasant notes to bread flavor. Much of the bread produced commercially is made by procedures which result in extreme blandness, for which reason the enhancement of flavor by soy enzymes assumes some importance (Ferrari 1959).

INHIBITORS OF MICROBIOLOGICAL SPOILAGE

The only form of microbiological spoilage with which the average baker has to contend is mold growth. A few decades ago, rope caused by *Bacillus mesentericus* or similar organisms, was a serious problem, but today's improved sanitary practices in the bakery combined with rapid turnover of the finished product have virtually eliminated this form of spoilage. Many bakers in the United States have never seen a true case of rope. Mold spoilage still remains a problem, however. No feasible amount of sanitation can prevent contamination of bakery products with the ubiquitous mold spores, and an abundant growth of mycelia and sporangia can appear on a loaf within three days if the conditions of humidity and temperature are right.

Over the years, a considerable number of chemical compounds have been proposed as fungicides or fungistats for use on, or in, food substances. Most of these materials are no longer heard of because they were shown to be either toxic to man or innocuous to molds—frequently both. However, the sodium and calcium salts of propionic acid and sodium diacetate have been used with good results for some time. Most of the organic acids having carbon chain lengths of 1 to 14 exert some fungistatic action but various objections, including that of inadequate supply have limited commercial applications of all but the two and three carbon compounds. It is the acid moiety of these substances which is effective, use of the salts being merely a convenience. However, some authorities have claimed that mixed salts have greater effectiveness than the combined acids.

According to the U.S. FDA (Anon. 1952), white, enriched, or raisin bread and rolls covered by the Standards of Identity may contain not more than 0.32% calcium propionate or sodium propionate (or a mixture) on the flour weight basis provided the label includes a statement that the compound has been "added to prevent spoilage." Whole wheat or graham bread and rolls may contain as much as 0.38% of the compounds on the basis of the whole wheat flour used as 100%.

Many persons claim that they can detect by odor or taste the presence of propionic acid in baked products, even when it is present in the small concentrations permitted by the federal government.

DOUGH IMPROVERS AND YEAST FOODS

These products are usually mixtures of several inorganic salts together with starch or flour as an extender. Most of them contain ingredients having these functions: (1) Gluten oxidizing agents such as potassium bromate, potassium iodate, or calcium peroxide; (2) calcium salts, usually phosphates or sulfates, which correct any lack of hardness in the dough water and provide a certain small amount of additional buffering action to partially offset unusually alkaline conditions of the water; and (3) ammonium salts to supply nitrogen in a form which can be used by yeast for protein building.

Some typical products are Arkady, Fermaloid, and Paniplus (these names are registered trade marks). Following are some typical formulations for three different types of dough improvers:

Type No. 1

	%
Calcium sulfate	24.93
Ammonium chloride	9.38
Potassium bromate	0.27
Sodium chloride	24.93
Starch and moisture	40.49

Type No. 2

	%
Potassium bromate	0.12
Potassium iodate	0.10
Ammonium sulfate	7.01
Sodium chloride	19.35
Monocalcium phosphate	50.06
Starch and moisture	23.36

Type No. 3

	%
Calcium peroxide	0.65
Diammonium phosphate	9.00
Dicalcium phosphate	90.00
Starch	0.35

Amounts of the first two types recommended for use in bread doughs are 0.25% on the flour weight basis in straight doughs, and 0.5% in sponge dough procedures. Type No. 3 is frequently used at the 0.25–0.50% level.

Oxidizing Agents

Some of the effects which have been attributed to the proper use of added oxidizers in dough are larger volume, brighter crumb, better texture, and improved appearance of the finished loaf as a result of greater symmetry and darker crust. The oxidizers have little effect on gas production, they affect principally gas retention. However, there is some controversy about their exact mode of action although the majority of cereal chemists incline to the view that they exert their effect chiefly as a result of the oxidation of sulfhydryl groups on the proteins. According to this theory, the number of —S—S— bonds between protein chains is increased by the oxidizing action and a more tenacious network of molecules is formed. The gross result is a tougher, drier, more extensible dough which gives rise to loaves having the improved characteristics cited above. An extensive discussion of this theory was given in the Osborne Medal address of Sullivan (1948). An opposing theory, put forth with much vigor for several years, was that of Jorgensen (1939) who believed that the effect of oxidizers such as potassium bromate was due to their inhibition of proteolytic enzymes present in flour.

By far the most commonly used oxidizing chemical applied to doughs (as contrasted with the gases used by mills for this purpose) is potassium bromate. Calcium peroxide and potassium iodate are used to some extent. Each of these compounds affect dough somewhat differently. Potassium iodate begins its action earlier in the baking process than bromate. It also acts at higher pH levels and gives a somewhat drier dough with improved machinability. Bromate does not exert much influence during the mixing period but works later in the processing cycle to shorten the fermentation time, among other effects. Calcium peroxide gives drier and more pliable and elastic doughs which have a greater oven spring and can be taken with a somewhat shorter pan proof. It increases absorption considerably and should be incorporated at the dough stage.

Not all flours benefit from the addition of oxidizers. Well aged flour or flour which has been treated with optimum quantities of oxidizers at the mill may not show any beneficial results from use of dough improvers and may, in fact, give doughs and bread of inferior quality when supplemented in this manner. Flours which react best to supplementation are likely to be long extraction, freshly milled flours from wheats of generally good baking quality. Short extraction flours from poor varieties of wheat may not be improved at all by the addition of oxidizers.

Mills frequently add from 1 to 4 gm of potassium bromate per 100 kg of flour. As a general rule, supplemented flours are underbromated by the mills which use this oxidizer so that a safety factor is present. Neither potassium iodate nor calcium peroxide is used to any appreciable extent by the flour mills.

According to Kirk (1959), bromate can be used to overcome some of the deleterious effects resulting from overmalting, and from use of milks having poor baking quality. Conversely, a flour or dough to which an excess of bromate has been added can be improved by the addition of extra malt.

According to Doose and Wolter (1955), overtreatment of doughs with oxidizers can sometimes be recognized by appearance of ruptures on the dough surface at the end of the fermentation period. As a result, the dough becomes rough and uneven during molding. At extremely high levels of supplementation the proofing period is also extended, i.e., the dough is "bucky." Loaves made from overtreated doughs show irregular grain, a rough surface, reduced volume, and gray crumb color. Doose and Wolter state that larger amounts of bromate are called for when short fermentation time, low dough temperature, soft doughs, small additions of yeast, short times of kneading, or milk doughs are encountered. Smaller amounts of bromate should be added with long fermentation time, high dough temperatures, firm doughs, large additions of yeast, and intensive kneading. Remixing of overtreated doughs will usually completely eliminate the deleterious effects of the excess oxidizer.

Ascorbic acid is not at this time allowed by the Definitions and Standards of Identity for bread and rolls, but there are reasons to believe this situation will change. Although it might appear from its formula and usual reactions that ascorbic acid would be a reducing agent, it acts as an oxidizing "mediator" where there is free access to oxygen of the air. Therefore, ascorbic acid is an efficient oxidizer in conventional breadmaking process. The compound which reacts with the gluten proteins is evidently dehydroascorbate. In closed systems, such as continuous mixing chambers, which do not have free access to air, ascorbic acid does act as a reducing substance, causing weakening of the gluten. Azodicarbonamide is a relatively new oxidant for doughs. It reacts rapidly, similarly to calcium peroxide, and its overall effect is also similar to that of peroxide. This compound does not donate oxygen atoms but instead exerts its effect by taking up two hydrogen atoms per molecule. Azodicarbonamide is frequently used in combination with bromate in continuous doughs at levels of about 20 ppm and 45 ppm, respectively.

TABLE 10.2
APPROVED OXIDATION MATERIALS

Chemical Name	Chemical Formula	Rate of Reaction	Reduced Form
Potassium iodate	KIO_3	Rapid	KI
Calcium iodate	$Ca(IO_3)_2$	Medium	CaI_2
Potassium bromate	$KBrO_3$	Slow	KBr
Calcium bromate	$Ca(BrO_3)_2$	Slow	$CaBr_2$
Calcium peroxide	CaO_2	Rapid	CaO
Azodicarbonamide	$H_2NCON=NCONH_2$	Rapid	Biurea

Yeast Foods

The use of ammonium salts, phosphates, and sulfates in dough improvers and yeast foods is based on the hypothesis that these substances improve the fermentation capacity of yeast in doughs. It should be recognized at the outset of this discussion that the growth or reproduction of yeast in bread doughs has not been shown to be either a necessary or a desirable accompaniment of the development of flavor or gas. Bakers' yeast as ordinarily supplied to the trade consists of very healthy, vigorous cells which can readily ferment at nearly the same rate throughout the entire dough processing cycle. If the gassing power is shown to be inadequate due to an insufficient supply of yeast at any stage, the proper remedy is to add more yeast, not to try to grow yeast in the dough.

Atkin et al. (1946) have shown that some of the substances commonly considered to be necessary for growth also have an accelerating effect on the gas production of yeast fermenting in artificial media. Potassium, magnesium, ammonium, sulfate, and phosphate are the principal inorganic ions found to be required. Vitamin B_1, thiamine, also can markedly increase the rate of fermentation. As these authors point out, most if not all, of the accelerating substances are present in doughs in sufficient amounts to support fermentation at optimum rates. For example, they state:

(1) "It is therefore probable that the phosphate content of flour is ordinarily sufficient to maintain yeast at its maximal fermentation rate, provided all other factors are present in adequate amount. (2) It seems probable from these data that sulfate, in adequate amount, is present in white flour. (3) As with phosphorus and magnesium, there is evidence that flour contains sufficient quantities of potassium and hence conceivably could make available adequate amounts for the nutrition of yeast. (4) Although a large proportion of the thamine of the wheat berry is removed in the course of the milling process which produces white flour, the amount retained is sufficient to exert maximal acceleration in most cases."

Minerals and Buffers

The effect of the cations of water on dough quality has been explained in some detail in the preceding chapters on water and yeast. If water is very low in such ions as calcium, the gluten may be adversely affected with resultant poor dough quality. Use of some of the salts which are included in most dough improvers is indicated in such cases. After an optimum level of concentration is reached, further additions have little effect.

If the water supply is alkaline, the buffering action of some of the salts used in dough improvers may bring the pH down slightly. Considering the small amounts of these substances which are customarily added to doughs, it is difficult to see how the effect could be very pronounced.

PROPERTIES OF GELATIN

Gelatin is a generic term used to identify a group of proteinaceous substances prepared by the partial hydrolysis of collagen, the latter being a material found in several animal tissues. Bones and pork skin are the two main commercial raw materials for gelatin manufacture. Type A, an acid-reacting gelatin, is produced from pork skin and has a pH range of 3.8–4.5 with an isoelectric point between pH 8.3 and 8.7. Type B, the alkaline-reacting gelatin, is prepared from bones and other animal by-products. Its pH range is from 5 to 7, and its isoelectric point is in the range of pH 4.7–5.0. The isoelectric point differences are chiefly responsible for the difference in behavior of the two materials (Kramer 1967). In this country, Type A, made from pork skins, is the commoner product.

The viscosity and other properties of a gelatin solution vary with the pH. The viscosity is lowest at the isoelectric point. As the pH is moved away from this point, the viscosity will increase to a maximum which will be several times the minimum. Selection of the proper bloom-strength of gelatin intended as an ingredient in a particular product will depend to some extent on transient economic factors. Although it is not strictly true that larger amounts of weaker gelatin can be substituted for high bloom-strength gelatin in a formula, there is an inverse relationship of bloom-strength and quantity which is reasonably valid in the intermediate ranges. Therefore, the selection of the bloom-strength which gives the lowest total cost for the amount required in a given formula must take into consideration the current market price of the available gelatins.

The bloom-strength of a gelatin refers to a measurement of the rigidity of a gel of standard composition as made by an instrument called the Bloom gelometer. This form of penetrometer determines the weight required to push a 12.7 mm diam circular plunger from the surface to a depth of 4 mm into the gel under standard conditions. Gelatins may be procured in the range of 50–300 bloom. The gel sample is prepared by dissolving 7.5 gm of the gelatin in 105 gm of distilled water at 140°F. The solution is gelled by holding it at 50°F for 18 hr prior to the penetrometer measurement.

Flavor and color of gelatin are also important but can be expected to vary only slightly in gelatins of similar bloom-strength obtained from different suppliers.

SALT

The ultimate sources of commercial salt are underground deposits of the crystalline mineral and saline water from the sea and certain lakes. The salt water is evaporated by solar energy. Underground deposits are mined or tapped by circulating water through bore holes. Crude salt obtained from these sources is further purified by recrystallization and other procedures to yield a material suitable for food use.

Nearly all salt offered for food use is of high purity. A typical analysis is given in Table 10.3. Principle variations among brands are crystal size and shape.

Granulated or common salt is made from brine which has been purified in a vacuum pan. The resultant cube-shaped salt crystal is extremely hard and has a medium solubility rate. Alberger flake salt is made from brine that has been treated to remove much of the calcium and magnesium from the brine. The Alberger method of crystallization gives small flake-like crystals which dissolve more rapidly than granulated salt.

The so-called dendritic salt is a form which results when crystallization is carried out in the presence of yellow prussiate of soda (sodium ferrocyanide decahydrate). A maximum of 13 ppm of the additive is permitted in the finished product. The particle is branched or star-shaped and filled with microscopic cavities. It has a relatively low bulk density, high specific surface area, resistance to caking, and a rapid dissolving rate. Because it is porous, this form of salt is a fairly good adsorbent for some nonaqueous liquids. Some manufacturers offer dendritic salt mixed with

TABLE 10.3
CHEMICAL COMPOSITION OF BAKERS' FINE FLAKE SALT

Sodium chloride (%)	99.95 ± 0.01
Calcium sulfate (%)	0.02–0.06
Calcium chloride (%)	0.00–0.02
Magnesium chloride (%)	0.00–0.01
Copper (ppm)	less than 1.5 avg
Iron (ppm)	less than 1.5 avg
Moisture (%)	less than 0.1
Insolubles (ppm)	less than 20

Source: Strong (1969).

antioxidants as a convenient means of retarding rancidity development in snacks, peanut butter, margarine, and sausage.

Other types of salt which can be obtained from certain suppliers include forms with reduced amounts of iron and copper (obtained by crystallizing the salt in the presence of EDTA), propylene glycol treated, enriched with vitamins and minerals for bread formulations, and with about 1.5% tricalcium phosphate for decreased caking and improved flow.

Caking of salt is a response to fluctuations in relative humidity around a critical point. The critical relative humidity is near 75%. Above this value salt becomes deliquescent and attracts moisture to form a saturated brine on its crystal surfaces. When the ambient relative humidity drops below 75% the water evaporates, leaving a recrystallized weld between individual crystals.

Particle size is an important part of the specifications for salt. A fine granulation is preferred for dough ingredient salt. Since many formulations (e.g., cookies) include only small proportions of water, the salt may not dissolve completely during mixing unless the particle size is small. The granulation is not as critical in high moisture formulations such as cake batters, but bakers making several types of doughs and batters will probably find it more convenient to use one type of salt for all doughs even though there may be a small cost advantage in favor of the coarser ingredient. Topping salt for depositing on saltines, pretzels, etc. should be of relatively uniform, large particle size. Fines should be at a minimum since they cause uneven feeding and poor appearance. A bulk density of 40 lb per cu ft is representative. A typical screen analysis would be 1% on a U.S. No. 16 and 90% on a U.S. No. 30, with 9% throughs.

Salt is available in multiwall bags containing 10, 25, or 100 lb net and in bulk. The bulk material is shipped in hoppered or top-loaded vans, or portable metal bins may be used.

BIBLIOGRAPHY

ANON. 1952. Bakery Products, Definitions and Standards of Identity. Federal Register 17, 4462–4463.

ANON. 1957. Cereal Laboratory Methods, 6th Edition. Am. Assoc. Cereal Chemists, St. Paul.

ATKIN, L., SCHULTZ, A. S., and FREY, C. N. 1946. Yeast fermentation. In Enzymes and Their Role in Wheat Technology, J. A. Anderson (Editor). Interscience Div., John Wiley & Sons, New York.

COOK, A. H. 1962. Barley and Malt. Academic Press, New York.

DOOSE, O., and WOLTER, K. 1955. The influence of flour treated with potassium bromate and ammonium persulfate upon dough produced by various methods. Trans. Am. Assoc. Cereal Chemists 13, 130–147.

FERRARI, C. G. 1959. Private communication.

JORGENSEN, H. 1939. Further investigations into the nature of the action of bromate and ascorbic acid on the baking strength of flour. Cereal Chem. 16, 51–60.

KIRK, D. J. 1959. Current and new uses for bromates, iodates, peroxides. Proc. Am. Soc. Bakery Engrs. *1959*, 153–157.
KOCH, R., STERN, B., and FERRARI, C. G. 1958. Linoleic acid and trilinolein as substrates for soybean oxidase. Arch. Biochem. 78, 165–179.
KRAMER, F. 1967. Gelatin—how it's made. Food Eng. *38*, No. 11, 74–77.
MONCRIEFF, J., and OSZLANYI, A. G. 1970. Development and evaluation of a new dough conditioner. Bakers Dig. *44*, No. 4, 44–46.
REED, G., and THORN, J. A. 1957. Use of fungal protease in the baking industry. Cereal Sci. Today 2, 280–283.
SHELLENBERGER, J. A. 1966. Basic differences in the oxidative responses of wheat flour. Proc. Am. Soc. Bakery Engrs. *1966*, 112–116.
STRONG, L. R. 1969. The functional properties of salt in bakery products. Bakers Dig. *43*, No. 2, 55–56, 59.
SULLIVAN, B. 1948. The Mechanism of the Oxidation and Reduction of Flour. Am. Assoc. Cereal Chemists, St. Paul.
WITT, P. R., JR. 1970. Malting. *In* Cereal Technology, S. A. Matz (Editor). Avi Publishing Co., Westport, Conn.

SECTION 2

Formulations and Procedures

CHAPTER 11

FORMULATIONS AND PROCEDURES FOR AIR-LEAVENED, STEAM-LEAVENED, AND UNLEAVENED PRODUCTS

Because it is difficult or perhaps impossible to make a clear separation between those bakery foods which are unleavened and those which are leavened by air or steam, discussions of all three types will be combined in this chapter. The range of products in the broad category under consideration includes such diverse types as angel food cake and pie crust, connected only by the fact that they are not deliberately or necessarily leavened by yeast or chemical reactants. In some cases, deviant formulas are known which include baking powder, further adding to the unclear boundaries of the classification. Although some products such as angel food cake are made by procedures which are intended to ensure the maximum contribution of air bubles to the leavening action, and others (e.g., pie crust) are virtually devoid of leavening action by any means, there are many doughs and batters which occupy an intermediate ground and benefit from the effect of leavening by air or steam without the use of procedures intentionally designed to accomplish that purpose.

During the mixing of doughs and batters in vessels exposed to the atmosphere, some air is inevitably entrapped in the form of bubbles. Gases are also dissolved in the fluid part of the mixture and adsorbed on the suspended solids. Among the procedures which lead to the incorporation of relatively large amounts of gas are: (1) Sifting of flour or air-conveying it under pressure. (2) Creaming the shortening with a particulate ingredient such as flour or sugar. (3) Whipping liquid egg products, especially egg whites. (4) Repeated folding and sheeting of dough, with or without interleaving of shortening. (5) Vigorous mixing of doughs or fairly stiff batters, particularly under pressurized conditions.

Air entrapped in the form of bubbles can be expected to increase in volume according to the well-known gas laws as the temperature of the dough or batter rises. For example, 100 ml of air at 70°F will expand to about 128 ml at 212°F. This relatively small increase in volume is not nearly enough to account for the expansion in the oven of air-leavened products such as angel food cake. It has been clearly shown that the additional gas volume comes from gases driven out of the liquid or dislodged from absorbents by the heat, and from the increase in water vapor pressure. The last named factor is undoubtedly the most important expansive factor in most cases since the change of water into steam involves a volume increase of about 1600 times. Steam is responsible for nearly all the expansion observed in puff pastry, popovers, and the like.

Although steam is the principal leavening force in many air-leavened products, it would not have the requisite effectiveness if small gas bubbles were not provided as foci for the evolution of water vapor: It can easily be shown that a deaerated dough loses water vapor in ways which do not contribute to the leavening action, especially as evaporation from the surface and in the form of large nonuniform bubbles which gradually coalesce and then rise to the surface and burst. The advantage of fine structured foams such as the meringues used for angel food cakes is that they have many small, uniform bubbles which retain their individuality throughout the baking process as gases are discharged into them from the liquid phase of the batter.

PROCEDURES HAVING A WHIPPING OR BEATING STEP

Cakes Based on Egg Foams

In a sense, meringues—baked shapes of foamed egg white and sugar—could be considered the simplest representatives of the class, but they are more closely allied to confectionery than to bakery products. The two basic types of cake in this category are angel food cakes, which are based on egg white foams and contain no shortening, and cakes such as pound, chiffon, and sponge, which do contain added fat and some egg yolk. These cakes represent slightly more than 10% of the commercially manufactured cakes sold in the United States (Borders 1968).

Angel Food Cakes.—The three basic ingredients of angel food cakes are egg whites, sugar, and flour. The usual proportions are about 20–40 parts flour, 100 parts liquid egg whites, and 80–100 parts sugar. Salt, cream of tartar (or other whipping aids and acidifiers), and flavor are also found in all formulas. The egg whites and flour act as "tougheners," i.e., they contribute to the strength or resilience of the foam structure, while sugar is the only "tenderizer" due to the complete absence of shortening. Increases in the percentage of egg whites or of flour in the formula will decrease the tenderness of the cake, while increasing the amount of sugar will make the finished product more tender. According to Lowe (1955), it is desirable to use a percentage of sugar just short of that which would cause the cake to fall because of excessive tenderness.

The sweetening agent is always sucrose. Although the regular granulated form can be used it is preferable to add a finer particle size of sugar to speed up the dissolving of this ingredient in the egg white.

Characteristics of the flour have a strong influence on the quality of the finished product. A weak soft wheat flour is desirable. Excellent cakes have been made from batters in which part of the flour was replaced by wheat starch.

The most critical ingredient is the egg whites. Both frozen whites and dried albumen can be used and both are equally satisfactory, if they have been properly processed from raw materials of good quality. The whiteness of the crumb, the crust appearance, the texture (closely associated with specific volume), and the flavor are strongly affected by the functional properties of the egg whites. Thinner egg whites whip to optimum volume quicker than more viscous whites and the final density of the foam is generally less, but the thicker whites give a more stable foam.

In some cases, bakers will add up to 10% of water to the whites during whipping to get additional moistness and closer grain in the finished cake. If the crusts are ordinarily too brown, the addition of water may lighten the color. A reduction in cake volume usually results when water is added.

It is common practice to add cream of tartar or some equivalent substance to improve the foam properties of the albumen. These whipping aids are important both in home preparation and in commercial manufacture. Cream of tartar, potassium hydrogen tartrate, is an acidic salt which adjusts the pH of the egg white to a level conducive to maximum solubility of the proteins and reduces their denaturation during whipping. Without it, the foam does not reach its maximum potential specific volume, and the cake is coarse in texture. Cream of tartar also decolorizes the flavone pigments of the flour, leading to a brighter crumb color although much of the color change is due to its effect on bubble size.

Acids such as acetic, malic, tartaric, and citric also have an improving effect on cake structure and color, but none are as effective as cream of tartar for improving the cake volume, and the latter substance is the additive of choice. It has the additional advantage of affecting flavor very little. About 1–2% (commonly 1.5–1.75%) based on the liquid egg whites is the accepted range of addition for cream of tartar. Eggs which have been in cold storage a long time have more alkaline whites than fresh eggs, and albumen separated from them may require increased amounts of acidifier.

Surfactants which have been suggested and used for improving the whipping properties of dried eggs are sodium desoxycholate (Kline and Singleton 1959), triethyl citrate (Kothe 1953), triacetin, sodium oleate, and oleic acid. Some of these applications are covered by patents.

The traditional procedure for making angel food cake is a two-stage operation. In the first stage, the egg whites (containing the acidic ingredient) are whipped with or without part of the sugar and the rest of the sugar is then mixed in with continued beating. The second stage consists of folding in the flour with the absolute minimum of disturbance needed to distribute this ingredient throughout the meringue. The reason for this sequence of additions is to keep to a minimum the bubble-collapsing effect which results from contact of the flour lipids with the protein solutions forming the cell walls.

A procedure in wide commercial use requires whipping the egg whites (containing cream of tartar and salt) at medium speed until the foam begins to exhibit a soft structure, after which 50–60% of the total sugar is added slowly while whipping is continued. When the meringue forms a wet peak, the flavor ingredients, the remainder of the sugar, and the flour are distributed over the surface while mixing is continued intermittently at the lowest possible speed. As soon as uniform distribution of ingredients is achieved, mixing is discontinued.

Angel food cake is very sensitive to changes in preparation method. There are few other bakery products which have so many critical points in their processing. The beating of the egg whites is the first critical step. If the aeration is insufficient, the cell walls are not extended to their full capacity during baking and suboptimal volume and texture result. On the other hand, excessive whipping of the egg whites causes coagulation of some of the proteins so that the bubble walls lose extensibility and may break during baking leading to a reduction in cake volume and a coarser crumb. The whipping end-point can be judged by appearance of the foam or by measuring the specific volume of a sample. Different samples of egg white will vary in optimum specific volume of their foams, but Barmore (1936) recommended beating (without sugar) until a specific gravity between 0.150 and 0.170 is reached. The temperature of the albumen affects the time required to reach maximum specific volume, but the final volume itself is not much affected by the initial temperature within the range of 45°–75°F. The higher the temperature, the more critical the whipping time, i.e., the easier it is to overwhip. Over-beaten egg whites generally lead to excess expansion during the initial period of baking followed by marked shrinking just before baking is completed.

Angel cakes are customarily baked in tube pans, not only because of the better heat distribution permitted by this design but also because the internal support allows a greater expansion of the cake without subsequent collapse. Perfectly acceptable cakes can be baked in many other kinds of pans. Obviously, the pans must not be greased and, in fact, must be entirely free of lipid material. Wetting the inside of the baking pans before they are filled with batter tends to lighten the crust color, probably because the dehydration of the surface is slightly delayed.

Satisfactory angel good cakes can be baked over a rather wide range of baking temperatures; however, there is an optimum set of oven conditions at which maximum volume will be obtained. Consensus of authorities seems to be that the best cakes result from baking at the highest temperature and for the shortest length of time consistent with the shape and weight of the cake. Examples would be about 350°–360°F for 1½ lb cakes and 375°–400°F for 12 oz cakes. A temperature can be reached which is high enough to set the crust prematurely, reducing the final volume and causing the crust to become dark and bitter flavored. If the temperature is unduly low, gas tends to be lost before the cake structure becomes rigid. Lowe (1955) recommended baking to a maximum interior temperature which will be constant for a given formula and altitude. Continued heating after this temperature is reached binds more water and increases the toughness and the apparent dryness of the cake. Aluminum or thin steel pans are recommended to reduce the heat capacity and prevent excessive drying out from postbaking heat retention.

The effect of altitude on cake baking times, which is primarily due to the difference in the boiling point of water, is particularly noticeable in angel food cakes. As shown by Barmore (1935), higher altitudes lead to greater expansion during baking, and the cake becomes more tender. The final cake volume changes and affects tenderness. The color of the crust becomes lighter.

Flavor variants of angel food are rather restricted because of the necessity for avoiding fatty materials. The customary or traditional flavors are vanilla and almond extract, while imitation rum extract is also fairly common. Fruit juices, especially citrus, can be used to good effect, but the cream of tartar should be reduced to compensate for acidic substances in the juices. Spices, alone or in combination with molasses, also lead to varieties liked by many people, and the small amount of spice oil apparently has little effect on the cake volume. Cocoa is frequently added, even though the flavor of cocoa is not at its best in acidic environments and the fat inevitably has a collapsing effect on the bubbles as it melts during the early baking period. If cocoa is to be used, it should be folded in with the flour. Nut pieces have been suggested as additives, but their texture hardly seems complementary to that of angel cake crumb.

A trouble-shooting guide for angel food cakes is given in Table 11.1.

TABLE 11.1
CAUSES OF FAILURE OF ANGEL FOOD CAKES

Defect	Cause	Remedy
Undersized cake	(1) Overbeating or underbeating egg whites	(1) Beat egg whites, sugar, salt, and cream of tartar to a wet peak
	(2) Overmixing after flour is added	(2) Fold in just enough to incorporate
	(3) Sugar content too high	(3) Balance formula
	(4) Oven too hot	(4) Regulate temperature
	(5) Cakes removed from pan too soon after baking	(5) Allow cakes to cool before removing from tins
	(6) Cakes underbaked	(6) Bake thoroughly
	(7) Greased pans or tins	(7) Do not grease tins for angel food cakes
Dark crust color	(1) Oven too hot	(1) Regulate temperature
	(2) Cakes overbaked	(2) Give proper bake
	(3) Excessive sugar content, causing cake to have sugary crust	(3) Balance formula
Light crust color	(1) Cakes underbaked	(1) Bake correctly
	(2) Cool oven	(2) Regulate temperature
	(3) Overbeaten or overmixed batter	(3) Mix properly
Tough crust	(1) Oven too hot	(1) Regulate oven temperature
	(2) Sugar content too high	(2) Balance formula
	(3) Improper mixing	(3) Exercise care in assembling batter
Thick and hard crust	(1) Overbaking	(1) Lessen baking time
	(2) Cold oven	(2) Regulate temperature
Strong flavor	(1) Off-flavored materials	(1) Check storage of materials for foreign material
	(2) Poor flavoring materials	(2) Use only top quality flavors
	(3) Cakes burned or overbaked	(3) Exercise care in baking
Lack of flavor	(1) Insufficient salt in formula	(1) Increase salt content
	(2) Poor flavor combination	(2) Use proper flavor blends
	(3) Poor quality flavoring materials used	(3) Use only top quality materials
Heavy cakes	(1) Over or underbeaten eggs	(1) Beat eggs to a wet peak
	(2) Overmixing after flour has been added	(2) Fold flour in just enough to incorporate
	(3) Too much sugar	(3) Balance formula
	(4) Too high in baking temperature	(4) Regulate temperature
Coarse grain	(1) Cold oven	(1) Regulate temperature
	(2) Overbeaten whites	(2) Whip to wet peak
	(3) Insufficiently mixed batter	(3) Fold until smooth
Tough cakes	(1) Overmixing ingredients	(1) Mix properly
	(2) Excessive sugar content	(2) Balance formula
	(3) Baked too hot	(3) Regulate temperature
	(4) Flour content high or wrong type flour used	(4) Balance formula. Use soft wheat flour
Cakes dry	(1) Low sugar content	(1) Balance formula
	(2) Overbaking	(2) Lessen baking time
	(3) Eggs overbeaten	(3) Whip to a wet peak
	(4) Flour content too high	(4) Balance formula

Source: Harrel (1960).

One of the common causes of failure is the presence of fats and oils, particularly glycerides. It is well known that lipids cause collapse of protein-based foams. Unsaturated fats seem to be somewhat more injurious than saturated lipids. According to Harrel (1960), mineral oil and cholesterol do not have any appreciable effect. Even barely detectable traces of liquid triglycerides will lead to significant decreases in volume. A common source of fat is egg yolk, but commercial frozen whites (or dried albumen) from reputable suppliers are remarkably free of yolk contamination. Whites prepared by breaking and separating fresh eggs in the plant are very likely to have some yolk in them. Inadequately washed bowls and agitators are often found to be covered with an invisible film of fat and for this reason many plants which make angel food have concluded that it is advisable to reserve a special set of utensils for these cakes.

Sponge Cakes and Allied Products.—Pound cakes, sponge cakes, and chiffon cakes are examples of products based on whole egg foams and containing shortening. They are always much more dense than angel food cakes.

Pound cakes were traditionally based on the very old formula of one pound each of flour, butter, whole eggs, and sugar. Modern formulas have departed considerably from this archetype. Most present-day commercial versions include at least some baking powder though the amount is usually considerably less than in layer cakes so as to retain the relatively dense and firm but tender and somewhat crumbly texture expected in pound cake. Other changes which have occurred in the formula have been decreases in eggs and butter accompanied by an increase in sugar to give the sweeter, more tender cake acceptable to modern tastes. Very frequently some or all of the butter is replaced by vegetable shortening to decrease the ingredient cost.

An example of a simple modern formula which does not rely on baking powder is:

	Lb
Cake flour	25
Shortening, emulsifier type	8
Sugar	28
Salt	1
Milk, liquid whole	12
Eggs, whole	17
Butter	9

Whipping improvers (other than emulsifiers) and acidifying agents are not used. The quality of the eggs has a marked effect on the volume, texture, and flavor of the finished product. Cake flour meeting the usual specifications is satisfactory for pound cake.

The usual procedure for making the batter involves the following steps: (1) Cream the flour, shortening, and butter. (2) Add the sugar, salt, and milk and mix well. (3) Gradually add the eggs, and beat for about 5 min.

There are many modifications of the mixing procedure which have advantages under certain circumstances.

Some minor variations in the formula include the addition of a few percentages of invert sugar syrup or a small amount of glycerine to increase moistness of the crumb, the use of additional yolks or additional whites to secure desired textural improvements, replacement of some of the sugar with corn syrup of high DE, use of MSNF and water instead of fresh whole milk, and addition of baking powder. Many flavor variations are possible. The most common flavors are vanilla with a trace of citrus. Butter flavor should be added if the shortening is predominantly vegetable. Excellent chocolate flavored cakes can be made by replacing a few percentages of the shortening with chocolate liquor, or by adding a good grade of cocoa. Marzipan cakes contain 5–8% of almond paste, or combinations of almond paste and kernel paste. Nutmeats can be added alone or in combination with almond and kernel pastes to give interesting flavor and texture variations. Raisin pound cakes are well-liked in some areas.

Major variations in the formula include:

(1) The Genoise, a specialty of the French cuisine, calls for melted and clarified butter as the shortening ingredient and requires a complicated mixing technique involving beating of the whites before they are mixed with the yolks and (in separate steps) with the flour and butter. This overrated cake can easily be replaced by pound or sponge layers wherever it is called for as a component of pastries.

(2) White pound cakes require only egg whites instead of whole eggs, and might be compared to angel food batters to which butter or other shortenings have been added.

(3) Fruit cakes, with a substantial part of the finished product consisting of nuts and glacé fruit. Pound cake formulas are regarded as preferable for this type of cake because the batter is viscous and relatively dense so that the fruit does not sink to the bottom during baking.

Pound cakes can be used as the basis for tortes, petit fours, jelly rolls, lady fingers, and trifles; but it is more common to use sponge cake for these purposes.

Sponge cakes can be regarded as a part of the continuum which starts with the original formula for pound cake and continues through sponge and chiffon cakes to layer cakes. It is very common to find baking powder or soda and some acidic ingredient in sponge formulas, and the shortening content is less than in pound cake (sometimes none). A formula not containing shortening is given below:

	%
Sugar, granulated	32.1
Whole eggs	20.0
Cake flour	26.5
Milk, whole or skim	21.0
Salt	0.4

For maximum volume, the eggs can be beaten separately, the sugar, milk and salt mixed in, and then the flour folded in with minimum agitation. If baking powder is to be used, it should be added in the final stage. Satisfactory results can generally be obtained by a one-stage mixing procedure, employing the wire whip at high speed to aerate the batter.

Many variations are possible. For loaf, sheet, and layer cakes, it is desirable to use substantial amounts of shortening.

Variations in flavors are similar to those suggested for pound cake. Sponge cake batters are well accepted as the basis for jelly rolls, lady fingers, tortes, berry shells, and the like.

Chiffon cakes are similar to angel food cakes in that leavening occurs mainly as the result of whipping the egg whites. In addition to the egg whites, flour, and sugar found in the batters of angel food, chiffon cakes contain egg yolks and added fat, the latter in the form of vegetable oil. Baking powder is often used to assist the oven spring. A typical formula is:

	%
Egg yolks	10.7
Salad oil	10.7
Egg whites	32.0
Salt	0.4
Granulated sugar	16.0
Cake flour	14.0
Powdered sugar	16.0
Cream of tartar	0.2

The egg whites and salt are whipped until they develop a soft foam, then the cream of tartar and sugar are added and beating is continued until a soft peak is obtained. The egg yolks are whipped in separate equipment until thoroughly blended and aerated. The egg yolk and oil mixture is carefully folded into the meringue using minimal agitation. The sugar and flour are sifted together and then folded into the eggs. If baking powder is to be added, it goes in with the flour.

Although chiffon cakes may be used in many of the same combinations suggested for pound and sponge cakes, the greater difficulty of making them and their somewhat coarser and less resilient structure reduces their utilization in these items. Flavoring preferences are similar to sponge cakes, although orange and lemon chiffon cakes seem to be the most common. Chocolate flavored varieties are also well accepted.

The preferred temperature for baking sponge-type cakes is around 350°F. Scaling weight, pan conformation, and batter characteristics will determine the baking time, but as first approximations, allow 40 min for tube cakes, 20 min for sheets, and 30 min for loaves.

PIE CRUSTS

The most important representative of the class of unleavened bakery foods is pie crust. Puff pastry and certain types of cookies are also unleavened in the sense that no chemical or biological leavening agents are included in the formula, although an appreciable volume increase occurs in puff pastry during baking. It is true that some formulas for pie crusts call for small amounts of baking powder, but the conventional and typical recipe omits such an ingredient and it is not required to secure finished products having desirable eating qualities.

Pie crusts are low in moisture and high in fat. The ratio of ingredients together with the method of preparation prevent the formation of a continuous gluten network throughout the dough mass and result in baked products that are more or less friable or flaky. A porous structure such as typifies all leavened bakery products is not desired because pie crusts must support and retain without leakage fillings of moderate viscosity and high moisture content.

Pie crusts are generally divided into three classes based upon their "flakiness." The latter term can be defined loosely as the tendency of the crust to separate into strata or layers when it is broken. Flaky or long-flake crusts when broken tend to exhibit fracture along different lines at different levels, and to show separation in layers parallel to the surface. Mealy crusts can be broken in a straight line and show a fracture surface more like that of a cookie. Short-flake or flaky-mealy crusts exhibit characteristics intermediate between the two extremes.

The flaky crust is esteemed by connoisseurs and by trade experts, but it shows the abuse of handling more quickly than the mealy type and it poses difficulties in serving. It is also more difficult to process than the mealy type. Mealy crusts can be cut readily, usually support fillings adequately, and are not particularly sensitive to processing conditions. Most manufacturers catering to the general public make pies with mealy-type crusts. Home recipes are generally designed to produce flaky crusts, but most packaged mixes yield the mealy variety.

The basic formula for pie crusts requires flour and water for structure formation, shortening to provide the desired textural qualities, and salt to enhance the flavor. Usually sugar is added to ensure adequate coloration. The amount of water used, the kind of shortening, and the method of mixing are the chief determinants of crust characteristics.

The weakest flour available is suitable for pie crusts. Any factor tending to strengthen the gluten structure is to be avoided. In practice, this means that the flour used in pie crusts should be unbleached with a protein content of 7.0–8.5, ash content of 0.38–0.48 per cent, and a MacMichael viscosimeter reading of 30°–40° (Cook 1953). Struckmann (1956) recommends even narrower limits of 7.0–7.25% for protein, and 32°–36° for viscosity. The flour should be milled from a soft white winter wheat and should be slightly granular. Soft red winter wheats yield somewhat stronger flours which may or may not be satisfactory for the purpose, depending upon how critical the finished product requirements are.

Shortening for pie crust doughs is used at a level of about 70–75% (FWB) in household recipes, about 50–60% in commercial pie crusts, 50% or less in doughs made with liquid shortenings, and as little as 35% in fried pie doughs. The type of shortening determines the amount which must be used. Elling (1952) listed the following shortening values for some common fats:

Totally hydrogenated shortening	100
Partially hydrogenated shortening as generally used in bakeries	110
Partially hydrogenated lard	110
Open-kettle plasticized lard	125
Special grainy type lard	130–135
Oil	150

These shortenings were evaluated by preparing crusts from a uniform recipe, varying only the type and quantity of fat. Woerfel (1959) claims that vegetable oils are generally lower in shortening value than is lard. Lard is frequently called for in household recipes and some prepared mixes include hydrogenated lard from which part of the lard oil has been removed. Lard is also much used commercially and the tough, fibrous variety is preferred over the soft, grainy type. The former gives a short and tender crust without greasy effect. Emulsifiers should not be used in pie crust shortenings.

Salt is used at levels of from 1.5–4% of the flour weight. It should be dissolved in the absorption water, otherwise its solution may be excessively slow at the temperatures and water concentrations present in pie dough.

Sugar, corn syrup, or dextrose are commonly used in proportions of about 3–8 lb per 100 lb of flour. These amounts give adequate coloration without contributing a sweet taste to the crust. Sometimes the sugars are dispersed in the absorption water along with the salt and the milk solids, if the latter are used. Whey or MSNF can be included for much the same purpose as sugar. That is, the lactose in whey and milk powder contributes to the browning. Spray-dried milk solids are preferred to roller-dried material. Wheat or corn proteins may be added to ensure good machinability of the dough and crispness of the finished product. Propionates are frequently included in the formula at about the 0.2% level to retard mold formation.

The flaky crust is obtained by mixing all of the shortening with all of the flour for a period just sufficient to reduce the shortening to small lumps. The recommended size for the fat pieces varies somewhat according to the authority consulted and the type of shortening employed. Generally all of the ingredients are refrigerated, and in any case the flour and water are brought to 35°–40°F before mixing. The doughs are invariably refrigerated before being rolled and cut in order to keep the shortening particles discrete.

In preparing doughs for mealy crusts, the shortening may be completely dispersed in the dough. Consequently, processing conditions are less critical. It is usually convenient to mix the flour-shortening blend until the fat is completely absorbed and the flour particles are coated. Refrigeration of ingredients and doughs is of no particular value in this case.

Large amounts of scrap dough are generated in the cutting of pie crust circles, and the problem of economically disposing of this scrap is of great concern to pie manufacturers. Most authorities recommend that scrap dough be blended into fresh dough in quantities not exceeding 50% of the total. Use of scrap dough in this manner is essential in most operations, but it does adversely affect texture. Some bakers restrict the use of scrap blends to bottom crusts, while other operators believe that it is more desirable to take advantage of the greater dilution of scrap which is possible when it is blended into both the bottom and the top doughs.

The two steps common to nearly all pie dough mixing processes are: (1) blending the shortening and the flour until the fat has reached the desired degree of subdivision, and (2) adding the water and water-soluble ingredients to the fat and shortening mixture and agitating until the water has been absorbed. As stated previously, flaky crusts require a short first stage which leaves the shortening in the form of discrete lumps while mealy crusts are thoroughly mixed during the first stage so that the flour particles are completely coated by the fat. Intermediate types of crusts may be prepared either by reducing the shortening to very small lumps, e.g., about the size of peas, or by a two-stage addition of fat during one stage of which the fat is thoroughly dispersed while in the other step mixing is carried only to the point where the fat has been broken down to fairly small uniform particles.

Most processing instructions call for the water to be chilled. Not infrequently the flour is also brought to refrigerator temperatures before use. In addition, the dough itself is usually chilled for several hours after mixing. This cool rest period allows the water to distribute itself more thoroughly in the dough mass and hardens the shortening so that it is less likely to liquefy during subsequent handling and shaping operations. These chilling steps are particularly important in the manufacture of dough for long-flake crusts. Mealy-type doughs should come out of the mixer at about 65°F and be held (covered, of course) at this temperature for about 3-4 hr.

Elling (1952) gives a formula and procedure for making a 221-lb batch of long-flake dough suitable for use during the warm weather months. He indicates that the same formula can be adapted for producing short-flake or mealy crusts if the processing techniques are changed appropriately.

Long-flake Crust

(1) Mix smooth but do not cream:
    45 lb steam rendered lard
    15 lb partially hydrogenated vegetable shortening
(2) Add the following ingredients to the above and mix until the fat is in pieces the size of walnuts:
    100 lb soft pastry flour at refrigerator temperatures
    6 lb nonfat milk solids
(3) Add the following to the flour, fat, and milk solids and mix just enough to blend thoroughly:
    38 lb ice water
    4 lb salt
    3 lb corn sugar

Struckmann (1956) described the production of doughs yielding a short-flake crust suitable for fruit pies.

Fruit Pie Dough

(1) Place in arm-type mixer and blend the following together until the shortening and flour are well incorporated:
    100 lb flour

25 lb margarine or low melting point shortening

(2) Continue to mix the flour and margarine until it attains the appearance of a coarse streusel with no raw flour spots in evidence, and then add 45 lb of lard.

(3) After mixing has reduced the lard to chunks about the size of eggs, add:
   4 lb spray skim milk powder
   3 lb salt
   2 lb corn sugar dissolved in
   28 lb ice cold water

(4) Continue the mixing until all of the ingredients are thoroughly dispersed. Stop mixing when the pie dough is dry with no wet spots evident and the shortening is in tiny lumps well distributed throughout the entire batch.

Struckmann also gave a formula and procedure for making a mealy-type crust especially suitable for small individual pies and custard shells.

Dough for Mealy Crusts

(1) Place in mixer and blend thoroughly:
   100 lb pie flour
   45 lb pie flour
   20 lb margarine or low melting point shortening

(2) When the above is thoroughly mixed and no raw flour spots are visible, add:
   3 lb spray dried nonfat milk solids
   4 lb corn sugar, and
   3 lb salt dissolved in
   24 lb ice water

(3) Continue to mix until the water has been completely taken up.

Frazier (1947) recommends using $6\frac{1}{4}$ oz dough for the bottom crust and $5\frac{1}{4}$ oz for the top crust of 9-inch pies containing 26–28 oz filling. Crusts for 9-inch cream pies should be scaled at 7 oz. However, Elling (1952) suggested a $6\frac{1}{2}$ oz scaling weight for both crusts of 9-inch pies and $4\frac{1}{2}$ oz for both crusts of 8-inch pies. The filled pies are baked 28–32 min at 450°F.

There is a considerable difference of opinion regarding the merits of "washes" for the top crusts of pies. Washes of egg or milk, or combinations of these, result in glossy and relatively dark crusts. Some bakers regard this appearance as highly desirable while others consider it to be somewhat artificial. Struckmann (1956) suggested the application of a spray of skim milk to the top crust of pies just before they enter the oven. This gives a golden brown crust color and a drier and crisper texture. Cook (1953) indicated that some bakers spray the crust with melted shortening to give a flake on top of the product.

Fried pie crusts present some special problems. The all-important characteristic in this case is structural strength since the crusts of fried pies are not supported by pans during their transportation from the factory to the point of consumption. According to Keathley (1956), the basic formula for fried pie dough is:

>100 lb pastry flour
>35 lb vegetable shortening
>35 lb water
>3 lb salt
>4 lb corn sugar

Lard is not recommended for the dough or as the frying fat. Mixing procedures and equipment are similar to those used for baked pies except that fried pie doughs may be mixed a little longer and to a smoother consistency than those used for baked pies. The securing of flakiness is generally not a primary consideration with these products.

Dietrich (1957) has given a specific formula and procedure for fried pie crusts.

Dough for Fried Pies

(1) Blend together thoroughly:
  100 lb pie flour
  25 lb hydrogenated shortening
  100 lb dough scraps from previous production
(2) Blend together the following, and then add to the above:
  30 lb water (variable)
  2 lb salt
(3) Add and mix until a smooth dough results:
  1 lb corn sugar (optional)
  3 lb wheat or corn protein
  3 oz. mold inhibitor

This dough can be made up immediately if desired, but holding does not cause it to deteriorate. After mechanical or hand scaling into pieces of desired size, the dough is sheeted by mechanical rollers or other means. Dietrich described some ingenious automatic panning and forming devices for preparing fried pie crusts, but these machines are apparently not available commercially.

About 1½ oz of dough to 2 oz of filling is the recommended scaling weight for fried pie crusts. The pies are fried submerged at a temperature of 375°–380°F for about 3 min and then are thoroughly cooled by forced air before wrapping.

Dietrich described variations in processing of fried pies which yield special characteristics. In one operation, fried pies were dipped into a kettle of constantly boiling water immediately after frying. This set the crust and floated off excess cooking fat. Such pies kept well during the summer months and had a slight gloss. In another variant process, the crusts were made up with high protein spring wheat flour. Then, prior to frying, the pies on the screen were dipped quickly into boiling water and then immediately transferred to the frying fat. Pies prepared by this method had less greasiness of crust than most.

Causes of Faults in Pie Crusts

For trouble-shooting crust problems, the following suggestions (Anon. 1958) may be helpful:

(1) Excessive shrinkage of crusts may be caused by: (a) Not enough shortening. (b) Too much water. (c) Dough worked too much. (d) Flour too strong.

(2) Crust not flaky. May be caused by: (a) Dough mixed too warm. (b) Shortening too soft. (c) Rubbing flour and lard too much (overmixing).

(3) Bottom crust soaks too much juice. May be caused by: (a) Insufficient baking. (b) Crust too rich. (c) Oven too cool.

(4) Tough crusts may be caused by: (a) Flour that is too strong. (b) Overmixing the dough. (c) Use of excess water.

(5) Soggy crusts may be caused by: (a) Not enough bottom heat. (b) Oven too hot. (c) Using a filling that is too hot.

PUFF PASTRY

Puff pastries, in their conventional form, are not very well adapted to mass production and so are, in the strictest sense, outside the scope of this volume. However, a brief discussion of these foods is included at this point for general information purposes.

The principle underlying the preparation of puff pastry is very similar to that on which the manufacture of true Danish pastry is based. Layers of fat are interleaved between layers of dough so that upon baking a separation of dough strata occurs. However, in Danish pastry yeast-leavening action plus the inclusion of auxiliary ingredients result in a relatively soft and porous structure in the baked dough layers. Puff pastry doughs yield a very open network of crisp and flaky layers. In the preparation of both of these products the main precaution to be observed is the maintenance of cool doughs so that the shortening will not melt and then be incorporated into the crumb.

A traditional method of preparing puff pastry dough is illustrated by the following method and procedure.

Dough for Puff Pastry

(1) Mix a dough consisting of:
 5 lb bread flour or a mixture of 8 parts bread flour and 2 parts pastry flour
 2½ oz. salt

2½ lb special puff paste shortening
1 lb water

(2) Roll the dough out into a rectangular shape and place it in the refrigerator. After the dough has cooled down, sheet it out to one-third inch in thickness, retaining the rectangular shape as much as possible.

(3) Spread 2½ lb of puff pastry shortening over ⅔ of the sheet and fold it over so that three layers of dough are separated by two layers of shortening. Roll the mass out to a thin sheet and again fold into three layers.

(4) Refrigerate for about 1 hr and then roll out and fold over as before. Repeat the sheeting and folding and then refrigerate once more. For best results, the sheeting and folding should be repeated once or twice after this refrigeration stage.

(5) After cooling down the dough, cut it into the desired shapes and bake at 350°–375° F for 35 min.

Development of highly specialized puff pastry shortenings has allowed the use of procedures which do not include the tedious rolling-in steps of the traditional method.

Rapid Puff Pastry Method

(1) Mix together just enough to incorporate the shortening:
  10 lb bread flour
  2 lb puff pastry shortening (cold)
  3 oz salt

(2) Add 6 lb (variable) of water at about 40° F. and mix with the batter beater at high speed until the dough forms a ball. Scrape the dough from the bowl sides.

(3) Add 2 lb of cold water and develop the dough.

(4) Scrape the dough away from the sides of the bowl and add 8 lb of cold puff pastry shortening. Mix at low speed until the shortening has just been blended in. This is the critical step and overmixing here will destroy the puff pastry characteristics of the product.

The special shortenings developed for puff pastries are generally compounds of meat fats, vegetable oils, water, and salt. Lecithin and monoglycerides may be included. Sometimes the water is replaced by skim milk or cultured milk. Butter was originally the shortening of choice for puff pastries, but many of the new compounds improve considerably on the performance characteristics of the dairy product.

AIR-LEAVENED BREADS

Matzos

Although matzos or matzoth, the Jewish specialty which is traditionally consumed at Passover, is an unleavened bread in the sense that no fermentation is permitted, it does undergo a moderate amount of oven expansion due to the entrapped air bubbles. If it were not for this leavening effect, the product would be much less palatable.

The formula for matzos is essentially flour, salt, and water, although some varieties flavored with onion and garlic have been offered commercially. The product is baked in very thin sheets at a moderately high temperature until a moisture level of about 2–5% is reached. It is desirable to have a substantial contribution of radiant (top) heat in the oven to brown the top of the wafers so as to produce some flavor in this otherwise quite insipid product.

Beaten Biscuits

Beaten biscuits are a southern specialty especially popular in Maryland. These biscuits have a crisp texture somewhat resembling that of soda crackers or ship's biscuits and the crust is pale in color, almost white. The method of preparation resembles in some respects the preparation of puff pastry without the use of roll-in shortening. They are prepared entirely without yeast or chemical leavening, the air bubbles being incorporated by repeated folding and thinning out of the dough piece. The "sheeting" is usually done by pounding the dough with a rolling pin or similar implement, although sets of rollers driven by a crank can be purchased for home use.

The formula is very simple, consisting of flour, salt, lard (a small amount), and water. A little sugar is sometimes added. The flour should be strong and a minimum amount of water added to make a very stiff dough. The dough should be developed before the beating and folding process begins. The dough piece should be folded and sheeted out perhaps 20–30 times. If sheeting rollers are used, the dough will break down and tear long before this many steps are reached unless rest periods are provided for it.

Small round pieces, about 1–1½ in. in diameter and ⅛–¼ in. thick, are cut from the dough sheet, an indentation is made in the center and the top is docked with several holes. The dough pieces are placed (separated) on an ungreased baking sheet and put in a 325°–350°F oven until substantially dried out (about 5% moisture remaining). They are generally consumed cold, and should be stored in a closed container to delay moisture absorption.

Home preparation has greatly declined in the last few decades because of the difficulty of preparation and lack of general appeal, apart from tradition. Attempts have been made to commercialize the product, which is inexpensive and easy to prepare using a dough brake, but there has been little demand for the product except as a novelty. When home recipes are used, the biscuits become rancid rather quickly, because of the instability of the lard at the low moisture levels.

Eclair Shells, Cream Puffs, and Popovers

These products typically have an extremely coarse grain, the interior being formed of a few large cells. Steam contributes the greater part of the leavening action. Popovers are a type of hot bread while eclair and cream puff shells are components of dessert foods.

Popover batters are made by a simple formula and procedure. In an average formula about 85–130 parts by weight of liquid whole eggs and 200 parts of milk will be used for each 100 parts of flour. Small amounts of shortening, salt, and flavorings constitute the remainder of the batter. Bread flour is generally used and it should be sifted.

To prepare popover batters, the eggs are beaten until light, the milk is added, then the flour is slowly added with moderate agitation until a homogeneous mixture is obtained. The butter or other shortening is melted and added last. The finished batter should be quite fluid, about the consistency of heavy cream.

Popovers can be baked in muffin tins or in specially designed pans. These utensils should be heavy walled to provide an initial source of heat. Before the batter is added, the pans are greased and placed in the oven to heat. The cavities are filled about one-third full of the batter.

The baking conditions are very critical in the successful production of popovers. The filled pans should be placed in a hot oven (about 450°–475°F) so as to form steam rapidly and expand the piece before the crust is set by radiant heat. After the expansion has reached its maximum, the temperature of the oven should be reduced to about 350°F to dry the popover and finish setting it without burning the crust. As the pastries are removed from the oven, the shells are punctured to allow steam to escape and drying to continue. When properly baked, the crust will be crisp in texture and medium dark brown in color, while the interior will be nearly dry but not tough or crumbly.

Grated cheese, rye meal, whole wheat flour or other flavoring materials can be added to the batter without ruining the popovers if the batter is kept at a very fluid consistency and the total fat content is low.

The preparation method for cream puffs and eclair shells is unusual in that the batter is cooked before it is deposited and baked. This so-called pâte à chou has a fairly simple composition of about 150–200 parts of liquid whole eggs, 100 parts flour, 100 parts shortening, and about 200 parts of water. Part of the whole eggs can be replaced by egg whites, but some egg yolk is needed because the eggs not only contribute to the structure of the finished shell, but also emulsify the fat so that it does not leak out of the batter during baking. The quality of the eggs has an important influence in both flavor and appearance of the cream puff.

The shortening (e.g., butter) and the water are brought to a boil, then the heat is reduced, and the flour and salt are added in one portion. The mixture is stirred until a ball of dough is formed. The source of heat is then removed, and the ball of flour paste is allowed to cool slightly so that it will not cause coagulation of the egg proteins. The eggs are added gradually with vigorous beating. At the completion of mixing the paste should be stiff enough to remain in a peak when a spoon is drawn out of it. The egg content may have to be adjusted to attain this consistency. The batter must be homogeneous, lumps being a distinct liability.

Mounds of the paste are extruded onto a lightly greased baking sheet from a pastry bag, or by any equivalent method. A hot oven temperature (450°F) is generally recommended although some authorities indicate 375°F is satisfactory. The pastries are baked until they are golden brown and beads of moisture are no longer seen, and then the heat is turned off and the shells are punctured to allow the escape of trapped steam. The puff cases are allowed to dry out in the oven for a few minutes.

Eclair shells are made in exactly the same way except that the paste is extruded in strip form.

COOKIES

Many kinds of cookies are made with only small amounts of leavening and several varieties contain none. Perhaps the most straightforward example of this type is the sugar wafer base cake. Small amounts of ammonium bicarbonate or soda are often added, but the major leavening action is due to steam.

Sugar Wafers

The base cake is entirely different from any other cookie. It has many similarities in texture and structure to puffed snack foods. Structurally, it is a foamed, dehydrated starch gel with a supporting gluten network. Most of the leavening action results from the evolution of steam during the baking process. The batter is closely confined so that the steam cannot readily escape, and its leavening effect under these conditions is much greater than it would be if the thin sheet were exposed to the atmosphere.

The basic principles used in making the flat, cream-layered sugar wafer are also used in manufacturing ice cream cones (waffle cones) and novelty cream-filled shapes such as circles, hemispheres, half-cylinders, peanut shells, etc. Some of the novelty shapes are filled with cheese-flavored or other savory fillings instead of sugar-shortening mixtures. All of the fillings are essentially fat based, however, since any appreciable amount of moisture completely ruins the texture of the base cake, causing it to collapse.

The batter is a very fluid mixture of flour and water to which small amounts of other ingredients are added. Generally, no sugar or other sweeteners are present. Table 11.2 summarizes six formulas found in the recent literature. To the base formula may be added colors and flavors selected to be compatible with the process. A yellow color, egg shade, is commonly added to the vanilla or plain base cake. Flavors should be added sparingly, since the predominant flavor is expected to come from the filling. Vanillin at the 0.025–0.05% level is a suitable flavoring. Chocolate or dark colored wafers sometimes do not contain any cacao products and are colored with caramel or food dyes. For a chocolate flavor, about 10% of cocoa (preferably the high fat or breakfast type) may be added to the formula. This addition will necessitate an increase of around 15% in the water.

Old-style formulas contained enriching ingredients such as milk or eggs, and sometimes even sugar, but batters made with these components tend to cause excessive build-up of carbon on the oven plates, especially at the corners. Carbon deposits will cause sticking of the wafer sheet with consequent difficulty in ejecting the sheet from the plates. Shortening, usually 76° coconut oil, is added to facilitate release of the wafer. The function of lecithin is to help prevent sticking, but its effectiveness in the simple batters must be questionable. Corn starch, when added, is intended to improve the texture, i.e., to make the wafer tenderer.

The flour should be a short extraction soft wheat flour. Flour from white wheat is sometimes used. Both bleached and unbleached flour

TABLE 11.2
SUGAR WAFER BATTER FORMULAS

	Average (Parts)	High (Parts)	Low (Parts)	Recommended (Parts)
Flour	100	100	100	100
Water, variable	135	150	125	140
Sodium bicarbonate	0.38	0.75	0.2	0.5
Ammonium bicarbonate	0.22	0.5	0	0
MSNF	1.8	5	0	0
Dried whole milk	0.5	3	0	0
Corn starch	1.7	5	0	0
Dried egg yolk	0.96	2.5	1.25	0
Salt	0.32	0.75	0	0.5
Lecithin	0.13	0.4	0	0.1
Coconut oil	0.8	2	0	1

have been used successfully. Any speckiness shows up clearly in white wafers. The amount and quality of gluten seem to have some effect on expansion, so that a very weak flour may give too dense or too close textured a piece. On the other hand, gluten also affects the texture so that a strong flour causes the wafer to be hard and flinty. The protein content or strength of the flour should be chosen to achieve a compromise between excess hardness and excess fragility or denseness. The precise specification will depend upon the kinds and amounts of other ingredients, the type of end product desired, and the characteristics of the equipment. As usual, water is varied, the amount being chosen to give a batter viscosity which will enable it to spread rapidly over the plate and between the plates while still retaining a substantially uniform internal structure without large voids or other defects.

Other ingredients which have been suggested for sugar wafer shells include heat-treated defatted cottonseed flour and degerminated white corn flour. Such materials add viscosity to the batter without increasing the possibility of gluten separation during mixing. Ammonium bicarbonate is often added in addition to soda. Leavening acids are rarely used, but the small amount of soda included in the formula is neutralized by the flour so that satisfactory pH's are attained. Color, especially of white shells, may be improved by adding cream of tartar or other leavening acid in an amount sufficient to bring the pH slightly below 7.0.

Mixing is a simple procedure. Any equipment which can produce a smooth, lump-free batter is suitable. The dry ingredients are first blended, then the water is added gradually while mixing. If shortening is used, it is blended in while the mixture is still of a doughy consistency. Some recommend using melted shortening. Eggs and milk solids can be added to the mixer at the start with about half of the water, and rehydrated before the remainder of the dry ingredients are added. Finally, the rest of the water is gradually brought in.

Batters are preferably mixed at high speed although there are numerous cases where low speed horizontal mixers have been used successfully. Under certain conditions, as when overmixed, the gluten may develop into strands and separate. Settling-out is also a problem and some agitation is necessary while the batter be being held for depositing. Mixing batches of the smallest possible size is highly recommended. Holding for longer than 30 min is definitely not recommended.

Batters of this type are ideal candidates for continuous mixing processes, but so far as the author knows, none has been developed for sugar wafers.

The baking devices for sugar wafer bases will be described and illustrated in a later chapter on ovens and baking. These are ovens through which travel pairs of plates (books) or continuous bands with the batter confined between them. The baking time is usually about 2 min. For maximum strength and crispness, the wafer should be at 2% moisture content or less at the time the cream is applied. The pH should be between 6.8 and 7.8, with the lower ranges preferred.

The original Scotch shortbread, actually a kind of cake or cookie, rather than the kind of "bread" we are familiar with, contained no liquid ingredients or leaveners in the formula, and was dense and very short in texture. Some formulas adapted to modern tastes include a small amount of egg and specify longer and more vigorous mixing to give a slight aerating effect. A traditional formula is

1 Cup butter
¾ Cup powdered sugar
1 teaspoonful vanilla
2 Cups sifted flour
½ teaspoon salt

The butter is creamed with the sugar and the vanilla added. The flour and salt are mixed in just enough to distribute them uniformly. The paste is rolled to desired thickness, usually about ½ in., cut in shapes, and baked at 300°F for 20–25 min.

There are many other kinds of cookies which contain little or no leavening substance. For a complete discussion, the reader is referred to *Cookie and Cracker Technology* (Matz 1968).

BIBLIOGRAPHY

ALLER, A. C. 1958. Wholesale pie production—quality necessary to meet today's consumer demand. Proc. Am. Soc. Bakery Engrs. *1958*, 298–303.
ANON. 1958. Baking Handbook. U.S. Navy Dept. Bur. Supplies and Accounts, NAVSANDA Publ. 342.
BARMORE, M. A. 1935. Baking angel cake at any altitude. Colo. Agr. Expt. Sta. Tech. Bull. *13*.
BARMORE, M. A. 1936. The influence of various factors, including altitude, in the production of angel food cake. Colo. Agr. Expt. Sta. Tech. Bull. *15*.
BORDERS, J. H. 1968. A look at foam cakes. Bakers Dig. *42*, No. 4, 53–55, 66.
BRODY, H. 1969. Fried pie production Tips. Food Eng. *41*, No. 5, 111, 113–114, 117.
COOK, W. C. 1953. Trouble shooting in pie bakeries. Proc. Am. Soc. Bakery Engrs. *1953*, 295–303.
DIETRICH, F. B. 1957. Production of fried pies. Proc. Am. Soc. Bakery Engrs. *1957*, 255–261.
Dow, W. T. 1958. Puff pastry—production fundamentals. Am. Soc. Bakery Engrs. Bull. *159*.
DUNN, J. A., and WHITE, J. R. 1939. The leavening action of air in cake batter. Cereal Chem. *16*, 93–100.
ELLING, J. W. 1952. Types of crust. Proc. Am. Soc. Bakery Engrs. *1952*, 275–280.

FRAZIER, B. M. 1947. Pie dough, pie crusts and their appearance. Proc. Am. Soc. Bakery Engrs. *1947*, 200–204.
HARREL, C. G. 1960. Air-leavened bakery products. *In* Bakery Technology and Engineering, S. A. Matz (Editor). Avi Publishing Co., Westport, Conn. (Out of print.)
HOOD, M. P., and LOWE, B. 1948. Air, water vapor and carbon dioxide as leavening gases in cakes made with different types of fat. Cereal Chem. *25*, 244–254.
HOWELL, S. 1954. Large scale production of pies. Proc. Am. Soc. Bakery Engrs. *1954*, 273–281.
KEATHLEY, M. F. 1956. New ideas in mechanized quality pie production. Proc. Am. Soc. Bakery Engrs. *1956*, 293–300.
KLINE, L., and SINGLETON, A. D. 1959. Improvement of egg albumen. U.S. Pat. 2,881,077. Apr. 7.
KOTHE, H. J. 1953. Egg white composition. U.S. Pat. 2,637,654. May 5.
LOWE, BELLE 1955. Experimental Cookery, 4th Edition. John Wiley & Sons, New York.
MATZ, S. A. 1968. Cookie and Cracker Technology. Avi Publishing Co., Westport, Conn.
SCHMIED, K. H. 1959. Fat distribution in puff paste prepared by different methods. Brot Gebaeck *13*, 225–233. (German)
SHEA, R. A. 1969. Single-stage angel food cakes. U.S. Patent 3,459,560. Aug. 5.
STINSON, C. G., and HUCK, M. B. 1969. A comparison of four methods for pastry tenderness evaluation. J. Food Sci. *34*, 537–539.
STRUCKMANN, E. 1956. The importance of good, tasty pie crust. Proc. Am. Soc. Bakery Engrs. *1956*, 300–306.
TAYLOR, W. F. 1963. Meat pie production. Food Trade Rev. *33*, No. 12, 65–76.
WOERFEL, J. B. 1959. Shortening for the production of pies. Bakers Dig. *33*, No. 1, 44–47.

CHAPTER 12

FORMULATIONS AND PROCEDURES FOR CHEMICALLY-LEAVENED BAKERY PRODUCTS

In the preceding chapter, some of the formulas included small amounts of leavening chemicals, but these reactants were added mainly for the purpose of establishing an accumulation of bubbles for later inflation by steam or other sources of gas which would furnish most of the leavening action. If we exclude bread and rolls from consideration, however, most bakery products depend upon the reaction of sodium bicarbonate and leavening acids for the expansive effect exerted during baking. Such products form the largest percentage of cakes and cookies prepared in the home or in bakeries.

CAKES

Function of the Ingredients

The gluten proteins of the flour serve as the basic structural element in chemically-leavened foods, just as they do in bread. However, the use of relatively smaller amounts of flour, the weaker (less extensible) protein in the soft wheat flours which are customarily employed, and the lower amount of protein in the flour result in a softer, crumblier texture in cakes and similar products. In most chemically-leavened foods, the protein of the flour is inadequate in quantity and quality to support an expansion of the extent found in bread so that they are of higher density than the latter product. Table 1.2 (Chap. 1) lists some specifications for soft wheat flours intended for use in particular types of chemically leavened foods.

In addition to their obvious function as sweeteners, sugars have a tenderizing effect on the crumb and promote the coloring of the crust. Sucrose is less effective in coloring the crust than are invert sugar and glucose. The situation is thus different than in yeast-containing doughs, where the invertase of the yeast rapidly converts sucrose to glucose and fructose. No such action is observed in cakes and cookies, and the sucrose remains intact and nonreducing throughout the oven stage. Sugars retain moisture in the crumb and thereby retard staling. Once again, glucose or invert sugar are more effective on a weight for weight basis than sucrose because of their lower molecular weight and consequently greater osmotic effect. As the concentration of sugars is increased, the batter has a tendency to become more fluid. Less air is entrained under these conditions, but the batter can be conveyed more easily.

An important function of the shortening component of batters is to entrap air during mixing. Not only do these air bubbles contribute directly to the leavening effect, but they also help to control grain size by serving as foci for gas evolution. Microphotographs of batters have shown that all of the air bubbles are enclosed in layers of fat. These observations demonstrate unequivocally the importance of the creaming function of shortening, regardless of whether or not the fat is creamed in a separate stage. Shortening also tenderizes the crumb and may contribute slightly to the flavor of the product. Emulsified shortenings increase the amount of water which can be used and thus contribute to the tenderness and resistance to staling of the finished product.

As mentioned before, the gluten of flours used in cakes has characteristics not conducive to the formation of large cells or thin cell walls. These deficiencies are remedied to some extent by using egg whites in the formula. Proteins of the egg form the vesicle wall in combination with gluten and permit the entrapment of air during mixing. In angel food cake the entire leavening effect is obtained from the air enclosed by the egg white during vigorous whipping. Egg white proteins themselves do not have sufficient mechanical strength, when in thin films, to withstand oven expansion or handling after baking and do not contribute the texture expected in cakes. These attributes must be obtained from flour. Eggs also contribute flavor, which may or may not be desirable, and are important sources of color. Egg yolks contribute emulsifying and tenderizing effects. Eggs are frequently the only material that can be used to compensate for an excessively weak flour.

Milk accentuates crust color as a result of its content of lactose, a reducing sugar. Skim milk appears to exert a toughening effect on the crumb, but with whole milk this effect is balanced by the lubricating or tenderizing action of the milkfat. The flavor contributed by milk is generally considered desirable, and the sugar it contains helps retard staling.

General Rules for Formulating Cakes

There exist more or less traditional rules for assuring "formula balance" or the correct proportioning of ingredients. These will be summarized here, but it should be understood that slavish adherence to their limitations is not necessary. They have worked well in practice in the past, but the development of new ingredients and new processing methods may very well allow the "rules" to be disregarded in some cases.

On a flour weight basis, sugar should be 110–160% in yellow layers, 110–160% in white layers, and 110–180% in devil's food and chocolate layers. Eggs as liquid eggs should be equal or exceed the shortening. Total liquid including the water in the eggs and milk should exceed the amount of sugar by approximately 25–35%. Shortening should fall in the range of 30–70%. Sodium bicarbonate should be 1.2–2% and salt 3–4% of the flour.

If the amount of sugar in a formula is increased, the egg content should be increased an equal amount. More shortening should be added when the percentage of eggs is increased. Additional water is usually not added when the formula contains dry milk, but if the formula water is not sufficient to equal the reconstitution water for the milk, add about 1% of water for each additional percentage of milk solids.

The following differences are usually found: Rich formulas need less chemical leavening because they incorporate more air during mixing, the batters display lower specific gravity for the same reason, and they perform better at a lower baking temperature. Batters baked in large piece sizes require less water and less leavener than those baked in small piece sizes.

Examples of Cake Formulas

Most authors consider the yellow layer cake as the basic type, but it is probably more logical to allocate this spot to the white layer cake since the yolk solids—the additional ingredient in yellow cakes—do not contribute any essential property to the cake or batter.

A formula for very lean white cake made in our American military installations for troop feeding (Anon. 1950) is shown below. Although this recipe is important as an approximate lower limit of "richness," cakes including considerably more enriching ingredients are desirable from a taste and texture standpoint. An example of a formula for a rich white layer cake which is considered basic from our point of view is also given. It is essential to use high emulsifying shortening in cakes which have a high proportion of sugar to flour, the so-called "high ratio" cakes. Of course, flavoring materials must be added to the basic formulas. In the case of white layer cakes, the flavor is nearly always vanilla. About ½ of 1% of single strength vanilla extract or artificial vanilla is a common level of addition.

White Layer Cake

	%
Flour	25.6
Sugar	25.6
Shortening, hydrogenated	11.2
Egg whites	16.0
Evaporated milk	10.2
Baking powder	1.6
Salt	0.6
Water	9.2

Rich White Layer Cake

	%
Sugar	29.5
Flour	21.0
Shortening, emulsified	11.5
Egg whites	16.0
Milk, whole	20.0
Baking powder	1.3
Salt	0.7

The author developed for the Armed Forces a "universal" cake mix which is very versatile as a result of its resistance to failure even when rather high levels of flavoring ingredients are added. It also performs fairly well even when considerable deviations from the recommended mixing procedure occur. The formula is given here as an example of a basic white layer cake prepared from all dry ingredients.

Universal Cake Mix

	%
Flour, 6% moisture	37.51
Sugar	41.00
Shortening, high stability with added emulsifiers	13.70
Dried egg whites	3.00
MSNF	2.50
Sodium bicarbonate	0.54
Sodium acid pyrophosphate	0.15
Monocalcium monohydrate	0.55
Salt	0.90
Powdered vanilla	0.15

About 35–40% water will be added to the above dry mix, the exact amount depending to some extent on the quality of the flour and the efficiency of the emulsifer.

The principle difference between yellow layers and white layers is that the former contain whole eggs instead of egg whites. In other words, the "additive" to our basic mix is egg yolks. A possible formula would be the rich white layer cake recipe given above to which 12–13% whole eggs are substituted for the egg whites and about 2–3% additional milk is included to supply necessary moisture. Rumsey (1959) gives a formula range which will include most satisfactory recipes. Below is a slightly modified version of his formula.

Formula Range for Yellow Layer Cakes

	%
Flour	21–23
Salt	0.5–0.75
Shortening	8–12
MSNF	2–3
Baking powder	1–1.5
Whole eggs	10–14
Water	22–25
Sugar	24–32

The recipe which follows was developed to take full advantage of the special properties of whole eggs.

Typical Yellow Layer Cake

	%
Flour	21.5
Sugar	30
Shortening, emulsifier added	11.5
Whole eggs	12.5
Whole milk	22.4
Baking powder	1.3
Salt	0.8

Yellow cakes are particularly adaptable to the addition of special flavors. Spice cakes are essentially yellow layer cakes to which, for example, mixtures of cinnamon, nutmeg, ginger, and allspice in the ratio of 8:6:1:1 are added. Pumpkin, applesauce, and mashed bananas may be added to spice cakes to furnish additional varieties. The above formula will support moderate additions of these adjuncts without failing. Larger quantities may necessitate increases in the flour and eggs.

Gingerbreads may deviate considerably in taste, texture, and appearance from yellow cakes, but they are usually formulated in accordance with much the same rules. The basic flavors in gingerbread are molasses and spices, and a coarser texture is acceptable and usually desired.

Typical Gingerbread Formula

	%
Cake flour	21.1
Sugar	8.4
Molasses	33.5
Shortening	9.4
MSNF	2.1
Whole eggs	8.4
Salt	0.5
Sodium bicarbonate	0.2
Baking powder	0.5
Cinnamon	0.5
Ginger	0.5
Allspice	0.2
Water	14.7

A small amount of soda in addition to that contained in the baking powder is included in the above formula in order to neutralize the natural acidity of the molasses.

Cakes containing cocoa (or chocolate liquor) can be divided into two classes, devil's food cakes and chocolate cakes. The difference is principally one of pH. Texture, color, and flavor are affected by the pH changes. Chocolate cakes may be considered as a basic cake to which cocoa or chocolate liquor has been added, and their pH is close to that of a yellow cake. Devil's food cakes are made with extra soda and have a crumb pH which is definitely alkaline. The next two formulas will illustrate the differences in preparation.

Chocolate Cake

	%
Flour	18
Sugar	27.5
Shortening	10.6
MSNF	2.5
Chocolate liquor	3.5
Baking powder	1.0
Salt	0.8

Whole eggs	15.0
Water	21.2

Cocoa takes up a considerable amount of water when added to a batter. This effect should be compensated by the addition of moisture to the base formula. As a rough rule of thumb, add water equivalent to 75–100% of the weight of the cocoa. Most authorities recommend reduction of the shortening by an amount equal to the cocoa butter contained in the cocoa or chocolate liquor. It is doubtful that this change is imperative in any but the most delicately balanced formulas. If it is desired to account for the cocoa butter in this manner, consider the chocolate liquor to contain 50% fat which has a shortening value ½ that of hydrogenated vegetable oils. Thus, addition of 10% chocolate liquor would call for a reduction of 2½% in the shortening.

Devil's Food Cake

	%
Flour	17.3
Sugar	26.8
Shortening	9.6
MSNF	3.8
Whole eggs	9.7
Egg whites	2.9
Water	24.1
Cocoa	3.8
Salt	0.8
Baking powder	0.7
Sodium bicarbonate	0.5

Foam type cakes, such as angel food, are properly included in the chapter on air-leavened bakery goods since they do not contain chemical leavening agents, at least in the original form. However, chiffon cakes, which derive a considerable portion of their leavening from an egg white foam, can be discussed here since they require chemical leavening agents to attain the required volume.

Chiffon Cake

	%
Flour	20.0
Sugar	26.5
Vegetable oil	9.5
Egg yolks	16.0

Baking powder	1.0
Salt	0.5
Water	6.9
Egg whites	19.5
Cream of tartar	0.1

The above formula indicates a separation of egg yolks and egg whites. In the usual batch mixing process, the egg whites and part of the sugar are beaten to a stiff foam and then the remainder of the ingredients are folded in. It is possible to mix and aerate the complete batter at one stage with some of the new continuous mixers. Flavors which can be added to chiffon cakes include vanilla, almond, and citrus flavors, particularly the latter.

Principles of Processing Chemically-Leavened Goods

There are perhaps five major categories of mixing methods for batters although, admittedly, what constitutes a minor modification is very much a matter of opinion. The five categories discussed here are: (1) single-stage mixing; (2) two-stage mixing, (3) creaming methods, (4) blending, or flour batter, method, and (5) sugar-and-water method.

The single-stage mixing process is the simplest of them all and consists of dumping all of the ingredients into the mixer bowl and beating them with the wire whip or batter beater until they are homogenous. Usually, the batter is beaten at low speed for 1–3 min, or until the dry ingredients have been wetted, and then the mixer is turned to high speed or second speed for 5–8 min. Variations of this method include adding the leaveners near the end of the mixing period, or adding the eggs near the end with a total mixing time much reduced from the normal. The obvious advantage of this process is the saving of time which results. Disadvantages are said to be poorer grain, texture, and volume in the finished product.

Two-stage batters are mixed by placing all of the dry ingredients and part of the liquid materials into the bowl and mixing until a homogenous or creamed mass results. The remainder of the liquid is then added, usually gradually, and the mixing completed. Variations in this method usually involve changes in the stage at which the eggs are added.

The creaming process requires that the sugar and shortening be beaten until a light and fluffy (creamed) mass is obtained. The eggs are then added while creaming is continued at medium speed, and finally the milk and flour are added alternately, in small portions. This method allows entrapment of a maximum number of small air bubbles in the fat with a consequent good effect on the grain in the finished product. It also does not develop the flour gluten as much as some of the other methods and this improves the texture of the cake somewhat.

The blending method requires the placing of flour and shortening in the mixing bowl and blending them together until the flour particles are thoroughly coated by the fat. The remainder of the dry ingredients is then added and the batter mixed until it is homogenous. Finally, the remaining liquid is added in portions and the mixing continued for a predetermined period. A modification which is frequently used requires that the sugar and eggs be beaten together to form a foam before they are added to the flour and shortening mixture. The chief advantage of the blending method is that it permits a very thorough dispersion of the shortening throughout the batter. This results in a very fine and uniform grain. On the other hand, the blending method does require more time and the use of more equipment than, for example, the single-stage method. Pyler (1952) says that cakes made by this method are tougher and have lower volume.

In the sugar-water method, all of the sugar and ½ of its weight in water are placed in the mixing bowl and beaten for 30 sec at medium speed in the first stage. Next, the shortening, flour, dry milk, salt, and baking powder are added and the bowl contents beaten at medium speed for about 5 min. The leaveners must be reduced by ¼ and superglycerinated shortening used for best results by this method. Advantages secured by this procedure are better crust color, tenderer crust, and improved volume as compared to cakes prepared by other methods.

As a general rule, layer cakes are baked at oven temperatures of 360°–400°F. Cooler ovens tend to give cakes which are flat on top and exhibit excess shrinkage around the circumference. The cakes may also be too tender. Higher temperatures result in peaked cakes with cracked centers. In addition, more holes and tunnels develop in the crumb and the products may be tough and low in volume.

Cake Faults and Their Remedies

Material in this section is attributable principally to Wihlfahrt (1953) and in part to Thelen (1951).

(1) Volume Too Low.—This can be caused by the use of insufficient amounts of leavening agents, in which case the remedy is obvious. If batters are allowed to stand too long at too high temperatures, an initially adequate leavening action may be lost as a result of premature reaction of the bicarbonate and the leavening acids. This can be true even when delayed action leaveners are used. Undermixing can cause low volume because of reduced aeration of the batter. An excessively high oven temperature can set the structure of the cake before the full effect of the leavening gases has been exerted. Improper balance of ingredients, or improper types of ingredients, especially the flour or shortening, can reduce the expected volume markedly.

(2) **Defects of Texture.**—Gumminess, doughiness, or chewiness are often the result of underbaking or improper cooling before packaging. Such faults are readily corrected by increasing the baking time slightly or by thorough cooling before wrapping. If these faults are due to improper formulation, the exact cause may be harder to spot although the percentage of water and the type and quantity of shortening should be checked first.

Toughness may be due to use of too strong a flour, overbaking, inadequate amounts of water, overmixing with consequent overdevelopment of the gluten, not enough sugar, inadequate amounts or wrong type of shortening, or underscaling.

(3) **Defects of Crust Appearance.**—Spotted crusts can be due either to a nonhomogenous batter or to bubbles in the crust. The former problem can be corrected by using a different sequence of mixing, longer mixing, or more severe mixing conditions. The latter difficulty may be the result of unsuitable types of leaveners, batters which are too viscous, or excessive oven heat.

Bursting of the crust may also be due to high baking temperatures, or to overmixing, too much flour, or flour which is too strong.

Pale crust color can result from a baking temperature which is too low. The oven as a whole may be set at too low a temperature or the heat distribution may be faulty with inadequate radiant heat reaching the crust. Conversely, crust colors which are too dark may result from undesirably high oven temperatures. In addition, pale crust colors can result from underscaling with resultant shielding of the top crust from radiant heat by the pan sides. Too much sugar, and particularly too much reducing sugars such as are found in corn syrups or in honey, can cause darkening of the crust even though baking conditions are correct as judged by the condition of the interior of the cake.

(4) **Coarse or Irregular Grain.**—Tunnels and large holes at the bottom of the cake may result from excessive bottom heat during baking. Too cold an oven can cause the grain to be open. Wet streaks are often due to underbaking. Undissolved spots of material in the crumb are not always the result of undermixing, although this is probably the usual cause. Some ingredients, particularly milk solids when improperly stored, will form agglomerates which are virtually indestructible by the usual mixing procedures.

Both undermixing and overmixing can create a coarse, open grain in the finished product. An excessively close or fine grain is more often due to overmixing.

COOKIES

The formulas for some types of cookies are very similar to those for layer cakes. In fact, some layer cake batters can be used to make quite acceptable cookies. For commercial production, however, the limitations of the equipment restrict the range through which the rheological properties of the dough can be permitted to vary, and these, in turn, limit the range of variations of the ingredients in the formula.

Functions of the Ingredients

Several workers have published lists showing the net effect of the common ingredients on the finished cookie. For example, the ingredients might be classified as binding or tenderizing materials depending upon their expected effect on the finished product (Thelen 1949):

Binding materials or tougheners: (1) Flour. (2) Water—because it assists in forming gluten. (3) Milk solids—not very effective in amounts found in cookie doughs. (4) Egg whites and whole eggs—the former more so. (5) Cocoa or chocolate products.

Tenderizing materials: (1) Sugars most important. (2) Shortenings. (3) Leavening—soften flour proteins, NH_4HCO_3, and $NaHCO_3$. (4) Egg yolks.

In addition, Flick (1964) lists baking acids, oat flour, and soy flour as tougheners and ground raisins, ground dates, etc., as tenderizers. Corn flour acts as a tenderizer, but more than minor amounts contributes an off-flavor. Starch (corn or wheat) is a convenient and inexpensive tenderizer. Generally, nonreactive substances act as tenderizers.

The continuous structure of the cookie arises from the flour. The basic framework is tenderized by sugar, invert sugar, egg yolk, ammonia, soda (or baking powder), and shortening. It is firmed or toughened by water, cocoa, egg white, whole egg, milk solids, and the leavening acids. Flavors and spices are usually not present in sufficient quantity to affect texture. Salt is usually considered to be a toughener.

Sugars and especially syrups in large amounts tend to make the dough sticky and hinder release from dies and wires. Shortening is one of the principal agents for increasing tenderness, at least so far as the rich, sweet biscuits are concerned. Too much shortening may lead to a greasy, smeary cookie which is susceptible to rancidity because the free fat soaks into the package, although these effects can be largely overcome by using plastic trays and cello overwrap. Too much sugar leads to hardness and excessive sweetness in the finished cookie.

Flours.—A wide variety of flours are being used, from a soft cookie flour to a rather strong sponge flour. The stronger the flour, the more shortening and sugar must be used to obtain an acceptable texture.

High protein contents lead to hardness of texture and coarseness of internal grain and surface appearance. Chlorine bleached flours are not recommended for soft type cookies where relatively large amounts of tenderizing and moisture-retaining ingredients such as sugar, shortening, and egg yolk are used (Flick 1964). If the percentage of flour is decreased too much, as when large amounts of enriching ingredients are added, the cookie will lack body and may become too fragile.

Eggs.—Whole frozen eggs contribute a better structure and a more delicate texture than do dried eggs, especially in semibatter wire-type cookies. Frozen eggs seem to give greater volume and a more open grain (Velzen 1963). Whole eggs either fresh or frozen cream readily and seem to provide better structure in drop cookies. Use of egg yolk as a part or complete replacement for whole eggs (using a smaller percentage than whole) will produce a tender cookie with excellent eating quality, but the grain or internal structure of the cookie may not be as good as with the whole egg (Flick 1963).

Shortening.—Velzen (1963) described the ideal relationship of shortening and sugar in three types of doughs as follows: cutting machine, 15% shortening and sugar variable; rotary, 30% of each of these ingredients; and wire-cut, 50% sugar and 50% shortening, all on a flour weight basis. Problems in machining are encountered when the shortening content is raised much above that indicated for rotary and cutting machine doughs, but this is not necessarily so for wire-cut doughs. Modern techniques have altered some beliefs; for example, it is possible to run certain shortening-free doughs on cutting machines.

Liquid shortening is in frequent use and oleo is the most common variety. For creaming, a hydrogenated vegetable shortening is recommended. Regular lard will not cream satisfactorily, but the rearranged types are acceptable. In rotary doughs, lard will tend to "oil off" on the back roll and may streak both light and dark doughs. Substitution of liquid shortenings for plastic usually calls for less shortening in the formula plus the addition of cold water or ice to adjust the dough temperature to the proper level.

Lecithin.—Lecithin seems to increase the shortening effect of fats. It also promotes a tendency for the fat to cover or spread among slightly moist particles of sugar, flour, etc., which would otherwise repel the fat. Because of the emulsification effect, lecithin makes rich sweet doughs seem drier, thereby improving their machineability. Especially on rotary pieces, better release from the die makes a clearer impression and cuts down cripples. Lecithin also speeds dispersion of the fatty and aqueous components of the dough so that mixing time can be reduced. In turn, the reduced mixing time improves tenderness by minimizing gluten development, especially when strong flours are used.

Salt.—Except for topping, a salt of small crystal size should be used. Most biscuit formulas call for about 1% salt (FWB) or even less. This seems to be on the low side of the acceptable range. The usual cracker dough or batter can take 1½% of salt (FWB) without the occurrence of an unpleasant saline taste in the finished product. Rich or nut-containing doughs may be able to use slightly more. One guideline which has been suggested is to add salt up to 3% of the fat weight.

Sugar.—Granulated, fine granulated, and powdered can be used alone or in combination to adjust spread and machining properties. For better uniformity of spread a specific granulation should be established. No two suppliers of sugar have the same screen analysis even though the nomenclature is the same. Finer sugars require less mixing than do the coarser varieties and they may reduce sticking to the band. A fine granulated sugar creams better than powdered. Dextrose can often be substituted for up to 20% of the sucrose. Invert syrup must be used with care. According to Wittenberg (1965), it makes wire-cuts, especially wafers, soft, light, and spongy, with an open texture. The crust color is often brighter and develops earlier in the baking.

Milk.—Milk blends or ameliorates harsh flavors without contributing much flavor of its own. About 5% of the flour weight as skim milk powder (MSNF) is a good average figure for securing the full benefits of the ingredient. Crust color and gloss are generally improved. The protein components bind water and make the dough stiffer and somewhat stickier. The toughening effect on the finished product is minor, in most cases.

Whey has similar results, except that the stiffening, water-binding, and toughening effects are negligible.

Proportions.—The range of contents of major ingredients in three kinds of cookie doughs are shown in Table 12.1. These data were accumulated by Wittenberg (1965) in a survey of most of the cookie producers in the United States.

Spread

The control of cookie spread is one of the most serious problems confronting the production man. Minor variations in appearance, flavor, and texture are usually accepted with little complaint, but a cookie which spreads so much that it cannot be filled in the package, or one that spreads too little, causing slack fill or excess height for the package, can create havoc on the packaging line and generate large amounts of scrap. Happy is the lot of the production man who is dump packing his cookies.

A great deal of study has been devoted to the elucidation of factors affecting spread. For example, Johnson (1965) examined the effect of various ingredients on characteristics of laboratory-prepared cookies.

TABLE 12.1
CONTENTS OF MAJOR INGREDIENTS IN THREE KINDS OF COOKIE DOUGHS

	Water %[1]	Shortening %[1]	Sugars %[1]	Syrups %[1]
Rotary molded	5–15	10–40	20–45	0–20
Cutting machine	10–25	5–20	15–50	0–20
Wire cut	10–40	10–50	30–85	0–20
Range	0–61	9–98	9–98	0–85
Average	22.2	33.7	43.7	16.9

[1] Based on flour as 100%.

Three flours were studied: (1) Michigan white, straight flour; (2) Indiana-Ohio soft, red straight; and (3) a cracker sponge version of the soft, red straight. He also increased and decreased sugar in 5% increments to a maximum change of 15%. For width and thickness, the curves were a straight line function of the percentage of sugar change, except at the increase of 15% sugar there appeared to be a slight regression of width. However, Johnson believed that at a slightly lower baking temperature the straight line relationship would have been retained. At the lowest sugar level, the tops showed fine hairline cracks and a light color, while at highest level wide deep cracks appeared.

When ammonia carbonate or bicarbonate increments were added in addition to the regular amount of soda, the spread was nearly a straight line function of the percentage of ammonia. Cracks became wider, and there was a faster bake-out as shown by darker color.

When ammonia (0, 0.25, 0.50, 0.75, 1.0 and 1.25%) was used without soda, the width was a straight line function of ammonia. Height was also directly related with the exception of the no-ammonia sample. With no ammonia *or* soda, a very thick nonspreading cookie, with large flat plateaus and heavy cracks was obtained. As ammonia was increased, finer cracks were observed, and spread increased. At the upper level cracks again deepened, spread increased, and color darkened.

With soda but no ammonia, a rapid increase in width occurred between 0 and 0.5% soda, then very little change between 0.5 and 1.1%. When 1.1% was exceeded there was again a rapid increase in width. Thickness was affected in a similar manner except that with *no* soda and *no* leavening a relatively thin cookie resulted. Appearance of the cookies was similar to those in the ammonia series except that at higher levels they became much darker in color. At 0.4% soda the pH was near the maximum considered desirable, yet added amounts of soda gave additional spread without seemingly hurting appearance. Johnson did not comment on the flavor of these latter samples.

The pH is a critical factor, and once the optimum pH for a particular piece has been established, any change in the leavening system should be balanced so as to maintain that level. Means leading to a change in the pH (as by addition of soda without compensating amounts of acid) should not be used to modify the leavening effect or spread.

In the experiments reported by Johnson, water gave no appreciable variation in width as it was increased (in the range considered). As water was decreased there was a fairly steady reduction in height. Stiffer doughs have a less well-developed system for retaining leavening gases plus a greater resistance to expansion. On the whole, it appears that changing the water content is a poor method for controlling spread though it does affect height. The water series showed little change in appearance throughout.

Temperature variations (dough) seemed to have minor effects on cookie width. Thickness, however, increased with increased temperature at lower levels, say to 75°-80°F; then at higher levels, to about 90°-95°F, thickness remained constant.

Finney *et al.* (1950), working with a simple sugar snap formula showed that the amount of shortening (25-35% range) affected spread very little. However, the spread was directly proportional to the amount of sugar added (50-80%) at each level of ammonium bicarbonate addition, and also directly proportional to the amount of ammonium bicarbonate added at each level of granulated sugar. Less than 55% sugar gave inferior top grain. An addition of 0.5% ammonium bicarbonate produced as much increase in diameter and change in top grain as 7.6% of granulated sugar. The optimum quantity of ammonium bicarbonate differed markedly for different wheat varieties. The pH of cookies increased from 7.3 with no ammonium bicarbonate to 7.9 at 2.25% of this leavener, but further increases were without effect on pH.

Based on the preceding evidence, and other studies, we can list some factors which might be varied to increase or decrease the spread. Those ingredients described as tougheners will usually decrease spread while tenderizers will often (but by no means always) increase spread. Increased spread will also result from increasing the amount of leaveners, using a finer granulation of sugar (within limits), or by adding more water or more shortening to the formula. However, powdered sugar will actually decrease spread and tenderness, while brown sugar contributes less to spread than does granulated. The spread can also be decreased by using stronger flour, increasing the mixing time, and bringing the dough from the mixer at a lower temperature (using chilled water or ice if necessary). Too much salt can reduce spread. An increase in the amount of sugar will often increase spread. Some authors have suggested the use of ⅛% potassium carbonate to increase spread when all else fails.

So far as oven control is concerned, increasing the temperature in the first zone tends to decrease spread, while closing the dampers in the first zone will often increase spread.

Types of Cookies

Cookies are generally classified according to the kind of equipment used to form the individual pieces. Stamping machines, rotary cutters, rotary molders, wire-cut machines, and depositing equipment are used for over 90% of the cookie production in the United States. The equipment has a strong influence on the texture of the cookie and limits the formula variations which can be used.

Deposit cookies are the machine-made counterparts of the hand-bagged cookie and many of the formulas for the latter can be successfully adapted to automatic production. Deposit cookies will contain about 35–40% sugar, 65–75% shortening, and 15–25% liquid whole eggs. The flour should be milled from soft wheat, and it should be unbleached, with 8–8.5% protein and 0.35–0.40% ash. It should have a viscosity of 40°M or more and a spread factor of 79–80.

Wire-cut cookie equipment permits a wider variation in dough composition than any other type of machinery. It is necessary to have the wire-cut dough sufficiently cohesive to hold together as it is extruded through an orifice, and yet it must be relatively nonsticky and short enough so that it separates cleanly as it is cut by the wire. Formulas may contain up to several 100% sugar based on the flour, and shortening up to 100% or more of the flour. Doughs may be almost as soft as some cake batters, or too stiff to be easily molded by hand. The very soft doughs overlap deposit doughs in consistency, while the other extreme is close to the texture expected in rotary molded type doughs. Advantages of the wire-cut cookie over rotary molded cakes are more open grain and softer texture, and, as compared to deposit goods, a more uniformly shaped cookie. Disadvantages over the rotary molded piece are the lack of potential for making a surface design and somewhat less uniformity of size and shape.

The principal distinguishing feature of stamping machine or rotary cutting operations is that the pieces are cut from a continuous web of dough by a cylindrical die or reciprocating-motion cutter. A rather large range of dough types can be handled by these types of equipment, but it is necessary that the dough be sufficiently cohesive to form the continuous sheet from which the blanks will be cut and to hold the scrap (if any) together as it is lifted from between the blanks. Reciprocating cutting machines, or stamping machines, are often discussed as though there were many points of similarity between them and rotary cutters. In fact, there are so many differences between the two types of equipment that it is not particularly informative to consider them together.

For rotary molded cookies, the dough consistency must be such that it will feed uniformly and readily fill all of the crevices of the die cavity under the pressures existing in the feeding hopper. The dough blank must be capable of being extracted from the cavity without undergoing distortion or forming tails of appreciable size, but it must adhere to the die roll long enough to prevent the piece from falling out before it reaches the extraction toller. The blank must have sufficient cohesion to hold together and not break up at any of the transfer points before or after baking. The dough must flow very slightly or smooth out during forming and baking so that woodiness or undesirable irregularities in the surface pattern are not apparent in the finished cookie. Usually, the spread and rise should be minimized so as not to blur or distort the design. Doughs formulated to meet these requirements are usually fairly high in sugar and shortening and low in moisture. Development of the gluten is definitely to be avoided.

Most manufacturers use flour of about 8.1–8.2% protein for rotary base cakes, although a range of 7.1–9.2% has been reported. Ash should be about 0.415, with a known range of 0.33–0.47% being used satisfactorily. Oleo shortening added in the liquid condition is suitable for most of these doughs, but vegetable shortening can also be used. Powdered sugar and sugar syrups are the preferred sweetening ingredients. MSNF are often added, but it is thought that condensed milk is preferable since the liquid ingredient removes any possibility of lumps appearing in the finished cookie. Lecithin at about the 0.4% level will improve machineability.

One-stage mixing is often perfectly satisfactory, but a creaming operation with most of the minor ingredients added before the flour goes in gives added assurance that lumps of undistributed ingredients will not appear in the cookie. Dough temperatures from 72° to 90°F are being used for rotary sandwich bases.

BIBLIOGRAPHY

ANON. 1950. Recipes. U.S. Army Tech. Manual *TM 10-412*.
BLAKES, A. 1954. Balancing cake formulas. Proc. Am. Soc. Bakery Engrs. *1954*, 244–248.
FINNEY, K. F., MORRIS, V. H., and YAMAZAKI, W. T. 1950. Effects of varying quantities of sugar, shortening, and ammonium bicarbonate on the spreading and top grain of sugar-snap cookies. Cereal Chem. 27, 30–41.
FLICK, H. 1964. Fundamentals of cookie production, including soft type cookies. Proc. Am. Soc. Bakery Engrs. *1964*, 286–293.
FORSMAN, J. 1951. Production techniques for producing uniformly good cookies. Proc. Am. Soc. Bakery Engrs. *1951*, 246–250.
FUHR, F. R. 1962. Cookie spread—its effects on production and quality. Bakers Dig. 36, No. 4, 56–58, 78.
GLABAU, C. A. 1958. Effect of pH on flavor, color and physical properties of cakes and cookies. Proc. Am. Soc. Bakery Engrs. *1958*, 256–262.

GLABAU, C. A. 1962. How much batter should cake pans take? Bakers Weekly *194*, No. 2, 44–48.
HABIGHURST, A. B. 1969. Quality factors in wire-cut cookie production. Bakers Dig. *43*, No. 1, 57–59.
JOHNSON, D. H. 1965. Correlating laboratory tests to production. 40th Ann. Training Conf. Biscuit Bakers' Inst. Apr. 7.
KISSELL, L. T., and MARSHALL, B. D. 1962. Multi-factor responses of cake quality to basic ingredient ratios. Cereal Chem. *39*, 16–30.
LAWSON, H. W. 1970. Functions and applications of ingredients for cakes. Bakers Dig. *44*, No. 6, 37–41, 66.
LIMBERAKIS, D. A. Control in quality cake production. Proc. Am. Soc. Bakery Engrs. *1959*, 265–269.
MCGEE, O. L. 1955. Soft cookies. Proc. Am. Soc. Bakery Engrs. *1955*, 251–260.
MOLLENHAUER, J. 1955. Lower cake production costs without decreased quality. Proc. Am. Soc. Bakery Engrs. *1955*, 293–302.
PYLER, E. J. 1952. Baking Science and Technology. Siebel Publishing Co., Chicago.
RUMSEY, L. A. 1959. Commercial baking procedures. *In* The Chemistry and Technology of Cereals as Food and Feed, S. A. Matz (Editor). Avi Publishing Co., Westport, Conn. (Out of print.)
SHUKIS, A. J. 1969. Chemical leavening systems. Bakers Weekly *216*, No. 13, 30–32.
THELEN, R. J. 1949. Cookie faults—their causes and helpful suggestions. Proc. Am. Soc. Bakery Engrs. *1949*, 265–272.
THELEN, R. J. 1951. Cake faults—their cause and cure. Proc. Am. Soc. Bakery Engrs. *1951*, 279–283.
VELZEN, B. H. 1963. Production of wire cut cookies. Proc. Am. Soc. Bakery Engrs. *1963*, 243–250.
WIHLFAHRT, J. E. 1953. A Treatise on Cake Making. Standard Brands, New York.
WITTENBERG, H. L. 1965. Wire cut cookies. 40th Ann. Training Conf. Biscuit Bakers' Inst. Apr. 7.

CHAPTER 13

FORMULATIONS AND PROCEDURES FOR YEAST-LEAVENED BAKERY FOODS

Yeast-leavened bakery products include not only those foods in which yeast is mainly an aerating agent but also those in which the leavening action is secondary in importance to the functions of dough-conditioning and flavor-enhancing. Examples of the latter types are Danish pastry and soda crackers. Some leavening action is unavoidable when live yeast is included in a formulation because gas production by the organisms is continuous in the presence of a suitable substrate (assuming the yeast is fully adapted to the substrate) and it would be difficult to formulate a dough which did not contain some utilizable carbohydrate. In fact, yeast of the kind used by bakers has a detectable endogenous gas production rate.

Some products in both groups, i.e., foods in which yeast is included primarily for its leavening action and foods in which the desired functions are other than gas production, will be discussed in this chapter, but primary emphasis will be placed on products such as bread where the leavening function is paramount, since the principles involved are also applicable to the other group.

The chapter was planned so as to present first some general considerations regarding the products, next to present some examples of formulas and procedures for the principal types of products, and finally to discuss some common defects and their causes. The initial discussion will deal with the sequence of reactions occurring in fermenting and baking doughs, and the function of the most important ingredients and processing steps. Actual recipes and preparation methods will follow, and, finally, some trouble-shooting hints will be listed.

FUNCTIONS OF THE PRINCIPAL INGREDIENTS AND PROCESSING STEPS

Yeast provides flavoring compounds, affects the texture of the dough and baked product, and supplies carbon dioxide which decreases the density of the food.

As yeast ferments the sugars in dough, it releases to the surrounding liquid dissolved carbon dioxide and ethanol, and metabolic by-products such as lactic acid, acetic acid, etc., as well as small quantities of unknown compounds. Bakers' yeast cannot hydrolyze proteins or even peptides and so, in its intact form, exerts no proteolytic effect on gluten. It cannot attack starch or dextrins and so does not affect dough viscosity by breaking down these compounds of large molecular weight. However, the acids such as lactic and acetic, which yeast elaborates, have a definite effect on some of the gluten proteins that is best described as solubilizing action. The net observable effect is a mellowing or weakening of the dough structure.

Carbon dioxide passes through the yeast wall as a dissolved compound, probably in the form of bicarbonate ion. As the concentration of carbon dioxide increases in the free liquid outside the cell, gas bubbles begin to form around foci in the dough. These foci have never been clearly identified although very possibly they may be small air bubbles incorporated into the dough during mixing. It appears certain that the foci are not the yeast cells themselves. The importance of this point is that fineness of grain, i.e., the number of gas vesicles in a given volume of bread, is not entirely controlled by the number of yeast cells present, and that uniformity of grain is not governed solely by the uniformity of yeast cell activity. These product qualities must be controlled by other methods and are usually determined in practice by the physical treatment accorded the dough, especially during mixing.

The substances contributing the major portion of the characteristic aroma of bread and similar foods undoubtedly arise either directly or indirectly from the activity of yeast. The responsible chemicals are mostly unknown, but it is to be hoped that the techniques of gas chromatography will enable investigators to identify most of them within the next few years. The substances are probably mostly extracellular. A simple proof of the latter statement can be obtained by baking a dough which contains yeast cells that have been washed to remove the extracellular metabolic by-products and then killed by heat. The odor of the baked product is not like that of bread. Furthermore, it is probably better to call the substances produced by yeast bread flavor precursors rather than bread flavors. It is a common enough observation that a well fermented dough does not have a bread-like smell, yet the same dough subjected to the baking process will yield during the later stages the characteristic and appealing odor of bread. It is the author's belief that many of the actual odorant compounds are created in or near the region of the crust as a result of nonenzymatic browning reactions. Participants in this reaction would be some of the unknown extracellular metabolities of yeast and nitrogenous substances orginating mostly from the flour. The author has shown that fermentation broths from which the cells have been removed are potent contributors of bread-like flavors to chemically-leavened baked goods. The flavor precursors in broth are subject to rapid deterioration at elevated temperatures or if access to oxygen is facilitated. They can be preserved to a limited extent by freeze drying the broth.

When yeast cells reach about 140°F, as they do shortly after baking commences, the semipermeability of the cell membrane is destroyed. As a result, the low molecular weight compounds in the cytoplasm may diffuse out through the cell wall. These substances may have a definite effect on the characteristics of the product since the gluten is not coagulated at this temperature and the vesicle walls are still extending as the heat continues to expand the contained gases. The effect of these reactions has never been adequately investigated, but purely qualitative observations would lead one to believe that the net result is an increase in the extensibility of the vesicle wall. Such compounds as reduced glutathione, known to be extractable from heat-killed yeast, might have such an effect.

The peculiar property of wheat flours which makes them indispensable for the preparation of light, well-aerated foods such as bread is the ability of the gluten proteins to form very thin continuous films which are rather impervious to carbon dioxide and moisture vapor diffusion. These films form the walls of gas vesicles. In them are embedded the starch granules and other particulate masses which are completely surrounded by the thin layer of hydrated protein. On the molecular level, the gluten films are probably composed of networks of protein molecules bound to each other by relatively strong ionic bonds such as—S—S—and by weaker hydrogen bonds, and surrounded by vast numbers of water molecules bound by forces of varying but relatively low strength. The water molecules undergo constant exchange with the "free" water which dissolves the sugars and other soluble dough constituents.

The dissolved gas emitted by the fermenting yeast cells eventually supersaturates the free water to an increasing distance from the cell until finally a discontinuity of some sort in the medium causes evolution of part of the dissolved gas at a restricted locus. The evolved gas forms a bubble in the gluten film which continually enlarges as further carbon dioxide diffuses into the open space. If this process were allowed to continue without interference, the dough would contain few vesicles and all would have thick walls. The mechanical punishment to which the dough is subjected at various stages in the processing procedure subdivides the bubbles, increasing their number and decreasing their size. Although most of the vesicle walls are ruptured by the pressing and beating steps, the breaks are quickly sealed as a result of the elasticity and cohesiveness of the gluten.

PROCEDURES AND FORMULATIONS FOR BREADS AND ROLLS

Limitations on the establishment of procedures and formulations for yeast-leavened bakery products are the result of both legal and technical considerations. The legal limitations arise from the provisions of the *Federal Definitions and Standards for Bakery Products* (Anon. 1952) with amendments which set forth requirements for white bread, enriched bread, milk bread, raisin bread, whole wheat bread and the equivalent rolls and buns. The technical limitations are due to the inherent characteristics and the interactions of the ingredients and the processing techniques which may be employed in the manufacture of the products.

The limitations established by the *Federal Definitions and Standards for Bakery Products* are, in general, quite lenient with respect to the types and relative proportions of flour, sugar, shortening, yeast, and salt which can be used. The only processing requirement is that the products be prepared by "baking a kneaded yeast-leavened dough." Although this latter limitation seems extremely easy to comply with, it does exclude any product leavened wholly by chemical agents.

Permissible ingredients for white bread are: flour, including bromated flour and phosphated flour; yeast; water, or an optional liquid ingredient; salt; shortening, including certain specified emulsifier additives; milk or milk products in quantities less than necessary to qualify the bread as milk bread; certain milk derivatives such as buttermilk, cheese whey, milk proteins, etc.; eggs, egg yolks, and egg whites; sugar, invert sugar, light colored brown sugar, honey, corn syrup, etc.; malted cereals and preparations made from malted cereals; inactive dried *Saccharomyces cerevisiae* in quantities of not more than 2% of the flour used; harmless lactic acid-producing bacteria; corn flour, potato flour, rice flour, certain starches, or soy flour in quantities equalling not more than 3% of the flour used; ground dehulled soybeans, optionally defatted, in quantities of not more than 0.5% of flour used; calcium sulfate, calcium lactate, calcium carbonate, dicalcium phosphate, ammonium phosphates, ammonium sulfate, or ammonium chloride in quantities not to exceed 0.25 parts for each 100 parts by weight of flour used; potassium bromate, potassium iodate or calcium peroxide in quantities not exceeding 0.0075% of the flour; monocalcium phosphate up to 0.75% of the flour; vinegar, not more than 1 pt of 100-gr vinegar per 100 lb flour; calcium propionate, sodium propionate, or any mixture of them in quantities totalling not more than 0.32 parts per

100 parts by weight of flour; sodium diacetate, not more than 0.4 parts per 100 parts of flour; lactic acid in amounts sufficient to bring the pH of the finished bread to pH 4.5 or above; and spice, spice oils, and spice extracts. In some cases, label declarations of some of the optional ingredients are required. In addition, the total solids of bread must be at least 62% of the total weight.

Anyone engaged in new product development should have a copy of the Standards readily available because it is essential to comply with them if the product is to be offered for sale under any of the above descriptive names. A copy can be obtained for 5¢ from the Superintendent of Documents, U.S. Government Printing Office, Washington, D.C.

Examples of Formulations

White Bread and Rolls.—Satisfactory white bread can be made from flour, water, salt, and yeast (or a "sour dough"). Italian bread is usually based upon this simple combination of ingredients, and French or Vienna breads are scarcely more complicated. Such breads have a hard crust which is light in color, a coarse and tough crumb, and a flavor which is excellent when fresh but considerably less attractive when the bread is a day or so old. Table 13.1 gives example of formulations which have been suggested for these products. Formulas may vary greatly from one bakery to another and between different sections of the country.

Of course, the formulas shown in Table 13.1 can be, and usually are, modified by the addition of dough improvers, yeast foods, mold inhibitors, vitamins, minerals, and small quantities of enriching ingredients such as milk solids. The sponge and dough process is usually employed in making these breads. The flours used must have good amylase activity or the lack of fermentable sugar production must be compensated for by added diastatic malt. Strong flours are desirable, and long extraction flours or even some or all clear flours may be used.

The standard low-density soft-crust breads which comprise the greatest proportion of white bread sold in this country include much greater

TABLE 13.1
FORMULATIONS FOR FRENCH, ITALIAN, AND VIENNA BREADS

	Italian (Parts)	French (Parts)	Vienna (Parts)
Flour	100	100	100
Water (variable)	60	60	60
Yeast (compressed)	1.75	1.75	1.75
Salt	1.75	1.5	1.75
Sugar	...	1.5	3
Shortening	...	2	3

quantities of enriching ingredients than the lean breads described above. Table 13.2 gives formulas for several white breads varying principally in the amounts of enriching ingredients required.

Home-style, army, egg, and bun formulas are usually made up by the dough process while it is more common to make the others by the sponge and dough process. It is customary to use yeast foods, dough improvers, mold inhibitors, etc., according to the convictions of the formulator or the conditions imposed upon him as final product requirements.

Whole Wheat and Other Specialty Breads.—Breads designed to take advantage of demands for unusual flavors or for special nutritional qualities can assume an almost unlimited range of forms and contents. In Table 13.3 are listed formulas for some of the more standardized varieties.

Several bread varieties of rather unusual composition which have been shown to have good commercial possibilities were recently described by Pickering (1956). A few of these formulas, adapted to the style used in this book, are given below to illustrate the possibilities.

TABLE 13.2
COMPARATIVE FORMULAS FOR SOME WHITE PAN BREADS

	Lean (Parts)	Home Style (Parts)	Premium (Parts)	Egg (Parts)	Army (Parts)	Buns (Parts)	School Lunch (Parts)
Flour	100	100	100	100	100	100	100
Water (variable)	60	65	60	60	60	65	74
Salt	2	2.25	3	2	2.5	2.5	2
Sugar	3	3	10[1]	2.5	3	16	4
Milk (MSNF)	2	3	4	4	6	10	12
Shortening	3	9	...	...	5	9	4
Malt syrup	1	...	...	2	2	1	0.5
Yeast (compressed)	2	3	1.75	2	2	4	1.75
Butter	...	...	8	3	...	...	...
Whole eggs	...	...	...	9	...	...	...

[1] Half honey and half invert sugar syrup.

TABLE 13.3
FORMULAS FOR WHOLE WHEAT, RAISIN, AND CHEESE BREADS

	Whole Wheat (Parts)	Cheese (Parts)	Raisin (Parts)
Flour	100[1]	100	100
Water (variable)	62	57	62
Salt	2	2	2
Sugar	3.5	2	2
Milk (MSNF)	2	2	4
Shortening	3	5	5
Malt syrup	0.5	...	...
Yeast (compressed)	3	3	3
Dehydrated cheddar	...	10	...
Raisins	...	...	50

[1] Must be 100% whole wheat flour.

Egg Twist Bread

	Lb
Bread flour (medium strength)	100
Water (variable)	62
Salt	2.125
Malt	0.5
Mineral yeast food	0.375
Shortening	5
Sugar	5
MSNF	5
Egg yolks	5
Compressed yeast	2

Vitality High Protein Bread

	Lb
Bread flour (high gluten type)	100
Water (variable)	70
Salt	2.25
Yeast	2.125
Mineral yeast food	0.25
Malt	0.5
Shortening	3
MSNF	4
Soya flour	6
Sugar	5.5
Wheat germ	1.5
Molasses	0.5

Old Fashioned Raisin Molasses Bread

	Lb
Bread flour (strong)	65
Whole wheat flour	35
Water (variable)	67
Salt	2.25
Yeast (compressed)	2.25
Mineral yeast food	0.375
Shortening	4
Molasses	3
Brown sugar	3
MSNF	3
Seedless raisins	55

Chuck Wagon Bread

	Lb
Bread flour (strong)	100
Water (variable)	76
Rolled oats	16
Salt	2.25
Yeast	2.25
Mineral yeast food	0.25
Honey or dark corn syrup	5
Sugar	1.5
MSNF	4
Shortening	4

Breads Requiring "Sours"

Bread doughs were originally leavened with "sours," or portions of old doughs which were kept over from preceding batches and used to inoculate a fresh batch with the mixture of wild yeasts and bacteria which had accumulated and stabilized during many transfers. Some specialty breads are still made with "sours" in order to achieve the more intense flavor and unusual texture characteristic of such fermentations.

From time to time, various types of sourdough breads acquire a regional popularity which leads bakers in other parts of the country to attempt to duplicate them. It is important to recognize that the typical flavors of these breads are quite dependent on the organisms present in the culture or sour and on the conditions of fermentation. The composition of the dough also has an influence on the flavor, of course, but it is futile to attempt to reproduce a specific sour dough flavor by manipulation of other ingredients, in the absence of the sour used in the original bread.

The culture may be composed of several different yeasts and bacteria which act in conjunction or in sequence in very complicated ways. Identification of the predominant species in the sour and duplicating the mix with pure strains of the organisms may not always provide results equivalent to the traditional system. Furthermore, transfer of the sour from one plant to another with inadvertent and unrecognized changes in conditions may result in loss of one or more of the necessary organisms and subsequent failure of the sour to perform satisfactorily. Additionally, inoculation of the sour with microorganisms present on the equipment (such as dough troughs) in the plant of the successful producer may be difficult to reproduce in new plants.

Rye Bread.—The most popular representative of this class is rye bread. It is true that rye bread of a sort can be made without using a sour dough, substituting in its place one of the special flavors distributed by bakery supply houses. These flavors consist usually of some organic acid plus caraway and other natural and artificial flavors. Most quality rye breads are prepared with commercially available dehydrated sours which contain viable microorganisms of the type found in natural sour doughs. A formula using such a preparation is given below.

There are many different types of rye bread. They differ from one another in the type of rye meal used, in the acidity of the crumb, and in the flavoring adjuncts such as spices which are included in the formula. A typical formula for American-style rye bread will include about 30–40% of white or light rye, and 60–70% of high protein spring wheat clear flour in addition to salt, malt extract or sugar, yeast food, shortening, caramel color, and yeast. It can be made either as a straight dough or a sponge. The processing is similar to that used for wheat bread, with care taken to avoid overmixing and overdevelopment. Sour or Jewish rye breads will be made with a sour or a commercial culture or a flavor which includes acid. A formula which yields a loaf that is relatively light in color and high in specific volume is shown below:

American Light Rye Bread

	Lb	Oz
Sour dough		
Light rye flour	23	6
Water	15	3
Dehydrated rye sour	1	7
Dough		
Sour dough	40	
Light rye flour	6	10
Clear flour	70	
Water (variable)	35	
Yeast (compressed)	2	
Malt syrup	5	
Salt	2	4
Whole or ground caraway	8	
Shortening	1	8

The sour dough comes out of the mixer at 80°F and is fermented 22–26 hr. The dough comes out of the mixer at 76°F and is given floor time of 1–1½ hr.

At the opposite end of the color and texture spectrum are such items as Westphalian pumpernickel which has virtually no leavening action and contains 100% whole rye in the form of slightly broken kernels. It is baked for hours in a slow oven with steam. Westphalian pumpernickel is a very dense, dark, and chewy loaf. It is rarely made in the United States; the breads called pumpernickel or even Westphalian pumpernickel being merely darker versions of the regular rye formulas, usually strongly colored with caramel.

Salt-rising Bread.—Salt-rising bread is a specialty product which owes its unusual texture and pungent aroma to a combined yeast and bacterial fermentation. It was formerly prepared by using a natural sour dough method, but practically all of the product now being made in this country contains a commercial dry "yeast" preparation or culture. As is the case with many strong-flavored products, it exhibits a dichotomous distribution of acceptance, many people finding it extremely desirable while others dislike it. The odor is said to be reminiscent of cheese. Since cheeses can be found with a wide variety of flavors, most of which are due to bacterial action, this similarity is perhaps not unexpected.

The formula and procedure given below are attributable to Kohman (1955):

Salt-rising Bread

	Lb	Oz
Culture rehydration step		
Water	6	
"Yeast" culture	1	
MSNF		12
Sponge		
Water	15	
Flour	20	
Dough		
Water	15	
Flour	40	
Salt		10
Sugar	1	4
Shortening	1	4
MSNF		10 (optional)

The salt-rising culture or "yeast" is mixed with the MSNF. The mixture is added to boiling hot water and stirred well. The rehydrated culture is covered and kept warm (90°–100°F) for about 9 hr. When gas begins to form, the preparation is stirred and allowed to stand until it is well aerated. It is then ready for the sponge. Do not allow the culture to ferment until it becomes sour and thin because it will lose much of its gas-producing ability.

The sponge is prepared from ½ of the total water (110°–130°F) and ⅓ of the flour required for the desired number of loaves. The flour is added first, then the fermenting culture, and the whole is lightly mixed. The sponge is made warm, about 95°–100°F, and kept at this temperature about 2 hr until it begins to drop. Care should be taken not to over age the sponge.

In making the dough, the remaining ½ of the water is heated to 120°–160°F and the shortening, salt, sugar, and MSNF are added. The dough flour is then added along with the sponge, and the mass mixed at slow speed just long enough to make a smooth dough. The dough should be warm (100°F) and stiff enough to handle well by machine or hand. Scale it within 15 min and mold the dough pieces as soon as they come from the divider. Avoid chilling the dough at any time. Fill small pans ½ full of the dough and grease the tops of the dough pieces. Proof approximately 1 hr at 100°–115°F until the dough doubles its bulk and bake at the usual temperature.

Salt-rising bread is close-grained and firm so that the volume is only about ¾ that of ordinary white bread. The loaves have a tendency to crack on the sides, so it is customary to mold the loaf in two parts or to pan as a double loaf so that the split comes in the middle.

It should be emphasized that this loaf cannot be made with ordinary bakers' yeast, either compressed or dry. The hot water reconstitution step would completely inactivate any preparation of *Saccharomyces cerevisiae*.

Potato Bread.—Potato bread can also be made using a primary ferment. Although a sour dough utilizing the action of wild yeasts on a potato mash was the former source of the typical flavor of potato bread, it is more common now to use a mixture of bakers' yeast, potato flour, and water. The following procedure has been suggested (Anon. 1952):

	Lb	Oz
Primary ferment		
Yeast (compressed)		2
Potato flour		12
Water (85°F)	3	8
Dough		
Bread flour	12	8
Water (cold)	5	
Yeast (compressed)		2
Sugar		8
Salt		5
Shortening		8
Malt extract		1
MSNF		8

Combine the ingredients in the primary ferment and beat well. Allow to stand until it rises and breaks (about 30 min) then mix in the dough ingredients using enough water to make a dough of medium stiffness. The dough should come out of the mixer at about 80°F. Let the dough come to a full rise. Take it out to the bench in 20 min. Round and mold as usual. The above formula will yield 22 lb.

Sourdough French Bread.—A type of bread sometimes called Pacific Slope sourdough French bread has achieved considerable popularity among the cognoscenti in recent years. It has a rather pungent aroma, a definitely acidic taste, a thick crust, and a dense, chewy crumb. Success in duplicating the desired characteristics in new locations has been spotty, evidently as a result of difficulties in starting and maintaining a satisfactory sour. Meigs (1967) recommended getting a supply of starter dough from a successful baker of the product when beginning the manufacture of this type of bread. Microlife Technics of Sarasota, Florida distributes a frozen culture concentrate which can be used to make an acceptable version of sourdough French bread.

According to Meigs, one modern procedure for making sourdough French bread includes the following basic steps:

(1) Mix 3 lb well-aged dough from a preceding batch, 2 lb water, and 4 lb clear or strong flour. Set at 80°F for 6 hr. This is the first "build."

(2) The second build is made from all of the first plus 6 lb water, and 12 lb clear flour, set at 80°F for 4 hr.

(3) The third build is all of the second plus 12 lb water, and 24 lb clear flour set at 80°F for 4 hr.

(4) The dough is made from all of the third build plus 60 lb strong flour, 38 lb water, 2 lb salt, and 8 oz yeast. Bring it out of the mixer at 78°F, and give it a floor time of 1½ hr. Makeup and give a proof time of 2½–3 hr in the proof box.

(5) Bake well, using some steam early.

PRETZEL PRODUCTION

Pretzel doughs are made very stiff so that they will withstand the punishment of machining without becoming sticky or misshapen. The sponge is fermented for a shorter time than cracker doughs, say 10 hr, and might consist of 20 lb of flour, 10 lb of water, and 1–2 oz of compressed yeast. At the dough stage, 80 lb of strong flour, perhaps 25 lb of water, 1.2 lb of salt, and up to 3 lb of shortening are added. Doughs may receive a short proof stage, but frequently are made up without additional fermentation. The machining steps, including formation of the pretzel, are handled automatically in all but a very few small plants. The characteristic gloss of the pretzel is the result of a lye dip. The dip solution contains about 0.5% sodium hydroxide or 2% sodium carbonate and is maintained at about 210°–212°F. Immersion time is about 10 sec. The solution may also be applied by spraying.

The two main manufacturers of pretzel equipment are the Reading Pretzel Machinery Company, which is owned by Quinlan Pretzel Company, and American Machine and Foundry.

In Reading Pretzel Machinery equipment the dough is placed in a hopper from which a helix forces it through a slot in the face plate of the extruder. The dough is cut into small strips as it is extruded. The dough drops on a canvas belt which carries it under a second belt. Between the two belts the dough is rolled to the desired thickness. At the end of the rolling process the string of dough has the ends clipped so that the length is uniform. The dough strip then enters the twister. As the shaped pretzel dough leaves the twister it passes under a roller which exerts a slight pressure that sets the knots.

The raw pretzels are placed across a proofing belt approximately 40 ft long, by means of a reciprocating conveyor. From the proofing belt the dough passes through a caustic bath.

The caustic section consists of two tanks. There is a smaller tank through which the pretzels travel and a larger make-up tank, usually at a lower level. The caustic solution is pumped from the make-up tank to the upper or immersion tank. The level in the upper tank is maintained by adjusting the overflow pipe. This system keeps the volume in the upper tank constant. The caustic solution of 1.25 ± 0.25% sodium hydroxide is maintained at 186°–195°F. If the caustic concentration becomes too high there is not complete conversion to sodium bicarbonate in the baking and drying cycles and the pretzels will be hot to the taste due to the residual sodium hydroxide. There appears to be no U.S. FDA regulation on the amount of sodium hydroxide in the caustic solution.

Immediately after the pretzels leave the caustic solution they are salted. The salter consists of a supply hopper from which the salt is dispensed by means of a grooved roller. It slides down a chute until approximately 2 in. above the pretzels and then drops the rest of the way. The general aim is 2% salt on the finished product, but it is necessary that the initial application be at the rate of 8–10% due to losses in processing.

The pretzels then enter the oven, which in the case of the Reading Pretzel Machine is usually a 50-ft oven. The bake section is the top portion of the oven and has burners over and under the band that carries the pretzels. The temperature of the bake section is quite variable; it might be 475°F as the pretzels enter and 425°F at the exit of the bake section. The time in the bake section is controlled by a variable speed drive and is between 4 and 5 min. The moisture at the end of the bake period should be about 15%.

The pretzels then go down a slide to the drying section which is underneath and separated from the bake section by heavy insulation. The pretzels that cling to the baking belt are removed by means of a doctor blade. The belt in the drying section travels in the opposite direction of the belt in the bake section. The speed of the drying belt is also variable but is run much slower than the belt in the bake section. The pretzels form a bed several inches deep and remain in the drying section from 25 min up to 90 min. The temperature is held in the range of 225°–250°F. There is much debate over the drying time and its total effect. Other than reducing the moisture to the desired 2.0–2.5%, many claim that the long drying time is needed to temper the pretzel so that it will not break too easily during packaging.

From the drying oven the pretzels are conveyed to the packaging machine. The sooner the pretzels can be packaged, the less breakage there is likely to be. Most companies strive to keep the breakage less than 15% at the time of packaging. Covering the drying belts to protect the pretzels from cold drafts and to facilitate equilibration of moisture vapor is a useful procedure for reducing checking. The relatively large amount of checking in twisted pretzels is due to the moisture gradients set up by the slower bake-out of the thicker knotted parts.

Stick pretzels are extruded using a group of 5 extruding heads containing 10 to 12 holes per extruding head. The dough is forced through the extruding head by means of a helix, and falls onto the proofing belt. As the dough nears the end of the proofing belt it is cut into the desired length by a group of reciprocating knife blades. These blades are circular and travel across the belt cutting the dough. When the knives reach the edge of the belt they raise and return to their starting point. The stick pretzels pass through a caustic and salting operation similar to that for twist pretzels. The temperature is usually kept at a constant 420°F and the time in the bake oven is between 4 and 5 min. The drying section is run at 225°-250°F with the sticks exposed for approximately 55 min.

Logs and nugget type pretzels are made similarly to the sticks except that they are cut off at the extruder head.

It should be noted that Reading pretzel machines also use a 25-ft oven for stick pretzels. All of their ovens are composed of modules approximately 5 ft long, so that ovens can be shortened or lengthened to the customer's specifications and available space. As supplied, the ovens require manual lighting and adjusting of each individual burner.

Water is adjusted to suit varying flour and climatic conditions. The stick pretzel can be made using almost any flour. However, the flour used in twisted pretzels is very critical.

On the American Machine and Foundry equipment the twisters work differently than the Reading Pretzel twisters. American Machine and Foundry have ovens similar to the Reading Pretzel ovens, but they also make or distribute a single pass oven that is approximately 90 ft long. In this oven the pretzels enter a bake section that is about 30 ft long and run at 450°F. The pretzels then enter a drying section that covers the remaining 60 ft and has a temperature range of 225°-250°F.

Typical Pretzel Formula

	Twist Lb	Stick Lb
Flour	160	160
Shortening	2	4
Malt (nondiastatic)	2	4
Yeast	⅖	⅖
Ammonium bicarbonate	1 (oz)	4 (oz)
Sodium bicarbonate	3 (oz)	—
Water	8 (gal.)	7.5 (gal.)
Yeast food	As required	

It must be stated that variations in any and all phases of pretzel production can be found in any operation that is visited. This is true not only between companies, but also between plants within any single company. At the present time the production of pretzels is more of an art than science, and therefore the pretzel manufacturer is very reluctant to discuss his operations with outside technologists.

SWEET DOUGHS

There are two major classifications of yeast-leavened sweet doughs. These are the remix sweet dough, which corresponds in a general way to a sponge dough product in the bread line, and the straight sweet dough. By varying the flavoring, filling, shape, and icing, an almost infinite number of kinds of cakes and rolls can be made by these two procedures.

Sweet doughs are much richer in shortening, milk, and sugar than are bread-type doughs, and in addition they usually contain whole eggs, egg yolks, or egg whites, or the corresponding dried products. Commonly used flavors include spices, vanilla, nuts and nut pastes, peels or oils of lemon or orange, raisins, candied fruits, etc.

A typical basic formula (Anon. 1953) is given below.

Straight Sweet Dough

	Parts
Bread flour	80
Cake flour	20
Sugar	20
Bakers' margarine	20
Whole eggs	20
MSNF	5
Nondiastatic malt syrup	2
Salt	1
Yeast (compressed)	8
Water (variable)	42

The sugar, margarine (for which emulsified shortening may be substituted), salt, eggs, malt, and MSNF are creamed together until homogenous and somewhat aerated. Then the flours are added slowly while mixing is continued. Finally, the water, in which the yeast has been dispersed, is mixed in and the dough developed. The dough should come out of the mixer at about 80°F. A fermentation period of about 1¾ hr is usually adequate.

To prepare a remix sweet dough, the above formula and procedure is followed in the initial stage. After fermentation, about 20–22 parts of a strong flour, 13–14 parts of sugar, 13–14 parts of butter, margarine, or emulsified shortening, and 13–14 parts of egg yolks (liquid) would be added to the dough. Mixing would be at a medium speed for the required length of time. No further fermentation is conducted, the dough is scaled as soon as it comes out of the mixer and made up after a short bench rest.

Some authorities suggest adding the eggs in a separate step after the creaming stage. Others add the flour before the water is added. Probably these changes do not alter the product character very much.

The basic formula given above is fairly rich although some increase in the enriching ingredients can be tolerated without destroying dough quality. The enriching ingredients can be reduced by at least half if a relatively lean dough is desired. As these ingredients are reduced, it is desirable to decrease the yeast also since the lowered osmotic pressure will tend to accelerate yeast activity. The absorption should be increased a few percentage points as the dough is leaned down.

The function of the enriching ingredients is to soften the texture and make it flakier, improve the taste and color, and increase the nutritional quality of the product.

Dried egg products can be used in sweet yeast doughs. Although whole eggs are called for in the preceding formula, egg yolks can be substituted with little observable change in the quality of the product. Liquid skim milk or whole milk in equivalent quantities can be substituted for the MSNF. Any nondiastatic malt preparation can be used to replace the syrup. In place of the bread flour and cake flour mixture, flours milled specifically for a sweet dough operation can be substituted with advantages in economy and convenience. Of course, various dough improvers and yeast foods can be added to the formula with the usual equivocal results.

Sweet Dough Faults

Volume Too Large or Too Small.—(1) Scaling weight wrong. (2) Undermixed doughs. (3) Underfermented doughs. (4) Chilled dough. (5) Oven too hot. (6) Improper roll-in of shortening.

Coarse Texture and Poor Grain.—(1) Too much pan proof. (2) Scaling weight wrong. (3) Excessive steam in proof box. (4) Proof temperature too high. (5) Improper roll-in of shortening. (6) Dough too old. (7) Mixing time wrong. (8) Underfermented dough.

Off-flavor.—(1) Unwashed pans. (2) Ingredients have picked up foreign odors during storage. (3) Doughs overfermented.

Gumminess and Poor Mouth-feel.—(1) Undermixing and underfermenting. (2) Insufficient pan proof. (3) Baked at too high temperature.

Gets Stale Too Fast.—(1) Lean formula. (2) Dough too stiff. (3) Dough too old. (4) Dough at wrong temperature. (5) Overmixing. (6) Overbaking.

DANISH PASTRY

The distinguishing feature of Danish pastry preparation is the interleaving of dough sheets with layers of fat. In this respect the process is similar to that used with puff pastry. However, the only leavening action occurring in puff pastry results from the water vapor evolved in the oven while Danish pastry dough contains enough yeast to give a porous structure to the crumb. When properly made, these doughs will yield baked products that are flaky and short. The three-dimensional lattice of gluten fibrils is interrupted by layers of fat so that a pile of dough strata is formed in the finished food. The shortening itself is liquefied by the heat during the final stages of baking and absorbed into the dough so that it does not appear in the finished product as separate layers or particles.

Since it is important to maintain separation of the dough layers until the product goes into the oven, Danish pastry dough is rolled while cold. The usual procedure is to spread shortening over a fairly thick piece of dough, fold the piece over, sheet it out, fold it over again, sheet out, and repeat these operations until a many-layered structure has been developed. Refrigeration is desirable after each sheeting operation to dissipate the heat resulting from the mechanical action. Accumulation of this heat would result in eventual attainment of temperatures sufficiently high to melt the shortening and allow the dough layers to merge.

Danish doughs do not ordinarily receive much fermentation. An initial short period of 20–30 min in the refrigerator before the fat is rolled in allows some gas and flavor to be developed. Then the dough is usually refrigerated between each series of sheetings and in each of these cases some fermentation will occur. Proof time is short, usually 20–30 min, and it takes place at temperatures below room temperature.

The following formula and procedure for making Danish pastry has been given by Wihlfahrt (1935).

Danish Pastry Procedure

	Lb	Oz
Cream until light:		
Sugar		12
Malt		4
Butter	1	
Vanilla		1
Add to creamed mixture:		
Whole eggs	1	
Egg yolks		8
Mix together and add to above:		
Milk (cold)	4	4
Yeast		10
Add while mixing:		
Hard wheat flour	5	
Soft wheat flour	2	
Blend together and roll in immediately after mixing:		
Butter	4	
Pastry shortening	2	

Wihlfahrt suggests rolling the above dough at 3 45-min intervals, making 4 folds each time and keeping the dough quite cold.

Special shortenings with a relatively high melting point are available for use in Danish pastries.

PROCEDURES—GENERAL

The Sponge and Dough Process

The sponge and dough method of mixing consists of two distinct stages, the first of which is called the sponge and the second the dough stage. The sponge usually contains from ½ to ¾ of the flour, all of the yeast, yeast foods, and malt, together with enough water to make a stiff dough.

Addition of all or part of the shortening may also be made at this stage although it is more common to add it later. ½–¾ of the salt may be added to the sponge to control fermentation. The sponge is fermented until it begins to decline in volume, a phenomenon called "the drop" or the "the break." The time required for this to occur is of course dependent upon too many variables (temperature, type of flour, amount of yeast, absorption, amount of malt, etc.) to permit any meaningful rule to be enunciated here. Frequently the variables are adjusted to give a drop in about 3–5 hr.

At the dough stage, the sponge is returned to the mixer and all of the remaining ingredients added. The dough is developed to a peak and then is returned to the fermentation room.

An extensive discussion of the techniques involved in judging adequacy of dough development would be out of place here. When tested by objective measuring techniques, optimum development is frequently taken to be the stage at which the dough mass exhibits maximum resistance to shear. Visually, the development is usually considered to be optimal when the dough mass exhibits a silky sheen and is thrown around the mixer bowl in one piece which stretches elastically from the mixer arm but does not break into pieces. When a piece of the dough is removed from the mixer and stretched with the fingers, a thin film can be formed which, when viewed by transmitted light, has a webbed appearance. Judging dough development with any degree of accuracy requires considerable skill which can be acquired only by experience. Frequently, mixing personnel achieve an ability to estimate the stage of development by the sound of the dough as it slaps the mixer bowl. This subject was discussed in detail by Swortfiguer (1950) who gave a good description of the various stages in development.

The second type of mixing, called simply the "dough method," requires that all of the ingredients be incorporated during the first mixing step. According to Pyler (1952), the advantages of the sponge method are:

"(1) There is a saving of approximately 20% in the amount of yeast used as compared with the amount required for a straight dough.

"(2) Bread produced by the sponge and dough method tends to have greater volume and a more desirable texture and grain.

"(3) The method possesses greater flexibility. Sponges can be held longer without marked deterioration of the final product, in contrast to straight doughs which must be taken up when ready."

Disadvantages of the sponge method result from the extra handling of the dough, the additional weighing and measuring, and the second mixing step. More labor, equipment, and power are required for the sponge and dough process.

Variations in the straight dough process which have been suggested to overcome some of its disadvantages include the remixed straight dough process in which the only ingredient added at the second mix is a small proportion of the water, and the no-punch method which involves extremely vigorous mixing. Continuous mixing processes can be considered either as straight dough methods or as sponge methods in which the "sponge" consists of the liquid ferment. From the standpoint of performance of the flour, it is more logical to consider them to be straight dough processes.

Special Processing Methods

Since both the straight dough and the sponge and dough processing methods are time-consuming, require much labor and space, and are sensitive to small changes in conditions, there has been a continual demand for procedures which can overcome these disadvantages. There would be little point in discussing the many proposals which have failed, but there are at least two which appear to have some merit and are still in commercial use. There are the Chorleywood process and the green-dough method.

The Chorleywood bread process (Axford et al. 1963) is a batch mechanical development process that has attained considerable popularity in England, and perhaps elsewhere. Some characteristics of the process are: (1) intense mechanical working of the dough in a fairly short period of time, say 5 min; (2) use of fast-acting chemical oxidation, by inclusion in the dough of either a low level of fast-acting, or a high level of slow-acting oxidizing improver; (3) addition of fat to the dough; (4) addition of extra water to the dough; (5) absence of any preferment or brew; and (6) increasing the yeast by a factor of up to two.

A requirement of 40 joules (energy input) per gram of dough during the mixing process means that special high intensity mixers are required if a reasonable output of product is to be achieved. It is generally thought that the appearance and texture of bread produced by the Chorleywood method are more suited to English tastes than to American preferences.

The green-dough method was designed to eliminate the many inconveniences of fermenting dough in troughs. It is used to a small extent in Europe, but apparently not in any commercial installations in the United States. A description of the method as used in a Holland bakery has been published (Anon. 1964).

Doughs equivalent to 440 lb flour are mixed by Artofex kneaders for about 30 min. Water goes in at 65°F and the dough comes out at 79°F. The dough is divided and rounded immediately after leaving the mixer.

The rounded pieces are deposited in an automatic proofer which holds them at between 82° and 84°F and at a relative humidity of about 80%.

After the first proof, the pieces are again rounded and proofed for about 55 min. Then they pass through a cross-grain panner-molder, and are pan-proofed at 89°F and 80% RH before baking.

By suitable control of ingredients and formulation, it is said to be possible to produce bread the equivalent in all essential details of conventional bread.

Calculating Dough Temperatures

The following empirical method has been suggested (Anon. 1950) for determining the temperature to which the ingredient water must be lowered (or the ice required) to yield the desired dough temperature.

Factors required to be known in order to make the calculations are: (1) desired dough temperature; (2) temperature of the flour; (3) temperature of the mixing room; and (4) machine allowance, which accounts for the heat accumulated during the mixing. The latter factor will vary with the type of mixer, the size of the dough, etc. It can be estimated by multiplying the exact temperature of a freshly mixed dough by three, and then subtracting from the product the sum of the exact temperatures of the flour, water, and mixing room.

Example:
Dough temperature = 80°F
80 × 3 = 240
Flour temperature = 70°F
Water temperature = 64°F
Mixing room temperature = 78°F
70 + 64 + 78 = 212
Machine allowance: 240 − 212 = 28°F

In order to determine the temperature of ingredient water which should be used in order to obtain the desired sponge or dough temperature, multiply the required temperature by three and subtract from this figure the sum of the exact temperatures of the flour and the mixing room, and the machine allowance.

Example:
Desired temperature = 80°F
80 × 3 = 240
Machine allowance   = 28°F
Flour temperature   = 70°F
Mixing room temperature = 78°F
　　Total   176
Necessary water temperature: 240 − 176 = 64°F

In order to determine the amount of ice required to reduce the temperature of tap water to the desired temperature, subtract the desired temperature from the measured temperature of the tap water, multiply this difference by the total weight of water to be used in the dough batch, and divide the product by 144 (1 lb of ice at 32°F absorbs 144 Btu). The resulting figure gives the number of pounds of ice required. Deduct this amount from the total pounds of water in order to determine the amount of tap water to be used with the ice.

Example:
Tap water temperature = 78°F
Water required for the dough: 240 lb at 64°F
78 − 64 = 14
14 × 240 = 3360
3360 ÷ 144 = 23⅓ lb of ice required
240 − 23⅓ = 216⅔ lb of tap water

CAUSES OF SOME DEFECTS IN BREAD AND ROLLS

In this section, an attempt will be made to summarize some of the fundamental causes of defects in bread and rolls. Bread will be the principal example because it seems to be more sensitive to small changes in formulation or processing than other yeast-leavened foods. Most of the points brought out here are also applicable to sweet doughs and similar products.

Defects of Volume

These are caused, of course, by unusually large or unusually small quantities of gas being present in the dough piece at the time it becomes "fixed" by heat. Although gases other than carbon dioxide are present in the dough, and may even contribute substantially to the final volume of the product, their amounts are relatively inflexible as compared to carbon dioxide; and where the amount of gas is the proximate cause of the defect of volume, it is almost certainly the amount of carbon dioxide which is the variant from the norm.

The amount of gas evolved during the final critical period (proofing) may be relatively normal, with the defect in volume being caused by abnormal retention, either on the high or (usually) on the low side. If the retention of gas is too high or too low, it is possible that the characteristics of the flour have changed. Use of an excess of protease will decrease the ability of the vesicle walls to retain gases. Excess distention of the gas cells during proofing may cause some of them to rupture, with consequent loss of gas. Changes in the size or shape of the pan can cause actual as well as apparent changes in specific volume. In addition, there are apparent defects in specific volume (volume divided by weight) which are the result of improper scaling. The most scientific criterion for this characteristic is the specific volume, and such standards as the height, width, or sales manager's opinion are of little value.

If the volume of evolved gas is the cause of the fault, the abnormality will usually have had its origin in one of the following four things: (1) wrong proofing conditions—time, temperature, or both; (2) wrong amount or quality of yeast; (3) different diastatic activity than usual; or (4) variation in the amount of substances which accelerate or inhibit the fermentative activity of yeast (salt, phosphates, thiamine, etc.).

Defects of Crust Color

The color of the crust originates from the reactions of nitrogen-containing substances with reducing substances in the surface layers of the dough piece. The speed of these reactions is dependent upon the relative concentration of the reactants and the physical conditions under which they react. The two most important of the latter are probably the pH and the temperature. The rate of dehydration of the crust layers is very important to the speed of color formation. Dehydration to very low moisture contents concentrates the reactants to high levels and permits the temperature to rise above the boiling point of water. Under these conditions the rate of browning increases enormously. Thus it is possible for the crust to take on a dark color while the crumb does not noticeably change in hue. As a rule, browning reactions of the type we are considering take place much more rapidly under conditions of alkaline pH than they do under the moderately acid conditions found in the crumb. It may be that the reactions in crust are self-catalyzed, since nitrogen, probably in the form of ammonia, seems to be released by the reaction. This ammonia, though transient, could temporarily raise the pH to high levels in the crust layers.

The concentration of the nitrogenous reactants in doughs should remain relatively constant unless a considerable difference in flour specifications is encountered. More of the reactive end groups can be released for the reaction by adding fungal protease to the dough. Deficient reducing sugars may be due to imbalance of yeast activity and yeast substrate. The reducing sugars can be increased by using lactose, either as skim milk solids or dried whey. Since lactose is not fermented by yeast, it can be added in required amounts without much affecting gas production (some effect due to increased osmotic pressure may be noted at very high addition rates). Increasing top heat in the oven, or decreasing bottom heat, will tend to darken the crust. If the baking container shields any part of the dough from the radiant heat of the oven, a lessened crust color can be expected.

Defects of Taste and Aroma

Flour is a remarkably good absorber of aromatic compounds. Paint, tobacco, solvents, and certain disinfectants are common odorous contaminants of flour. Contacts rarely occur in the mill under present conditions, but may occur during shipment or storage. Musty odors due to the use of inferior wheat or overlong storage of the flour are possible but rarely occur in practice. Any of these odors present in the flour will carry through in some degree to the finished baked goods.

Other ingredients in which off-flavors may occur are the shortening, especially butter, milk, and even the water. Any raw material procured from a reliable manufacturer can be expected to be of good flavor quality. Only in very unusual circumstances will this be found to be untrue. More likely sources of off-flavor are the means of transportation, storage areas, and equipment used in the bakery.

Deficient flavor is usually due to the use of insufficient salt or to inadequate fermentation. The remedy for the former is self-evident, and the latter can be corrected by increasing the time or the temperature of fermentation at any of the stages. Care should be used in accepting a diagnosis of deficient flavor, since it is rather clear that the great majority of consumers actually prefer a bread of bland flavor. Sour or acid flavor may be due to over fermentation and the corrective measures in this case are obvious.

Defects of Grain

Gross unevenness of grain, e.g., holes, streaks, and lumps, is due to inadequate sealing of the dough layers by the molder or to excessive dusting flour or divider oil. Formation of an unusually thick and dry crust during intermediate proofing will also cause such defects.

Coarse grain can be caused by doughs which are too old or too slack, overproofing, pans which are too large or too small for the weight of the dough, or too low a temperature in the oven. Grain which is too close or tight can be caused by underproofing or overmixing. Out of balance formulations or weak flour can cause defects in grain. Some emulsifiers have been shown to cause relatively thick cell walls.

The crumb color is greatly affected by the grain. Small and uniform cell size are attributes contributing to whiteness of crumb, regardless of the background color of the cell walls. A dark or grayish cast may be due to use of long extraction flour with its higher content of bran fragments. The creamy or slight yellowish coloration which may or may not be desirable is due primarily to the fat soluble pigments of the wheat endosperm.

Defects of Symmetry

Defects in the shape of the loaf generally originate during molding or during placement of the dough in the pan. If the molder is compressing the dough cylinder too much, a loaf which is enlarged at the ends may result. If the compression is too slight, the loaf may be peaked in the center. Dough which is overproofed or made from weak flour may be the cause of misshapen loaves.

Defects of Bread and Shred

Lack of shred may be due to: (1) excessive pan proofing; (2) excessive proof room humidity; (3) extremely young or extremely old dough; (4) too little steam in the oven; or (5) slack dough.

A very ragged break or shell tops may be caused by: (1) slightly young or slightly old dough; (2) crusting during pan proofing; (3) stiff dough; (4) excessive salt; (5) underproofing; (6) excessive top heat; (7) chilled doughs; (8) lack of salt; (9) over bromating; (10) too much dough in the pan; or (11) insufficient milk or shortening.

Defects of Texture

In this category it is desirable to consider not only the usual texture judgement arrived at by feeling the crumb with the fingers, but also the "mouth feel" or what some authors call "mastication." These characteristics are closely related. No doubt the mouth feel is the more sensitive of the two judgments.

Texture is partly a function of the grain size and uniformity and partly a function of the inherent elasticity and resistance to shear of the basic material. The adhesiveness of the crumb may also play a part. Doughiness or similar qualities should cause suspicion of excess absorption, wrong shortening or emulsifier, insufficient baking time or temperature, or excess fermentation. Crumbliness might be caused by insufficient absorption, very weak flour, excessive baking time or temperature, or insufficient fermentation.

SODA CRACKERS

Six published formulas for soda crackers are summarized in Table 13.4. There are few secrets in soda cracker composition. An economical formula is essential in order that a competitive item may be marketed. In effect, this means use of the maximum percentages of flour and salt consistent with acceptability.

Ingredients

Flour.—Since flour may be present to the extent of 80% or more of the finished product, its qualities are the principal controlling factors in machining quality of the dough. It is also an important texture determinant. However, due to the bland flavor, it does not supply, except in unusual circumstances, the dominant flavor note, even in unsalted crackers. Appearance, insofar as it can be separated from machining response, is also considerably affected by ingredients other than flour.

The specifications of flours suitable for cracker production are narrower than those for flours intended for cookies. Some very general recommendations can be made for flour specifications. The reader should understand that the limits can be exceeded in special cases without adverse effects and also, that some flours meeting the requirements will be found to be wholly unsuitable for cracker production.

The sponge flour should be relatively strong, unbleached, with an ash of 0.39–0.42%, a protein content of 8.5–10.0%, and an acid viscosity value somewhere in the range of 60°–90°M, the exact value depending upon the product and the conditions. The dough flour should be weaker, with an ash of about 0.40%, a protein content of 8.0–9.0%, and an acid viscosity reading of 55°–60°M.

Cookie bake tests are suitable for evaluating some of the properties of cracker flours, but they do not give enough weight to the gluten strength factor since the conditions of the test allow little opportunity for gluten development. Mixograph and pup loaf tests may be valuable, especially

TABLE 13.4
SODA CRACKER FORMULAS

	Average	Range High	Range Low
Sponge ingredients (lb)			
Flour	70	80	60
Yeast	0.23	0.5	0.06
Water	30	34	28
Shortening	4	8	0
Diastatic malt	0.02	0.1	0
Sponge time (hr)	18	20	16
Dough ingredients (lb)			
Flour	30	20	40
Shortening	5.8	10	0
Salt	1.4	1.6	1.25
Sodium bicarbonate	0.63	0.7	0.52
Malt syrup	0.92	1.5	0
Water	0.8	2	0
Totals (lb)			
Flour	100	100	100
Yeast	0.23	0.5	0.06
Water	31	34	29.5
Shortening	9.5	10.5	8
Malt	0.02	0.1	0
Malt syrup	0.92	1.5	0
Salt	1.4	1.6	1.25
Sodium bicarbonate	0.63	0.7	0.52
Fermentation			
Time (hr)	4	5	3
Temperature (°F)	82	84	80

if a long series of results from supplies by the same miller are available for comparision.

The influence of the type of flour on cracker flavor is little understood. Some authorities have indicated that hard wheat flours have superior flavor potential (as compared to soft wheat flours) in lean goods such as crackers. Long extraction flour is said to give a superior, wheatier flavor. However, long extraction flour may lead to a grayish color or even to specks in the product.

Strong flours tend to increase oven spring but the crackers are often tougher. Weak flours lead to lesser amounts of spring, and to a tender, more friable cracker. The effect of fermentation is to mellow the gluten. Weak flours and strong fermentation combine to yield flat, tender crackers.

Flour for thick saltines (120 count) should be stronger than that for thin crackers (160–170). The thicker crackers need a sponge flour of about 9.0–10.5% protein, 0.41–0.45% ash, and a viscosity of about 95°–125°M. Thin saltines require a weaker flour in the doughs—a protein content of 8.0–8.5%, 0.43% ash, and 55°–60°M viscosity. Alternately, a certain percentage (determined by trial) of the strong flour is replaced by cookie flour.

Shortening.—Lard and oleo are widely used. The flavor of crackers containing lard is probably superior to those made with oleo. Plastic shortenings are not essential, so liquified fats handled by bulk transfer and measuring systems are common. Hydrogenated shortenings have the advantage of improving spring while lard contributes tenderness and frequently detracts from the oven expansion. Emulsifiers are commonly added.

Water.—The effect of this ingredient on fermented doughs has been fully discussed in a preceding chapter. These doughs are generally more susceptible to changes in water supply than are cookie doughs. Water supplies very high in pH call for supplementation with some sort of buffering system, such as that found in some yeast foods.

Yeast Foods.—The reader must satisfy himself as to the value of a given yeast food under his conditions of use. In formulas containing very small amounts of yeast, as found in soda cracker sponges, yeast foods probably do not have much of an effect on fermentation, contrary to some statements in the literature. However, many yeast foods also contain oxidizers and buffers which may prove valuable in certain situations.

Salt.—The amount of topping salt is not shown in the quoted formulas. Based on dough weight, about 2.5% is a good average figure. Salt suppliers sell a size specially intended for this purpose. Different brands are probably distinguished mainly by the percentage of fines, which should be at the minimum it is feasible to obtain. Dough salt should be of a finer granulation, though this is not as important in crackers as in cookies. It has been said that flake salt, used in the dough, causes crackers to have slightly more spring in the oven.

Processing

All crackers of the type discussed in this chapter are made from laminated doughs. Formerly, this step was performed on reversible dough brakes. At present, automatic laminators, to be described in detail in a subsequent chapter, are used throughout the industry. The number of layers formed is somewhat variable, but must be at least 6 or 7 to secure any benefit from this operation.

Laminating of cracker doughs is usually done without the benefit of an interleaving ingredient such as is used in puff pastry. In cream crackers, a mixture of flour and shortening is added between the dough sheets.

Shortening is shown as being added to the sponges. One of the advantages of this alternative is that the shortening is certain to be adequately distributed. If any crust forms on the sponge, it is made softer by the shortening. Some authors also say that resistance to rancidity is increased as a result of including the shortening in the sponge. The fermentation rate is probably not affected appreciably by the fat.

Fermentation.—The process of yeast fermentation has been discussed in considerable detail in the section on yeast. However, there are special considerations involved in cracker sponge fermentations which need to be examined more fully.

Micka (1955) showed that the yeast added to cracker sponge and the bacteria from ingredient flour or from deposits retained in the trough from previous doughs will grow for 10–15 hr. After this period, both the yeast and the bacteria are retarded, but the bacteria are inhibited more than the yeast. Acidity increases are largely due to bacteria and are favored by low percentages of yeast. The converse is also true. Sterile troughs retard bacteria and yeast fermentation as well as development of acidity. When the yeast addition is greater than 0.50% or the trough is sterile, acidity is retarded to such an extent that the finished cracker is of high pH and has an undesirable flavor.

The rapidity of gas and acid development is obviously related to the temperature of the sponge, and for a given formula is a function of the temperature at which the sponge is set and the temperature of the fermentation room. It is also related to dough composition, as follows:

(1) Absorption—the greater the percentage of ingredient water, the faster the fermentation.

(2) Salt—this ingredient inhibits fermentation.

(3) Amylolytic enzymes—the yeast first uses up the monosaccharides in the dough. After these are exhausted, a more or less quiescent adaptation period ensues, and then maltose split off from starch by amylolytic enzymes can be metabolized. Amylases are found in flour, but are present in much larger quantities in malt and fungal supplements. Most bacteria can utilize maltose but some strains cannot.

(4) Added sugars—sugar, whether in the form of corn syrup, sucrose, or invert syrup is consumed rapidly by both the yeast and bacteria. Bakers' yeast does not utilize lactose. Many bacteria do so, however.

The soda percentages shown in the formulas are only estimates, and are not constant. The correct amount of sodium bicarbonate to be added to the trough contents at the doughing-up stage is the quantity necessary to assure the obtaining of a predetermined pH in the baked cracker. The addition therefore will be related to the amount of acid produced during fermentation.

As indicated by the above discussion, the amount of acid produced cannot always be predicted.

One problem which has still not been solved to everyone's satisfaction is that of insuring uniform fermentation in all the troughs of sponges or, if it is not possible to achieve this goal, the compensating for the different levels of acid produced in different troughs. The difference in rate of fermentation between troughs is evidently due to varying levels of inoculation left by preceding batches. The difference is particularly noticeable when some troughs have been left idle for a time while others have been in constant use. Furthermore, some troughs seem to retain a heavy inoculation better than others. Some technologists have attempted to overcome the uncertainties of predicting proper fermentation time and proper soda addition by numbering both the troughs and their usual location in the fermentation room. Assuming the temperature and time are kept constant and the troughs are in continual use, the development of a known amount of acidity in a given trough can be expected. The soda addition should then be predictable from day to day.

The acidity which must be compensated for by addition of soda can be measured. It is related in a general way to pH, and the pH readings on the dough can be used as a rough guide for adjusting the soda supplementation. A better and more direct indicator is the total titratable acidity. This figure is more difficult to determine accurately and the analysis is more time-consuming than is the pH test and it is not much used in practice. The pH determination, though it is only indirectly correlated with the amount of acid which has been developed, is probably the most useful index for actual fermentation room practice. Sturdy, accurate pH meters, requiring only daily standardization by quality control personnel, can be placed near the mixer used to dough-up the sponges. Measurements with temperature-compensated electrodes can be taken directly on the sponges immediately prior to the remix, and the amount of soda determined by reading the appropriate figure from a chart.

Other procedures which have been suggested are pH tests on lumps of dough or sponge sent through the oven ahead of the rest of the trough contents. This technique can be expected to compensate for some of the unknown responses of fermentation-derived chemicals in the oven which might not be accurately predicted on the basis of raw dough pH.

As the dough ferments, it rises in temperature. The rate and extent of heat production are undoubtedly related to the same processes by which acids are elaborated. However, quantitation of this relationship is uncertain at best. The basing of soda addition on degrees of rise in sponge temperature is likely to lead to some undesirable variations in pH of the cracker.

Material is lost through fermentation. Ethanol and other volatile materials are produced from starch and sugars. Carbon dioxide is also lost, both from the trough and in the oven. The losses may amount to between 2 and 3% in a normal operation. In a low profit item such as soda crackers, it is important to keep these losses at a minimum. However, reduction in loss without reducing flavor or other desirable changes is very difficult. One thing that can be done is to keep the fermentation time at the shortest possible length consistent with a quality cracker. Overfermenting for convenience of scheduling should be avoided, if possible. Adding ripe sponges or a fermented broth for flavor purposes are possible approaches to minimizing fermentation losses. No doubt we will ultimately see the widespread use of pure bacterial cultures and chemical dough modifiers employed in conjunction with a short (perhaps continuous) dough fermentation to yield flavorful crackers with minor fermentation losses in a perfectly controlled system. Such systems are already widely used in bread manufacture, and only the limited market for equipment is delaying their modification to cracker production.

BIBLIOGRAPHY

ALESCH, E. A. 1970. Alternate methods of batch processing. Proc. Am. Soc. Bakery Engrs. *1970*, 69–74.
ANON. 1950. Fleischmann's Part in Baking Bread. Standard Brands, New York.
ANON. 1952. Specialty Breads and Basic Sweet Doughs. Borden Food Products Co., New York.
ANON. 1953. Fleischmann's Bakery Tested Formulas. Standard Brands, New York.
ANON. 1964. New Dutch bakery. Biscuit Maker Plant Baker *15*, No. 6, 448–452.
AXFORD, D. W. E., CHAMBERLAIN, N., COLLINS, T. H., and ELTON, G. A. H. 1963. The Chorleywood process. Cereal Sci. Today *8*, 265–266, 268, 270.
BAYERLEIN, F., and KOLBECK, W. 1970. Process for producing bread and baking products. U.S. Pat. 3,520,703. July 14.

BAYFIELD, E. G., and LANNUIER, G. L. 1962. The effect of fermentation from remix to out of oven, upon bread yield. Bakers Weekly *203*, No. 9, 33-37.
BRADLEY, W. B., and TUCKER, J. W. 1964. Bakery processes and leavening agents. *In* Encyclopedia of Chemical Technology, 2nd Edition, John Wiley & Sons, New York.
CAIN, E. O. 1966. Formulation and production of wheat bread varieties. Proc. Am. Soc. Bakery Engrs. *1966*, 63-69.
DE MUYNCK, E. P. L. 1968. Bakery products of the European economic community. Proc. Am. Soc. Bakery Engrs. *1968*, 144-158.
DENK, H. 1965. Production of rye bread. Proc. Am. Soc. Bakery Engrs. *1965*, 66-75.
GORDON, J. 1970. Basic production aspects of rye bread. Bakers Dig. *44*, No. 5, 38-39, 67.
HARDING, E. T. 1968. Influence of principal ingredients on bread quality. Proc. Am. Soc. Bakery Engrs. *1968*, 68-74.
JACKEL, S. S. 1969. Fermentation—today and tomorrow. Proc. Am. Soc. Bakery Engrs. *1969*, 91-98.
KAMMAN, P. W. 1970. Factors affecting the grain and texture of white bread. Bakers Dig. *44*, No. 2, 34-38.
KOHMAN, H. A. 1955. Formula for Salt-rising Bread. H. A. Kohman, Pittsburgh.
MARINI, J. L. 1964. Production of Italian type breads. Proc. Am. Soc. Bakery Engrs. *1964*, 65-72.
MCNICHOLL, C. 1967. Fine breads of the past and present. Proc. Am. Soc. Bakery Engrs. *1967*, 47-54.
MEIGS, H. T. 1967. Pacific Slope sour dough hearth breads. Am. Soc. Bakery Engrs. Bull. *183*.
MEIGS, H. T. 1968. Sweet doughs. Am. Soc. Bakery Engrs. Bull. *186*.
MEIGS, H. T. 1970. Quality white bread by sponge and dough procedure. Am. Soc. Bakery Engrs. Bull. *192*.
MICKA, J. 1955. Bacterial aspects of soda cracker fermentation. Cereal Chem. *32*, 125-131.
PAUL, H. E., SR. 1970. Sour dough French bread: Production. Proc. Am. Soc. Bakery Engrs. *1970*, 91-96.
PEDERSON, C. S. 1971. Microbiology of Food Fermentations. Avi Publishing Co., Westport, Conn.
PICKERING, C. S. 1956. The how of quality variety bread production. Proc. Am. Soc. Bakery Engrs. *1956*, 127-137.
POMERANZ, Y., and SHELLENBERGER, J. A. 1971. Bread Science and Technology. Avi Publishing Co., Westport, Conn.
PYLER, E. J. 1952. Baking Science and Technology. Siebel Publishing Co., Chicago.
SWORTFIGUER, M. J. 1950. Dough development. Proc. Am. Soc. Bakery Engrs. *1950*, 94-101.
WIHLFAHRT, J. E. 1935. A Treatise on Baking. Standard Brands, New York.

CHAPTER 14

FORMULATIONS AND PROCEDURES FOR MAKING ADJUNCTS

Icings, fillings, frostings, toppings, sauces, cremes, streusels, marshmallow, jellies, and the like are more closely allied in formulas and processing to confections than they are to most bakery products, but they are essential elements in the composition of many kinds of sweet goods and so form a pertinent subject for discussion in this book.

STREUSELS

Streusel toppings are characteristically in the form of dry lumps and powders of nonuniform particle size, and are applied to the tops of unbaked goods by sprinkling. Upon baking, they partially coalesce and adhere to the base cake while at the same time retaining their soft crumbly texture. The simplest version is cinnamon topping which is typically composed of about 93% sugar, 6% shortening, and 1% cinnamon.

True streusels generally are made with slightly less than ¼ shortening, slightly more than ¼ sugar, and about ½ flour. If the shortening is all or part margarine or butter a flavor improvement is obtained. Because the latter shortenings contain about 15% water, they make the flour slightly sticky and lead to the formation of larger lumps. Bread, pastry, or cake flours all make satisfactory streusels although each contributes slightly different qualities to the finished product. Because of its blander flavor, cake flour is generally preferred. The sugar is usually of the granulated type, although some brown sugar may be added for flavor and color. Honey can also be added up to the 10–15% level to give a flavor variation and to contribute a slightly glazed appearance to the topping. Some formulas recommend adding egg yolks or whole eggs up to 4–5% of the total formula for the binding effect, but these ingredients are not really necessary in most streusels. Salt from 0.2 to 0.7% is desirable.

The most common flavor is cinnamon. The amount to be added is entirely dependent upon the strength of the spice, the amount of streusel on the cake, and the taste of the consuming public, but levels of 0.5–1.5% have been given by various authors. Chocolate style streusel can be obtained by replacing about 6% of the flour with a good flavored alkalized cocoa of 10–12% fat. Vanilla improves most streusels and because of the high heat treatment the topping receives, addition at a high level is recommended to ensure adequate retention.   Lemon extract or lemon oil may be used to point up the basic flavor of the streusel.   Rum and almond are popular flavors in some areas.

Nuts are often added to streusels though they can easily double the ingredient cost with little effect on texture and not much improvement in flavor. Chpped peanuts or pecans are among the most common, but macaroon coconut is also used when the characteristic flavor and texture can be tolerated.   Addition levels are 10–25%.

In place of the flour, a similar or larger percentage of stale cake crumbs of compatible flavor can be used, often giving a texture advantage.

Peanut butter streusel can be made by adding enough peanut butter to a basic streusel formula to make a mix of slightly softer consistency than pie dough.   The mixture is pressed through a potato ricer or run through a food chopper. Because the soft, oily nature of the peanut butter tends to make the mixture cohere, the riced streusel should be well chilled in the refrigerator before it is applied to the dough or batter.   Freezing temperatures will make it even easier to use.   When this material is baked on the top of coffee cakes, it takes on a fine flavor and resembles small brown nuggets of peanut butter.

Table 14.1 contains several representative formulas which can be flavored and otherwise modified to give unique products fitting individual tastes.

Preparation methods for streusels are simple. Generally, the sugar and shortening are creamed, and then the flour is mixed to form a light paste which is chilled and rubbed through a very coarse (¼ in.) sieve. When eggs are used, they should be creamed with the sugar and shortening.   For small quantities of streusel, the shortening can be cut in or rubbed into the pulvurelent materials, as in making a dough for flaky pie

TABLE 14.1
REPRESENTATIVE STREUSEL FORMULAS

	Plain Streusel (%)	Deluxe Streusel (%)	Honey Streusel (%)	Chocolate Nut Streusel (%)
Flour	45	47	46	40
Butter or margarine	—	21	10	—
Shortening	25	—	11	12
Granulated sugar	15	17	23	24
Light brown sugar	14	11	—	—
Salt	0.5	0.3	0.7	0.5
Cinnamon	0.5	—	—	—
Egg yolks	—	3.7	—	5.5
Honey	—	—	9.3	—
Chopped pecans	—	—	—	12
Cocoa, dutched	—	—	—	6

crust. Some streusels are baked in sheet pans until they become dry and are then broken up and crumbled to the right size, but this extra processing step is not needed for the preceding formulations.

Somewhat similar to streusel in composition are the pastes which are used to form the pan linings or glazes for sticky buns, pineapple upside down cakes, etc. A pecan caramel pan glaze can be prepared from the following formula:

	Lb
Medium brown sugar	43
Granulated sugar	11
Honey or invert syrup	9
Corn syrup, about 42 DE	8
Margarine	16
Apple jelly	13

Enough baking soda should be added to the above to neutralize some of the acid (about 2 oz should be sufficient) and the quantity of water needed to obtain a spreadable paste must be added. The paste is used to coat the cups before the dough or batter is deposited, and chopped or whole nuts are often sprinkled on top of the paste. After baking, the pan is inverted to allow the hot syrup to flow onto the rolls.

ICINGS

Icings, frostings, glazes, and the like constitute a large and complex group of bakery adjuncts. Composition and processing methods vary widely. If there is a unifying characteristic of the group, it is that all, or nearly all, of the members are at some stage of their manufacture plastic masses made up of fine sugar crystals suspended in saturated sugar syrup. Fats, colors, flavors, gums, emulsifiers, and other ingredients are usually added to modify flavor, appearance, texture, and functional properties.

The simplest type of icing is the sugar glaze, flat icing, or water icing consisting essentially of confectioners' sugar to which enough water has been added to give a consistency suited to the application at hand. These icings may be pourable or plastic, and are colored and flavored to suit the intended purpose. Such glazes are commonly used on doughnuts, petit fours, specialty cakes, etc. Because they lose moisture readily, water icings become dull and flake off in a very short time. Improvement of storage stability can be achieved by adding stabilizers and more hygroscopic sweetners. An example of a formula for chocolate doughnut glaze is given below.

Chocolate Pouring Icing for Doughnuts

	Lb
(1) Mix together:	
Fondant (12% moisture)	70
Boiling water (variable)	10
Glucose	6
Melted chocolate liquor	14

(2) Heat above ingredients to 100°F while stirring.
(3) Temper slowly down to 85°F before using. The water content is adjusted to give proper consistency. Yield 100 lb.

Glazes made with ordinary powdered sugar are often grainy in texture and to improve quality it is preferable to use fondant as a base.

The term "fondant" is a generic designation for a mixture of sugar crystals and sugar syrup ranging in its visible, physical state from a nearly dry, granular mass to a creamy or pasty semifluid material. It is traditionally made by establishing conditions leading to the precipitation of very fine crystals from a strongly supersaturated solution of sucrose. The texture or consistency of the mass is affected by the ratio of syrup to solid particles, by the size and uniformity of the crystals, and by the dissolved materials other than sugar remaining in the syrup. The soft, creamy fondants can be used directly as centers for chocolate creams and the like and for icings, fudges, and similar confections and bakery adjuncts. The other types of fondants can be used as bases to which other materials can be added to form the finished icings, etc.

The fondant bases or stock fondants can be made with coloring or flavoring compounds. If pasty fondant stocks are to be flavored or colored, the incorporation of the added materials is carried out by a carefully controlled heating of the stock followed by mixing to uniformity. The pasty fondant stocks normally contain about 11–12% water and further dilution is often not necessary or desirable, although more fluid can be added if essential.

The fondant stocks are somewhat difficult to prepare in a repeatable manner and undergo changes in storage related to crystal growth. Dry fondant bases have been developed to overcome these difficulties (Harding et al. 1970) and some have had reasonable commercial success.

Illfehlder (1964) suggested the following guide for trouble shooting icing problems in yeast-raised sweet goods:

Icing too dry: Check (1) amount of moisture used, (2) boilout loss, (3) temperature at which icing was applied, (4) time elapsed between icing and wrapping, (5) wrapping material, and (6) dough formula.

Icing too soft: Check (1) moisture content, (2) amount of granulated sugar, and (3) temperature of icing at the time of application.

Icing becomes discolored: Check (1) bun for overbaking, (2) raisins for excess moisture, and (3) icing consistency (it should not be too dry).

Icing sticks to wrapper: Check (1) moisture, (2) formula balance of invert syrup and corn syrup, (3) stabilizer type, (4) bun dough formula, and (5) wrapping material.

MARSHMALLOW

There are several kinds of marshmallow. Some are sold as firm candy pieces, soft ice cream toppings, or the traditional cylindrical cuts. This discussion will be restricted to varieties suitable for use in cookies or other bakery foods.

Marshmallow is frequently used as an adjunct with cookies. It can be placed between base cakes to form a sandwich or it can be placed on a single base cake. In the latter case, it is either enrobed with chocolate (or other fatty base coating) or covered with particles such as flaked coconut. The purpose of enrobing or covering with coconut is two-fold: it allows the packers to handle the material without coming into contact with sticky marshmallow and it avoids presenting the consumer with a crusty dehydrated layer of marshmallow: in the case of coconut coating by concealing the defects of the existing layer in the textural qualities of coconut and, in the case of enrobed goods, by the actual prevention of evaporation and dehydration.

Even enrobed marshmallow tends to dehydrate somewhat by vapor phase translocation of moisture, and by draining and capillary absorption. In each of these cases, the base cake is the recipient of the lost moisture. The extent to which dehydration will occur with resultant toughening is controlled to a large extent by the relative proportions of the base cake and the marshmallow deposit. However, the equilibrium relative humidities (water activities) of the two components must also be considered. All other things being equal, drier base cakes will cause the marshmallow to dehydrate to a greater extent, but the composition of the marshmallow and of the base cake are also influences affecting the final equilibrium moisture.

Formulation

The fundamental structure in biscuit marshmallow is a gelatin foam strengthened by the dehydration effect of a concentrated sugar solution. Other types of marshmallow are based on foamed egg white or processed proteins derived from soybeans, milk, etc. All marshmallows are aqueous systems and should be distinguished from the fluffy white fillings used in certain cake goods sold in single service packages, and in cream horns for vending distribution, etc. These fillings are made by whipping mixtures of low melting fats and powdered sugar, and are not subject to microbiological spoilage.

A typical formulation for cookie marshmallow will include granulated sugar, corn syrup, neutralized invert syrup, gelatin, and water. The types and amounts of sugars and the moisture content have a distinct effect on the texture of the finished piece. In a given solids system, decreasing proportions of water lead to a firmer, harsher texture. Relatively large amounts of sucrose or invert sugar tend to give a shorter, less elastic structure, while increasing the amounts of corn syrup, particularly if it is the low-conversion type, leads to a stringy, elastic texture. Most marshmallow formulations use both sucrose and corn syrup, often with some invert syrup, to obtain an intermediate texture thought to be most acceptable to the majority of consumers. The response to whipping of these mixtures differs as the proportion of ingredients is changed. The formulas commonly recommended for biscuit marshmallow have the following composition:

Granulated sugar: average 30%, range 0–60%
Corn syrup, 43° Baumé: average 25%, range 20–83%
Invert syrup, 76% solids: range 0–85%
Gelatin, 200 bloom-strength: range 1.25–2.25%
Water, added as such: range 10–20%

Occasionally, formulas will be found which depart from the usual range. Larger amounts of gelatin tend to give greater stability of the foam, but also restrict aeration somewhat giving a heavier deposit (if volume is held constant) and firmer texture. The granulated sugar or the invert syrup, or both, may be omitted, with corresponding increases in the corn syrup. Corn syrup has the undeniable advantage over sucrose and invert syrup of being cheaper per pound of solids. Use of too much corn syrup in the formula results in a marshmallow that is not as sweet and is heavy and gummy. When the higher conversion, i.e., higher DE, syrups are used, these defects are not as pronounced. Lactose can be substituted for some of the sucrose when a less sweet marshmallow is desired.

It may not be possible to use all corn syrup as the sugar component if a vertical mixer is used, but these marshmallows can be whipped on an Oakes. The highest conversion corn syrup will be required and it is often necessary to add $\frac{1}{8}$–$\frac{1}{4}$% whipping protein in addition to the gelatin. Sometimes dextrose (dry corn sugar) may be used (with an additional amount of water) instead of corn syrup, but this substitution usually is not economically advantageous.

Whipping proteins, such as Gunther D-100 and Hyfoama do not heat coagulate, like egg white does, and they have similar viscosities hot or cold, contrary to gelatin performance. These proteins should be used to supplement the gelatin, not replace it. They are helpful at low levels to influence the texture of marshmallow and to improve the whipping properties. Their characteristic flavor may become evident at higher use levels. Texture improvement results from the development of smaller, more uniform cells and from improved moisture retention. Their long-term contributions to strength or maintenance of volume and shape are probably small.

Much effort has been devoted to finding moisture-retaining substances which will decrease the rate of hardening of exposed marshmallow deposits. The most hygroscopic substance available for this purpose is glycerin. All other solutions, including those made with low-conversion corn syrups, and sorbitol, will lose moisture to atmospheres of 50% RH or less, at normal temperatures. Getting a soft marshmallow to the consumer, in an open deposit, requires relatively fast turnover, a moisture-proof package, and an initial moisture content as high as possible consistent with acceptable shelf-life.

Preservation of marshmallow from fungal, yeast, and bacterial attack is a function of the osmotic pressure of the solution, essentially of the sugar concentration, and of any inhibitors, such as sorbic acid, which are added. The inoculum at time of preparation can also be a factor and the highest standards of sanitation are necessary if maximum shelf-life is to be obtained. Most plants making crackers have large numbers of yeast and mold spores floating in the air. Use of sterilizing lamps in the skinning tunnel will kill most surface yeast or mold cells. These lamps can also be used in the head space of tanks containing finished syrup. Spoilage can become apparent through visible mold growth, but the most common evidence of microbial deterioration is bursting of an enrobed piece as a result of the accumulation of fermentation gases. The presence of an alcoholic aroma is another characteristic indicator of spoilage in enrobed marshmallow.

The heat treatment given marshmallow syrups is inadequate to produce sterility and the material is often deposited under conditions conducive to massive contamination. Holding finished syrup in the kettle for 30 min at 150°–160°F is a valuable pasteurizing procedure. If frequent and thorough cleaning of the equipment, including routine use of sanitizing solutions, is not done, pockets of osmophilic yeast can become established with disastrous results. Errors in making up the batch with addition of too much water or too little sugar is the other frequent cause of spoilage. Quality control determinations of the moisture content of each batch of syrup by refractometer will prevent these errors.

In order to take maximum advantage of the moisture content it is possible to start with under a given set of conditions, it has been the practice to vary the moisture content of biscuit marshmallow according to seasons of the year and geographical location of the distribution area. These considerations are more important in open marshmallow, of course, where the relative humidity, varying with the seasons, affects the rate of drying. It has been customary to increase the moisture content of open marshmallow deposits about 1–1.5% in winter months.

A minimum total solids content of about 68% is required in order to assure protection against spoilage. Higher proportions of solids may be necessary if the base cake is relatively small or other adverse conditions exist. As a matter of fact, most marshmallows, as made, contain between 28 and 32% moisture. This will decrease on storage to perhaps 22%. The requirement also varies according to the climate and weather as previously stated. The way in which one manufacturer changes formulas with the season is illustrated by the following recipes:

	Winter %	Spring and Fall %	Summer %
Granulated sugar	5.5	10	20
Dextrose	5	10	13
Corn syrup, 43° Baumé	25	27	30
Invert syrup, 76%	55	36	18
Water	8.25	15.5	17.25
Gelatin, 200 bloom-strength	1.25	1.50	1.75

Starchy ingredients are often used, primarily to firm up the structure while retaining shortness, but also to reduce the amount of gelatin required. For example, about 1.5% cassava flour or cornstarch can be added.

Various hydrophilic gums can be used to improve, or at least change, the structure of marshmallow. Gum arabic in amounts up to 10% of the gelatin can be added. Gum tragacanth has also been included in formulas for marshmallow specialties, but probably not in biscuit toppings.

If the marshmallow has an acidic reaction, as it usually does, soda is sometimes added to raise it to near neutral pH. If the pH is too high, color will suffer because of the appearance of yellowish tints. The higher pH levels are thought to be better for some flavors, particularly cocoa. There may be a very slight increase in resistance to microbial attack below pH 4.5.

Formulas may call for the addition of a small amount of phosphoric acid or other substance to reduce pH. In foams based on egg white, acids have a definite improving action on the response to whipping. This is probably not as apparent in gelatin marshmallow. Continuous whipping machines seem to require syrup of pH 5.5 or lower. Phosphoric acid will cause some inversion, thus aiding in moisture retention and hindering sugar crystallization.

Any amount of fatty substance present in marshmallow mixtures will seriously interfere with the whipping and will break down the foam already formed. It is best to have certain items of equipment restricted to preparation of marshmallow syrups and whipping since films of fat left on beaters, bowls, etc., due to inadequate cleaning after making doughs and batters can markedly increase the density of marshmallow. Small amounts of sodium lauryl sulfate, food grade, (restricted to 0.1% of the gelatin used) have a slight improving effect on whipping properties when traces of fat are present.

The usual flavorings for marshmallow are vanilla, vanillin, ethyl vanillin, or combinations of the last two compounds. The sensitivity of marshmallow to fats and oil seriously restricts the flavoring possibilities. The citrus oils, mint, chocolate or cocoa, and other lipid-type flavors can be incorporated, if at all, only in very minor amounts and even then with considerable loss of overrun. Some emulsified forms of these oils can be used with greater success. Small amounts of low-fat cocoa can be used for color, but the flavor contributions of practicable additions will be negligible. Fat soluble colors are, of course, not recommended. Many emulsifiers have been suggested to overcome the susceptibility of marshmallow to fatty substances, but successes have been minor. The polyglycerides are thought to be the most effective of the emulsifiers investigated so far. It is often found that a marshmallow made with one of the emulsifiers and another fatty substance will appear to have considerable mechanical strength or stiffness when first made but will gradually collapse and drain on storage.

Either enrobed or open-faced marshmallow should be stored for at least 48 hr at about 72°F in order to allow the deposit to firm up before it is shipped.

Preparation of Marshmallow

Biscuit marshmallow manufacture begins with the preparation of a syrup containing all of the ingredients in an unwhipped form. If the sucrose content is high and there is very little corn syrup or invert syrup in the formula, the batch may be made by the cooked process, in which all of the ingredients except the gelatin and flavor are brought to boiling in order to ensure the complete solution of the sugar. The semicooked process, suitable for syrups of intermediate sucrose content, involves bringing the ingredients to 180°F to obtain a clear solution. In either the cooked or semicooked process the syrups must be cooled to 140°F or less before adding the soaked gelatin. In the cold process, the sugars and water are agitated at about 120°F or slightly less for sufficient periods of time to ensure complete solution. The soaked gelatin must be heated before adding to cold process syrups.

Gelatin is prepared for syrups by adding it slowly to at least four parts of cold water. The more water that can be used, the better. Complete wetting of the granules must be obtained. Unless care is used, agglomerates are formed which will remain dry on the inside indefinitely. The gelatin must be allowed to soak for at least 30 min. If the syrup temperature is lower than 140°F at the time the soaked gelatin is added to it, the gelatin must be melted by gentle application of heat until it becomes fluid enough to pour like a liquid. As the bloom-strength of the gelatin becomes higher, the difficulty of soaking it and dispersing it completely becomes more pronounced.

After the gelatin and flavors have been thoroughly blended into the sugar solution, the syrup is beaten or whipped. Batch or continuous equipment can be used. Batch equipment consists of vertical mixers with bowls of various sizes and a wire whip, or the special horizontal beaters for marshmallow. The latter, which are more common in the confectionery industry than in biscuit factories, yield about 200 lb of marshmallow with 20 min of beating. Continuous equipment is more effective in increasing overrun, easier to control, and more efficient in terms of labor requirement per pound of marshmallow produced.

The three types of continuous foam developers differ in the way in which turbulence is developed. All kinds require the injection of air under pressure and a pump to force the syrup. The Oakes type relies on mechanical agitation to produce turbulence as the syrup is sheared between a stator with many fixed projections and a rapidly moving rotor with intermeshing projections. The scraped film type of whipper relies on a somewhat similar action in a cylindrical shaped chamber enclosing an elongated beater element. The Whizzolater whipper forces the air and syrup through a column packed with small balls or the like. As the syrup rushes through the many irregular channels, an intense turbulence is set up. This turbulence causes the syrup to envelop volumes of air which are then broken down to small bubbles by the same forces.

The overrun or the volume of air whipped into the marshmallow syrup is related to texture or mouth-feel in that the apparent resistance to chewing of a given volume of product (i.e., in pieces of uniform size) is less with increased overrun. The overrun obtained from a marshmallow syrup varies inversely with the viscosity of the syrup and directly with the moisture content. Other factors influencing the overrun, such as the temperature of optimum whip, change with variations in moisture content. A very thorough analysis of the fundamental physical factors contributing to perceived texture in marshmallow, and their relationship to processing variables has been published by Tiemstra (1964 A, B, C, D).

The whipping equipment and method should be such as to produce: (1) small air cells; (2) air cells of uniform size; and (3) thin cell walls (this characteristic being a function of average cell size). Such a foam holds up better than one composed of larger or irregular cells and it is firmer and shorter in texture.

COATINGS

Coatings of chocolate or simulated chocolate as well as pastel colored coatings of similar texture are used to enrobe cookies and cake goods of the Swiss roll type. Enrobed goods also constitute a large percentage of the cookie market. The coating may be a true chocolate (sweet or milk), or it may be a compound coating. The fatty materials in compound coatings are hardened vegetable oils instead of cocoa butter. Compound coatings may be chocolate-flavored, white, or any color for which a suitable food dye is available. Much research work has been done in attempts to develop compound coatings which would have the same mouth-feel as those coatings made with cocoa butter, but success has not yet been achieved. Even the best compound coatings tend to have a rather waxy texture, especially in colder weather.

The principal ingredients in a coating are sugar and a fat. Corn syrup solids, flavors (such as cocoa), colors, and emulsifiers are often used. Moisture must be held to a very low level. The sugar must be finely powdered, with all particles preferably below 40 μ in their largest dimension. The fat must have a melting point above the highest temperature expected to be encountered before the product is to be consumed. Coconut oil fractions are favorites because of their bland flavor, but hydrogenated cottonseed and soybean oils, or even animal fats can be used. There are proprietary compounds of treated and mixed fats which have exceptionally good melt-down properties. The proportion of fat to solids, the melting point of the former, and the particle size of the latter, are major determinants of texture.

The total amount of fat necessary to give the desired texture in vegetable coatings is related to the particle size of the sugar. The so-called 6X sugar can be used in coatings that are intended for crisp or chewy pieces, such as grahams, butter-cookies types, caramel-base cake combinations, coconut creams, etc. For enrobing marshmallow, the coating must be made with sugar of smaller particle size. Marshmallow also requires lower melting coatings for optimum eating quality.

Although it is perfectly feasible to make acceptable coatings using preground sugar, the texture (smoothness) of coating will be ensured by refining (i.e., grinding on roller mills) even when coarse sugar is used.

It is extremely important that the vegetable butters used have completely bland flavors. Any taste or aroma whatsoever is likely to be perceived by the consumer as an off-flavor with consequent rejection of the food. Evaluation for this characteristic must be done organoleptically, and it is good procedure to taste not only the solidified fat but also a melted sample.

Most presently available commercial coatings have adequate shelf-life provided the initial flavor is satisfactory. A rough test of storage stability can be made by storing the material at 140°F for a couple of weeks in an open jar. Contact of the material with copper lines or vessels is very undesirable, since traces of this element greatly accelerate oxidative reactions and the development of rancidity. A small amount of citric acid will reduce the effect of traces of copper. Lecithin, often added as an emulsifier, also has an antioxidant effect.

Some authorities recommend the addition of a small percentage of glycerin to coatings to partially offset the adverse effect of the presence of moisture.

The amount of coating applied to a piece should, ideally, be adjusted to give optimum eating quality in the finished cookie. Since the coating is almost always considerably more expensive per unit weight than the enrobed part, there is a temptation to reduce the amount of coating to a bare minimum. These thin coatings to not provide adequate protection against moisture transfer and are easily fractured. It has been stated that a coating percentage of less than 28% is undesirable. On the other hand, excessive amounts of coating, especially hard butter coatings, can lead to unpleasant texture effects when the cookie is eaten. The exact percentage must, however, be related to the size and conformation of the enrobed part, i.e., smaller or irregular pieces take a higher percentage of coating than do larger or smooth and uniform bases.

The amount of coating that will adhere to a given piece is related to the viscosity of the coating. This is controlled by varying the percentage of fat added, or, occasionally, by temperature (in the case of hard butter coatings only).

If colors are to be used, fat soluble forms are preferable. If it is necessary to use water-soluble lakes, a refining step is almost essential to prevent speckiness and uneven distribution of the colored particles.

Corn syrup solids, starches, and the like, are sometimes used to reduce sweetness. They also tend to reduce the cost of coatings. Particle size of common commercial materials may not be small enough to give the required mouth-feel. This defect can be remedied by refining. In Table 14.2 are given formulas for six different types of coatings.

All ingredients must be low in moisture content. Moisture in the finished product should be around 0.5% and never over 1.0%. The coatings in Table 14.2 are intended to be refined. If microfine ingredients can be obtained, it may be possible to make satisfactory coatings without milling the solids.

Viscosity can be lowered to get the proper enrobing consistency, if necessary, by adding more of the appropriate fat—cocoa butter or hardened vegetable oil. Adjustment of the amount of lecithin is also useful for viscosity control, but present-day coating formulas generally call for full lecithination (0.3–0.35%) because of the economics involved.

Pastel- and fruit-colored coatings can be based on the vanilla formula.

Chocolate coatings when described as such on the label, are covered by federal standards and definitions. These regulations specify with exactitude the types and amounts of ingredients which must be used in coatings identified by one of the standard names.

Many chocolate-colored or -flavored coatings used to enrobe cookies do not meet these specifications. Some manufacturers feel that the standards result in coatings that are too strong in flavor to be compatible with certain fillings. Also, the large proportion of cocoa butter causes the coating to be too expensive for popularly priced lines. Cheaper, less highly flavored coatings are prepared by using cocoa as the flavoring ingredient with fat having a suitable melting point. Sugar or other fat-insoluble material is also added to maintain approximately the same texture.

All of these fat-based coatings have the desirable property of sealing the enclosed material off from the atmosphere (providing it is completely enclosed) so that loss or uptake of moisture is prevented. Marshmallow can be kept soft and base cakes can be kept crisp indefinitely. Of course, when marshmallow and base cake are stored in contact, there

TABLE 14.2
COATINGS FOR ENROBING COOKIES

	Vanilla (%)	Dark Chocolate (%)	Light Cocoa (%)	Dark Cocoa (%)	Coconut (%)	Peanut (%)
Natural chocolate liquor	...	41.3	...	...	...	...
Hardened vegetable oil	33	...	30	34	33	28
Sugar	57	41.3	48.2	39.5	52	32
MSNF	...	...	14.3	6	...	12
Lecithin	...	...	0.3	0.3	...	...
Vanillin	0.1	...	0.1	0.1	...	...
Salt	0.1	0.1	0.1	0.1	0.1	0.1
Natural cocoa	...	...	7.0	20	...	...
Cocoa butter	...	17.2	...	...	...	...
Coconut flour	...	...	...	...	15	...
Peanut flour, 12–14% fat	...	...	...	...	...	28

will be a transfer of water vapor from the marshmallow to the base cake. In most cases, loss of volatile flavors is markedly reduced from marshmallow or base cake enclosed in coatings. Oxidation is also reduced.

Loss of color and flavor from coatings is often a problem. Many food dyes are light sensitive and will fade on continued exposure to light. In the case of colors made of a combination of dyes, fading of one of the dyes at a faster rate than the other can cause very undesirable changes in hue: brown changing to green, for example. Flavors are not firmly held in the coating and will volatilize from the large surface area at a fairly rapid rate. For this reason it is advisable to add the flavors to the base cake or filling, or if this is not possible, to flavor the coatings with nonvolatile compounds.

Coatings made with chocolate liquor and combinations of this ingredient with other fats of similar melting point require careful handling during application if fat bloom or low gloss is to be avoided. A strict tempering procedure must be followed. The fat is fully melted by bringing it to 110°F and then cooled with constant stirring to a mushy consistency at a temperature of from 80°–85°F, typically 84°F. This establishes a seed or crystallization nuclei of fat crystals. The coating is then brought back up to 88°–90°F to melt unstable crystal forms. Subsequent cooling should result in formation of stable crystals only.

The cookies should be at a temperature of 68°–72°F when they pass through the enrober. The excess chocolate is blown and shaken off. Coverage, or thickness of the coating layer, is related to the cookie temperature, the viscosity and temperature of the coating, and the vigor and duration of the shaking and blowing process. The enrobed pieces pass into a tunnel through which chilled air is blowing. Radiation coolers are also in use.

After the pieces emerge from the far end of the tunnel, they are stored at 72°F for at least 48 hr. During this period, various fractions of the fats continue to solidify and the relatively low temperature prevents remelting due to release of the heat of crystallization. Under unfavorable conditions, a thin layer of fat may rise to the surface and cause a dull appearance or even white specks of the fat, the so-called fat bloom.

With vegetable coatings of higher melting point than cocoa butter, different enrobing conditions must be used. Cocoa butter is incompatible with some of these hard butters and transfer of this fat from a cooling tunnel belt to the cookies has been the cause of fat bloom developing on the bottoms.

When cocoa powder is used as the flavoring ingredient instead of chocolate liquor, higher enrobing temperatures are necessary. Coatings made with cocoa and hard butters generally retain gloss longer and under more adverse conditions than liquor coatings.

FORMULAS AND PROCEDURES FOR MAKING ADJUNCTS 251

PIE FILLINGS

Most pie fillings can be categorized as either fruit or cream style, although there are varieties which do not fit into either category as well as combinations of the two main types. In any case, the filling should have a gel structure to retard the rate at which liquid soaks into the crust and to simplify serving. The gel is usually based on starch. Although ordinary corn starch gives reasonably good results in home baking, the modern trend in commercial pie plants is toward the use of waxy maize starch or modified starches which give good clarity and do not retrograde. Other gel agents, such as low methoxyl pectin (Moyls and Strachan 1957), have suggested but not widely adopted. Fillings relying on gelled egg protein for their structure are traditional for certain types of pies (custard, cheese, pecan, etc.) but are expensive, very sensitive to changes in mixing and baking procedures, tend to shrink and crack, and have a limited textural range.

Fruit Fillings

Fruit pie fillings generally consist of pieces of the fruit suspended in sweetened, flavored (and sometimes colored) juice thickened with starch. The most popular variety of fruit pie is apple. The apples may be fresh, frozen, canned, evaporated, or dehydrofrozen. A typical formula for a good quality filling based on canned fruit is given below.

Canned Apple Pie Filling

	Lb
(1) Bring to a boil:	
Solid pack canned apples, firm texture	54
Sugar	15
Cinnamon	2 (oz)
Water	15
(2) Make a slurry of:	
Water	4
Waxy maize starch or modified pie starch	1½–2
(3) Cook until clear and add to apple mixture.	
(4) Add:	
Sugar	9
and heat until completely dissolved.	
(5) Turn off heat and mix in thoroughly:	
Lemon juice	12 (oz)

An alternate preparation which maintains the shape and texture of the apples better is to cook the other ingredients separately, then pour them over the apples.

Some fruit pie fillings such as mince meat have a structure composed almost entirely of fruit pulp (in this case, apples and raisins) so that the small amount of viscous interstitial fluid needs no additional thickener. Deluxe open-faced pies and tarts can be made by arranging whole strawberries (uncooked) or the like in baked shells and pouring over them a glaze such as the following.

Fruit Glaze for Open-faced Fresh Fruit Pies and Tarts

	Lb
(1) Bring to a boil:	
Sugar	10
Water	8
(2) Mix the following together and add to the syrup:	
Water	2
Starch, such as waxy maize	1
(3) Cook until clear, then add:	
Corn syrup	1
(4) Bring to boil again, remove from heat, and add:	
Lemon juice	4 (oz)
Appropriate food coloring	

Cream Fillings

There are undoubtedly thousands of recipes for cream pies but there is no space here to give more than the briefest introduction to filling formulation. Custards are differentiated from creams in that the former are baked in the crust and form a firm gel, while cream fillings are cooked outside the shell and form a somewhat softer gel when completely set. Formulations are somewhat similar, however. A good quality cream base which can be flavored with butterscotch, vanilla, or other flavors, or used with bananas, coconut, cherries, etc., can be made as follows:

	Lb	Oz
Whole milk	29	3
Salt		1
Granulated sugar	10	
Corn starch	2	
Egg yolks	2	8
Butter, melted	1	4
Whipping cream	5	
Vanilla		qs

Slurry the corn starch into part of the milk, bring remaining milk, sugar, and salt to a boil, then add the starch slurry. Cook with continual stirring until smooth and thickened. Combine egg yolks, vanilla, and butter. Add some of the cooked milk to the yolks, beat well, and then combine with the rest of the filling beating until well blended. Cook for about 4 min over hot water.

Pumpkin pie fillings are custards, as the recipe below indicates.

Pumpkin Custard Pie Filling

	Lb	Oz
(1) Blend together the following ingredients:		
Pumpkin (about 4 No. 10 cans)	25	
Granulated sugar (or half granulated and half brown)	16	
Corn syrup	2	
Starch		12
Mixed spices		4
Melted butter	2	8
Whole milk	32	
Whole eggs	8	8
(2) Beat slightly and fill into unbaked pie shells.		

Many so-called cream pies are strictly starch-based gels, very similar to cooked starch puddings, and the following banana formula can be considered representative.

Banana Cream Starch-based Gel Filling

	Lb	Oz
(1) Bring to a boil:		
Water	8	
Sugar	3	
Margarine	2	
(2) Add, while mixing, a slurry of:		
Starch	2	
Water	5	
Vanilla		2
(3) Cook until thick, shut off heat, and mix in:		
Mashed bananas (1 No. 10 can)	7	4
Add other flavors and colors as desired		
(4) Fill into prebaked pie shells		

Although filling weights will vary depending upon the depth of the pan and the quality of pie desired, it is customary to scale 19–21 oz of fruit filling in an 8-in. shell and 28–32 oz in a 10-in. pan. Creams or custards will require somewhat less.

FILLINGS FOR SWEET YEAST-LEAVENED PRODUCTS

The fillings and spreads used in or on sweet dough products are similar in many respects to pie fillings but are often formulated to be more intense in flavor and color because they are used in small proportions relative to the dough and they may be stabilized differently so as to retain their shape and reduce syneresis under the conditions of baking.

Fruit-flavored Fillings

Jams, jellies, and preserves are covered by Federal Standards of Identity which restrict their composition within fairly narrow limits. For example, pure preserves and jams must be made with a minimum of 45 parts of fruit to 55 parts of sugar, by weight. The soluble solids content, which comprise the dissolved solids after processing, including sugar, natural fruit sugars, acids, and salts, must be not less than 65% for some fruits and 68% for others. With the exception of pure mint jelly and pure spiced apple jelly, artificial color and flavor may not be added. The fruit-flavored fillings and toppings used by bakers are almost always imitations not meeting the Standards of Identity. There is nothing wrong with using these materials as long as they are not described, or implied to be, as fruit jellies or other foods covered by the Standards.

All pure jellies rely on the gelling power of pectin. From a technological rather than a legal point of view, satisfactory gels require a sugar content of 60–70%, a water content of 30–40%, a pectin content of 0.65–1.25%, and acid sufficient to produce a pH of 2.2–3.5 in the finished product. Within these limits, gels are formed with textures ranging from very tender to very tough. Part of the pectin, acid, and sugar and all of the water are obtained from fruit juices. Sucrose, corn syrup, dextrose, or honey may be used as the sweetener additive.

If pure jellies are to be used in bakery foods, it is best to obtain them already made from a reliable supplier. The convenience, reduced labor requirements, and more uniform quality more than offset the small saving in ingredient cost that might be achieved by making jellies in the plant. There may be a considerable economic advantage in making imitation jellies and similar fillings from the basic ingredients, however. Some of these artificial materials are based on pectin gels while others use agar or some other gelling agent instead of pectin. Pectin gels tend to break down readily and become thin and fluid when pumped or otherwise vigorously agitated. Separation of fluid then occurs and the filling will bake out or soak into the pastry. A desire is frequently expressed to have a fruit-flavored gel which will go through the oven without melting down. Although perfection has not been achieved in meeting this goal, some formulations approach it rather closely.

Table 14.3 provides formulas for three quality levels of strawberry-flavored fillings for coffee cakes, sweet rolls, jelly rolls, puff dough, and doughnuts. The premium quality filling will hold up better than pure preserves or jelly during transfer and application in production equip-

FORMULAS AND PROCEDURES FOR MAKING ADJUNCTS

TABLE 14.3
STRAWBERRY-FLAVORED FILLINGS FOR YEAST-FILLED SWEET GOODS

Premium Quality	(%)	Medium Quality	(%)	Low Quality	(%)
Frozen sliced strawberries	26.00	Frozen sliced strawberries	25.84	Sugar	9.32
Sugar	23.81	Sugar	28.00	Corn syrup, 43° Bé, 62 DE	59.65
Corn syrup, 43° Bé, 62 DE	42.08	Water	37.80	Water	27.96
Rapid setting pectin, 150 grade	0.65	Waxy maize starch	5.81	Pectin, slow set, 150 grade	0.62
Algin	0.13	Modified tapioca starch	1.91	Algin	0.12
Water	5.12	Salt	0.26	Artificial color	0.25
FD&C Red No. 2	0.02	Citric acid anhydrous	0.22	Artificial flavor	0.03
FD&C Yellow No. 5	0.02	FD&C Red No. 2	0.06	Phosphoric acid, 8% solution	2.05
Phosphoric acid 8% solution	2.13	FD&C Yellow No. 5	0.06		
Natural strawberry flavor	0.04	Natural strawberry flavor	0.04		

Source: Rumminger (1968).

ment, but it may exhibit slight syneresis and soaking. The medium quality filling, which is stabilized with starch, holds up well under normal handling but may thin out if recycled excessively. It should not show syneresis in the oven but the eating quality or final texture may not be as good as a pectin-set filling. The cheapest formulation given in the table is strictly artificial but it is stabilized with pectin and algin, leading to fair finished texture but having a strong tendency to separate or collapse when pumped or heated. Such inexpensive fillings can be used for striping or topping low cost coffee cakes and Danish, or for filling doughnuts. The general method of preparation is to cook the fruit with sugar, water, stabilizers, coloring, and corn syrup until the desired soluble solids content (68, 43, or 65%, respectively for the 3 strawberry fillings) is reached, then add the acid and flavor.

Use of a considerable amount of puréed fruit, practically restricted to apple, in fillings, gives a product which has a distinctive mouth-feel and holds up very well during handling and baking. The following formula was developed (Rumminger 1968) for use in breakfast tarts to be heated in toasters, or in fruit-filled soft cookies. The combination of stabilizers is intended to give a gel structure which breaks cleanly at the depositor head and spreads smoothly.

Breakfast Tart Filling

	%		%
Evaporated apples	12.50	Agar	0.16
Sugar	31.25	Water	20.83
Corn syrup, 43° Bé, 62 DE	25.00	FD&C Red No. 2	0.008
		FD&C Yellow No. 5	0.008

Frozen strawberry puree	8.32	Citric acid anhydrous	0.33
		Sodium benzoate	0.08
Dehydrated citrus pulp	0.83	Imitation flavor	0.014
Carboxymethylcellulose	0.33		
Algin	0.21		
Locust bean gum	0.13		

Cream-style Fillings

Many variations of cream-style fillings are possible. The basic filling can be either cooked or uncooked. The uncooked filling base depends on fat and sugar for its structure and it can be made according to the following formula.

	%
Powdered sugar or brown sugar	46
Margarine or butter	36
MSNF	9.75
Egg whites	9
Salt	0.25

The dry ingredients are scaled into the mixer bowl, the paddle is started at low speed, and the egg whites are added and blended until the mixture is smooth. To the base are added nuts, fruits, honey, cheese, cocoa, flavors, spices, or other materials to give the desired variety. An example of one of these is:

	%
Basic filling	60
Almond paste or kernel paste	12
Cake crumbs of compatible flavor	16
Honey	12

The basic cooked filling is a starch stabilized water system which can be prepared according to the following formula:

	%
Water	37
Waxy maize starch	2.5
Granulated sugar	27
Cake crumbs of a compatible flavor	27
Margarine	6.5

About ⅔ of the water is placed in the kettle and brought to a rolling boil. The starch, which has been slurried in the remaining water, is added to the boiling water and cooking continued until the mixture becomes clear, showing that the starch has become completely gelatinized. Add the sugar, heat to boiling again, then mix in the crumbs and the margarine and mix until smooth. Cool before using.

A cheese filling can be made by mixing about equal amounts of bakers' cheese and either of the basic fillings. Lemon flavor, raisins, cinnamon, or chopped nuts may also be added to set off the cheese flavor.

BIBLIOGRAPHY

ANON. 1960. A Guide to Better Marshmallow Toppings. Swift & Co., Gelatin Dept., Kearny, N. J.

ANON. 1962. Gelatin. Gelatin Mfgs. Inst. Am., New York.

BABAYAN, V. K. 1970. Tailor-made fats and oils for bakery, confectionery, and cereal uses. Cereal Sci. Today 15, 214-217, 225.

BECK, W. 1961. Gelatin. Biscuit Cracker Baker 50, No. 8, 26-27, 37.

BOLLENBACK, G. N. 1954. Latest formulas and techniques for fondant and icing production. Proc. Am. Soc. Bakery Engrs. 1965, 266-272.

CHARTRAND, G. 1965. Sandwich creme fillings. Biscuit Cracker Baker 54, No. 12, 30-32.

GOODMAN, A. H. 1970. Doughnut finishings. Proc. Am. Soc. Bakery Engrs. 1970, 174-181.

HARDING, F. H., HOROWITZ, R., and MONTI, A. 1970. Dry fondant and method of making same. U.S. Pat. 3,518,095. June 30.

ILLFELDER, B. 1964. Preparation and application of icings for sweet yeast-raised products. Proc. Am. Soc. Bakery Engrs. 1964, 254-260.

JOHNSON, O. 1935. Marshmallow formulas are founded on basic principles. Biscuit Cracker Baker 24, No. 12, 21-22, 38.

KAVANAGH, J. 1969. Fillings for sweet yeast-raised products. Proc. Am. Soc. Bakery Engrs. 1969, 189-200.

LACHMANN, A., and VOLL, H. 1969. Structure and behavior of icings. Bakers Dig. 43, No. 2, 40-41, 44-45.

MOYLS, A. W., and STRACHAN, C. C. 1957. Improved formula for canned fruit pie fillings. Food Can. 17, No. 7, 18-19.

RUMMINGER, A. 1968. Formulation and application of fillings and toppings. Proc. Am. Soc. Bakery Engrs. 1968, 272-281.

SHAFFER, J. R., BRUNNER, G. F., and LAWRENCE, B. 1970. Process for preparing icing. U.S. Pat. 3,526,517. Sept. 1.

TIEMSTRA, P. J. 1964A. Marshmallows. I. Overrun. Food Technol. 18, 915-920.

TIEMSTRA, P. J. 1964B. Marshmallows. II. Viscosity and elasticity. Food Technol. 18, 921-927.

TIEMSTRA, P. J. 1964C. Marshmallows III. Moisture. Food Technol. 18, 1084-1091.

TIEMSTRA, P. J. 1964D. Marshmallow. IV. Set and syneresis. Food Technol. 18, 1091-1096.

WHITELY, P. R. 1965. Ingredient proportions of jams, jellies, and cream fillings. Biscuit Maker Plant Baker 16, 390, 393-394.

SECTION 3

Equipment

CHAPTER 15

BULK HANDLING OF INGREDIENTS

INTRODUCTION

The question of a few years ago as to whether bulk handling of bakery ingredients was feasible is no longer pertinent, the practicality of such systems having been proven in hundreds of installations. In the first flush of enthusiasm some unsuitable equipment was installed and it became clear that bulk conveying is not an infallible answer for every handling problem; but use of bulk receiving, storage, and in-plant conveying of ingredients can often be justified on the basis of elimination of the cost of disposable containers, reduction in waste, lower labor costs for material handling, and other economic advantages. Additional benefits are frequently observed in the form of improved sanitation, better control over measuring, and reduction in size of storage areas. Although it is technically feasible to handle in bulk virtually all of the ingredients normally used in bakeries, it is usually not economically advantageous even in the largest plants to construct such facilities for more than 7 or 8 of the raw materials. A few factories handle nearly all the ingredients, including such materials as ammonium bicarbonate, in automatic bulk handling systems (Hagedorn 1965).

Bulk storage facilities can be classified into two categories based on the state of the product—whether it is liquid or solid (granular). Flour is, of course, always handled as a powder and it is usual to handle sucrose, corn sugar, and salt in this form. Shortenings, corn syrups, invert sugar, and eggs are more frequently handled as liquids in bulk systems. When milk is received in bulk, the liquid form is preferred, in spite of the negative factors in this procedure.

There are some general principles applicable to the design of all bulk handling facilities. Sanitation should be a primary consideration in the design. The ingredient contacting surfaces should be nonporous and resistant to corrosion and abrasion. They should be nontoxic and should not transfer odor, taste, color, or particles to the ingredient. They must not accelerate deteriorative changes in the food material. Physical changes (as in particle size) during transfer or storage should be held to a minimum consistent with necessary design limitations. Tubes carrying powders should be grounded to prevent the buildup of static electricity.

Sampling and testing of bulk loads present some problems. The receiving department is generally anxious to unload the shipment quickly in order to avoid demurrage and other costs and complications, while the quality control department will not want to risk contamination of tanks or old stocks of ingredients with unsatisfactory material and will insist on completing the necessary tests before unloading is started. There is usually no provision for returning unsatisfactory material which has already been taken into the system, an additional reason for caution. The interests of the two departments necessitates close coordination of effort and maximum speed in sampling and testing incoming shipments.

Sampling of liquid loads for physical and chemical tests can be performed with a simple bottle-on-a-stick type of device inserted through the loading hatch or by collecting fluid from an appropriate port. Sampling of dry materials such as sugar and flour is accomplished by inserting a long trier or specialized sampling equipment through the opened manhole at the top of the car, and withdrawing and combining portions taken from several directions. There are automatic sampling devices which divert a certain portion of the ingredient as it flows into the plant. The sampling problems resulting from stratification of either liquid or powder loads must be kept in mind constantly in order to avoid unpleasant surprises on the production line.

Assurance should be obtained that an adequate supply of delivery conveyances will always be available. Shortages of trucks and cars are commonplace and are more common in some parts of the country than in others. Sources of supply are more restricted for bakers who must rely on bulk delivery.

Scheduling of deliveries is much more difficult for bulk receiving because the storage space is absolutely limited. It is nearly always possible to find a place to put a few hundred bags of sugar, but, if the syrup tank is nearly full, nothing can be done to remedy the situation. "Running out" is also more serious, since it is often quite difficult to introduce bagged or drummed material into bulk systems.

PNEUMATIC FLOUR HANDLING SYSTEMS

Although it is possible to design a bulk handling system for flour based entirely on mechanical conveying, nearly all modern large-scale

BULK HANDLING OF INGREDIENTS

Courtesy of Baker Perkins, Inc.

FIG. 15.1 A PNEUMATIC HANDLING SYSTEM FOR RECEIVING BAGGED FLOUR.
Bagged flour is dumped into the hopper in the foreground. The compressor is in the left foreground. Back of the compressor and hopper are two double-compartment flour bins.

equipment uses pneumatic transfer principles. Mechanical conveying of flour is inherently less sanitary, requires greater capital expenditures (for complete large-scale installations), and is not as reliable or versatile as pneumatic conveying; but many pneumatic systems do include one or more mechanical conveying steps. Movement of flour by gravity, as in some mill operations, is not generally applicable to bakery operations.

There are no product changes of importance caused by pneumatic conveying of flour. Moisture loss may be somewhat greater in bulk flour as compared to sacked flour. There have been no verified reports of stratification by particle size; and fragmentation is not a problem in flour, contrary to the experience with sugar. Oxidation or aging of flour reaches an equilibrium stage much sooner in product handled by these systems than in sacked flour.

Pneumatic handling can be applied within the bakery to flour received in bags (Fig. 15.1), but it is more efficient to receive the material from

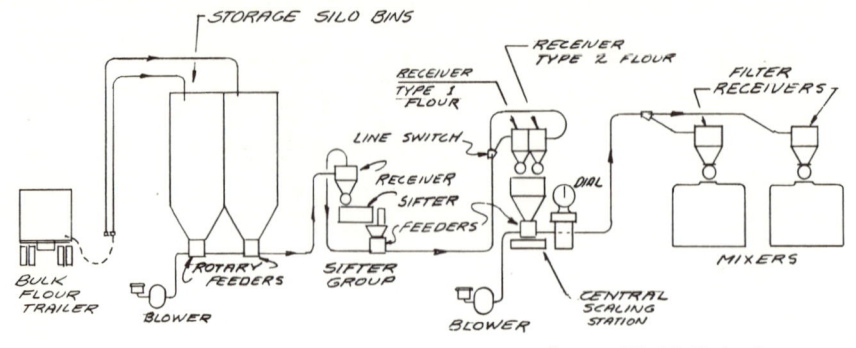

FIG. 15.2 A BULK FLOUR HANDLING SYSTEM.

bulk cars or trucks. Pneumatic flour handling installations are classified as either negative pressure systems or positive pressure systems. There are also combination systems embodying both principles. Although there are fundamental design differences between the two types, in either case their operation depends upon fluidizing the flour, i.e., by air flow causing each particle to be surrounded by turbulent gases. In positive systems (Fig. 15.2), the conveying air stream is at a pressure higher than atmospheric and the pumped air pushes the flour through the line. Normal operating pressures do not exceed 10–11 psig and the required air volume seldom exceeds 100 cfm. Negative pressure systems can be regarded as vacuum systems, where a low pressure is created by pumping air out of the last storage or surge tank downstream from the receiving part. That is, air entering at atmospheric pressure is pushing the flour through the lines. It is possible to design systems combining these two basic types of air conveying.

There are at least seven groups of equipment in pneumatic bulk flour handling installations (Pfening 1958). These are:

(1) A mill-to-bakery transporting vehicle with unloading means compatible with the bakery receiving system.

(2) Equipment for receiving flour from the vehicle and transferring it to bins.

(3) Storage bins sufficient in number and capacity to hold the different types and required amounts of flour.

(4) Sifters and conveying means leading from storage bins to sifters and from sifters to subsequent points.

(5) Surge or service bins feeding the scale hoppers.

(6) Scale hoppers and conveying means to and from them.

(7) Filter receivers discharging to mixers.

Connections between the different pieces of equipment are conveying

BULK HANDLING OF INGREDIENTS 263

tubes of necessary diameter and made of metal (frequently aluminum) or plastic. The interior walls should be very smooth to reduce friction, facilitate air flow, and minimize abrasion of the particles. Bends, turns, and elbows should be made on a wide radius. Grounding is essential to prevent the buildup of static electricity.

The system should include quick-disconnect joints at critical points so that blockages may be easily corrected.

In positive pressure systems, there will be blower-feeder groups at the car or trailer discharge point, storage bin discharge, central scaling unit, and use or service bin. The blowers are of the positive displacement type, in which two close-fitting impellers rotate against each other like gears. Air is discharged through filters and it is important that plenty of filter area be provided to prevent pressure from building up in the bins. An arrangement which has been suggested for eliminating the necessity for an expensive dust collector is to have all storage bins vented into a common system so that the individual dust bags will relieve pressure. Although the passive exhaust system is satisfactory, a more efficient means of exhausting the air is by suction blower and filter.

Delivery and Unloading

The delivery vehicle may be either a specially equipped freight car (see Fig. 15.3) or a truck. In the case of the truck, unloading equipment is carried as part of the vehicle. Pneumatic unloading equipment

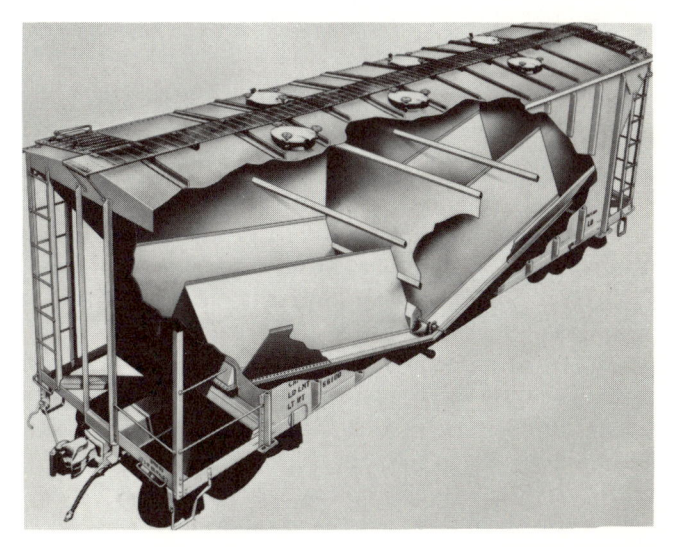

Courtesy of General American Transportation Co.
FIG. 15.3 CUTAWAY VIEW OF 2600 CUBIC FOOT AIRSLIDE CAR.

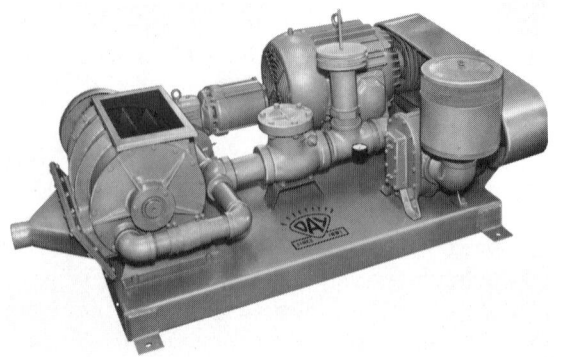

Courtesy of J. H. Day Corp.
FIG. 15.4 AIR INJECTION UNIT WITH VALVE.

for freight cars may be either the pressure or the suction type, with the pressure type probably the most common. There is a self-contained wheeled unloader for GATX Airslide cars which provides air for activating the slides of the car and empties the flour at the rate of 600 to 1000 lb per hr. Mechanical equipment (screw-conveyors) is also in use. In the pressure system, flour is fluidized by injecting air (Fig. 15.4) and transported to the top of the flour bin. Capacity of railroad cars is 90,000 lb while most trucks will carry 40,000 lb. Unloading rates will vary, but may reach 40,000 lb in 15 min. Unloading points may be located as much as 500–600 ft from the storage silos. Power and equipment costs become prohibitive for longer distances.

Bins

Flour bins can be horizontally or vertically aligned and, in either case, are of circular cross-section. The availability of floor space in relation to ceiling height usually dictates the style of bin construction. They must be air and dust tight. It is often necessary to install flour storage bins outside the main building in order to conserve valuable processing areas. When outside, the bins are exposed to rapid changes in temperature. There is a possibility of condensate forming on the inner wall and running down into the flour if the temperature drops rapidly outside the bin. Insulation can be applied on the exterior to slow down the rate of heat exchange in the empty portion, but some suppliers have expressed doubts about the efficacy of this measure. A better arrangement in extreme climates is to enclose the bins in an inexpensive shelter, as shown in Fig. 15.5. Condensation can be prevented by installing an air circulation system to exchange the air above the flour so that its relative humidity is always in equilibrium with the outside atmosphere.

In horizontal bins, leveling of the contents so as to get a complete fill becomes more difficult as the length and width of the bin increases.

Coatings are usually not recommended for the interior flour-contacting of bins, clean polished metal surfaces being preferred. Flour has an abrasive effect which tends to keep the surfaces polished and to remove coatings.

Hopper slopes should be as steep as bin height allows, and never less than a 60° angle. Even at this angle, vibrators may be required to expedite flow (see Fig. 15.6). Both horizontal and vertical bins can be unloaded either by screw conveyors or inclined air chutes.

Where blending is required, the bulk system may include storage bins for flour, blending screws, and daily usage bins.

Provision should be made for withdrawing dusting flour from a bulk system. Two methods are: (1) provide an additional flour scale weigh hopper in the air-line loop, or (2) return the residue from the flour scale air line and divert it to a flour dust receptacle.

A weak point in some bulk handling systems for flour is the difficulty of adequate inventory control. None of the methods currently used for measuring bin contents are completely satisfactory. Both volumetric and gravimetric devices are being used. Among the gravimetric types

Courtesy of J. H. Day Corp.

FIG. 15.5 SHELTER FOR FLOUR STORAGE BINS.

Fig. 15.6 A Bin Activator Assembly for Facilitating the Outflow of Ingredients.

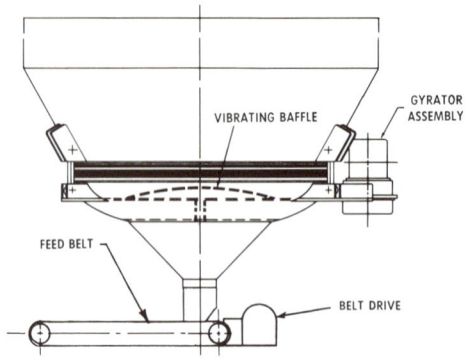

Courtesy of Vibra Screw, Inc.

are strain gauges operating as part of an electronic indicating circuit and liquid load cells based on a combination of hydraulic and mechanical principles (Haile 1960).

BULK HANDLING OF SUGAR

In bakeries where bread, cake, and sweet dough products are made, the bulk sweetener installations are predominantly of the liquid type. In cookie plants, however, there is a need for granular sugar to control cookie spread and permit formulations of low moisture doughs so that bulk handling systems for dry sucrose, or combinations of dry and liquid systems, are more common. Many cookie manufacturers prefer to receive all of their sucrose in the bulk granulated form.

Most modern bulk handling systems for dry sugar are pneumatic, at least in their long transfer sections, but there are some older installations which are entirely mechanical. Mechanical conveying is more frequently used in sugar than in flour installations because attrition or particle breakdown is a more significant factor with air-conveyed sugar supplies.

Mechanical Systems

These set-ups are based on assemblages of conventional transfer devices (Fig. 15.7). Trucks used to supply mechanical bulk systems are either bottom- or end-dump type and discharge contents by gravity. The receiving unit usually consists of a hopper and a standard screw conveyor feeding a bucket or chain elevator that terminates slightly above the level of the top of the storage bin. Sugar may also be discharged directly from the delivery conveyance into a receiving pit under the roadway or railroad tracks. There will be a conveyor leading from the pit to transfer the sugar to the elevating means. At the terminus of the elevator, another screw conveyor carries the sugar to the entrance part of the bin. The sugar is reclaimed from the storage bin at the bottom by a screw, belt, or other type of mechanical conveyor and then discharged into a surge bin feeding an automatic weigh scale that delivers the selected amount of sugar into the mixer (Meeker 1957).

Bins are made of many different kinds of material, but the usual choice for new construction is mild steel lined with a plastic coating. The cone at the base of the bin should have a minimum angle of 50° from the horizontal and the discharge opening should be at least 8 in. in diameter. There should be properly gasketed side and top manhole inspection plates about 22 in. in diameter. Insulation is required.

Pneumatic Systems

A pneumatic system consists of, at a minimum, a compressor or a vacuum pump, a rotary airlock (Fig. 15.8) at the discharge point from the storage bin to feed the sugar into the air stream, conveyor tubing, and a sugar-air separator (equipped with a sugar dust collector) dis-

Courtesy of C and H Sugar Refining Co.

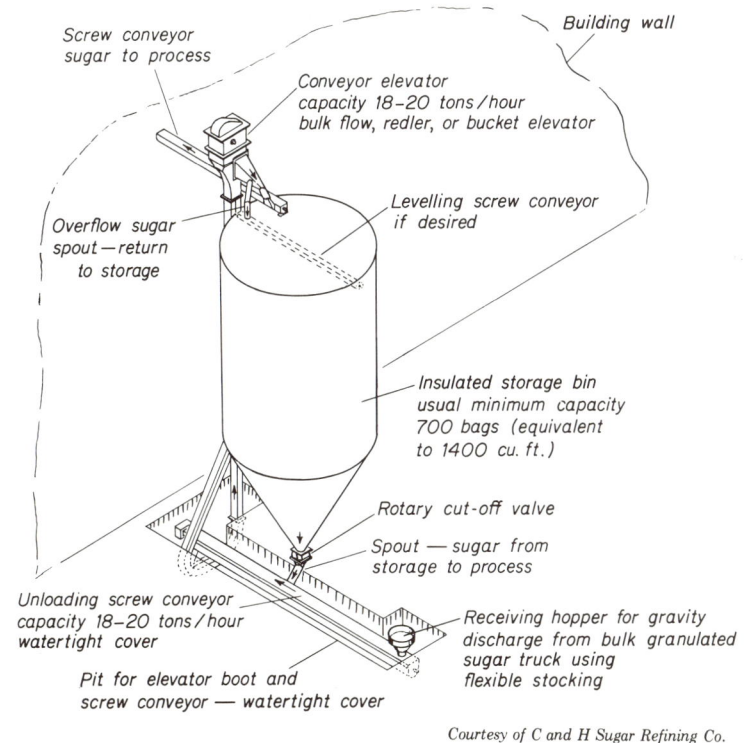

FIG. 15.7 A BULK GRANULATED SUGAR STORAGE INSTALLATION USING MECHANICAL TRANSFERS.

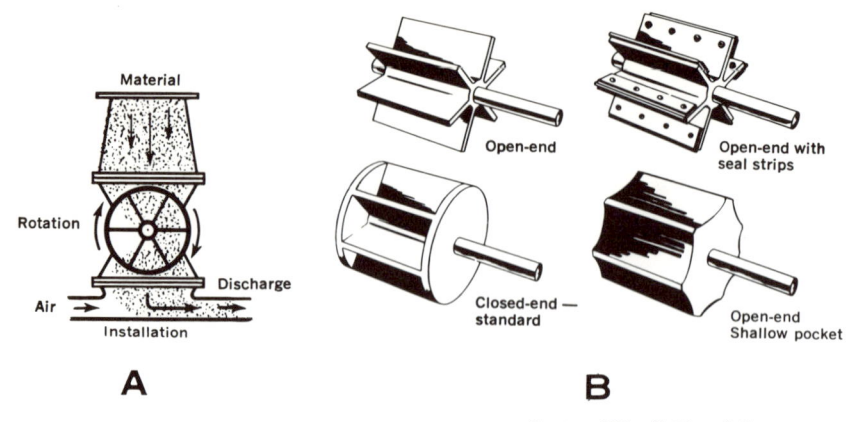

FIG. 15.8 ROTARY AIRLOCK FEEDER (A) AND ROTOR DESIGNS (B).

Courtesy of Wm. W. Meyer & Sons

charging into a supply hopper which feeds the weigh scale assembly. Delivery is by truck or rail cars similar to the vehicles used for flour.

The remainder of the system is somewhat simpler than for flour because no sifters are required. More air volume is required to move sugar and therefore larger filters are needed to exhaust the used air. Reuse of the air (closed system) helps to maintain a constant relative humidity in the storage and conveying circuit and may reduce caking problems.

Bins should be of sanitary construction with a minimum number of cracks and crevices. They should be of steel construction, cylindrical in shape, and vertically oriented. The minimum capacity is around 50,000 lb. The bin can sometimes be placed at an elevation such that gravity feed can be used to the process area since the delivery truck can elevate and convey sugar for a considerable distance.

The principal problem in sugar handling is caking due to moisture absorption. This can lead to bridging in the silo. Suppliers should load sugar at a maximum moisture content of 0.2% and a maximum temperature of 95°F (Hagedorn 1965). Bins should be kept as small as possible and contents should be recirculated during plant shutdowns. Use of multiple screws at the bin discharge will facilitate movement of sugar agglomerates (Fig. 15.9). The bins should be completely emptied at convenient intervals so that any sugar caked on the sides can be removed.

The tubes through which sugar is transferred to the silo, and through which the air with its entrained sugar dust is returned for filtering and reuse are ordinarily 6 in. in diameter. Straight sections can be made of thin-walled aluminum tubing, but the elbows should be of stainless

BULK HANDLING OF INGREDIENTS 269

steel and bend at a radius of at least 8 ft. The inside of the tubing should be smooth and without projections.

Attrition of sugar crystals during transfer from one point to another in the pneumatic system can be a serious problem in cookie production. If the particle size distribution remained the same at all times, the attrition could be compensated for, and very little notice would be taken of the phenomenon. In some systems, however, there appears to be a fluctuation in the amount of fines produced, related perhaps to variations in air velocity, temperature, and unknown factors.

If the bin is properly insulated or if it is maintained in a heated space, caking of sugar should be minor. It is good practice, however, to completely empty the tank every six months or so and remove any caked material by manual chipping.

Liquid Sugar

Water was the first ingredient received and conveyed in bulk and other liquid handling systems are based to a considerable extent on water distribution systems (Fig. 15.10). Corn syrups, sucrose syrups,

Courtesy of J. H. Day Corp.
FIG. 15.9 A STORAGE BIN SUITABLE FOR STORAGE OF SUGAR OR FLOUR.
The powdered material is brought into the bin pneumatically and taken out by screw conveyors.

270 BAKERY TECHNOLOGY AND ENGINEERING

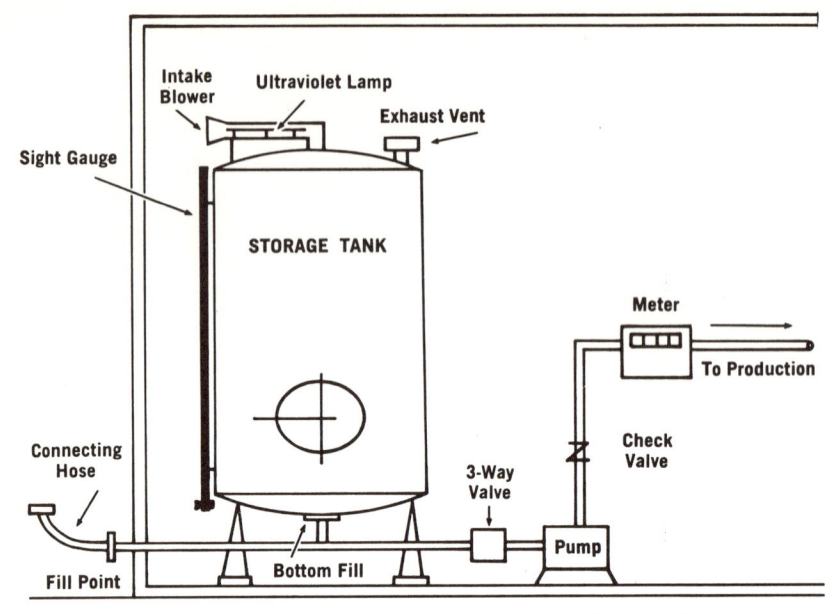

Courtesy of SuCrest Corp.

FIG. 15.10 SCHEMATIC DIAGRAM SHOWING THE BASIC COMPONENTS OF A SIMPLE LIQUID SUGAR HANDLING SYSTEM.

invert syrups, and various combinations of these are widely used by the baking industry in bulk systems. Molasses, refiners' syrups, and other specialty items as well as unorthodox mixtures are available for bulk delivery by special arrangement in many sections of the country. The economic advantages of buying sucrose in syrup form vary in different regions of the country and a careful analysis of the financial aspects of this method of handling the sugar supply should be made before a commitment is made to change. Anyone purchasing large volumes of corn hydrolysates (dry or syrup), however, would almost certainly save money by installing a bulk system for this material. Invert sugar, being available only in syrup form, is also cheaper to receive in bulk.

Pure cane or beet sugar syrup at the 66% solids concentration will occasionally spoil. Good sanitary conditions and occasional cleaning of the tank with sterilizing solutions are essential. The ultraviolet lights installed in the tops of the tanks are effective only in the air space and in the top layer of liquid. The penetrating power of their rays is very poor in aqueous solutions. Consequently, osmophilic yeasts may become established in the bulk of the liquid and begin a slow fermentation. Sucrose syrups of higher concentration are not feasible, but combinations of sucrose and invert with solids up to 76% are available and are definitely more stable. It is good practice to have plate counts run on the syrup at least every month, and, preferably, weekly.

A single tank for each type of corn syrup is the usual arrangement (Fig. 15.11). Fresh loads are mixed with the remnants of previous deliveries. For sucrose-based syrups, the two-tank system is used, each tank being completely emptied before a new load is placed in it. Storage tanks are usually fabricated of mild steel with an inside baked-on lining (Wadsworth 1957).

Corn syrups are supplied at 76% solids or higher. These will not be subject to microbiological attack unless diluted by condensate or water from other sources. Most corn syrups will have to be heated before they can be handled satisfactorily in a bulk system, since corn syrups of low DE and the high solids syrups now being produced are extremely viscous at low temperatures. Although it is possible to use the type of heating arrangement described for shortening tanks, it is not really essential to raise the temperature of the entire tank. Electric strip heaters with thermostatic controls can be placed under the tank end nearest the discharge port. A temperature of about 105°F is suitable. The tank should have a screened vent, a circulating blower of 40 cfm capacity on top, and a manhole access at least 18 in. in diameter to allow cleaning and inspecting of the interior (Kollman 1961).

Positive displacement, low rpm pumps are preferred. Rotary positive displacement pumps should have iron casings and bronze or hardened steel trim. Reciprocating piston pumps should have iron casings with bronze trim including metal snap rings on the piston. Rod and shaft packing should be of a reasonably impervious material.

Dispensing of sugar syrups can be accomplished by volumetric meter or by constant rate pump and time controller.

Liquid sugar, but not corn syrup, can be refrigerated down to about 45°F as a means for adjusting dough temperatures. Corn syrup can be heated, either for simplifying processing steps (as in confectionery manufacture) or for reducing the viscosity so as to simplify handling. In either case, it is desirable to accomplish the temperature change shortly before the ingredient is used to minimize undesirable changes such as crystallization or caramelization.

Pumps, pipes, valves, and meters should be made of stainless steel, if possible. In practice, most piping is found to be galvanized iron because of the cost factor and occasionally copper is used. Piping must be installed so as to allow complete drainage of the system for cleaning. The entire system is normally kept full of liquid sugar. Pipes in corn syrup installations are sometimes traced with heat tapes or steam pipes in order to permit use of less powerful pumps. This

272   BAKERY TECHNOLOGY AND ENGINEERING

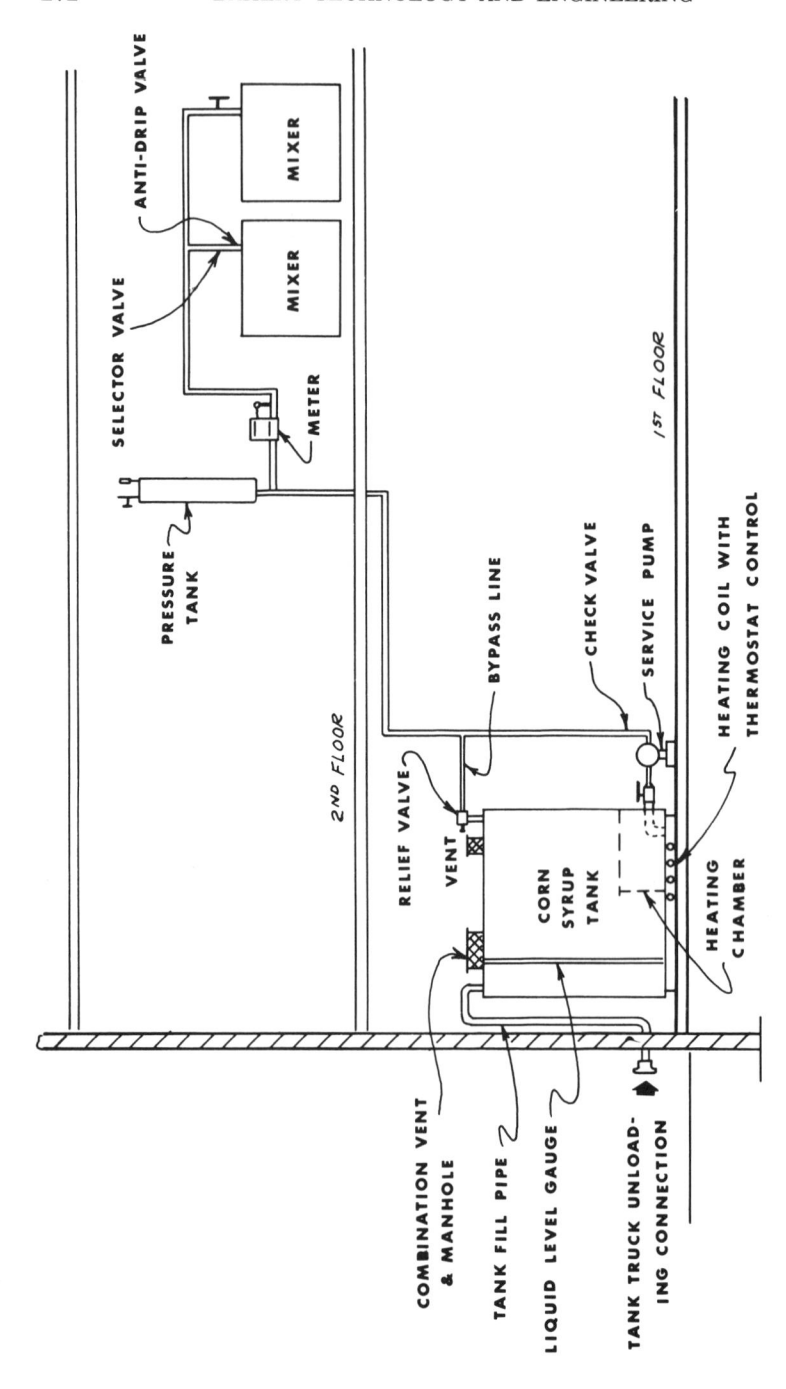

FIG. 15.11 DIAGRAM OF A BULK SYSTEM FOR HANDLING CORN SYRUP.

Courtesy of Corn Products Sales Corp.

BULK HANDLING OF INGREDIENTS 273

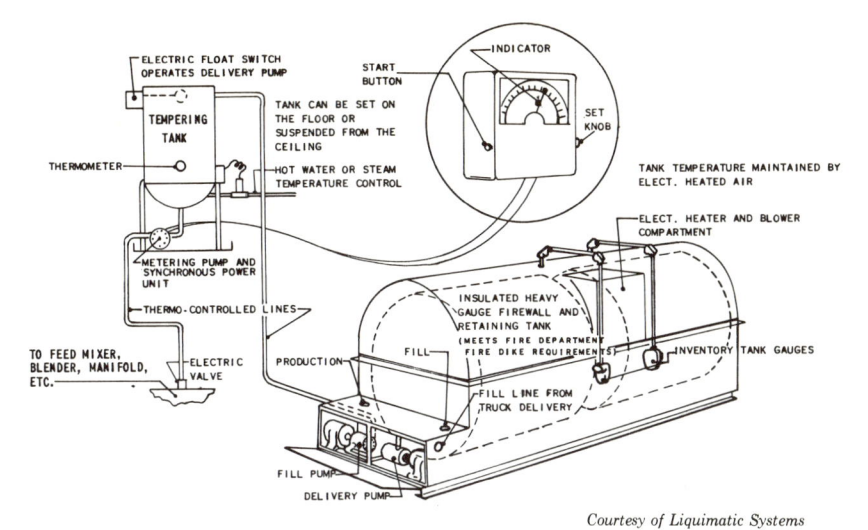

Courtesy of Liquimatic Systems
Fig. 15.12 A Self-Contained Portable Package Unit and Metering System for Melted Shortening.

may lead to discolored and off-flavored syrup being delivered (due to overheating), especially after a shut-down.

LIQUID SHORTENING

Bulk shortening installations consist essentially of pumps, pipes, and tanks (Fig. 15.12). Bulk oil shipments are usually made in 60,000 lb tank cars or in 20,000 or 30,000 lb tank trucks.

Both round and rectangular tanks are used. A convenient arrangement consists of 2 or more tanks of 65,000–70,000 lb capacity for each type of shortening. Since each tank will hold a full tank car of oil, it will not be necessary to mix fresh oil with residues left in the tank from previous shipments. Tanks of 35,000 lb capacity are more convenient for truck deliveries.

Stainless steel, type 302 or 304, is the preferred material for constructing storage tanks. These metals have no adverse effect on fats and oils and are not affected by common cleaning solutions, but they are high in cost and difficult to fabricate. Consequently, most tanks are made of mild steel plate or even of black iron. The configuration of the tank and the location of the outlet should be such that complete drainage of the contents can be obtained. Vertical tanks can be made with dished or cone-shaped bottoms and rectangular tanks can be slightly tilted toward the outlet to achieve this result. The tanks must be equipped with gauges, manholes, etc. The inlet pipe should be brought to within a few inches of the bottom to minimize splashing.

Liquefied fats should be held at about 10°F above the AOCS capillary closed-tube melting point (not the Wiley melting point). Lard will be completely liquid at 120°F, but some vegetable shortenings or oleo may require slightly higher temperatures. The fat can be heated by internal coils of pipe carrying hot water or steam or by external coils or jacket. Hot water heating is preferred since steam may cause localized overheating with damage to the fat. Nonaerating agitators should be installed if steam is to be used for heating. Side-entering propeller-type agitators or recirculating pumps are satisfactory. Thermostatic controls must be provided. Tanks may also be installed in a heated room or a separate heated enclosure, in which case, no additional temperature-adjusting equipment is necessary.

Liquid level gauges can either be sight tubes or float type indicators. The latter can be arranged to operate signals or controls. Sight tubes are not suitable for use with high temperature installations. The installer should calibrate the tank in terms of depth versus volume (or weight) of contents.

Some suppliers recommend installation of stainless steel screens at the inlet, others indicate that this is not required. Lines and valves may be of standard iron or steel. No copper-containing alloys such as brass, Monel, or bronze should ever be allowed to contact the fat. Gate-type valves are recommended. Welded construction is highly desirable since few pipe compounds and gaskets are compatible with edible fats and oils.

Transfer pipes within the plant are almost always heated and insulated. A convenient method of heating is by means of an electrical heating tape wrapped around the pipe. Steam tracing or hot water tracing is also used. Unloading lines are not heated. They are freed of fat after use by draining or by blowing nitrogen or air through them.

It is good practice to incorporate in the system a holding tank located close to the use points. A float switch in this tank is connected to a pump which maintains the liquid level within a narrow range. The temperature is thermostatically controlled. Maintaining the head and temperature constant increases the accuracy of the dispensing meters and confers other advantages.

Recommended turnover is a tank every 2–3 weeks. Many operators take four weeks to use a tank. The tanks should be thoroughly cleaned at least every six months or at the first sign of sediment or off-odors suggestive of rancidity. A new shipment of shortening should never be dumped on top of the residue from a preceding shipment. Antioxidants should be used up to the legal limit.

Nitrogen blanketing is sometimes recommended as a means of increasing the storage life of bulk shortening. Melted shortening will absorb oxygen during manufacture and transport to the user's plant. Blanketing the shortening under a layer of nitrogen while in the user's tank will retard further uptake of oxygen, but the amount already present can cause sufficient deterioration to make the shortening unusable. Oxidation at the surface is small compared to that due to entrained and dissolved oxygen. Therefore, the nitrogen blanket is not a sure preventive of rancidity, but it is a further precaution which, in combination with other good practices including prompt turnover of stock, will assure a constant supply of shortening having excellent organoleptic qualities. Cost of the equipment for nitrogen blanketing in only a few hundred dollars while the expenditure for gas should not exceed $10 per month per tank. To hold down condensation in the head spaces of tanks held in a room where the temperature fluctuates, a worthwhile precaution is to blow air across the surface of the liquid with a fan of about 90 cfm capacity.

Bubbling nitrogen through fat in short bursts is a good method for preventing stratification or settling of higher melting point fractions. This is probably not needed for vegetable oils, but may be helpful for maintaining uniformity in hydrogenated shortening, oleo, or lard held near the melting point or if the required temperature is not being maintained in all regions of the tank.

Some varieties of gear-type single or double-lobe pumps have been used to dispense liquid shortening. However, these pumps have a high degree of slip and do not accurately measure low viscosity liquids if any fluctuation in head occurs. Positive displacement pumps can be used. There are pumps expressly designed for this application. According to Abbott (1959), a packed type, ball check, reciprocating pump will give good accuracy with low viscosity liquids.

The fluid shortenings consisting of oils with added stearine flakes and emulsifiers do not need to be heated and, in fact, heating above the melting point of the stearine can lead to separation on subsequent cooling. These fluids should be kept under continuous agitation with a slow moving blade that circulates all the way around the outside of the tank. At temperatures within the range of 70–87°F, the shortening should retain good odor and flavor for at least 3–4 weeks.

Plastic shortenings can be produced from liquid fats by chilling and working them to the proper texture in equipment such as the Votator.

BIBLIOGRAPHY

Abbott, J. A. 1959. Weighing and mixing procedures. *In* Bakery Technology and Engineering, S. A. Matz (Editor). Avi Publishing Co., Westport, Conn. (Out of print.)
Anon. 1955. This is Liquid Sugar. Refined Sugars and Syrups, Yonkers, N. Y.
Anon. 1959. Conveying flour by air. Food Process. 20, No. 9, 37, 39, 43.

ANON. 1963. Store syrup—reduce yeast count to zero. Food Process. 24, No. 9, 127.
ANON. 1964. Bulk handling of shortenings and oils. Durkee Technical Bull. 110A.
ANON. 1967. Vibra Screw bin activator. Vibra Screw, Totowa, N. J. Bull. BA-67.
BORDEN, B. 1958. Bulk liquid sweeteners—engineering and economics. Proc. Am. Soc. Bakery Engrs. 1958, 79-84.
COLEMAN, J. E. 1963. Recent developments in conveyors. Proc. Am. Soc. Bakery Engrs. 1963, 163-169.
DAVIS, L. B. 1953. Pneumatic conveying systems. Proc. Am. Soc. Bakery Engrs. 1953, 123-128.
Dow, W. T. 1963. Pumpable shortening. Biscuit Maker Plant Baker 1963, 404, 406, 408, 410.
FARRAND, W. J. 1962. Flour packing, warehousing and bulk transport. Biscuit Maker Plant Baker 1962, 407-412.
FILIPPON, A. E. 1946. How to handle corn syrup. Food Ind. 18, 1686-1687, 1830, 1832.
FISCHER, J. 1959. Conveying flour by air. Food Process. 20, No. 9, 37-39, 43.
HAGEDORN, H. G. 1965. New practices in bulk handling of materials with special emphasis on instrumentation controls. Proc. Am. Soc. Bakery Engrs. 1965, 148-152.
HAILE, F. 1960. Bulk handling of ingredients. Proc. Am. Soc. Bakery Engrs. 1960, 104-110.
HOWARD, R. M. 1956. Bulk flour. Proc. Am. Soc. Bakery Engrs. 1956, 78-84.
KOLLMAN, W. C. 1961. Some engineering and economic aspects of bulk systems. Proc. Am. Soc. Bakery Engrs. 1961, 199-206.
MEEKER, E. W. 1957. Progress through bulk granulated sugar. Paper presented to Chicago Sec. Am. Assoc. Candy Technologists, Sept. 17.
MILLER, G. E. 1957. Bulk handling of dry sugar. Am. Soc. Bakery Engrs. Bull. 155.
OTOCKA, E. 1948. Pneumatic handling of flour. Proc. Am. Soc. Bakery Engrs. 1948, 102-107.
PFENING, F. D. 1958. Pneumatic bulk flour handling systems. The Fred D. Pfening Co., Columbus, Ohio.
SASSEMAN, R. 1956. Liquid sugars. Proc. Am. Soc. Bakery Engrs. 1956, 91-102.
SCHROEDER, W. F. 1956. Bulk fat handling. Proc. Am. Soc. Bakery Engrs. 1956, 85-90.
SPANGLER, E. G. 1958. Storage and automatic dispensing of bulk lard and shortening. Proc. Am. Soc. Bakery Engrs. 1958, 71-78.
TUBB, G. O. 1966. The use of liquid shortening in bread. Proc. Am. Soc. Bakery Engrs. 1966, 102-107.
WADSWORTH, D. V. 1957. The Bulk Handling of Liquid Sugar in Plants Manufacturing Products for Human Consumption. Refined Sugars and Syrups, Yonkers, N. Y.

CHAPTER 16

WEIGHING AND MEASURING EQUIPMENT

The measurement of ingredients is obviously one of the most critical operations in bakery processing. Not only is the accuracy of measurement related directly to the quality of the finished products, but it also affects costs. Since composition is regulated by Federal, State, and local laws in the case of standardized items such as bread, and must, in any case, conform to the label declaration of ingredients, bakery management must be certain that the amount of each component found in the finished product will fall within acceptable tolerances.

The hand scaling of individual ingredients has been replaced at an ever increasing rate in recent years by automatic weighing and metering. Some of the advantages which may result from such changes are greater reproducibility (not necessarily greater accuracy), lower manpower requirement, and improved sanitation. In addition, automatic measuring is almost essential in a bulk-handling system.

Designers of automatic measuring equipment for ingredients, doughs, and finished products have borrowed freely from other industries. Water meters of various kinds have proved to be adaptable, with changes of varying degrees of complexity, to the measuring of other liquid ingredients. Weighing devices originally used in other food industries or in nonfood applications have been modified for bakery use. A great deal of ingenuity and expertise has gone into these adaptations and modifications, however,

Powders and granular materials are generally measured by gravimetric techniques while liquids are more commonly measured volumetrically. Volumetric equipment is the least expensive, as a rule, but is also inherently less accurate and dependable since the feed rate necessarily depends upon the density and flow characteristics of the material being measured, and these factors cannot be expected to be perfectly uniform, especially in powdered materials. As a practical matter, volumetric feeders function perfectly satisfactorily in many bakery applications for sugar and other relatively free-flowing ingredients. Gravimetric measurement is inherently more difficult to automate but is theoretically capable of greater accuracy, at least for powdered and granular materials which may vary considerably in density.

The next two sections of this chapter describe the equipment which has been developed for the automatic weighing and the automatic metering (i.e., volumetric measuring) of ingredients. A subsequent section will cover dough dividers and other dough measuring equipment.

WEIGHING

The two major categories of weighing devices are balances and force-deflection systems. The simplest weight, or force, measuring system is the ordinary equal-arm balance. It operates on the principle of moment comparison. The moment produced by the unknown weight is compared with that produced by a known weight. If the 2 arms are equal in length, the 2 weights will be equal when a null balance is obtained. Obviously, such equipment is unsuitable for most practical applications. Some industrial equipment is based on the principal of an uneven-arm scale, of which the ancient steelyard is the simplest example. An unknown weight on a short moment arm is balanced by moving a poise of known weight along a calibrated long moment arm. Multiple beam industrial scales introduce additional levers between the unknown weight and the beam to increase the ratio of unknown to poise. Small capacity bench balances are examples of the uneven arm scale while many platform scales and suspended hopper scales make use of the multiple beam construction.

Pendulum balanced scales use one or more "pendulums" (weights mounted on one end of a rigid rod which rotates about a pivot at its other end) to balance increasing loads as they move from vertical to horizontal. Because the weight which the pendulum will balance varies as the sine of the displacement angle, cams are used to give linear movement of the scale pointer. Metal tapes transmit the motion from pendulum to platform. These scales are commonly used where a dial indication of weight is required. They are available in recording and printing models, and with electric cutoff.

Because the deflection of a spring or any other elastic element is directly proportional to the applied force, within the elastic limit, a calibrated spring, tube, rod, or plate can serve as a weighing device. This principle is applied in the spring scale and the torsion balance. They are subject to hysteresis, fatigue, and temperature errors, but when properly designed and used can be valuable weighing devices.

The torsion principle of weighing is incorporated in the Thayer Flexure-Plate Leverage System. The weighbeam is connected to the sensor or indicator by a series of levers and steel plates which are calibrated to flex the desired extent. When the weighbeam is in the null position, all flexure plates are plumb and in tension and transmit no movement within the system. When the beam moves out of the balance position, the flexure plates are very slightly deflected and tend to urge the system into a balanced position. Advantages claimed for these systems include (1) no knife-edge or other friction surface to wear, (2) shockproof, (3) require no maintenance, and (4) not affected by dust, dirt, or vibration. An example of equipment using this principle is shown in Fig. 16.1.

Other force-sensing elements adaptable to weight measurement include strain-gage load cells and pneumatic pressure cells. In a sense, strain gages are deflection scales, but the deformation is measured as a change in an electrical signal rather than directly as a change in dimension.

Continuous and automatic operating scales utilize the same weight-comparison principles used in manually operated unequal arm balances. Sensing means are used to energize the mechanisms that start and stop the flow of material into the weighing hopper. For example, weighing of flour in most modern bakeries is accomplished by a special automatic flour scale located immediately above the dough mixer (See Fig. 16.2). In some cases, the hopper is on a trolley, and can be moved over several mixers, as required. The usual model consists of a conical steel hopper mounted on four-point suspension bearings of knife-edged

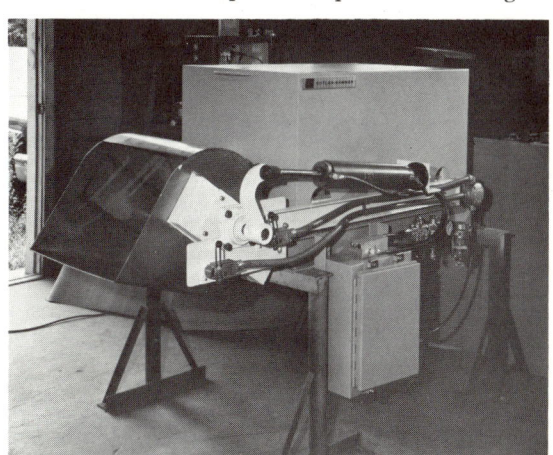

Courtesy of Thayer Scale Div., Cutler-Hammer Co.

FIG. 16.1. AUTOMATIC BATCH SCALE FEATURING FLEXURE PLATE LEVERAGE SYSTEM.

At left front of machine is seen the sanitary weigh hopper with a pneumatic actuator for tipping bucket (center) and the flexure plate scale (center back).

280   BAKERY TECHNOLOGY AND ENGINEERING

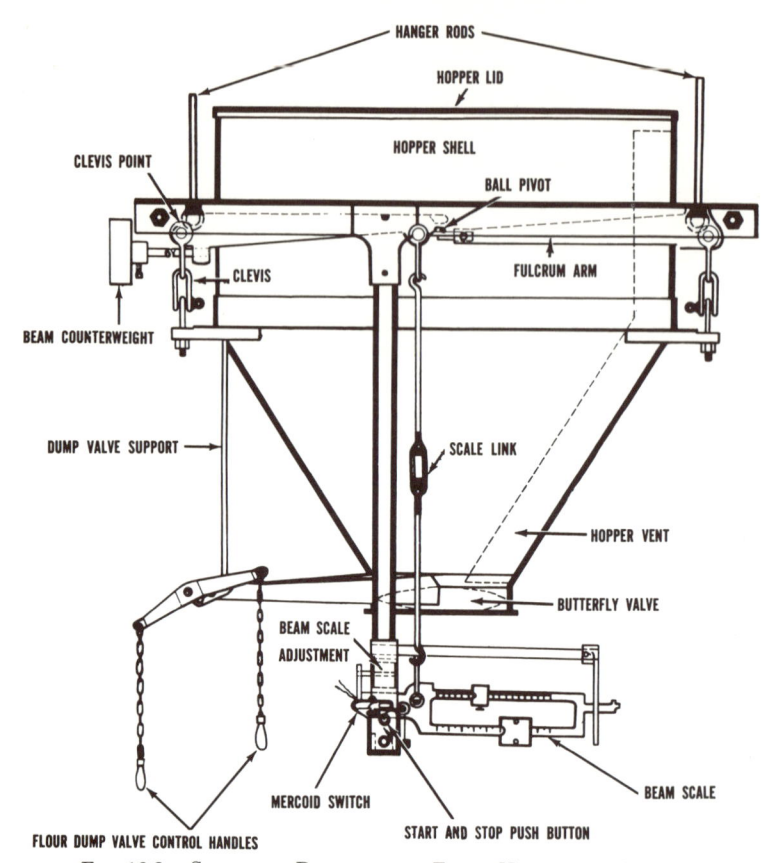

FIG. 16.2. SCHEMATIC DIAGRAM OF A FLOUR HOPPER AND SCALE.

pivots made from case-hardened steel. Once the scale beam is set for the necessary amount of flour and the switch is activated, operation is completely automatic. A mercury switch activated by the scale beam shuts off the flour input when the preset weight has been reached. At the proper time, the operator discharges the contents of the hopper directly into the mixer. Capacities range from 200 to 1000 lb of flour. Transfer operations are dustless, the outlet of the hopper being connected to the mixer inlet by a sliding sleeve. Air displaced as the flour goes into the mixer is conducted to the upper section of the hopper by a venting tube. The scale must be adjusted by the operator or automatically compensated for conveyor overrun to obtain satisfactory accuracy.

In another type of automatic scale, a balancing weight is positioned by a reversible electric motor. Deflection of the beam makes an electrical contact which causes the motor to move the weight in the direction necessary to restore balance, and the final balance position is translated by means of a potentiometer or digital encoding disc into a signal which can be used for recording or control purposes.

Automatic batch scales are adaptable to continuous flows of liquids (Fig. 16.3), granular materials, or powders. If dry materials are being measured, the ingredient flows from a feed hopper through an adjustable gate into the scale hopper until the preselected weight is reached and a trip mechanism closes the gate and opens the outlet. When the scale hopper is empty, the weight of the tare forces the door closed, resets the trip, and opens the gate for another cycle. A dribble feed, resulting from a partial closing of the gate as the set weight is approached, reduces the rate of inflow so that the extent of overshooting the mark is reduced. A counter can be used to record the number of cycles and the total amount of material which has been dumped.

For systems in which continuous addition of dry ingredients is required, automatic gravimetric feeders are preferred.

Weighers Using Moving Belts

The simplest forms of this type of measuring equipment weigh the delivered ingredient but do not adjust the delivery rate to maintain a constant flow (i.e., no feedback). They are useful in automatic batching, but are not readily adaptable to continuous processing where the rate of delivery and not the total weight is important. In one semicontinuous model, the scale belt runs continuously but is fed intermittently with loads that do not extend its full length so that a definite increment is being weighted at any given time. Since the increments are depos-

Courtesy of Thayer Scale Co.
FIG. 16.3. AN AUTOMATIC LIQUID BATCHING SCALE.
Drum at center is the weigh tank connected (above center) to the liquid control valve. Flexure plate scale is at left.

ited at short intervals, they approximate continuous flow. The weigh belt is mounted on a scale mechanism which records and sums the amounts removed.

A second type, the continuous conveyor scale, uses a scale-supported section of a belt conveyor to totalize the load which is being constantly deposited on it. The forms of weighing devices used in such equipment include spring-balanced beams, strain gages, and pneumatic load cells.

Fully automated belt weighers with feedback to control rate of delivery are useful in continuous or intermittent weighing.

The most common type utilizes a conveyor belt balanced on a weighbeam. When the belt is driven at constant speed and the total weight of the belt, material, and associated mechanisms is held constant, the rate the material comes off the end of the scale is also constant and total weight for any known time interval can be computed. Imbalance of the beam actuates a change of the rate of material deposit onto the belt in the direction of restoring balance, by mechanical adjustment of the feed gate or by varying the speed of a belt or screw feeding the weighing conveyor (Fig. 16.4). Accuracies are said to be as high as 0.0001% for certain products and equipment, but a more likely figure is about 0.1% for continuous measuring scales used in the bakery.

In another design of automatic belt gravimetric feeder, variation in the amplitude of vibration of a feed tray is used as a means of controlling the rate of delivery to the belt. A cam-operated mechanism driven off the belt transmission oscillates a driving plate at constant frequency in the direction of an opposing receiving plate connected to the feed tray. A rubber control wedge suspended from the scale beam transmits the vibration from the driving plate to the receiving plate. The amplitude of vibration is thus regulated by the position of the wedge between the plates. If the weight on the belt is excessive, the wedge is raised, the vibration is diminished, and less material is fed, and vice versa.

Loss-in-weight Feeders

In a typical design, the entire feed hopper is mounted on a scale which controls the rate of removal of material from the hopper. The hopper may be discharged, for example, by a rotating valve driven by a variable speed motor. If the scale beam counterpoise is retracted continuously by a constant speed drive, the rate of delivery will be constant and the equipment will be suitable for continuous processes.

Loss-in-weight feeders are of several design types. Vibratory, screw, pneumatic, and belt methods may be used to remove material from the hopper which is mounted on a multiple-beam scale mechanism. The hopper is filled and the scale beam balanced by manually adjusting the

WEIGHING AND MEASURING EQUIPMENT   283

poise. The control dial on the rate setter is set to the desired rate of feed in pounds per hour. The setter, operated by a synchronous motor, retracts the poise by a lead screw at the exact feed rate desired. As long as the feeder delivers material from the hopper, causing it to lose weight at the same rate the poise is being retracted, the scale beam will stay in balance. If the feeder delivers too much or too little, causing loss in weight faster or slower than the poise is retracted, the beam will tip and operate controls which cause the feeder to correct its rate. Only a very small beam movement is required for control, and the scales are so sensitive that the beam is essentially in balance at all times (Anon. 1968).

Where the loss-in-weight feeder is electronically controlled, it can be coupled to the flow from another loss-in-weight feeder or from variable liquid flows through a Venturi tube, orifice plate, or other flow measuring device. The metering can be continuous or intermittent, and in the latter case, the sensing of a predetermined amount of one

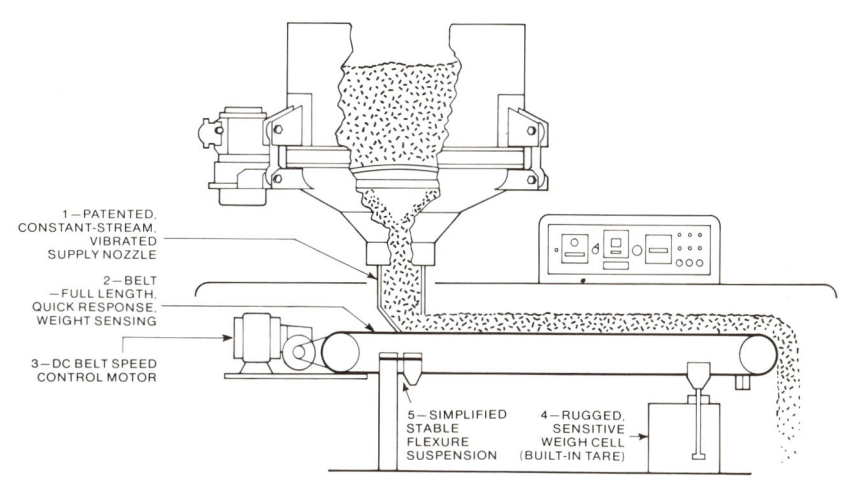

FIG. 16.4. PRINCIPLES OF OPERATION OF THE VIBRA METRIC FEEDER.
1. Patented vibrated supply nozzle attaches to vibrated bin bottom. This assures positive, unfaltering supply to the weigh belt with deviation limited to 1–2% at the supply point. 2. Teflon-coated weigh belt speeds up or slows down instantly in response to any deviation from the set point, maintaining a constant weight-per-minute discharge off the belt. Accurate to better than 0.25–0.5% of set rate, minute-to-minute, at 2 sigma. 3. TENV motor ($\frac{1}{15}$ hp) with integral tachometer for continuous monitoring of belt speed. 4. Weigh cell is rugged Linear Voltage Differential Transformer (LVDT) with 500-lb overload capacity. Provides built-in tare system which eliminates counterweights. Dust and water tight, temperature compensated. 5. Inconel "X" flexure plates provide a sturdy pivot for conveyor, insensitive to accidental or shock loading, but highly sensitive to the slightest weight changes on belt.

284　BAKERY TECHNOLOGY AND ENGINEERING

Courtesy of Thayer Scale Div., Cutler-Hammer Co.

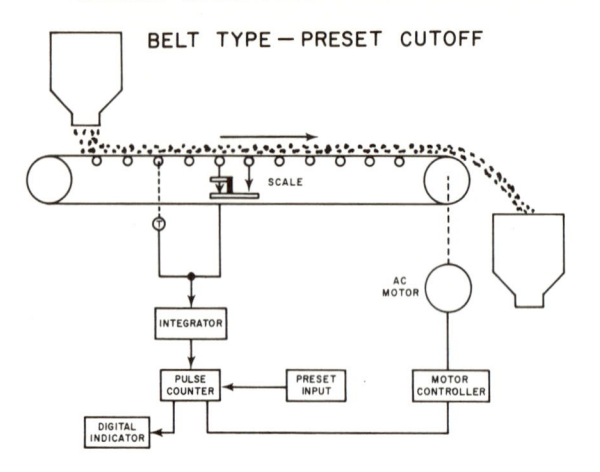

FIG. 16.5. PRINCIPLES OF OPERATION OF AUTOMATIC BELT AND HOPPER FEEDERS.

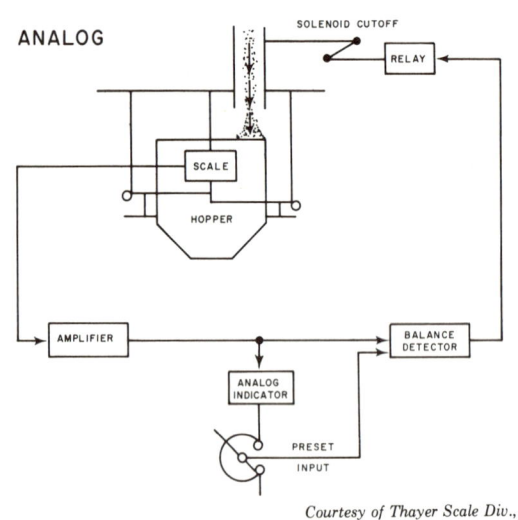

ingredient leads to the operation of the feeder for a fixed number of seconds.

Principles of Control of Gravimetric Feeders

Principles of the controls for belt type and hopper type gravimetric feeders are illustrated in Fig. 16.5. Belt gravimetric feeders can be

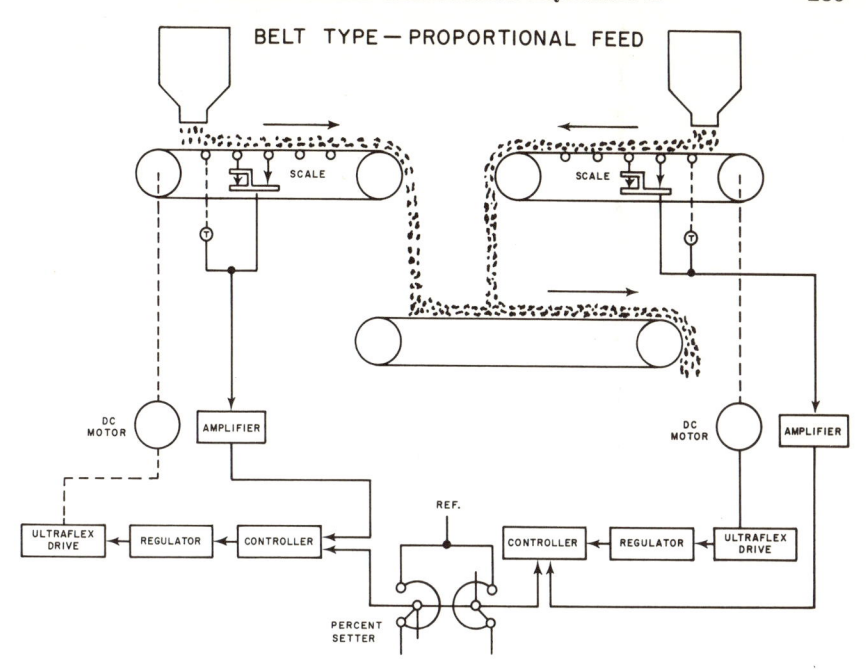

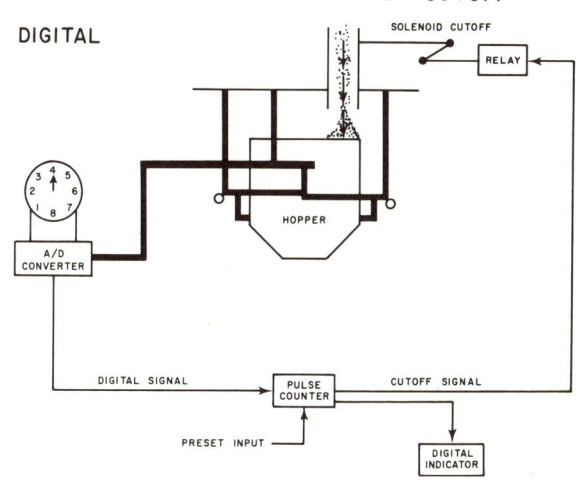

WEIGHING AND MEASURING EQUIPMENT 285

Fig. 16.5 Con't.

mechanically, pneumatically, or electronically controlled. Operation of belt gravimetric feeders is based on the principal of maintaining a constant weight of material on the moving belt by actuation of a positive-acting gate on the feed hopper. The rate of feed may be changed by varying the belt load and/or changing belt speed. Net weight of belt load may be sensed directly by a force balance pneumatic transmitter and load cell or by a differential transformer which transmit any variation from set load to the solid-state electronic controller. The feedback system actuates the control gate to maintain belt load at the set point and weigh platforms in a null position. Electronically controlled belt gravimetric feeders are available with capacities from about 0.1 lb per min to over 60,000 lb per hr and accuracies of $\pm 1\%$. The belt type with preset cutoff uses a scale and tachometer signal to provide an instantaneous indication of rate of material flow by weight per unit of time. The resulting analog signal is converted into digital form through an integrator. A pulse counter records the digital information to provide visual indications of the total flow of material. The pulse counter can also be provided with a stop-point setting which will cause a contact to close and halt the conveyor when the prescribed amount of material has been transferred.

The proportional feed belt feeder also relies upon a scale and tachometer output to provide instantaneous rate of flow measurement. In this case, however, the resultant signal is electronically compared with that from a percent-setter to regulate conveyor speeds. The system can be designed to have a stop-point similar to the arrangement described above. One illustration in Fig. 16.5 shows two ingredients being measured at proportional rates and blended on a conveyor. In belt type systems, one of the chief factors affecting overall accuracy is the location of the sensing device in relation to the discharge point; the closer together, the greater the accuracy.

Hopper weighing systems can provided with either analog or digital controls. The analog system shown in Fig. 16.5 employs a scale and a conventional sensing arrangement. Other types of weighing devices such as load cells can be used as sensors, provided their output is electrical. The amplified signal is compared with the present input through the balance detector. When the signals balance, indicating that hopper weight is at the desired level, the solenoid cutoff closes the feeder. The analog indicator (e.g., a large scale head graduated in 1000 increments) continually supplies progressive weight information.

The digital system employs a mechanical weighbeam and lever arrangement and a conventional scale head. The basic sensor can assume a variety of configurations and use several kinds of components, but a pulse signal giving a number of pulses which are proportioned to the material weight must be obtained. The remaining portion of the system features a preset counter with digital weight indication.

Fuller (1970) discussed the importance of receiving scales. He points out that without checking all ingredient receipts for weight (including bulk shipments), no control can be exerted over the shipper's errors or intentional fraud. Certified public scales and railroad scales are usually accurate but do not allow positive and direct control of the weighing operations by the purchaser. According to Fuller, many suppliers do not even have shipping scales and do not weigh their shipments, but only estimate them. Some of the weighing equipment used for receiving are railroad track scales, motor truck scales, bulk handling scales, bag check weighers, and dock platform scales. By installing an automatic bulk handling receiving scale in the unloading line leading from the truck or rail car to the storage bins and by installing automatic tank scales under the liquid storage tanks, the shipping weights can be verified and inventory of bulk materials can be closely controlled. In one type of bulk receiving scale, the material is air-conveyed to an overhead surge hopper, and then fed through a weigh hopper on a scale until a preset weight is reached at which time the fill feeder stops and the weight is recorded. The weigh hopper then discharges the lot of material to a selected storage hopper. When the weigh hopper is empty, the residual weight is recorded, and the cycle begins again. The computer adds each batch weight and subtracts each residual weight so that the contents of the shipping vehicle are known exactly at the termination of the receiving process.

METERING

A volumetric measuring device in its simplest form is a container of known volume, such as a tank, barrel, pipette, or volumetric flask. The container may be calibrated at various points, as in the burette, graduated cylinder, or some storage tanks. Volumetric measurements can be applied to solid materials as well as liquids; for example, in home cooking procedures where nearly all proportioning is done volumetrically in spoons and cups. But large scale manufacturing processes do not customarily include volumetric measurements for powders and the like because of difficulty in controlling density.

Location of the liquid surface, and hence the amount, of liquid in a tank, can be determined by several methods. Simplest of these is the tape or chain connected to an indicator and attached to a float on the liquid surface. A calibrated or plain glass tube attached to taps at the top and bottom of the tank can also be used for direct indicating of liquid level. The dielectric, conducting, or absorption properties of the liquid can be the basis of measurement. If the liquid rises between two plates of a condenser, a capacitance change will be produced pro-

288 BAKERY TECHNOLOGY AND ENGINEERING

Courtesy of Baker Perkins, Inc.
FIG. 16.6. TOTALIZING FLOW METERS FOR WATER AND SHORTENING.

portional to the depth. The absorption of radiation between a radioactive source and a sensor located above the liquid and at the bottom, respectively, will be proportional to the depth of the liquid.

In modern bakery practice, liquid ingredients are measured by totalizing flow meters wherever possible (Fig. 16.6). This equipment is almost essential in bulk-handling systems.

Much engineering work has gone into the construction of water meters, and virtually all fluid control and measuring systems are based on instruments initially designed for water. Although we rarely think of it in this way, water is a classical example of an ingredient handled and dispensed by bulk transfer methods.

Several accurate versions of flow meters are commercially available. These have been classified as (1) inferential meters, in which the liquid actuates a screw, a vane, or some other inertia-dependent mechanism, and (2) the positive displacement type in which a definite volume of water is allowed to pass during each complete cycle of the mechanism. Both types are accurate to a few percentage points of the total reading at high rates of flow. At low rates of flow, the displacement meters are generally more reliable.

Head meters (orifice plates, Venturis) relate the flow rate through a constant area to a variable pressure difference. It is also possible to relate the flow rate to the area change needed to obtain a constant pressure drop. Rotameters, a variety of inferential meter, are the most common type of variable area meters in the food industry. They consist of a gradually tapered vertical tube, usually of glass, with the fluid flowing upward through it, and a float capable of unrestricted movement up and down the tube. The float will assume an equilibrium position such that fluid drag and buoyancy just equal the downward force of gravity. The fluid drag is related to the area of flow between the float and the sides of the tube. If the flow rate increases, the bob moves upward to increase the area and keep the drag constant. The pressure drop through the instrument remains almost independent of the flow rate.

The calibration will vary with float dimensions, tube taper, and fluid properties such as viscosity and density. Special float designs are available which are relatively insensitive to viscosity effects; but in the bakery these meters will normally be used for one ingredient only, so viscosity fluctuations should not be a major problem. Means for compensating fluid density changes can be obtained. The mathematical treatment of fluid flow measurement is detailed in many texts on chemical engineering and hydraulics, but a good summary of this aspect of metering has been given by Rothfus (1968). By affixing a magnet or armature to the float and placing a sensing device outside the tube, rotameter readings can be transmitted for recording and control purposes (Fig. 16.7).

Turbine meters (another type of inferential meter) have come into use for measuring such liquids as water, invert syrup, and ammonium bicarbonate solution (Hagedorn 1965). Their small size and weight permit installation at any convenient point. These meters consist essentially of a rotor located in a tubular housing (inserted as part of the pipe line) and a sensing device.

The flowing liquid impinges upon the turbine blades which freely rotate about an axis along the center line of the surrounding tube. The angular velocity of the turbine rotor is directly proportional to the fluid velocity through the turbine. The angle of the rotor blades to the stream governs the rotor velocity. Blade angles are usually between 20° and 40° because larger angles result in excessive end thrust and bearing friction while smaller angles cause undesirably low angular velocity and loss of repeatability.

Sensing of the rotation is done by magnetic interaction between the blade tip and a pickup coil located outside the tubing. The rotor blades are made of paramagnetic material and the pickup coil contains a permanent alnico magnet. Because the surrounding pipe is stainless steel, it does not interfere with the interaction. Frequency of the magnetic pulses is proportional to the flow rate. Pulses per unit volume may be varied in meters of small capacity by using some nonmagnetic

290   BAKERY TECHNOLOGY AND ENGINEERING

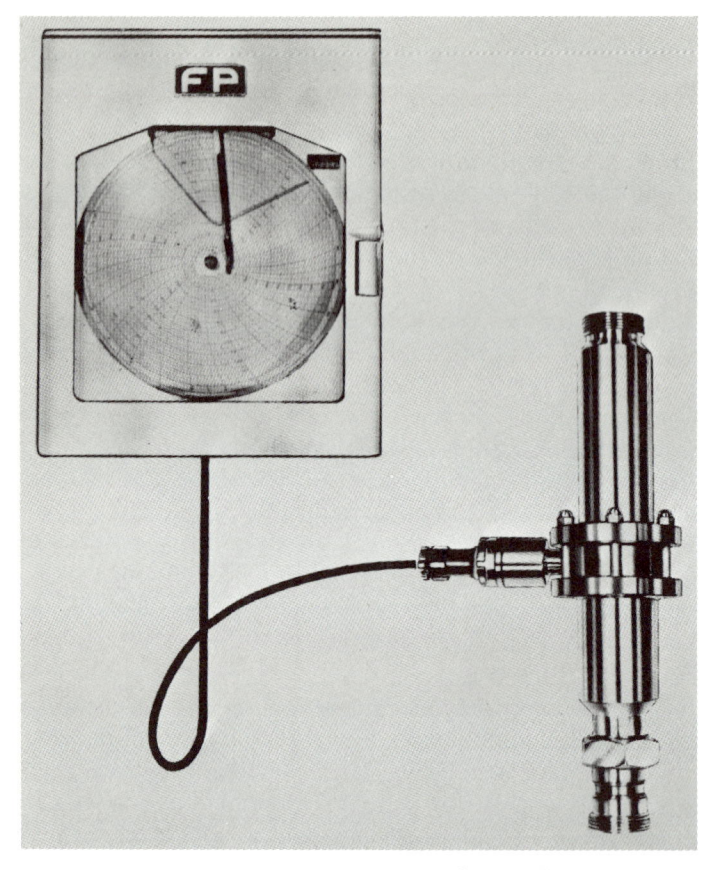

Courtesy of Fischer & Porter Co.
FIG. 16.7. AUTOMATIC RECORDING FLOWRATOR FOR METERING LIQUIDS CONTINUOUSLY.

blades. In large diameter meters, resolution is increased by installing a large number of small magnetic buttons on a rim which rotates with the turbine.

In addition to the wide range through which accurate measurements can be made (on the order of 10:1), a major advantage of the turbine meter is that each electrical pulse is proportional to a small incremental volume of flow. This incremental output is digital in nature, and so can be totalized with a maximum error of one pulse regardless of the volume measured. Accuracies of ± 0.5% of the actual flow rate or ± 0.25% over selected flow ranges have been claimed for these systems.

Continuously flowing streams of material can be measured volumetrically by displacement meters. There are several types, based on nutating discs, reciprocating pistons, rotating vanes, etc.

The piston meter is like a piston pump operated backwards and it is capable of accuracy to 0.1%.

For precise volume measurements, corrections for temperature must be made because of its effect on the density of the material being measured and the dimensions of the volumetric device. Pressure is generally not a factor since common liquids are noncompressible under the conditions of measurement.

The principle of nutating meters is as follows (Fig. 16.8): A disc piston fits approximately horizontally in a chamber defined by truncated cones top and bottom (the apexes facing each other). A vertical diaphragm also separates the chamber. Liquid flows into the chamber on one side of the vertical diaphragm and pushes the disc up and down with a nodding or nutating motion (it does not rotate). At each complete cycle, the piston discharges a volume of liquid equal to the capacity of the measuring chamber. A spindle affixed to the ball-like bearing which supports the piston describes a circle as a result of the disc's nutation,

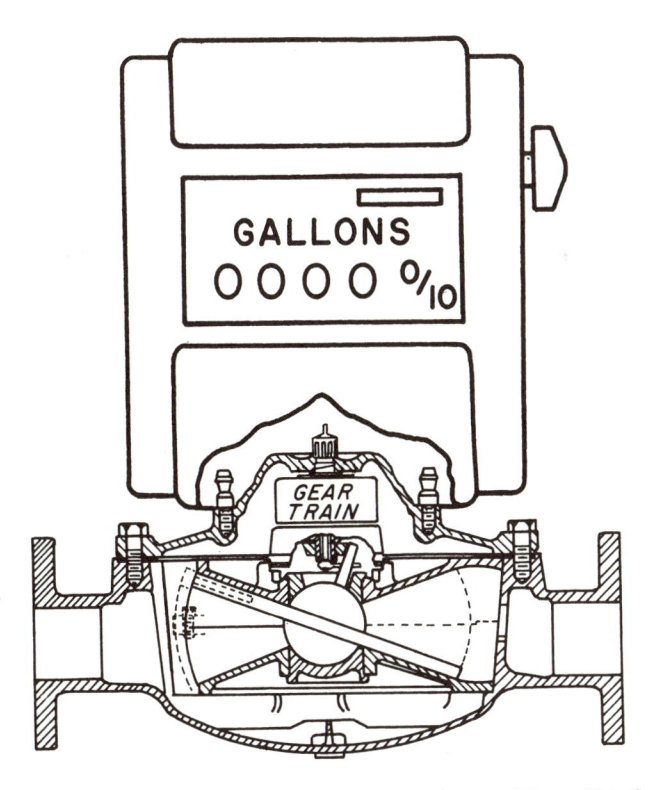

Courtesy of Neptune Meter Co.

FIG. 16.8. PRINCIPLE OF THE NUTATING METER.

and this motion is transmitted through a gear train to a register. The only moving part in the measuring chamber is the piston (Anon. 1963).

The meters previously discussed measure the volume of a liquid under a head of pressure applied at some other point. A calibrated pump can also serve as a measuring and dispensing device for supplying ingredients to batch or continuous processes.

The positive-displacement metering pump is electrically actuated by a controller which has a synchronous motor drive unit. The drive moves the hands on an indicator which can be preset for the quantity desired. The metering cycle continues until the synchronous motor in in the controller has counted the predetermined number of revolutions of the metering pump, after which the controller stops the two motors at the same time. The metering pump is also driven at a constant speed by a synchronous motor, and, since both the controller drive and the pump motor are energized by current of the same frequency, their motions will always be proportional. Control of metering can also be accomplished by micro-switches activated by digital counters operated by cams on the pump shaft.

When the shut-off point is reached, the meter automatically resets itself to the original amount, ready to dispense the ingredient for another batch. Accuracy of 0.1% has been claimed for positive displacement flow meters utilizing a system of oval gear wheels to measure the liquid.

Metering pumps must be fed at a pressure (rate) sufficient to avoid cavitation. Piping must be assembled so that the meter does not "pump air." If these conditions are not met, accuracy of any degree cannot be relied upon.

Volumetric feeders for pulverulent materials can be classified on a basis of their action as: (1) a belt, disc, roller, or screw moves the ingredient through a gate which is usually adjustable in height, (2) a helix moves the material through a tube at a rate governed by the speed or "on time" of the screw, or (3) pockets are filled with the powder and then rotated to dump their contents, the speed of movement of the pockets past the release point governing the rate of delivery.

Volumetric feeders relying on helical feed devices are typified by the device shown in Fig. 16.9. In this feeder, two concentrically mounted and independently driven augers rotate in the same direction but at dissimilar speeds. The larger outer helix tends by its slower rotation to create constant motion in a zone of material surrounding the faster speed smaller inner auger (or metering auger). An optimum ratio of the two speeds is selected to give a constant uniform density in the material surrounding the metering screw. If product characteristics require it, a reverse helix can be added to further stabilize the flow pattern. Since the metering screw operates in an environment of uniform density, it can deliver a constant rate of ingredient at any given speed. Metering accuracy of ± 1% of set rate is claimed for most materials.

Figure 16.10 is a Sterwin feeder, which uses volumetric principles and is useful for low addition rates, such as vitamins and oxidizers. The feeding range can be varied from 4 oz to 60 lb per hr. The principle is that a vertically-movable slide or gate controls the depth of powder on a horizontally rotating feed disc which is drawing the material from a hopper. The powder, after it is removed from the disc by a screw, falls down a chute to the mixing area. Addition rates are controlled by varying the speed of the disc or the height of the opening in the hopper. Disc speed can be varied by changing the gears or the speed of the motor. The gate is adjusted by a micrometer screw to give a 1:20 variation in the height of the opening. As in all equipment of this type, feed rate is not necessarily directly related to the dimensions of the opening or the speed of the disc, and it is important to check the settings by weighing the material discharged during a given time interval.

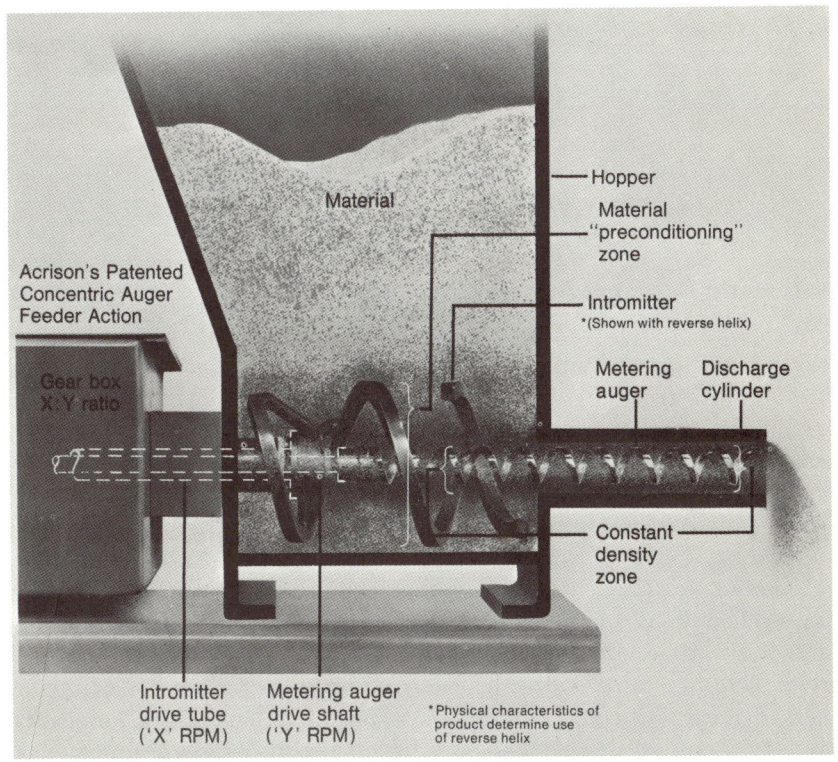

Courtesy of Acrison, Inc.

FIG. 16.9. CUT-AWAY VIEW OF DRY MATERIAL FEEDER.

Courtesy of Sterwin Chemicals, Inc.

FIG. 16.10. VOLUMETRIC FEEDER FOR LOW ADDITION RATES OF DRY INGREDIENTS.

Automatic Batching Systems

Weighing operations for flour, sugar, and some other ingredients are integral parts of the bulk-handling systems. Other ingredients can be dumped into receiving hoppers daily or more frequently. Bag unloaders, sifters, and conveying systems (mechanical or pneumatic) will precede the receiving or surge hopper. Automatic conveying and metering or weighing devices eliminate manual transfer thereafter.

Automated bakeries generally use a central control panel registering and controlling many remote scales (Fig. 16.11). In one form of the automated weighing system, formula weights are set in advance of each day's schedule by a supervisor who adjusts the weight selector dials behind the console. When the mixer operator signals readiness, the central control operator starts the material by pressing a button. A further advance is the computerized system, in which recipes for several kinds of products are recorded on tape, on circuit boards, or on punched cards. After the mixer operator signals for his ingredients, the computer takes over all other functions. Changes, as to compensate for differing flour moisture contents, can be made at will by typing them on the input station which is part of the computer circuit.

The advantages claimed for automatic batching include: (1) elimination of human errors, (2) more consistent weights, (3) better sanitation, (4) less labor, and (5) reduction in loss of costly ingredients.

The automatic scale or meter is a system, or part of a system, made up of material handling devices, the weighing or metering equipment, data handling read-outs, and the controls which program the entire series of functions for automatic operation. All automatic scales transfer materials from some type of storage to a scale and from the scale to some destination. From the scale comes information in the form of electrical signals which controls the weights of ingredients and which can also be used to print out weight data for quality control, inventory control, and other management requirements.

The simultaneous coordination of all feeders can be achieved by powering each of the critical drives with an induction motor receiving its electrical power from a central adjustable frequency source, such as a U.S. Varidyne Power unit used on the blender. The higher the frequency, the faster an induction motor revolves.

A typical digital blending system will include: (1) a master unit with integral controls for setting system demand rate, batch size, valve ramp rates (up and down), and preshutdown point. Automatic shutdown will be initiated either by measured or demand total. (2) Ratio unit

Courtesy Thayer Scale Co.

FIG. 16.11. CONTROL CONSOLE WITH DIGITAL CARD READER FOR AUTOMATIC BATCHING.

(one or more) for setting individual component ratios by manual thumb-switches. Multicomponent ratios are available, and 3 or 4 digit settings are optional. (3) Individual component controllers, either pacing or memory, to provide control of the addition rates of the separate ingredients. Standard features include integrated total flow indication, manual valve control, and a low flow alarm to warn the operator when the measuring device is functioning below the linear flow range.

Computers can be made part of the system to control any of the functions and coordinate their operation. Automatic temperature compensation units can be used to continuously adjust quantity measurements for variations in density due to temperature fluctuations of liquid ingredients.

MEASURING DOUGH PIECE SIZE

Since dough dividers are measuring devices, it is appropriate to discuss them in this chapter even though their usual location in the processing sequence would place them after mixing, which is covered in the next chapter.

Bread doughs present unusually severe problems in uniform measuring of pieces. The elastic, cohesive nature of the material does not adapt it to gravimetric procedures, and the constantly varying density that results from fermentation interferes with accurate volumetric measurements. Of the two approaches, volumetric scaling has proven to be the most practical and economical, however, and all successful dough dividers have been based on such measurements.

Dividers

The simplest type of divider is the bench top roll divider which separates a large dough piece into 18 or 36 portions of more or less equal weight by a cutting head actuated through a lever assembly. The lever may be operated by hand or by a hydraulic system receiving its energy from a motorized pump. These dividers are of no importance in large commercial bakeries, where pocket dividers are used without exception for conventional batch processed bread and rolls. In the following discussion, the operation of pocket dividers will be described.

Transporting the Dough to the Divider

After the dough has completed its fermentation in bulk, the filled trough is transported, usually by man power, to the divider area or to the floor above the divider. Transfer of the trough contents is effected by gravity to the divider hopper or to a chute leading to the hopper. The trough contents may be transferred to the raised hopper of the divider either as one mass or as chunks, depending upon the capacity of the hopper and the available equipment for handling the trough. Usually, the trough is elevated and then tipped so that the dough falls into the divider chute. The trough, which is on casters, is rolled along the floor and into the brackets of the elevator and the elevator motor is started, first raising the trough above the divider and then turning it through a 90° angle to dump the dough into the divider hopper.

Function of the Divider

In brief, the function of the divider is to cut the dough into loaf-sized pieces. The important factor to the baker is the loaf weight, but it has proved to be difficult to design an apparatus which will subdivide dough on a weight basis. Consequently, all dividers presently used operate on a volumetric basis. The dough is forced into spaces having a known volume, the pocket contents are cut off from the main dough mass, and the pieces of constant volume are ejected onto a conveyor leading to the rounder. As long as the dough density is kept constant, the weight as well as the volume of the pieces will be the same.

Figure 16.12 is a schematic diagram of the most common type of divider. The dough flows from the hopper into the underlying compression chamber. At the start of the cycle, a knife moves horizontally to cut off the piece of dough near the hopper bottom. Next, the ram or piston moves forward pressing the severed dough piece into a chamber contained in a rotatable cylinder. At the end of the ram stroke, the cylinder turns, cutting off the excess dough, and, finally, the discharge lever ejects the measured dough piece. In the return cycle, the emptied cylinder is turned back so that the cavities face the compression chamber, and the knife and compression piston withdraw, allowing more dough to be drawn into the chamber by gravity and suction.

Commercial models are available which have from 2 to 8 pockets in the cylinder and operate at speeds up to 25 strokes per minute. Scaling range is from 6 to 36 oz, and motors up to 7½ hp are used. An eight-pocket divider is shown in Fig. 16.13. This machine will scale dough pieces at a speed of 2400 to 9600 loaves per hour. It is 5 ft 3½ in. high, 5 ft 6½ in. long, and 3 ft 5 in. wide. A special feature of this model is the variable speed drive on the discharge conveyor.

Some dividers use a reciprocating division box instead of the rotating cylinder to measure and cut off the dough pieces. In these machines, the box containing the pockets is forced downward after they are filled, shearing off the excess dough as a result of the movement of the pockets past the chamber edge.

A warm air current is sometimes provided on the conveyor leading from the divider to the rounder in order to partially dry the cut surfaces.

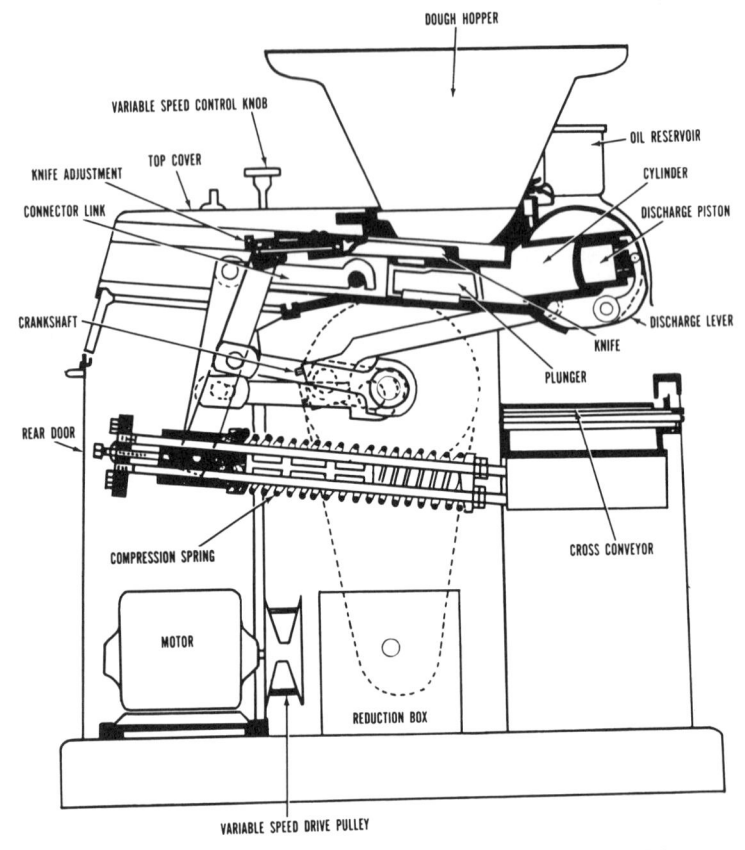

FIG. 16.12. SCHEMATIC DIAGRAM OF A COMMON TYPE OF DIVIDER.

Courtesy of U.S. Dept. Defense

Controlling and Adjusting the Divider

The volume of the pockets which scale the dough piece is adjustable to allow variation in the weight of the finished loaf and to permit compensation for changes in dough density. Volume adjustment is made by trial and error changes of the piston depth in each individual pocket. The pistons are adjusted by different mechanisms in different models. Lock nuts or shims are the usual means. Any change in the density of the dough will be reflected in an alteration of the piece weight measured at any piston setting. Therefore, it is essential to set the machine using a representative sample of dough. Allowing the dough to stand around for a considerable period while making adjustments is a sure way to create troublesome conditions later on.

The speed of the apparatus must be coordinated with the speed of other elements in the forming machine complexus. However, top speed

WEIGHING AND MEASURING EQUIPMENT

of the divider is established as frequently by dough characteristics as by machine limitations. A variable speed drive is provided on all dividers for the adjustment of scaling rate. Changing the speed is simply a matter of adjusting the wheel or lever controlling the variable speed drive.

Dough dividers have a special lubrication system which provides an important variable in machine adjustment. Oil used in this sytem has two functions: it lubricates the mechanical parts of the divider which come in contact with the dough, and it forms a seal between the dough box and the divider head. It is usually a special grade of mineral oil since it has been found that vegetable oils leave a gummy film which may cause excessive friction or even bind the close tolerance moving parts of the machine. Divider oil should be as colorless, odorless, and tasteless as possible. Specifications commonly call for a technical white grade mineral oil with a viscosity of 85–120 at 212°F and a flash point of 662°F. Lubrication systems are either pressure-fed or gravity types. Adjustment of either is simple. The correct setting is that which uses the least amount of oil to secure proper functioning of the divider. Ma-

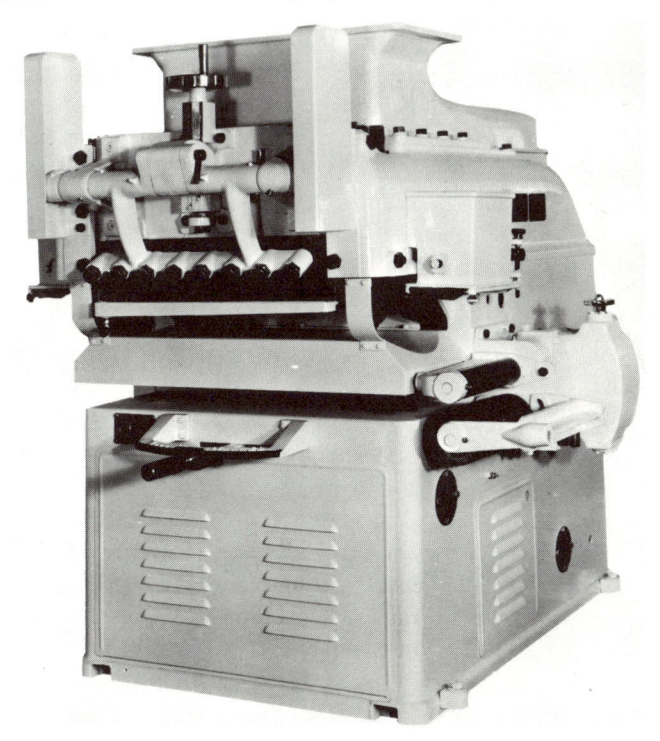

Courtesy of Baker Perkins, Inc.

FIG. 16.13. AN EIGHT-POCKET DIVIDER.

chine bearings and other moving parts which do not contact the dough are lubricated by the usual petroleum oils and greases.

Since divider oil is taken up by the dough and appears in small quantities in the finished loaves, it falls under certain provisions of the Federal regulations governing use of food additives. White mineral oil has been cleared for use as a release agent and lubricant in bakery products at a level not to exceed 0.15%. It must meet the following requirements: (1) it is a mixture of liquid hydrocarbons, essentially paraffinic and naphthenic in nature, obtained from petroleum; (2) it meets the test requirements of USP XVI for readily carbonizable substances; (3) it meets the test requirements of USP XVI for sulfur compounds; (4) it meets the specifications prescribed in the J. Assoc. Offic. Agri. Chemists, Vol. 45, p. 66, after correction of the ultraviolet absorbance for any absorbance due to added antioxidants; and (5) it may contain any antioxidant permitted in foods by regulations issued in accordance with Section 409 of the act, in an amount not greater than that required to produce its intended effect. The limitation of 0.15% applies to the total of all petroleum hydrocarbons used in the food, including divider oil.

Maintaining the proper clearances between the knife and the ram and between the dough box and the divider head is very important in assuring proper operation of the machine. Excessive clearance will cause dough leakage, and insufficient clearance will cause the machine to overheat with consequent bad effects on the dough and extra demands on the motor. Consult the manufacturer's recommendations for maintaining the proper clearance between these parts.

The ram and the knife control the amount of dough that enters the dough box, and they are adjustable. If an insufficient amount of dough is taken in, the weights of the pieces will usually be erratic, while an excessive amount of dough will receive unnecessary punishment which may cause poor performance of the dough in the later stages of processing. The former condition is frequently accompanied by a knocking sound in the divider as the partially empty pockets allow gas to be compressed in them. An up and down movement of the dough in the hopper is considered a symptom of poor adjustment, or of dough which is not pliable enough. The adjustments which will produce the best results for any particular dough must be determined empirically.

According to Trautman (1951), breaking of the dough between the divider chamber and the dough hopper is a certain indication of improperly conditioned dough. He also states that it is important for the chute to have the proper pitch so the dough will be given an even pressure at the chamber at all times. Other authorities indicate the chute should have an angle of at least 45° if possible, and under no circumstances should the angle be less than 30°. The surface finish on the dough chute and divider dough hopper is quite important and should be in the neighborhood of 125 disc grind finish. It is sometimes possible to solve problems of proper dough feed to the compression chamber by applying a Teflon coating to the high friction surface.

The amount of flour dusted on the conveyor belt can be controlled, and should, of course, be kept to the minimum capable of promoting adequate performance of the divider.

Maintenance

Cleaning the divider is a rather difficult job which must be performed whenever the machine is shut down for more than an hour in order to prevent caking of the retained dough. Proper cleaning requires removal of the ram, knife, dough hopper, and pistons.

Following is a recommended sequence for cleaning: (1) Stop the divider with the knife and the ram all the way back. (2) Remove the housing covering the knife connecting links and release the knife. Draw the knife out of its guide slots and, if possible, remove it from the machine. (3) Disengage the ram from its connecting shaft, and draw it out of the dough chamber. (4) Remove nut holding plunger in cylinder and remove the plunger. Since the pistons are usually not interchangeable, they should be plainly marked if the manufacturer has not provided an identification symbol. (5) Remove the excess dough from the parts with a hardwood or plastic scraper and finish cleaning with water and soda or detergent. After rinsing and drying, cover the parts with a thin film of divider oil. (6) Place the oil catch pan under the divider head to protect the conveyor belt and vacuum or blow out all flour from the divider proper, the conveyor belts, motor, drives, and switch boxes. (7) Clean the inside and the outside of the divider housing. (8) Replace the plungers, ram, and knife.

So far as sanitary problems are concerned, divider oil will not support insect, rodent, or microbial life. Dusting flour is subject to the usual infestation problems if not carefully watched. Dirty or hardened dough pieces, if allowed to accumulate, can end up in the finished loaves as readily detectable contaminants.

Serious accidents can be caused if the hazardous nature of the divider is not fully recognized. The American Standard Safety Code for Bakery Equipment[1] (Anon. 1947) lists the following desirable safety features for bakery equipment.

---

[1]This material is reproduced from the American Standard Safety Code for Bakery Equipment, Z50.1-1947, copyrighted by ASA, copies of which may be purchased from the United States of America Standards Institute, 10 East 40th St., New York, N.Y. 10016

Pinch and Shear Points.—All pinch points and shear points from rotating or reciprocating parts of the divider shall be enclosed or guarded, to protect the operator's hands and fingers from these hazards.

Front Guards.—Guards at the front of a divider shall be so arranged that the weight of dough can be adjusted without removing the guard.

Rear of Divider.—The back of the divider shall have a complete cover to enclose all of the moving parts, or each individual part shall be enclosed or guarded to remove the separate hazards. The rear cover shall be provided with a limit switch in order that the machine cannot operate when this cover is open. The guard on the back shall be hinged so that it cannot be completely removed and if a catch or brace is provided for holding the cover open, it shall be designed so that it will not release due to vibrations or minor bumping whereby the cover may drop on an employee.

Oil Holes in Knife.—The oil holes in the knife at the back of the divider shall be of such size that an employee's finger cannot go through the hole.

Knife Actuating Arm.—There shall be a saddle guard or other protective device on any elongate hole in the knife actuating arm at the back of the divider.

Shear Pin.—Dividers shall be equipped with mechanical overload release devices such as shear pins.

In addition to the above, the Code has a general discussion concerning the hazards of dividers which brings out the following points:

(a) In some dividers the division box goes up and down, causing pinch points.

(b) On another type of divider the cylinder division box revolves and if a man reaches in to grab a "double" he is subject to a shear hazard. A transparent shield is suggested across the front.

(c) At the start of a run the operator grabs the first piece of dough to weigh it. On some machines there is not sufficient clearance between the bottom of the divider and the primary conveyor belt.

(d) Rotating division boxes on some dividers are cylindrical, but with a segment cut off from one side. There is a shear point under the divider drum where this flat side rotates past the edge of the machine.

(e) The pocket adjustment on some dividers is a knurled round knob on the end of a reciprocating bar. There is a pinching hazard between the side of this knob and the side of the box.

(f) There is a shear hazard on some machines where the division box connecting rod end passes the side of the machine.

(g) There is a pinch point on some machines where the top of the division box passes the edge of the hopper.

(h) There is a hazard on some machines where the division box lever is pulled up past the bottom of the division box by the division box connecting rod.

(i) On the primary conveyor of some dividers where the conveyor belt goes over the pulley, there is an exposed pinch point where the belt makes contact with the pulley because the end of the pulley is exposed.

(j) Conveyor-belt connections should be checked for pinch points.

(k) At present certain dividers have relatively large oil holes which sometimes fill with dough and when the employee tries to push out the dough with his fingers there is a shear hazard with the frame below.

Interaction of Doughs and Divider

Anything which affects the dough density will change the weight of the scaled pieces. Since the dough continues to ferment in the hopper, with the gas production contributing to a lower density, a slight decrease in scale weight can be expected as each batch of dough is processed, with a rise as a new batch starts to flow into the compression chamber. If the batches are small enough and divider operation is rapid enough, the changes in piece weight will probably be within limits that can be tolerated. If the divider must be shut down for even a few minutes with dough in the hopper, a considerable error in weight must be expected. Frequent tests of the weight of dough pieces from each pocket should be made by the operator with the aid of an "over-and-under" scale placed adjacent to the conveyor.

Excessively bucky doughs may not fill the divider pockets completely, with resultant erratic scaling. Wide variations in piece weights may also be observed if the dough is full of large gas pockets. Some dividers have been equiped with compression pistons which have rods projecting from their faces so that large gas pockets in the dough will be punctured.

The divider has a pronounced effect on dough properties. The compression and cutting result in a considerable loss of gas, not only initially, but continuing through the cut and torn surfaces of the dough piece as it is transported to the rounder. Furthermore, the compression and cutting actions disorient the gluten fibrils, changing the dough qualities. A temperature increase is observed as the dough passes through the divider, and this affects the fermentation speed, among other things. The temperature change is due to contact with hot divider surfaces and to the mechanical work performed on the dough. The dough also picks up divider oil and flour during its passage through the machine, although, if adjustments are properly made, the amounts should not be great enough to cause a significant change in the dough properties.

Automatic check weighers are often installed to verify the weights of the dough pieces coming from the divider. They may follow the rounder in some bakeries. The dough ball is passed over a short belt attached to a weighing device. If the dough piece is within the preselected range, it is transferred to a conveyor leading to the overhead proofer. Out-of-standard pieces are diverted to a reject conveyor from which they may be returned to the divider or used in other ways. The weights are recorded in a computer which periodically compares the average to the target weight and signals when the average is out of tolerance. In the most sophisticated systems, a feedback loop allows the signal to adjust the divider so as to correct for the erroneous weights.

The FMC Bread Weight Controller, which was first offered around 1958, was an approach to closer weight control of dough pieces, especially for bread doughs (Fig. 16.14). The basic principle was the addition of small pieces of dough to the large chunks coming from the divider (which had been set to deliver pieces slightly on the light side) to make the required weight. Heavy and extremely light chunks were re-

Courtesy of FMC Packaging Machinery Div.
FIG. 16.14. THE FMC BREAD WEIGHT CONTROLLER.

turned to the divider or mixer by the checkweigher which was an integral part of the equipment. The following decisions could be made by the electronic computer after the basic dough piece was measured: (1) If the weight was correct within the limits of accuracy selected by the operator, the dough piece was passed without modification. (2) One small increment of dough was added to pieces which were slightly underweight. (3) A larger increment was added to dough pieces which were moderately underweight. (4) Two increments of dough were added to pieces considerably underweight. (5) Dough pieces which were excessively overweight or grossly underweight were rejected.

The divider was automatically adjusted by the feedback signal from the computer so that most dough pieces were underweight when they left the pocket. A push-button mechanism allowed the operator to override the adjuster when changing loaf sizes.

The increments of dough added to make up weight were formed in pockets located in intermittently revolving heads within a pressurized hopper (Fig. 16.15). The vacuum formed by pistons in each pocket combined with slight positive pressure in the hopper forced the dough

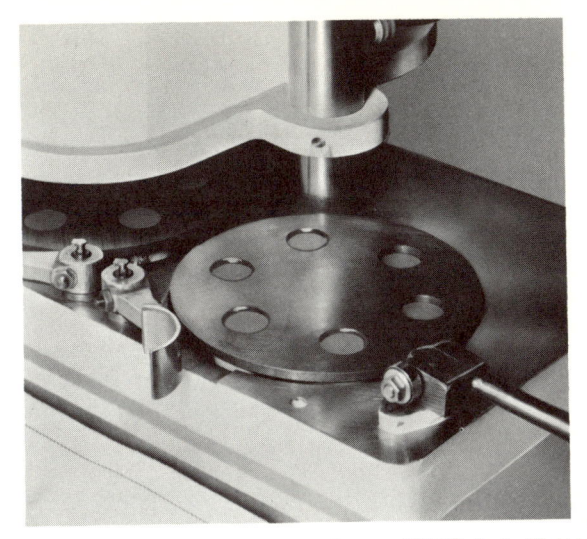

Fig. 16.15. The Increment Forming Devices and Flip Arms on the FMC Bread Weight Controller

Courtesy of FMC Packaging Machinery Div.

into the cavities. Two formers, one for large increments and the other for small increments, were used. When an increment was called for as a result of an underweight dough piece passing the electronic scale, the increment was brought into a position outside the hopper where a flipper arm could push it onto the main dough piece at the right time.

The hopper, with its locking cover to retain pressure, was charged at the beginning of the run with the first pieces from the divider, and replenished with rejected dough.

According to a test described in a company brochure, standard deviation of the loaf weight was reduced from 0.32 to 0.20 oz., and the average weight per loaf was reduced from 23.16 to 22.89 oz, a saving of 0.27 oz.

BIBLIOGRAPHY

Abbott, J. A. 1959. Weighing and mixing procedures. *In* Bakery Technology and Engineering, S. A. Matz (Editor). Avi Publishing Co., Westport, Conn.

Anon. 1947. American Standard Safety Code for Bakery Equipment. United States of America Standards Institute, New York.

Anon. 1956. Bread Baking. U.S. Dept. Army Tech. Manual *TM 10–410*.

Anon. 1963. Neptune meters. Neptune Meter Co., Long Island City, N.Y.

Anon. 1965. Conveyorized Weighers. Food Eng. 37, No. 12, 67–71.

Anon. 1968. Omega gravimetric dry materials feeders and weighers. BIF, Providence, R.I.

Fuller, W. S. 1970. Automatic weighing and dispensing of wet and dry sundry ingredients. Proc. Am. Soc. Bakery Engrs. *1970*, 145–151.

HAGEDORN, H. G. 1965. New practices in bulk handling of materials with special emphasis on instrumentation. Proc. Am. Soc. Bakery Engrs. *1965*, 148–152.

MILLEVILLE, H. P., and GELBER, P. 1964. Sanitary design of food processing equipment. Food Process. *25*, No. 10, 93–102.

ROTHFUS, R. R. 1968. Working concepts of fluid flow. V. Flow measurement. Instr. Control Systems *41*, No. 7, 105–108.

SANDERS, A. 1963. Accurate weights protect your profits. Bakers Rev. *126*, No. 4, 24–26.

SPANGLER, E. G. 1958. Storage and automatic dispensing of bulk lard and shortening. Proc. Am. Soc. Bakery Engrs. *1958*, 71–78.

TRAUTMAN, E. 1951. Dough development and its relation to divider, rounder, and intermediate proofing. Proc. Am. Soc. Bakery Engrs. *1951*, 50–53.

WILLIAMS, J. C., JR. 1955. Instrumental weighing and control in the baking industry. Baking Ind. *104*, No. 3, 62–65.

ZIEMBA, J. V. 1965. Conveyorized weighers. Food Eng. *37*, No. 12, 67–71.

CHAPTER 17

MIXERS AND MIXING

Mixing, in its most general form, can be defined as an operation by which two or more materials having some distinguishable characteristic are brought, through the application of external force, into closer relationship to one another, i.e., the average distance between particles of one material and particles of the other material becomes less. This result is generally achieved by causing random movement of two or more materials in the presence of each other so as to result in a more or less uniform distribution of the particles throughout the mass. Blending or mixing can be accomplished by many different types of equipment, but they all rely on one of the following types of action: (1) devices using blades, paddles, ribbons, etc. to push portions of the mix through other portions, (2) devices relying on the elevation and dropping of all or a portion of the mass so that the random rebounding of individual particles during the gravitational stage results in mixing, and (3) devices creating turbulent movement by injecting currents of gases or liquids.

There are many changes occurring during the mixing of doughs and batters which are not encompassed by the preceding definition. For example, gluten development is a separate phenomenon which happens to occur simultaneously with mixing when certain conditions are present. On the other hand, creaming and whipping fit the definition, since they involve the entrapment and reduction in size of bubbles of gas within a mass of other material.

According to Abbott (1960), mixing is the only bakery operation classifiable as a chemical engineering unit operation. It has been thoroughly studied in the simpler manifestations by many investigators. Based on these investigations, the relation of power input to mixer design and operating variables is fairly well understood, at least for the mixing of Newtonian fluids with simple equipment and other uncomplicated systems. Chemical Engineers' Handbook (*Perry et al.* 1963) is a basic reference on the subject.

As materials become more complex and the means of applying force becomes more sophisticated, the technologist finds himself increasingly dependent on art and on dubious extrapolations from meager amounts of data. Therefore, mixer function and the response of doughs and batters to design changes still cannot be discussed in a truly scientific or quantitative manner, and judgments must frequently be based on cursory observations and qualitative evaluations by individuals of doubtful expertise. Adaptation of these data to the particular circumstances existing when a specific dough is mixed in a specific piece of equipment must, unfortunately, be based on cut-and-try procedures.

MIXING

Theory of Mixing

When classified on the basis of the mixing action required, most bakery products fall into two categories: (1) extensible doughs, generally but not always yeast-leavened, including those for products such as bread, rolls, sweet doughs, saltines, pretzels, and puff pastry, and (2) flowable or friable mixtures such as cake batters, icings, streusels, most cookie doughs, and premixes of powdered or granular materials with shortening. The mixing of extensible doughs presents the more complex problem and is discussed in the following section.

As mentioned previously, the two most important functions accomplished by the dough mixer are the blending of ingredients and the development of the gluten. The hydration of the flour, or more correctly, of the gluten proteins, is an essential precursor of the development process. It is generally agreed that the hydration of the gluten proteins occurs rapidly and does not vary a great deal between flours, while dough development is relatively slow and requires the input of a considerable amount of ordered force. The mixing response of a flour is determined by the amount and quality of the gluten, to a large extent.

The kind of mixing action which appears to be the most effective in promoting gluten development is a repeated stretching and folding action. If the stretching and folding are always performed in the same direction, the mixing will be particularly efficient. Although no completely satisfactory explanation of the changes happening at the molecular level has been published, the chief result of the folding and stretching actions may be an orienting of many of the gluten molecules so that they become extended and lie side by side, rather than randomly coiled and interlaced in a brush-heap structure. When so positioned there would be ample opportunity for disulfide bonds and hydrogen bonds to form between adjacent protein molecules, leading to maximum strength of the gluten network. It can be postulated that the intermolecular bonds are constantly breaking and reforming under the conditions existing in a normal dough.

As the dough approaches the peak, it will start to enfold considerable amounts of air. As a result of the gas entrapment, density is markedly reduced just before the maximum power requirement. This phenomenon apparently marks a major change in the status of the gluten (Fortmann 1967). There are also measurable changes in plasticity, viscosity, adhesiveness, cohesiveness, elasticity, and extensibility throughout the mixing cycle.

The success of the mixing operation in forming a continuous gluten network which will have the maximum gas holding capacity has a large influence on the quality of the finished product. Well-developed doughs can result in loaves with high specific volumes, a soft, silky, and uniform grain and texture, and good keeping qualities. If the dough has not been mixed to its optimum state, it is difficult if not impossible to compensate for the deficiency by changes in subsequent processing conditions.

Some factors other than quality and amount of gluten tending to increase the mixing requirements are: (1) short fermentation of sponges, (2) high salt level, (3) fast acting oxidizers, and (4) low dough temperature. Factors decreasing the mixing requirements are: (1) long fermentation of sponges, (2) higher dough temperatures, (3) proteolytic enzymes, (4) reducing substances, (5) alcohol, and (6) inactive yeast.

Practice of Mixing

Mixing Bread and roll doughs.—The two principal plans for mixing bread and roll doughs are the straight dough process and the sponge process. With the straight dough process, all of the ingredients are mixed together at one time and the complete dough is fermented. Only a part of the total ingredients is bulk fermented in the sponge method, and the fermentation step is followed by adding and mixing the remaining ingredients. Advantages of the sponge method are tolerance, flexibility, and better opportunity to achieve optimal mixing. Disadvantages are additional scaling steps, repeated handling of the dough, and the necessity for two mixing stages.

There are other mixing procedures which rely on intensive mechanical working of the dough or chemical modification of it to substitute for the desirable changes which occur during bulk fermentation. These "no punch", "no time", or "mechanical development" processes will be discussed in a subsequent section.

The flexibility of the sponge procedure, which has been one of the principal reasons leading to its predominance over a long period of time in spite of the serious disadvantages inherent in the repeated handling of the same batch, is due to the adjustments in time, temperature, and ingredients which are possible at the dough stage. It is also generally possible to obtain finer and more uniform grain in sponge bread.

Marked degassing of the sponge takes place as it is remixed. The existing gas cells, which are large and not uniform in size, are repeatedly subdivided as the dough is stretched, folded, and compressed. It is this action which furnishes the basic structure of the dough in later stages. The structure can be destroyed by subsequent processing, or it can fail to develop as a result of defects in the physical properties of the dough, but failure to establish a proper vesicular structure at this stage cannot be compensated by any form of treatment in the subsequent processing, and the finished loaf will not have a fine grain and silky crumb.

During mixing the dough undergoes three more or less distinct phases of development. The first phase, from the beginning of the mixing until the so-called cleanup, consists primarily of a blending together of the various ingredients. The soluble materials are brought into solution, the gluten hydrates, the yeast and the fatty ingredients are thoroughly dispersed, and some air is occluded. At the end of the blending stage, sometimes called the "pickup" stage, the dough will have little cohesiveness and elasticity and will consist of large wet pieces which tend to stick to the mixer parts.

With the continuation of mixing, the dough gradually begins to attain elastic properties, the free water disappears, and the dough forms a single mass which does not adhere strongly to the mixer bowl. This is the "cleanup" stage.

Further mixing leads to development of the dough. A peak of extensibility is reached and the dough can be stretched into thin films which show a fibrous structure with transmitted light. The dough feels soft and relatively dry. It obviously contains considerable gas and is silky in appearance. When torn, it tends to show strands. The length of time the dough remains in good condition during continued mixing, after development has been completed, is called mixing tolerance and is primarily a function of protein quality, although other dough constituents can also have a significant influence.

If mixing is continued beyond the peak, gradual breakdown is observed. Apparent wetness is again noticed and the dough becomes sticky. Extensibility is lessened and stringiness of the stretched dough can be seen.

Mixing stage is usually judged by the operator using auditory, visual, and tactile clues such as the slapping sounds of the dough as it is thrown around the mixer bowl, the appearance of the dough as it is stretched, and the wetness and elasticity of the dough.

Mechanical development.—The elimination of the bulk fermentation or sponge stage would be highly beneficial in terms of processing efficiency, since it would drastically reduce labor and equipment needs, as well as the requirement for air-conditioned space. It also would probably reduce the percentage of ingredients lost through fermentation. Satisfactory flavors in the finished loaf can evidently be obtained in the absence of bulk fermentation if the ingredients are properly adjusted (primarily by an increase in the proportion of yeast) and the conditions of intermediate proofing and pan-proofing are appropriate. Doughs are more difficult to machine and the texture of the bread is not satisfactory, however, unless special techniques are used to mature the dough. Several approaches to this problem have been made. With the exception of the continuous dough systems, to be described in a later chapter, the most widely used scheme in mass production bakeries is probably the "mechanical development" method now quite popular in England. In essence, mechanical development is a dough modification or ripening process which depends for its success upon high inputs of energy during the mixing stage.

According to Hall (1965), the following points are essential to the process: (1) a specially designed high speed mixer-developer, (2) a minimum fat content of 0.7%, flour weight basis, (3) chemical oxidizing agents, (4) a relatively large amount of work must be expended on the dough in a short period of time, (5) about 3–4% extra water (FWB) must be added to the dough, and (6) extra yeast is necessary to keep the proof time constant.

When these factors are properly applied, bread resembling the conventional English product can be obtained without a bulk fermentation step. English bread normally has a specific volume of about 6 cu in. per oz, as compared to a typical 10–11 cu in. per oz in the United States and is tougher and firmer than the U.S. product.

By this technique, process times as short as 5 min from metering of ingredients to dividing are said to have been achieved in some instances (Hall 1965). Total mixing and development times of less than 5 min are said to be customary. The method demands that a large amount of work be expended on the dough in a short period of time. The energy needed is at least 6–8 times greater than the amount required for conventional mixing. Commercial success of mechanical dough development awaited the availability of automatic batch mixers which were capable of completing the charging and mixing cycles within about 6 min. The mixers currently in use have relatively small capacities to keep within reasonable limits the structural strength and motor size needed for the high torques which are encountered.

The mixers designed for mechanical development do not resemble the horizontal mixers used for nearly all batch processing in U.S. bakeries. Hall (1965) describes three types of mixer-developers. One has a portable shallow bowl into which the ingredients are scaled before it is pushed beneath a mixing head where it engages with gears for rotating the bowl while the head is lowered into the ingredients. Another type produces a ring of dough about 3 ft in diameter by a kind of radial cutting action. The third type allows for mixing under vacuum conditions. A separate vessel receives and holds the charge of ingredients until it can be discharged into a cylindrical mixing chamber. A revolving base plate causes the ingredients to travel through a vortex so that the dough reaches the work area at the periphery of the mixing plate. The mixer circuits incorporate a meter which measures the consumption of electrical energy and switches the mixer off after the preset number of watt-hours.

Chemical oxidizers are used at higher levels than in conventional breadmaking, and the faster-acting compounds are preferred. The oxidizing agents most used in England are ascorbic acid and potassium bromate at levels of 35–75 ppm, and 15–20 ppm, respectively.

Premixing

Premixing is an operation which can contribute significant benefits under certain conditions. By premix is meant a blend of certain ingredients which must be combined with other components to yield a complete dough or batter. The usual purpose of premixing is to ensure uniform distribution of ingredients which are to be added in very small amounts. Vitamin enrichment tablets, yeast foods, and baking powders are examples of proprietary premixes frequently seen in bakeries.

Premixing is particularly advantageous when fixed proportions of some of the ingredients in formulas are used repeatedly within a relatively short time period, such as a day. Under these circumstances, many weighing steps can be eliminated. For example, suppose it is necessary every working day to make up 38 batches of dough, of which 6 mixes each contain 4 lb of salt, 6 lb of soda, 8 lb of leavening acid, and 2 lb of dry flavor; 12 mixes each contain 8 lb of salt, 12 lb of soda, 16 lb of leavening acid, and 4 lb of dry flavor; and 20 mixes each contain 2 lb of salt, 3 lb of soda, 4 lb of acid, and 1 lb of flavor. It would seem to be advantageous to prepare a premix composed of 20% salt, 40% leavening acid, 30% soda, and 10% flavor. This would reduce weighing operations by 110 per day, assuming only one batch of premix was made each day, and would probably lead to increased uniformity in the finished mix. Storage for the premix would be a disadvantage the importance of which would have to be evaluated for each individual case.

An essential requirement for premixes is that the ingredients do not interact or undergo accelerated deterioration when in contact with each other. In the example given above, the premix would not have been feasible if the flavor had been an aqueous solution, for the soda and the leavening acid would react prematurely under these conditions. On the other hand, aqueous solutions of some ingredients might be a very satisfactory form of premix. Salt, some oxidizers and preservatives, and ammonium bicarbonate are frequently added as aqueous premixes.

Mixing of Cracker and Cookie Doughs

Kramer (1953) classified mixing methods for wire-cut cookie doughs into three categories: (1) the multistage or creaming method in which several steps are used, with different ingredients or sets of ingredients added at intervals during the procedure; (2) the simplified single-stage, in which all, or nearly all, of the ingredients are added at one time even though different combinations of speeds and times are used; and (3) the continuous, in which there is no variation in speed or distinct separation into phases in the mixing operation. Continuous equipment is being used for true batters such as vanilla wafers and has the advantage of delivering a uniform mixture at all times. The classification is valid for other cookie types as well.

There are few guidelines applicable to development of mixing procedures for new products. Generally, the first approach is to draw up a proposed mixing method based on a procedure which has been found to be satisfactory for a somewhat similar product, and then make such changes as observations indicate are necessary. The method of mixing is more important for wire-cut doughs than for cutting machine or rotary doughs. For the former type, creaming is widely used.

Creaming usually requires the initial introduction into the mixer of shortening, and sometimes the syrups, then the addition of the granulated sugar and some or all of the other dry ingredients. Mixing is continued at a slow or medium speed until the components are thoroughly blended together and the mixture has taken up air in the form of minute bubbles. Excessive speed or time in the absence of refrigeration will tend to break down the cream as the fat liquifies, although use of high speeds for short periods of time may be beneficial. In some procedures, the cream is emulsified or broken down by adding the water before the flour is dropped in. Good creaming is impossible if ingredients are too hot or too cold. For optimum creaming, shortening should be at a temperature causing it to be firm but not hard.

The beneficial effects of creaming, as opposed to other mixing schemes, lie in the fat-coating effect which delays solubilization and hydration of sugar and flour, and in the incorporation of small air bubbles which assist in leavening and establishing the structure of the finished cookie.

For drop-type cookies, a creaming very much like that for layer cake batters is used. Regular soft cookies can be mixed by a creaming procedure although a one-stage process is also reasonably satisfactory. One of the greatest dangers is overmixing; the gluten should not be allowed to develop. Slow speed mixing is preferred, 25–35 rpm. The semibatter wire-cut cookies can be creamed for about 5 min before the eggs and water are incorporated, then the flour and leaveners are added. The doughs should come out at 70°F ± 2°. Some of the factors affecting length of mixing are: strength of the flour, type of product, machinability of dough, temperature of dough, speed of the mixer, and size of the batch (Velzen 1963).

Ingredients intended to be present in the finished cookie as visible pieces, such as nuts, raisins, and chocolate bits, should be added at the end of the mixing cycle and blended at slow speed for the minimum time consistent with adequate distribution throughout the dough.

The single-stage technique provides greater mixing tolerance for most cookie doughs. Less skill is required on the part of mixing personnel. At lower total mixing times, there is more opportunity for spots of unincorporated ingredients to show up in cookies made from creamed doughs. Experience seems to indicate that the single-stage procedure is satisfactory for a wide variety of formulas. Short breads can be mixed in a single-stage, but unduly prolonged or vigorous mixing may cause the fat to work out. Wire-cut cookies made from single-stage processes will, in general, exhibit a coarser texture and rougher surface than similar formulations made by creaming.

Cracker sponges are mixed just long enough to wet the flour. Flour, yeast, water, and sometimes malt and shortening make up the sponge. Overmixing tends to develop the gluten and cause problems during fermentation. In some plants, mixing is stopped before complete wetting of the flour occurs, but this is probably undesirable from the standpoint of obtaining a uniform fermentation.

Cracker doughs made with strong flour should be mixed a few minutes at high speed to incorporate ingredients, but full development of the gluten in this stage will cause difficulties in machining. If the doughs are made up with relatively weak flours, full advantage can be taken of the limited gluten extensibility by developing the flour completely in the dough stage. This technique will tend to improve gas retention and therefore, oven spring.

MIXERS

Types of Mixers

There are several possible methods for classifying mixers. The classification given here is useful in analyzing the different types of bakery mixers for their value for dough mixing: (A) Horizontal—fixed bowl and tilting bowl: (1) high speed; (2) low speed. (B) Vertical: (1) planetary action; (2) fixed spindle. (C) Reciprocating agitator (Artofex type). (D) Continuous: (1) agitator-in-tube; (2) rotor and stator heads.

For use in blending premixes or preparing adjuncts, a considerably wider choice is available. Ribbon blenders, twin-cone, or V-shell mixers are suitable for preparing premixes of dry ingredients. A large number of different designs for liquid blending are available, most of them being based on the propeller-in-tank principle. For mixing air in batters, devices such as the Whizzolator (continuous) and the Morton pressure whisks (batch) can be used.

Horizontal Mixers.—This type of equipment (Fig. 17.1 and 17.2) can be used for a wide variety of mixtures ranging in consistency from thin batters to extremely tough or dry doughs. They are almost essential when gluten development is desired since vertical mixers are too inefficient and slow in this operation and spindle mixers do not have the right kind of action. Six or more American manufacturers construct

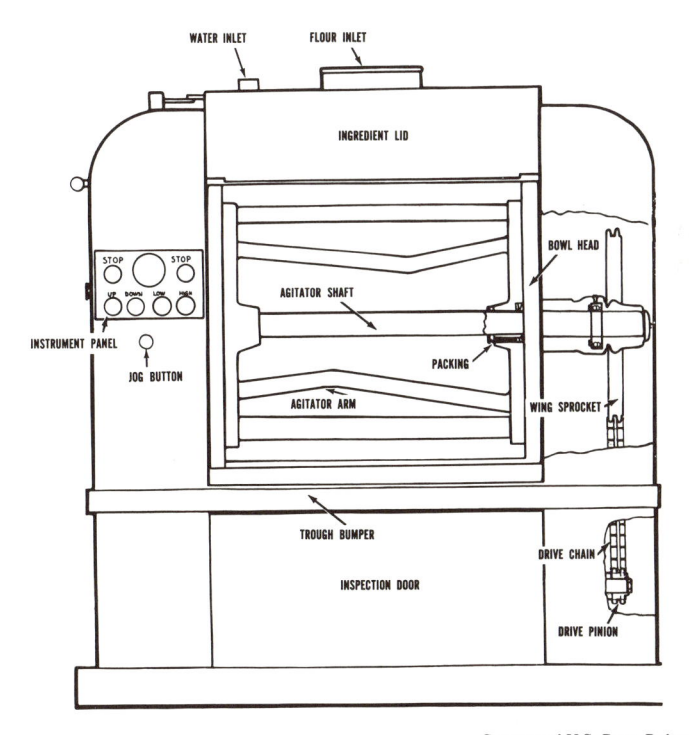

Courtesy of U.S. Dept. Defense
FIG. 17.1. FRONT VIEW DIAGRAM OF HORIZONTAL DOUGH MIXER.

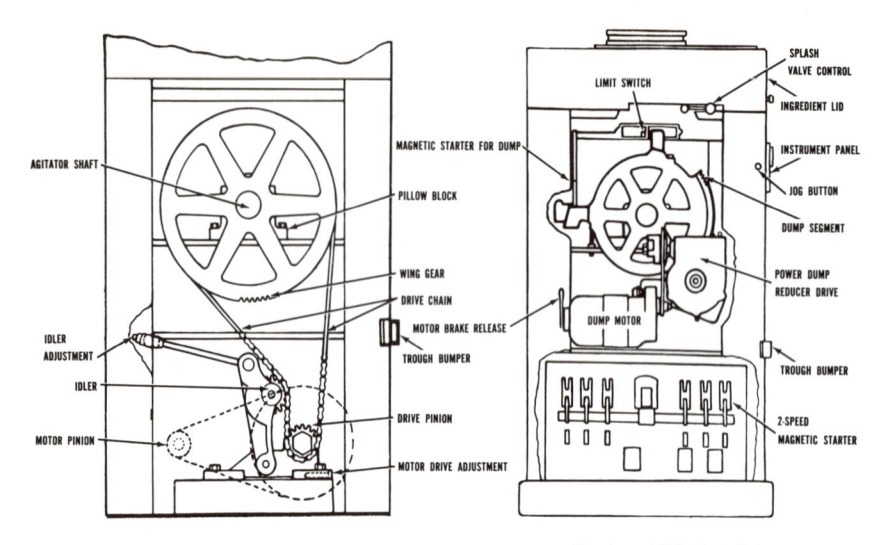

Courtesy of U.S. Dept. Defense

FIG. 17.2. SIDE VIEWS OF HORIZONTAL DOUGH MIXER.

TABLE 17.1
TYPICAL SPECIFICATIONS FOR HORIZONTAL DOUGH MIXERS

Capacities					
Final doughs (max lb)	800	1000	1300	1600	2000
Sponges (max lb)	480	600	780	960	1200
All doughs (min lb)	400	500	650	800	1000
Usable bowl volume (cu ft)	25.5	30.7	38.6	47.2	59.6
Power units					
Agitator (hp)	15/30	15/30	20/40	25/50	38/75
Door (hp)	0.75	1.0	1.0	1.5	1.5
Compressor (hp)	10.0	20.0	20.0	20.0	25.0

horizontal mixers suitable for mixing the usual types of bakery products. All of this equipment has in common a horizontal mixing bowl, U-shaped in cross section, mounted in a heavy rigid frame enclosing the drive motor and transmission. Capacities from 200 to 2000 lb, based on flour weight, can be obtained, although the larger sizes (1800 and 2000 lb) are constructed only on special order (Table 17.1).

There are two methods used for discharging dough. In some models, the bowl can be tilted so that the top is brought to a forward facing position. In the others, the front of the bowl consists of a tightly fitting door which can be raised and lowered independently of the other immobile section of the bowl. Figure 17.3 shows large mixers of both types. A separate, low-horsepower motor is used to activate the opening mechanism. Most bowls are either stainless-clad mild steel or solid stainless steel though mild steel surfaces have been used.

MIXERS AND MIXING 317

Mixer bowls are usually provided with jackets in which a refrigerant can be circulated (Fig. 17.4). Some jacekts are equipped to utilize direct expansion of a refrigerant such as ammonia or Freon for cooling, while others make use of a cooling liquid such as propylene glycol, brine, or water. Chilled water may not provide enough cooling capacity for

Courtesy of Baker Perkins, Inc.
FIG. 17.3. STATIONARY BOWL MIXERS (LEFT) AND ROTATING BOWL MIXER (RIGHT).

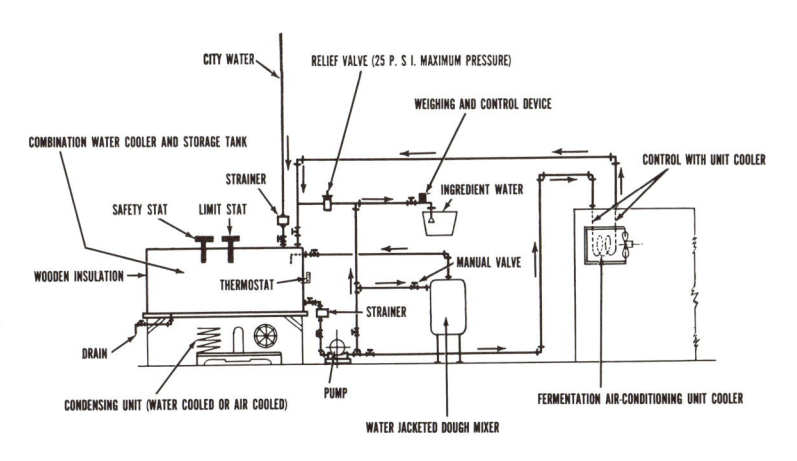

Courtesy of U.S. Dept. Defense
FIG. 17.4. CHILLED WATER SYSTEM FOR MIXER AND AUXILIARY EQUIPMENT.

all purposes, but use of this refrigerant does ensure against ice formation on the inside of the jacket, either from ingredient water or condensate. Occasionally, there are encountered situations in which it is desired to warm the dough or batter without overmixing it. Direct expansion jackets are not suited for this application, but jackets using liquid coolant can be modified rather easily to circulate hot water as well as refrigerant. The usual practice is to jacket the mixer shells (front, back, and bottom) only, but it is possible to have the trough ends jacketed also. The latter arrangement is not frequently used in the baking industry.

Agitators take a variety of forms. In the high speed mixers designed for developing gluten, a set of 2, 3, or 4 cylindrical bars (parallel to the front of the mixer) may be mounted on spiders which are connected to the axles at the point where they enter the jacket (Fig. 17.5). These bars may be attached by bearings allowing them to rotate, or they may be rigidly affixed. The limited clearance of the jacket wall by the agitator bars causes the dough mass to be repeatedly stretched and

Courtesy of American Machine & Foundry Co.

FIG. 17.5. HIGH SPEED HORIZONTAL DOUGH MIXER SHOWING ARRANGEMENT OF AGITATOR ARMS.

kneaded in a single direction with the result that gluten fibers tend to become oriented and the dough develops. In some cases, stationary bars or baffles are affixed to the jacket to intensify the mixing or developing action. The power train in these machines is equipped for 2-speed rotation, generally 35 and 70 rpm, with ranges of 30–60 to 40–80.

Slow-speed horizontal mixers employ agitators of various forms. They may be equipped with 1 or 2 sets of axles. The configuration of the mixer arm as well as the speed affects the action. Double-armed mixers of the type shown in Fig. 17.6 were formerly called creamers because they were used specifically for batters. They are now used for stiffer doughs, although these may require heavier drives and motors. Air is incorporated by agitator arms of this conformation, as distinct from the action of the figure-eight type arms (see Fig. 17.7). The latter type reduces gluten development and heat buildup. The range of speeds in commercial mixers of this type will be from about 14 to 60 rpm, with an average of about 25 rpm.

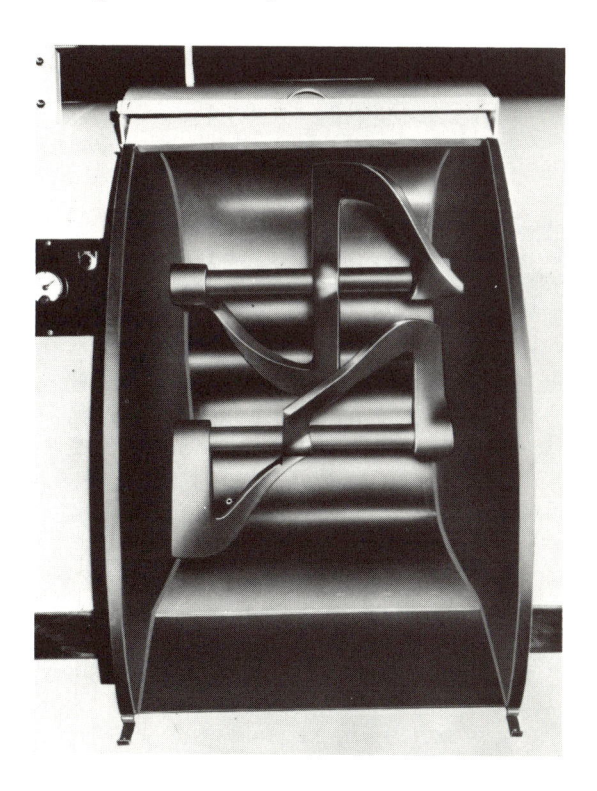

Courtesy of Peerless Mixer Co.

FIG. 17.6. DOUBLE-ARM MIXER.

320   BAKERY TECHNOLOGY AND ENGINEERING

Courtesy of Peerless Mixer Co.
FIG. 17.7   "FIGURE EIGHT" AGITATOR CONFIGURATION.

Vertical Mixers.—A unifying feature of vertical mixers is the use of movable bowls or troughs. The other characteristics may be quite diverse; that is, there may be one or more beater shafts, the beater shafts may move in a planetary design or remain stationary, and the designs of the agitators can be varied over a wide range. The main types of interest to the baker are the planetary mixers capable of mixing batters and some doughs but most often used for adjuncts such as icings, and the spindle mixer used in the cookie and cracker industry primarily for mixing saltine and graham cracker doughs.

The planetary mixers (see Fig. 17.8) are made in bowl sizes of 20, 40, 60, 80, 120, 140, 160, and 340 qt capacity (Table 17.2). The agitator movement is called planetary because it not only revolves around its own vertical axis at relatively high speed, but the axis also moves in circles as it is rotated around the bowl. These compound motions ensure that all of the mixer bowl volume receives beater action. Usually, a small part of the bowl at the bottom center is raised so that this blind spot does not become a collecting point for unmixed material.

Some mixers have a geared transmission to provide a choice of 3 or 4 speeds while others have variable speed drives permitting the selection of any desired speed within the limits of the equipment. The bowl is raised or lowered by an auxiliary motor in the larger units.

Courtesy of American Machine and Foundry Co.
FIG. 17.8. A 160-QUART PLANETARY MIXER.

TABLE 17.2
TYPICAL SPECIFICATIONS FOR PLANETARY MIXERS

	Model A	Model B	Model C
Bowl capacities (gal)	10; 20; 30	10; 20; 40	85
Bowl capacities (cu ft)	1.3; 2.7; 4.0	1.3; 2.7; 5.3	11.3
Mixing speed range (rpm)	70 to 370	40 to 320	45 to 325
Agitator motor (hp)	2	5	10
Lift motor (hp)	0.25	0.33	2

A fairly large selection of agitator types is available, making this type of mixer the most versatile of all in this respect. The dough hook is a single curved arm which provides the stretching, kneading action necessary for developing gluten with a minimum of tearing. The wirewhip is an assembly of wires, wide at the top and coming to a point at the bot-

322   BAKERY TECHNOLOGY AND ENGINEERING

TABLE 17.3
TYPICAL SPECIFICATIONS OF KNEADING-TYPE MIXERS

	Model					
	A	B	C	D	E	F
Rating (in barrels)	0.75	1.0	1.25	1.5	1.75	2.0
Capacity (lb) (FWB)	176	265	385	441	551	661
Capacity (gal)	46	64	78	102	116	130
Agitator motor (hp)	1.5	2.5	2.5	3.0	3.0	4.0

Courtesy of Simon-Vicars

FIG. 17.9. A SPINDLE MIXER.

tom. The design is intended to give the maximum air incorporation and bubble dividing action. Regular batter beaters have 2 or 4 wings shaped to fit the inside of the bowl. They may be cast or formed of bars and a frame. Sometimes a plastic or rubber scrapper is fitted into the edge of the beater to wipe batter from the inside of the bowl.

Bowls may be fitted with baffles to restrict the swirling motion of very thin batters. Bowl covers are available to cut down on splashing or dusting.

Spindle mixers (Fig. 17.9) are most often used for cracker doughs, both soda and graham types. They can be used for cookie doughs, but have few advantages for these purposes. Their principal advantage for saltine doughs lies in their adaptation to mixing in the special mobile trough used for fermenting sponges. Because of this feature, the sponges and doughs do not have to be transferred in and out of the mixer and trough between the various stages. The troughs, which can be regarded as a part of the mixer, are of 5–6 barrel capacity and have flat bottoms and rounded ends conforming to the arc made by the blades. They are proportioned so that the blades on the mixing spindles traverse nearly the whole volume of the trough. The action imparted by the blades is a tearing, cutting, and churning action which is not conducive to dough development. A typical speed was 18 rpm in the old-style mixers and the speed was not usually adjustable. Newer equipment includes variable speed drives.

The spindles can be raised to allow the trough, which is fitted with casters, to be rolled into place under them. The trough is locked into place, the spindles lowered, and mixing started. A mixing time of about 2–4 min has been recommended for cracker sponges and 4–6 min for the doughs when the blades are rotating at 18 rpm. For graham cracker doughs, considerably longer times are required unless the mixer has a variable speed transmission allowing the use of higher revolutions per minute.

Since the mixer blades are designed to give a cutting action rather than a kneading or stretching action, it is possible to get prolonged and more or less intensive mixing action without the toughening effect on crackers which might result from the formation of an extensible dough.

Modern versions of spindle mixers have automatic timers and the variable speed provision mentioned previously. Raising and lowering of the spindle is also governed by limit switches. Equipment is available for dumping the trough contents directly into hoppers of processing equipment (Fig. 17.10).

Reciprocating Agitator Mixers.—In these mixers, a pair of agitator arms travels through intersecting elliptical paths in a shallow, slowly-revolving bowl. Because of the relatively slow rate of energy input, temperatures can be held near that of the room without the use of bowl jackets. These mixers are useful in mixing temperature-sensitive doughs when an intensive blending action is not required. Breakdown of adjuncts such as nuts and raisins is probably less in this mixer than in any other type, for equivalent mixing times. It has been used for pie doughs, where it is desired to retain discrete shortening lumps and it should have value for making blitz-method puff pastry. Dough output per unit time is relatively small as compared to horizontal mixers.

POWER REQUIREMENTS FOR DOUGH MIXING

During the mixing operation, the power requirement increases gradually until it reaches a peak after which it declines as the dough starts to

Courtesy of Thomas L. Green Co.
FIG. 17.10. DOUGH TROUGH OF SPINDLE MIXER IN DUMPING POSITION ON PROCESSING LINE.

break down. The power requirement is affected by mixer load, ingredients, temperature, and mixer efficiency. In a given mixer operating on a given weight of dough, the flour strength and amount of water are probably the most important factors affecting power consumption. Addition of salt causes an increase in power demand and the time required to reach the peak. For this reason, the procedure of delayed salt addition was developed. By developing the dough nearly to the optimum before the salt is added, overall mixing time and power requirement can be reduced considerably.

There have been many attempts to adapt recording wattmeters or other power-measuring instruments which would show objectively the dough development in the mixer, as replacements for the "art" of judging the status of the batch by the sounds the dough makes while moving around inside the mixer or by its appearance or "feel." None of the instruments has become very popular, perhaps because it has been difficult to equate the measurements with dough condition, especially if several different kinds of dough are being mixed. The problem is much simpler if all of the doughs are of the same type. One of the most satisfactory devices is the Mixatron (Whittle 1963) which measures and records dough consistency during the mixing cycle. Extraneous measurement of power consumption by the mixer motor is filtered out and only those electrical characteristics directly related to the dough consistency are measured. Results are presented as a graph of consistency versus time, and proper mixing time is supposed to be indicated by the peak in the graph. The shape of the ascending curve is related to absorption characteristics. Errors in ingredient addition can sometimes be detected by examination of the curves.

TEMPERATURE AND MIXING

One undesirable result of the intense shearing action of high speed mixers, is the generation of heat in the dough. Most of the work done by the mixer can be shown to end up as sensible heat, and if this heat is not removed during mixing, many doughs would leave the mixer at temperatures in excess of 100°F. At these elevated temperatures the dough would not have the physical properties to handle satisfactorily in conventional makeup equipment and the fermentation rate would be excessive. To keep the temperature within workable limits, it is necessary to cool the dough in high-speed horizontal mixers.

There are several methods of reducing dough temperatures. Refrigerated jackets are common on horizontal mixers. The mixer bowls are double-walled for the circulation of chilled water, propylene glycol, or brine in some designs and for direct expansion of refrigerants such as ammonia or Freon in others. The direct expansion units seem to be more popular and are available in sizes up to 40 hp for the largest mixers. Such equipment is very helpful for maintaining dough temperatures within the desired ranges. The problems of freezing of ingredient water on the jacket or nonuniformity of temperatures within the dough mass, which are sometimes troublesome when direct expansion jackets are used, can be alleviated or eliminated by careful control of the temperature gradient.

Prechilling of flour is good in principle but difficult to achieve if the flour comes from a bulk handling system. Bulk flour can be chilled in a jacketed mixer before the other ingredients are added, but this expedient is rarely practicable. Sugar solutions can be chilled before adding to the mixer. This is a satisfactory means of holding dough temperatures down if substantial amounts of sucrose or invert syrups are part of the batch and a suitable means for refrigerating them is available. Chilling is not suitable for corn syrup because the resultant increase in viscosity makes the syrup virtually impossible to handle. Sacked sugar and cubes or drums of shortening can be chilled before use, if ingredients in this form are available. Chilled ingredient water reduces temperature with few disadvantages if there is enough water in the formula to provide the necessary reduction. Ingredient water-chillers using vapor compression refrigeration equipment can be obtained from mixer manufacturers.

Temperatures affect the response of cookie doughs to machining, as well as the spread, texture, and surface appearance of the finished piece. For best results, the temperature should be below the upper limit of the plastic range of the shortening, and preferably between 68° and 75°F, or even lower if the shortening content is high. It is known, however, that under proper conditions satisfactory products can be made from batter-type doughs having temperatures of 62°–80°F, and from regular wire-cut doughs at the extreme temperatures of 65° and 80°F.

Most wire-cut cookie doughs should come from the mixer in the range of 70°–80°F or slightly less for best results. Higher temperatures can produce sticky, fast-working doughs which are difficult to deposit uniformly and which cause fluctuations in scaling weights. Wire-cut cookies seem to be more susceptible to temperature changes than are other types and the softer doughs are generally more sensitive than the stiffer ones. Kramer (1953) ran vanilla wafer batters, using both multiple-stage creaming and single-stage mixing procedures, varying temperatures from 50° to 80°F, and found yield to be definitely related to batter temperatures, increasing in linear fashion as temperature is increased. He indicated 65°F was a good temperature for this batter.

BIBLIOGRAPHY

ABBOTT, J. A. 1953. Continuous mixing. Food Eng. 25, No. 8, 64–65, 134.
ABBOTT, J. A. 1960. Weighing and mixing procedures. In Bakery Technology and Engineering, S. A. Matz (Editor). Avi Publishing Co., Westport, Conn.
ANON. 1937. Mixing—a unit operation seldom discussed but widely used. Food Ind. 8, No. 2, 109–116.
ANON. 1963. Batching and Mixing. Food Eng. 35, No. 6, 75-90.
AXFORD, D. W. E., and ELTON, G. A. H. 1960. The mechanical development of bread doughs. Chem. Ind. (London) 1960, 1257–1258.
BUSHUK, W., TSEN, C. C., and HLYNKA, I. 1968. The function of mixing in breadmaking. Baker's Dig. 42, No. 4, 36, 38–40.
CONDO, M. S. 1970. Principles of mechanical dough mixing. Proc. Am. Soc. Bakery Engrs. 1970, 46–52.
COPPOCK, J. B. M. 1969. Accelerated mechanical dough development. Proc. Am. Soc. Bakery Engrs. 1969, 79–90.
DEMPSTER, C. J., and HLYNKA, I. 1958. Some effects of the mixing process on the physical properties of dough. Cereal Chem. 35, 483–488.
FLICK, H. 1964. Fundamentals of cookie production, including soft type cookies. Proc. Am. Soc. Bakery Engrs. 1964, 286–293.
FORTMANN, K. 1967. Theory of mixing. Proc. Am. Soc. Bakery Engrs. 1967, 64–69.
HALL, C. H. 1965. Accelerating batch process bread production. Proc. Am Soc. Bakery Engrs. 1965, 51–57.
HLYNKA, I. 1964. Some experiments on the development of a continuous system in heavy batters or thin doughs. Cereal Chem. 41, 243–251.

INGLETON, J. F. 1966. Dry powder mixing in confectionery. Confectionery Production *32*, 602–603, 624.
KIRK, D. J. 1963. Water in the dough. Bakers Weekly *197*, No. 11, 80–82.
KOVAC, G. M., and ZIEMBA, J. V. 1964. Solids blending. II. Food Engr. *36*, No. 6, 69–72.
KRAMER, B. R. 1953. Cookie doughs: new approaches to the mixing operation. Proc. Am. Soc. Bakery Engrs. *1953*, 259–265.
LARSEN, R. A. 1964. Hydration as a factor in bread flour quality. Cereal Chem. *41*, 181–187.
LUDWIG, J. B. 1965. Liquid mixers, agitators—how to select them. Food Eng. *36*, No. 6, 54–58.
MCCARTHY, F. W. 1949. Modern food mixing. Food Ind. *21*, 1577–1586.
PAULES, C. E. 1964. Jacketed dough mixer. U.S. Pat. 3,126,054. Mar. 24.
PARKER, H. B. 1960. Continuous bread making processes. *In* Bakery Technology and Engineering, S. A. Matz (Editor). Avi Publishing Co., Westport, Conn.
PERRY, R. H., CHILTON, C. H., and KIRKPATRICK, S. D. 1963. Chemical Engineers' Handbook, 4th Editon. McGraw-Hill Book Co., New York.
SMITH, D. E., and MULLE, J. D. 1964. Studies on short and long mixing flours. II. Relationship between solubility and electrophonetic composition of flour proteins and mixing properties. Presented at 49th Ann. Meeting Am. Assoc. Cereal Chemists, Toronto, Canada, Apr. 27–30, 1964.
VALENTYNE, P. H. 1959. Practical aspects of heat balance in dough mixing. Bakers' Dig. *33*, No. 1, 40–44.
VELZEN, B. H. 1963. Production of wire-cut cookies. Proc. Am. Soc. Bakery Engrs. *1963*, 243–250.
WHITTLE, O. W. 1963. The Mixatron—more uniform doughs through controlled development. Baker's Dig. *37*, No. 2, 78–81.

CHAPTER 18

MAKEUP EQUIPMENT

After the dough pieces leave the divider, they are processed by a series of devices rather loosely classified as makeup equipment. In the manufacture of pan bread, this category is comprised of the rounder, the intermediate proofer, and the molder. The divider, which has previously been discussed in the chapter, "Weighing and Measuring Equipment," is often considered to be makeup equipment. Except for the intermediate proofer, these devices have the common function of changing the size or shape of the dough piece. Together they form an integrated group (Fig. 18.1) and must be discussed together for maximum clarity. Problems involved in operating and maintaining the various machines are similar, and they must operate in unison and at the same rate for maximum efficiency. Furthermore, the dough is at approximately the same state of chemical and physical development throughout the processing in the makeup equipment.

Although the intermediate proofer is discussed in this chapter, it is certainly not "makeup" equipment in the usual sense, because it does not change the shape of the dough piece. It is included here because it is a necessary connecting link between the other parts of the complex, and consideration of the processing sequence would be more difficult and less understandable if a description of the intermediate proofer were not included.

The subject of dough forming and shaping is so complex that it was mandatory to adopt some plan for limiting the contents of this chapter. The largest amount of space has been devoted to bread-making equipment. Special forming equipment for some other bakery products will also be discussed, but not in the same detail used for bread makeup machines. It is believed that this limitation is justified not only by considerations of available space but also by the relatively greater importance of bread-making devices.

Discussions will be limited to equipment suitable for wholesale or large retail bakeries. There are several good books on retail shop practices and procedures available to technologists who are interested in that aspect of the bakery arts, and there would be little justification for duplicating such coverage in the present volume. On the other hand,

MAKEUP EQUIPMENT 329

Courtesy Baker Perkins, Inc.
FIG. 18.1. THE DIVIDER (LEFT), ROUNDER (CENTER), AND INTERMEDIATE PROOFER (RIGHT) ILLUSTRATING THE USUAL POSITIONING.

the lack of organized discussions of mass production equipment dictates the fullest possible use of the available space for consideration of this type of machinery.

Current procedures and machinery are emphasized but some historical material is included when it is considered necessary for a better understanding of the present state of the art. Trends and the reason for trends in equipment design are discussed in relation to the past.

Examples are chiefly confined to U.S. practices. It is recognized that these are not the most advanced in every case, but they are likely to be the most important to the reader. Where important and instructive deviations from U.S. practices are thought to be readily applicable to situations existing in this country, they are discussed briefly.

ROUNDERS

Function of the Rounder

When the dough piece leaves the divider, it is irregular in shape with sticky cut curfaces from which the gas can readily diffuse. The gluten structure is disoriented and so not in suitable condition for molding. It is the function of the rounder to close these cut surfaces (giving the dough piece a smooth and dry exterior), to make a relatively thick and continuous skin around the dough piece, to reorient the gluten structure, and to form the dough into a ball for easier handling in subsequent steps. It performs these functions by rolling the well-floured dough piece around the surface of a drum or cone while moving it upward or downward along this surface by means of a spiral track. As a result of this action, the surface is dried by an even distribution of dusting flour as well as by dehydration occurring because of exposure to the air, the gas cells near the surface of the ball are collapsed forming a thick layer which inhibits the diffusion of gases from the dough, and the dough piece assumes an approximately spherical shape. After this processing step, the dough ball passes to the intermediate proofer.

Types of Rounders

Rounders may conveniently be classified as bowl-, umbrella- or drum-type. The conical or bowl variety consists of a rotatable cone-shaped bowl around the interior of which is placed a stationary spiral track or "race." Figure 18.2 schematically illustrates such a device, while Fig. 18.3 is a photograph of a commerically available machine. From the conveyor leading from the divider, the dough pieces fall into the feed hopper of the rounder and then drop to the bottom of the rotating bowl. The pieces are tumbled and rolled along the dough race until

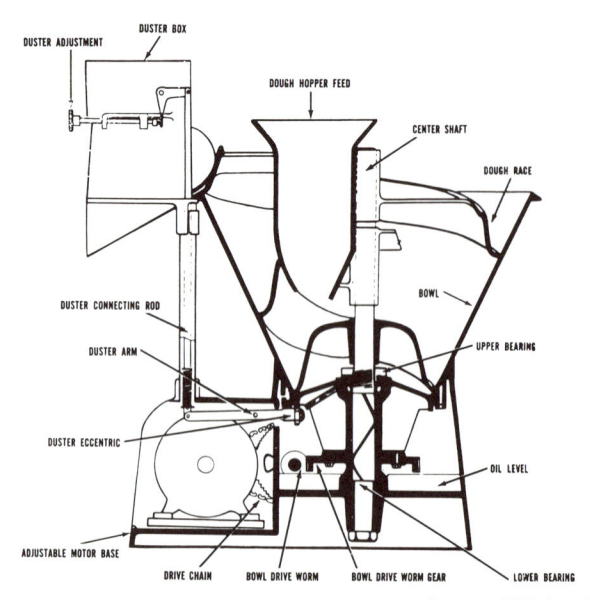

Courtesy of U.S. Dept. Defense
FIG. 18.2. SCHEMATIC DIAGRAM OF A BOWL-TYPE ROUNDER.

Courtesy of American Machine & Foundry Co.
FIG. 18.3. A COMMERCIALLY AVAILABLE BOWL-TYPE ROUNDER.

they emerge from the top of the bowl and fall onto the belt leading to the intermediate proofer.

A second popular type of rounder is the so-called umbrella or inverted cone variety. These machines differ from the preceding kind in that the dough piece is carried around the outside surface of a cone which has its apex facing upwards. Since the dough enters the rounder at the larger diameter of the cone, as shown in the schematic diagram of Fig. 18.4, its initial movement is more rapid than it would be in the bowl rounder. Opinions vary as to the relative merit of the two types of machines. It is certain, however, that many examples of both types have been performing satisfactorily for many years.

A third type of rounder is the drum type. These machines differ from the bowl and umbrella varieties in that the cone segment has very little slope to its sides, i.e., the sides are almost vertical. The dough piece enters near the bottom of the drum. It is obvious that the ball travels at a more uniform rate in these machines than in the other two types. Among the advantages claimed for the drum rounders is that they require less floor space, allowing greater latitude in positioning the machine with respect to other makeup equipment. Figure 18.5 illustrates positioning of the divider with respect to three different types of rounders.

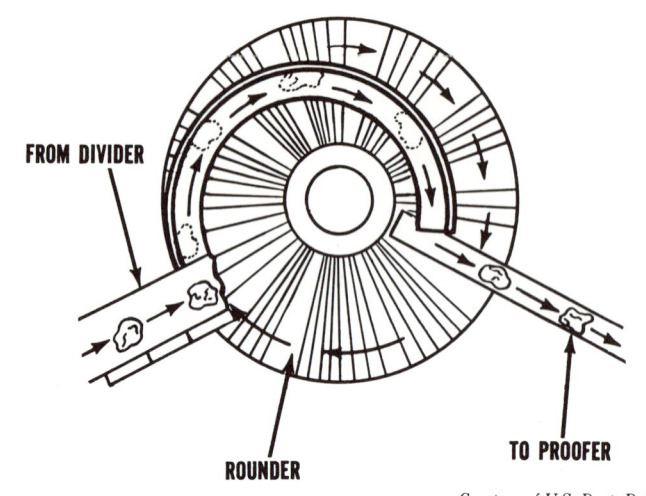

FIG. 18.4. PATH OF DOUGH PIECE IN UMBRELLA-TYPE ROUNDER.
Courtesy of U.S. Dept. Defense

A fourth style of rounder has concave sides. The round dough race is constructed in two or more sections on different planes. The dough pieces feed in at the top, move through the sections of the dough race, and are discharged into the feed drum of the intermediate proofer.

In addition to their form, rounding machines may vary in the texture or composition of the rotating surface, in the means provided for adjusting the relationship of the dough race to the drum or cone, in the method of applying dusting flour, etc. The rotating surface is usually corrugated vertically or horizontally, but the design and size of the ribs varies considerably from one manufacturer to another. The surface may be waxed or it may be coated with a plastic such as Teflon to reduce sticking. Frequently, a device to shunt aside oversize dough pieces (doubles) is fixed at the exit chute.

Controlling and Adjusting the Rounder

Most rounders provide a means for adjusting the distance of the race from the rotating surface. This furnishes a method for controlling the formation of "pills" or small pieces of dough which are pinched off between the race edge and the drum. As a rule, the race should be just as close to the drum as it can be placed without creating friction. It should be recognized that a film of dough builds up as the rounder operates, reducing the amount of clearance between the race and the drum.

The speed at which the rounder rotates is usually not easily changed, a constant speed sufficing for all applications. The amount of dusting

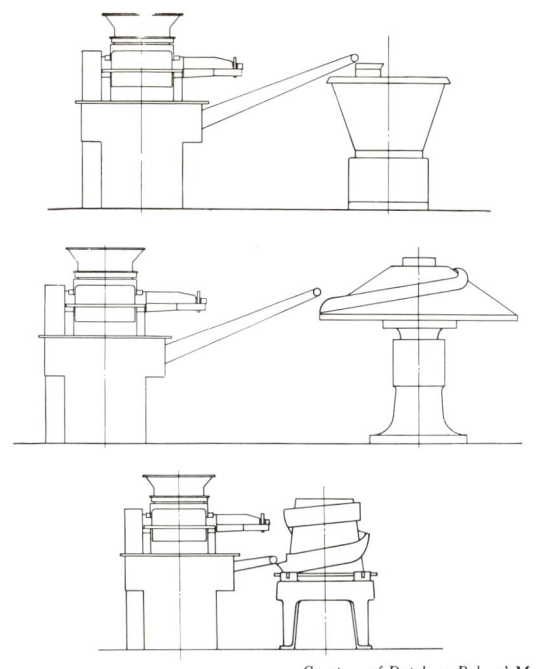

Courtesy of Dutchess Bakers' Machinery Co.

FIG. 18.5 POSITIONING OF DOUGH DIVIDERS AND THREE DIFFERENT STYLES OF ROUNDERS.

flour which the machine applies is capable of adjustment in most cases. Another important variable is the rate at which pieces are supplied to the rounder. Indications of a need for adjustment are the formation of doubles, tearing of dough pieces (usually due to an accumulation of dough film on the drum surface), cores in the finished loaves (too much dusting flour), and stick-ups.

Maintenance requirements for rounders are relatively simple and consist fundamentally of proper lubrication and adequate cleaning. Dusting flour accumulations should be removed at every convenient opportunity. Accumulations of dry dough on the cone surface are particularly harmful and should be carefully removed during each shutdown. To avoid scoring the surface, hardwood or plastic scrapers should be used. If special maintenance procedures are necessary for any machine, the manufacturers service booklet will list them.

Rounders are inherently less dangerous to operate than are dividers and molders, nonetheless an occasional operator will find some ingenious way to get a finger or hand caught in the mechanism. As in the case of all other machines involving moving parts, the operator should be directed to keep his hands away from shear points and pinch points and to assure himself that the power will remain off while he is cleaning the device.

INTERMEDIATE PROOFERS

Function of the Intermediate Proofer

When the dough piece leaves the rounder, it is rather well degassed as a result of the punishment it received in that machine and in the divider. The dough lacks extensibility and tears easily. It is rubbery and would not mold satisfactorily. To restore a more flexible, pliable structure which will respond well to the manipulations of the molder, it is necessary to let the dough piece rest while fermentation proceeds. This is accomplished by letting the dough ball travel through an inclosed cabinet for a few minutes. The physical changes other than gas accumulation which occur during this period are rather obscure, but apparently there are some alterations in the submicroscopic structure of the dough which render it more responsive to the subsequent operations. When the dough leaves the intermediate proofer, it is found to be larger in volume due to gas accumulation, the skin is firmer and drier, and the piece is more pliable and extensible.

Types of Intermediate Proofers

Most intermediate proofers used at the present time are the overhead type in which the principal part of the cabinet is raised high enough above the floor to allow space for other makeup machinery beneath it. When overhead space is not adequate, one of the floor types may be installed.

Intermediate proofers may be conveniently divided into the belt type and the tray type, the latter variety having many subtypes. The former style consists essentially of endless belts running in a closed cabinet. The dough pieces are carried forward to the end of the cabinet, then dropped down on the next lower belt traveling in the opposite direction, and so on until they reach the exit conveyor. The principles of operation of such a machine are illustrated in Fig. 18.6.

Tray-type conveyors—and in this class are included all conveyors which have segmented areas for carrying dough pieces—are composed of equipment which moves the dough in metal pans, troughs or buckets, wooden trays, or canvas loops. Figure 18.7 illustrates schematically the intake section of an overhead tray-type proofer which has perforated metal troughs or tubes in which the dough pieces are dropped. Each of the types has its special virtues and evils and consequently has proponents and detractors. Attributes of the dough carrying unit which are of importance in evaluating the relative worth of an intermediate

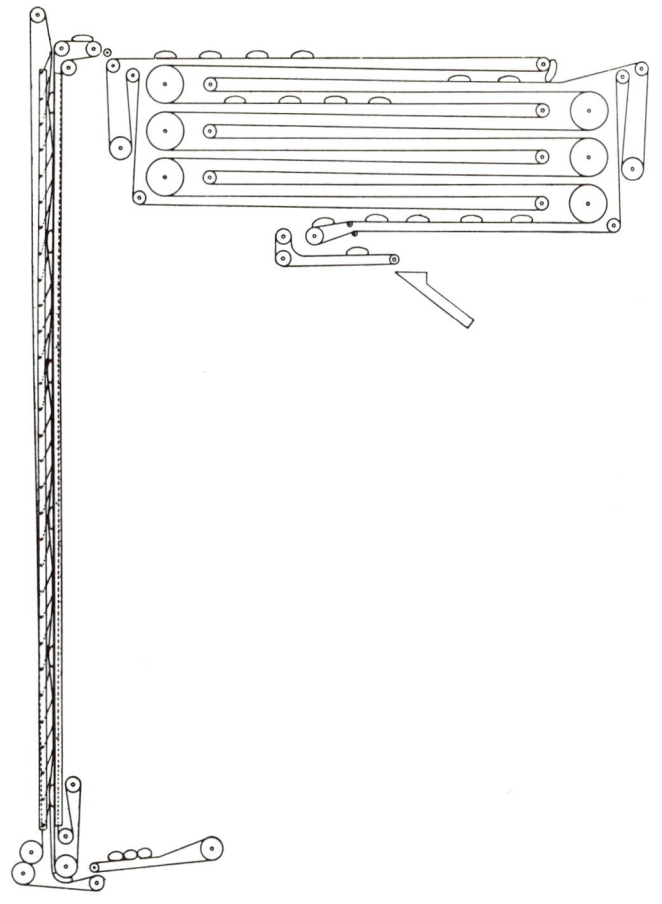

Courtesy of Dutchess Bakers' Machinery Co.
FIG. 18.6. DIAGRAM OF A BELT-TYPE INTERMEDIATE PROOFER.

proofer are: (1) the ease of cleaning and of keeping it clean; (2) ease of replacement and economy of repair; and (3) its adequacy in preventing doubles and retaining the proper form of the dough piece.

Figure 18.8 illustrates a tray type of intermediate proofer which uses canvas loops over metal frames as the carrying means. Location of overhead proofers of this, and other types, must be carefully planned. They should be easily accessible from all sides for cleaning and maintenance. The foundation should be level and capable of giving a firm base to the proofer. They should not interfere with free movement of personnel beneath or around them, or with placement and function of other makeup equipment.

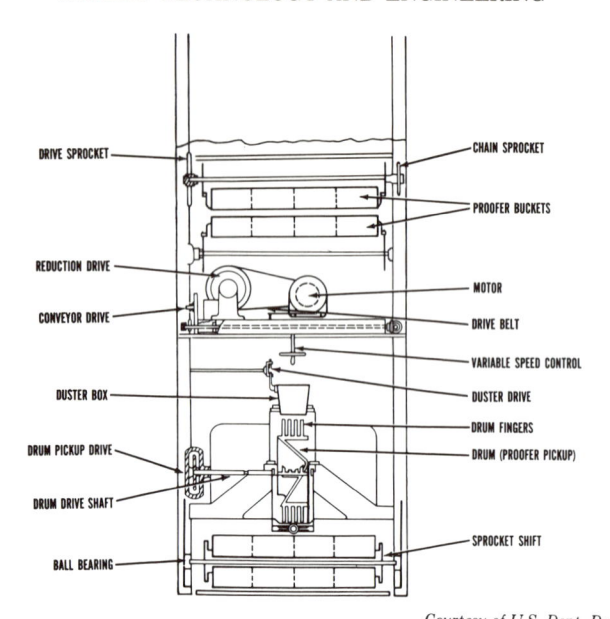

FIG. 18.7. DIAGRAM OF THE INTAKE SECTION OF A TRAY-TYPE INTERMEDIATE PROOFER.

An important part of the intermediate proofer is its loading mechanism. This machinery takes the dough pieces which come along the conveyor belt in single file, and arranges them in rows in the receptacle of the intermediate proofer. The proofer trays may contain spaces for 2 to 8 dough pieces placed across the tray.

Controlling and Adjusting the Intermediate Proofer

Intermediate proofers of all types are equipped with variable speed controls which can be used to determine the length of time dough pieces spend within the cabinet. An absolute maximum of dwell time is dictated by the maximum capacity of the proofer and the rate of output of the divider and rounder. If an attempt is made to slow the machine below this point, doubles will accumulate in the dough pockets or on the belts. Below this maximum level of capacity, the correct time for the dough piece to stay within the cabinet is determined by the period necessary to condition the dough properly.

No large capacity (over 3000 lbs per hr) intermediate proofers are available with air-conditioning equipment built in. Temperature and relative humidity are thus at the mercy of room conditions and the state of the dough pieces entering the proofer. Fortunately, an absolutely uniform and carefully controlled treatment at this stage is not essential

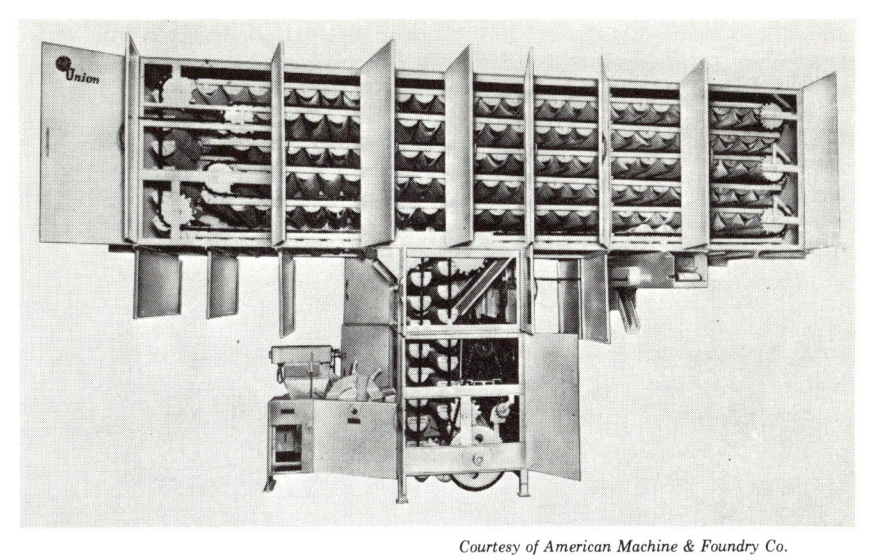

MAKEUP EQUIPMENT 337

Courtesy of American Machine & Foundry Co.
Fig. 18.8. Overhead Intermediate Proofer Using Canvas Loops Over Metal Frames as the Conveying Means.

for the dough. A moderate range of variation can be tolerated without causing significant observable differences in the finished loaf. Since room conditions usually remain fairly constant over extended periods, and since the temperature and equilibrium relative humidity of the dough do not usually vary a great deal, the former being largely determined by the temperature in the fermentation room and the latter by dough composition, insuperable difficulties in adjusting the intermediate proofer seldom occur. It is certainly desirable to have means for controlling the temperature and relative humidity of the interior of the intermediate proofer, however. Some modern cabinets of relatively low capacity do have air-conditioning units, or provision for ventilating with air from an outside source. Others could be improved by the addition of steam outlets to provide additional moisture. Opening the doors of the cabinet to reduce the humidity or temperature is inadvisable because it creates drafts with resultant erratic behavior of the dough pieces, e.g., crusting, insufficient proof, etc.

Maintenance of intermediate proofers is a matter of keeping the machine cleaned and lubricated. The pockets or belts accumulate coatings of dusting flour and dough and must be cleaned frequently. This process requires removal of the trays, buckets, or belts, and thorough washing of them. The schedule for cleaning is dependent upon the climate, the susceptibility to infestation of the plant, and other factors.

The Baking Industry Sanitation Standards Committee has enunciated the following general principles of design and construction for mechanical (intermediate) proofers:

Product Zone

(1) All surfaces in contact with the dough piece shall be impervious to flour, dough and resist the effect of the acids and other products of dough fermentation, and capable of being readily cleaned and sanitized. This shall not apply to fabric liners or belts that can be removed for cleaning.

(2) All surfaces shall be smooth, of non-toxic material and free from loose scale, pits, cracks, crevices, and other imperfections and not contain stampings or embossings.

(3) All surface and areas within the product zone should be readily accessible to both sight and reach.

(4) All inside corners and intersections, other than in parts that can be readily removed for cleaning, shall be rounded or cone shaped, with not less than one-sixteenth inch minimum radius of curvature, to minimize retention of flour, dust or other material.

(5) Set screws, keys and/or other projections, also inside threads, tapped holes, keyways, sockets or other recesses, should be avoided. Nuts shall not be placed so as to form pocket patterns.

(6) All product zone enclosures shall be so designed that they may be readily opened for inspection and cleaning, and reclosed securely with a minimum of time, with fewest possible loose parts, and by use of only simple tools.

(7) Solder shall contain not more than 5 per cent lead and other toxic material. Silver solder, consisting mainly of silver, copper and zinc, shall not contain cadmium or other toxic materials.

(8) When sheets or plates are permanetly joined they should preferably be butt welded with the welds ground smooth in the product zone. If horizontal lap joints are necessary the upper sheet shall lap over the lower sheet. All lapped joints shall be scarfed and the joint filled and smoothed.

(9) Bearings shall be of the sealed or self lubricating type wherever possible. If the bearings cannot be removed for cleaning, they should be pressed into the housing and sealed to prevent flour from seeping into the space betwen the bearing and the housing. Where it is possible, the bearings shall be out-board. Where lubrication is required, the design and construction shall be such that lubricants cannot leak, drip, or be forced into the product zone.

Non-Product Zone

(1) All bolt heads and nuts shall be set so that they do not form pocket patterns or areas hard to reach for cleaning.

(2) Housing or guards around sprockets, chains, shafts, pulleys, etc., shall be removable, or be fitted with easily removable covers to provide for access and cleaning. These may be fitted with hinges.

(3) All joints and edges where two members are permanently joined or lapped shall be properly filled, welded, or smoothed to prevent cracks or recesses that may retain flour and dust, or harbor contamination.

(4) All surfaces shall be accessible to both sight and reach.

(5) Metal or other non-absorbent, odorless, non-splinterable material shall be used.

MAKEUP EQUIPMENT 339

(6) Hinges shall be of the loose pin or take apart type and shall not contain cracks and crevices that cannot be cleaned.

(7) Surfaces shall be reasonably smooth with castings free of coarse sand impressions or blow holes. The base frames and supporting members shall be designed to be cleaned easily and shall be free of pockets, crevices and other inaccessible spaces where flour may collect or insects develop.

Function of the Molder

In the bread-making plant, the molder receives pieces of dough from the intermediate proofer and shapes them into cylinders (loaves) ready to be placed in the pans. There are several types of molders, each of which will be described later, but they all have four functions in common: sheeting, curling, rolling, and sealing. Some writers consider the last two as one function, since they are performed simultaneously.

Figure 18.9 is a schematic diagram of a simple type of molder in which these functions are illustrated. The dough as it comes from the intermediate proofer is a flattened spheroid. The first operation of the

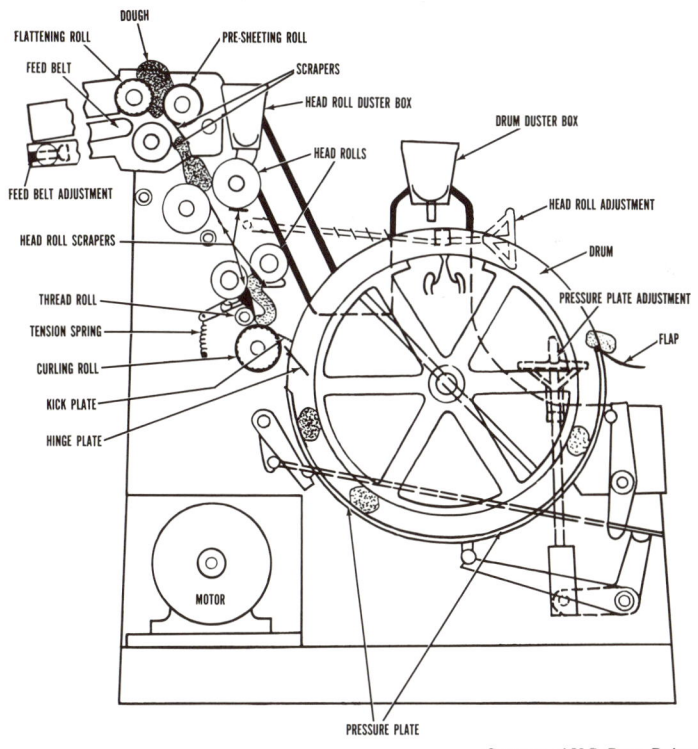

Courtesy of U.S. Dept. Defense

FIG. 18.9. DIAGRAM OF A SIMPLE DRUM MOLDER FOR BREAD DOUGHS.

molder is to flatten this spheroid out still more into a thick sheet which can be properly manipulated in the later stages of molder operation. This effect is usually achieved by 2 or more (usually 3) consecutive pairs of rollers, each succeeding pair being set more closely together than the ones which precede it. The first pair of rolls, called the head rolls, exerts only a relatively slight pressure on the dough piece. The second set of rolls, the center rolls, operates at an intermediate pressure. The last set, which may be called either the sheeting rolls or the lower rolls, exerts the maximum pressure on the dough sheet. In the case of a reverse sheeting molder, there are two single rolls, the reversing roll and the receiving roll, which intervene between the center rolls and the lower rolls. The gradual reduction in thickness effected by this multiple roller system minimizes the punishment received by the dough so that tearing and similar problems are reduced. Sometimes a single "flattening" roll is located above the infeed conveyor to the molder. The flattening roll performs an initial slight reduction in thickness of the dough piece which facilitates its engagement by the first pair of rolls.

In the past few years, it has become fairly common to encase the sheeting rolls with Teflon sleeves in order to render them resistant to adhesion to the dough pieces. When the molder sheeting rolls have not been treated in this manner, scrapers are placed so as to assure the separation of the dough sheet from the rollers.

After the dough has been sheeted out, it is curled up into a loose cylinder. This operation is conventionally performed by a special set of rolls, as indicated in Fig. 18.9. Alternately, it is accomplished by a pair of canvas belts. The lower conveyor belt moves the dough piece forward until the upper curling belt or mat engages the front end of the piece, brings it back, and curls it up into a loose cylinder. A more advanced development substitutes a short length of woven metal mat or linked thin metal bars for the upper curling belt. In these machines, the metal curling device is affixed just above the conveyor belt, with one end resting on the belt. As the dough piece passes under the curling device, the weight of the latter creates enough drag to pull the forward end of the dough piece up and delay it while the conveyor belt rolls the piece into a cylinder.

The layers in the cylinder of dough are not tightly adherent when it leaves the curling section. The next function of the molder is to thoroughly seal the dough piece so that it will expand into the typical loaf shape when it is proofed. In addition, the cylinder of dough is lengthened so that its axial dimension is somewhat greater than the length of the pan, and entrapped air between the dough layers is expelled. The conventional molder achieves these results by rolling the dough cylinder between a large drum surfaced with canvas and a semicircular compression board having a smooth surface. Clearance between the drum and board is gradually reduced along the route of dough travel so that the piece is constantly in contact with both surfaces and gradually becomes compressed.

An alternate arrangement is a flat pressure board and a powered belt which gradually squeeze the dough cylinder into shape as a result of the gradually decreasing distance between them. At high speeds, say 80 pieces per minute, dusting flour is usually applied just before the dough piece goes under the pressure board. Pressure boards range in length from 24 to 48 in. The surface of the pressure board is often altered by some kind of "buildup" to give better control over the shape of the dough piece. A layer of sponge rubber covered by canvas is a common expedient. Angles made of metal or wood strips or half-cylinders are sometimes attached to the pressure board, with the points of the angles pointing toward the intake, and the whole structure covered with canvas. Thick pieces of canvas belting are also used to build up the pressure board. These pressure board modifications are intended to permit use of a loose pressure board without getting pointed ends on the dough pieces. They leave the ends of the dough pieces rather loosely sealed so as to allow gases to escape, the end result being a more even grain the length of the loaves (Olmstead 1970).

An integral component of most modern molders is the automatic panning device. The empty pans are carried by a conveyor past the end of the molder, and the loaves are transferred from the molder and positioned in the pans by an apparatus operated by compressed air.

Types of Molders

As the dough piece passes through the sheeting rolls, there is a tendency for the moisture content of the trailing edge to become increased at the expense of the leading sections. This redistribution of moisture results from the effect of compression on the dough structure. In the normal course of events in a conventional molder, the trailing edge, which is of relatively high moisture content, ends up as the outside layer of the cylinder. It has been thought for many years that it would be preferable, from the standpoint of loaf performance during proofing and baking, to have the wetter portion of the dough sheet folded into the center of the loaf. Observations on hand molded doughs formed in this manner seemed to confirm the superiority of "reverse molded loaves."

The major modifications which have been made in molder design in the last few years are the result of attempts to avoid folding the dry end of the dough sheet into the center of the loaf. Successful developments have included the cross grain molder and the reverse sheeting molder. The former type curls the dough sheet at right angles to its direction of travel through the sheeter rolls. As a result, the wetter edge of the dough forms one end of the loaf rather than the outside layer. The crossover effect is achieved by changing the direction of travel of the dough 90° after it leaves the sheeting rolls. According to Hunter (1949), the first machines developed used a turnover or "flip-flop" method of transfer, while a slide transfer or "shoot-over" method later came into use. Figure 18.10 illustrates a cross-grain molder-panner which uses the slide transfer system.

The reverse sheeting molder was devised to curl the sheet of dough so that the wet end of the piece would be folded into the center of the loaf. The dough piece is turned over or reversed between the second or third set of rolls (between the center rolls and the sheeting rolls) thus placing the original trailing end (or wet end) in the leading position. Figure 18.11 is a diagram of a molder-panner which includes these operations.

Another type of molder that was developed primarily to give loaves with more uniform cell structure twists the dough pieces after they have been rolled into cylinders. Twist bread has been very popular in some sections of the country for many years. The twisting was formerly done entirely by hand, an obviously uneconomical practice in this highly competitive industry. Machines are now available which will perform the twisting at a rapid rate and with results as good or better than those achieved by hand twisting. Figure 18.12 illustrates a combination molder-twister-panner. The dough cylinder falls into the U-shaped cups shown at the end of the machine and then is twisted by a rotary movement of the cups.

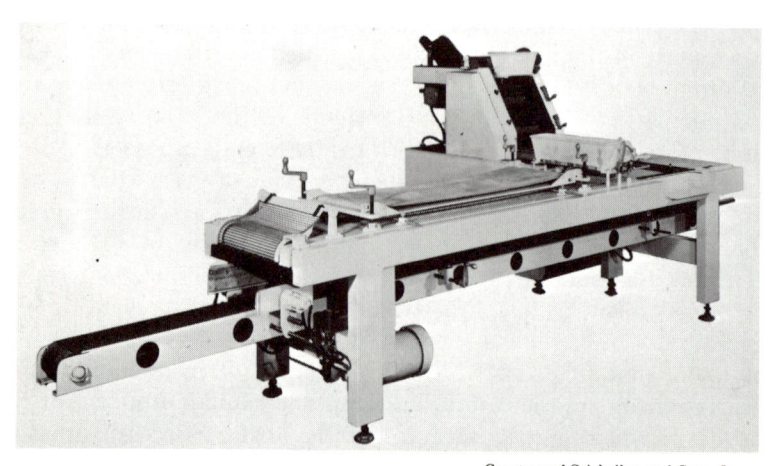

Courtesy of Stickelber and Sons, Inc.

FIG. 18.10. CROSS-GRAIN MOLDER-PANNER.

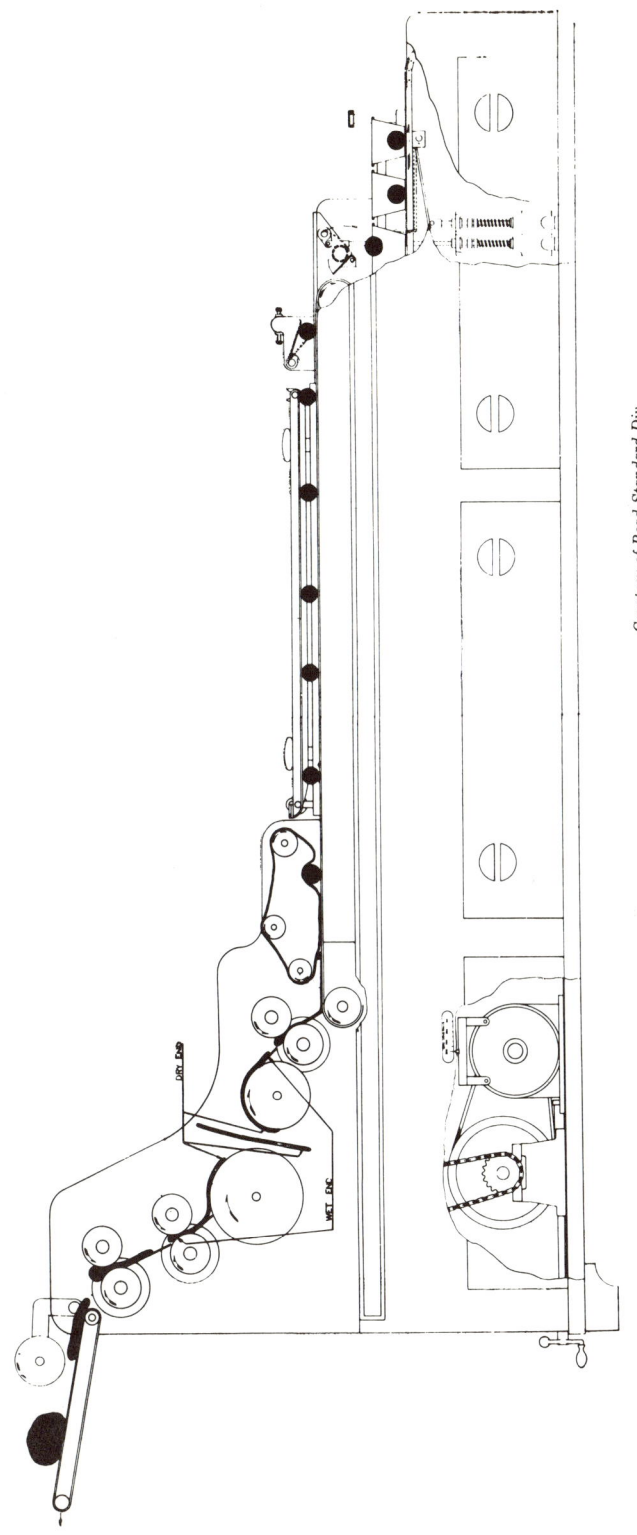

Courtesy of Read Standard Div.

FIG. 18.11. DIAGRAM OF A REVERSE-SHEETING MOLDER-PANNER.

Courtesy of Baker Perkins, Inc.

FIG. 18.12. DISCHARGE END OF TWO MOLDER-TWISTER-PANNERS WITH PAN CONVEYORS.

Controlling and Adjusting the Molder

The first adjustment (in terms of sequence of the processing) possible on the molder is the setting of the head rolls. According to Mohr (1949), most steel head rolls are run with an opening of 0.140–0.180 in. With plastic covered sheeting rolls of equivalent size, it is possible to reduce the opening to 0.060 in. Many authorities seem to feel that the closer these rolls can be set without tearing the dough, the better will be the grain in the finished loaf. In any case, the optimum setting will be determined by the conditions existing in each particular plant. It is evident that the lower sets of rolls should be set more closely than the upper set, and that the difference between the first pairs should be greater than the difference in settings of the last two pairs.

Adjustment of the scrapers on the head rolls (if plastic covered rolls are not used) should be just sufficient to prevent stick-ups. Too close settings create friction and may even result in scoring of the roll surface.

The speed of the molder can be adjusted, and should be sufficient to allow adequate space between the dough pieces arriving from the intermediate proofer.

The length of the dough cylinder discharged from the molder is governed by adjusting rails or guides lying between the compression surfaces. These guides should be far enough apart so that the dough piece is just slightly longer than the pan.

Clearance between the compression surfaces is another variable which can be controlled in molders. Enough pressure should be exerted on the piece to seal thoroughly the contacting layers of dough. Too much pressure will result in dumbbell shaped pieces and consequent misshapen loaves of bread. Too little pressure, in addition to causing inadequate seals with holes in the bread, may give dough pieces an oval longitudinal section which bakes into a misshapen loaf. Gradual application of pressure is necessary to efficiently remove air bubbles from between the dough layers.

Dusting flour applicators should be controlled to give the minimum rate of addition consistent with the prevention of stick-ups and other malfunctioning of the machinery. Too much flour added at this critical stage will result in spots and streaks in the bread, holes due to poor sealing, and other defects.

Maintenance requirements include lubrication of the mechanical parts, cleaning away dough particles and flour from the working surfaces, and application of divider oil to the rolls after cleaning.

The molder is a relatively hazardous piece of equipment. The American Standard Safety Code for Bakery Equipment (Anon. 1947) establishes the following requirements for safe operation of the molder:

(1) **Hoppers**—Mechanical feed moulders shall be provided with hoppers so designed and connected to the proofer that an employee's hands cannot get into the hopper where they will come in contact with the in-running rolls.

(2) **Hand-Fed Moulders.**—Hand-fed moulders shall be provided with a belt-feed device or the hopper shall be extended high enough so that the hands of the operator cannot get into the feed rolls. The top edge of such a hopper shall be well rounded to prevent injury when it is struck or bumped by the employee's hand.

(3) **Stopping Devices.**—There shall be a stopping device within easy reach of the operator who feeds the moulder and another stopping device within the reach of the employee taking dough away from the moulder.

(4) **Clean-Out Holes.**—Machines shall be so designed that there is no shear point in close proximity to the clean-out holes.

(5) **Rear of Moulders.**—At the rear of moulders all revolving shafts shall have

round corners or cylindrical surfaces, and all bolts shall be flush. Tie rods shall be far enough from revolving parts to prevent a shearing or pinching hazard.

(6) **Adjustment Crank**.—Where a removable crank is used to adjust the moulder for different sizes of loaf, brackets shall be provided on the side of the machine for holding the crank when it is not in use. The brackets should be connected to a limit switch so that when the crank is removed the current is broken and the machine cannot run unless the crank is returned to the resting position on the machine.

The Code brings out the following additional points about safe practices in molder operations:

(a) Where the moulder is designed for direct feed from proofers a few pieces of dough at the end of the run are frequently fed into the hopper by hand. The hopper being designed for mechanical feed does not give the necessary protection for hand feed. In such cases it is recommended that the dough pieces be dropped on the in-feed conveyor.

(b) During hand-feed operations dough is apt to be sticky and cling to the operator's fingers. It is, therefore, much easier for the operator, if he is able to throw the dough into a hopper that is deep enough and has a rounded edge which will allow him to hit the hopper regularly with each stroke of his hand thereby releasing the sticky dough.

(c) Some moulders have been installed so that the delivery end is at the wrong elevation. The operators have to stoop in order to pick up the dough and this is very fatiguing. It has been suggested that all installations should be so arranged that the delivery point is 35 inches above the floor.

SPECIAL MOLDING AND FORMING EQUIPMENT

Sweet Goods

The multiplicity of shapes and dough types found in sweet goods leads to the use of many different combinations of the relatively few automatic devices available to the baker. Some of the most common pieces of equipment required for shaping sweet dough products are sheeters, applicators, curlers, and cutters. These units are usually combined in pastry benches, automatic sweet goods machines, etc., which process the dough after it has been sheeted or extruded.

Dough extruders for sweet doughs move dough from a hopper through a large orifice by means of a screw or auger. Since the dough is not forced through a small opening, little harm is done to its cell structure. A cut-off mechanism is controlled by a variable electronic timer to give the desired weight. This equipment is particularly useful for extruding large (e.g., 15 lb) dough pieces to be sheeted out as Danish pastry.

If a layered dough or roll-in dough is to be prepared, as for puff pastry or Danish pastry, repeated sheeting and folding of the dough and fat combination is required. Dough brakes have been used for sheeting doughs for many years. These are quite simple in principle, being a

Courtesy of Simon-Vicars, Ltd.
FIG. 18.13. DOUGH BRAKE.

set of long horizontal steel cylinders with provision for adjusting the clearance (Fig. 18.13). The cylinders turn at relatively high speeds and are supported by heavy springs. A set of plates or chutes is provided for guiding the dough into and out of the rolls. Usually the brakes include automatic return devices which bring the dough back into the hands of the operator. A revolving circular plate in front of the operator simplifies the task of folding the strip and turning it 90° for the next pass. Braking or reversing switches or other effective safety devices are essential on this dangerous equipment.

Reversible sheeters perform functions similar to those of dough brakes but they are slower. This can be a real advantage in preventing dough breakdown but it is, of course, more expensive in terms of labor. Reversible sheeters consist of 2 conveyor belts, 1 on each side of a set of rollers which can be brought closer together in a series of steps as the dough sheet is gradually reduced in thickness (Fig. 18.14). The conveyor belts move at different speeds to accomodate the extension of the dough as it passes through the rollers. Machines are available with electronic programming of the reduction steps.

Danish products can be made by a continuous flow system which starts with the extrusion of the dough as a strip onto the conveyor belt. The dough strip is thinned and widened by one or more pairs of reduction rollers. Subsequently, a number of narrow bands of shortening, covering perhaps ½ of the surface, are extruded onto the surface of the dough. The roll-in fat should equal at least 25% of the dough weight. A curling roller forms the dough and fat into a cylinder which is then flattened out by other sets of rollers. This is similar to a three-fold operation. A cutting wheel cuts the strip of dough in lengths to fit a

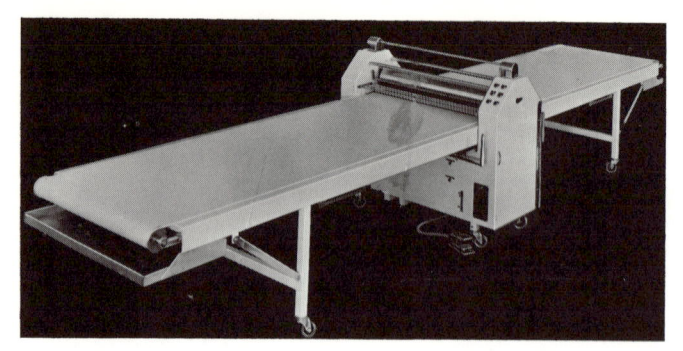

Courtesy of Moline, Inc.

FIG. 18.14. MEDIUM-DUTY REVERSIBLE SHEETER WITH AUTOMATIC PROGRAMMING OF REDUCTION STEPS.

bun pan which is then placed in a retarder. Some operators give the dough a little floor time (room temperature rest) before sending it to the retarder. After 1-4 hr rest in the refrigerated room (about 34°-38°F) the dough pieces are folded in 4 layers, sheeted out, then folded and sheeted again. The dough can now be retarded until it is scheduled for makeup, or it can be cut and shaped immediately. The pieces are filled, formed, and topped, as required for the particular item being made, and then proofed. Room temperature Danish should be proofed for about 50 min to 1 hr and 20 min at approximately 95°F dry-bulb and 85°F wet-bulb temperatures.

The baking time and temperature depend on the piece size and, to some extent, the shape. A 2½ oz roll should bake in 11-13 min at 385°-410°F (Davey 1965).

Automatic Sweet Goods Machines.—These "mechanical benches" are assemblages of several types of devices connected by conveyor belts. They may be either specialized for the manufacture of one type of product or convertible for several products. They are used primarily for yeast-leavened sweet goods, such as cinnamon rolls, coffee cakes, Danish pastries, doughnuts, bismarcks, and long johns but may also be used for baking powder biscuits, shortcakes, soft rolls, etc. Production rates are intermediate between fully automated lines and hand work. A description of a typical bench suitable for general production follows (Fig. 18.15).

The infeed conveyor carries the dough to three sets of sheeting rolls by which it is brought to the desired width and thickness. The dough strip is then delivered to the makeup conveyor where oil or any other kind of liquid can be applied to it by a spray, drip, or roller applicator. A powder dispenser then applies cinnamon-sugar or any other kind of pulverulent spice or seasoning. Next in line is a curling roll which can

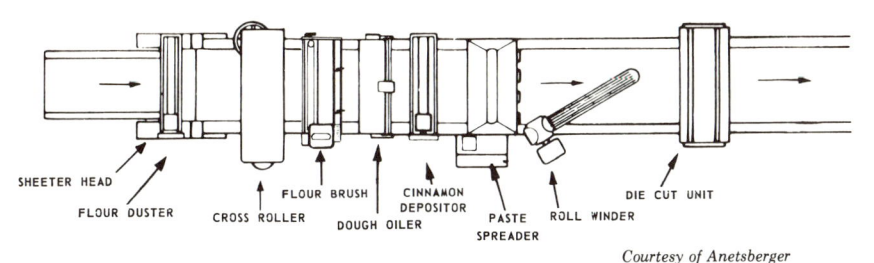

FIG. 18.15. ARRANGEMENT OF PROCESSING DEVICES ON AN AUTOMATIC SWEET GOODS MACHINE.

Courtesy of Anetsberger

automatically wind the strip into an endless helical coil. Adjustments can be made so that the straight seam lies along the bottom. A sealing and guide thimble (also called a bell) moves the cylinder back to the center of the belt. The dough may now be flattened by rollers, slit by disc cutters, and chopped into segments by a guillotine cutter. Finally, the pieces emerge into the panning section of the conveyor where they may be hand panned, automatically panned, or dropped into a proofer or fryer.

Piecrust Formers

There are two popular methods for forming piecrusts: (1) sheeting the dough and cutting out the crusts, and (2) pressing the dough to shape between two dies (Fig. 18.16). Satisfactory crusts can be formed by both methods. The sheeting and cutting method is said to permit the achievement of better texture but it generates a certain amount of scrap. The stamping method should be essentially free of reworking scrap.

The sequence of operations in a commercially available pie production line using the sheeting and cutting approach is: (1) Metering the dough. An automatic dough divider converts bulk dough into two rectangular dough pieces which will ultimately become the bottom and top crust. Weight adjustments can be made while the line is running. (2) Conveying the dough from the divider to the crust rollers. (3) Sheeting the bottom crust. One dough piece is automatically cross-rolled and deposited over a moving pie tin. Size and thickness can be varied by adjusting the roller settings. (4) "Docking" the bottom crust. The dough sheet is pressed down into the pan so it closely fits the sides and bottom of the cavity. (5) Wetting the rim. A simple dispenser and applicator wets the upper rim of the bottom crust so that the top crust will adhere to the lower dough piece after the trimming operation. (6) Forming the rim. Planetary spinning heads form and trim the edge of the dough sheet. (7) Filling the shell. A measured quantity of fruit filling is deposited into the bottom crust. Adjustments of delivery rate

Courtesy of Ekco

FIG. 18.16. A SMALL PIE-SHELL PRESS ILLUSTRATING THE PRINCIPLE USED FOR PRESSURE-FORMING DOUGHS IN PANS.

can be made at this point. (8) Sheeting the top crust. The second dough piece is automatically cross-rolled and deposited over the moving pie pan containing the bottom crust and fitting. (9) Sealing. The bottom and top crusts are sealed together around the rim, and excess dough is trimmed off. Plain or fancy crimps can be formed at this stage. (10) Spraying. A wash or glaze can be automatically sprayed on the top crust if desired. (11) Recovering trimmings. The excess dough from the shaping operations is returned to the dough divider (Jahn 1964).

It is said that the production rates of 600 2-crust fruit pies per hour can be achieved with a labor force of 3 people with equipment of the type described above.

A pie-making machine in which the dough is not rolled and sheeted but press-formed into the desired shapes was described by Gageant (1964). A metered amount of the blended ingredients is fed through a series of stations where it is formed and placed in a pan and various filling materials dispensed into it. After filling, a die-formed pastry cover is placed over the pan and its edges crimped to the bottom crust. The porous metal dies release dough from the forming surface by slight air pressure without using any dusting flour. In some cases, the crust molding die may be heated, say to 250°F, to facilitate the dough flow (Atwood 1964). Since the shortening is substantially liquified by this technique, air-injection or other means must be used to release the dough from the molds.

Roll-forming Equipment

Bun dividers, rounders, proofers, and molders are often part of an integral unit which maintains dough piece registration throughout processing (Fig. 18.17). Frequently, an automatic panning unit is also part of the complex.

The bun divider is somewhat similar to the dividers for bread previously discussed. A horizontal cylinder containing cavities rotates beneath a hopper filled with dough. Hoppers normally have a capacity of 250–500 lb of dough. The dough is sucked into the cavities (usually four) by retracting pistons, which then cut off and expel the dough pieces onto the rounder conveyor as the cylinder completes its rota-

Courtesy of American Machine & Foundry Co.
FIG. 18.17. A ROLL-FORMING ASSEMBLAGE INCLUDING DIVIDER, ROUNDER, INTERMEDIATE PROOFER, MOLDER, AND PANNER.

tion. A scaling range of 1–4½ oz can be achieved. Since a dough trough will contain enough dough for at least 15 min running time, and usually longer, the change in dough properties with time can create serious problems in maintaining uniform weights. Attempts have been made to overcome the density change by constant working of the dough during the time it is being held, or by placing the dough under pressure while subjecting it to a slight mixing action (Euverard 1970).

The most common type of bun rounder in this country consists essentially of a conveyor belt and a set of concave bars set at an angle to the line of belt travel. The contacting surfaces of the bars are lined with Teflon. Dough pieces are positioned on the belt, as they drop from the divider, so that they are pulled along by the belt while the bar applies a sidewise force. The action of the belt and the restriction on forward motion imposed by the bars causes the dough pieces to rotate. If the dough has suitable physical properties and the piece size is in the correct range, this is a very effective and reliable rounding method in spite of its simplicity. Such rounders do not have as positive a placement control as certain other types and their action may result in imperfect registration at the proofer intake, but on normal runs this is seldom a major problem. Production rates of up to 320 pieces per minute can be attained with the divider and rounder combinations.

At the end of the rounder belt, the pieces fall into Teflon-lined chutes which release four dough pieces simultaneouly into the trays of the proofer.

The dough pieces leave the intermediate proofer and enter the molder, where they are formed into the desired shapes, such as hamburger buns, hot dog rolls, club rolls, etc. A typical molder will consist of: (1) A molder chute having a gate operated by a cam mounted on a cam shaft synchronously driven from the proofer section. (2) A set of adjustable molder rollers. (3) A molding belt with an auxiliary curling mat. (4) A standard auxiliary pressure board unit for forming hot dog rolls. (5) A set of hot dog dough gates. (6) An indexing mechanism for synchronizing the release of the formed dough pieces with the cavities in the pans.

Attachments can be obtained for making twin rolls, clover leaf rolls, hard rolls, pull-apart bread, etc.

English Muffin Equipment

Crumpets, English muffins, and similar products are customarily cooked on a hot griddle rather than baked in a pan. For mass production, the dough or batter may be deposited in ring-shaped forms which rest on a heated plate. After cooking on one side, the product is inverted for the final stage of baking.

The operations in an automatic plant are: dividing, rounding, dusting (with corn meal), proofing, dusting of trays with corn meal, transferring of dough pieces to griddle, first stage of grilling, inverting muffins, second stage of grilling, conveying to cooler infeed, cooling, discharging to packaging line, and packaging (Noel 1962). Lines with capacities of up to 750 dozen per hour are said to require the attention of only 1 man between the mixing and packaging steps. The cups can be varied in diameter and height to give a product suiting local preferences and they are Teflon-coated so that the dough will not adhere to them. Forrester (1963) described a crumpet-making machine in which the mold rings are placed on moving hot plates at one end, taken off at the other end, but rest only on the hot plates during the cooking part of the cycle. The mold ring carrying apparatus rises free of the rings while the latter are on the hot plates so that jarring of the rings will not disturb the crumpets while they are cooking.

Biscuit-forming Equipment

Cookies are formed or shaped by three major types of mechanisms: (1) die-forming, in which the dough is pressed into shaped cavities in the surface of a metal cylinder, (2) extrusion procedures, which may take several forms, and (3) cutting, in which pieces are severed from a continuous strip of dough by rotating or reciprocating (up and down motion) dies. There are also procedures not fitting into any of these categories, such as sugar wafer production, which involves the baking of a thin batter in the confined space between two metal plates.

Soda crackers, club crackers, saltines, and the like are formed by a reciprocating die which cuts pieces out of a continuous strip of dough that has been formed by laminating and sheeting. The scrap is pulled off the belt and returned to the laminating section. These doughs are "docked" or perforated by pins in order that the cracker will not expand excessively during baking. A few kinds of cookies, in particular the so-called hard sweets, are also made by cutting machines (Fig. 18.18).

Extrusion equipment can be used for wire-cut, deposit, and fig bar type cookies. In any case, the dough or batter is pushed through an orifice by cylinders rotating in the hopper. For deposit cookies, the individual pieces are separated from the constantly extruding strand of batter by moving the band (baking surface) up and down beneath the orifice (Fig. 18.19). In the wire-cut method, the strand of dough is severed by a wire or tape that is moved back and forth across the face of the orifice. Fig bars, and some other cookies, involve the simultaneous extrusion of two types of pastes which are baked in continuous strips and then cut by disc knives moving across the band.

354   BAKERY TECHNOLOGY AND ENGINEERING

Courtesy Simon-Vicars, Ltd.
Fig. 18.18. A Cutting Machine Making "Hard Sweets" from a Sheet of Cookie Dough.

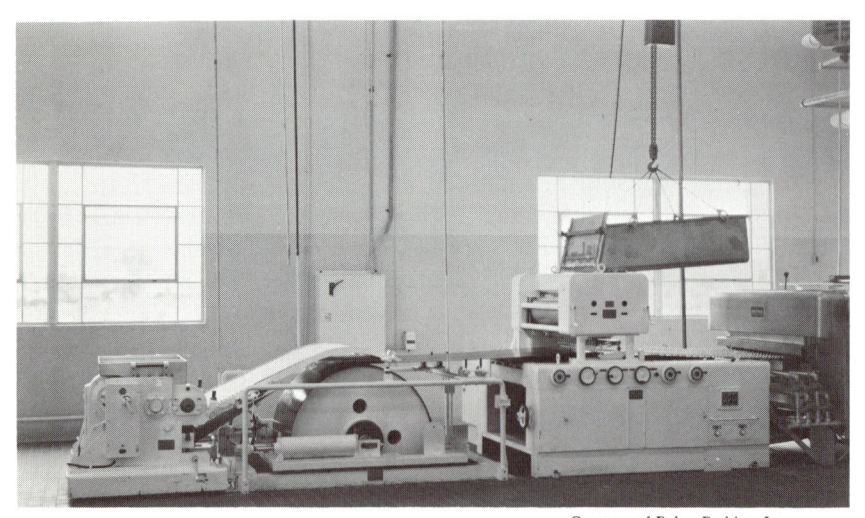

Courtesy of Baker Perkins, Inc.
Fig. 18.19. Making Deposit Cookies.

Cookies produced on rotary molding cylinders include the baked component of sandwich cookies and all those with embossed designs. A metal (brass, stainless steel) cylinder having a surface covered with engraved pockets rotates past the opening in a hopper filled with cookie dough. The pockets fill with the dough which is sheared off the main mass as the cylinder continues its revolution and the pieces are ejected onto a conveyor belt leading to the band oven. Figure 18.20 is a diagram of a rotary molder used in cookie production.

Pretzels are formed by highly specialized equipment. In the AMF machine, a dough ball is extruded and then formed into a thin cylinder which is grasped at the ends by metal clamps and twisted into the characteristic shape. In another make of equipment, the dough is extruded from a hopper through a slotted face place. The dough is cut into small strips as it is extruded. The strips are rounded and lengthened by passing them between two canvas belts. After the ends are clipped so that the lengths are uniform, the strings of dough enter the twister which makes the pretzel shape. A roller then applies slight pressure to set the knots. Pretzel sticks, rods, and nuggets are usually formed by simple extrusion techniques.

Further details on biscuit shaping and forming can be obtained from *Cookie and Cracker Technology* (Matz 1968).

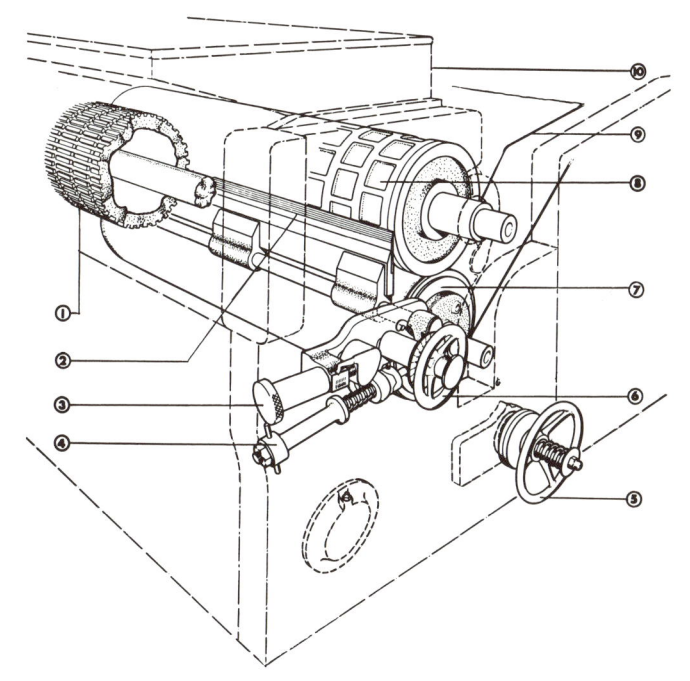

Courtesy of Simon-Vicars, Ltd.

FIG. 18.20. DIAGRAM OF OPERATING FEATURES OF A ROTARY MOLDER FOR BISCUIT DOUGHS.

1. Feeding roller. 2. Scraper blade. 3. Forward and backward movement of scraper. 4. Scraper quick release control. 5. Extracter roller adjuster. 6. Control for upward and downward movement of scraper. 7. Extraction roller. 8. Molding roller. 9. Extraction web (edge). 10. Dough hopper.

Doughnut-forming Equipment

Automatic doughnut production can be divided into seven basic operations in a linear system. These are: (1) scaling ingredients, (2) mixing, (3) extrusion forming, or sheeting and cutting, (4) proofing—for yeast-leavened doughs, (5) frying, (6) finishing, and (7) packaging. The efficient production of doughnuts requires specialized equipment subsequent to the mixing stage. Generally, conventional horizontal or vertical mixers can be used for yeast-raised and cake-type doughnuts.

Yeast-raised doughnuts can be formed either by cutting (usually) hexagonal pieces from a dough sheet or by extruding the dough through a circular orifice. Although the extrusion method is potentially the most efficient since it is scrapless and deposits the scaled doughs directly onto the infeed conveyor of a continuous proofer, it does require certain characteristics in the dough to operate satisfactorily. Extrusion can be either vacuum or pressure driven.

Cake doughnuts are generally extruded from a mass of dough held in a hopper. Both vacuum-mechanical or pressure-extrusion systems are in use. In pressure extrusion, a rotary valve delivers batter from the hopper into a chamber where it is subjected to 4–10 lb of air pressure. Several tubes lead from the chamber and are closed by cutting valves. When these valves are opened, the pressure forces batter down the tubes and around the cutting dies which sever the rings of dough. The simple vacuum system uses negative pressure to draw batter into a chamber when a sliding gate of the hopper opens. Then this gate is closed, and air pressure forces the dough through another valve into the dies.

In the preceding methods, product weight is affected by the batter viscosity, the pressure on the batter, and the length of time the die is open. Product size cannot be varied at the individual orifices because a single pressure chamber feeds all the cutters.

The vacuum-mechanical method uses individual plungers or cutters to create a vacuum which draws batter from the hopper into individual cylinders. The batter is measured volumetrically and extruded in doughnut shape. Very uniform dough weight can be maintained because a precise amount is measured at each cycle.

A recent development in vacuum-mechanical equipment has been the introduction of multispaced cutter heads. Since both the die shapes and the center-to-center spacings can be changed, several varieties and sizes of doughnuts can be formed simultaneously. When smaller pieces are being made, more pieces can be extruded on the same belt width, eliminating empty proofer spaces and low utilization of fryer capacity.

The three types of automatic proofing systems for yeast-raised doughnuts are:

(1) The proofing cloth system in which the pieces are cut from a sheet of dough on the bench or makeup table and then transferred to a proofing cloth, screen, or proofing board. The dough pieces are then transferred on their supporting material to a conventional proof box. After a proof time of 25–35 min, the proofing cloths are taken to a feed table from which the dough pieces are transferred to a conveyor-type fryer.

(2) A second type of production system involves the manual transfer of the raw doughnuts from a conventional makeup table to the flights or baskets of an automatic proofer. Humidity and temperature are maintained by automatic controls. The uniform proof imparted to the prod-

Courtesy of Belshaw Bros.

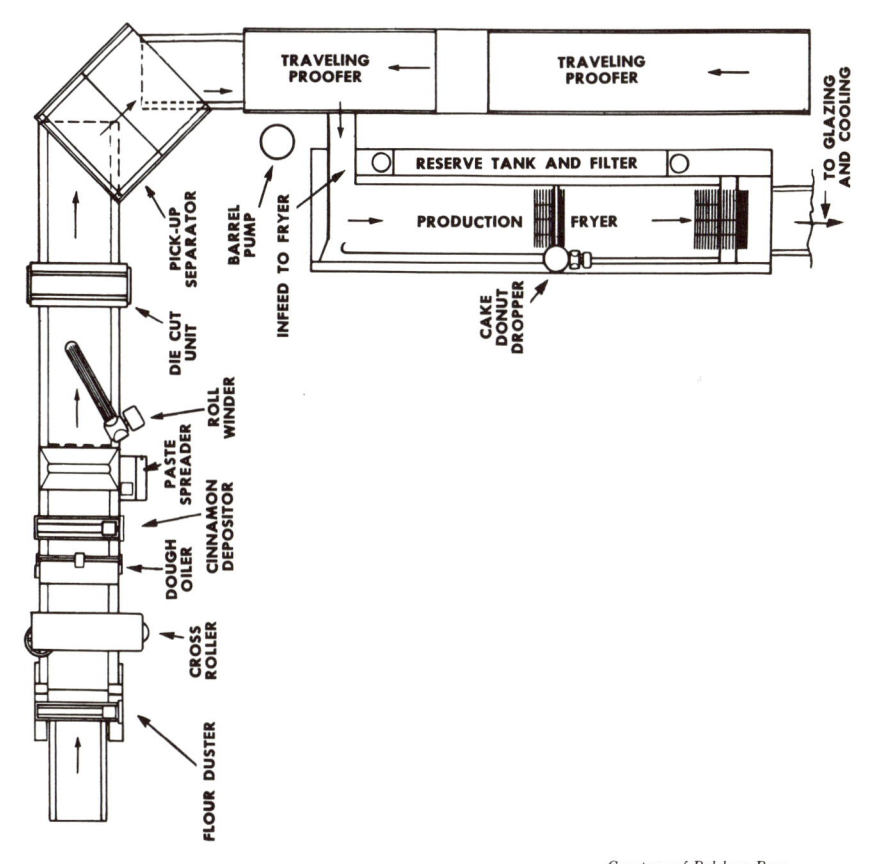

FIG. 18.21. LAYOUT OF AN AUTOMATIC PRODUCTION LINE FOR DOUGHNUTS.

uct by the controlled conditions in the cabinet permits close control of product size and quality. Since a constant load is being sent to the proofer, and there are no doors to open or close, uniform temperature and humidity conditions can be maintained.

(3) The third type of proofing system uses microwave heating to speed the leavening action. Microwave proofers cause a substantially uniform temperature rise throughout the dough piece, eliminating the slow transfer of heat by conduction or convection which must occur in conventional systems. As a result, the dough pieces expand to the desired extent within 3–6 min in continuous microwave proofers. Conveying means is a belt rather than the trays or pockets used in conventional systems. Some formula modification may be required when

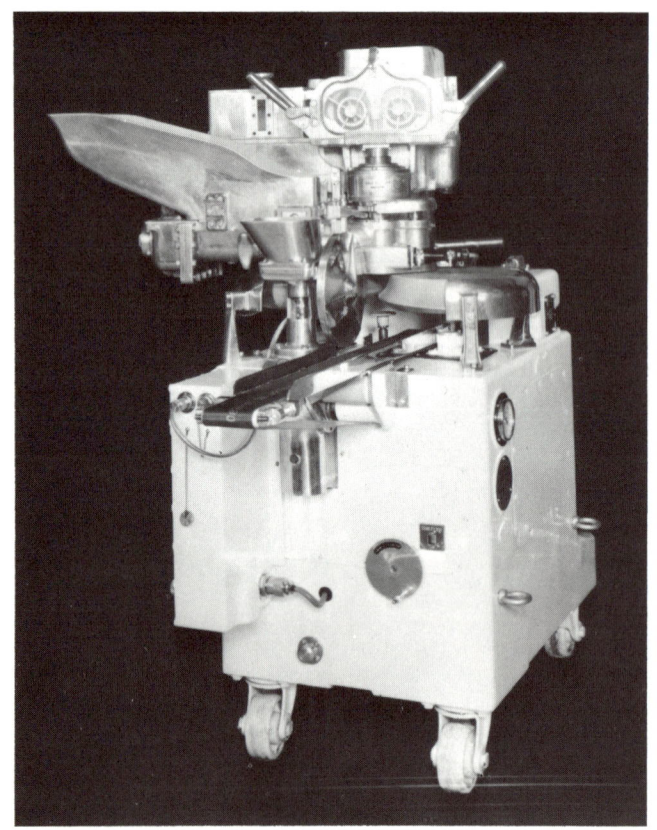

Courtesy of Lea-Fi International, Inc.

FIG. 18.22. THIS INGENIOUS DEVICE ASSEMBLES A NUMBER OF TINY DOUGH BALLS AROUND A FILLING TO MAKE MANY KINDS OF FILLED DOUGH PRODUCTS.

switching from conventional to microwave proofing, since reactions other than gassing may not proceed at the same enhanced rate.

A completely automatic production system for doughnuts would include an extruder for yeast-raised dough, an automatic proofer, an automatic cake doughnut cutter, an automatic fryer, a fat melter and leveler, a sweep conveyor, an automatic glazer, and a screen loader (Belshaw 1970). A typical layout is shown in Fig. 18.21. With commercially available equipment, 1 such line should yield up to 600 regular-sized doughnuts per hour, using a 90-sec fry time.

Miscellaneous Equipment

An automatic dough-molding and filling machine of unique design (Fig. 18.22) is said to eliminate conventional dividing, rounding, intermediate proofing, molding, and filling operations in the production of many kinds of yeast-raised products. It is said to produce 2400–3000 pieces per hour in the $½-5½$ oz scaling range. The machine extrudes dough from the hopper by means of a set of two worm conveyors and a roller. The dough is extruded in ring (doughnut) shapes which are formed into spherical pieces about $⅜$ in. in diameter at the rate of about 200 per min. These dough balls are further shaped by a helical rounder which also conveys them to a pocket formed around the orifice of the filling extruder. The filling is enrobed and the dough covered, sealed, and formed into a ball by horizontal rotating discs.

Bagels.—Regular bagel dough is too stiff to be cut into shapes as doughnuts sometimes are, since the edges do not round off during proofing. In a machine patented by Paitchell and Goldberg (1963), a piece of dough is forced onto the tip of a cone and then rolled up the cone by mechanical fingers until it assumes the proper size and shape.

BIBLIOGRAPHY

ANON. 1947. American Standard Safety Code for Bakery Equipment. United States of America Standards Institute, New York.
ANON. 1959. Paterson introduces ful-flavor bread. Baking Ind. *111*, May 16, 36–37.
ATWOOD, H. T. 1964. Mold for pie shells. U.S. Pat. 3,124,083. Mar. 10.
BAKER, G. L. 1967. Conditioning of sweet yeast dough for mechanical make-up. Proc. Am. Soc. Bakery Engrs. *1967*, 179–188.
CACKLER, H. 1957. Bread twisting techniques. Proc. Am. Soc. Bakery Engrs. *1957*, 68–77.
CADWELL, C. C. 1956. Continuous operation of all variety coffee cakes and sweet yeast goods. Proc. Am. Soc. Bakery Engrs. *1956*, 137–151.
DAVEY, V. F. 1965. Make-up procedures for roll-in coffee cake production. Proc. Am. Soc. Bakery Engrs. *1965*, 281–287.
ENOCH, D. W., SCOTT, G. L., HUBER, M. M. AND KIEFFABER, C. A. 1964. Loaf coiling bread molding machine. U.S. Pat. 3,116,703. Jan. 7.
EUVERRARD, M. R. 1970. Evolution of bun production systems. Baker's Dig. *44*, No. 1, 74–79.
FAGERLIND, B. 1959. Custom built for automation. Baking Ind. *111*, Mar. 21, 76, 79.

FORRESTER, C. W. 1963. Machine for making crumpets and the like. U.S. Pat. 3,093,062. June 11.
GAGEANT, L. M. 1964. Automatic pie machine. U.S. Pat. 3,136,268. June 9.
HANCOCK, M. B. 1958. Automatic bun production—plant layout. Proc. Am. Soc. Bakery Engrs. *1958*, 112–117.
HUNTER, C. L. 1949. Conventional molding vs. loose curl cross-molding. Proc. Am. Soc. Bakery Engrs. *1949*, 91–93.
JAHN, M. C. 1964. Automatic pie machine. U.S. Pat. 3,129,674. Apr. 21.
KUNSTMANN, W. O. 1969. New production methods for yeast-raised sweet products. Proc. Am. Soc. Bakery Engrs. *1969*, 174–181.
LUBER, S. V. 1959. Mechanical production of sweet yeast goods. Proc. Am. Soc. Bakery Engrs. *1959*, 183–191.
MATZ, S. A. 1968. Cookie and Cracker Technology. Avi Publishing Co., Westport, Conn.
MOHR, J. 1949. Conventional molding versus loose curl straight molding. Proc. Am. Soc. Bakery Engrs. *1949*, 93–96.
NOEL, E.M. 1962. Fully automatic production of English muffins. Bakers Weekly *194*, No. 9, 33–35.
OLMSTED, J. P., JR. 1970. Fundamentals of mechanical make-up. Proc. Am. Soc. Bakery Engrs. *1970*, 54–57.
PATERSON, A. C. 1957. Mechanical cake baking, mixing through finishing. Proc. Am. Soc. Bakery Engrs. *1957*, 273–277.
PAITCHELL, H., AND GOLDBERG, I. 1963. Apparatus for automatically forming dough rings for making bagels. U.S. Pat. 3,080,831. Mar. 12.
PERGIEL, L. J. 1958. Synchronization of make-up equipment—so that capacities of individual units are related, eliminating costly bottlenecks. Proc. Am. Soc. Bakery Engrs. *1958*, 124–129.
PFROMMER, P. 1954. Mechanical production of roll-in Danish type coffee cake and sweet rolls. Proc. Am. Soc. Bakery Engrs. *1954*, 200–208.
PRESCOTT, S. E., AND HAVIGHORST, C.R. 1956. Engineering reaches new high in this ultra-modern bakery. Food Eng. 28, No. 11, 45–50.
ROHRBACH, I. O. 1957. Sweet yeast dough sheeting methods. Proc. Am. Soc. Bakery Engrs. *1957*, 278–286.
SCHIEB, W. M. 1959. New gadgets for you. Proc. Am. Soc. Bakery Engrs. *1959*, 209–222.
SPOWART, S. J., GOODMAN, D., AND SUTHERLAND, D. 1963. Doubles deflector for dough rounding machine. U.S. Pat. 3,115,250. Dec. 24.
STILES, L., JR. 1958. Mechanized coffee cakes—Danish and sweet dough types. Proc. Am. Soc. Bakery Engrs. *1958*, 200–209.
VALENTYNE, P. H. 1959. Calculable approaches to bread dough cooling. Baking Ind. *111*, June 27, 38–39, 87.
WAGNER, J. 1955. Automatic equipment—its operation for profit. Proc. Am. Soc. Bakery Engrs. *1955*, 144–150.

CHAPTER 19

CONTINUOUS PROCESSING OF BAKERY PRODUCTS

Many of the operations required for making bread were converted to continuous flow several decades ago. It was not until the 1950's, however, that satisfactory equipment for automatic mixing and depositing of bread dough became available. Although many critics said that bread made by these installations would never be accepted by the consumer because the grain was too uniform, the texture too soft, and the flavor somewhat blander than most conventional bread, they were proved wrong and great success was achieved in gaining public acceptance of the new product.

The two types of continuous plants which dominate the U.S. market are the Baker Do-Maker and the AmFlow process. The principles are somewhat similar. In both cases, automatic metering of ingredients into fermentation tanks leads to the development of a brew, broth, or liquid sponge which is mixed with the other ingredients, developed into the form of a dough by a special mixer, and then deposited in pans.

Continuous processing is not restricted to bread and rolls. Cake batters and many adjuncts such as marshmallow and icings can be prepared by continuous mixing techniques. In fact, some of this equipment predates the AmFlow and Do-Maker introductions.

FORMULATIONS AND INGREDIENTS

Although the ingredient specifications and rules of formulation are generally similar to those applicable to conventionally processed bread and rolls, there are several notable differences.

An obvious formulation difference is the necessity for dividing the ingredients into brew and dough ingredients. Composition of the brew has been a source of controversy for many years. The differences of opinion chiefly concern the amount of flour to be added to the ferment (Table 19.1). It is generally agreed that addition of some flour to the brew tends to open the grain and improve slicing, stacking, and spreading characteristics of the loaf; and it also gives more chewiness to the bread and reduces gumminess.

The recent trend has been to increase the amount of flour in the

TABLE 19.1
CONTINUOUS MIX FORMULAS

Ingredient	No Flour Brew (%)	30% Flour Brew (%)
Brew, Stage 1		
Water	67.0	67.0
Flour	—	30.0
Dextrose, db	8.0	2.0
Yeast	2.62	2.62
Salt	2.10	2.10
Nonfat dry milk	1.00	1.00
Yeast food	0.50	0.50
Calcium propionate	0.10	0.10
Oxidizers[1]		
Brew, Stage 2		
Dextrose, db	—	6.00
Dough		
Flour	100.0	70.0
Brew	81.3	111.3
Liquid shortening	3.0	3.0

Source: Adapted from Redfern et al. (1968).
[1] Potassium bromate 50 ppm, and potassium iodate 10 ppm.

liquid ferment. Some of the advantages of using high levels of flour in preferments are said to be (Bare 1969): (1) increased bread volume, (2) a firmer texture, (3) longer retention of crumb resiliency, (4) better accommodation of enriching ingredients such as nonfat dry milk, (5) sugar can be decreased somewhat without decreasing the residual sugar level of the bread, (6) mechanical energy required to develop the dough is reduced, and (7) less cooling of the ferment is required. Use of high levels of flour requires specialized equipment for mixing the ingredients to provide a continuous flow of properly blended ferment.

The mixing of high levels (up to 70% of the formula amount) of flour into water without developing the gluten requires rapid addition of the flour during vigorous agitation so as to immediately wet and disperse the flour. In this way, formation of agglomerates is prevented and the gluten does not develop and separate. Agitation is stopped at once when all the flour is dispersed to minimize foaming. After a 30-min rest, the mixing action may be resumed to prevent excessive expansion of the sponge as the yeast begins to emit gas. At an appropriate time, from the scheduling point of view, the liquid is transferred to a holding tank where it is held at 80°F for about 2–2½ hr. A deviation of up to 40 min is said to be within the acceptable range.

A ferment supply system for a continuous mixing operation might consist of 2 blending ranks, 2 holding tanks, metering devices, a continuous blender, and a ferment tank (see Fig. 19.1). Water and yeast

Courtesy of American Machine & Foundry Co.

FIG. 19.1. A SMALL CONTINUOUS UNIT (AMFLOW 300).
Brew tanks are at extreme left and developer is at extreme right

would be mixed in 1 of the blending vessels and transferred to 1 of the holding tanks. Water, yeast-food, salt, and sugar would be blended in the other mixing vat and transferred to the second holding tank. From this point, the operation is automatic and continuous with the flour and the two solutions being metered into the continuous blender. After mixing, they pass into the ferment tank.

There are two types of arrangements for ferment holding tanks—the parallel system (see Fig. 19.2) and the in-line (or series) system. In the series system, there are perhaps four tanks into which the ferment is pumped in sequence as the final vessel finishes discharging into the mixer. In the parallel arrangement, each tank receives a batch from the blender and holds that batch until it is called for at the dough-mixing unit. The advantage of the series arrangement is that some mixing of the batches occurs during the transfer and this tends to smooth out differences in composition or stage of fermentation which may have developed prior to that time.

From the holding tanks, the preferments go to a tempering tank

364   BAKERY TECHNOLOGY AND ENGINEERING

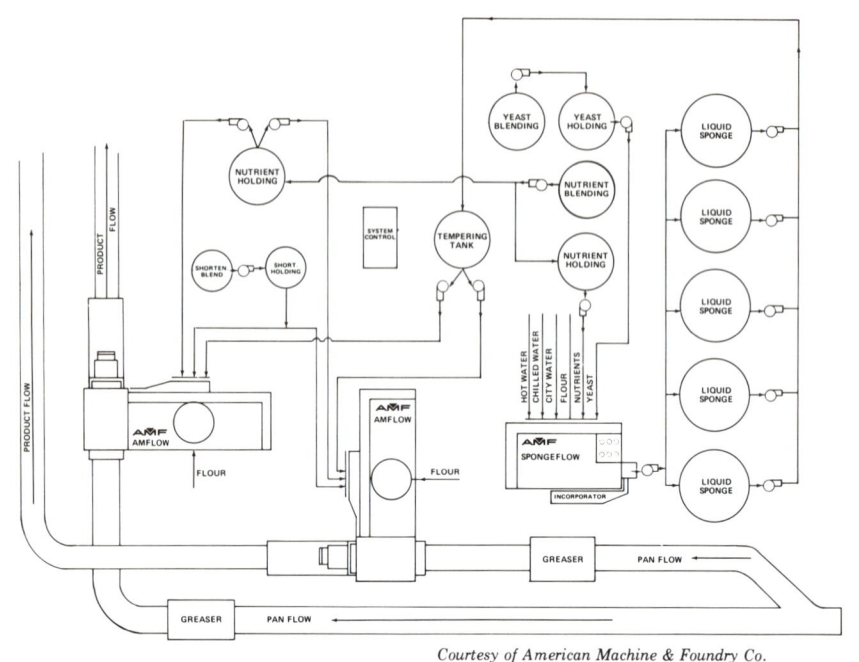

Courtesy of American Machine & Foundry Co.
FIG. 19.2. LAYOUT OF CONTINUOUS BREAD DOUGH PRODUCTION SHOWING ONE SPONGEFLOW UNIT FEEDING TWO AMFLOW UNITS.

for adjustment of temperature and density. The tempered ferment along with a nutrient slurry, a shortening mixture, and the remaining flour is metered to the continuous incorporator and developer.

The preferment system of the continuous mixing plant can be considered as replacing the sponge mixer, the dough troughs, the fermentation room, and the trough hoists of the batch plant. According to Euverard (1969) there are three basic types of preferments—concentrated, no flour, and high flour. Examples of formulas for the doughs are shown in Table 19.2. Principal differences other than the content of flour are the higher amounts of yeast and sugar in the concentrated and no-flour preferment doughs, and the higher level of milk in the high-flour preferment and the conventional sponge doughs. The preferment portions of the formulas are compared in Table 19.3. The high-flour preferment approaches sponge formulas in composition, except that all of the water is used in the ferment to give a viscosity that can be tolerated by available equipment.

Continuously mixed doughs usually require higher oxidant levels. This is probably due to the smaller amounts of oxygen incorporated into continuous doughs, and the shorter times available for oxidation to occur. Potassium iodate, potassium bromate, calcium iodate,

TABLE 19.2
TYPICAL FORMULAS FOR PREFERMENT AND CONVENTIONAL DOUGHS

Ingredient	Concentrated Preferment (%)	No Flour Preferment (%)	High Flour Preferment (%)	Conventional Sponge Dough (%)
Flour	100.0	100.0	100.0	100.0
Water	64.0	64.0	64.0	64.0
Yeast	3.5	3.5	2.75	2.75
Yeast food	1.0	0.625	0.625	0.625
Salt	2.25	2.25	2.25	2.25
Sugar	9.0	9.0	7.0	7.0
Skim milk solids	1.5	1.5	3.0	3.0
Inhibitor	0.125	0.125	0.125	0.125
Shortening	3.5	3.5	3.5	3.5

Source: Euverard (1969).

TABLE 19.3
TYPICAL FORMULAS FOR PREFERMENTS

Ingredient	Concentrated Preferment (%)	No flour Preferment (%)	High Flour Preferment (%)
Flour	—	—	60.0
Water	16.0	63.5	55.75
Yeast	3.0	3.0	2.75
Yeast food	1.0	0.625	0.625
Salt	1.0	2.25	0.25
Sugar	5.0	9.0	0.5
Skim milk solids	1.5	1.5	—
Inhibitor	—	0.125	0.125
Totals	27.5	80.0	120.0
% of total formula	15.0	43.0	66.0
% of formula solids	9.5	13.7	53.80
Liquids to solids ratio	1:0.72	1:0.26	1:1.15

Source: Euverard (1969).

and calcium peroxide are probably the most common oxidants used today. According to surveys, total oxidant levels range from 60 to 75 ppm, with a ratio of potassium bromate to potassium iodate of from 4:1 to 6:1 (Redfern et al. 1965). As the oxidant level is raised, developer speed must be increased and the power required for optimum development also increases. If the oxidant level is too low, a weak crumb structure is produced.

Continuous mix formulations often contain from 2 to 5% of added shortening, and usually this is a mixture of fat and emulsifiers. Much of the fat system combines in some way with either the protein or the starch during processing. Adding a hard fat fraction (hydrogenated fat flakes) to the shortening results in improvements in grain and specific volume. Baldwin et al. (1963) showed in their experiments that all fats which were completely liquid at the dough temperature (104°F) produced poor quality bread, but each of these oils produced good bread when hydrogenated cottonseed oil flakes or tallow flakes were added in amounts (about 10%) sufficient to congeal the fat at dough temperature. Better results were obtained with hydrogenated cottonseed and tallow flakes than with soybean or lard flakes presumably because the latter promote formation of the larger beta crystals in lard systems while the former tend to produce beta prime crystals. It appears that neither the degree of unsaturation nor the fatty acid composition of fats is extremely critical to dough properties as long as solid fats are present during dough preparation and proofing. Flour fat may be essential. Flour from which a substantial part of the lipids had been removed by ether extraction gave complete failures.

Milk has caused trouble in continuous bread production. Addition of more than 1% skim milk powder can result in loss of volume and of the uniform grain, bright crumb, and soft texture which are characteristic of the normal product. These quality defects can be remedied to some extent by other formula adjustments and particularly by the use of higher strength flours or higher percentages of spring wheat flour (Cotton 1963). In any case, high heat treatment of the milk before drying is essential.

Yeast, sugars, and mold inhibitors can be the same types used in batch bread production. Some special additives are said to improve the tolerance and quality of the doughs. For example, sodium stearyl fumarate at levels of 0.25–0.5% apparently extends the range of developer speeds at which continuous mix bread of uniformly high quality can be produced (Geminder et al. 1965).

EQUIPMENT AND PROCEDURES[1]

The AmFlow and Do-Maker procedures, as currently practiced, are similar in most respects. In its original form, the AmFlow process put the developed dough through a conventional rounder and molder before panning. This was soon changed to direct panning, as with the Do-Maker equipment.

Preparation of the Broth

The Do-Maker broth is prepared at a definite time in advance of its need for mixing with the flour, shortening, and oxidizing agents (Fig. 19.3).

The time of fermentation begins when the yeast is added to the solution of sugar, milk, salt, yeast food, vitamins, and mold inhibitor and ends when the fermenting liquor is pumped to the premixer—an

---

[1] Part of this section was written by Dr. Hugh K. Parker, consultant, Glen Ridge, N.J.

FIG. 19.3. FERMENTATION TANKS FOR A DO-MAKER OPERATION.
Courtesy of Wallace and Tiernan, Inc.

average time of from 2 to 2½ hr. The expected conversion of sugar to carbon dioxide and alcohol amounts to about 1½–2% during this period. At the end of 2½ hr the yeast is fermenting at a lively rate, and its action will bring the hydrogen ion concentration down to pH 4.7, which is more or less controlled by the buffering action of the milk content of the broth. The Do-Maker ferment conditions the yeast for optimum dispersion of gluten, which is another way of describing mellowing of the dough due to good yeast condition. To maintain continuity each broth is "set" (yeast is added) 30 min after the yeast addition to the preceding broth.

The properly fermented Do-Maker preferment contributes to the flavor of the finished bread. Additional sweetness can be obtained by use of enough sugar to satisfy the baker and his particular market. A long fermentation would produce a sour type of bread, but could not be used if dough properties were adversely affected. Some of the so-called "sours," cultures of acid-forming bacteria, could be used if conditions of time and temperature were favorable, and here, again, the effect would have to be controlled so that dough properties would not be adversely affected.

The characteristics of these preferments influence the resultant dough properties when mixed with flour and the other ingredients, i.e., shortening and oxidizing agents. In general too long a fermentation may weaken the doughs, whereas too short a fermentation will not sufficiently mellow the dough for best mixing and for good machining in the extrusion process which is to follow. These effects are somewhat similar to those found in conventional sponge processes, except that in the latter at dough-up, the addition of fresh flour may correct for some difficulties and create slightly more tolerant conditions in the bake shop. The preferment acts upon all fresh flour, so to speak, and thus continuously-produced dough resembles the straight-dough process.

The Do-Maker broth is pumped from the fermentation tank to the transfer tank, where it is held for some minutes to allow emptying of the fermentation tank, and level out the feed rate. Then it flows through a constant level tank. A two-speed pump takes the liquid from the constant level device and forces it through a heat exchanger to the premixer.

Since there is the usual temperature rise of 10°–12°F in the yeast action of the ferment (corresponding to about the same amount of temperature rise in the conventional sponge) there may be times when the ferment should be cooled, so a heat exchanger is installed between the pump and the premixer. This arrangement makes it possible also to adjust for flour temperature, and thus bring dough out at the right temperature.

The flow of this liquid, as well as other liquid and the dry constituents, must be under exact control and must never stop once the machine is started. In the Do-Maker system the problem is solved by use of 2-speed motors for the pumps and 2-speed motors for the flour feeders. These are actuated by the load in the balanced premixer. Too much load, for example, calls for the use of the motor at two-thirds its normal speed while too little returns the pump and feeder rates back to full speed.

The pump and feeder speeds are at the full speed rate 95% of the time and at ⅔ of the speed rate 5% of the time. While this is an automatic feature, the operator has the opportunity of changing each individual ingredient rate or all of them by increasing or decreasing speed rates from the main Do-Maker control panel where each ingredient feed rate is also indicated and adjusted.

The AmFlow procedure for preparation of the preferment can be best described by referring to the schematic diagram of Fig. 19.2 and the illustration of equipment, Fig. 19.4. Major components of the fermentation system are the blending tank, two holding tanks, and the fermentation trough each of which is equipped with special agitators.

The preparation of the liquid sponge begins with the addition of yeast, yeast food, liquid sugar, and dry ingredients to water in the

Courtesy of American Machine & Foundry Co.
FIG. 19.4. DUAL AMFLOW INSTALLATION PRODUCING UP TO 16,000 POUNDS OF DOUGH PER HOUR.

blending tank, into which is also recycled some of the liquid sponge. After about 1 hr, salt, milk and 10–16% of the flour are added and the mix is pumped to 1 of the 2 holding tanks to develop the liquid sponge (before the addition of flour the liquid is called the "brew") which is about the consistency of high-solids milk. The remainder of the water is added at this point. A four-pronged horseshoe agitator holds the flour in suspension while fermentation continues.

From the holding tank the liquid sponge is pumped to the horizontal tank where more sugar is added according to the baker's need for sweetness, and to be sure that the yeast is sufficiently fed. The liquid sponge continues to ferment for about 1 hr before it is pumped to the incorporator where the assembly of oxidizing solution, shortening, and major part of the flour occurs. As previously noted, some of the liquid sponge is recycled to the blending tank in order to take advantage of some enzyme and fermentation products which may occur in flour and other ingredients to improve yeast activity and final flavor.

Preliminary-mixing Apparatus

The premixer of the Do-Maker process functions as an assembly point for the liquid ingredients; i.e., fermented broth, melted shortening, and solution containing the oxidizing agent as well as for the dry ingredients—the flour. Here also occurs the first wetting of the flour with liquids and consequent homogeneous admixture to form the dough. The ingredients are admitted to the head end of a two-shafted mixing conveyor, each shaft of which has a series of blades. The dough is discharged to the dough pump at the exit end. By measurement of the torque required to mix this mass of forming and moving dough, it is possible to record consistency—which some might term viscosity. At any rate, such readings are useful in observing slight changes in flow of ingredient rate, and more especially to help keep absorption levels at a steady state. The assembled dough thus prepared has no structure and little gas retaining property; since no kneading work has been done, no development has occurred. In the Do-Maker the premixer is mounted on a pivot, and overweight and underweight of the "through-flowing" dough is corrected as described earlier. Moreover, it should be pointed out that a light on the panel indicator changes with the full-to-$\frac{2}{3}$ pump rate.

In the AmFlow Incorporator (Fig. 19.5) the design is such that a manual adjustment must be made to maintain the dough flow to the pump ahead of the developer at constant pressure.

Courtesy of American Machine & Foundry Co.

FIG. 19.5. AMF SPONGEFLOW INCORPORATOR (DISASSEMBLED).

Dough Pump

The dough pump functions as a regulator of dough flow, and as a means of forcing dough under pressure to the developer. The control of the dough flow is necessary for exact dividing, and the regulation thereof comes from the main panel by changing the speed of the pump. Besides this control, the speed of the divider can be changed, if conditions warrant, so that dough-piece weight can be adjusted. Naturally, for a major change in dough-flow rate, as called for from the panel, ingredient-flow rates must also be changed accordingly. For example, a small adjustment of ¼–½ oz of dough per dough piece would be taken care of with a change of dough pump speed alone, but a change from 90 lb of dough per minute to 100 lb of dough per minute would require ingredient feed rate adjustment of 11.1%. The dough pump is indirectly concerned with the shaping of the developed dough piece, since the pressure of the dough incoming to the developer and outgoing from the developer is a function of the dough pump, and pressure is required to maintain through-put and extrusion.

The Developer

The developer is really one of the most interesting and important elements of continuous operation, for at this point the dough is changed from an assembled mass with no structure, no strength, and no property of gas retention to a smooth film-forming body (the dough at this stage can be stretched out into fine coherent and extensible films), which has superior strength and characteristics for holding the leavening gas which will be generated in the subsequent proof stage. The kneading work done in this part of the apparatus is done on a substantially degassed dough, and because of the 20–60 lb pressure involved and the comparatively high speed mixing action, carbon dioxide is driven into solution and into the gluten matrix as indicated by Dr. Baker's (1954) studies. Such effects can, in part, explain the fine grain and texture of continuously produced bread. Due to mechanical work, kneading, folding, stretching, etc., there will be a temperature rise in the finished dough of 18°–24°F depending upon the flour used, consistency of dough, through-put rate, and other conditions. Roughly, this heat rise is the same as shown in conventional batch mixers of 600–1200 lb capacity indicating that mechanical work required to develop 1 lb of flour is about the same in either case, but the efficiency difference is in favor of the continuous operation.

In conventional operation 1000 lb of dough may require 10 min to develop, and the dough, in some cases, must be cooled by ice or refrigeration during mixing. In contrast, the continuous operation can be compared on a per minute basis: 100 lb of dough per minute are developed in 90 sec. In other words, the work is done on smaller dough increments in the continuous processes.

The work in the Do-Maker developer is accomplished by two vertical impellers which turn at a speed which will do the best work. Doughs of flours from different wheats or different manufacture require different impeller speeds (rpm) to get the necessary work done. In general, the stronger flours of higher protein content require more revolutions per minute than do the medium strength flours. A northern spring standard patent of about 12% protein might require 160 rpm whereas a southwestern bakers patent of 11.4% protein might require 120 rpm. Naturally, speeds also are adjusted to take care of throughput.

Other factors which may influence the mixing requirements of the dough may be the amounts of some of the ingredients besides flour as well as the amount of absorption; for, while high absorption increases mixing time in conventional operation, a slight increase in revolutions per minute is usual in the Do-Maker. The higher milk or shortening levels tend to call for more revolutions per minute, possibly to allow for more contacts between flour particles separated by the dilution effect of the inert materials.

Oxidizing agents can affect mixing requirement. It has been found that best continuous operation requires roughly 10-fold as much oxidation as conventional. Part of this increase in requirement may be due to lack of atmospheric oxygen in the closed system of continuous operation, and possibly part may be due to removal or change in some flour constituent due to yeast fermentation as practiced in the sponge and dough method. Oxidation seems to be necessary for good gluten development during mixing, and such action improves gas retention and stabilizes conditions. Oxidation of flours tends to lengthen mixing time in the conventional and increase revolutions per minute in the continuous methods.

Most of the changes in mixing requirement, if these occur, will be seen on the power curve. The amount of power used in mixing the dough is continuously shown by means of a recording wattmeter, so the operator can check deviations and make adjustments on the panel in cooling water at the heat exchanger, etc. In addition to the recording wattmeter control, an experienced operator can usually pick up differences in appearance of the extruding dough piece to detect improper mixing. Undermixed doughs show striations or laminations; overmixing is indicated by a glossy surface and tackiness. In start-up operations these observations are helpful in proper adjustment of mixing speed. The feel of the dough and its capacity to stretch and be drawn into films also helps the operator judge development progress and arrive at proper mixing speeds. The usual test is to run a mixing curve, to find a point of undermixing, then overmixing, and finally arrive at an optimum. With a flour of critical mixing performance the lower limit of mixing speed may be 115 rpm, for example; the upper limit 125 rpm; and the optimum would be 120 rpm. A flour with good mixing tolerance would have somewhat more spread in these requirements; for example, a very tolerant flour with an optimum of 120 rpm might have a lower limit of 110 rpm and an upper limit of 130 rpm.

The dough is continuously developed as it progresses downward to the exit of the developer, and should be fully developed as it passes through a narrow slit opening to the extruder. After passing this point, it is shaped so that an elongated cylindrical dough piece is cut off by opposed knives as it is extruded from the divider. The knives are actuated in synchronization with the panner, and this in turn is timed to catch the falling dough piece in a properly placed pan below. The timing of the panner and the knife stroke is adjusted so that dough pieces of the desired weight are cut off. When the operator desires to change the length of the dough piece, adjustments are quickly made to lengthen or shorten the cut-off orifice. To increase the weight of the dough piece the time of the cut-off is lengthened. Some of these adjustments call for a short period of time during which the developed dough is run through the panner into a trough below. This dough is fed back into the premixer at a low rate of addition, so no waste of material occurs nor is the time schedule seriously affected. The dough extruding and panning operation in the Do-Maker is shown in Fig. 19.6.

The AmFlow and Do-Maker developers are similar in many respects. However, the AmFlow impeller is driven hydraulically rather than electrically and is mounted in a horizontal position in contrast to the vertical alignment of the Do-Maker impeller. Extrusion is accomplished in a somewhat similar manner with both processes.

Once panned, the dough is conducted to the proof box or chamber, where it is allowed to ferment to height or time if a continuous proofer is used. From the proof the dough is delivered to the oven as usual. These steps are not very different from conventional operation. The exceptions will be noted and discussed. For instance, one finds the panned, continuously produced dough is somewhat more sticky since no dusting flour is used in the processing; it can, and usually does, carry more absorption than conventional. The proof time is approximately the same. The dough of the continuous operation will not tolerate a dry proof box, so careful attention is paid to humidity control.

Courtesy of Wallace and Tiernan, Inc.
FIG. 19.6. DO-MAKER DEVELOPER-DIVIDER-PANNER HEAD.

In general the doughs are lively and very uniform in their rise in the proof and in the oven. If lack of uniformity is noted the operator checks for cool or hot spots which result from uneven heating or poor circulation.

The baking of the continuously-made dough may require some oven adjustment when the process is first installed. As in all good operations, even heat application to every loaf alike is the ultimate goal. In a well-adjusted continuous operation, it is indeed an impressive sight to view the uniformity with which the baked loaves come out of the oven, hour after hour.

Buns and Rolls

Bun and roll doughs can be continuously mixed and developed in much the same way as bread doughs and with similar equipment. Makeup requires special automatic dividers and forming equipment

(Fig. 19.7). Because of the excessive stickiness resulting from dough temperatures, it is difficult if not impossible to shape dough at 100°F so some provision must be made for cooling the dough coming from a continuous mixer. Additional cooling capacity can be supplied to the heat exchanger so that colder sponge can be metered into the incorporator. One successful operator has wrapped the developer head with copper tubing through which cold water is circulated. A representative layout for a bun department producing 2400–4800 lb per hr is shown in Fig. 19.8.

OTHER CONTINUOUS EQUIPMENT

The Konpetua system for continuous dough mixing is made in West Germany. Former versions were the Kontinua and the Perpetua (for the cookie industry) which used different mixing systems. The maker claims the present model will mix nearly all kinds of doughs including bread, rolls, sweet doughs, pretzels, bagels, pizza, crackers, crisp bread, and cookies.

The Konpetua continuous dough mixing system consists of: (1) An automatic scaling unit which measures dry, pasty, and liquid ingredients and mixes solutions (if necessary). (2) A mixing machine with kneading (developing) section. (3) An electrical control panel. (4) An automatic water chiller. The mixing and kneading machine comes in 3 sizes with single chambers and 3 sizes with double chambers.

Courtesy of American Machine & Foundry Co.
FIG. 19.7. CONTINUOUS DOUGH MIXING UNIT FEEDING TWO ROLL DIVIDER-ROUNDER MACHINES (AMFLOW).

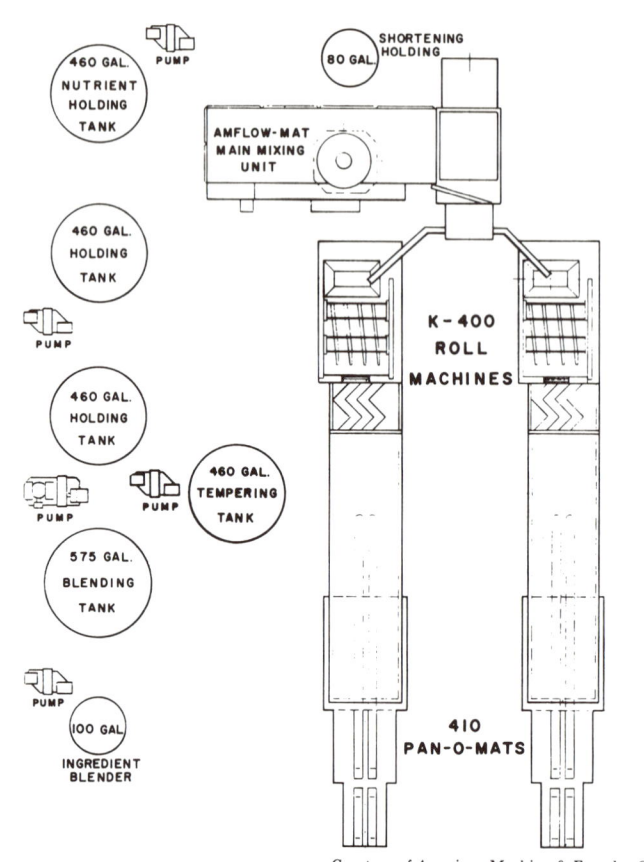

Courtesy of American Machine & Foundry Co.
FIG. 19.8. LAYOUT OF CONTINUOUS ROLL PRODUCTION PLANT.

The double barrel machines (see Fig. 19.9) have the mixing section in the upper barrel. Ingredients are fed into the hopper, thoroughly mixed while passing the mixing section, and then transferred to the lower chamber where developing of the dough takes place. Single barrel machines combine mixing and kneading sections in one tube. The barrels are jacketed for water cooling.

Output ranges from 500 to 12,000 lb per hr depending upon the model and type of dough.

Oakes Continuous Dough Machine

Although the Oakes equipment for continuous mixing of marshmallow, cake batters, and other flowable mixtures is better known than their mixing equipment for extensible doughs, they have offered two models of a mixer-developer for use in bread production. These models

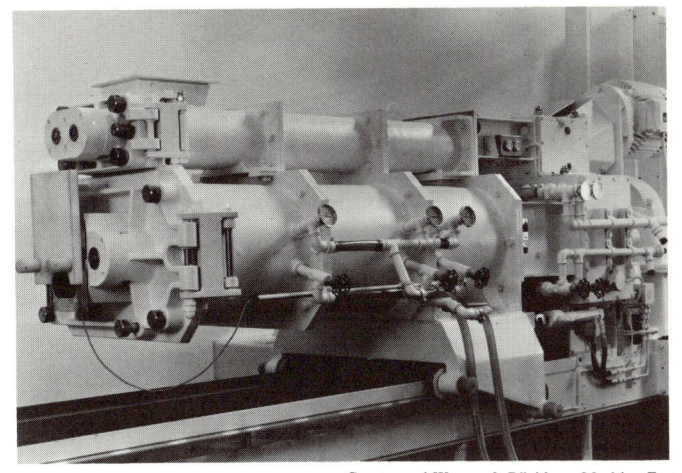

Courtesy of Werner & Pfleiderer Machine Factory
FIG. 19.9 THE KONPETUA CONTINUOUS MIXING AND DEVELOPING UNIT.

have nominal maximum through-puts of 1800 lb and 3150 lb per hr, respectively.

The processing approach is said to be based on the Chorleywood Mechanical Development concept. The required energy input per pound of dough is imparted at an optimum rate, an important factor in the production of high quality bread by mechanical development. Variable speed controls on the rotor drive shaft and a wattmeter permit adjustment of the energy input to the desired level. The rheological properties of the dough produced by the mixer-developer enable the unit to be operated in conjunction with existing makeup machinery. The internal design features make the unit self-cleaning and minimize dough loss.

Ordinary tap water can be used for ferment preparation, eliminating the heat exchange equipment needed for chilled water. Temperature is controlled by water cooled jackets on the modification zone of the unit.

A typical layout is shown in Fig. 19.10.

Strahmann

A continuous dough preparation machine called the Strahmann 35 was offered by Simon Engineering of Stockport, England (Anon. 1963). It consists of: (1) a flour feeder of the band weighing type, (2) a control panel monitoring all the operations from feeding to dividing, including regulation of dough consistency, (3) pumps which feed controlled amounts of prepared liquid from sponge and liquor tanks and, (4)

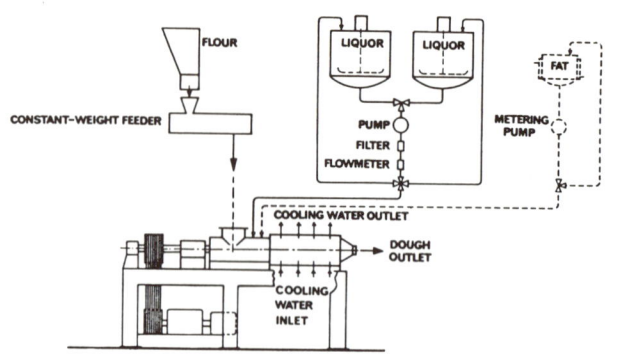

FIG. 19.10. LAYOUT FOR AN OAKES CONTINUOUS BREAD-MAKING UNIT.

mixing chamber with divider. The agitator and mixing chamber are designed to continually cut and reunite the dough, which finally emerges ready for immediate scaling. The divider is pneumatically operated and said to allow very accurate scaling. It has been recommended for breads, cookies, rusks, and pie doughs.

The original Strahmann continuous mixer was put in operation about 1960. It was driven by a 10 hp motor through an in-line gear box, and it consisted of a segmented jacket holding static shear plates and a shaft on which were affixed a simple flour-feeding worm and 16 mixer-impellers. The dough extruded from the machine was fed into a conventional divider. The rest of the processing was also more or less conventional. The dough obtained from this unit was not considered suitable for full-scale commercial production and further improvements were made in order to get an acceptable loaf. The changes included the introduction of a specially designed volumetric divider and a shortening of the relaxation time before molding to about 2 min. The mixer later consisted of 20 segments, numbers 1 to 4 having open stators and coarse pitch impellers which hydrate the flour and consolidate the dough, numbers 5 to 10 having static plates with 1-¼ in. holes and fine pitch impellers which complete the mixing and force the dough forward, while numbers 11 to 20 have static plates with holes of varying size and coarse pitch impellers for developing the dough. Restrictor plates with holes of different diameters have been used in the distal half of the barrel to increase the working of the dough (Eggitt and Coppock 1965).

Continuous Mixing of Cakes

Continuous batter processing can be applied to nearly all varieties of cakes: angel food, layers, pound, chiffon, etc. It is not suitable for batters containing particles such as nuts and candied fruit.

CONTINUOUS PROCESSING OF BAKERY PRODUCTS 379

The basic equipment for a continuous processing plant for cake batter would include: (1) a premixer into which the ingredients are metered and given an initial blending, (2) a holding tank for the premix, (3) the continuous mixer, and (4) a hopper depositer or continuous closed system depositer. Figure 19.11 illustrates such a system.

The slurry mixer can be either a vertical batch mixer or an automatic slurry mixer. In either case, the ingredients are blended only enough to insure uniform dispersal, and there is no attempt to incorporate air. If a batch mixer is used, the bowl contents are simply dumped into the slurry hopper, but the premix is transferred to the tank by pump and piping if an automatic slurry mixer is part of the system.

The slurry blending time is much less than for conventional batter mixing and the specific gravity at this stage is lower. Table 19.4 details some of these relationships. Because of the greater density, considerably larger batch weights can be prepared in bowls of equivalent size.

The batter premix is fed into the mixing chamber at a constant rate. Pressurized air is also metered in at the velocity required to give the desired specific gravity in the finished batter. Continuous mixers

Courtesy of American Machine & Foundry Co.

FIG. 19.11. MACHINERY ASSEMBLY FOR CONTINUOUS MIXING OF CAKE BATTER.

The initial blending step takes place in the planetary mixer at extreme right.

TABLE 19.4
COMPARISON OF CONVENTIONAL BATTERS AND CONTINOUS SLURRIES

Cake Variety	Batch Weight Batter (Lb)	Batch Weight Slurry (Lb)	Specific Gravity Batter	Specific Gravity Slurry	Mix Time Batter (Min)	Mix Time Slurry (Min)
Angel food	212	580	0.30	0.82	18	4.5
Sponge	459	670	0.65	0.95	18	4.0
Chiffon	248	670	0.35	0.95	20	5.0
Pound	496	672	0.71	0.98	17	5.0
Chocolate layer	637	700	0.93	0.99	15	5.0
Yellow layer	637	672	0.90	0.98	15	4.0
Devils food	670	785	0.95	1.11	17	5.0

Source: Adapted from Bonavia (1967).

consist of a circular chamber having the inner surfaces (stators) fitted with projections, and an inner disc-shaped rotor with many teeth. The Oakes and the AMF differ somewhat in the design of the rotor and stators. Both are capable of doing a satisfactory mixing job on cake batters.

There are several advantages in using continuous mixers for batters. Chief among these is the ability to furnish an exceptionally uniform batter filled with fine bubbles of consistent size, provided that due care is taken in the metering of all ingredients including air. The resultant cakes should have a uniform texture and improved brightness of the crumb. Mixing time is, of course, reduced. It may be possible to reduce the leaveners and the emulsifiers by a moderate amount to give a cost saving. The main disadvantage of the system is its relative inflexibility and the necessity for making extended runs in order to utilize it efficiently.

The batter depositer consists of an assembly of piping, nozzles, and cut-off devices which extrude a given amount of material into each pan. Pressure is supplied by the pumps placed between the premix hopper and the mixer. Metering is based on time rather than measured volume. Because flow is continuous through the nozzles as long as the pumps are functioning, it is necessary to continue extruding the material while the mixer is in operation.

SANITATION

The sanitary considerations involved in designing and installing continuous mix equipment, including ferment tanks, were well summarized by the Baking Industry Sanitation Standards Committee. The Standards are given below, and additional copies can be obtained at a nominal charge from the Committee at 521 Fifth Avenue, New York, N.Y. 10017.

STANDARD NO. 20 FOR LIQUID FERMENT AND CONTINUOUS MIX PROCESSING EQUIPMENT

The requirements of this standard apply to the design, construction and installation of liquid ferment and continuous mix processing equipment including processing tanks, storage tanks, piping, dispersing equipment, pumps metering and measuring devices, pre-mix tanks, developers, extruders, and other accessories as may be required in the process.

This standard shall become effective on and after January 1, 1968.

The General Principles of Design and Construction shall apply to all equipment covered in this standard and shall be considered as a part of this standard except where specifically exempt. Special or Specific Requirements for equipment covered in this standard follow, and shall also be considered a part of this standard.

SPECIAL PRINCIPLES OF DESIGN AND CONSTRUCTION, DEFINITIONS AND INSTALLATION OF EQUIPMENT OR MACHINERY COVERED BY THIS STANDARD.

4.1 Definitions

 4.1.1 Liquid Ferment Process—The liquid ferment process is that in which a part of the ingredients for bread-making is fermented in a liquid medium with or without all of the required water.

 4.1.2 Continuous Mix Process—The continuous mix process is that of mechanically combining and developing the ingredients of bakery products on a continuous basis.

 4.1.3 Processing Tanks—Processing tanks shall include such tanks as pre-mix, blending, broth, brew, liquid ferment, fermentation, retention, holding, constant level, and storage tanks other than those used for the storage of a single ingredient.

 4.1.4 3-A Sanitary Standards—The term 3-A Sanitary Standards refers to the sanitation standards formulated jointly by the Milk, Food and Environmental Sanitarians, Inc., the U.S. Public Health Service, and the Dairy Industry Committee.

4.2 Specific Design Requirements

 4.2.1 All components of the system shall be constructed and installed to facilitate complete drainage. When connected by piping, valves and other fittings, the system shall not be cleaned in place unless it shall have been especially designed, constructed, and installed for this method of cleaning.

 4.2.2 The inner lining of processing tanks shall be so constructed that it will not sag or buckle under full load to prevent complete drainage when operated in accordance with the manufacturer's recommendations.

 4.2.3 The breast, or that portion of the metal used to join the inside tank lining proper to the outer vertical wall, shall be integral with or welded to the inside lining, and shall be sloped or so arranged that all drainage will be toward the outer edge of the tank.

 4.2.4 Tank bridges shall be pitched to the outside of the tank for complete drainage, and shall have a minimum of $\frac{3}{8}$ in. raised flange where edges meet covers. Bridges shall be installed so that the underside thereof shall be readily accessible from outside the tank.

4.2.5 If the lip or edge of a tank, cover or bridge is rolled, the arc of roll shall not exceed 180 degrees and the returned edge shall be at least ¾ in. from the adjacent surfaces to provide access for cleaning.

4.2.6 Valves shall comply with 3-A Sanitary Standards for Fittings and Valves.

4.2.7 Inlet, agitator shaft, thermometer or control openings in the cover or bridge to which connections are not permanently attached shall be flanged upward at least ⅜ in. All sanitary pipelines, agitator shafts, or accessories entering through cover or bridge shall be fitted with a sanitary umbrella deflector that overlaps edges of openings through cover.

4.2.8 Discharge openings of the water inlet shall be located at least one inch, or twice the diameter of the inlet pipe, whichever is greater, above the flood level rim.

4.2.9 Permanently installed inlet, outlet lines, or thermometer wells, either through the bridge or the side walls, shall be made of corrosion-resistant material, welded in place with the weld ground to a finish equal to the surrounding surface. These fittings shall comply with 3-A Sanitary Standards for Fittings and Connections.

4.2.10 If a guard or support in the product zone is necessary for the operation of an agitator, it shall be of a packless bearing type and the agitator shall be removable.

4.2.11 Agitators permanently mounted through a bridge are not required to be removable if they do not interfere with drainage from the tank and are readily accessible for cleaning. Drip protection shall be provided to prevent lubricant from entering the product zone.

4.2.12 The outer edges of covers shall overlap the tank shell. The cover shall, if in two or more parts, be designed with drip protectors; if in one piece, it shall open on hinges which pivot outboard.

4.2.13 In totally enclosed tanks for the storage of liquid ferment, a hooded air vent of not less than three square inches in free open air shall be installed at the top of the tank. The air vent shall be equipped with a perforated metal screen having openings no greater than 1/16 in. in diameter, or slots no wider than 1/32 in. All parts shall be readily accessible and, except for the housing, shall be readily removable for cleaning.

4.2.14 Unless other comparable means of egress are provided, a manhole shall be provided at the drainage end or side of the tank. The dimensions of the manhole opening shall be not less than 15 in. vertical and 20 in. horizontal, or 18 in. in diameter. The cover shall be of the inside-outside swing-type and shall be readily removable for cleaning.

4.2.15 If openings to the tanks are more than five feet above floor level, a permanent ladder or platform shall be provided and installed at the tank to facilitate access.

4.2.16 Pumps for shortening shall meet the requirements of BISSC Standard No. 28 pertaining to shortening pumps.

4.2.17 Pumps for sweetening ingredients shall meet the requirements of BISSC Standard No. 27 pertaining to sweetening ingredient pumps.

4.2.18 Product contact surfaces of pumps for oxidant solution shall be constructed of corrosion-resistant materials and shall be accessible for cleaning; but, because of low volume characteristics they shall not necessarily conform to 3-A Sanitary Standards, but shall conform to the requirements of 3.1.

4.2.19 Pumps for liquid ferment shall meet the following requirements: Parts forming the space between the motor and the pump body shall be constructed in such a way as to be readily accessible for cleaning and to drain freely.

Shaft seals shall be readily removable for inspection and cleaning. Either single service gaskets or readily removable multi-use gaskets shall be used.

Inlets, outlets, and impeller fastenings shall conform to 3-A Sanitary Standards for Pumps.

4.2.20 Piping, valves and fittings for products of fermentation shall conform to 3-A Sanitary Standards for Piping, Fittings and Valves.

4.2.21 Piping, valves and fittings for shortening and liquid sweetening ingredients shall conform to BISSC Standards No. 27 and No. 28.

4.2.22 Piping, valves and fittings for oxidant solution shall be constructed of corrosion-resistant material. The fitting where the oxidant solution is introduced in the process mixture shall conform to 3-A Sanitary Standards for Piping, Fittings and Valves.

4.2.23 Air used in connection with liquid gauges shall be filtered through single service filters which are connected to the gauge by means of sanitary piping.

4.2.24 Liquid meters for liquid ferment shall meet the requirements of BISSC Standard No. 26 for Liquid Measuring Systems.

4.2.25 Heat exchangers shall conform to 3-A Sanitary Standards for Heat Exchangers.

4.2.26 Sanitary piping inlets and outlets shall conform to 3-A Sanitary Standards for Fittings.

4.2.27 Panner conveyors shall comply with BISSC Standard No. 7 for Conveyors.

4.2.28 All materials in the non-product zone shall be suitable for the purpose intended and shall conform to the requirements of cleanability. The exterior of processing tanks shall be of corrosion-resistant material. (3.2.2 Modified)

4.2.29 Equipment installed on the floor shall provide a floor clearance of at least 6 in. or shall be accessible for cleaning. Structural members shall be so arranged as not to form traps, recesses or pockets.

If made of hollow stock, frame members shall have the ends closed. Tanks with a horizontal diameter greater than 72 in. shall have a minimum clearance of 8 in. from the floor. (3.2.6 Modified)

4.2.30 The electrical wiring system shall be dust-tight. Conduit terminal boxes, relay boxes, fuse boxes and switch boxes shall either fit tightly against the supporting members so that open cracks or crevices are not formed, or shall be mounted so that the back of the box shall not be less than ¾ in. from their supporting members. Conduit piping shall be so installed that it does not form hard-to-clean areas or crevices against adjacent surfaces, and should be self-supporting. If flexible conduit is used, it shall have a smooth external surface. The electrical system shall be water-tight in areas where wet cleaning may be carried out. (3.2.12 Modified)

4.2.31 Lubricated transmissions shall be housed so that no leakage occurs.

4.2.32 Openings of sufficient size and proper arrangement shall be provided to permit access to all internal surfaces that require periodic inspection or cleaning. Covers or doors for these access openings shall be capable of being readily opened and, if hinged, the hinges shall be of the take-apart type.

4.2.33 All hollow members, such as frame castings, shall be sealed.

4.2.34 Base supports shall provide a 6 in. minimum clearance between the lowest horizontal surface and the floor.

4.2.35 If pumps are mounted on legs, the legs shall be smooth with round ends and no exposed threads. Legs made of hollow stock shall be sealed. On pumps with legs designed to be fixed to the floor, the minimum clearance between the lowest part of the base and the floor shall be 4 in. If pump is mounted on a base, a minimum clearance of at least 2 in. shall be provided between the pump belly and the base. Readily portable pumps not permanently attached shall have leg heights of not less than 2 in. (3.2.6 Modified)

4.2.36 All exterior surfaces shall be pitched to permit complete drainage away from the product zones.

4.2.37 All exterior seams of the outer shell of tanks shall be sealed by welding.

4.2.38 Electric motors shall conform to the requirements of BISSC Standard No. 29 for Electric Motors.

4.3 Installation

4.3.1 A minimum of 18 in. clearance shall be provided between equipment or structures except where the equipment is integrated with other equipment. In such case, the attachment shall be made in such a way that all parts are accessible for cleaning.

4.3.2 Accessory conveyors shall be so installed as to permit cleaning.

4.3.3 All flour bins, hoppers, feeders or chutes shall be so installed that they do not hamper cleaning.

4.3.4 Liquid ferment and continuous mix processing equipment should be installed on tile, concrete or other equally non-absorbent floors, properly pitched with at least ¼ in. per foot to a trapped drain. Such non-absorbent floor should extend at least five feet beyond the equipment and preferably should be surrounded by a curb to retain drainage.

4.3.5 All structural bracing attached to walls or ceilings shall be properly grouted or sealed.

4.3.6   Dough hoppers and reservoirs, either integral or supplemental, shall be provided with covers.
4.3.7   Control panels or cabinets shall be installed so as to be readily cleanable with a minimum clearance of 6 in. from adjacent walls or structures, or shall be sealed or grouted to such structure or wall. Isolated installations or thermostats, pressure reducing valves, or other similar equipment shall either be sealed to the supporting surface or spaced ¾ in. from such surface.
4.3.8   Where gaskets are used, they shall be flush with the inside edges to avoid ledges and crevices.
4.3.9   All supports or fixed equipment resting on floors shall have sanitary feet. All structural bracing attached to walls shall be sealed at point of attachment.
4.3.10 The electrical wiring system shall be dust-tight, except it shall be water-tight in areas where wet cleaning may be carried out. Conduit, terminal boxes, relay boxes, fuse boxes, and switch boxes directly associated with the equipment shall be so located that uncleanable pockets are not formed and that there is sufficient space between each accessory unit to permit easy cleaning.
4.3.11 Motors shall be mounted on the equipment and off the floor.
4.3.12 Equipment shall be installed with tops not less than 18 in. from ceiling, and shall have sufficient clearance for inspection and cleaning.
4.3.13 Fixed equipment shall be installed to provide a 6 in. minimum clearance between the lowest horizontal surface and the floor; or where the size of the equipment dictates, this dimension shall be increased to provide access for inspection and cleaning.

BIBLIOGRAPHY

ANON. 1963. New unit for continuous dough preparation. Food Process. Packaging *32*, 292.
BAKER, J. C. 1954. Continuous processing of bread. Proc. Am. Soc. Bakery Engrs. *1954*, 65–79.
BAKER, D. K. 1964. Manufacture of bread dough. U.S. Pat. 3,125,968. Mar. 24.
BALDWIN, R. R. et al. 1963. The role that fat plays. Cereal Sci. Today *8*, 273–274, 276, 284, 296.
BALDWIN, R. R. et al. 1964. Progress report—effects of milk components on continuous mix bread. Cereal Sci. Today *10*, 284, 287–288, 290, 308.
BALDWIN, R. R. et al. 1965. Fat systems for continuous bread. Cereal Sci. Today *10*, 452, 454, 456–457.
BARE, S. 1969. Pre-ferments—concepts and engineering. Proc. Am. Soc. Bakery Engrs. *1969*, 63–69.
BORTHWICK, J. T. 1971. Automatic liquid sponge production. Baker's Dig. *45*, No. 1, 50–51, 54.
COFFMAN, J. R., MEISNER, D. F., and TERRY, D. E. 1964. Aroma of continuous mix bread—a preliminary study. Cereal Sci. Today *10*, 305–306, 308.
COLLYER, D. M. 1966. Flavor of bread. J. Sci. Food Agr. *17*, 440–443.
CONDO, M. S. 1970. Principles of mechanical dough mixing. Proc. Am. Soc. Bakery Engrs. *1970*, 46–52.
COTTON, R. H. 1963. Dairy products in bread. Cereal Sci. Today *8*, 12, 14.
CRONEN, C. S. 1959. Chemical engineering updates dough making. Chem. Eng. *66*, No. 3, 98–101.

EGGITT, P. W. R., and COPPOCK, J. B. M. 1965. An approach to continuous mixing. Cereal Sci. Today *10*, 406–408, 410, 474–475.

EUVERARD, M. R. 1969. Pre-ferments—production techniques. Proc. Am. Soc. Bakery Engrs. *1969*, 71–79.

FORTMANN, K. L., GERRITY, A. B., and DIACHUK, V. R. 1964. Factors influencing work requirement for mixing white-bread dough. Cereal Sci. Today *10*, 268, 270, 272.

GEMINDER, J. J., THOMAS, P. D., and HETZEL, C. P. 1965. Sodium stearyl fumarate—effects in continuous process bread. Cereal Sci. Today *10*, 425–428, 430.

HENIKA, R. G. 1965. Cysteine, whey and oxidant reactions in continuous mix. Cereal Sci. Today *10*, 420, 422, 424.

JACKEL, S. S. 1964. Evolutionary operation (clinical) research in the continuous bread bakery. Cereal Sci. Today *10*, 310–311.

KAMMANN, P. W. 1967. State of the art in continuous breadmaking. Cereal Sci. Today *12*, 354–356.

MASELLI, J. A. 1958. Brew processes: Theory and fundamental principles involved. Bakers Weekly *168*, No. 6, 30–32; No. 7, 40–43.

MAUSETH, R. E., NEES, J. L., and JOHNSTON, W. R. 1965. Milk and flour in the broth in a continuous dough system. Cereal Sci. Today *10*, 431–432.

REDFERN, S., BRACHFELD, B. A., and MASELLI, J. A. 1964. Laboratory studies of processing temperatures in continuous breadmaking. Cereal Sci. Today *9*, 190–191.

REDFERN, S., GROSS, H., and BELL, R. L. 1965. Effect of type and level of oxidant. Cereal Sci. Today *10*, 438, 440–442.

REDFERN, S., GROSS, H., BELL, R. L., and FISCHER, F. 1968. Effect of brew fermentation time and make-up on flavor of continuous-process bread. Cereal Sci. Today *13*, 324–326, 360.

SCHILLER, G. W., and GILLIS, J. A. 1964. Laboratory studies of flour for continuous mix bread production. Cereal Sci. Today *9*, 256, 259–263.

SCHILLER, G. W. 1968. Continuous mixing production of buns and rolls. Proc. Am. Soc. Bakery Engrs. *1968*, 58–68.

SNELL, P. E., TRAUBEL, I., GERRITY, A. B., and FORTMANN, K. L. 1965. Flour—effect of high levels in liquid ferments for continuous dough processing. Cereal Sci. Today *10*, 434–436, 457.

TRUM, G. W. 1964. The AMF pilot plant in continuous bread experimentation. Cereal Sci. Today *9*, 248, 250, 252, 254.

WALDT, L. M. 1965. Fungal enzymes—their role in continuous process bread. Cereal Sci. Today *10*, 447–450.

CHAPTER 20

FERMENTATION AND PROOFING ENCLOSURES

Fermentation of dough either as a sponge or straight dough, has as its principal objects: (1) saturating the liquid phase with carbon dioxide, (2) forming the gas bubbles which will be, in the later processing, subdivided to form the basic structure of the baked product, (3) developing the fermentation products, such as lactic acid, which mellow or soften the gluten, making it more extensible, (4) providing some flavoring substances and flavor precursors, and (5) adapting the yeast to the fermentation of maltose. Doughs are proofed for many of the same reasons and, additionally, to form a shape-retaining skin, to allow gas to expand the existing vesicles, and to permit relaxation of the structural protein network after the violent stretching and pressing it undergoes during molding.

To maintain a uniform rate of fermentation, it is necessary to control the temperature of the dough piece. Control of the relative humidity of the atmosphere in contact with the dough is desirable in order to prevent drying out, crusting, and loss of weight. Control of the velocity of air flowing through the fermentation or proofing enclosure determines the rate at which the contents approach an equilibrium status.

In the conventional method of producing bread and rolls, enclosures (rooms, boxes, cabinets) providing a more-or-less controlled environment for dough conditioning are used at the stages of (1) sponge fermentation, (2) intermediate proofing, i.e., proofing of the rounded dough piece, and (3) proofing of the dough piece after it has been molded and (if applicable) panned (Table 20.1). In continuous processing, only the final panned dough piece is proofed, while the brew tanks take the place of the sponge room. In the most primitive installations, special enclosed spaces are not provided at any of these stages and the dough is allowed to proof in some handy container, either exposed to the atmosphere or covered with a cloth or board.

Failure to control temperature and humidity at the fermentation and proof stages results in extreme variability of products. Some compensation can be made for variability in sponge fermentation rate if the conditions are not closely controlled, but even in the older bakeries, it is customary to control both temperature and humidity in the proof box,

TABLE 20.1
REPRESENTATIVE PROOFING CONDITIONS

	Temperature (°F)	Relative Humidity (%)
Bread		
Sponge doughs	110	75
Straight doughs	105	80
Continuous process	115	85
Rolls		
Sponge doughs	105	85
Straight doughs	105	90
Continuous process	100	85
Sweet goods		
Basic sweet doughs	105	75
Danish, high butter	90	70
Danish, low butter	95	70

since it is well recognized that the dough piece is at a very critical stage and it is important to maintain the volume increase at a uniform rate. The atmosphere in the intermediate proof cabinet is often adjusted, if at all, only by opening some of the panels in the sides, there being no air-conditioning system (Fig. 20.1).

Measurement and Control of Humidity

The effectiveness of fermentation rooms, intermediate proof cabinets, and proof boxes for their intended purposes depends upon the control of humidity and temperature. To be sure, in practice the controls may be crude and poorly susceptible to adjustment, but the value of maintaining the humidity and temperature within fairly narrow ranges is well recognized. In these enclosures an atmosphere of high humidity is required in order to prevent drying out or crusting of the surfaces of dough pieces during the fermentation or proofing periods. On the other hand, if the humidity is allowed to rise to near the dew point, there will exist the danger of water condensing on the dough with the resultant development of a sticky or spotted surface. The solution lies in the careful control of the relative humidity within a narrow, high range. Control is made more difficult by the fact that, in some of these installations, only a limited choice of dry-bulb temperatures is available to the operator because artificial cooling of the air is not provided. The preferred situation is to have both cooling and heating means available.

Humidity Measurement.—The amount of water vapor which can be contained in a given space is affected by the temperature and pressure. At ordinary pressures, the maximum content is independent of the kinds and amounts of the other gases which are present, for all practical purposes. Absolute humidity is the mass of water vapor present per unit of space. Specific humidity is the weight of water per unit weight of gas. Absolute humidity and specific humidity, though fundamental measurements of importance to the scientist, are probably less useful and certainly less often used by the bakery technologist than is relative humidity. The latter datum is the partial pressure of water divided by the saturated vapor pressure of water at the same temperature. It is always expressed as a percentage.

If two or more solids or liquids containing water are present together in a closed system, a transfer of moisture will occur until the water con-

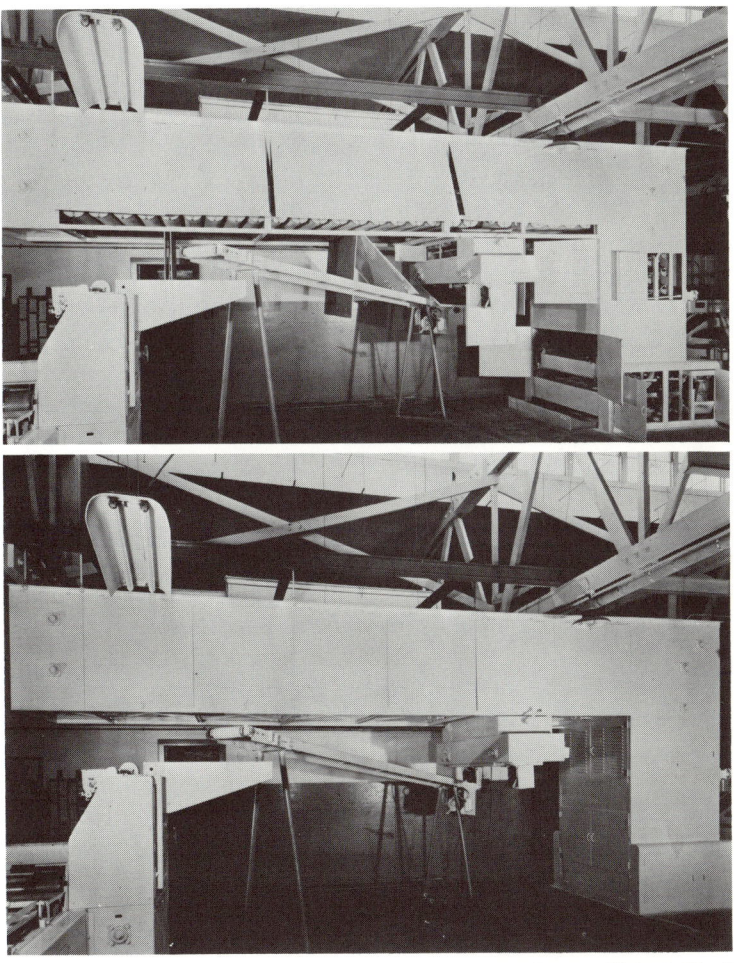

Courtesy of Baker Perkins, Inc.

FIG. 20.1 OVERHEAD INTERMEDIATE PROOFER SHOWING ALL ACCESS PANELS OPEN (ABOVE) AND CLOSED (BELOW).

tents of all of the system's components are in equilibrium with the same relative humidity. The rate at which equilibrium is approached in such systems depends on many factors among which are temperature, surface area of the solids, gas currents inside the container, separation of the components, and spread between the initial equilibrium relative humidities. It is this effect which permits the adjustment of relative humidity within an enclosure as well as the measurement of relative humidity.

The most reliable means for determining the quantity of water vapor in a known volume of air is to collect it and weigh it directly. Although it is possible to collect water vapor as ice on surfaces held at temperatures so low that the vapor pressure of the water is negligible, it is much simpler to remove it by passing the gas mixture through efficient desiccants such as phosphorus pentoxide. If sufficient contact between the gases and the desiccant is obtained, all water within the usual limits of accuracy of weight measurement will be removed. When temperature and volume of the gas sample are known, the difference in weights of the desiccant before and after the experiment will be sufficient information to permit the calculation of absolute humidity. Practical difficulties of instrumentation and procedure are encountered in this technique.

For most purposes, there are methods of sufficient accuracy which use less sensitive and elaborate instrumentation than gravimetric hygrometers. The psychrometer has been much used in food studies and especially in measuring the relative humidity of bakery proofing rooms. When based on mercury thermometers, it is not readily adaptable to automatic feedback control, but versions using electronic temperature sensors (thermistors, thermocouples) can be so employed (Atkins 1964). A psychrometer consists essentially of 2 thermometers, 1 of which is operated in the normal manner, while the other is mounted so that its bulb is constantly in contact with a film of evaporating water. The reading of the wet-bulb thermometer is depressed through the loss of latent heat and will be less than that of the dry-bulb thermometer at all relative humidities below 100%. The extent of this depression is dependent upon the rate of evaporation of water from the film surrounding the wet-bulb thermometer and this, in turn, depends upon the relative humidity of the ambient space. The difference between the two readings and the temperature of the dry-bulb thermometer are translated into relative humidity by consulting a psychrometric chart (see Fig. 20.2).

Usually, the required contact of the "wet bulb" with water is obtained by inserting the lower part of the thermometer into a cloth tube which extends into a container of distilled water. The tube or wick is kept wet by capillary action. The water reservoir must be maintained at the

FERMENTATION AND PROOFING ENCLOSURES 391

FIG. 20.2. TABLE FOR CONVERTING PSYCHROMETER READINGS TO RELATIVE HUMIDITY.

temperature of the dry-bulb thermometer, i.e., at the temperature of the gas being measured. Use of colder or warmer water, even though the difference is only a fraction of a degree, will introduce appreciable error into the determination. The wick should be changed frequently, since accumulation of soil will affect its performance.

Means for ensuring a rapid flow of air over the sensing region of the psychrometer must also be provided. It has been found that a stream of air having a velocity of about 600 fpm causes the water held by the wick to evaporate at a rate sufficient to yield an accurate and stable wet-bulb reading. In fixed permanent installations, fans are used to move a stream of air over the thermometer bulbs. If the fan is mounted on a motor shaft, it should be placed so that the air is sucked over the wick rather than blown over it, since heat radiated from the motor will otherwise affect the temperature of the air.

Although the psychrometer is sufficiently accurate for the purposes of measuring humidity in the bakery, it is subject to several sources of error. The two thermometers double the chance of misreading and, at low temperatures, misreading by a few tenths of a degree can lead to gross errors. Insufficient air flow, dirty wicks or wicks that are too thick, and impure water lead to inaccurate observations.

When approximate indications of relative humidity are acceptable, hygrometers based on measurements of the contraction or relaxation of hair or certain other animal tissues can be used. They are relatively sturdy and inexpensive, function over a wide range, and give direct readings. The principle is simple. Strands of hair are brought from a fixed point around a spring-loaded cylinder or lever which has an indicator attached to it. As the humidity changes, the hair lengthens or contracts, exerting greater or lesser torque on the cylinder. These devices are subject to appreciable error. The hair expands with increasing temperature, and its response to changes in humidity is not strictly linear and is rather slow, the lag time increasing with decreasing temperature.

Another approach to hygrometer construction utilizes a diaphragm of hygroscopic animal membrane clamped between two aluminum retaining rings, forming a flat truncated cone surface. Changes in the humidity of the air surrounding the assembly cause directly proportional changes in dimensions of the diaphragm. Movements at its apex are communicated to the indicating or recording mechanism by a multiplying linkage connected to a small ring affixed to the center of the diaphragm.

There are also hygrometers depending for their action on the changes in electrical parameters of certain substances which occur as the relative humidity of their environment varies. Most of these devices are readily adaptable to use in automatic control of humidity generation equipment. The basic electrical hygrometer consists of an insulator supporting two metal electrodes joined by a film of hygroscopic salt which absorbs moisture in amounts dependent upon the temperature and relative humidity of the air. The quantity of water absorbed by the film governs the electrial resistance of the system.

A typical electrical sensor for humidity has a hygroscopic film of lithium chloride coating a bifilar-wound noble-metal (e.g., gold) resistance element (Quinn 1963). The resistance of the hygroscopic film responds to small changes in the vapor pressure. In another form, the wire electrodes may be wound on a textile sleeve impregnated with the hygroscopic substance. Honeywell's (Anon. 1962) humidity sensor is constructed of two intermeshing gold grids stamped on plastic. It is coated with a complex film containing hygroscopic salts and plastic. As the relative humidity of the surrounding air becomes greater, the film becomes more conductive and electrical resistance between the grid is lowered. The variation of electrical resistance is interpreted by a recording or controlling unit. This sensor is said to be capable of detecting a change of a small fraction of 1% in relative humidity.

For further details on psychrometry consult *Water in Foods* (Matz 1965).

Dew point is the temperature at which the partial pressure of water in a gas is equal to the saturated vapor pressure of water. In other words, a gas at its dew point would have a relative humidity of 100%; it would be saturated. A further release of moisture into the space, or a decrease of temperature, would cause condensation, or "dew" to form. The dew point of a gas is thus a measure of the moisture in the gas in terms of the partial pressure of the water vapor. It is independent of the temperature, and, in almost all situations, independent of the type of gas. Dew point or frost point hygrometers measure the temperature at which dew or frost is deposited on a cooled (relative to the ambient air) surface, usually a highly polished mirror. The measurements can be entirely automatic and used to feed back signals to a humidity controller, but these devices are necessarily more elaborate than the common psychrometer.

Humidity Adjustment.—When a stream of air of controlled humidity is required, as in environmental cabinets for testing storage stability, accurate results can be obtained by mixing appropriate quantities of 2 streams of air, 1 of which has been thoroughly dried and 1 of which has been saturated with water vapor, as by bubbling through a reservoir of water. By varying the relative amounts of the two streams it is possible to obtain any desired relative humidity. In proof cabinets and fermentation rooms, the usual problem is to maintain the relative humidity at a sufficiently high level. Reducing the humidity is not often a concern for most bakeries. Humidity is maintained at the desired level by the intermittent injection of low pressure steam or of atomized water.

In the simplest type of humidity control, as in the small cabinet proofing boxes used in some retail shops, the air is conditioned by a manually adjusted heating coil and a valve or cock permitting steam to be injected for raising the humidity. In larger fermentation and proofing installations, both the temperature and relative humidity are automatically controlled.

CONSTRUCTION DETAILS[1]

The principal goals of the designers of proof boxes and fermentation rooms are: (1) to provide for the efficient delivery and removal of the dough containers, (2) to maintain the relative humidity at a uniform level, (3) to maintain a uniform temperature, (4) to provide sanitary conditions, and (5) to minimize the physical shocks to dough pieces.

A major design problem is the selection of the proper capacities for the air-conditioning unit which will control humidity and temperature (Fig. 20.3 and 20.4). The demands on the unit are expected to be heavy and cyclic since it will be called upon to compensate for the sudden changes occurring as dough and pans are moved into and out of the enclosure.

The major unwanted causes of temperature changes in proof boxes are: (1) infiltration of air as doors are opened or through other openings, (2) addition of pans, racks, and dough, (3) heat flow through the insulated walls, ceiling, and floor. Cold air infiltrating into the conditioned room or contacting the walls subtracts from the sensible and latent heat and can result in condensation, loss of heat, and a reduction of the humidity. Flow of heat through the walls, roofs, floors, doors, etc., depends upon the area, the difference in temperatures, and the heat-conducting properties of the wall. The pans and their contents, when moved into the enclosure, will not be at the same temperature as the atmosphere. Heat must be added or subtracted to bring the dough to the desired temperature. Steel has a specific heat of 0.12, dry air of 0.24, and dough has an average of about 0.88. Generally speaking, the weight of the straps will exceed the weight of the dough, but the higher specific heat of the latter makes it an important contributor to the heat exchange. All of these factors must be considered in calculating the capacity of the air-conditioning unit which will be required.

---

[1] Part of this section was written by Fred D. Pfening, Sr. (deceased), Founder and former Chairman of the Board, The Fred D. Pfening Co., Columbus, Ohio.

The design temperature is the temperature which the system is expected to maintain under the most difficult conditions expected to be encountered. It will be affected by the load placed on the system by the dough and pans, the climatic conditions (which influence the temperature of the infiltrating air and the temperature differences between the cabinet and the environment), and the effectiveness of the insulation.

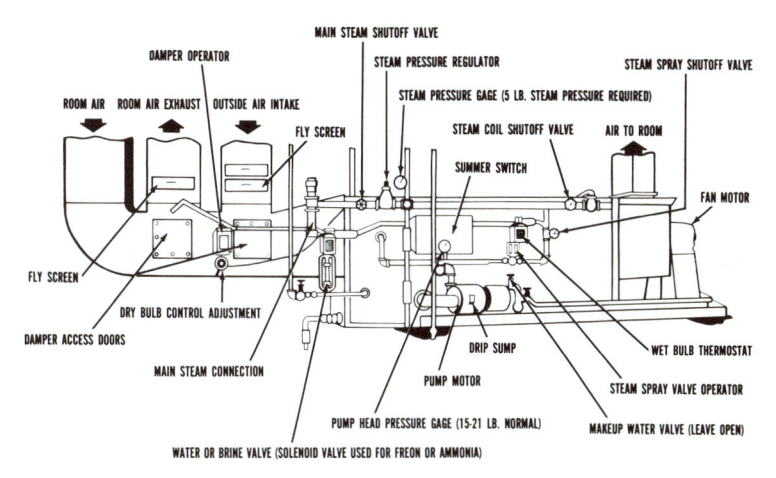

Courtesy of U.S. Dept. Defense

FIG. 20.3. AIR-CONDITIONING SYSTEM FOR FERMENTATION ROOM.

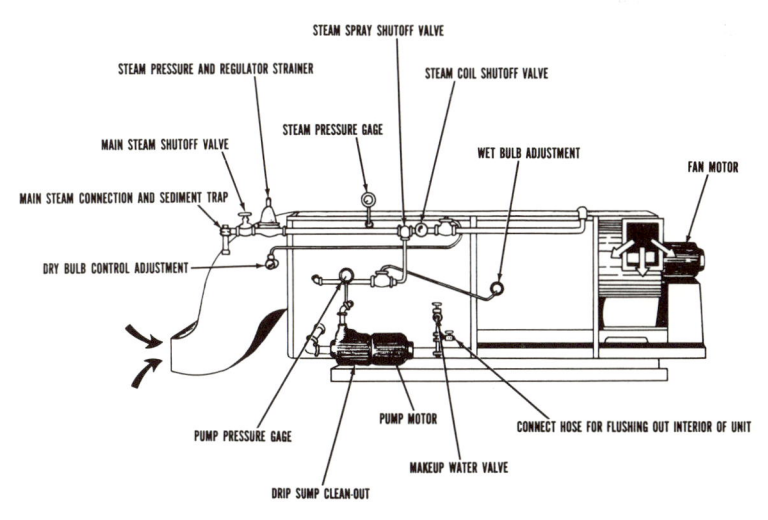

Courtesy of U.S. Dept. Defense

FIG. 20.4. AIR-CONDITIONING UNIT FOR PROOF ROOM.

Room Enclosure

An air-conditioned room must be of such construction that it excludes unwanted temperatures. To accomplish this goal a room should be built with steel structural members which support insulated steel-covered panels. This room should be made as airtight as possible to prevent loss of heat from within and to exclude heat gains and infiltration from without. The floor area is of such dimension that it accommodates the number of troughs of a capacity required to satisfy the production rate of the bakery. Heat accumulates from warm floors, walls, equipment, motors, people, troughs, dough, light bulbs, and infiltration. The designer has control over these heat gains only to the extent he can insulate. The total quantity of chilled air to be supplied to the conditioned room is determined solely by its internal sensible heat gains. The entire basis for the design of the air-conditioning system rests on the calculation of these heat gains. The survey of the premises and the calculations must be made with care and accuracy. Undersized air-conditioning systems are never satisfactory; oversized systems are to be avoided.

Location Liabilities

The fermentation room must be located between the mixer and a point where the sponge can get back to the mixer and the dough can get to the dough chute and into the divider. Perhaps only in a newly designed bakery can each piece of equipment be ideally located. In any event, the fermentation room exterior should not be exposed to heat

Courtesy of Fred D. Pfening Co.
FIG. 20.5. FERMENTATION ROOM ASSEMBLED FROM MODULAR PANELS.

from an oven, to sun heat through a roof, or to a large glass area in a west or north building wall. The western sunload at 4:00 P.M. can be the peak load for the cooling system, necessitating a larger investment. Generally, windows parallel with adjacent fermentation room walls should be bricked-in, insulated, and sealed against outside elements. It costs money to heat more than is necessary and, equally, to cool an area from a high temperature down to 80°F. In many existing bakeries there is no choice concerning the most favorable location of the fermentation room, if the building walls must be a part of the fermentation room.

Insulation

A definite key to the required capacity of the conditioning unit lies in the amount of insulation used in the walls, ceiling, and sometimes the floor. The better the insulation used in the room, the less cooling capacity from the cooling coil is required. If more and better insulation is used in the construction of the room itself, less evaporator temperature is required and, therefore, less dehumidification occurs. If we dehumidify less, we also need to humidify less. If we spend more for insulation, we spend less for conditioning equipment and, at one and the same time, improve the controllability of the room.

Height

A prevailing belief among the uninitiated is that the lower the fermentation room ceiling height, the easier the job of maintaining proper temperature and humidification because the volume of the room is less. This might be true generally, but is a fallacy in fermentation room design. High air velocity has a marked drying effect on dough. More height is a distinct advantage because it permits dispersion of the air and permits additional air changes required to obtain the necessary cooling.

Temperatures

A good air-conditioning system should positively circulate air and provide heat, moisture, and refrigeration to the air in sufficient quantities.

Lower relative humidity is available by a three-position toggle switch; on center position all humidity is cut off. The lower humidity is preferred for use with silicone-coated pans, or glazed pans, and for other purposes. On the optional lower range, the 98°F dry bulb setting provides no humidity. This setting is often used for the proofing of raised doughnuts, where a dry atmosphere is preferred to obtain a crusty surface.

A "humidity lockout" feature prevents the humidity from coming on when a "cold" proof box is started up after a shutdown period. The humidity is "locked out" until the previously selected dry-bulb temperature is reached. Thus, an undesirable dew point and the accompanying condensation are automatically avoided. The air heats more quickly than the steel and panels; the thermostat reflects the air temperature only until the steel equals it.

Floors

All floor areas on which the structure is to rest should be of equal elevation, particularly the perimeter where the major portion of the load is carried. The elevation points should be established by a transit level. A sound floor must be provided under the proof box. The floor must not only support the structure, but also must have sufficient insulation and moisture-excluding qualities to prevent a constantly wet floor surface. Water vapor which condenses is lost and, necessarily, must be replaced. Laying new floor, rather than the use of a doubtful old floor, is advisable when a new proof box is to be installed, or when an old box is moved to a new location.

Floors laid directly on the earth will rapidly condense overlying vapor to water. The remedy is to insulate properly the floor area under, and for 2–3 ft beyond, the perimeter of the proof box. The higher the dry-bulb temperature at which an air-conditioned enclosure is operated, carrying approximately 82% relative humidity, the greater the flow of heat to and through the concrete floor. The condensation potential under such conditions is great. Insulate as the manufacturer recommends, not only to prevent condensation, but also to prevent the loss of heat. Where proofing temperatures are up to 120°F, we suggest that heat conductors be installed under the floor surface to maintain a floor temperature of 112°F.

The ideal proof box floor has: (1) A tile surface to take the wear of caster mounted racks, and provide the utmost in sanitation. (2) A surface slab of solid concrete or slab used as a sub-base for tile should be a minimum of 3 in. thick in order for the lag screws to have secure anchorage. (3) Under this slab a Zonolite insulating concrete of not less than 8 in. in depth and extending 24 in. beyond the outline dimension of the proof box, on all 4 sides. This should be a 1 to 6 mix, being 1 bag of cement and 1½ bags of Zonolite stabilized concrete aggregate. (4) If proof box is less than 10 ft away from an outside building wall, the wall and floor should be separated with 12-in. width and 8-in. to 12-in. depth of Zonolite insulating concrete to prevent "crawl" of cold to the floor and wall panels of the box. If the box is close to a cold wall, the separation strip is a positive "must."

Where the soil on which the concrete is to be laid has recently been disturbed and there is danger of settling, a reinforcing steel mesh should be placed in the concrete. Where the slab is below grade, in a poorly drained location, or where there is a high water table, the soil should be stabilized by raking dry cement into the top inch of soil, sprinkling it with water, and rolling it to a hard crust. Over this, mop down two layers of waterproof paper with hot asphalt. This membrane should be turned up against the outside wall to the height of the concrete.

When the slab goes over a well-drained area, the insulation would probably remain drier if no vapor-seal membrane is installed. When the proof box temperature is 110°F dry bulb and 104°F wet bulb, and the earth temperature is approximately 55°F, the tendency is for the moisture to go toward the earth. It is, therefore, important to ascertain the moisture condition, or probability of what will occur, in order to decide whether or not to use a vapor-seal membrane between the earth and the insulation. This phenomenon is true regardless of what type of insulation is used. A vegetable material insulation will in time decay. It should be remembered that a wet insulation material loses its insulating quality.

Humidification

For a fermentation room there should be two separate systems. One system cools or heats the recirculating air to maintain the 80°F dry-bulb temperature. The other provides moisture to maintain the relative humidity at 75.7%. When the wet-bulb thermostat causes moisture to be injected, a certain amount of evaporation occurs, dropping the dry-bulb temperature of the atmosphere as much as 3°. Where the thermostatic control is sufficiently sensitive, the momentary cooling effect will cause the heating coil to react to restore the heat, if required. When the water supplied for humidification is the same temperature as the room atmosphere, superior results are obtained.

Dehumidification

It is neither economically nor atmospherically desirable to dehumidify the air in a fermentation room. However, the cooling coil condenses moisture out of the air to an extent dependent on the temperature of the coil. The excessive elimination of moisture from the atmosphere, passing through the coil face area, causes the humidifying system to operate more nearly continuously to restore the cyclically eliminated water. A normal fermentation room will have 6 air changes per hour; therefore, the cubic feet of air in the room will pass through the cooling coil 6 times an hour. In a room with ceiling height greater than 8 ft, the volume increases for the same floor area and more air changes per hour

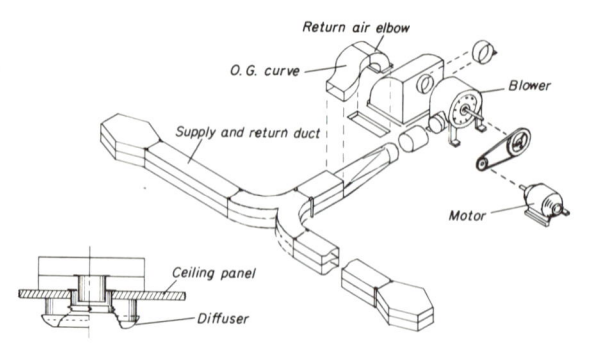

FIG. 20.6. FERMENTATION ROOM DUCTWORK.

are permissible. In the event the cooling load is above normal, this condition will prove of advantage since the velocity through the cooling coil may be increased and more Btu's are obtained at a lower discharge temperature, thus decreasing the elimination of water.

Air Distribution

The reconditioned atmosphere should be released to the room and distributed equally to prevent drafts or stratification (Fig. 20.6). The number and nature of air-diffusing outlets depends on the height of the room. In no event should an air stream pass over a dough surface since it would have an evaporating effect and, therefore, would crust the dough. The fewer the air changes the more beneficial the atmosphere remains. A contradictory situation arises between setting up fewer air changes per hour and, at the same time, obtaining sufficient air velocity over the coil to transfer heat at a rate sufficient to maintain room temperature at 80°F. In comfort conditioning, the engineer provides a coil and air velocity to obtain the necessary cooling or heating, letting the number of air changes be what they will. However, the designer for fermentation conditioning requires, also, a knowledge of bakery processing.

Air Washer

It is our belief that the spray air-washer evaporative type of conditioning is detrimental to the fermentive process. So-called "fresh air" is continuously introduced through the washer and into the fermentation room. The expelled air continuously removes carbon dioxide as rapidly as it is released from the dough.

Carbon Dioxide

The influence of carbon dioxide should be discussed in more detail. Since carbon dioxide is 1½ times heavier than air, a blanket of gas (generated by the yeast) lies over the dough surface until the dough rises to the top of the trough. Then, the gas spills to the floor level or to the previous top level of the gas itself. This gas has a beneficial effect on fermentation. However, if the surrounding atmosphere is permeated with carbon dioxide, breathing becomes difficult for the personnel who must enter the room. This situation is easily remedied by providing an opening, say 10 in. in diameter, in the room doors, at a level a little higher than the highest trough. This method permits the gas to flow to the outside at this level and prevents it from rising to the breathing level. Moreover, it eliminates bringing in outside air, which would lower the concentration of the carbon dioxide.

Conditioning Unit

The air-conditioning components may be assembled in a relatively small housing, which should be made of stainless steel in all instances (Fig. 20.7). The radiator and the cooling coil may be located in the same housing about 12 in. apart, the most preferable distance depending on the relative face area of each. Sometimes a damper is installed to divert the air stream over one or the other of the coils, as either is activated. However, since the radiator face area is smaller than the face area of the cooling coil, and since the room requires considerably less heating than cooling, it would appear that dampers are not worth their cost. The cooled air temperature is so comparatively moderate that coil Btu capacity, whether from chilled water or Freon-12 cooling medium, demands calculated consideration. All the cooling permissible

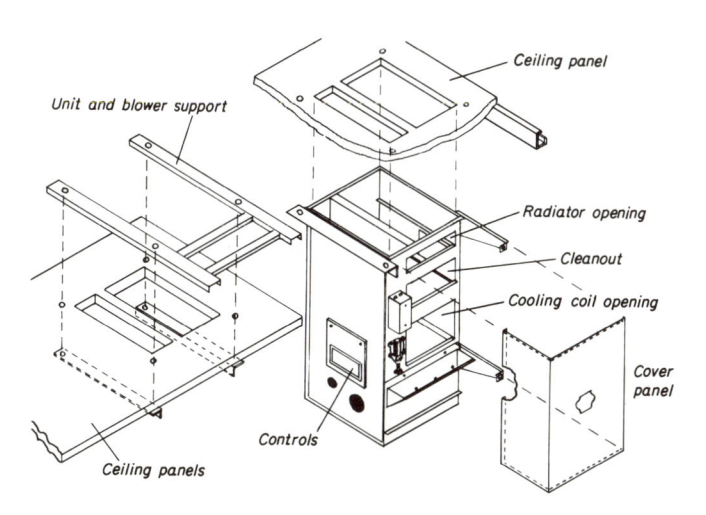

FIG. 20.7. FERMENTATION ROOM CONDITIONING UNIT SHOWING CONSTRUCTION DETAILS.

with as little dehumidification as possible is the objective. A blower size is determined by calculation to obtain the desired velocity at the static pressure of the system. The blower runs continuously, the heating or cooling functions intermittently, subject to the direction of the thermostatic controls.

PROOF BOX HEATING AND HUMIDIFICATION PREREQUISITES[2]

The purpose of a proof box is primarily one of heating and humidifying to maintain wet- and dry-bulb temperatures which will cause a dough piece to proof within a scheduled time period. Many contributing factors influence performance success or failure. The process is essentially air-conditioning and subject to the vagaries of psychrometric deviation.

Heat Transfer

If a temperature control apparatus is to perform its assigned duty in a proof box, then sensible heat must be available. When steam pressure drops below 15 psig, sufficient heat is not transferred from the heating coil or radiator to the recirculating air to maintain the desired dry-bulb temperature. Normally, the humidification, or wet bulb control, continues to add moisture to the atmosphere resulting in an overly humidified atmosphere. Without protective circuity in the thermostatic complex to avoid a dew point, condensation will appear on cold surfaces. Steam pressure itself is not enough to supply the necessary sensible heat. Steam in volume is also required.

Pressure

Pressure of any fluid will be reflected regardless of the diameter of the conveying pipe. To obtain greater volume a larger diameter pipe and pressure are required. A pound of water, when vaporized, will produce less than 1000 Btu. If it takes up to 12,000 Btu per hour to maintain 110°F of heat per proof rack, pans, and dough, there will be 12 lb of condensate draining from the radiator. A simple test is to collect the condensate for 1 hr as it drains through the trap and then weigh it.

The pressure of steam indicates its temperature; at 10 psig it is 240°F, at 15 psig it is 250°F, and the higher the pressure the higher the temperature. This is the reason why steam from a high pressure boiler must have a pressure reducer in the line and also why bare pipe should be provided for a distance of at least 25 ft to the proof box humidification unit to obtain wet steam.

---

[2] Part of this section was written by Fred D. Pfening, Sr. (deceased), Founder and former Chairman of the Board, The Fred D. Pfening Co., Columbus, Ohio.

Capacity

A proof box needs ample heating capacity to be drawn on for quick reaction to counteract infiltrated cold air. This occurs particularly when a door is opened to admit a cold rack, pans, and dough. Adding to this burden is the fact that with an open door the ambient air volume and temperature rush into the proof box at the lower part of the open door; and at the same instant, the conditioned atmosphere from inside the box rushes outward. Considering the number of doors involved and the rate of their opening and closing, we encounter quite a heat and humidity loss. The recovery rate is dependent on the sensitivity of the thermostat and the heat capacity of the conditioning equipment.

Steam

A proof box does not consume steam continuously; the demand is intermittent and, for a great volume, is at short intervals. If a proof box were a totally closed space without air infiltration or ambient heat-subtracting influences, wet- and dry-bulb temperatures could be maintained to fractional degree values. As it is, a proof box has many doors, many cracks, and many cold racks loaded with cold pans and cool dough entering and leaving only a few minutes apart.

Trough Handling

Automatic handling in the proof room moves troughs in a line down the feed side of the enclosure, laterally across the end of the room, then back to the discharge door. A carriage, powered by a hydraulic ram, moves incoming troughs forward on their own casters and between two horizontal guides along the sides. Upon reaching the end of the room, the cross-carriage powered by a hydraulic motor moves the end trough transversely and positions it in the discharge line. At this point another carriage, identical with the feed unit, moves the procession toward the discharge door. Troughs are moved onto and off of the carriages by hand.

FINAL PROOFERS

The mechanical aspects of the intermediate proofer have been discussed in a preceding chapter and it is evident that the factors affecting temperature and humidity control are very similar to those described for fermentation rooms and proof boxes. Final proofers, which receive the shaped and panned dough piece and deliver it to the oven, are of several types. The most primitive example in commercial bakeries was a shallow box or drawer which controlled humidity and temperature only by sealing off the dough piece from the bakery air for a short period.

Courtesy of Baker Perkins, Inc.
FIG. 20.8. A TEMPLEX RACK PROOFER.
Rear of proofer shows view of control panels and recorders. Note access doors for rack removal.

Eventually, the advantages of better control became apparent and special rooms were designed for final proofing. At first, the dough was introduced manually, sometimes by pushing racks of pans into one end of the room and removing them from the other. Injection of steam from a pipe leading to the boiler was the means of both heating and humidification. Adjustment was manual and based on occasional reading of the wet- and dry-bulb thermometers, if such a sophisticated instrument was available.

The high labor requirements for conducting the proofing operation led to the design of several different conveying methods. In the floor-type proof box, racks mounted on casters are used to hold many pan straps. There may be several lanes through the proof box, with a series of racks being moved through each. The racks are manually pushed into one end of the box and pulled out of the other at a rate calculated to give the necessary proof time. The enclosure is a steel frame covered with insulated panels and provided with an automatic air-conditioning system (Fig. 20.8). Overhead rails or floor rails may be used to guide the manually moved racks.

Pan conveying systems somewhat similar to those used in traveling hearth ovens have been built. Other automatic conveying means which have been suggested or designed include belt- and chain-driven mechanisms. Relatively large amounts of floor space are required and construction costs tend to be high. Whatever the method used for conveying the racks, it should not cause undue vibration, shock, or impact. At least toward the end of the proof period, the extended condition of the gluten network and the relatively relaxed state of the proteins render the structure readily subject to collapse.

Modern proofers for large-scale operation automatically load pan straps onto racks which are integral parts of the proofer. In a multitray proofer, pans are grouped automatically and fed to the loading section. The loading conveyor is coordinated with the tray unit, both operating intermittently. As each tray is loaded, the tray unit indexes upward one tray pitch while the loading conveyor delivers another load. When filled, the tray unit is indexed upward once more and then pushed one space down the length of the proofer by the top ram. This action also causes the movement of one tray unit onto the elevator at the other end of the proofer. The elevator lowers the tray to the lower level where a bottom ram pushes it one space in the return direction. This movement automatically forces another tray unit onto the front-end elevator which indexes it upward through the unloading position and then back to the loading position. Where plenty of floor space is available, the multitray proofer is the simplest, most economical type.

In multitier proofers, each tray after it is loaded is raised individually to the top tier of the proofer. Drive chains on each side of the loaded trays convey them back and forth throughout the length of the proofer, dropping them to a lower tier at each turning point until they have reached the unloading station. The trays then continue through the bottom leg to the loading station (see Fig. 20.9). In all types of automatic proofers, the dwell time can be varied within predetermined limits so as to fit production requirements.

Another type of automatic proofer is shown in Fig. 20.10. This unit comprises eight principal functions: feeding, grouping, and discharge conveyors, automatic loader, unloader, elevator, Lowerator, and double-deck tracks upon which racks are conveyed by hollow-stud roller chains. The racks are equipped with flanged wheels that roll along the rails. Each rack would have, for example, 7 shelves, each holding 8 straps of 5 1½ lb pans. Four endless conveyor chains are powered by sprockets at the ends of each of the four rails. Uniformly spaced projections engage slots at both sides of the racks and move them laterally on the upper rails, then transfer them to the Lowerator at the rear of the proofer. The Lowerator engages slots at the sides of each rack and moves it to the lower rail where the slots are caught by dogs on the conveyor chains. The Lowerator and the elevator consist essentially of a set of two endless chains powered by sprockets. The chains operate in the vertical plane and are located on both sides and at the ends of the two sets of rails. Each set of chains is fitted with short lengths of rail, properly spaced to match the trucks. The elevator is more complex than the Lowerator, since it must index the shelves at proper intervals, keeping them level with both the feed and discharge conveyors. The loader and unloader consist of two steel pusher bars

Fig. 20.9. An Automatic Proofer of the Multitier Design.

Courtesy of J. W. Greer Co.

Courtesy of Baker Perkins, Inc.
FIG. 20.10. COMPLETELY AUTOMATIC FINAL PROOFER.

on rams mounted at opposite ends of heavy steel rods. As they move in a horizontal plane, they simultaneously sweep straps off the feed conveyor and onto a shelf and off a shelf onto the discharge conveyor.

A proof box about 18 ft wide, 12 ft high, and 68 ft long could accomodate about 8120 loaves at 1 time. Similar equipment is used for rolls.

Recently, microwaves have been used as the heat source for proofing doughnuts. The entire doughnut can be heated to proof temperature in a few seconds by this means, but about 4 min are allowed for adequate yeast action and dough relaxation. Comparable time in a conventional proofer would be 30–35 min.

The doughnuts are carried through the tunnel on a canvas belt. The system is not applicable to doughs which must be proofed in pans because of the interference with the microwaves by the metal. A 2½ kw magnetron tube operating at 2450 MHz is housed in a console at the side of the tunnel and the microwaves fed through a waveguide into the cavity. Air, heated and humidified by conventional techniques, is blown through the cavity to retard evaporation from the dough pieces. The doughnut mix must be specially formulated for this type of proofing to be satisfactory, according to Russo (1971).

DOUGH TROUGHS

The trough is an important piece of equipment, but is rarely given much consideration by the bakery technologist because it seems to have little direct effect on product quality. The production man is most concerned with the sanitary aspects and manpower requirements for trough handling. In conventional saltine fermentation the trough has an effect on product quality since it serves as a source of inoculation for the sponge, furnishing bacteria which give the characteristic flavor and some of the gassing power to the dough.

Considerable variation is possible in trough design. Most of the modifications are intended to afford better control over the removal of sponge from the trough. A few of the better-known types are described below.

Slide-end

The whole of one end of the trough can be raised to give an opening through which the sponge can flow. Ordinarily, there will be no mechanical provision for removing the gate or raising it in increments.

Sloping Bottom

This design feature can be applied to most of the other variations described here, and has an obvious function.

Gate-end

The bottom part of one end is formed into a gate hinged at its upper edge. Spring action keeps the gate sealed until it is released to allow the dough to run out.

Chute-end

The lower ⅓ (approximately) of 1 end can be opened leading the sponge to an inclined pan or chute which guides it into the mixer. While the sponge is fermenting, the chute can be turned up, out of the way.

Drop-side

Approximately the top ⅓ of 1 side is hinged and can be dropped down to facilitate removal of the contents.

Controlled Flow

Troughs designed primarily for overhead hoist operation, having a gated end which can be raised in increments by a rack and pinion arrangement.

Troughs are customarily made from 10-gage steel, either standard or stainless. They should be welded, with polished seams, and the rims rolled and sealed for sanitary reasons. Capacities range from about 13.5–56.5 cu ft to hold from 180–750 lb of sponge or 400–1680 lb of straight dough.

Various accessories can be obtained. Top extensions, or domed covers of aluminum, stainless steel, or plastic are examples. Bails can be provided on the sides for hoist hooks.

BIBLIOGRAPHY

Anon. 1962. Humidity—How it Affects your Industry and What You Can Do About It. Honeywell Corp., Minneapolis.

Arnold, J. H. 1933. The theory of the psychrometer. Physics 4, 255–262, 334–340.

Atkins, R. M. 1964. Wet-dry bulb thermistor hygrometer with digital indication. Instr. Control Systems 73, No. 4, 111–114.

Bohringer, R. 1952. Quality of bread as affected by underproof and overproof. Proc. Am. Soc. Bakery Engrs. 1952, 88–92.

Flanigan, F. M. 1960. Comparison of the accuracy of the humidity measuring instruments. ASHRAE J. 2, 56–59.

Fuhrmann, D. 1955. Principles of dough fermentation. Proc. Am. Soc. Bakery Engrs. 1955, 118–123.

Gardner, H. D. 1957. Today's concept for final proofing of bread and rolls. Proc. Am. Soc. Bakery Engrs. 1957, 127–132.

Gralenski, F. M. 1964. Automatic dewpoint hygrometer. Instr. Control Systems 37, No. 5, 124–125.

Hildebrand, H. E., Jr. 1952. Proof boxes—their design and operation. Proc. Am. Soc. Bakery Engrs. 1952, 83–87.

Jackel, S. S. 1969. Fermentation—today and tomorrow. Proc. Am. Soc. Bakery Engrs. 1969, 91–97.

Matz, S. A. 1965. Water in Foods. Avi Publishing Co., Westport, Conn.

May, L. 1962. Spaulding's three streamlined production lines for bread, rolls, and doughnuts. Bakers Weekly 195, No. 9, 40–49.

Morris, V. B., Jr., and Sobel, F. 1954. Some experiments on the speed of response of the electric hygrometer. Am. Meteorol. Soc. Bull. 35, 226–229.

Pfening, F. D., Sr. 1955. The Fermentation Room. Baker's Digest, Chicago.

Prescott, S. E., and Havighorst, C. R. 1956. Engineering reaches new high in this ultra-modern bakery. Food Eng. 27, No. 11, 88–93.

Quinn, F. C. 1963. Equilibrium hygrometry. Instr. Control Systems 36, No. 7, 113–114.

Russo, J. R. 1971. Microwaves proof doughnuts. Food Eng. 43, No. 4, 55–58.

Schaffer, W. 1946. A simple theory of the electric hygrometer. Am. Meteorol. Soc. Bull. 27, 147–151.

Schmidt, B. 1952. Pan proofing. Proc. Am. Soc. Bakery Engrs. 1952, 78–82.

Schiffmann, R. F., Stein, E. W., and Kaufman, H. B., Jr. 1971. The microwave proofing of yeast-raised doughnuts. Baker's Dig. 45, No. 1, 55–57, 61.

Sullivan, B., and Richards, W. A. 1946. Open trough and cabinet fermentation of bread sponges. Cereal Chem. 23, 365–387.

CHAPTER 21

OVENS AND ASSOCIATED EQUIPMENT

The oven is the most conspicuous and characteristic piece of equipment in the bakery. With its associated loaders, unloaders, coolers, depanners, and conveyors, it dominates the layout and determines, in large part, the arrangement of the other pieces of equipment. Baking is also the operation which limits the output in most bread plants. For this reason, selecting an oven, maintaining it properly, and operating it at a maximum rate are key elements in the sucessful management of the bakery.

The oven has an important influence on product quality. It cannot compensate for errors committed earlier in the processing sequence, but a well-adjusted oven of the proper design can bring out the potential of a well-processed dough piece. The elements of oven design and operation which govern its effectiveness in optimizing product quality are not completely accessible to scientific analysis. The mechanical details of oven construction are, of course, important in that they are related to labor requirements, efficiency of fuel utilization, frequency of product damage, and sanitation. But of more fundamental importance and less well understood are the effects of heat transfer mechanisms on product quality. All ovens transfer heat by conduction, convection, and radiation. It is the differences in the percentage of heat transferred by each route that accounts for the variation in baking results in different ovens.

HEAT TRANSFER MECHANISMS

Heat may be transferred from one location to another by convection, conduction, or radiation. The relative effectiveness of each of these means of transfer varies with oven design as well as with the distribution and conformation of dough pieces. The response of the dough pieces, and thus many of the qualities of the finished product, is affected by all of these factors.

Radiation

Transfer of energy by electromagnetic radiation is a significant factor in most ovens. These radiations are not in themselves heat, but are converted into heat through absorption by and interaction with absorbing molecules. Light, which is an electromagnetic radiation, is an extremely poor means of transferring heat. Invisible infrared radiation is quite effective. The radio frequency waves generated by electronic ovens are also efficient transmitters of energy. The quantity of heat transmitted between two bodies by radiation is directly proportional to the differences of the fourth powers of the absolute temperatures and inversely proportional to the square of the distance between the two bodies.

Radiation has two characteristics different from the other means of heat transfer which affect its action on dough blanks: (1) it is subject to shadowing, and (2) it is very responsive to changes in absorptive capacity of the dough, e.g., to changes in coloration in the case of infrared radiation or to changes in water content in the case of radio waves of certain frequencies.

Changes in color affect baking principally through increases in the absorption of infrared rays. The darkening accompanying baking indicates an increase in the absorption of visible wavelengths. An increase in absorptive capacity for infrared rays, though not apparent visually, is an almost invariable concomitant of the visible change. As a result of the increase in heat absorption in the darkening areas, there is a tendency for the color changes to accelerate after the first browning appears. This means that ovens relying on radiant energy for a relatively large proportion of the heat transfer will tend to accentuate color differences. Such effects may be either good or bad, depending upon the characteristics desired in the finished product.

The shadowing effect is most apparent with radiation near the visible range (i.e., infrared) and is much less with radio frequency waves. The infrared radiation comes from all angles in the oven, although its intensity will vary. The source of the radiation is from burner flames and all the metal parts in the oven sides, top, band, etc. Radiation from below the band is completely intercepted by the band and partly reradiated as infrared inergy and partly converted into conducted heat. The sides of the pan also shadow the top of the dough piece until it rises above them, at which time radiation becomes much more effective in promoting color development in the crust.

If a dough piece is shaped approximately like a segment of a sphere, with a relatively smooth surface, the reception of radiation during its trip through the oven will be approximately equal over all parts of its surface. Absorption will also be approximately equal as long as the color (related to absorptive capacity in the infrared) remains the same over the entire surface. This also applies to flat-surfaced pieces covering most of the band. Products with irregular surfaces, such as wire-cut cookies with holes in the middle, twist bread, fancy pastry shapes, etc., will have some parts of their surfaces in a better position than other parts to intercept radiant energy. If these surfaces are sufficiently absorptive, heating will occur at an accelerated rate in the prominences. The shadowed areas will receive less energy and will tend to heat slower and brown slower. It must be understood that all of these effects of radiant energy can be offset by complementary inputs of conducted or convected heat.

The specific effects of microwave radiation will be discussed in the section on electronic ovens.

Convection

Convection is the transfer of heat from one part to another within a gas or liquid by the gross physical mixing of one part of the fluid with another. In the oven, molecules of air, water vapor, or combustion gases heated by whatever means, circulate throughout the oven, constantly mixing with the other gases and transferring heat by conduction when they contact solid surfaces. Within the dough piece, convection occurs as the result of the movement of water vapor and other gases. Furthermore, some translocation of liquid water, melted shortening, and other liquids cause a transfer of heat from one region of the dough to another.

If the overall results of convection can be generalized, it would be as a smoothing or evening effect of heat distribution. The gases within the oven mix readily as long as there are no mechanical barriers and tend to make more uniform the temperature throughout the chamber. When different temperatures are required in different zones of the oven, it is necessary to isolate these zones in some manner to retard heat transfer between them by convection.

Within the dough piece, one of the principal effects of convection is also a smoothing or blurring of temperature differentials. The hotter areas of the dough give off more water vapor than the cool ones, and the loss of this vapor in some areas and its gain in others, tends to minimize the differences.

Convection affects exposed areas only, of course. The bottoms of the dough pieces, protected as they are by the band, do not participate directly in this type of heat exchange. It is doubtful that much convective transfer occurs at the bottoms even when mesh bands are used. All exposed parts probably participate about equally in convective heat exchange. No doubt some protective effect of protuberances could be shown, but the high degree of turbulence of the gases known to exist above the band and the relatively low relief of most dough pieces suggest that variations in reception of convective heat by the different parts cannot be very great. On the other hand, products at the edge of the band may receive substantially more heat because of more rapid flow of hot gases and higher temperatures in this area.

Conduction

Conduction is the transmittal of heat from one part to another part of the same body, or from one body to another in physical contact with it, there being no appreciable displacement of the particles of the bodies. The fundamental differential equation for heat transfer by conduction is called Fourier's law:

$$q = \frac{dQ}{d\theta} = -kA \frac{dt}{dx}$$

where q is the rate of heat flow in Btu per hr, Q is the quantity of heat transferred in Btu, θ is the time (hr), A is the area normal to the direction in which the heat flows (sq ft), and dt/dx is the rate of change of temperature (°F) with the distance (ft) in the direction of flow of heat, that is, the temperature gradient. The factor k is called the thermal conductivity and is dependent upon the material through which the heat is flowing and upon temperature. The negative sign indicates that the net flow of heat is in the direction of lower temperatures. The thermal conductivity of water at 32°F is 0.343 and at 100°F is 0.363 Btu per sq ft per °F per ft.

When baking in a band oven, conduction of heat of the dough occurs only through the band. The band receives its store of energy from radiation, from convection, and from heat conducted through the supports on which it rides. Because of the localized nature of conductive transfer, steep gradients of temperature are set up within the dough piece, the hottest areas being the ones in contact with the pan and particularly where the pan is in contact with the band. Unwanted differences in the rates of heat-catalyzed reactions can easily occur unless these gradients are carefully controlled. Conduction from one part of the dough to another is a force tending to reduce temperature differentials.

To summarize the effects of the three types of heat transfer during baking, it can be said that conduction and radiation tend to cause localized temperature differentials, conduction acting to raise the temperature of the bottoms and radiation acting to raise the temperature of exposed surfaces (and especially darkened areas or protuberances), while convection tends to even out temperature gradients within the oven.

TYPES OF OVENS

Although it is not within the scope of this volume to give extensive discussions of the history of equipment development, a brief description of some older types of ovens should contribute to a better understanding of the advantages of modern tray and band ovens.

The most primitive oven was a chamber of mud or brick in which a fire was built. When the oven had been thoroughly heated, the ashes were scraped out and dough pieces inserted into the chamber. The same general pattern applied to both large and small ovens. A great advance was achieved when it was discovered that the baking compartment could be isolated from the fire chamber. Then the heating could be carried on continuously during baking and while the dough pieces were being transferred into or out of the oven. The peel oven, in which a fixed hearth is surrounded by a fire box, was the predominant type in commercial bakeries until fairly recent times and is still in use in some parts of the world. The "deck" oven, used for small-scale roasting and baking in some food service operations is similar to a peel oven except that it may be heated by electricity or gas and the convection assisted by fans. Peel ovens are generally of massive construction, with very thick brick walls to serve as a heat sink and to minimize temperature fluctuations. Sand was sometimes used between brick walls for the same purpose.

The baker uses a peel, or long wooden spatula, to insert dough pieces into the baking chamber and to remove the loaves. Since the back part of the oven is loaded first and unloaded last, there may be several minutes difference in baking time between the first and last loaves. Somewhat greater uniformity was achieved through the use of a portable metal hearth which was completely loaded with dough outside the oven before it was pushed into the baking chamber. The problem of uneven temperatures in different parts of the baking area remained, however, and was alleviated only by the invention of the moving hearth.

The first type of moving hearth was a circular metal plate which rotated in a horizontal plane about a pivot or axle placed approximately in the center of the oven (Fig. 21.1). Since each dough piece was carried in a path around the oven, temperature differences were more-or-less equalized. Baking times could also be kept constant because different parts of the hearth could be loaded and unloaded in the proper sequence. The motion of the hearth and its load created some air movement in addition to that normally resulting from temperature differentials, and thus increased the contribution of convection to the total heat transfer—as a result, baking times decreased. One of the chief disadvantages of these ovens is the large amount of floor space required. Rotary ovens are rarely, if ever, used in commercial installations today, but some laboratory ovens for test baking use this principle.

The reel oven was a considerable improvement in that it not only allowed horizontal (front to back) movement of the dough pieces but also moved them vertically, further leveling out differences in temperature distribution within the chamber (Fig 21.2). In addition, it increased the amount of hearth area within a given floor space. Convection was greatly increased. Some manufacturers designed ovens to give a steam trap through which the pans moved. Because of its many advantages, the reel oven became very popular and many of them

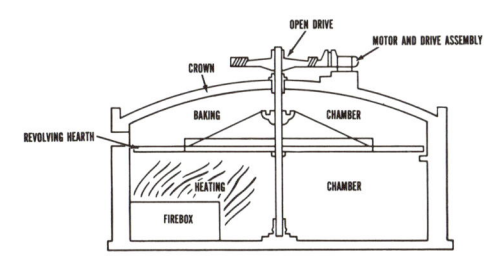

Courtesy of U.S. Dept. Defense

FIG. 21.1. SCHEMATIC DIAGRAM OF A ROTARY OVEN.

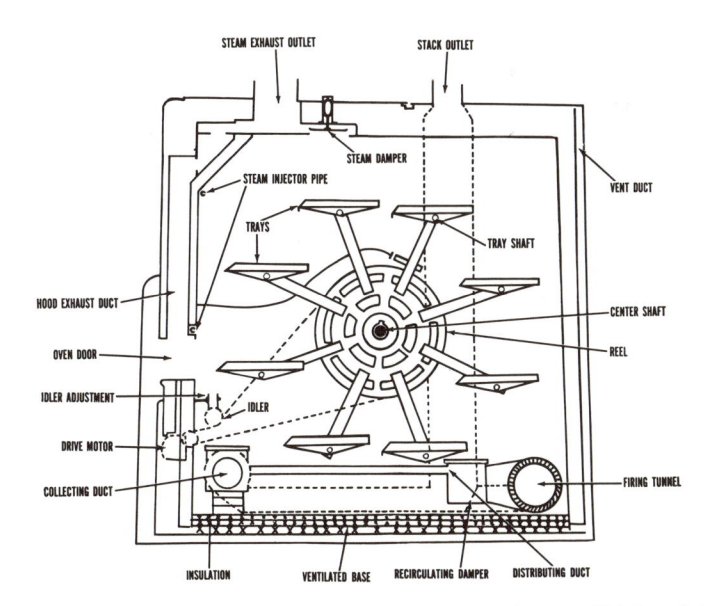

Courtesy of U.S. Dept. Defense

FIG. 21.2. SCHEMATIC DIAGRAM OF A REEL OVEN.

are in use today. The chief disadvantages were the difficulty in automating the loading and unloading operations and the inability to provide zone heating. Tray and band ovens gradually superseded peel ovens in large commercial bakeries.

Because provision can be made for long horizontal runs, traveling tray ovens are more efficient than reel ovens in space utilization. Each tray holds several pans or straps and is permanently fixed to a conveying chain. The trays are pulled by the chain from front to back of the oven, then moved to a lower track and continue baking on the return trip to the front, where they are unloaded (Fig. 21.3). In the early designs, problems were encountered in obtaining a smooth, vibrationless transfer as the trays were moved from the upper to the lower track. The jarring and vibration sometimes encountered were not

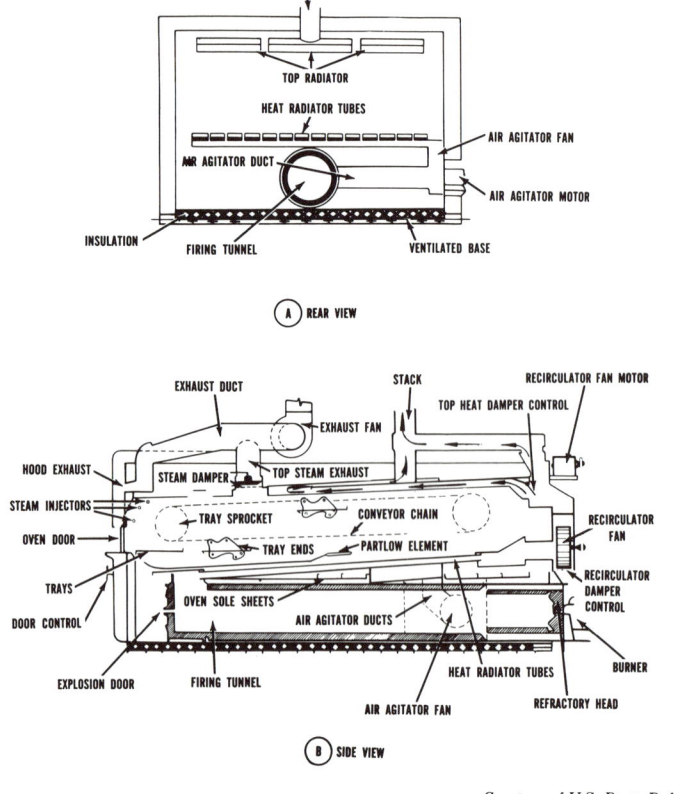

Courtesy of U.S. Dept. Defense

FIG. 21.3. TRAVELING TRAY OVEN.

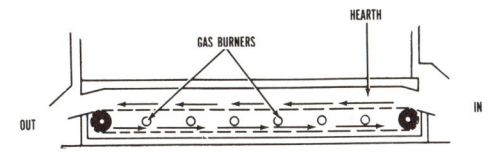

FIG. 21.4. TRAVELING HEARTH OVEN.

Courtesy of Baker Perkins, Inc.

FIG. 21.5. A DIRECT GAS-FIRED TRAVELING HEARTH OVEN.
This traveling hearth oven is 120 ft long and 10 ft 8 in. wide with automatic side loader and automatic unloader.

particularly harmful to bread, but could cause damage to delicate or fluid products such as pies and sheet cakes. Various methods of stabilization were invented, among them the shoe or chain system and the transfer arm.

Small sized traveling tray ovens may be operated as batch or multicycle equipment. After the oven is loaded, the pans are permitted to make two or more round trips before they are unloaded. In longer ovens, however, the travel time required for one complete cycle is sufficient to complete the baking so the oven can be operated continuously, and automatic loaders and unloaders can be used.

In tunnel ovens or traveling hearth ovens, the baking hearth is made of steel segments which move through the baking chamber on conveying chains (Fig. 21.4 and 21.5). Loading and discharging are at opposite ends of the tunnel, which is frequently a considerable advantage when positioning the auxiliary equipment. Straps, individual pans, or even unpanned dough pieces can be placed on the hearth. Because the baking surface is not divided into relatively small compartments, as in the traveling tray oven, it is more flexible in the size of pans it can accept and is often more efficient in capacity, especially where several sizes of straps are utilized. If pans are not at the loading area at the precise time a tray becomes available, the whole tray remains empty, but a traveling hearth oven can accept pans at any place on the hearth, and additional efficiency may accrue when timing is somewhat irregular.

Band ovens carry the continuous concept one step further and make the hearth one uninterrupted strip of metal. The band may be solid, perforated, or woven. Doughs can be deposited directly on the hearth, as in the case of crackers and cookies, or pans can be used.

Design Features of Traveling Tray Ovens

Construction details will be given for single-lap, direct gas-fired tray ovens for commercial pan bread.

The shell of the oven consists of a steel frame, resting on a level concrete foundation. The frame supports the steel lining sheets which form a rectangular baking chamber. Expansion joints allow the lining to expand and contract as the temperature changes without affecting the outer shell. A horizontal baffle divides the baking chamber into upper and lower compartments. The oven can also be divided in "zones" along its length, to allow application of a sequence of temperatures.

The top, bottom, and sides of the oven are insulated with about 2 in. of rock wool, and then plastered with asbestos cement to meet sanitary standards. The insulation is covered and concealed by the exterior finish sheets which are usually enameled white. Generally, the exterior sheeting is designed so as to be readily removable for inspection and servicing of the mechanical components located between the inner and outer walls.

Rows of direct gas-fired burners extend into the oven cavity below and above the tray conveyor. The burners are arranged in groups to form control zones for regulating the temperatures in different parts of the oven. Every zone has a separate air and gas supply, a modulating temperature controller, and a group of burners. To permit adjustment of the heat balance across the oven, some or all of the burners are constructed so as to allow variation in flame intensity along their length. Each burner has a fuel mixing inspirator where gas at 0 psig and air are combined. Ignition is continuous in ovens made by this manufacturer.

Indirect fired ovens have a more complex heating system. They will have one or more heating units located outside the chamber area. A heating unit will consist of a burner, combustion tunnel, heater body, radiator tubes, delivery and return ducts, circulating blower, exhaust stock with damper, controls, and safety devices.

Safety devices are of three types: (a) controls regulating the mechanical functions of the loader, unloader, and tray conveyor, (b) controls regulating the heat in the baking chamber, and (c) devices to protect against damage to the conveyor system, loader, and unloader and to prevent overheating of the oven and flues.

The conveyor drive is protected by three safety devices. If a pan or some other object jams the conveyor, it will either break a shear pin to disengage the main drive sprocket or activate an overload clutch which shuts off the motor. In the event these do not operate, the excessive current will cause the overload-protected magnetic starter to interrupt the electricity flowing to the motor.

There is ordinarily a safety bar mounted across the top of the oven loading door, and it will cause the conveyor to stop if it is contacted by a pan or lid overhanging the edge of the tray.

Pressure relief panels are held in place by thin strips or special bolts which release the panel when a sudden increase in pressure occurs. This arrangement may prevent serious damage to the oven as the result of an explosion.

Temperature limit controls shut down the fuel supply when the heat becomes excessive. Pressure switches also stop gas flow when the blowers fail. Gas pressure safety controls function when the pressure is too high or too low.

Design Features of Band Ovens

The following description is applicable to band ovens for cookie and cracker baking. In these ovens, raw dough pieces are dropped onto a flexible steel strip at the entrance and baked cookies taken off at the other end.

The original models consisted of substantial tunnels of brick in which moved a motor-driven traveling conveyor. Production was placed on top of the conveyor as in later designs. Heat was supplied by banks of steam tubes above and below the baking conveyor, the steam being produced in furnaces outside the ovens. These steam tube ovens were very satisfactory and were used for a long time.

The modern band oven is an outstanding triumph of engineering and technology. With very little maintenance, an oven 300 ft long and 39 in. (1000 mm) wide will routinely bake 2000–3000 lb of cookie dough per hour continuously for long periods. On certain doughs, much higher outputs can be obtained. Assuming proper adjustment, the millions of units put out in 24 hr of operation will be uniform enough to satisfy the most discriminating of consumers. The feeding and removal of dough pieces is routinely automated so as to require minimal attention by the operators.

In a survey of the types of continuous band cookie ovens being used in commercial bakeries (Light 1965), the following information was obtained: (1) The ovens ranged from 100 to 400 ft in length, and the bands were from 26 to 60 in. in width. (2) Direct-fired, indirect-fired, and infrared means of heat generation were being used. (3) Energy sources were natural gas, manufactured gas, propane, oil, and electricity. (4) Ovens had been manufactured by Baker-Perkins, Thomas L. Green, J. W. Greer, Spooner, Vicars, Werner, etc. (5) There were single-ribbon, double-ribbon, high intensity, and double-flame burners, with premix, inspirator, and aspirator means for combining air and fuel. Sometimes blowers and heat tubes were used, as well as various types of baffling, dampering, and exhaust systems. (6) The baking surfaces were solid or perforated continuous steel bands, and several types of wire mesh varying from very open (for some types of pretzels) through continental types, with smaller wire but still with open mesh, to heavy cord-weave bands utilizing both straight- and crimp-wire designs. (7) Basic adjustments which could be made included variable band speed, number of burners in top and bottom of each zone, pressure valves to regulate top and bottom burner flames separately in each zone, and dampers to remove or retain moisture in specific areas, vertical baffles between zones, and controllable exhaust systems.

Baking Chamber Construction.—The oven chamber consists of a frame supporting the necessary rollers, guides, burners and the like, together with insulation on top, sides, and bottom. Vents with dampers, clean-out doors, and observation ports are included as necessary (Fig. 21.6).

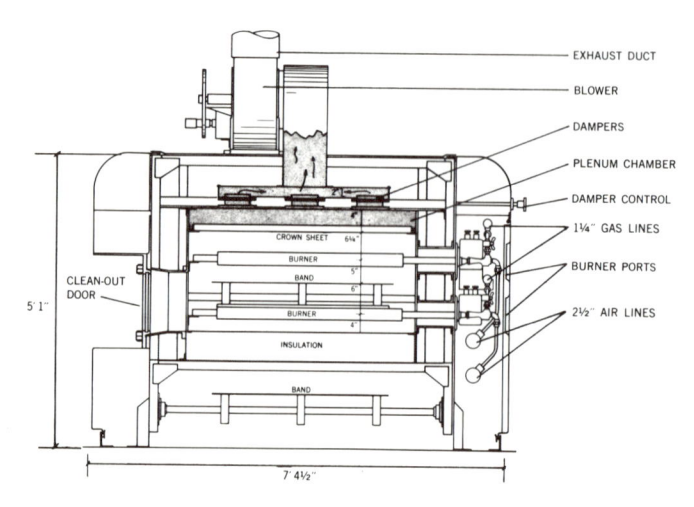

Courtesy of J. W. Greer Co.
FIG. 21.6. CROSS-SECTION OF A BAND OVEN.

Fiberglass wool is a common insulating material. When this is used, the oven is cased in enameled metal such as 10 gage steel with a white vitreous enamel. A representative arrangement would be 10 in. of 3 lb density fiberglass on top, 8 in. on the sides, and 6 in. on the bottom. Sheet material, composed essentially of asbestos fibers and binders, can be used both as an insulation and structural component. In this case, an outer covering is not necessary.

The baking chamber is usually provided in modular units, for example, 10-ft lengths. Ovens up to 400 ft are in operation, while ovens as short as 60 ft are used for special items.

Bands.—The baking surfaces can be either solid steel bands, perforated steel bands, or wire-mesh bands. The earlier mesh bands had a fairly open weave, but the more recent versions have had a finely textured closely-woven structure. Perforated bands and wire mesh allow steam to escape from the bottoms of dough pieces and help prevent gas pockets and distortions. They also tend to retard spread. The unbaked dough or batter is either deposited directly on the oven band, or formed on auxiliary equipment and then transferred to the band by conveyors.

According to a survey reported by Suarez (1963), solid steel bands now being used range in thickness from 0.032 in. to 0.092 in. but most are 0.062 in. Thinner bands allow use of smaller drive drums and assure rapid transmittance of heat. Wire mesh bands reported in this survey had an average thickness of 7/32 in.

Most steel bands are low carbon alloy steels which have been cold rolled according to given specifications. The cold working process generally increases the yield strength and tensile strength, and reduces ductility. The hardened steel is tempered to restore the ductility (Lugar 1962). The necessity for a straight, flat band is obvious. When properly made and maintained, a split band provides satisfactory service. Patched bands are highly undesirable. Uniform thickness is also essential. The expansion and contraction of the band caused by temperature changes is compensated for by pneumatic cylinder adjustments (Fig. 21.7) or by heavy counterweights on one of the drums.

On occasion, cookies may stick to the band. Presence of particles of sugar or milk solids in contact with the band will inevitably lead to sticking. Certain doughs are much more troublesome than others. Lean doughs which are relatively high in water are more prone to sticking. Sticking can also be accentuated or alleviated by band characteristics.

Dirty bands with built-up carbon deposits and bands with numerous pits and scratches are conducive to sticking. The band should be slightly oily from previous runs of rich cookies. If it is not, it may be

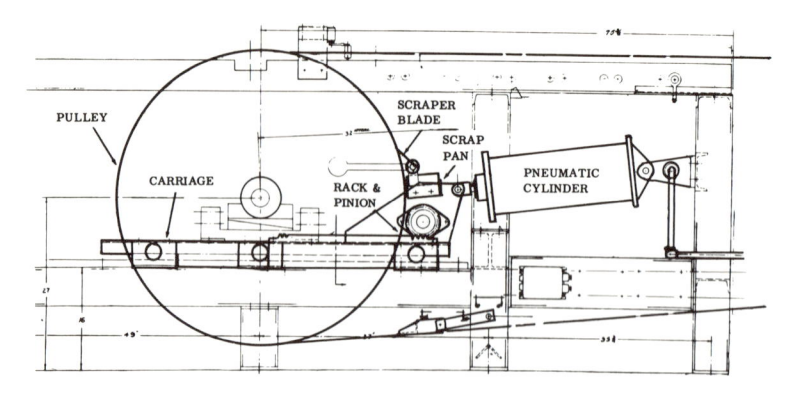

FIG. 21.7. RACK-AND-PINION ASSEMBLY FOR MAINTAINING TENSION ON THE BAND.

Courtesy of J. W. Greer Co.

necessary to grease it lightly or dust it with flour. Use of liquid shortening in the dough helps to eliminate sticking, though it may cause other difficulties.

New bands are usually conditioned by applying sufficient shortening to thoroughly saturate the surface. Sometimes beeswax or other special materials are used. The shortening is usually rubbed on at the inlet and the excess rubbed off at the exit end of a warm oven (300°–350°F). Temperature is then increased in 100°F steps until the highest operating temperature is reached. Lard, lard plus lecithin, corn oil, and coconut oil are some of the band conditioning materials which have been used.

The band is powered by a variable speed motor. Relatively low horsepower units are required. The time of baking is adjusted by varying the speed of the band.

Band Guides.—In long band ovens, even a slight amount of sideways movement will soon accumulate to the point where the band will be damaged and the oven jammed unless corrective measures are taken. This sideways movement is prevented by band guides which may be of several kinds. The simplest, and least satisfactory, are angle irons welded at strategic places along the band length. They will force a wandering band back into place, but they can also cause serious damage to the band in the process. Friction quickly wears out these simple guides.

Spring-mounted vertical spools fixed at numerous places along the band are reasonably satisfactory. They do cause edge wear. Canting the rollers supporting the band will guide it without edge wear, but this system requires close attention by the operator. Overcompensation or failure to correct the faulty condition soon enough, can ruin the band and damage the oven. A combined system utilizing spools as a sensing device to warn the operator when to adjust the support rollers is probably the best compromise solution. A recently-patented system may be even better: the spools themselves cant the rollers when the spools are driven off center by a wandering band.

Electronic Ovens

Electronic ovens generate heat within the product as a result of vibrations set up in some of its molecules by absorption of electromagnetic radiation of high frequency. The radiation is created by electronic circuits resembling radio transmitters in a very general way. There are two principal types of electronic ovens, the dielectric heating variety using frequencies in the range of 30–40 Mc, and the microwave or radar types using frequencies of 915, 2450, 5800, or 22,125 Mc per sec. This type of baking can be very efficient because the oven cavity is not held at a high temperature and therefore does not lose large amounts of energy to the environment as do conventional ovens. Since electricity rather than gas must be used as the energy source, the economics may not be as favorable as the efficiency, however. Microwave systems are the basis of the electronic ovens used in homes and restaurants for the rapid heating of miscellaneous foodstuffs. The installations in cracker and cookie plants have been principally the dielectric heating type because the economics appear to be considerably better at high heat transfer rates. Some microwave baking units have apparently been used for bread and similar products.

Because electronic heating will not give normal crust coloration, and for other reasons, there has never been a large-scale installation for bread baking. It can be useful for rapidly thawing frozen prebaked bread and rolls and unbaked dough pieces. Its most important commercial application has been in the final stage of baking soda crackers where it is used to reduce moisture content.

Use of electronic heating during the early stages of the baking process seems to offer no significant advantage over more conventional techniques. In the first or development stage, the dense dough can be rapidly heated on the band. In the second stage when spring occurs, the application of electronic heat leads to an excessively vigorous evolution of gases with some distortion of the structure. It is in the final stage, where a delicate balance between coloration and moisture reduction must be maintained, that electronic heating is most valuable. Moisture can be reduced with little or no browning because the localized dehydration with rapid temperature rise which occurs during conductive, convective, or infrared heating does not occur. Regions with the most moisture are heated most and the heat input drops as the moisture approaches zero. By bringing the entire piece to very low moisture content, a slight internal coloration can be induced.

This relationship of the moisture content of the piece to energy input is a very important feature of electronic ovens. The wetter the dough the more heat is generated in it. Because of this relationship, the ovens are self-compensating for variations in moisture content. The final moisture contents of the baked cookies and crackers tend to be evened out by this effect. Not only can excess or uneven browning be alleviated, but checking can also be reduced.

According to several published reports, installation of electronic heating in existing ovens, though possible, has many disadvantages. The heat tends to break down insulation and the accumulation of deposits on the conductors and electrodes cause current leakage. Furthermore, any unevenness in the band, which must form part of the electronic system, causes nonuniformity in the current flow. The solution to these problems has been to place the electronic heating unit just beyond the terminus of the band oven, using a plastic conveyor or belt.

Other Types of Ovens

The equipment used to bake the crisp sheets that form the base of sugar wafer cookies is a highly specialized oven. There are two basic types, the traveling book and the continuous band oven. The former type is by far the most common.

In the traveling book oven, sets of two plates each are mounted on traveling chains (Fig. 21.8). The bottom plate is fixed solidly to the carrier chains, and the top plate is hinged to the bottom plate. The books open automatically to accept a charge of batter, then close and lock. The closed books are carried through the baking chamber. When they again reach the front of the oven, the books open, the baked sheet is ejected, and the book receives its next charge of batter.

Wafer ovens are made in 12, 18, 24 and 30 plate models. Some manufacturers offer 36 plate models. The plates are usually 11 by 18 in., but double-sized books with baking surfaces 18 by 22 in. have also been offered. The bearings in the hinges of the books require frequent lubrication. In a 30-plate oven 330 points should be greased every 8 hr. By a relatively recent development, maintenance has been reduced through the use of self-lubricating bearings made of porous metal.

Plates can be adjusted to vary wafer thickness by means of shims located between the top and bottom plates, and the use of screwed sleeves and lock nuts.

Chrome plated oven books give better release of baked wafers than do

Courtesy of Simon-Vicars, Ltd.
FIG. 21.8. THIRTY-PLATE GAS HEATED WAFER OVEN.

untreated books. Oven books are cured by the application of vegetable or animal fat to the hot plates, similar to the treatment used for other baking surfaces.

Production rates vary depending on the thickness of the sheets, extent of baking, etc., but 1 oven manufacturer estimates a yield of 323 lb from a 24-plate gas-fired oven in 5 hr (including 35 min preheating).

A modification of the traveling plate oven utilizes two sets of books conveyed through a common baking chamber to increase output per unit of floor space and per dollar of capital expenditure.

The continuous band oven is designed in such a fashion that the batter is deposited on the surface of a reeded drum similar in construction to the drive drums of band ovens. A reeded steel band forms the top plate, heat being applied to the inside of the drum and to the outside of the band. Batter is injected between the drum and band, and a continuous wafer sheet is withdrawn from the outlet.

HEATING THE OVEN

Fuels

The great majority of commercial bakery ovens are fueled by natural gas. Oil, manufactured gas, and electricity are other fuels used because of some special situation or requirement. Electricity has many advantages as an energy source, such as the cleanliness, low maintenance requirement, and ease of control, but its cost is prohibitive in all but a few locations. There may be some installations where coal or coke is still being used but they have so many disadvantages as compared to natural gas that they can be expected be to phased out. Average theoretical Btu per unit for the various fuels has been reported to be: electricity, 3142 per KWH; natural gas 1000 per cu ft; manufactured gas, 550 per cu ft; light fuel oil, 140,000 per gal.; and coal, 13,500 per lb.

From 150–250 Btu will be required for baking 1 lb of bread to completion. In addition, heat will be required by the pans, and some will be lost from the oven to its surroundings, so a considerably larger amount of fuel will be required than is indicated by the preceding figures. The heat taken up by the pans will obviously vary depending upon their weight and composition, but an average figure of 40 Btu per lb of dough is often used in calculations of oven capacities.

Efficiency of the oven in utilizing fuel depends upon the details of construction, such as type and thickness of insulation, method of transferring the heat, etc. Skarin (1964) estimated that 400 Btu of gas were consumed per pound of bread in direct-fired ovens equipped with air-agitating systems. With gas burning at 85% efficiency, 340 Btu are delivered into the oven, of which about 50 Btu are lost through the walls or through other routes. Indirect-fired ovens require an additional 20% fuel because of the loss of efficiency in supplying heat to an enclosed system. For oil, about 80% of the theoretical heat content can be recovered in an efficient combustion system.

Burners

The two main types of conventional ovens are those with ribbon burners in the baking chamber itself and those with combustion chambers located outside the oven proper. Ribbon burners are placed approximately 2 ft apart (Fig. 21.9) while the recirculating ovens have a heating unit about every 50 ft. There has been a great deal of controversy about the relative desirability of these two systems, but it is well known that both types are being used satisfactorily. Figure 21.10 shows a cross section of a typical oven using ribbon burners. Open flame or surface combustion (ceramic) elements have been used, but the former type is more common.

Several burner systems have been devised to obtain maximum safety and control of the heat sources within the oven. The open inspirator system uses gas at 1–5 lb pressure and room air drawn into the inspirator by the Venturi effect. Good combustion is obtained at or near the

OVENS AND ASSOCIATED EQUIPMENT

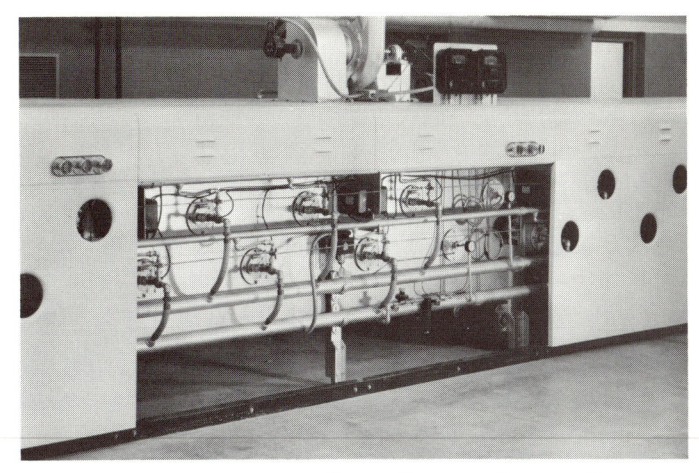

Fig. 21.9. Oven With Trim Sheets Removed Showing Combustion Piping Supplying Ribbon Burners.

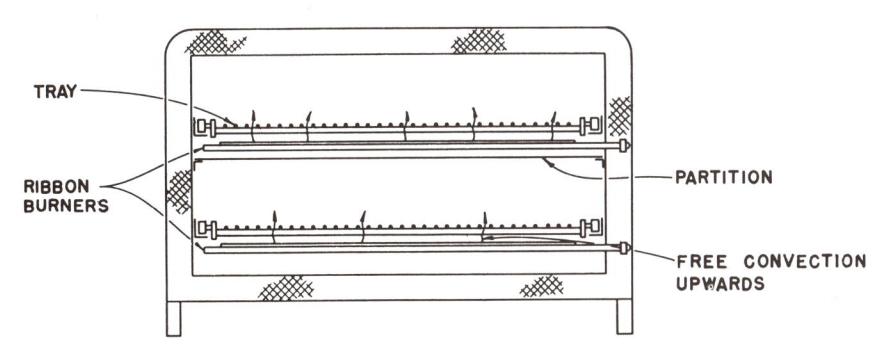

Fig. 21.10. Direct Natural Convection Heating System With Ribbon Burners.

maximum output, but at lower settings adequate air for complete combustion may not be entrained. The question arises as to the fate of solid particles drawn in with the room air. Smaller particles will undoubtedly pass through the jets and be burned without causing any problem. Large particles which might clog the burner can be entrapped by filters fitted over the intakes to the inspirator. Even so, some accumulation of deposits inside the burner occurs, and these systems are designed for easy and fool-proof cleaning of the inspirator and other critical parts.

The zone proportional mixer system uses air pressurized to approximately 1 psig to draw gas at substantially atmospheric pressure into a proportional mixing unit. This gas is depressurized to zero gage by a special valving arrangement. The combustible mixture is distributed to several burners, usually to a complete zone. Control is effected by changing the volume of air going into the proportional mixer. Any change made affects all of the burners in the zone, making this system rather inflexible. The air is filtered before being pressurized.

A modification of the zone proportional system mixes the air and gas in proper ratio at each burner. It is necessary to lead a zero pressure gas line and low pressure air line to each burner and to have a separate proportional mixer and gas valve for each burner. This system provides excellent flexibility although it may be questioned as to how often the high level of control achievable by it is actually necessary.

Gas and air for all the burners in an oven are premixed in a special device in the premixed gas system. The disadvantage of this method is the presence of an explosive misture in relatively large quantities throughout the distribution system. Each burner must be fitted with a fire check to prevent backfiring. The system is flexible because each burner can be adjusted separately, but because of the potential dangers is not much used. Some ribbon burners can be adjusted so as to give different flame height in three sections across the band.

In the exterior-combustion chamber type of oven, several arrangements are possible. Generally, there is one combustion chamber per zone, which restricts the number of adjustments which can be made (Fig. 21.11). On the other hand, relatively close control of the temperature of the circulating gases can be achieved. The type of burner is more-or-less immaterial so far as the effect on the dough piece is concerned.

Courtesy of J. W. Greer Co.

FIG. 21.11. AN INDIRECT COMBINATION GAS- AND OIL-FIRED TRAVELING HEARTH BREAD OVEN.

Steam can be used to transfer heat from the combustion chamber to the baking tunnel. In one steam system, metal tubes sealed at both ends and partially filled with water or some other suitable liquid extend from the fire box into the oven. The flames vaporize the liquid, and the turbulent gases under high pressure carry heat throughout the length of the tube. Since heat is transferred to the product mainly by radiation, very high temperatures must be attained by the tube before satisfactory baking conditions are reached. This system is no longer used to any great extent in bakery ovens.

The Rhodes Acceletron consists of a high voltage direct current supply connected to a series of grids within the baking chamber. A high potential electrostatic field is produced between the grids and the grounded oven hearth, but the energy consumption is low. It is claimed that the difference in potential causes a concentration of steam near the hearth, baking pans, and product. As a result, heat transfer is facilitated and the baking time is reduced. Kilborn and Tipples (1970) showed the Acceletron caused a significant increase in the rate of temperature rise inside the loaf. In their laboratory oven, total baking time was reduced by about 17%. Crust color tended to be darker and loaf volume larger when the Acceletron was used. Fuel consumption per unit time appeared to increase by about 11–16% as compared to an increase in product throughout of 22%, suggesting that a slight saving in energy costs might be achieved.

Zone Control

Traveling hearth ovens have the advantage that baffles can be placed in the baking chamber to restrict heat circulation so that different temperatures can be applied to the product at different times in its baking cycle. This provides the baker with much more flexibility in adjusting the baking conditions to an optimum for a given product. Generally, the burners can be regulated separately for the top and bottom of each zone and the exhaust control dampers are separate for each zone. The use of zone control is particularly important in baking crackers and cookies.

The number of zones in an oven will vary according to the specifications established by the engineer based on the kinds of products to be baked in the oven, but will rarely exceed eight. In setting up baking conditions, it is often constructive to consider the oven as being divided into 3 sections even though more than 3 zones are present.

The recommended temperature pattern for most wire-cut cookies is a fairly low temperature in zone 1, where the spread and rise of the dough takes place; a considerable increase in temperature in the intermediate zone(s) to set and bake the cookie; and a slightly lower temperature in the final zones to give the desired color and dehydration. Relatively low bottom heat, as compared to the top heat, is used in the first zone to promote good spread and a finer, more even cell structure.

In baking saltines, the first zone (or section) of the oven is adjusted for high bottom heat and relatively low top heat. This arrangement leads to proper bottom development and starts the gas evolution necessary for adequate spring while at the same time maintaining a soft uncrusted top which will allow moisture and gases to escape. Shelliness and premature development of blisters result from excess top heat in the first zone. In the middle section, the top heat is brought up and the bottom heat is usually reduced somewhat. The top of the cracker is set, and the final shape of the biscuit develops, although moisture is still being driven off. In the third section, the moisture is reduced to the point where dehydration can be satisfactorily completed during cooling, and the coloration is begun.

Rotary goods and some rich wire-cut doughs require low heat in the first zone, slightly increased heat in the middle section, and the correct intensity of heat for bake-out and coloration in the final zone. This provides the gentle, slow development necessary for these doughs, and prevents excessive or premature rise. Higher bottom heat in the early zones tends to set the bottom early and may facilitate the removal of sticky doughs from the band.

Steam

Steam is introduced into ovens primarily to modify crust characteristics. It tends to reduce the rate at which the dough surface dehydrates. Consequently, the crust remains elastic for a longer time, preferably during the entire period of dough expansion, and ragged breaks are avoided. The delay in crust stiffening may allow the development of greater volume. The crust becomes smoother throughout leading to a glossier appearance. Browning reactions are also modified so as to give better crust colors, in most cases.

In order to achieve the desired results, it is necessary that moisture condense on the dough surface. Injection of high pressure steam is worthless for this purpose. Authorities agree that saturated steam of 2–5 psig should be injected with orifice velocities of 200–500 ft per min. Violent turbulence is not desired, since it would tend to reduce the opportunities for moisture vapor to condense.

As the crust temperature approaches 212°F, steam has little effect since condensation will not occur. The major effect occurs in the first 1–2 min in the oven, as the temperature of the crust is rising from about 90°F to near the temperature of boiling water.

According to Dersch (1960) the steam in a typical oven comes from the following sources: vaporization of water in the dough, 2.7 cu ft per lb of dough; product of combustion 0.9 cu ft per lb of dough; and steam injectors 9.25 cu ft per lb of dough. It is obvious that far more steam originates from steam injection than from the other two sources.

AUXILIARY EQUIPMENT

Ovens can, of course, be hand loaded with pans or straps. This arduous task is accomplished by mechanical means in nearly all large volume shops, however. The principle of operation of loading devices is relatively simple. Pans move over roller conveyors from the final steam proofer to a point in front of the oven loading door. Their momentum carries them onto a series of rollers at right angles to the previous conveyor and parallel to the oven door. When a series of pans the width of the tray or hearth has collected, they are pushed into the oven. A retractable metal bar prevents additional pans from coming onto the loading platform while the pusher bar is operating.

The moving element in the loading device is synchronized with the travel of the oven trays (if it is a tray oven). Design variations are seen mostly in the actuating mechanism of the pusher bar and the way in which it is returned to its starting position. For example, it may go back and forth on the same level. In this arrangement, movement of pans onto the loading platform must be held up during the retraction cycle leading to some waste of time. Another version is designed to raise the pusher mechanism to a higher level as it is retracted, so that it passes over any pans which are coming onto the loading platform. In a third design, the pusher bar moves back under the loading platform, rising again as it passes the front end of the loading plate. This method of operation also clears the path of incoming trays during the return cycle.

In tunnel ovens, pans can be loaded as soon as a set comes into position, but the loader on a tray oven must wait until the tray is correctly situated inside the loading door. If a tray starts to pass out of the loading area before pans are available, a substantial amount of hearth space will be wasted.

Loaders are customarily fed from the side of the oven (Fig. 21.12). Side-feed loaders operate best at about four cycles per minute. Higher rates cause too much mechanical disturbance of the dough pieces as a result of the sudden acceleration. On the other hand, slower speeds do not confer any added benefits.

Unloaders

On some models of tray ovens, provision is made for tilting the trays carrying the baked bread just before they reach the loading position,

Courtesy of Baker Perkins, Inc.
FIG. 21.12. A TRAY OVEN WITH PAN GROUPER AND AUTOMATIC SIDE FEED.

so that the pans slide by gravity onto a cross conveyor at a lower level. This conveyor carries the pans through an opening in the side of the oven. High production rates and simplicity of operation are features of this design.

Level plane or horizontal unloaders use pusher bars to move the pans off the trays. Mechanical damage to the bread is likely to be less with this method of unloading. Gentler methods of unloading may be required for pies, products in foil pans, etc. Pie unloaders have a special fork lift that picks up a row of pans and transfers them to a take-away conveyor. Walking finger unloaders will handle almost any type of panned or foil product with minimal damage.

The slide plate unloader for hearth goods and some pan goods simply allows the product to slide off the oven hearth and down the plate to a take-away conveyor (Fig. 21.13).

Depanners

Depanners are of two major types, the gravity models in which the loaf is dislodged by dropping the inverted pans a short distance and vacuum depanners which rely on a multitude of suction cups to lift the loaves or rolls out of the pans. Vacuum depanners will function properly only with certain types of pans.

In the AMF Model F Depanner (which is combined with a packing unit), the vacuum pick-up head swings on an arc and is driven from a continuous crank motion (Fig. 21.14). The machine picks up 12 rolls simultaneously and gently deposits them into formed boxes. Roll-filled pans are placed on the pan infeed conveyor, which has a positive indexing finger to properly situate the pans in the depanning area. Empty pans are than returned to infeed area or storage. Vacuum is supplied from a 3 hp turbine pump. In addition, a compressed air supply at 50 lb pressure is required.

Conditions which are required to ensure the best operation of the depanner-packer are (1) uniform make-up at Pan-O-Mat; (2) uniform pan greasing for good release; (3) uniform proofing to hold even size; (4) uniform production flow from oven to cooling; (5) uniform cooling, approximately 94°F inside roll temperature; (6) good box forming; and (7) quality boxes to lay reasonably flat when formed.

Pans coming from the depanner will usually be at a temperature between 250° and 300°F. They must be cooled to about 90°F before dough is placed in them.

Coolers

After loaves have been removed from the pans, they must be cooled before being sliced and wrapped. The bread may be stacked on racks and exposed to the cooling effect of the atmosphere, either aided by fans or not. Since racks occupy a great deal of floor space and require

Courtesy of Baker Perkins, Inc.

FIG. 21.13. TRAY OVEN SHOWING UNLOADING ARRANGEMENT AND CONVEYOR LEADING TO HAND DEPANNING STATION.

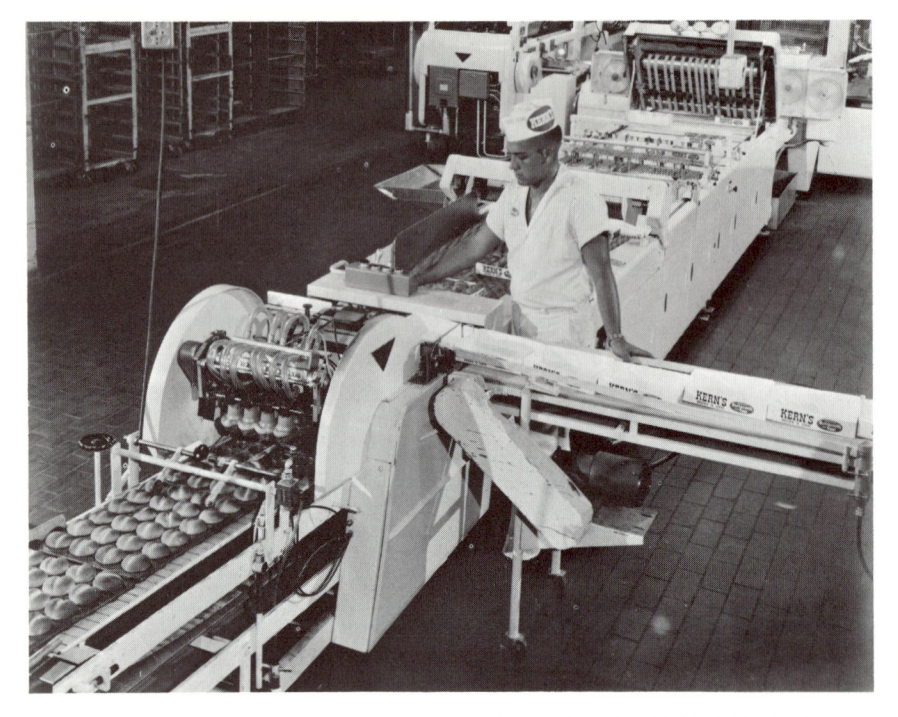

Courtesy of American Machine & Foundry Co.
FIG. 21.14. A VACUUM DEPANNER SHOWING PICKUP HEAD IN FOREGROUND.

considerable manual labor to load, unload, and transfer, high volume bakeries make use of conveyorized coolers which are suspended from the ceiling, leaving space underneath for installation of other equipment. These coolers are equipped with a fan system which draws in air at the discharge end and moves it past the loaves, exhausting it at the top. More elaborate coolers make use of air-conditioning units to refrigerate the air current and cut down on the time required for reducing the temperature to the desired level.

Vacuum bread conditioners first precool the bread by passing it through a tunnel in which it is contacted by an air current of controlled humidity and temperature. The loaves are then placed in a vacuum chamber for 2 min, where accelerated heat loss occurs as a result of the vaporization of some of the moisture. Vacuum cooling leads to a uniform temperature throughout the loaf.

May (1962) described an automatic rack-type cooler installed in a large commercial installation. It has the form of an enclosed box 13 ft high, 16 ft wide, and 38 ft long. The bottom perimeter is bordered by washable aluminum filters, each 25 in. wide by 16 in. high. Filtered air is circulated by 4 30-in. fans mounted on top of the cooler. Each fan has a capacity of 7500 cfm and is driven by a ⅝ hp dust-proof motor. Fans are individually controlled by pushbutton switches. Bread is placed on 44 racks, each with 8 shelves 16 in. deep and 12 ft wide. Rack travel is the same as in the proof boxes, namely front to rear on the upper level and rear to front on the lower level. Cooling time may be varied from 59 to 70 min.

Pans

Baking pans can be considered as interacting with the oven and the dough during the baking process. It is generally recognized by both practical bakers and technologists that the conformation, construction, and surface characteristics (color, reflectivity, and adhesive qualities, for example) affect not only the finished product, but also the handling efficiencies, speed of baking, etc.

Interaction occurs as a result of the guiding effect of the pan on the expanding dough, the support offered the baked piece as it sets up, the rate of heat transmission to the product, the shading effect on product surfaces, among other mechanisms. Some of these effects are not easily modified, but dimensions (i.e., relation of volume to height and width) and slope of sides can frequently be modified more or less at will. Once the pans have been purchased, however, the large investment strongly tends to restrict the options of the baker in future planning.

Pans are made of black iron, tinplate, aluminum, aluminized steel, and stainless steel. Black iron is covered by an oxide coating which has good rust resistance as long as it remains intact. It also absorbs radiation very well and heats up rapidly in the oven. Tin-plated steel is a common pan material. New pans of tin-plated steel must be oxidized before use by heating for several hours at temperatures near 400°F. An alternate method is to coat the tinned surface with a material which simulates the surface of heat-treated pans for a time long enough for the oxide to develop. Aluminum conducts heat well but is very subject to mechanical damage. Aluminized steel was developed to give greater strength while retaining the desirable surface characteristics of aluminum. Stainless steel has the advantages of resistance to corrosion and mechanical damage, but it is very expensive, rather difficult to fabricate, and does not conduct heat well, so it has never become a popular metal for pan construction.

The costs of pans for a bread bakery represent a considerable percentage of the total capital investment. About 6–8 times the oven's capacity will be required: 2 sets in the proof box and 3–5 sets in the cooling, greasing, and panning operations in addition to the set in the oven.

Usually 3–4 pans are held in a unit by metal strips. These pan sets, or "straps," serve to separate the pans an optimum distance. Spacer lugs are attached to the side and end bands to give spacing between the straps as they go into the oven.

Sticking of the baked product to the pan is a serious problem, leading to difficulties in depanning and excessive cripples. Pan greasing is the oldest solution to the problem. Treatment with silicones which are intended to last through a great many baking cycles has been widely accepted. Teflon coating is excellent but expensive.

There are some general rules which can be applied to estimate the scaling weights of batters and doughs suitable for pans of any given dimension. Table 21.1 gives general guidelines for various kinds of cakes. As stated by Glabau (1962), optimum scaling weights will be affected by (1) the type of cake, (2) the formula variations within the type, (3) the specific gravity of the batter, (4) amount of leavening, (5) the altitude, and (6) oven characteristics and baking temperature.

For bread baked in open top pans, 5.8–6 cu in. of pan volume for each ounce of dough is considered satisfactory. Pullman breads will require 6 cu in. of pan volume for a closely grained loaf and 7 cu in. per oz of dough for the loaves of higher specific volume.

TABLE 21.1
AMOUNT OF BATTER REQUIRED FOR PANS OF DEFINITE DIMENSIONS

Diameter (In.)	Depth (In.)	Capacity (Cu In.)	Cake Batter			
			Pound (Oz)	Layer (Oz)	Angel (Oz)	Sponge (Oz)
6	1	28.4	6¾	5½	3½	3¼
7	1	38.5	9⅓	7½	4¾	4¼
8	1	50.4	12⅓	10	6¼	5⅓
9	1	63.8	15⅓	12½	7½	6¾
10	1	78.5	19	15½	9½	8½
11	1	95.3	22¾	18¾	11½	10
12	1	115.0	27½	22½	14	12½
6	1¼	35.3	8½	7	4⅓	4
7	1¼	48.2	11½	9½	6	5⅓
8	1¼	63.0	15⅓	12⅓	7¾	6¾
9	1¼	80.0	19⅕	15¾	9½	8½
10	1¼	98.2	23¾	19⅓	12	10½
11	1¼	119.0	28⅓	23½	14½	12½
12	1¼	141.0	34½	28	17½	15½
6	1½	42.4	10¼	8½	5¼	5
7	1½	57.7	14	11½	7¼	6½
8	1½	75.4	18⅓	14⅔	9½	8
9	1½	95.2	23	18¾	11⅓	10
10	1½	118.0	28½	23⅓	14⅓	12¾
11	1½	142.0	34¼	28	17⅓	15
12	1½	170.0	41¼	33¾	21	18¾

BIBLIOGRAPHY

ANDERSON, R. C. 1970. Oven maintenance. Baker's Dig. *44*, No. 8, 58–62, 76.
ANON. 1963. Direct-fired and wire-mesh ovens. Greer Tech. Inform. Sheet *BT-101*. J. W. Greer Co., Wilmington, Mass.
BAUMEISTER, T. 1958. Mechanical Engineers' Handbook, 6th Edition. McGraw-Hill Book Co., New York.
DERSCH, J. A. 1960. Bakery Ovens. *In* Bakery Technology and Engineering, S. A. Matz (Editor). Avi Publishing Co., Westport, Conn.
DIXON, F. R., and CLEMENTS, R. G. 1963. Improvement in heat treatment of baking ovens. British Pat. 924,071. Apr. 24.
GLABAU, C. A. 1962. How much batter should cake pans take? Bakers Weekly *194*, No. 2, 44, 46, 48; No. 4, 45–46, 48; No. 8, 74, 78, 79; No. 10, 51–53; No. 12, 52, 54, 60.
HOLLAND, J. M. 1963. Foodstuffs baking apparatus. U.S. Pat. 3,082,710. Mar. 26.
KELLEY, H. N. 1969. A Brief Encyclopedia of Commercial Ovens. Middleby-Marshall Oven Co., Morton Grove, Ill.
KILBORNE, R. H., and TIPPLES, K. H. 1970. Studies with a laboratory scale "acceletron" heat and steam accelerator. Baker's Dig. *44*, No. 6, 50–52.
LIGHT, H. J., JR. 1965. Baking principles by zone. Biscuit Bakers' Institute 40th Ann. Training Conf., Montreal.
LUGAR, T. R. 1962. Economic Biscuit and Cracker Baking. Thomas L. Green & Co., Indianapolis.
MAY, L. 1962. Spaulding's three streamlined production lines for bread, rolls, and donuts. Bakers Weekly *195*, No. 9, 40–49.
MORINE, R. L. 1965. Effective preventive maintenance schedule with emphasis on ovens. Proc. Am. Soc. Bakery Engrs. *1965*, 97–104.
NUTTALL, J. M. 1963. Detinning bakery goods. U.S. Pat. 3,099,345. July 30.
PERRY, R. H., CHILTON, C. H., and KIRKPATRICK, S. D. 1963. Chemical Engineers' Handbook, 4th Ed. McGraw-Hill Book Co., New York.
PETERSEN, C. W., and HEIDE, H. A. 1963. Depanning apparatus. U.S. Pat. 3,099,360. July 30.
PIRRIE, P. G. 1934. Use of steam in bakers' ovens. Am. Soc. Bakery Engrs. Bull. *98*.
PONTE, J. G., JR., TITCOMB, S. T., and COTTON, R. H. 1963. Some effects of oven temperature and malted barley level on breadmaking. Baker's Dig. *37*, No. 3, 44–48.
RHODES, I. 1968. Processes of cooling foods, and apparatus therefore. Can. Pat. 783,385. Apr. 23.
SKARIN, R. 1964. Selecting an oven for maximum performance. Proc. Am. Soc. Bakery Engrs. *1964*, 88–93.
SMITH, W. H. 1966A. Steam, humidity, and damper control in bakery ovens. Biscuit Maker Plant Baker *17*, 730–732.
SMITH, W. H. 1966B. What happens in the baking oven? Biscuit Maker Plant Baker *17*, 652–656.
SUAREZ, P. E. 1963. Oven bands—their use and maintenance. Biscuit Cracker Baker *52*, No. 9, 74, 76.

CHAPTER 22

SLICERS

Sliced bread was a major advance in convenience foods. Slices of uniform thickness are highly desirable for toasting and making sandwiches, but obtaining uniform slices with kitchen utensils is difficult and tedious. The development of automatic slicing also permitted the offering of very soft loaves which would be difficult or impossible to slice satisfactorily in the home.

Slicers for bakery products can be classified into three categories based upon the type of cutting mechanism employed: (1) slicers using circular blades; (2) slicers using straight blades; and (3) slicers using continuous band blades. The first type is used only on rolls, buns, and similar pieces. Today, most white pan bread is sliced on machines using endless blades, but a considerable number of reciprocating slicers (using straight blades) are in use, particularly for specialty breads and in small retail bakeries.

SLICING THEORY[1]

The secret of good slicing lies in the cutting band. It is made from a $7/16$-in. wide, carbon-chromium-vanadium-steel strip, especially selected for its strength. These strips are cut into lengths with tolerances of about $1/1000$ of an inch. The ends of the strip are ground to form an overlapping joint, which is then silver-soldered on a special electronic induction heating unit. This heating unit allows the joint to be formed without exceeding the critical temperature of the steel. If the critical temperature of the steel is exceeded, the strength will be reduced, inviting breakage.

On these bands, as they are now called, are ground the desired tooth forms and the necessary bevels. The bands are then honed to razor sharpness. At the bakeries, the bands are mounted on 2, 4, or 6 drums (depending upon the type of slicing machine) and crossed as in Fig. 22.2. From one drum to the other, each band is twisted through an angle of 180°. Midway between the two drums, is a point at which the two bands are perpendicular to the axis of the drums.

---

[1] Part of this section was written by John Hansen of the Hansaloy Manufacturing Co., Davenport, Iowa, and David Diehl.

FIG. 22.1. BREAD COOLER CONVEYORS SUSPENDED ABOVE A ROW OF BREAD SLICERS.

Courtesy of Baker Perkins, Inc.

Since there must be no twisting on that portion of the band which is doing the cutting, guides are introduced above and below the loaf to be cut.

Since the guides are exerting a force on the bands, the guides are subject to constant wear and must have extremely hard wearing surfaces. However, even with these hard surfaces, the friction between the bands and the guides will eventually cause wear. As a result, shoulders form in the guides as shown in Fig. 22.3. This situation can be helped by using new $7/16$-in. bands for a time, and then using reground $5/16$-in. bands for the rest of the time. This helps to distribute the wear more evenly over a greater area. If the depth of the shoulder becomes greater than $1/2$ the width of the band, the teeth of the band will be knocked off. When this condition develops, the guides must be replaced.

To keep guide wear to a minimum, these six rules should be followed: (1) Distribute wear over the greatest possible area. (2) Allow a very small amount of play between the backup roller and the band (if a backup roller is used). (3) Run the bands with the least possible tension for good slicing. (4) Do not allow crumbs to accumulate in

440 BAKERY TECHNOLOGY AND ENGINEERING

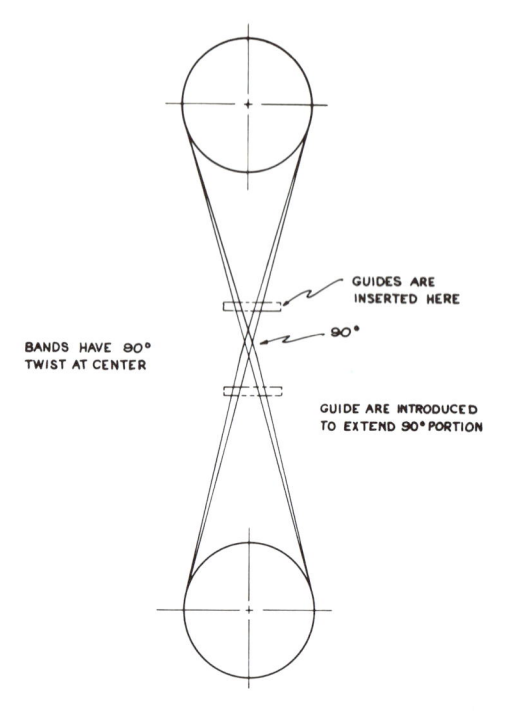

FIG. 22.2. TYPICAL ARRANGEMENT OF DRUMS, BANDS, AND GUIDES IN BREAD SLICERS.

the guides to such an extent that the band cannot move freely. (5) Put a drop or two of divider oil on the guides occasionally. (6) Alternate the direction in which the band points are directed in successive set installations. In this way the guides will wear on both sides alternately. All points in the same set must, of course, be in the same direction.

There are, at present, three basic types of tooth forms being used. The three types are illustrated in Fig. 22.4. The first type is the alternating scallop-flat type. The second is the two bevel serration, and the third is the scallop type. The most common type is the scallop type.

It was stated earlier that, to be efficient, a band must cut smoothly without crushing. It has been found that crushing becomes less as the penetration becomes better. It has been observed that penetration becomes better and crushing is decreased as the scallops are made deeper. More tearing and a rougher slice result, however. Conversely, as the scallops are made shallower, a smoother slice results but the penetration becomes less and more crushing is obtained. From these observations, it can be concluded that the efficiency of slicing is somewhat dependent on the depth of the scallop.

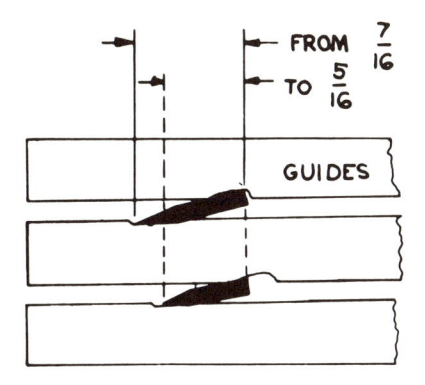

FIG. 22.3. DEVELOPMENT OF SHOULDERS ON BAND GUIDES.
Long, continued abrasion by the blades wears channels in the hardened steel guides.

ALTERNATE SCALLOPS & FLATS

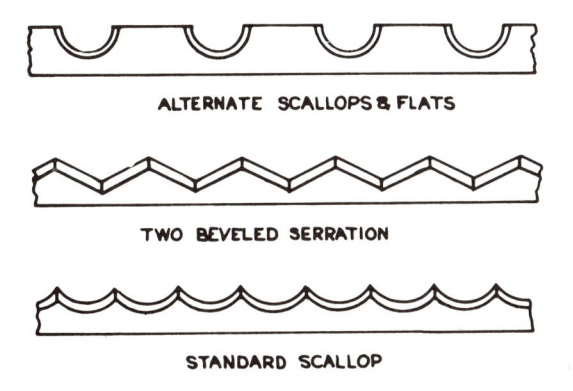

TWO BEVELED SERRATION

STANDARD SCALLOP

FIG. 22.4. TYPES OF TOOTH FORMS USED ON BANDS.

The relationship described above can best be explained in terms of what is called the "shear angle." The shear angle is formed by the line drawn tangent to the scallop and a line drawn across the top of the scallop. It is illustrated in Fig. 22.5.

Many experiments have been run using different shear angles and the results showed that it was necessary to work within fairly close limits. It has been proved experimentally that the upper and lower limits should be between 30° and 45° for efficient slicing. This, of course, means that any saw-tooth type of band would not work because the shear angle is greater than 90°. When the shear angle is less than 30°, crushing will occur sooner than with a greater shear angle. When the shear angle is greater than 45°, tearing occurs resulting in a rough slice.

Several other angles are also important to slicing. These are

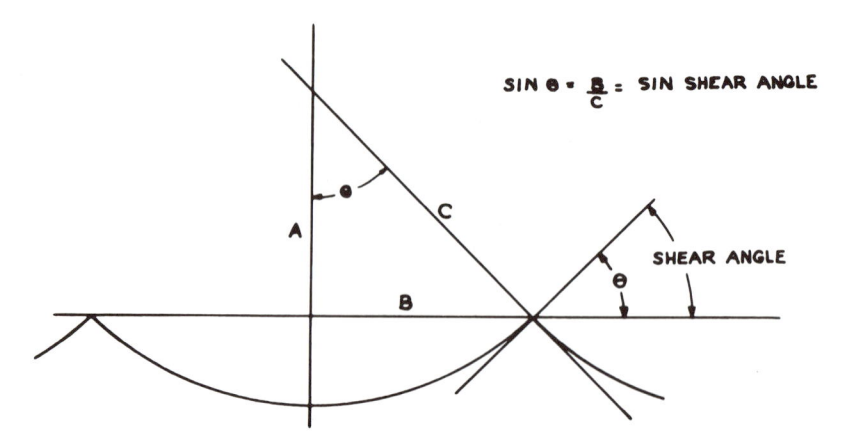

FIG. 22.5. DETERMINING THE SHEAR ANGLE.

illustrated in Fig. 22.6. The first is the cutting angle. The tangent of the cutting angle is equal to the depth of the cut divided by the distance between each tooth minus the distance from the point of contact with the bread. The smaller the cutting angle the smoother the slice.

Another important angle is the resultant angle. The tangent of the resultant angle is equal to the infeed divided by the band speed (both in feet per minute). The greater the resultant angle the less crushing will occur. The effective shear angle is then referred to as the shear angle minus the resultant angle. The effective shear angle must be great enough to accommodate the infeed plus the compression of the loaf due to the dullness of the edge, or crushing will again result. It has been concluded that if the effective shear angle is made smaller, without exceeding the limits previously established, a smoother slice will result.

There are various methods used in grinding the scallops or serrations forming the cutting edge. The scallops are produced by grinding two bevels in such a way that the resulting cutting edge is exactly in the middle of the steel. These two bevels are the "primary bevels."

The primary bevel is usually at about a 6° angle with the side of the steel. This form has the strongest support of the cutting edge and is the most efficient cutting edge. The primary bevel will retain sharpness longer than either a 3- or 4-beveled edge. The main disadvantage of this type is that it is difficult to hone since much steel must be removed to sharpen the cutting edge. It is commonly used for slicing relatively firm loaves of bread. It makes a high pitched or hissing sound as it passes through the guides.

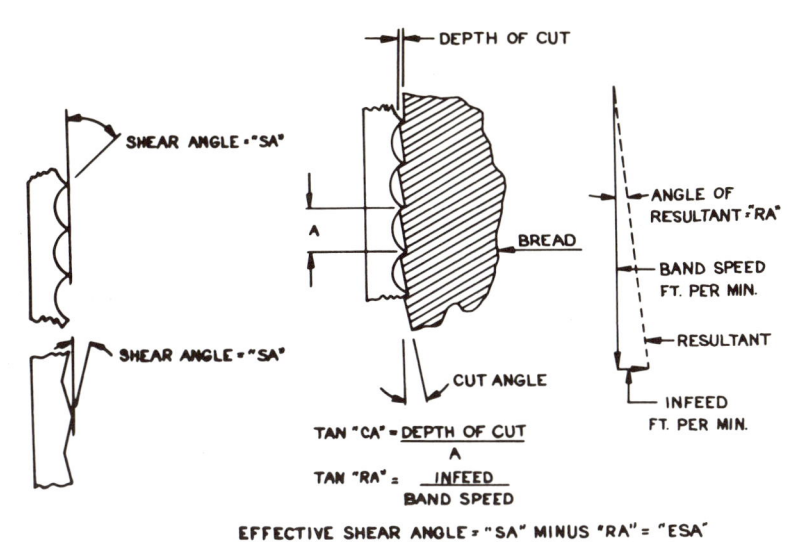

FIG. 22.6. ANGLES IMPORTANT IN SLICER PERFORMANCE.

The next type of band is the three-beveled band. This type of band has 1 primary bevel and 2 secondary bevels, 1 on each side. The secondary bevels usually form an angle of about 1° with the side of the steel. This type of band is generally used where a special type of honing is employed. It has the disadvantage that the cutting edge is at an angle with the cutting action.

The four-beveled form is the type which is becoming more and more popular with the bakers who are slicing soft or "super-soft" loaves. This type has 2 secondary 1° bevels in addition to the primary bevels. The 4-beveled type has 2 distinct advantages over the other 2 types. The main function of the secondary bevel is to reduce the amount of steel to be honed off in order to sharpen the cutting edge. Also the vibrations and hissing sounds caused by the two-beveled band moving through the guides are eliminated. A disadvantage is the loss in strength due to the removal of some of the steel supporting the cutting. edge. This type of band is not recommended for the firmer loaves because it sometimes has a tendency to weave when it hits the crust resulting in uneven slicing. The four-beveled bands are excellent for slicing soft loaves.

So far, only the tooth forms and the various beveled edges have been considered. The smoothness of the cutting edge itself has not been considered. For many years the finished cutting edge was always ground at a 90° angle with respect to both primary and secondary bevels. Cross-grinding does not produce the smoothest cutting edge because the minute grooves or ridges that are left by the grinding wheel cause microscopic serrations where the two intersecting bevels form the cutting edge.

When a tool grinder wants to put the best possible edge on a tool, he grinds and hones it parallel to the cutting action. Thus, when the best possible cutting edge is desired on a bread-slicing band, the final grinding and honing should be done parallel to the cutting action.

Experimentally, it has been found that the parallel-ground band does a much better job of slicing softer, more delicate loaves, than does the cross-ground band. Efficient cutting is not done by burrs. The smoother the cutting edge, the more efficiently it will do its job. Therefore, for slicing extremely soft, delicate loaves, it is recommended that parallel-ground bands be used.

Probably the most important single factor determining efficient slicing is the cutting edge thickness. When bands are new, for all practical purposes, the cutting edge may be considered to have no width. By flash electroplating various thicknesses of chrominum on the cutting bands, it was found that when the cutting edge was 0.0003 in., the band was too dull to give satisfactory results. Wear causes this thickness to occur after about 300,000 loaves or 100 hr of slicing.

Band tension is a very elusive quantity. Many bakers have the impression that uneven slicing can be corrected by increasing the tension. This is not the case. A loaf of bread is so soft that it does not deflect the band to any appreciable degree. Uneven slicing is caused by either guide wear or play developed in the guide supports.

It is very difficult to establish the exact amount of tension in the bands in a slicer. It is impossible for the slicer manufacturer to produce a drum that has exactly the same diameter all the way across. It is equally impossible for the band manufacturer to make every band of exactly the same length.

If we assume that the drum is 0.0001 in. smaller in diameter where 1 band runs than it is where an adjacent band is running, this band has to advance about 1 in. farther for every 400 revolutions. The band traveling the greater distance will increase its tension (in the trailing course) until 1 of 2 things happen: either the band breaks or it must slip on the drum, equalizing the tension. If the band cannot slip before the ultimate strength of the band is reached, the band will break.

Guide wear is also increased by too much tension. When the tension is lessened, the guide wear will be reduced to a minimum.

Several gages are available to measure the tension in the band, but they measure tension only; they do not allow for torsion, twisting, rubbing, and traveling. Although the steel band will break at about 2000 lb straight tension pull, it is recommended that the tension not exceed 80 lb. When the tension is measured both courses of the same band should be tested, often they will be different. Neither course should be allowed to exceed the maximum 80 lb.

Slicer and band manufacturers are not the worst offenders with respect to variation of drum and band diameters. If crumbs are permitted to accumulate on the band or on the drum in such a way that they can get caught between the band and the drum, increasing the diameter, the tension will be increased. To prevent this, the slicers should be kept as immaculately clean on the inside as they are on the outside. No heels should be on the top of the lower drum after cleaning because when the slicer is started, they will ride around the drum between it and the band. If this happens chances are that the band will break because the steel used for the band is made of an alloy that has very little capacity for elongation. Crumbs and heels should be kept away from the lower drum to prevent breakage.

Factors contributing to the variation in tension are as follows: (1) the drums are not exactly the same diameter from end to end; (2) the drums are not perfectly round; (3) the two drums are not exactly parallel; (4) the bands are not in their proper slot in the guides; and (5) crumbs have been allowed to accumulate on the drums.

There are several basic requirements that must be met in order to obtain maximum efficiency from a slicing machine. The right bands for the right type of loaf being sliced must be selected. The 2-beveled edge should be used for the firmer loaves and the 4-beveled edge for the softer loaves. The blades should be honed correctly and as often as necessary to maintain maximum smoothness of slice. The slicer should be kept clean inside as well as out and checked to make sure that the bands are not under too much tension. There is probably not another piece of equipment or machinery in the bakery subjected to more complex stresses and loads than that thin band of steel which does the slicing in a band slicer. It deserves the best of care.

Most slicers of today are of the two drum type using crossed bands. Because of the characteristics of the two drum machines the cross is quite open (see Fig. 22.7).

The texture of the "whipped batter" or "continuous mix" bread is such that it has a tendency to cling to the bands. Assuming that 20 bands are used to slice a given loaf and that each band is 0.015-in. thick, then the thickness of the steel forced into the loaf is 20 × 0.015 or 0.300 in. everywhere except at the cross where we have 40 bands or 40 × 0.015 in. or 0.600 in. of steel.

Since the bands are running in opposite directions and it is often assumed that this equalizes the forces within the loaf, such is not always the case. If the friction of one band going into the cross for

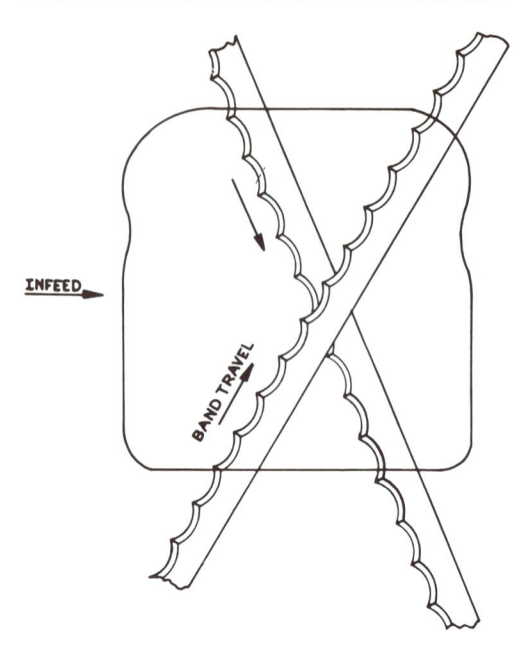

FIG. 22.7. RELATIONSHIP OF BANDS AND BREAD IN A TWO-DRUM SLICER.

some reason is increased over the adjacent band going away from the cross, equilibrium has been destroyed and all the bands going into the cross in the same direction will cause the loaf to collapse. Sometimes the loaf is collapsed against the upper plate and sometimes against the lower plate, depending upon which direction got the upper hand. Collapsing is also apt to happen with Pullman loaves.

The theory has been developed that forces of slicing should be equalized within the loaf being sliced and not transmitted to supports and hold-down plates.

To prove this theory, many tests have been conducted on multiple drum slicers with bands practically parallel in the cutting zone. Extremely soft bread has been sliced at 150°F, 300 loaves per minute (4-in. loaves), band speed of 1200 ft per min, 4-beveled cutting edge, with no crushing, and with extremely smooth slices. When the infeed was slowed down to less than 100 loaves per minute, excessive roughness of slice occurred. Since a noncrushing, smooth slice was obtained, we assume that the theory is correct.

The success of this fast slicing must, no doubt, in some measure be attributed to the resistance ot motion of the bread crumb itself. The time element of slicing is so short that the texture does not have time to move. It is on the same order as pulling a table cloth from under dishes and having them remain on the table.

It appears as if the effective shear angle and tooth form has less effect than in conventional slicing. Also sharpness of the cutting edge is perhaps of greater importance.

SLICERS

According to Hartman (1948), bread has been sliced on a commercial basis since the late 1920's. The first production scale slicers were based on the reciprocating blade principle and would slice about 20–25 loaves of bread per minute. After the bread was sliced, it had to be placed in a cardboard tray or bound with a paper circlet to keep the slices together through the wrapping cycle. It took about 2 yr for the manufacturers of wrapping machines to make improvements in their devices so that they could wrap sliced loaves not held together by trays or bands.

The first slicing machines were rather crude machines, made a lot of noise, and readily developed mechanical troubles. Because they were slow, there was a tendency to crush the loaf as it was pushed through the blades. A large amount of crumbs were generated, and it was necessary to cool the bread to about 90°F.

Wrapping machines could handle the output of two of these early slicers, so the initial improvements were directed toward improving the speed. Slicers were finally developed which could process 40–50 loaves per minute, or about the capacity of 1 wrapping machine. The principle of slicing the loaf with a parallel set of steel blades spaced about ½ in. apart and moving at high speed has remained the same. Some models with reciprocating blades are still being made, particularly for use with specialty breads or for retail bake shops, but all high-capacity machines for white pan bread now use endless steel bands for cutting.

Automatic slicers for bakery products can be classified into three categories based on the type of blade they employ: (1) slicers using disc-shaped blades; (2) slicers using straight blades; and (3) slicers using continuous bands as the cutting element.

Reciprocal Slicing Machines

When band slicers are used for cutting raisin bread, the sticky substances from the interior of the fruit are collected by the blades and deposited on the drums. Eventually, the deposit may become thick enough to interfere with the operation of the machine and the bands may break. Any bread with a soft and sticky crumb can cause a similar accumulation of material on the band. Although there are difficulties in slicing these breads with reciprocating blades, the problems do not reach such a severe state and the blades will not break from product buildup. Reciprocating slicers are also used for slicing hard-crust breads such as French or Italian, heavy rye and health breads, and iced loaves (Willson 1948). They are also useful in low volume applications such as small retail bakeshops where loaves are sliced at the customer's requests, etc., the lower capital cost making them more acceptable in these outlets. On the whole, machines of the reciprocating type can be said to be more versatile but less efficient than band slicers.

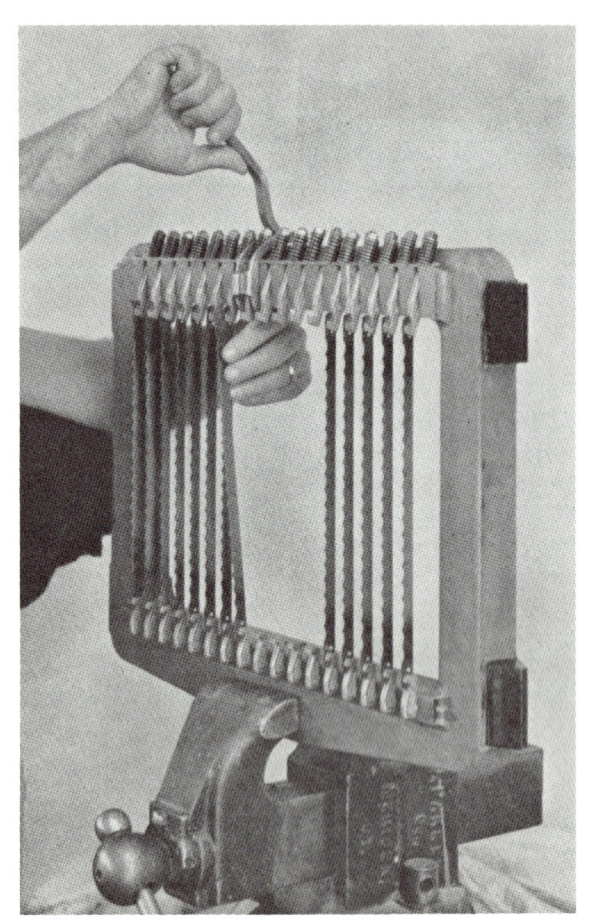

Courtesy of Battle Creek Bread Wrapping Machine Co.

FIG. 22.8. PLACING A BLADE INTO THE FRAME OF A RECIPROCATING SLICER.

The up-and-down motion of the blades in this type of equipment is transmitted from the motor to the blade frame by a crankshaft and levers. The vibration and noise created by the frame movement have been the most objectionable features in the use of reciprocating slicers. Machines of modern design are constructed so as to minimize the noise and vibration, however, and these factors should no longer be considered major objections to their use.

Figure 22.8 illustrates the method of inserting blades in the frame of a reciprocating slicer. Each of the blades is held taut by the force exerted by a heavy spring. When a blade is to be inserted in the frame, its spring is compressed by a special tool, allowing the blade pin to be slipped into the appropriate retaining notch.

The procedure for fitting the blade frame into the machine is shown in Fig. 22.9. The frame in the picture is made of cast magnesium permitting achievement of satisfactory strength with a weight

Courtesy of Battle Creek Bread Wrapping Machine Co.

FIG. 22.9. INSERTING THE BLADE FRAME INTO A RECIPROCATING SLICER.

Courtesy of Battle Creek Bread Wrapping Machine Co.

FIG. 22.10. THIS CAKE SLICING MACHINE ILLUSTRATES THE CUTTING ZONE OF A RECIPROCATING SLICER.

of about 10½ lb. A different frame must be obtained for each slice thickness and models are available for thicknesses of ⅜, ⁷⁄₁₆, ½, and ⁹⁄₁₆ in. The time required to replace a frame is about 5–8 min.

Figure 22.10 illustrates the slicing zone and compressor of a typical reciprocating slicer. In this model, the knife frames are tilted 20° toward the top crust of the bread to provide angle cutting and to accommodate the natural flow of loaves through the knives. Other manufacturers arrange the knife frames perpendicular to the floor but have the entrance conveyor slanted so that the top crust of the loaf encounters the knives first.

A disadvantage encountered in using reciprocal slicers for soft white loaves is that the surface of the bread slice may exhibit slight waves or corrugations. This is usually objectionable to the salesmen and may even be so to the consumer. The effect is much less noticeable on denser varieties such as rye and whole wheat breads.

According to Hartman (1948), knives in reciprocating slicers attain a maximum lineal velocity of 35 ft per min. They will slice from 10,000 to 20,000 loaves of bread without resharpening. Much longer service can be obtained between sharpening of continuous bands. There is no way of providing automatic honing on reciprocal slicers.

Also, the parts of the blade which cut the crust undergo more abrasion than the other parts, so that wear is not uniformly distributed over the blade length.

Band Slicers

Slicing machines using continuous blades are the preferred type for slicing uniform loaves of white bread at high rates of speed. They are also usable for many other types of bakery foods, but as the products begin to assume irregular shapes or to have sticky or heavy crumb their efficiency decreases. Some of the advantages of band-type slicers are: (1) no vibration, (2) greater cutting speed, (3) less frequent need for blade sharpening, and (4) continuously variable slice thickness, within limits.

One type of endless blade slicer requires that the bands be placed around steel cylinders and crossed in the center so that they form a figure eight as viewed from the side of the machine. The bread contact area is at the point where the blades cross. Another type, which will be discussed later, uses four drums to give an approximately parallel orientation of the blades in the slicing area. Since the blades must pass over the drums in a flat position and yet must present their serrated edges to the bread, it is necessary to turn them through a 90° angle between the time they leave the drum surface and the time they contact the bread. This turning function is performed by hardened steel guides located above and below the line of travel of the bread. Three types of elements are found in all band slicers: (1)

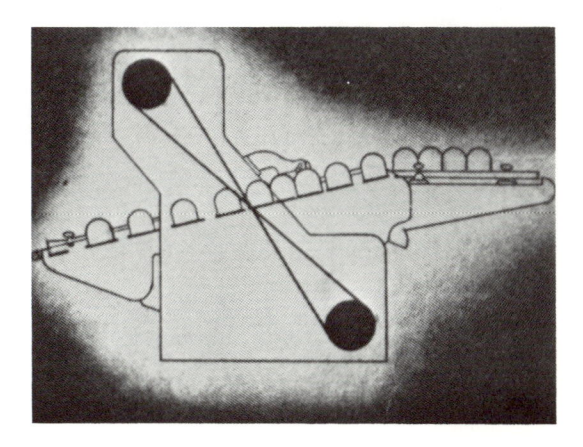

Courtesy of the American Machine & Foundry Co.
FIG. 22.11. ARRANGEMENT OF DRUMS AND BLADES IN A SLICER HAVING OFFSET DRUMS.

rotating drums which power the bands, (2) slicer blades, and (3) blade guides.

According to Hartman (1948), the first band slicer had 2 drums with relatively close centers and an overall height of about 6 ft. After these machines had been in operation for some time, it was found that the drums were too close together, causing a too abrupt twist in the blades as they were turned through a total of 180° between the upper and lower drums. Too much pressure was exerted on the knife guides. As a result, the guides and bands overheated and suffered excessive wear and breakage. Experimentation with various band lengths resulted in the conclusion that drum centers about 7 ft apart would give a band twist sufficiently gradual to eliminate excessive heat generation in the knife guides. Slicers with drums placed far apart also have the advantage that the longer blades require replacement or resharpening less often, saving labor costs and material. In addition, the blades are more nearly parallel at the position where they cross, creating better cutting conditions. The disadvantage of the arrangement is that the machine becomes quite tall. Unless an unusually restrictive head space situation exists, however, a height

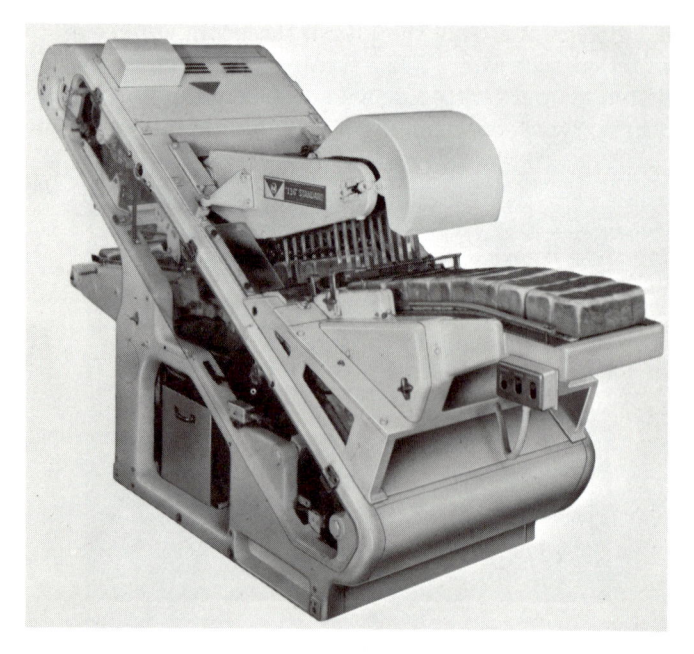

Courtesy of American Machine & Foundry Co.
FIG. 22.12. A CONTINUOUS BLADE SLICER USING OFFSET DRUMS.

SLICERS 453

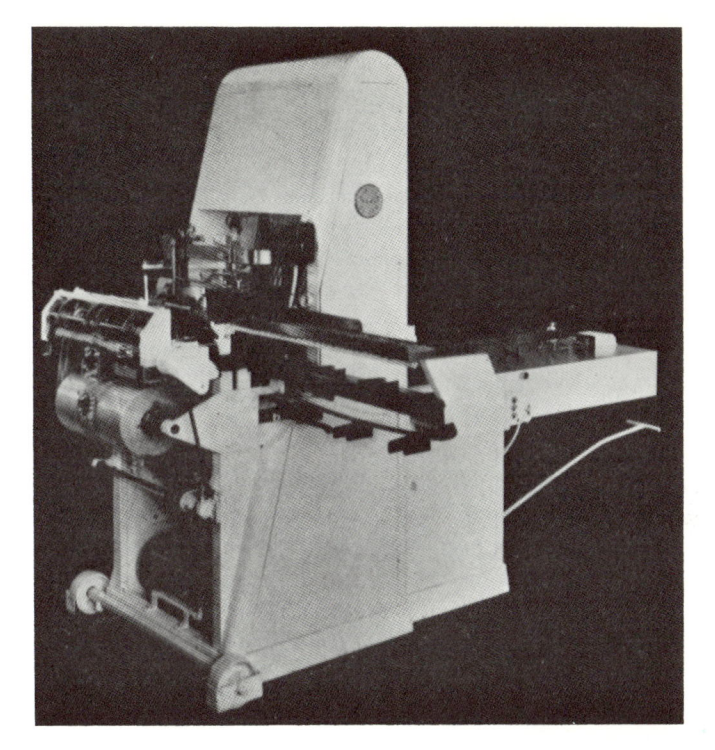

Courtesy of Maine Machine Works
FIG. 22.13. A SLICER-WRAPPER FOR ROUND LOAVES ILLUSTRATING A NEARLY VERTICAL ALIGNMENT OF DRUM CENTERS.

of 8 ft or so should not create any major problem. The floor space is not increased appreciably and this is usually the critical factor.

Some manufacturers have decreased slicer height while maintaining band length by placing the blades at an angle to the floor. An arrangement of this type is diagrammed in Fig. 22.11. A photo of a commercial device using offset drums is shown in Fig. 22.12, while a machine using almost vertically aligned cylinders is illustrated in Fig. 22.13. The chief operational difference between the two arrangements is that the vertical alignment permits an almost perpendicular approach of the blades to the loaf, resulting in the exerting of a constant force on the bread at all times.

With offset drums, the blades contact a corner of the bread first and the force on the loaf continually increases until the blade crossover point reaches the center of the loaf. In most practical situations, it is debatable whether or not a difference between the two methods would be detectable. Machines designed with offset drums may have the product approach conveyor (or slide) changed from the horizontal to a descending slope as the slicing zone is reached so that the blades are almost at a right angle to the line of travel of the product, even though they may be at a considerable angle to the perpendicular.

In another machine designed for use on soft bread, such as continuous process loaves, four drums are positioned to give the blades an obtuse angle and keep them in a nearly parallel alignment in the slicing zone (Fig. 22.14). Balanced forces, low blade speed, and reduced rate of loaf travel in the illustrated model (Fig. 22.15) tend to minimize tearing, keyholing, and crushing of side walls. Loaves from 6 to 17 in. long, 3 to 5½ in. high, and 3 to 6 in. wide can be handled. Slice thickness of about ⅜ in. can be obtained. As in most machines, thickness is adjusted by a simple hand wheel control which moves the blade guides farther apart or closer together.

The knife speed in modern slicers is usually from 900 to 1200 ft per min. There is a trend to lower blade speeds since this minimizes loaf distortion and temperature rise in the bands. Hot bands accelerate dough buildup on bands and drums. Blades are capable of slicing 500,000 to 2,000,000 loaves of bread between resharpening periods if they are properly rehoned at intervals.

There has existed a considerable amount of disagreement among blade manufacturers regarding (1) the desirability of honing blades on the slicer while the machine is operating and (2) location of the cutting surface responsible for the slicing operation. Simmons (1953) forcefully stated his view that the danger of bread contamination by metal particles and dirt is a sufficient reason for avoiding automatic honing. Simmons also stated that the cutting action is due primarily to the burr on the blade edge and that efficient slicing cannot occur in the absence of this structure.

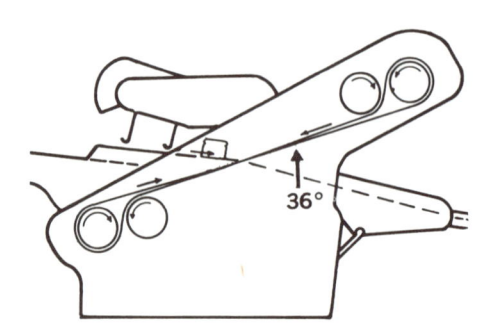

Courtesy of American Machine & Foundry Co.

Fig. 22.14. A Slicer in Which Four Drums are used to Guide the Bands into Parallel Position in the Slicing Zone.

Courtesy of American Machine & Foundry Co.
FIG. 22.15. PARALLEL BLADES SLICING LOAF OF BREAD.

As a practical matter, most band slicers do include automatic honing devices and these are often activated while slicing is in progress. It has been claimed that the operation of slicing adds about 0.2 mg of foreign material per pound of bread, the impurities resulting from abrasion of the cutting edge in the loaf, wear by the guides, wear on the drums, etc. This is about 0.4 ppm. Honing while slicing adds an approximately equivalent amount.

The two types of hones are the rotary and the fixed. Different grit sizes and different hardnesses of the binder are obtainable. Grits up to 600 are available in rotating hones, while the nonrotating variety is offered in fine, medium, or coarse grits. Automatic hones are often activated by a timing device which applies the hones after every hour or half hour of slicer running time. Overhoning causes excessive wear and reduces band life.

In most slicers, the hone is located about 5–6 in. below the point where the band meets the upper drum. At this point the band is vibrating with sufficient amplitude that the hone contacts all parts of the cutting surface. In the absence of this vibration, a stationary hone would not be able to process the complex beveling in a modern blade.

Blades.—The useful service life of a blade is determined by the quality of the steel from which it was fabricated. Most, perhaps all, slicer bands are made of chrome-vanadium-steel conforming to close specifications for uniformity, hardness, dimensions, smoothness, accuracy of the rounded edges, and the camber or straightness of the steel over the 20 ft or so required for the band. This relatively high priced alloy contains chromium to improve its hardness, so that the edges will maintain sharpness for a relatively long period of time, and vanadium to increase its toughness, so that the band can undergo repeated twisting and bending without breaking.

The effectiveness of the blade in performing its intended function is determined by the design of the cutting edge and the accuracy of the manufacturing method in implementing that design. The standard shape is a scalloped tooth of specific dimensions and angles. Dunn (1964) said, however, that angular teeth are better. The depth of the curve affects the smoothness of the sliced surface, deeper scallops giving better penetration and less crushing of the loaf but also causing more tearing so that the sliced surface is rougher. The type and direction of beveling also affect the smoothness of the slice.

Courtesy of American Machine & Foundry Co.
Fig. 22.16. Bread Being Discharged from AMF Model 75 Slice-Master into a Wrapping Machine.

According to Fitzmaurice (1970), blade types are generally differentiated into three categories on the basis of the relative softness of the bread which they are best adapted to slice. Firm bread (e.g., French, rye, and whole wheat breads) require a ½ in. scallop having a cross-ground primary bevel. This bevel tends to produce relatively rough surfaces. A variation in which the cross grind marks have been removed by parallel grinding provides a smoother bevel with a reduced tendency to tearing the crumb. Conventional pan loaves with fairly soft crusts and a medium firm texture are best sliced with blades having a secondary bevel applied to each side so as to remove some metal at the cutting point. Still smoother slicing results when the secondary bevel is ground parallel to the cutting action. Very soft breads, such as continuously mixed bread, require a four-beveled cutting edge in which all the bevels are ground parallel to the cutting action. This provides the thinnest possible cutting edge.

In an earlier section, it was stated that reciprocating slicers are preferred for raisin bread and loaves with soft sticky crumb. Some simple modifications can adapt band slicers to the efficient processing of these products. The usual procedure is to continuously dampen the blades with a wet sponge or the like. Frequent cleaning of the bands, drum, guides, and sponges is absolutely essential. Teflon coating of blades has been used to accomplish the same purpose. The principle is basically good, but it has proved to be difficult to put into practice. Teflon itself is very subject to mechanical erosion and the extremely abrasive conditions encountered by slicer blades causes the material to wear off very quickly. The combination coatings which have been developed to simplify the method of application and to retard wear are not as stick-proof as pure Teflon.

A Typical Band Slicer.—The following description is of the AMF Model 75 Slice-Master (Fig. 22.16), but many of the points are applicable to other slicers as well. In this slicer, bread is received from racks or a cooling conveyor and deposited on a horizontal woven metal belt which transports it up against a rigid stop. An elevator releases loaves one at a time and delivers them into the flights of an infeed conveyor. The flights move down the infeed conveyor and then retract so that the gentle pressure of the accumulating bread moves the leading loaf toward the slicing area. A cushion of two loaves is set up between the blades and the positive feed.

Blades rotating around steel drums in a figure-eight pattern tend to pull the loaves forward, thus minimizing the need for force feeding. The sliced loaves are brought by a flighted discharge conveyor to the packaging machine.

The blade drums are all steel and chrome-surfaced. They are precision ground and balanced. The supporting shafts are fitted with removable screw plugs on the operator's side to facilitate blade changes.

A heel control adjustment permits changes to equalize heel thickness after the bread guide rails have been set to the proper loaf length. Slice thickness control handle allows change of slice thickness from $3/8$ to $5/8$ in., the setting being indicated by a pointer and scale having $1/16$ and $1/64$ in. graduations.

Disc Slicers

Slicers with horizontal disc blades are used primarily for slicing hamburger buns and hot dog rolls so that the bread can be readily spread apart for inserting the meat. These slicers consist of two motor-driven discs with serrated edges. These saws are placed in a plane horizontal to the bun conveyor and are separated by a short distance so that they leave hinges in adjacent edges of the pair of rolls which they are slicing. The distance between the blades and the distance between the blades and the table or conveyor are usually adjustable.

In the different designs of this general type, the characteristic operating element (the toothed disc) remains the same while the methods of orienting the rolls and moving them through the slicing area differ. For example, a series of belts, moving in the same direction as the incoming conveyor but raised an inch or so above it, grasp a cluster of buns as they travel down the conveyor belt and carry them past the blades. There are two vertical knives immediately in front of the saws for splitting the clusters so they can pass by the spindles of the saws. The belts have rows of tiny spikes to firmly hold the buns. Such equipment will process up to 35 clusters of 8 buns per minute.

Another device carries an entire pan of individual buns or clusters, on or off pans, through a slicing head where the circular blades slice each bun. A special rimless pan similar to a cookie sheet must be used. An advantage is obtained by having the buns kept in a fixed relationship when the entire pan is conveyed through the slicer. Rates of 1200, 2400, and 3200 doz buns per hour can be obtained when individual buns and clusters are sliced in the pan, while a rate of approximately 1200 doz buns per hour is possible when slicing clusters out of the pan.

Still another arrangement uses a circular table rotating at high speed to bring buns to its outer periphery where they pass under a revolving paddle wheel called an unscrambler. The wheel rotates in a direction opposite to that of the table and separates the buns so that they can be individually fed between two horizontal belts. The belts carry the buns past a disc saw where they are sliced before being ejected onto a packing table. This equipment will slice up to 1500 doz sandwich buns per hour. It is not as satisfactory for wiener buns because some of the pieces go through the slicer on their sides and receive cuts on their top or bottom.

A roll slicing machine, patented by Lecrone (1963), includes an air jet to partially open the bun as it is cut, and to cool and clean the knife blade.

BIBLIOGRAPHY

Dunn, L. D. 1964. Blade for slicing bread. U.S. Pat. 3,132,677. May 12.
Fitzmaurice, D. T. 1970. Selection and care of slicer blades. Baker's Dig. *44*, No. 3, 52–53.
Hartman, W. W. 1948. The Story of Bread Slicing. Maine Machine Works, Los Angeles.
Hauswald, C. C., Jr. 1964. Bread slicing problems and their remedies. Proc. Am. Soc. Bakery Engrs. *1964*, 130–135.
Lecrone, D. S. 1963. Roll slicing machine. U.S. Pat. 3,112,780. Dec. 3.
Simmons, H. C. 1953. Bread slicing. Proc. Am. Soc. Bakery Engrs. *1953*, 82–90.
Tolley, A. E. 1958. Automatic bun production—formulation, make-up, proofing, baking, cooling, and slicing. Proc. Am. Soc. Bakery Engrs. *1958*. 118–123.
Tuzin, C. 1953. Automatic conveying, cooling, and slicing of plain rolls and buns. Proc. Am. Soc. Bakery Engrs. *1953*, 102–114.
Willson, A. M. 1948. What is the best solution for slicing soft bread. Proc. Am. Soc. Bakery Engrs. *1948*, 64–68.

CHAPTER 23

PACKAGING EQUIPMENT AND MATERIALS

Attractive packaging of foodstuffs is an indispensable requirement for successful marketing. A neat, colorful package which gives the potential customer a first impression of wholesomeness and freshness goes a long way toward making a sale at the point of purchase. In general, bread and other baked goods are attractively packaged. It is much rarer to see a truly repellent package design in the bakery display than in other sections of the supermarket. Perhaps this is due to the fact that most bakery foods have inherent visual appeal, and transparency is much easier to achieve than compelling graphics.

Cost is another important factor. Bakery foods have relatively large dimensions per unit of price. Inexpensive packaging materials applied at low labor costs are essential if a profit is to be made. Suppliers of packaging machinery and materials have done a good job in achieving these goals. There are very few food products that are being packaged as inexpensively as bread. Yet the package is usually attractive and gives adequate, though not outstanding, protection to the product. Suppliers have had the advantage that the bakery industry is a large volume outlet for their equipment, and a heavy outlay for development and design can be justified.

PACKAGING EQUIPMENT

Loaf Wrapping and Bagging Equipment

According to Manno (1966), the first commercial bread package (tied with a string) appeared in 1899, the first nonadjustable overwrap machine appeared in 1912, and the adjustable machine in 1925. Sliced bread appeared about 3 yr later between 1928 and 1930, along with the first use of Cellophane as a wrapping material. End labels were added in 1937. Ten years later, fortified waxes became available as improved coatings for paper and, in 1958, plastic films were first used commercially for wrapping bread. In about 1964, some bakers started packaging bread in premade bags closed by tying or clipping the open end. Then came the simulated bag, which was a folded package sealed at one end, formed on a modified bread wrapper to which had been added an attachment for clipping or tying the unsealed end.

In almost all bakery layouts, the bread wrapper is closely connected to the slicer. Not only does this arrangement avoid unnecessary conveyor lengths—always a good principle—but the transfer of sliced loaves is kept to a minimum, thus reducing the opportunity for the slices to become disorganized. Units in which the slicer and the wrapper are combined on one framework provide the ultimate in integration of these functions. Flexibility of layout is not impaired by such designs, since a loaf is never sliced without being wrapped.

The simplest of these units is a hand-wrapping machine, in which the loaf passes through a reciprocating slicer and then is delivered to the hands of the operator, who uses a folder jig and hot sealer plates to package the bread. Such units find some application in small retail bakeries. The equipment used in wholesale bakeries is completely automatic and operates at a high rate of speed.

The basic kinds of mechanisms found in all automatic bread wrapping machines are the feed conveyor and guides, the elevator or lifter table, the folding mechanism, the heat sealing stations, and the cooling plates. Figure 23.1 shows the arrangement of these operations in one type of automatic wrapper.

The infeed conveyor consists of flight plates supported and advanced by a pair of chain belts or link belts. It receives the loaf from the slicer and carries it into the wrapping machine. Most firms manufacturing

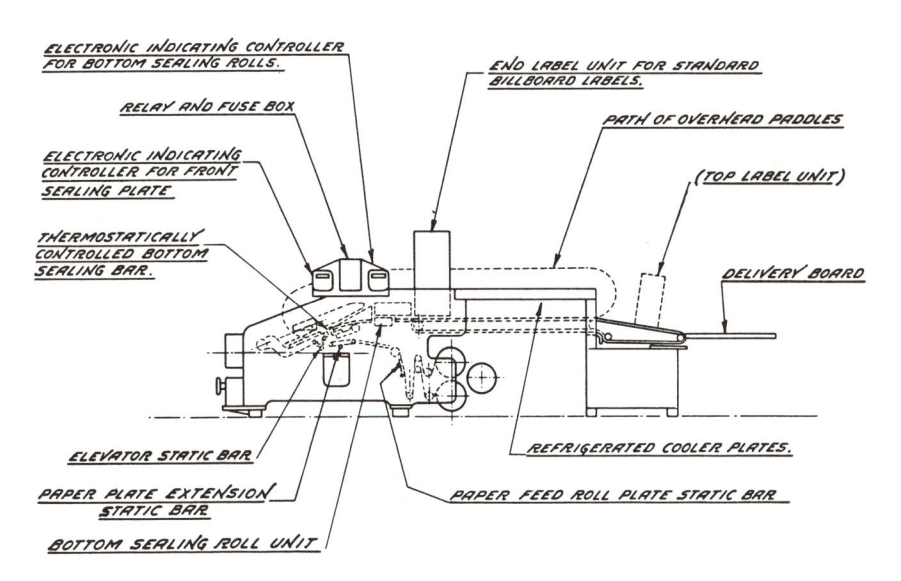

Courtesy of Package Machinery Co.

FIG. 23.1. RELATIVE POSITIONS OF THE FUNCTIONAL ELEMENTS OF A BREAD WRAPPING MACHINE.

wrapping machines offer infeed conveyor lengths of 6, 9, 12, or 15 ft. If the slicer and wrapper are combined, the need for a separate conveying unit is eliminated. Sliced loaves may be held together either by adjustable railings or by flexible metal plates which are set to compress the loaves slightly as a means of assuring a tight wrap.

The lifter table or elevator (Fig. 23.2) receives the product either directly from the infeed chains or as the result of the action of a pusher plate and arm. As the loaf advances onto the elevator, it moves into a pocket of packaging film which has been formed by retractable fingers. At this time the film is cut to a predetermined length. The elevator now lifts the bread so that the paper or film is drawn across the top and passes down the trailing edge of the loaf. Subsequently, the direction of travel of the loaf is reversed and the loose edge of the packaging material is drawn beneath it so that it overlaps the outer cut edge. Figure 23.3 illustrates the sequence of wrapping movements.

End folds are made by tuckers. The first fold is made by tucker blades or plates which are attached to and sit astride the elevator on which the loaf goes up for the final heat-sealing operation. The bread is

Courtesy of American Machine & Foundry Co.

FIG. 23.2. A LOAF OF BREAD ON THE ELEVATOR.

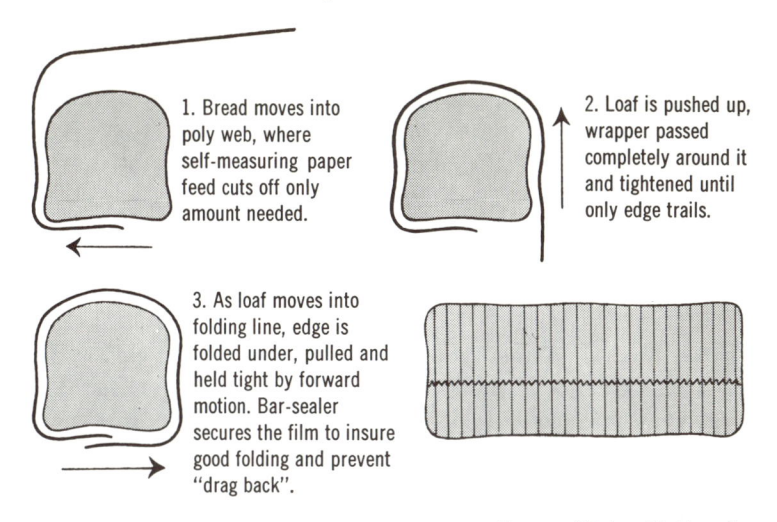

1. Bread moves into poly web, where self-measuring paper feed cuts off only amount needed.

2. Loaf is pushed up, wrapper passed completely around it and tightened until only edge trails.

3. As loaf moves into folding line, edge is folded under, pulled and held tight by forward motion. Bar-sealer secures the film to insure good folding and prevent "drag back".

Courtesy of Package Machinery Co.
FIG. 23.3. SEQUENCE OF WRAPPING OPERATIONS.

carried up from 6 to 12 in. while being held by the initial tuckers and pressure plate, for action by the second set of tuckers. Three other folding operations follow to complete the wrapping operation, the third set of tuckers fold the side, while the fourth set folds up the bottom of the end folds.

The sealing stations consists of electrically heated platens, rollers, or belts. Resistance heating is usually employed, but recent advances have led to infrared heating of platens or Teflon-covered mesh belts which contact the wrapping material.

There are other ways of sealing plastics, as by impulse devices or adhesives, but they are not used in ordinary loaf wrappers. Transfer of heat to the wrapping material causes the wax or plastic on contiguous surfaces to melt and run together. The sealant may be polypropylene, polyethylene, or wax. The underfold is sealed first, usually before the tucks are made. One method of sealing the ends involves making all four folds and then heating them simultaneously. This procedure has been largely supplanted by the progressive method in which each fold is sealed as it is made. Progressive sealing eliminates the necessity for heat penetration through several layers of paper with the resultant danger of overheating and excessive flow of wax or plastic. Neubauer (1953) says that the soft loaf is wrapped most effectively by using relatively high temperatures on the inner fold and relatively low temperatures on the sealer plates. Less wax is melted or burned off by this method.

The heat applied at the sealing plates is controlled by one or more thermostats. Most wrapping machine thermostats are of the "off-on" type and are adjustable within the range of 150°–500°F. St. Arnaud (1959D) described a method for calibrating thermostats by using "Tempilsticks" and gave the following common causes of thermostat malfunctioning: (1) loose or broken heat-sensitive section (the part attached to the sealing plate); (2) leak in tubing or actuator, permitting gas or liquid to escape; (3) loose terminal posts; (4) faulty wiring; (5) loose connections on electric heating elements; and (6) burned out elements.

Preheated second folders improve the inner seals of heavy opaque material. Heated second folders or tuckers should not be used if Cellophane or synthetic coated papers are used as wrapping material. When second folders are to be heated, 4-inch elements of 200-watt capacity are the proper size to use. In all cases, sealing plates should be heated by elements of equal size and a grooved element should not be paired with a smooth element.

At the cooling station, plates through which cold water or refrigerant is circulated contact the hot areas on the package and bring the wax or plastic to a solid state, completing the seal. The heating and cooling plates, as well as other parts of the equipment which come into contact with hot packaging material, may be coated with Teflon to eliminate sticking and the buildup of carbon deposits.

To the basic wrapping machine may be added various attachments, such as end-seal applicators (Fig. 23.4), coders, label printers, equipment for inserting coupons, etc. If, as is frequently the case, an inner paper band is required, it is formed simultaneously with the wrapping operation, and from roll stock (Fig. 23.5). Some machines have an inner band heater shoe which tacks the band automatically to the outer film. It is probably more common to buy from the converter stock combining band and wrapper in one roll.

End labels, which can give valuable added strength to the end seal, are attached before the package reaches the cooling plates. These labels can be affixed by heat or by a pressure-sensitive adhesive. The latter materials are of two types, adhesives which are activated by heat and can be applied by conventional end labelers, and permanently tacky substances which are protected by a release backing until the moment of application and require the use of auxiliary equipment.

Top labels, coupons, and similar inserts are deposited on the loaf as it enters the conveyor leading from the slicer.

Wrapping speeds of 65 loaves per minute, even more under very favorable circumstances, are possible with modern machines. The rate of packaging is governed to a large extent by the type of product and its size. As the dimensions increase, lower speeds are recommended. The rate must be reduced when wrapping extremely soft loaves. In general, the speed of the wrapping machine is limited by the output of the slicer. Recent improvements in this equipment have centered around facilitating cleaning, improving the precision of temperature control, and giving greater ease of access to the operating field.

The following guidelines for preventive maintenance of wrappers should be followed.

Keep the rollers and rubber surfaces that touch the wrapping material free of wax or plastic deposits. Rollers in the paper feed system must turn freely, and they must be uniform in size and parallel to one another.

In the product zone, all of the sealing plates, belts, and rollers must

Courtesy of American Machine & Foundry Co.
FIG. 23.4. BREAD WRAPPER END LABEL DEVICES.

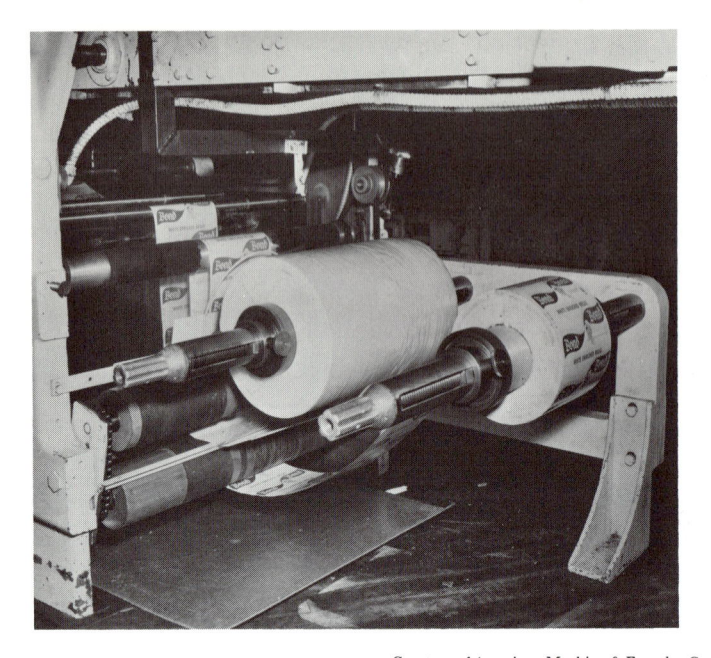

Courtesy of American Machine & Foundry Co.
FIG. 23.5. FEEDING INNER PAPER BAND AND WRAPPER SEPARATELY.

be smooth and free of deposits. Accumulations of wax or plastic should be removed before they carbonize on the hot plates. The sealing plates must be clean and smooth to minimize surface friction between the sealing plates and material.

All knives must be kept free of wax deposits. Dull or dirty knives contribute to fluctuations in the cut-off length. End labeler knives must be set to manufacturer's recommended settings to assure positive label cut-off.

The drive and timing chains must be kept at the proper tension. The speed of the friction drive on the paper feed must be properly set to assure minimum force on the loaf during the initial drawing of material around the loaf.

Tuckers should be clean, free of marks, and of proper width. Blow crumbs out of the finger assembly several times a day.

Keep machines adjusted so as to give a bottom overlap very close to the predetermined length. According to Panuline (1964), excessive overlap due to poor machine adjustment and maintenance can increase material costs as much as 5%, loose wrap can add up to 2%, and rewraps can easily amount to 3%.

The product configuration is an important factor in efficient operation of the wrapper. Concave bottoms can lead to poor sealing or even failure to seal on the overlap. Loaves that are too large or too small, or which have irregular or concave ends cause poor folding.

The following guide for trouble-shooting AMF bread wrappers (Panuline 1963) is useful for other makes of equipment as well.

(A) Losing heels: (1) Check the infeed flight spacing. (2) Center line of material in-feed flights may be off center with pusher plate. (3) Improper pusher plate or pusher plate may not be cut symmetrical about the central holding pin. (4) Heel guides may be out of line with in-feed pusher and follower flights. (5) Check tucker setting and timing. (5) Check loaf center on slicer.

(B) Paper weaving (front to rear): (1) Check center of paper supply roll with machine center line. (2) Reverse arm rubber may not be parallel or seated properly on the backup roller, or may be off center. (3) Paper arbors may not be parallel with paper drive rollers. (4) Lap roller and drape table roller may not be parallel with each other.

(C) Bottom lap variation: (1) Dull paper knives. (2) Loose wrap set too tight. (3) Rubber rollers on the lifter table may be eccentric or distorted. (4) Uneven pressure between the rubber rollers on the lifter table and pump roller. (5) Variable spacing between top transfer pusher flights.

(D) Tuck fold pullback: (1) Improper width of paper. (2) Dirty tuckers, distorted tuckers. (3) Improper size of tuckers.

(E) Open bottoms: (1) Improper setting of loose wrap. (2) Bottom heater temperature may be too high or too low. (3) Timing of bottom conveyor heater with top transfer. (4) Delivery bottom canvas belt may be dirty. (5) Heater covers may be frayed and dirty.

(F) Label centering: (1) Dirty plunger rollers. (2) Plunger roller action may be sluggish. (3) End labeler top and bottom knives may be dirty. (4) Side belt temperature may be too high. (5) Poor label adhesive.

(G) Losing labels: (1) Side belt temperature may be too low or too high. (2) Machine setting too wide. (3) Dirty canvas belt. (4) Label index. (5) Knife opening.

(H) Loose wrap variation: (1) Dirty ratchet and pawl. (2) Worn ratchet and pawl. (3) Loose drive chain. (4) Eccentric rubber rollers on lifter table. (5) Improper pressure between lifter table rubber rollers and pump rollers.

(I) Tight wrap: (1) To maintain a uniform bottom overlap, the loose wrap cannot be set for an extreme tight wrap. (2) Improper setting of loose wrap will vary the outside bottom wrap.

(J) Distorted folds: (1) Improper tucker. (2) Improper folder setting. (3) Dirty folders.

(K) Heel guide malfunction: (1) Screw threads may be filled with bread crumbs and wax. (2) Improper alignment of the heel guide with the infeed bottom plate. (3) Improper position of the double idler sprocket in the drive system. (4) Loose drive chains.

(L) Wrinkled outside bottom lap: (1) Uneven pressure between lifter table rubber rollers and pump roller. (2) Replace knives in pairs. (3) Dirty bottom extension plate. (4) Improper machine setting (length of package).

(M) Inside lap variation: (1) Dirty or worn reverse arm rubber. (2) No rubber on back tension plate. (3) Improper back tension plate pressure. (4) Lifter table fingers may be too high. (5) Rubber on paper clamp may be dirty.

(N) Temperature variations (heater): (1) Poor sensing contact. (2) Voltage variation. (3) Carbonization buildup on folders. (4) Loose heater mounting. (5) Poor receptacle contact. (6) Dirty probes. (7) Controller malfunction.

(O) Crushing of loaf on lifter table: (1) Paper feed speed control. (2) Wedging of reverse arm rubber. (3) Back tension spring pressure. (4) Malfunction of the back tension slide. (5) Lifter table pressure against the pump roller may be too low. (6) Improper alignment of the pump roller with the rubber rollers on the lifter table.

Bagged bread has taken over a large part of the market from wrapped loaves. The fundamental difference between these two kinds of packages is that the wrapped loaf has the film heat sealed at both ends while the bag has one end closed by a clip or wire tie which bunches the material together 3–4 in. from the end.

Bags may be purchased ready-made in wickets, or be made in the bakery from preprinted roll stock. The wicket is simply a bundle of bags held together by a metal fastener. Bags are pulled off the metal clip as required by the packaging device. Among the differences in design between machines is the manner in which the bag is removed from the "wicket" or guides which hold the stack of bags. One design lets the loaf pusher thrust the bag from the wicket after the loaf has bottomed. Another style depends upon the loaf itself pushing the bag off the wicket, while a third type removes the bag before the loaf is inserted.

There are manually operated and automatic baggers. Since the former equipment is relatively simple and found mostly in retail bakeries, it will not be discussed further.

Equipment for automatic loading of preformed bags costs in the neighborhood of $10,000. Plastic clips or other types of closures are automatically applied. A snug-fitting minimum size bag can be used provided the loaf circumference can be closely maintained. The bag circumference must be large enough to take the maximum size loaf expected, however. The wickets of bags are easily and quickly changed. Recent advances have included a double bag magazine which moves a new stack of bags into place without stopping the machine.

The equipment for automatic loading of bags fabricated at the packer from rolls of folded film costs about $20,000. A saving on packaging material usually results and it eliminates the small torn area where the bag has been torn from the wicket.

Bags are opened by an air jet and held by fingers or scoops while the loaf is pushed into the scoops. Needless to say the compressed air should be free of oil droplets, water, or odor. Pushing of the bread may be performed by overhead continuously moving arms or by reciprocating plates. While the bag is being filled, it is held in place by temporary adherence to metal scoops. When the loaf contacts the end of the bag, it pushes the film loose. Bags made for these machines must have well-defined requirements for slip and side weld strength. For example, the coefficient of friction should lie between 0.15 and 0.20 at 140°F. Another system pulls the bag over the product after the air-inflated pouch has been removed from the wicket by a set of guides.

So far as the bagging machine is concerned, the quality of the air and the settings for loaf size and bag size are important factors in assuring a satisfactory performance.

The bag characteristics which tend to affect efficiency are: (1) physical properties—slip, static charge retention, and tackiness; (2) bag construction—uniformity of the lip and strength of the weld; and (3) bag dimensions—symmetry and uniformity of width. If wicket packs are used, the following factors are also important: (1) the size of the hole and its location relative to the lip and the tear slit; and (2) alignment of the bags at the wicket.

A variant of the bagging process uses conventional wrapping equipment to form a container folded and sealed at one end and open at the other. The open end is then gathered or twisted and tied or clipped. Polyolefin materials can be used, as in existing wrappers, but a wider web is required to give the 3–4 in. of loose film past the tie.

The plastic clip has been the most widely accepted closure, because it is easy to apply and remove, and it is economical. There are self-contained units for applying plastic clips held in a continuous roll. These can simultaneously print code dates or prices. The units are fairly simple pieces of equipment which convey the bagged bread through a gathering device and into the clip affixing station. In tying units, the bag flaps are flattened and gathered by a rotating brush. Bag closing problems have resulted from heavy applications of ink in the neck area which caused slipping during the tying step.

Portion Packaging

Slices of bread and cake, cookies, Danish pastries, fried pies, cupcakes, doughnuts and many other kinds of baked goods are being packaged as individual servings for distribution through hospitals and other institutions, cafeterias, vending machines, lunch counters, and the like (Fig. 23.6). Packaging in portions has many things to recommend it; for example, it is eminently sanitary, it generally keeps the baked goods fresher, and it permits a good display of the product. The disadvantages are mainly the added cost for labor and materials and the inconvenience to the consumer of opening the pouch.

Machines for packaging individual pieces are either simple sealers for closing preformed bags into which the baked goods have been inserted by hand, or horizontally-aligned form-and-fill equipment which envelope the piece in film drawn from a roll (Fig. 23.7). The manual baggers can be purchased for less than $800 and will seal up to 20 packages per minute when operated by experienced personnel.

The automatic equipment most often used for portion packaging can be further subdivided into (1) machines which draw film from two rolls, one web forming the top and the other the bottom of the package (seals must be made on all four sides), and (2) equipment which forms a single sheet of plastic into a V-shape (with the open end either toward bottom, the side or the top) before sealing it on three sides or with a fin seal at bottom and cross seals at the ends. There is also a design utilizing a roll of tubular film from which bags are formed. Speeds in excess of 200 packages per minute can be attained. Although vertical form-fill

FIG. 23.6. MANY TYPES OF BAKERY ITEMS CAN BE OVERWRAPPED AUTOMATICALLY.

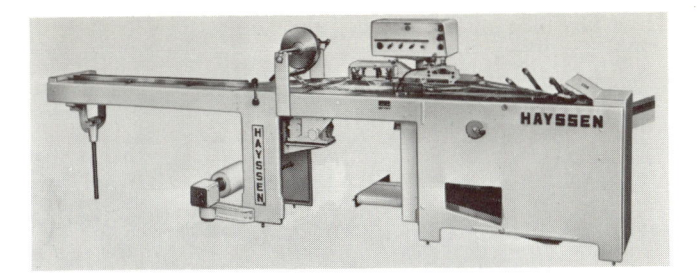

FIG. 23.7. PORTION PACKAGING MACHINE.

machinery is widely used for snacks such as potato chips and popcorn. It is not very common in the baking industry because the filling mechanisms are difficult to adapt to large pieces. Some are being used, however, for croutons, bread crumbs, and stuffing mixes.

Small cakes (cupcakes, cookies, doughnuts, etc.) are often placed on flat cards, or V-boards before being overwrapped with transparent film (Fig. 23.8). The board may be coated with wax or polyethylene to make it more greaseproof. Cards can be precut and fed from a stack, or be cut from roll stock at the time of wrapping. The overwrapping may be done on a horizontal form-fill-seal machine, or on a tray overwrapper, although these two types of equipment cannot be used interchangeably on all bases.

Bulk Packaging of Buns

There are three kinds of packages which have been widely used for bulk buns delivered to restaurants and institutions, particularly to the franchised hamburger outlets. These are: (1) returnable cardboard boxes or bins, (2) disposable box and bag, and (3) pillow or pouch pack, which may be automated. Both the returnable and one-trip boxes are relatively expensive, and the reusable type creates the sanitary problems always associated with repeated use of a food container.

Semiautomatic packagers for bulk buns (Fig. 23.9) require 2 operators for placing the buns in proper positions, and 1 man for taking off the packaged goods and stacking them. Capacities range from 300 to 340 buns per minute. Fully automated machines pack buns between 2 layers of 1 mil polyethylene film which are then heat-sealed on all 4 sides to form a pillow-type package. Speeds of up to 530 buns per minute can be reached with 3 people on the line. It is common practice to pack 12, 20, or 30 buns in a single layer in these pouches, although many other arrangements are possible without equipment modification. The pouch is transported to the user multipacked in corrugated or plastic trays, returnable in most cases.

Courtesy of Crompton and Knowles Corp.
FIG. 23.8. OVERWRAPPING MACHINE FOR PACKAGING SIX SMALL DOUGHNUTS ON A BASE CARD IN A CONTROLLED DIE FOLD WRAP OF CELLOPHANE.

PACKAGING MATERIALS

The packaging films most often used for bakery products are waxed paper, foil, Cellophane, glassine, polyethylene, and combination structures. Not so many years ago waxed paper was practically the only film used for bread packaging. It is still used in considerable quantities, but first Cellophane, then polyethylene, and finally polypropylene took over some of the market. Each of these films has some desirable features and some disadvantages.

The requirements for an ideal packaging material for bakery products might be summarized as follows:

(1) It should protect the product from drying out during its normal storage life. Not only must the film itself have a low rate of moisture-vapor transmission, but it must also be capable of forming seals which are as impervious as the intact film. If the film protects adequately against moisture-vapor transmission, it can also be expected to satisfactorily protect the product from adventitious mold spores, dirt, dust,

and other foreign particles, and it will give some protection against off-odors.

(2) The package should contribute to the dimensional stability of the product. Since most bakery foods are very susceptible to crushing, some mechanical strength must be added by the container if the product is to survive storage, transportation, and merchandising without undergoing an unacceptable amount of distortion.

(3) The film should be capable of being applied easily and quickly by mechanical means, and preferably by existing machines. A fundamental requirement is that the material heat-seal readily. It should be capable of undergoing rapid transfers and foldings by the wrapping device without cracking, tearing, or stretching.

(4) The package should assist in selling the product. For bread this usually means that the product can be squeezed so that the customer can assure himself of its softness and freshness. In cases where visibility of the product is important, transparent films are imperative. A glossy surface is a definite advantage. Adaptability to printing is necessary in most instances.

(5) The film should be relatively low in price. It must have a favorable cost per square inch, and the supplier's factory or warehouse must be located so as to make transportation costs relatively low. It must be

Courtesy of American Machine & Foundry Co.
FIG. 23.9. BULK BUN PACKAGER INSERTING TWELVE BUNS BETWEEN TWO ROLLS OF FILM AND SEALING ALL FOUR SIDES.

capable of being stored under reasonable conditions without loss; and it must machine with minor waste.

Few, if any, films possess all of these qualities in the desired degree. Shortcomings of one film may be compensated for by using combinations of materials. Thus, the lack of strength and rigidity in some transparent films may be overcome, at least partially, by using bands or trays of tougher materials. Laminations, particularly of aluminum foil, are another way of taking advantage of the best qualities of several materials in one film.

Transparent Cellulose Films

When Cellophane was first offered to the baker, he had only a few types available. Today, suppliers offer many varieties of this type of film with a wide range of properties. The letters used in the combination letter and number symbols which identify the films are indications of some of the properties of the material. For example, S denotes heat sealable coatings, P indicates a plain film without coating or heat sealing properties, M denotes moistureproof qualities, T indicates transparent or clear, C means it is a colored film, A indicates an anchored coating which can be used for frozen foods, and K informs us that the Cellophane has a vinylidene chloride coating.

The so-called PT films (plain transparent) were never of value to the baking industry because they would not heat seal and they retained moisture-vapor very poorly, contributing to rapid staling of the product. Coated films of certain types overcame these disadvantages and have been widely used for bakery food packaging. Coated films with yields of 19,500 to 21,500 sq in. per lb in 300 gage thickness and of 14,500 sq in. per lb in 450-gage thickness have been especially useful (see Table 23.1). Recently, vinylidene coatings have been used, and they have generally proved to be of excellent value in that they increase the shelf-life of bakery products by decreasing moisture loss. Originally, this film was available only in a 450-gage weight due to the coating process but it is now obtainable in a 300-gage weight free of fish eyes or nonuniformities of coating.

Cellulose film has a grain direction resulting from the manufacturing process. It is weak across the grain and relatively strong in the other direction. In use, it is run through the wrapping machines so that minimum stress is placed in the cross-grain direction. This procedure provides a strong package. Weakness may result from loss of moisture-vapor or pickup of moisture-vapor by the film with resultant shrinkage of the product and stretching of the film. On lengthy unsupported products such as 12-, 13-, or 14-in. loaves of bread, the foregoing character-

TABLE 23.1
APPROXIMATE YIELD AND THICKNESS FACTORS FOR CELLULOSE FILMS

Gage No.	Square Inches per Pound	Thickness, (In.)
	Plain Types	
300	21,500	0.0009
450	15,000	0.0013
600	12,400	0.0016
	Moistureproof Types	
300	19,500	0.0010
450	14,000	0.0014
600	11,600	0.0017

Source: Graw (1956).

istics can cause trouble in the form of tearing or bursting. In carton overwraps or in bags few difficulties are observed from this source.

During very low humidity periods the film can lose part of the 5.7–6.0% moisture content it needs to keep it reasonably limp and pliable. If this situation is coupled with a wrapping machine that has dull cut-off blades, fracturing of the film may become excessive.

Cellulose films accept printing inks readily and have an unexcelled transparency which adds to the attractiveness of the package contents. They are inexpensive and available in forms suitable for use in all types of package machinery. They will seal at a fairly wide range of temperatures producing a continuous and indestructible seal.

Greaseproof Paper and Glassine

These papers are not often employed for bread packaging although a few bakers use bags made of them for enclosing French bread and the like. Cookies, crackers, pastries, and brown'n serve rolls are frequently packaged in greaseproof paper or glassine. Greaseproof paper is formed from cellulose fibers which have been digested for a relatively long time during the pulping process and consequently have a high moisture content. Glassine is prepared from greaseproof paper by a procedure which includes a supercalendering step. The application of heat and pressure in this step makes the fiber mat denser and more or less transparent. Greaseproof paper is similar in appearance to parchment, being opaque or translucent. The so-called manila glassines range from a deep to a very light amber in color, while bleached glassine is virtually colorless.

Neither glassine nor greasproof paper offer much resistance to the transmission of water-vapor. Of course, coatings to improve this characteristic can be applied. As indicated by the name of the basic product, the papers are quite resistant to the absorption and transfer of fatty materials. This property is attributable to the high degree of hydration of the cellulose fibers. Protection against the transmission of off-odors and off-flavors is said to be very good.

Greaseproof paper and glassine are not heat-sealable. Coatings of wax or lacquer can be applied to remedy this defect. The papers can be printed by the usual methods, except when coated. The basic papers are obtainable in a weight range of 20–45 (laminated) lb per ream as continuous rolls or sheets. The 45-lb laminated sheet is more commonly used in the snack food industry than in the baking trade.

White Bakery Stock Paper

Bleached sulphite paper (usually 28 lb basis) is used for bakery bags for both retail and wholesale operations, principally to package crisp crusted breads such as French or Italian. In the wholesale trade, an untreated paper is used for gluing into bag form on bag making machines. This paper has no heat-sealing properties. In retail operation, the material is treated with hot-melt wax to retain freshness of product. This treatment is done on one side only and penetrates the rather porous paper. Bleached sulphite paper cannot be printed in bright and vivid colors due to the porosity. The chief advantages of bags made from this type of material are the rather low cost, the high breathing value, and its wide and traditional acceptance for certain types of breads when unwaxed, and its low cost, whiteness, and good quality retention characteristics when waxed.

Polyethylene

Polyethylene is made in two forms, high density and low density. The manufacturing methods and the properties of the two kinds are different. Within these two classes are ranges of products with varying characteristics, but, in general, high density polyethylene, sometimes called "linear," is stiffer, tougher, denser, and more opaque. Low density, sometimes called "conventional," is softer, more flexible, less crystalline, and more permeable to gases and moisture. Medium-density polyethylene is made the same way as the low-density plastic and its properties are somewhat similar.

Low-density polyethylene finds its greatest use in preformed bags. It is not stiff enough in the economical thicknesses to run satisfactorily on most bread wrapping equipment. Medium-density films combine good heat sealability with good stiffness, while the high-density films offer superior stiffness but poor heat sealability.

Cast polyethylene is the form in which this plastic is used for bread packaging. The term "cast" means that the molten substance is extruded through a very narrow slit and immediately cooled by passing over chilled metal drums. This method produces film with good optical properties and stiffness. Oriented forms are available for other uses. They are extruded by a different method and have been stretched in either 1 or 2 directions as they solidified.

The trend of costs for polyethylene has been toward lower levels in recent years, but in an irregular pattern. At present it is probably the cheapest of the plastics on a per pound basis. Since it can be drawn into very thin films and is satisfactory as a bread wrap at 1 mil or less in thickness, it is also the cheapest on a square inch basis. As a rule of thumb, 30,000 sq in. of 1 mil film can be obtained from 1 lb of plastic. Some equipment can run 0.85 mil films, while others require 0.95 mil or even thicker material.

Roll stock can be obtained as flat sheeting or tubular film, in the so-called U-sheets and J-sheets, which are folded configurations, gusseted tubing, and centerfold sheeting. Bags are made in the bottom seal design, which is normally flush cut, and in the side-weld pattern, usually with a projecting lip.

Rotogravure printing can be used on polyethylene, but the normal decorating process is the flexographic or rubber-plate process because of the lower plate costs of the latter.

Although the greatest demand is for transparent packaging materials, there are some uses and markets for which opaque films are thought to be more suitable. Waxed paper is the most widely used opaque packaging material, and it is the least expensive. Pigmented polyethylene can be used alone or in combination with other materials, or plain polyethylene can be overprinted with one or two layers of opaque ink (though the latter procedure may cause sealing problems). Another fairly common structure is paper coated on the back with white opaque polyethylene and then waxed on both sides. This material costs about 50% more than standard waxed paper per unit area, but it provides excellent protection for the bread. A third alternative uses 2 webs which are wrapped simultaneously—waxed paper and a plastic film such as ¾ mil polyethylene.

Polypropylene

Polypropylene is a polyolefin, as is polyethylene, and the two substances have somewhat similar properties. Polypropylene is, however, considerably stiffer and much tougher than either high-density or low-density polyethylenes in equivalent thicknesses. The major advantage of polypropylene is its superior machinability.

Polypropylene has been made available as cast oriented, cast coated printed, oriented coated, and laminated combination films. Cast unoriented film, the form in which polypropylene has been available for the longest time, is available in 0.87 and 1 mil calipers. It has outstanding toughness and a stiffness which makes excellent end folds that hold throughout the wrapping operation to give a package of neat appearance. The higher sealing temperature and the wider sealing range of this plastic simplifies equipment control. Because of its toughness, heated knives, preferably with tempeature controls, are required for the cutoff operation. Cracking of the film at low temperatures was a negative feature observed in some early applications, but formulations were modified to give better strength in the cold.

The oriented sheet can be obtained in very thin films which have excellent clarity. When coated with a sealant, this material can be run without special machine conversions. It seals at lower temperatures than the cast films but higher than the coated cast films.

The coated films can be sealed in the printed areas, which are otherwise resistant to adhesion.

The cast films are the least expensive, per pound, of the propylene structures but they cannot be printed without the addition of a heat seal coating compatible with the ink system. Coated oriented film has a glossier appearance and gives a neater, sharper fold but is more expensive than plain cast films. The cast, coated, and printed film seals best and is the most expensive of the types discussed here.

Foil Laminations

Laminated foils are not much used for bread wrappings except for some of the higher priced specialty loaves, but they have found a place as wrappers for other bakery products and may in time take over some of the market now held by waxed paper, Cellophane, and polyethylene. A suitable foil lamination is virtually impervious to moisture-vapor and grease and can be quite attractive, though of course not transparent. Unsupported aluminum foil puckers and tears easily, and for this reason, as well as to obtain a seal, it must be laminated with other materials when it is to be used as a wrapping film.

A foil lamination which was probably the original one used for bread wrapping consisted of a combination of wax-foil-adhesive-sulfite paper-wax. Some users found that excess wax melted from the foil side and accumulated on the wrapping machine, necessitating frequent downtime for cleaning. Subsequently, a lamination of foil-wax-sulfite paper-wax-strikethrough tissue paper was offered. The tissue, being porous, allowed the hot wax to flow through it to make the seal. At the same time, the flow of wax was retarded sufficiently to prevent accumulation of the substance on the machine. A different approach to the problem resulted in the development of a film consisting of heat-sealing transparent lacquer-foil-adhesive-sulfite paper-wax-tissue. This tissue was a resin impregnated paper. A line of pinhole perforations about 1 in. in width on each side of the web allowed sufficient wax to flow out onto the adjacent surfaces to accomplish sealing, usually with the aid of a thermoplastic coated end label to add structural strength to the end.

A fourth type of lamination consisted of layers of lacquer-foil-wet adhesive-sulfite paper-wax-tissue. In this combination, the lacquer was a heat-sealing type. Since it has to be applied at a very high temperature to the foil and sulfite paper layers (the wax and tissue being mounted later) the latter must be cemented together by a high-melting wet adhesive rather than wax.

Recent technological advances have permitted the production of films coated with very thin layers of metal which have been deposited from the vapor state or by buffing with metallic dusts. These vacuum coated materials, usually called metallized papers, are being used extensively for candy packaging and have been suggested for use on bakery products. The principal advantage of these films lies in the added attractiveness which they contribute to the package. The metal layers do not contribute significant resistance to moisture-vapor transmission as do foils.

Rigid Packages

Shape-retaining containers are suitable for certain kinds of cakes and pastries, as well as some premium breads. Foil has been the major construction material used for rigid containers. Many sizes and shapes of pans are available from 3 or 4 major converters. In addition to size and shape, containers vary in foil thickness, whether the side walls are smooth or crimped, the finish on the exterior (natural, anodized, or printed), and the rim construction. Products are usually, but not always, baked or iced directly in the pan. For example, single layer cakes of the most expensive type are being packaged in aluminum pans in which they have been baked and iced. They are covered by a crimped-on flat paperboard, usually polyethylene coated. This seems to be the preferred package for frozen cakes. Auxiliary equipment includes pan dispensers, board top dispensers, and crimpers to fix the tops to the pans.

Some of the advantages claimed for aluminum foil containers when used as pie plates and baking pans are: (1) save capital investment in reusable sheet metal pans, (2) eliminate labor and materials costs of greasing, washing, drying, straightening, and refinishing, (3) are more sanitary, (4) do away with cripples from the depanning operation, and (5) eliminate the need for equipment and labor for depanning.

Foil pans for pizzas and pies are frequently given a black coating on the bottom to make them absorb the radiant heat, rather than reflect it. Perforations in the bottom allow moisture to escape and reduce the formation of concavities in the crust.

The water-vapor transmission rate of the foil container itself is zero, but in practice the moisture transfer is controlled by the type of lid or overwrap and the way it is applied.

A method of packaging large or premium cakes is to use thermoformed plastic blisters combined with board trays or foil pans. The excellent display properties and product protection afforded by these containers often justify the greater expense.

There is increasing use of polystyrene trays for cookies, partially baked rolls, doughnuts, and cupcakes. Regular oriented polystyrene is glass-clear, but the impact plastic is opaque or translucent as a result of the additives required to give it increased resistance to cracking. These plastics will not stand oven heats, so the products must be baked and cooled before they are inserted in the containers. Both the impact and the regular polystyrene compare favorably in cost with other materials used for rigid and semirigid plastics. The trays are thermoformed, that is, heated sheets of material are drawn by vacuum or pushed by air pressure into molds and then cut to shape. Nearly all bakeries using these trays buy them from plastic converters.

Expanded polystyrene has been used mostly for egg cartons, and meat produce trays, but is gradually finding a place in bakery goods packaging. It is relatively inexpensive and lightweight. Although it holds its shape well, it does not have much mechanical strength. Printing is considerably more difficult than on film.

Metal cans and boxes are rigid containers which have been used for bakery foods. A fairly interesting market exists for bread and cake baked in tin cans and hermetically sealed. This will be discussed in greater detail in another chapter. It has been the custom to bake fruitcakes in the pan in which they are offered for sale. Consideration must be given to the effect of oven conditions on the exterior finish, and to the interaction of product and lining during the baking period.

BIBLIOGRAPHY

CLEMENTS, R. B. 1963. Feeding machine for biscuits or the like laminar articles. U. S. Pat. 3,113,660. Dec. 10.
DAVIS, R. E. 1964. Packaging ideas. Baking Ind. *1532*, 76, 78.
DE RAFFELE, F. 1964. The design advantages of the waxed bread wrapper. Bakers Weekly *202*, No. 4, 42–43.
DILNO, G. 1949. Packaging of sweet goods and soft rolls. Proc. Am. Soc. Bakery Engrs. *1949*, 158–161.

FISHER, L. L. 1959. Effect on sealing and wrapping techniques of polyethylene, Cellophane, waxed, foil, and combinations thereof. Proc. Am. Soc. Bakery Engrs. *1959*, 125–131.

GRAW, F. P. 1956. Modern packaging materials. Proc. Am. Soc. Bakery Engrs. *1956*, 160–165.

HARMON, K. E. 1964. Progress report on films for wrapping cake and sweet yeast raised products. Proc. Am. Soc. Bakery Engrs. *1964*, 202–207.

HARRIS, R. G. 1962. A study of the flavor retention qualities of various flexible packaging materials. Bakers Weekly *195*, No. 8, 40–42.

HERRICK, J. H. 1958. Advances in cake and sweet goods packaging. Proc. Am. Soc. Bakery Engrs. *1958*, 278–287.

HUMPHREY, J. P. 1965. Progress in bread wrapping. Proc. Am. Soc. Bakery Engrs. *1965*, 185–191.

HUNGERFORD, G. P. 1964. Bread wrapping today. Bakers Weekly *204*, No. 5, 30–32.

JENSEN, C. J. 1970. Specific requirements for the performance of packaging materials. Proc. Am. Soc. Bakery Engrs. *1970*, 132–136.

JENSEN T. 1960. The importance of loaf shape when wrapping with plastic films. Bakers Weekly *186*, No. 9, 18–21.

JENSEN T. 1968. New developments in bagging. Proc. Am. Soc. Bakery Engrs. *1968*, 92–97.

JOHNSON, G. R. 1954. Handling and storage of packaged materials. Proc. Am. Soc. Bakery Engrs. *1954*, 123–127.

LINGELBACH, C. J. 1953. Packaging of plain rolls and buns. Proc. Am. Soc. Bakery Engrs. *1953*, 114–122.

LINGELBACH, C. J. 1964. Progress report on bread wrappers. Proc. Am. Soc. Bakery Engrs. *1964*, 110–117.

MANNO, F. 1966. The packaging of bread. Proc. Am. Soc. Bakery Engrs. *1966*, 69–75.

MCDONALD, W. J. 1970. Line paces product flow, ends fill errors, cuts costs. Package Eng. 15, No. 12, 58–61.

MCKEE, J. 1966. Successful methods of packaging and handling quality cakes. *1966*, 240–246.

MEYER, H. A. 1954. What the production department can contribute to the profit picture: wrapping, packaging, and shipping. Proc. Am. Soc. Bakery Engrs. *1954*, 159–161.

MONAHAN, E. J. 1964. Method for continuously wrapping biscuits. U.S. Pat. 3,127,273. Mar. 31.

MUELLER, E. 1963. How to determine your true bread packaging cost. Bakers Weekly *197*, No. 9, 30–33.

MURPHY, L. A. 1962. New product developments in packaging films. Bakers Weekly *196*, No. 2, 34–36.

NEUBAUER, W. 1953. Bread wrapping. Proc. Am. Soc. Bakery Engrs. *1953*, 90–95.

PANULINE, G. 1963. Maintaining and Operating AMF Bread Wrappers. American Machine and Foundry Co., Richmond, Va.

PANULINE, G. 1964. Organizing an efficient wrapping department. Proc. Am. Soc. Bakery Engrs. *1964*, 137–142.

PILE, L. 1955. Foil and paper baking containers vs. re-use baking pans. Proc. Am. Soc. Bakery Engrs. *1955*, 185–190.

ROCKWOOD, F. 1952. Cooling and wrapping. Proc. Am. Soc. Bakery Engrs. *1952*, 124–128.

ROSEN, S. 1949. Packaging of breads. Proc. Am. Soc. Bakery Engrs. *1949*, 155–158.

ST. ARNAUD, L. 1959A. Compression wrapping of bread. Bakers Weekly *184*, No. 6, 52–54.

ST. ARNAUD, L. 1959B. Preventive maintenance to reduce packaging costs. Bakers Weekly *183*, No. 6, 29–30.

ST. ARNAUD, L. 1959C. The care and feeding of paper in packaging machines. Bakers Weekly *184*, No. 2, 31–33.

St. Arnaud, L. 1959D. The thermostat—watchdog of the bread-wrapping machine. Bakers Weekly *184*, No. 11, 28–29.

St. Arnaud, L. 1960. Faulty machine packaging in film: the causes and cure. Bakers Weekly *185*, No. 1, 24–26.

Sherwood, W. 1964. Permeability in packaging. Biscuit Maker Plant Baker *15*, No. 8, 624, 628.

Suess, T. 1967. Evaluation of newer types of bakery foods packaging. Proc. Am. Soc. Bakery Engrs. *1967*, 55–62.

Turiello, J. A. 1969. Up-to-date information on packaging materials and packaging machinery. Proc. Am. Soc. Bakery Engrs. *1969*, 210–217.

CHAPTER 24

AUXILIARY EQUIPMENT

This chapter contains descriptions of finishing and decorating equipment, special plants, and some auxiliary devices which do not properly fit into any of the preceding discussions. The extremely broad scope of this category made it impossible to include all of the types of equipment which manufacturers have made available within recent years.

Although all types of production lines may use auxiliary equipment, perhaps the greatest number and variety are found on cookie lines, as in Fig. 24.1.

APPLYING GRANULAR MATERIALS, POWDERS, AND OIL

Although topping applicators are used with all sorts of bakery goods, they are especially prominent in cookie production where they can be found at many places along the production line. Salters are usually placed after the cutter and in front of the oven. Depositers of coconut, nonpareils, and the like are often placed following a marshmallow depositer and before the skinning conveyor. This ensures maximum stickiness of the marshmallow. Most of this equipment is portable so that it can be brought in or out of the line as needed.

An automatic coconut topper is shown in Fig. 24.2. The rate of dispensing of coconut or other topping materials is controlled by the stroke length of an eccentric. The eccentric shaft drives a screen which controls the rate at which coconut drops from the hopper onto two rotating dispersing wheels. Screens of different mesh size are used for different granulations of topping material. A gate is provided at the bottom of the feed hopper to control the amount of topping material fed to and by the Syntron feeder to make up for the topping material consumed on the product. A stainless hopper for replenishing the topping furnishes material to a Syntron feed, with variable control, feeding a bucket conveyor. The collecting hopper under the recovery unit also has vibrators. A blower is furnished for removal of excess coconut from cookies at the discharge end. With proper adjustments, this feeder can be used for chocolate sprinkles, nonpareils, etc.

Figure 24.3 is a photograph of a salt applicator with automatic recovery system for depositing on a noncontinuous product (such as round crackers). Uniform distribution is achieved by proper adjustment of

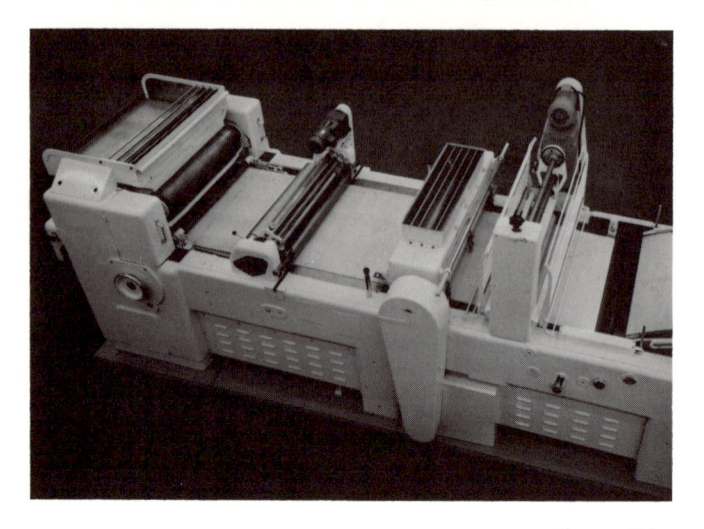

Courtesy of Hecrona
FIG. 24.1. COOKIE MACHINE WITH SEVERAL TYPES OF AUXILIARY EQUIPMENT: EGG WASHER, DECORATING DEVICE, AND GUILLOTINE CUTTER.

the pitch and reciprocating strokes of accumulating and distributing plates. The metering valve deposits measured amounts of the topping material on the accumulating plate. On the latter, the discontinuous deposit is spread out to a continuous and more-or-less uniform layer which then drops onto the distributor plate. The latter further disperses and spreads the material so that it is released onto the product as a uniform curtain. Sugar applicators operate on similar principles (Fig. 24.4).

Dough Oilers

Dough oilers are of three different designs: (1) oil flowing from a hopper through a slit or gate is deposited on a roller which transfers it to the surface of a continuous dough strip, (2) oil is sprayed in a fine mist onto a sheet or pieces of dough as they pass through an enclosure, and (3) dough pieces or baked goods pass through a curtain of oil, as in an enrober.

Since oil is relatively expensive, application by enrober is usually nonfeasible from a cost standpoint, more oil being applied by these devices than necessary to achieve the desired result. Oil-spray equipment is composed essentially of a pumping unit, atomizing heads, wire belt conveyor, and a housing. A satisfactory unit must create a mist of small and uniform droplets near the object to be coated; it will collect, filter, and recycle all excess oil, and will prevent emission of more than traces of oil to the atmosphere. There are several available units which will accomplish these aims (Fig. 24.5).

Close control of oil temperature and pumping pressure are necessary if uniform coverage is to be obtained. Design of the sprayer orifice is critical, and the nozzle must be kept free of debris so that partial clogging does not occur.

Flour Brushes

This equipment brushes excess loose flour (or starch) from the top of dough sheets as they travel on a conveyor to a cutting or forming operation. Construction is usually very simple: a motor and a brush mounted on a frame which attaches to the conveyor. The brush may be cylindrical in cross-section but the bristles are frequently set in the form of two or more strips. Bristles are white nylon in the majority of cases. The equipment may include a small conveyor belt to catch flour removed by the brush and convey it to a container for sifting and reuse.

Flour Dusters

Many operations require the application of dusting flour to continuous strips of dough. The simplest designs have small hoppers extending across the width of the conveyor, the bottom of the hopper being a

Courtesy of J. W. Greer Co.

FIG. 24.2. COCONUT TOPPER ON MARSHMALLOW LINE SHOWING PORTABLE RETURN ELEVATOR.

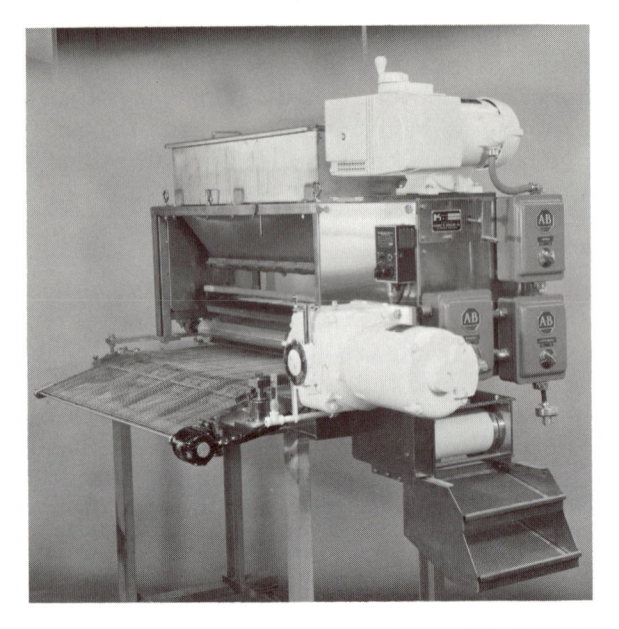

Courtesy of Stuart P. Kessler Co.

FIG. 24.3. SALTER WITH AUTOMATIC RECOVERY SYSTEM FOR NONCONTINUOUS PRODUCT.

perforated plate through which flour is encouraged to flow by a rocker arm. A rotary spindle may be attached below the perforations to improve the uniformity of the deposit. Both the spindle and the rocker arm are actuated by a motor mounted above the hopper. Provision is made for adjusting the amplitude of the rocker arm motion, this being the means by which the rate of flour deposit is controlled.

Starch dusters which surround pieces with a cloud of the powder in a slightly vacuumized chamber are also available.

APPLYING FILLINGS

There are many ways of applying icings, fillings, frostings, jams, jellies, and the like, varying to suit the properties of the material being applied and the base product. Especially in the larger plants, equipment is constructed in the shop, or commercially available devices are greatly modified resulting in a large number of different designs being in existence. Fluid and semifluid icing compositions (water icings and fondants) can be extruded continuously through a perforated pipe to give striping on coffee cakes, Danish pastry, and similar sweet dough products. Generally, no attempt is made to control flow through the individual nozzles. The baked goods can be iced as depanned products directly on a wire belt conveyor, or in their foil pan. The motive power is usually a rotary pump in line from the supply tank. Electric eyes, microswitches, or other sensing devices can be used to restrict the flow to the time when a product is in place beneath the dispenser. In one variation, the perforated pipe can be moved back and forth to lay down wavy lines on the product.

When it is necessary to extrude stripes of jams, jellies, and the like onto sheets of dough, the depositer may rely on several spiral screws operating in cylindrical chambers to force the material out of a hopper and through simple spreading attachments riding just above the dough. Wiper blades (spatulas) smooth and spread the deposit to give continuous coverage. If an intermittent or semicontinuous deposit is satisfactory, fruit depositers as shown in Fig. 24.6 can be used. The pistons beneath the hopper are actuated by the vertical rods seen in the picture.

Multiple rosettes of whipped topping can be extruded through die plates by air pressure in the closed hopper (see Fig. 24.7). Similar devices can be used for jellies, in which case it may be necessary to apply a brief pulse of negative pressure to prevent tailing of the deposit.

If the filling is stringy in consistency, but still coheres slightly, it can probably be extruded from large cylindrical pistons, and cut off by a wire as discs which are then deposited on the cake. Hare (1966) described application of buttercream filling by a horizontally-aligned rotating drum fitted with four plungers or pistons which retract as they pass beneath a hopper. This motion draws the required amount of filling into the chamber where it is held while the drum rotates until the chamber is directly above the cake. At this point the piston ejects the

Courtesy of Stuart P. Kessler Co.
FIG. 24.4. SUGAR APPLICATOR.

Courtesy of T. & T. Vicars, Ltd.
FIG. 24.5. OIL SPRAY UNIT.

creme deposit so that it lies above the surface of the drum, and a wire slices it from the piston face and allows the disc of filling to fall on the cake. The weight of creme deposit can be controlled by adjusting the length of the piston stroke.

The deposit of creme filling onto sandwich cookie bases is accomplished somewhat differently. The filling is pumped through pipe lines into the center of a rapidly rotating cylinder of relatively small diameter. Extrusion is through orifices in this cylinder and usually the dies are ring-shaped to give a deposit with a central hole. The extrusion process is continuous and the amount of deposit is controlled by adjusting the speed of the pump. The extruded material is sliced off by a stationary wire as the orifice passes above the base cake. Centrifugal force plays a part in detaching the disc of filling from the extruding mass.

In all cases where the deposit is measured volumetrically, (and this includes virtually all filling depositers) density of the filling must be maintained within narrow limits if acceptable package net weights are to be obtained. This is not difficult with jams and jellies, unless air has been inadvertently whipped into them during preparation; but aerated toppings, buttercream frostings, etc., may require frequent adjustments of the dispensing apparatus.

SANDWICHING MACHINES

These devices are designed to assemble two base cakes and a layer of creme filling to form a sandwich cookie. The following description applies to the more modern design of equipment.

Base cakes are received from the cooling conveyors or fed from base cake boxes by hand. Automatic converging units can be used to converge multiples of the desired number of rows emerging from the oven cooling conveyor. Vibrating conveyors jog the rows (up to eight) into a stacked-on-edge position. Half of the rows have the embossed design leading while the other rows contain cookies with the design trailing. Cakes enter the magazines in the proper position for sandwiching and are removed from the magazines, one at a time, by means of double pins on double chains.

As the bottom cakes travel through the machine with the design facing down, they receive deposits of creme extruded through a rotating sleeve with shaped orifices. Extrusion pressure is supplied by the pump which moves the creme from the hopper to depositer. The creme deposit is cut off by adjustable stationary wires. Deposits can be adjusted by changing the speed of the Reeves variable speed motors driving the auger paddles and the Moyno pump. An air valve stops the creme delivery in case the sandwiching machine stops for any reason.

At the second set of magazines, the top cakes are dropped onto the deposit. Subsequently, the sandwich is gently pressed together to assure adherence of the components and establish uniform thickness of the finished cookie.

Courtesy of Moline, Inc.
FIG. 24.6. FRUIT-FILLING DEPOSITER.

Courtesy of Quality Machine Co.
FIG. 24.7 WHIPPED TOPPING DEPOSITER DECORATING FOUR-INCH PIES.

A typical sandwiching machine will take round base cakes from 1½ to 2⅝ in. in diameter or rectangular, square and finger-shaped base cakes up to 3¼ in. long and as narrow as 1⅙ in. Speeds are variable up to 1600 sandwiches per minute on a 2-row machine. Operation on these machines can be made automatic except for replenishing the creme hopper. Peanut-butter-and-cracker sandwiches are made on a somewhat different machine, which, in Fig. 24.8, is shown combined with a vend pack wrapper.

The rows of sandwiches are conveyed to the packing area in stacked or flat array, depending upon the type of package to be used. Several machines may feed one packing conveyor. In recent developments, sandwiching machines have been combined with tray loaders and overwrap equipment to give a completely automatic packing operation.

In the old stencil machine, the base cakes were pressed against a stencil plate. Filling was forced by gravity into the stencil holes, and the cakes with filling were knocked away from the plate.

JELLY ROLL (SWISS ROLL) PLANT

The integrated Swiss roll plants which have been designed in recent years are further examples of the increase in specialization characteristic of modern bakery design. There are sufficient unique finishing operations in an automated Swiss roll line to justify describing the entire operation in this chapter on auxiliary equipment.

Batter may be mixed in a two-speed pressurized whisk or in more conventional equipment. When the whisk is used, an automatic flour-feeding attachment makes it possible to fold flour into the aerated pre-mix without losing pressure. With two whisks, a continuous supply of batter is available.

A typical jelly roll plant utilizes a continuous oven with a steel band 32 in. wide. Ovens are usually gas-fired, but other heating sources can be used. The length of the oven may vary from 40 to 70 ft, depending mainly upon the output desired. The entire plant consists of a greasing machine, which applies a layer of fat and flour to the band, a roll-fed batter depositer, a steel band oven, an inclined lowering conveyor (if a two-floor plant is desired), a steel band cooling belt, a sugar duster, jam and/or creme depositers, a rotary cutting unit, and a packing section.

The greasing machine and sponge depositer operate as a unit. A quantity of the greasing mixture is continuously measured out on the band and a side-to-side reciprocating brush distributes it uniformly. A sponge batter is laid down on the greased band and spreads until it is the proper width. The batter is continuously deposited, either in 2 broad strips or 5 narrow strips from a hopper with feed rollers and a die plate which meters the flow of batter. The machine which deposits the batter has a variable-speed drive, permitting adjustment of the rate of extrusion.

At the delivery end, the baked cake is stripped from the band after the layer has passed halfway around the drum. This arrangement results in the cake being placed upside down on an inclined lowering conveyor. Oven band and conveyor speeds are synchronized. The lowering conveyor is not necessary if a one-story plant is constructed. Two-floor plants are more common.

Cooling takes place on a second steel band, which is about twice as long and slightly wider than the baking band. Prior to receiving the cake from the lowering conveyor, the band is lightly sprinkled with

Courtesy of Vend Pack Machine Co.
FIG. 24.8. SANDWICHING MACHINE FOR PEANUT BUTTER AND CRACKERS.

sugar, which keeps the cake from sticking to the cooling band. The cake strip is carried through a humidified tunnel, which adjusts its moisture content and temperature to the required levels.

After it leaves the tunnel, the cake is spread with jelly or creme, which is applied by a depositer. The last mechanical operation is that of cutting the roll, and this is accomplished by two sets of cutters. A reciprocating blade or guillotine divides the cake into lateral strips, and a revolving cutter separates the strip longitudinally when this is required. Operators manually roll the strips into jelly roll configuration. The individual rolls may be conveyed to a chocolate enrober and then cooled in a refrigerated tunnel. They are automatically wrapped. For layered gateaux and triangular (Alpine) sandwich forms, appropriate cutting arrangements are available.

Estimates of the production of a 2-floor Swiss roll unit with a 32 in. by 50 ft band are in the neighborhood of 12,000–14,000 of the small bar-sized rolls, or about 5000–7000 of the large rolls per hour. The baking time would approximate 4 min at these yields.

CHOCOLATE CONDITIONERS AND ENROBERS

Enrobing lines for applying fat-based moisture-free coatings to small baked goods are common in cookie plants and some other parts of the baking industry. Chocolate-flavored coatings are the most common, but other types are occasionally used.

The initial handling of chocolate coating will depend upon whether it is received from the supplier in melted condition or in slabs. All but the largest users will obtain the material in solid form. The slabs must be melted. In one type of conditioner (Fig. 24.9), a melting drum maintained at a predetermined temperature (about 100°F) by a thermostatic control continuously rotates against a block of coating (or irregular pieces) and melts a thin film of chocolate from it. The film is scraped from the roll and drops through a strainer into a water-jacketed storage tank. A specially-designed agitator in the storage tank thoroughly mixes the melted chocolate. Continuous delivery eliminates the need for large holding tanks for liquid coating.

The melted chocolate must be cooled to the proper temperature to establish stable seed crystals. Various types of heat exchange equipment are used for this purpose. In one type, chocolate is pumped through a spiral-shaped, close-tolerance gap between inner and outer water-cooled jackets of a heat exchanger. Use of thin layers allows complete equilibration of the chocolate because of the minimum temperature differentials necessary to reach the desired level.

The piping, which may be of black iron, must be wound with industrial heating cable and insulated.

AUXILIARY EQUIPMENT 493

Courtesy of J. W. Greer Co.
FIG. 24.9. CHOCOLATE MELTING AND CONDITIONING UNIT.

Properly tempered coating supplied by the conditioning unit is delivered to the enrober as required. An enrober or coater will consist of a jacketed coating tank with an agitator, a flow pan, a wire mesh conveyor belt for carrying the product through a curtain of coating, an agitator device for the take-away section of the conveyor belt, a water-jacketed heat exchanger, a bottomer, a detailer rod, a blower, and the necessary pumps, piping, motors, and controls (see Fig. 24.10).

A specific design of enrober is described in the following section. Most of the details are applicable to enrobers in general. The coating tank and drip pan extension, which form an integral machine frame, are made from continuously formed and welded stainless steel sheet. Surrounding this frame is a stainless steel air jacket. Thermostatically regulated, electrically heated air circulates continuously within this jacket to maintain the temperature of the tank. During shutdown periods the hot air system increases the temperature within the jacket to maintain the coating in a liquid state.

A stainless steel wire mesh belt with a ¼ in. pitch conveys the product through the coater. A shaker system of variable frequency and amplitude is provided to agitate the enrobed product. This action distributes the coating more evenly over the product and also contributes to the removal of excess coating. The detailer rod affixed at the end of the wire belt can be adjusted up or down to eliminate trailing bits of coating.

Stainless steel flow pans allow a double curtain of coating to flow

494   BAKERY TECHNOLOGY AND ENGINEERING

Courtesy of J. W. Greer Co.
FIG. 24.10.   CHOCOLATE ENROBING LINE FOR MARSHMALLOW COOKIES.

onto the belt. The melted coating either flows through a slit at the bottom of the pan or over one edge of the pan. The latter design is less likely to clog up at the point along the stream. The height of the pan can be adjusted in some models, while in others it is fixed at about a 5-in. product clearance. Coating is pressure fed from the coating tank across the width of the pan. Pans can be designed to pour many evenly separated narrow streams of coating over the product for striped goods.

Beneath the belt, a bottoming pan receives the excess coating. An additional supply of coating is also piped into this pan when bottomed goods are being made. The pan can be moved toward or away from the belt to affect the extent of bottoming. A bottoming roller can be placed in the pan to pick up the coating and apply it to the bottom of the cookie.

Excess coating is removed by a high-pressure blower system. A damper on the blower intake controls the flow of air through the nozzle. The nozzle, which is a tubular plenum chamber, gives uniform air distribution across the width of the belt. Nozzle height and angle, and width of air discharge are adjustable. The detailer, a simple powered roller of small diameter, removes tails of coating which drop down from the pieces as they leave the enrober belt.

It is necessary to have precise control of chocolate temper if glossy coatings are to be obtained and bloom avoided. Temperature control is assisted by the use of a water-jacketed heat exchanger of the swept-wall type in the coating line subsequent to the sump. Automatic tempering cycles can be programmed. The coating is heated high enough to destroy all crystal structures, cooled to the temperature at which stable crystals develop, then reheated to production temperature and maintained there during the run. Overnight holding is preceded by a heating step to melt all crystals present, when the pump is reversed to clear all lines of the seed forms.

Cooling tunnels are necessary to solidify the coating so the pieces can be packed. Sufficient cooling capacity must be available to solidify all of the fat if bloom is to be avoided. If the coating is not firm, it will smear or retain fingerprint impressions from the packing operation. Lack of adequate refrigeration capacity can limit the output of the entire enrobed goods line.

Multizone cooling tunnels are preferred. Some makes are in module form with each section being self-contained and automatically regulated. The product is carried through the assembled modules on a belt with nonstick surface. Single- or double-row evaporator coils and the air-circulation means are placed between the belt supports in the illustrated design. Inspection doors should be installed at frequent intervals to permit observation of the product and withdrawal of samples.

BIBLIOGRAPHY

HARE, R. W. P. 1966. Fully mechanized cake production. Proc. Am. Soc. Bakery Engrs. *1966*, 175–185.

ILLFELDER, B. 1964. Preparation and application of icings for sweet yeast raised products. Proc. Am. Soc. Bakery Engrs. *1964*, 254–259.

WELCH, R. C. 1968. Chocolate and hard butter coatings. Proc. Am. Soc. Bakery Engrs. *1968*, 252–263.

CHAPTER 25

FREEZING AND OTHER SPECIAL PRESERVATION METHODS

The preservation methods for bakery foods which have received substantial experimental effort are low temperature storage (refrigeration and freezing), exposure to ionizing radiation, dehydration, heat treatment in hermetically sealed containers (metal cans or film pouches), and microbiological inhibition by chemicals. Of these approaches, only freezing has achieved appreciable commercial success, although some canned baked goods are sold. Perhaps packaged melba toast and zweibach could be regarded as dehydrated products since they are often prepared by baking twice, the second heat treatment resulting in dehydration as well as toasting. But dehydration of items for later reconstitution by the addition of water is not practiced, though it has been considered by the Armed Forces. The propionates added to retard mold growth and the various starch complexing agents used for softening the crumb certainly have a preservative effect, but affect only a narrow aspect of the storage life.

FREEZING AND FROZEN STORAGE

General Considerations

As a food processing operation, freezing is conducted for one of two reasons: (1) the promotion of desired texture changes, as in the production of ice cream, or (2) the improvement of storage stability. For bakery foods, the second reason is of primary importance.

The commercial success of frozen bakery foods is too well known to require emphasis here. Every variety of bakery goods has been offered in frozen form at one time or another, with the possible exception of low moisture products such as crackers and common cookies. The technology is not quite as simple as it seems, however, and many failures have been recorded. Freezing is not a simple process and it is important to understand the many changes that occur in order to process top quality products having maximum potential storage life.

In the freezing range, the moisture in a foodstuff undergoes a change of state. A relatively large amount of energy, called the latent heat of fusion, must be removed in order to change liquid water to ice at essentially constant temperature. For this reason, graphs of temperature of a product versus the time it has been in a freezing environment will show a leveling off of the temperature drop as the freezing range is reached. After all the latent heat of fusion has been removed, the temperature again begins to drop.

Although the freezing temperature of pure water is about 32°F, the moisture in bakery products will not become entirely solid until considerably lower temperatures are reached. For most bakery products, the freezing point is between 20° and 28°F. The freezing point depression is due to the presence of dissolved gases, liquids, and solids in the water. Leaner doughs freeze at the higher end of the range while the richer products require lower temperatures. Some adjuncts such as jams and certain frostings do not freeze solid until very low temperatures (in the present terms) are reached.

It is reasonably certain that enzymatic and microbiological reactions in foodstuffs come to a complete halt when all of the water is converted to ice. Deteriorative chemical changes such as the development of oxidative rancidity (of course, enzymes can also mediate the development of rancidity) and physical changes such as the growth of ice crystals and the loss of water through sublimation, as well as strictly mechanical damage through breakage and the like, can continue in the absence of liquid water.

One reason for the effectiveness of the freezing process in promoting storage stability is that it removes water from participation in chemical reactions. For maximum effectiveness, substantially all of the water must be present as ice since partial freezing may result in a concentration of reactants which tends toward acceleration of changes. For most foodstuffs, the completely frozen state requires temperatures much below the freezing point of pure water. There can be a very substantial reduction in spoilage reactions even though some liquid water remains, but the effect is not as great as that which occurs when freezing is complete.

There are disadvantages as well as advantages in the freezing of bakery products. Not all of the reactions are desirable. The principal objectionable changes affect mainly the textural characteristics and the appearance of the products. Nutritive value, taste, and odor are seldom damaged. Some of the undesirable changes which occur are: (1) dehydration as the result of the removal of water from intimate association with hydrocolloids into ice crystals with the collapse of the gels when thawed, and (2) mechanical damage to the microscopic structure as a result of the formation and growth of ice crystals.

The size of the ice crystals formed during the freezing process is generally recognized to be related to the extent of textural damage observed in a foodstuff after it has been thawed. Slow freezing tends to yield large crystals while fast freezing usually results in the formation of relatively small crystals. The rate of freezing may be considered to be, for most practical purposes, a function of the temperature of the fluid (gas or liquid) by which the object is surrounded or the solid surface with which it is in contact, although it is certainly true that the rate of heat transfer is the fundamental controlling process and this includes factors other than the temperature differential. If the air surrounding a product is not continually changed, it can assume a temperature quite different from the air circulating in the main channels.

The time required to freeze a product can be reduced by: (1) Lowering the air temperature in the freezer. (2) Improving cold air circulation by (a) exposing more product surface to the air current, or (b) increasing air velocity and (to some extent) turbulence. (3) Reducing the distance-to-center in the product, i.e., making it thinner in one of the dimensions. (4) Reducing the moisture content. (5) Minimizing the free air space in the package, using foil for the package, or, preferably, freezing the product unwrapped.

There are, however, conditions not directly related to the rate of heat transfer which have an effect on the textural damage undergone during freezing. For example, the number of ice crystal foci and their distribution within the foodstuff are influential in this regard. The ease with which water molecules can diffuse to crystallizing sites is important, this being controlled not so much by the extent of binding (in the molecular sense) as by the actual physical discontinuities such as air pockets, fatty deposits and other relatively dehydrated regions, pools of eutectics, and, perhaps, cell walls.

Water will pass in the vapor state between crystals in a frozen food. Large crystals will gain molecules at the expense of smaller crystals. Crystal growth is considered undesirable. When most of the crystals formed during the freezing process are relatively large, the net translocation of moisture is slow. The surface energies of large crystals do not vary over a sufficiently wide range to cause pumping of water molecules at an appreciable rate. In such cases, the amount of water tied up in small crystals is insufficient to cause much growth even if all of it is transferred to the larger crystals. Growth will be most rapid and noticeable when the bulk of the water is in the form of very small crystals with a generous sprinkling of substantially larger crystals.

A second important reason for rapid freezing is the existence of a rapid-staling range between 70° and 20°F. Between 32° and 36°F, firmness increases about 3 times as fast as at room temperature. In this range, gelatinized starch retrogrades at a relatively rapid rate and the crumb gains a harshness and firmness which it will retain in all subsequent steps unless it is reheated under certain conditions. Staling of this type does not have much effect in rich cakes, but it can be very important in bread and similar products. It has no effect in raw dough products intended to be baked after thawing.

If the baked product is frozen relatively slowly, then it will spend considerable time in the 20°–70°F range and undergo texture changes which will adversely affect its acceptability even though all other processing steps have been optimal.

Products[1]

Bread and Rolls.—Because of the short storage life of freshly baked bread, any method of preservation which makes possible the holding of loaves for long periods is of great importance as a possible means of reducing stale returns and permitting the distribution of specialty loaves to distant or relatively inactive markets.

Cool bread (unfrozen) becomes stale in much less time than warm bread. Using only physical characteristics as criteria, Katz (1928, 1934) found that at 140°F bread would stay "fresh" indefinitely (flavor deteriorates rapidly at this temperature); and, further, that at ordinary room temperatures the rate of staling was most rapid during the first 12 hr. His observations indicated that the maximum rate of staling occurred at temperatures of +27° to +29°F, and that the rate decreases as the temperature is raised or lowered.

Many research workers have demonstrated that, although bread stales very rapidly at its freezing point, if it is stored at 0°F and below the rate of staling is very slow. At −30°F, the bread is still palatable after approximately 1 yr of storage.

Cathcart and Luber (1939) drew the following conclusions from a careful, comprehensive, detailed study of changes in commercially baked bread held in a commercial freezer at +12°, −8°, and −31°F:

According to swelling power tests, bread staled rapidly at temperatures as low as −8°F. This test showed that it was about half stale when placed in the freezer (8 hr out of the oven) and nearly completely stale after 24 hr in the freezer. At about −31°F, the bread was kept in its original fresh condition for a period of about 4 days and required 8–10 days to become nearly stale, according to the swelling power test. When the tests were continued for 60–70 days, a refreshing of the bread was observed; the sediment returned to values in the neighborhood of those for unfrozen bread 8 hr out of the oven.

According to aroma and taste tests, bread frozen at −8°F remained good for 20 days and saleable for approximately 40 days. At −31°F it has a much better keeping quality and remained in a saleable condition for much longer periods of time.

Although the change in the starch, which the swelling power test measures, is important it does not tell the whole story about staling.

---

[1] Based on an article by Tressler (1960).

The development of an off-aroma was the limiting factor for the time the bread could be kept saleable by freezing at the temperature used.

At −8°F, carbon dioxide in the freezing chamber did not improve the keeping qualities.

When bread frozen at −8°F was removed from the freezer, it staled at about the same rate as ordinary bread....

Although bread does not keep indefinitely at the temperatures employed, freezing offers an excellent means of keeping commercial bread in a saleable condition for 40 days or longer. It must be remembered that all frozen products deteriorate slowly during storage, when comparing the practicability of freezing bread with other food products.

Pence *et al.* (1955C) studied the effect of storage temperature on firmness increases in frozen bread and reported that firmness increases fairly rapidly at 15°F, more slowly at +10°F, and very little or not at all at 0°F or below. Since staling takes place most rapidly during the first few hours after baking, bread should be frozen as soon as possible after it comes from the oven. This was shown by Pence *et al.* (1955C) in a study in which they used a taste panel and determined the firmness of bread frozen 4, 11 and 34 hr after baking. Their results are shown in Table 25.1.

These workers also studied the effect of variations in the storage temperature on the firmness of bread frozen at −20°F and noted that, when the temperature was fluctuated between 0° and 20°F (on a 24-hr cycle), the bread soon lost its compressibility (Table 25.2).

Pence *et al.* (1955C) also indicate the value of rapid thawing. If the frozen bread is thawed and held at ordinary room temperatures it retains its freshness about as long as fresh bread which has not been frozen.

Work by Cathcart (1941) indicated that the packaging of freshly baked bread in hermetically sealed cans prior to freezing greatly in-

TABLE 25.1
EFFECT OF AGE OF BREAD AT TIME OF FREEZING ON FIRMNESS AND TASTE-PANEL EVALUATION OF FRESHNESS AFTER DEFROSTING

Age at Time of Freezing (Hr)	Firmness (Gm/4 Mm Compression)	Mean Rank by Taste Panel[1]
	Freshly Defrosted	
4	92	1.3
11	109	1.8
34	131	2.9
	48 Hr After Defrosting	
4	172	1.2
11	183	2.3
34	201	2.5

Source: Pence *et al.* (1955C).
[1] Judges were asked to rate samples in order of freshness so that the freshest sample would receive the rating of 1, the next freshest 2, and so on. Comparisons in rank cannot be made between results obtained at separate testing times.

creased the length of time that the frozen product can be kept without marked staling. In fact, bread sealed in a normal atmosphere remained saleable in cold storage for approximately 1 yr. That which was vacuum packed not only remained saleable, but was quite similar to freshly baked bread at the end of the year's storage.

Pence *et al.* (1955B) compared the rate of freezing of wrapped and unwrapped bread in an airblast freezer at −20°F and observed that the unwrapped bread froze in much less time (Fig. 25.1). The unwrapped fresh bread loses little weight during freezing in an airblast. These workers reported that loaves of unwrapped bread placed in the freezer 3 hr after leaving the oven lost an average of only 4 gm (approximately $\frac{1}{7}$ oz) during freezing in a −20°F airblast with 1200 fpm velocity. However, they found that the loaves of unwrapped bread continued to lose moisture during storage at 0°F at the rate of approximately 2 gm ($\frac{1}{14}$ oz) moisture per day. They concluded that freshly baked bread can be safely frozen unwrapped, but a wrapper is necessary to prevent serious moisture losses during storage.

TABLE 25.2
EFFECT OF A VARIABLE STORAGE TEMPERATURE ON FIRMNESS IN FROZEN BREAD
(TEMPERATURE FLUCTUATED BETWEEN 0° AND 20°F ON A 24-HR CYCLE)

Days in Storage	Firmness (Gm/4 Mm Compression)
0	94
7	123
14	131
28	165

Source: Pence *et al.* (1955C).

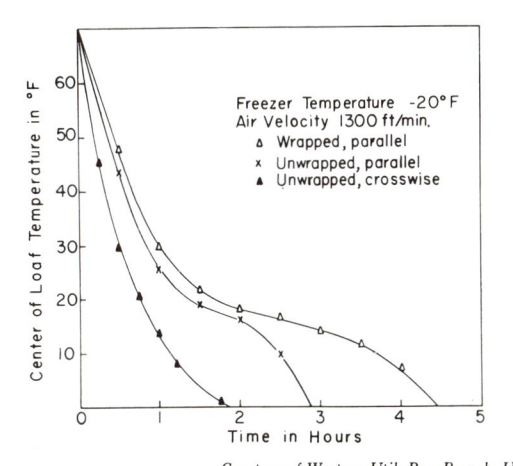

FIG. 25.1. RATE OF FREEZING OF WRAPPED AND UNWRAPPED BREAD AT −20°F.

Despite the advantage gained by the more rapid freezing of the unwrapped bread, followed by prompt packaging of the frozen bread, most bread frozen commercially is wrapped before freezing.

Points to be taken into consideration in choosing a wrapper for bread to be frozen include the following: Bread shrinks about 6% during freezing; so, if the bread is wrapped before freezing the wrappers fit loosely. During defrosting, moisture usually condenses on the wrapper. A desirable wrapper should be both sturdy and flexible to minimize wrinkling and cracking due to handling of the frozen or partially defrosted bread. The wrapper should not absorb moisture and soften as otherwise it may be marked by the fingers during handling after defrosting. A heat-sealable wrapper which seals securely and does not fall apart after moisture has condensed on it, is required.

Pence *et al.* (1955A) studied the effects of various factors on the rate of freezing. As a result of their studies of the effects of air velocity and temperature, freezing with and without a wrapper, and the position of the loaf in the airblast freezer, they concluded:

Freezer temperature was found to be the variable with greatest effect on freezing rate of wrapped bread. With unwrapped bread, air velocity and position of the loaf in the airblast were factors of major importance. The most rapid method of freezing bread in the present experiments was by means of a high-velocity, low-temperature blast of air at right angles to the long dimension of an unwrapped loaf. Individual loaves could be frozen in less than 30 min by this method and no significant loss of moisture was incurred.

The wrapper on a loaf of bread slowed the rate of freezing about as much as using a freezer temperature 10° higher. Wrapped bread packed in pasteboard cartons froze several times more slowly than individual loaves under similar freezer conditions.

The effect on the rate of freezing of unwrapped bread in varying air velocity is shown in Fig. 25.2. The effects of varying the temperature from −20° to −40°F and the velocity at −30°F from 700 to 1300 fpm are shown in Fig. 25.3. They tried freezing wrapped bread in a fiberboard delivery carton in an air-blast at −20°F (Fig. 25.4), and found it impossible to effect rapid freezing.

These workers also compared the freezing rates of unwrapped 1-lb loaves of whole wheat, raisin, and sour French bread. They found that whole wheat and white bread freeze at substantially the same rate despite a considerable difference in loaf density. Raisin bread freezes at a lower temperature than white bread, whereas French bread freezes at a higher temperature. Because of the shape of the loaf, French bread freezes more rapidly than the other breads studied.

In Fig. 25.1 are presented the curves obtained by Pence *et al.* (1955B) in studying the relative rate of freezing of wrapped and unwrapped

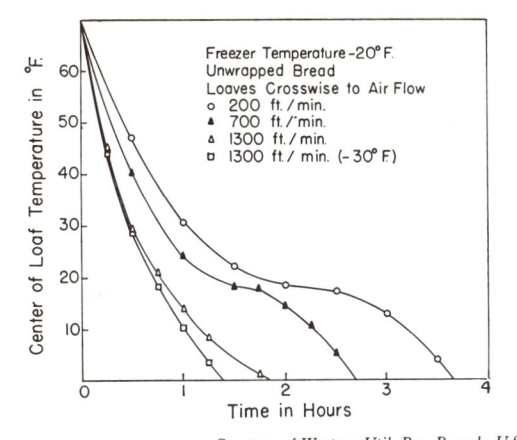

FIG. 25.2. EFFECT OF AIR VELOCITY AT LOW TEMPERATURES ON RATE OF FREEZING OF UNWRAPPED BREAD.

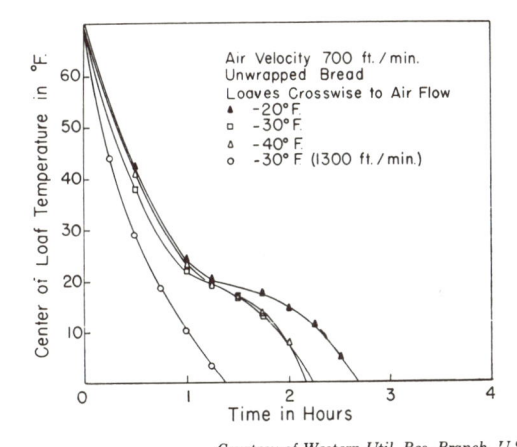

FIG. 25.3. EFFECT OF AIR TEMPERATURE AT INTERMEDIATE AND HIGH AIR VELOCITIES ON RATE OF FREEZING OF UNWRAPPED BREAD.

bread when placed parallel to the airblast, and unwrapped bread placed parallel and crosswise to the direction of the air current. This work clearly indicated the advantages of placing the loaves crosswise to the airblast and the importance of freezing the bread before wrapping if rapid freezing is to be obtained. Contrary to what might be expected, they found that unwrapped bread loses little weight during freezing in an airblast, but loses moisture during subsequent storage at 0°F at the rate of approximately 1/14 oz per day.

The comparable rates of freezing for another bakery product are shown in Fig. 25.5.

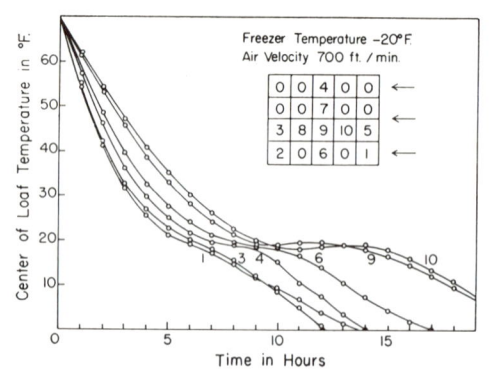

504   BAKERY TECHNOLOGY AND ENGINEERING

Courtesy of Western Util. Res. Branch, U.S. Dept. Agr.
FIG. 25.4. RATE OF FREEZING OF WRAPPED BREAD, PACKED IN A PASTEBOARD DELIVERY CARTON, AT LOW TEMPERATURE AND INTERMEDIATE AIR VELOCITY.

Numbers indicate position of test loaves in carton and order in which they froze. Arrows indicate direction of air flow.

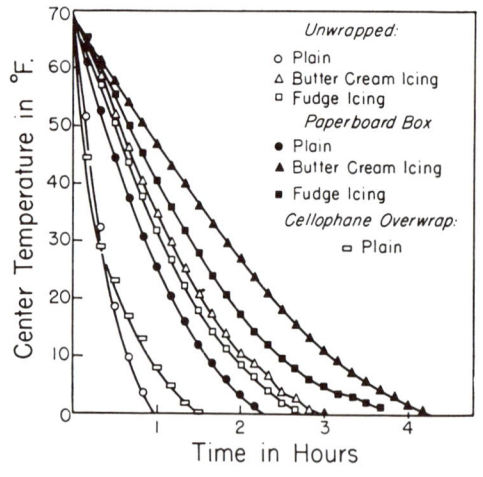

Courtesy of Western Util. Res. Branch, U.S. Dept. Agr.
FIG. 25.5. COOLING CURVES FOR 7-INCH LAYER CAKES IN FREEZER AT −20°F AND 650 FPM AIR VELOCITY.

As has previously been indicated, frozen bread becomes stale very slowly indeed. The lower the storage temperature the more slowly it becomes stale. Early workers reported that bread quick frozen immediately after baking and held 1 yr at 0°F was equivalent in freshness to bread held 1 day at 70°F. This is probably a slight exaggeration. In order to retain freshness as well as this, the storage temperature should be −20°F or below.

During storage of bread in the frozen state, a whitened or opaque ring about ¼ in. in width sometimes develops in the crumb just beneath the crust. When bread is stored at +15°F, rings may begin to appear in 2 weeks; at +10°F rings may be noted in about 5 weeks. At 0°F, 10 weeks or longer elapse before the rings are noted. This whitening is associated with the movement of moisture by sublimation and diffusion from the interior of the crumb to a region of lower moisture content just beneath the crust. Fluctuating temperatures, especially at 10°F or above, may accelerate this movement of moisture. Because of the danger of the formation of these abnormal white rings when bread is held for a few weeks, it is of importance to maintain bread at a low storage temperature.

Rapid defrosting with moving air of low humidity is of great importance in maintaining the quality of frozen bread.

All are agreed that defrosting conditions should be such that no moisture condenses on the cold bread. In still air, the rate of heat transfer is slow and consequently defrosting is very slow. Further, it is likely that moisture will condense on the bread, unless the relative humidity of the air is very low. At temperatures just below 32°F, staling is rapid; therefore, it is important to thaw the bread and bring it rapidly to room temperature or slightly above. This can be done best with air of low humidity which circulates freely and uniformly around the product.

Yeast-leavened dough products intended to be frozen and held for baking at some later time are often formulated and processed according to conventional guidelines. Some adjustments to the usual procedure which have been suggested are: (1) Doughs are taken out of the mixer cooler, in the range of 65°–70°F. (2) Stronger flours are used. (3) Absorption is slightly reduced. (4) More yeast is used at the dough stage (5–7%) though sponge yeast addition is kept normal or even slightly lower. The purpose of these changes is to give a stiff, bucky dough containing a considerable proportion of yeast cells that have not been actively fermenting at the time of freezing. Such doughs will maintain quality during longer periods of frozen storage and will have good proofing and oven spring.

Others recommend the straight dough system, with only 15–20 min of floor time. Some plants use the L-cysteine and whey formulation, develop it at high speed, and bring it from the mixer at 68°–70°F.

Budding of the yeast is thought to bring it to an undesirably sensitive state, susceptible to rapid loss of viability during freezing, and this is the reason for keeping fermentation times short.

Pies.—As is obvious after a glance into the freezer of your local supermarket, pies of all kinds can be frozen satisfactorily. There are few tricks involved.

Pies which are frozen before baking, can generally be baked without

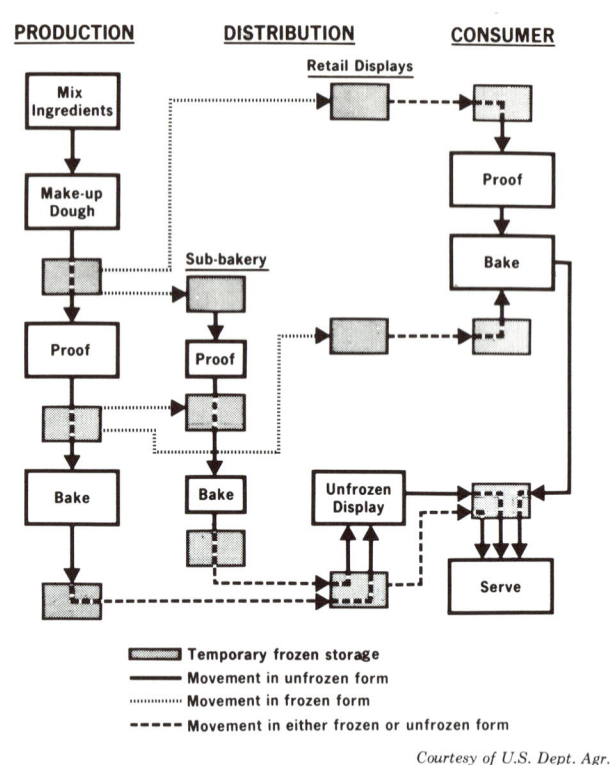

FIG. 25.6. ALTERNATIVE USES OF FREEZING IN THE PRODUCTION AND MARKETING OF BAKERY PRODUCTS.

Courtesy of U.S. Dept. Agr.

defrosting. Prevention of soggy crusts depends on getting sufficient heat to the bottom so that it is completely baked by the time the top crust is suitably browned. Heat transfer to the bottom crust is influenced by the oven characteristics and the kind of pie tin. Pans with perforated and blackened bottoms are helpful.

Rapid freezing is not essential for top quality. One study (Anon. 1962) showed that pies frozen over a period of as long as 28 hr remained in satisfactory condition throughout the usual length of frozen storage. Storage at temperatures no higher than 0°F is desirable, however, since the study mentioned above showed that pies stored at 20°F became unacceptable after 2 weeks, while 10°F storage allowed deterioration in about 4 weeks.

Baked or ready-to-eat pies in pastry crusts or graham cracker crusts are sold in large quantities. Pie dough is very little affected by freezing, but may become soggy through accumulation of ice crystals during lengthy frozen storage. Selection of the proper thickening agent for the filling and the whipped toppings is critical, since some of the commonly-used stabilizers will not stand up under freezing.

Cakes.—When frozen cakes first entered the market, most bakers tried to use the same formulas for batter and icing that they had been successfully using for cakes distributed in the usual manner. Complaints about the dryness of the cake crumb and unsatisfactory icing were received. Improvement was obtained when the moisture content of both icing and cake was raised. Moisture levels of 27–32% in layer cakes and 17–20% in buttercream icing are considered normal. Pregelatinized starch can be used to hold this additional moisture in bound form in both cake and icing.

The high sugar and soluble protein content and small percentage of "free" water in the cake crumb reduces the freezing point of most cakes to 15°F and under. Pence and Hanamoto (1959) estimate the nominal freezing points of cakes as follows: chiffon, 15°F; angel-food, 12.5°F; yellow layer, 3°–5°F; and pound, 2°F. However, they indicate that "it must be emphasized that these nominal freezing points apply only to cakes having the same or closely similar composition to the ones used."

Freezing does not damage either the flat or fondant type of icings. Unless the frosted cakes are properly packaged, however, moisture will condense on the surface of the frozen cake and damage the icing when it is brought into a warm room. The colder the cake, and the higher the humidity, the greater the condensation on the cake, other conditions being the same.

Equipment[2]

Commercial freezing of bakery products is accomplished either by subjecting them to blasts of mechanically refrigerated air or by contacting them with liquid nitrogen (or the cold gas from this liquid). Blast freezing is the oldest and by far the most common type, but cryogenic methods have definite advantages for certain applications. Among the important differences between the different types of freezers is the freezing heat transfer coefficient (Table 25.3).

Mechanical Freezers.—Blast freezers consist essentially of an enclosed insulated area containing some arrangement for holding and conveying the bakery goods while exposing their maximum surface area to the cold air currents, a mechanical refrigeration system, and blowers to distribute the cold air throughout the chamber. The principal elements of a mechanical refrigeration system are a compressor, a condenser, an evaporator, and the refrigerant. In this system, the refrigerant

---

[2] Part of this section was adapted from an article by Tressler (1960).

TABLE 25.3
FREEZING HEAT TRANSFER COEFFICIENTS

Freezer Type	Heat Transfer Coefficient Btu/(Hr) (Sq Ft) (°F)
Naturally circulating air	1
Air blast	4
Plate contact	10
Circulating brine	15
Immersion in liquid nitrogen	30
Cold gaseous nitrogen	60
Spray liquid nitrogen	75

Source: Liquid Carbonic Co.

is alternately expanded and condensed, taking up heat from the surroundings in the one case and giving it up in the other. The evaporator has an expansion valve, a coil of tubing in which the refrigerant vaporizes, and metal fins or other means for absorbing heat from the air and transferring it to the coil. The evaporator coil must also be provided with some means of defrosting to keep its heat transfer efficiency at a high level. This may involve spraying the coils with a liquid of low freezing point, such as brine or propylene glycol, by blowing over it hot air obtained from the compressor discharge, or by occasionally heating it electrically.

The function of the compressor is to pressurize the refrigerant so that it will rise to a temperature considerably above that of the condenser surface. Compressor types are: (1) reciprocating piston, (2) rotary vane, and (3) rotary screw. Piston compressors, which are the oldest and most common type, have from 4 to 16 cylinders, and can be obtained in high-speed and low-speed designs.

The condenser liquefies the highly compressed refrigerant gas by cooling it with water or air. If water is used, the refrigerant passes through a tube surrounded by flowing water. In the case of air cooling, the refrigerant flows through many feet of coils, on which room temperature air is blown. In evaporative condensers, the air cooling effect is assisted by sprays of water directed onto the coils.

Few of the common types of equipment used for freezing fruits and vegetables were designed to accept bread, cake, pies, and other bakery products. None of the multiplate freezers (e.g., the Birdseye, the Amerio and the Food Machinery freezer) is advantageously adapted to freeze bakery products. These units are designed so that metered groups of products or packages are pushed onto plates contacting refrigerant coils. After loading is completed, another refrigerated plate is brought down on top of the products so that the product contacts freezing surfaces on both sides. This equipment is mostly restricted to hardening ice cream, freezing packaged fruits and vegetables, etc.

FREEZING AND OTHER SPECIAL PRESERVATION METHODS 509

They have been tried with some bakery products and may be in use for those products.

Mechanical freezing systems used for bakery foods vary in complexity of design from simple holding rooms to fully automatic conveying arrangements. The simplest method of freezing baked goods is to place the products on large wheeled racks which are moved into a freezing room or a tunnel provided with powerful fans that blow cold air over and around the goods. A common airblast temperature is −20°F. The lowest practical temperature for a mechanical freezer system is about −40°F. Probably the simplest type of semiautomatic freezing is the buggy tunnel through which racks are pulled at a fixed rate by a lugged motor-drawn chain. The continuous belt freezer consists of a long metal belt located in the freezing room. Other belt-type freezers carry the product under a large number of cold air outlets. In this design, product is fed onto the conveyor from the makeup line. It is said to be practical for use only with products having a very short freezing time (Smith 1966). Another type of freezer automatically positions product on moving trays which travel through the freezer compartment before discharging the product onto conveyors leading to the packing area (Fig. 25.7).

Arnold Bakers of Port Chester, N.Y., place freshly baked wrapped bread on wheeled racks, each 2 ft wide and 6 ft long holding 450 1-lb loaves. As soon as the temperature of the bread falls to about 80°F, the wheeled racks are pushed into a −22°F freezing room equipped with "No-Frost" Niagara Blower coolers. Cold air is delivered into a plenum

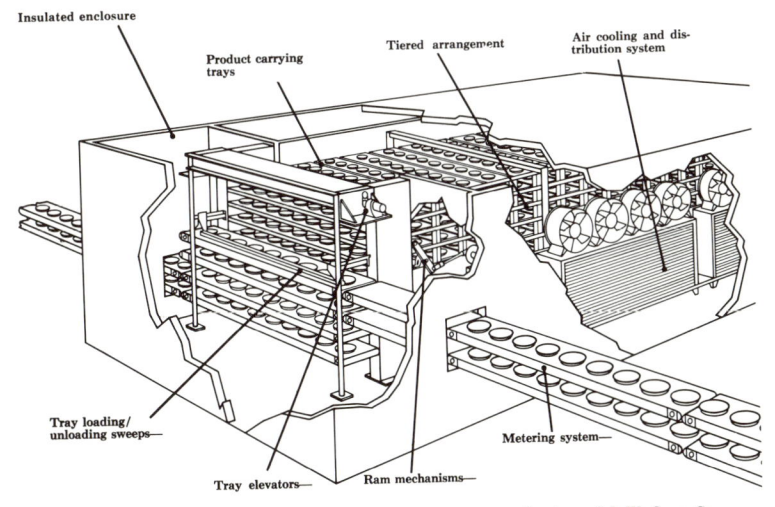

Courtesy of J. W. Greer Co.

FIG. 25.7. A FULLY AUTOMATIC MULTITRAY FREEZER.

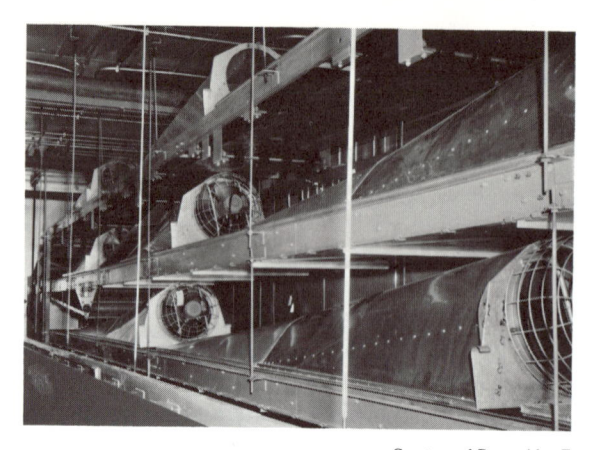

Courtesy of Pepperidge Farm, Inc.
FIG. 25.8. BLOWERS AND DUCTS IN A YORK FREEZER DESIGNED FOR THE FREEZING OF UNBAKED PASTRY.

over a false ceiling. Fans located at the corners of the aisles formed by the bread racks distribute the air uniformly through the racks. When this room, which measures 40 ft by 40 ft, is fully loaded with bread, 4-6 hr are required for freezing.

When the bread is frozen, the racks are wheeled out into a packing room where it is packed into sealed cartons for shipment or storage. This packing room is dehumidified and maintained at about 45°F so as to prevent condensation of moisture on the wrapped bread.

The York Corporation has cooperated with Union Steel Products in the development of a freezer (no longer available) capable of handling simultaneously a variety of baked goods (Fig. 25.8) (Anon. 1956). The use of this continuous automatic freezer eliminates most of the labor required for the handling of bread frozen on racks. Wrapped or packaged baked goods roll onto the conveyor entering the freezer, move slowly through the freezing tunnel until frozen, and then leave the freezer on a conveyor which transports them into cold storage.

Figure 25.9 shows the rate of reduction of temperature of bread conveyed through the York-Union freezer operating at $-30°F$; both the temperature of the "core" (center) and the "skin" (crust) of the loaf are given. As ordinarily operated, temperature of the bread is reduced to 15°–20°F in the continuous freezer, then packed in fiberboard shipping containers and placed in 0°F storage until needed for shipment. Here the temperature of the bread drops to that of the storage room within a few hours.

The York-Union freezer is also used to freeze wrapped doughnuts, cinnamon rolls, finger rolls, Danish buns, and pound and other small

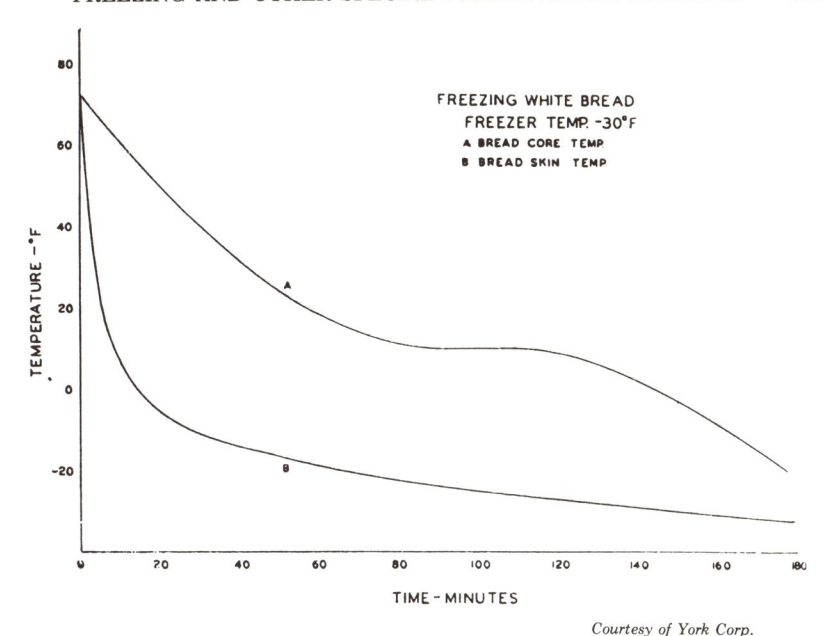

FIG. 25.9. RATE OF FREEZING OF WRAPPED BREAD IN YORK-UNION CONTINUOUS FREEZER.

Courtesy of York Corp.

cakes. The freezing rates of these specialties are indicated in Fig. 25.10.

Another type of freezer loads metered groups of pans or trays by pushing them onto trays or racks with rams (Fig. 25.7). The shelf or rack is then carried through the freezer by a conveying system and returned to the vicinity of the loading station where removal is accomplished by rakes and a cross-conveyor. The loading and conveying systems are very similar to those used in certain continuous proofers.

Cryogenic Freezing[3]

The second major category of food freezing equipment is the so-called cryogenic type, which relies on liquid nitrogen as the source of cold. The nitrogen is purchased from firms which liquefy air and separate the oxygen for use in steel mills, welding, etc. Liquid nitrogen is to some extent a by-product. If the nitrogen were relied upon to cover all the charges of its production, its cost would probably be excessive for most food freezing applications.

Other low temperature liquids have been suggested, but only nitrogen has attained widespread use. Oxygen is out of the question be-

---

[3] Most of this section is based on material supplied by Conroy (1971).

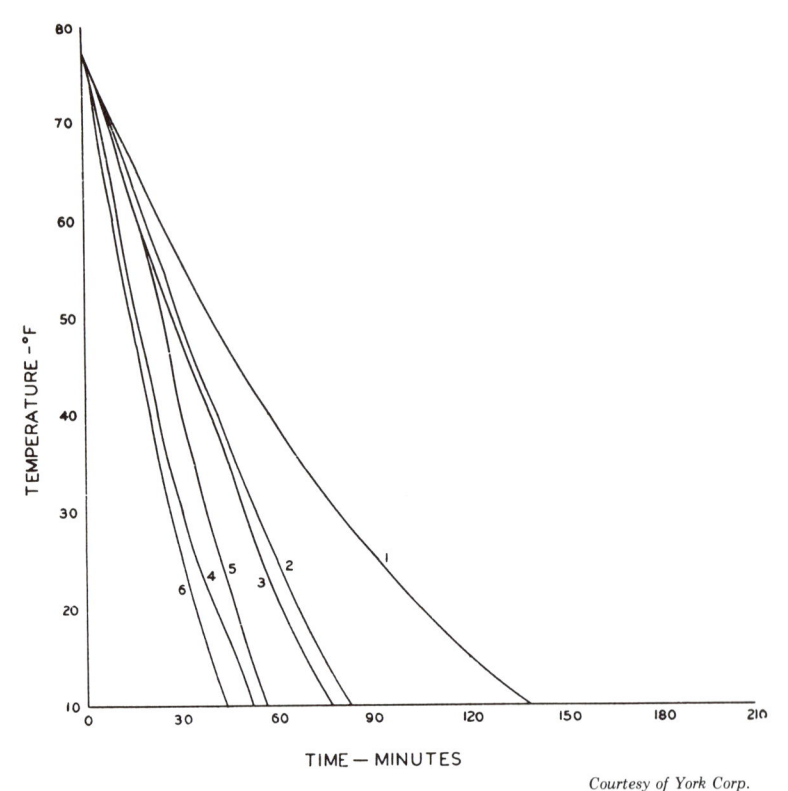

FIG. 25.10. FREEZING RATES OF WRAPPED DOUGHNUTS, CINNAMON ROLLS, AND OTHER SPECIALTIES IN A YORK-UNION CONTINUOUS FREEZER AT $-30°F$.

cause of its extreme reactivity. Carbon dioxide cannot be made a liquid at atmospheric pressures, and application in solid form (as snow) is very difficult to implement. Carbon dioxide in gas form requires pressure vessels which are expensive. None of the other gases or liquids which might be used are cheap enough to apply in a system which does not have recycling means, and the introduction of recycling increases capital costs tremendously. Nitrogen also has another clearcut advantage for use on foods since it is obviously nontoxic, constituting about ⅘ of the atmosphere.

Cryogenic freezing depends upon the initial low temperature and high evaporation rates of liquid nitrogen. Nitrogen has a boiling point of $-320°F$ at atmospheric pressure, but it can be stored and transported in specially constructed Dewar-type containers with only moderate losses from evaporation. In going from a liquid to a gas at $-320°F$, a pound of nitrogen absorbs 86 Btu. Each pound of gas takes up 80 Btu in going from $-320°F$ to $0°F$. The total available freezing capacity obtained by bringing a liquid at $-320°F$ to a gas at $0°F$ is roughly equivalent to the amount needed to freeze 1–2 lb of food. Liquid nitrogen currently costs about $1.75–$2.50 per cwt depending on location and volume.

In some of the original experiments on freezing with liquid nitrogen, the food was immersed in the fluid. Although extremely rapid freezing occurred, some disadvantages were noted. Violent boiling at the interface resulted in reduced contact between the article and nitrogen. Products cracked and surface layers peeled off because of thermal shock and the violent contraction of the outer surface. The refrigeration available in the gas was not fully utilized.

These observations led to the development of systems in which the products were precooled with nitrogen gas and then either sprayed with liquid nitrogen or completely frozen by the gas.

The mechanical part of the installation consists of a conveying system, usually a wiremesh belt, operating inside an insulated tunnel. In order to take full advantage of the refrigerant capacity of the cold gas, a recirculating system is used to move it at high velocity over the product. The point of exhaust of the gaseous nitrogen is toward the entrance. It is not economical to recycle the gas, i.e., reliquefy it, so the relatively warm gas is vented to the atmosphere. Actually, the exhaust gas is often near $-100°F$ even from fairly efficient freezers.

As the product travels through the freezer, it encounters continually colder gas temperatures until it passes through the spray zone which is held near $-320°F$. One measure of the process efficiency is the temperature of the exhaust gas. Experience has shown that efficiency is improved by insulating the inlet and exit conveyors and by cooling the food with gas directly from the recirculation blowers. The length of the conveyor system is not as critical for products with a large surface-to-volume ratio as it is for dense products; but even so, some precooling is required.

One type of installation which has been commercially successful is the Cryotransfer process of the Liquid Carbonic Co. (Fig. 25.11 and 25.12). In this equipment, liquid nitrogen from the supply tank flows directly into an external, vacuum-insulated nitrogen reservoir or sump at the exit end of the freezer. Liquid is usually pressurized at 10–20 psig at the storage tank, sufficient to transfer the liquid under conditions existing in the usual installation. A centrifugal pump in the external reservoir pressurizes the liquid nitrogen (now at $-320°F$ and atmospheric pressure) to 5–7 psig and pumps the liquid into spray manifolds above and below the product. Nitrogen which remains liquid after spraying is accumulated in a collector pan and flows back into the external reservoir for recirculation. Integration of this unit into a pie processing line is shown in Fig. 25.13.

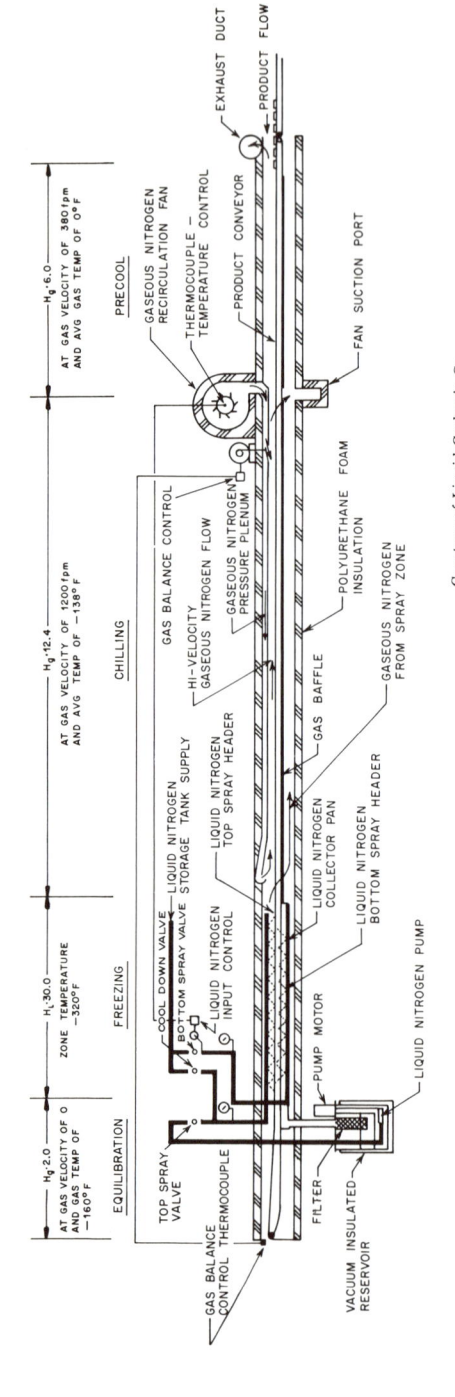

514   BAKERY TECHNOLOGY AND ENGINEERING

FIG. 25.11. Schematic Diagram of Cryotransfer Freezer. 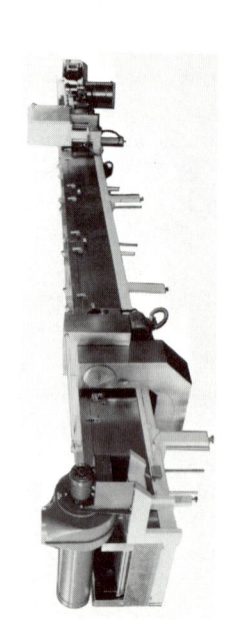
Courtesy of Liquid Carbonic Co.

FIG. 25.12. A Cryotransfer Freezing Unit.
Courtesy of Liquid Carbonic Co.

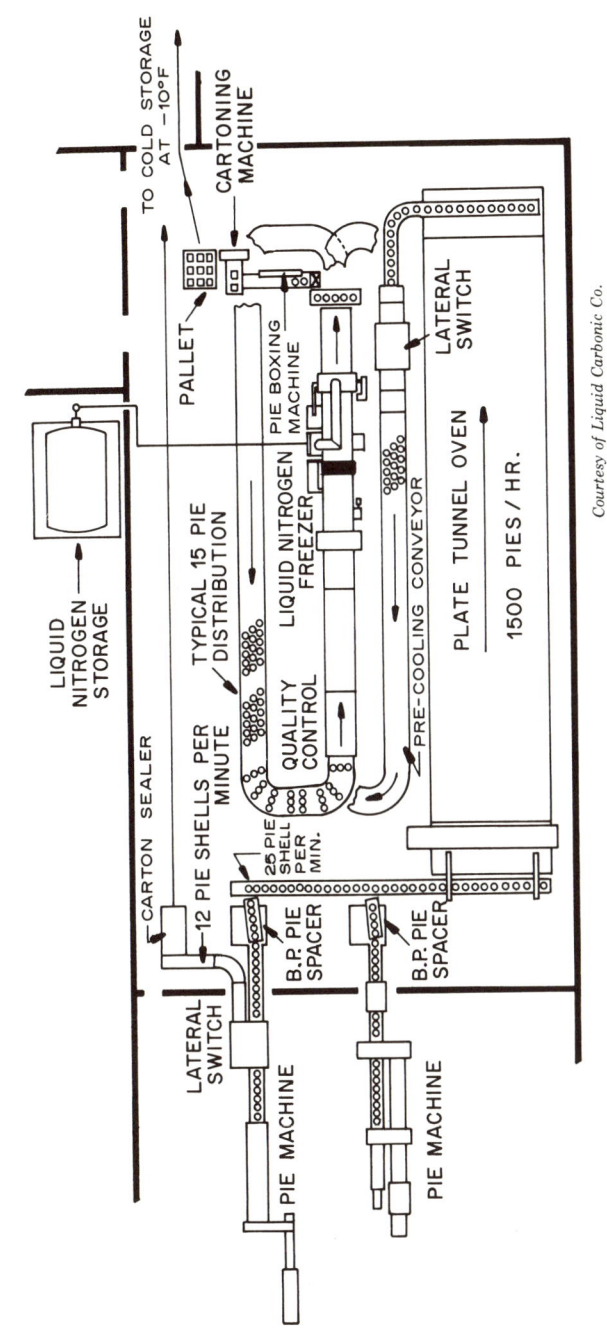

FREEZING AND OTHER SPECIAL PRESERVATION METHODS 515

FIG. 25.13. LIQUID NITROGEN PIE FREEZING OPERATION.

Courtesy of Liquid Carbonic Co.

Certain advantages are claimed for this manner of introducing the refrigerant. The nitrogen is allowed to reach a saturated liquid state at a pressure of one atmosphere prior to being pumped into the spray headers. The small amount of heat introduced by the pump is extracted by heat exchange to the low pressure liquid in the external reservoir as a result of the submerged discharge line of the pump acting as a heat exchanger. The subcooled liquid nitrogen eliminates vapor formation in the spray headers within the chamber. The resulting single phase liquid spray keeps the surface of the food product enveloped with liquid nitrogen droplets, achieving rapid heat transfer. Complete separation of the liquid and gaseous phases is accomplished and the flashed gas is employed in a separate high velocity circulation system.

A device for accurate metering of refrigerant to the system is not required. As liquid nitrogen is vaporized by the freezing process, the level of liquid drops in the external reservoir and additional refrigerant is added to the system. In effect, the heat load of the product entering the freezer automatically determines the demand for liquid nitrogen.

One of the major cost considerations in operating a cryogenic freezing system is the amount of refrigerant required to cool the equipment down to the desired temperature at the start of operations. This can represent a substantial percentage of the total refrigerant usage if the system is operated intermittently; and it is advisable to operate the equipment around the clock seven days a week, if possible.

There has been much disagreement about the difference in cost (per pound of product frozen) between mechanical blast freezing and liquid nitrogen freezing. Some estimates seem to show an advantage for nitrogen freezing in certain circumstances, but it is generally agreed that costs of operation per pound of product frozen are less for mechanical freezing installations. For example, Drake (1970) claimed a cost of 0.324¢ per lb of dough for blast freezers versus 0.751¢ for liquid nitrogen spray, based on 1 million cases per year and taking all known factors into consideration. The cost of nitrogen is the major variable and it is highly dependent on location and volume. On the other hand, capital expenditures for liquid nitrogen freezers are much less than for blast freezers of equivalent capacity. Space requirements are also less.

The real advantage of cryogenic processing is the improved product quality which results from extremely rapid freezing (Table 25.4). Although the advantages of rapid freezing may be greater for particularly sensitive products such as shrimp and strawberries than for bread and similar baked products, the improvement in quality is demonstrable even in the latter. For example, cryogenic freezing confers the following benefits: (1) The product is rapidly brought through the zone of maximum texture staling, 70°–20°F, so that minimal starch retrogradation occurs and the original softness is retained. (2) Proliferation of spoilage microorganisms, such as can occur in cream fillings, is greatly reduced. (3) Original flavor is sealed in by rapid surface hardening. (4) Dehydration is reduced. (5) Crystal size of the ice is smaller and more uniform.

It is known that the faster heat is removed, the smaller the ice crystals which form. Although this phenomenon is very important in such natural cellular material as fruits and muscle tissue because of the destruction of the texture caused by the large ice crystals, it is not as important in products such as bread and cake. Not only is the structure less subject to texture damage because of the absence of semipermeable cell walls, but the amount of free water is so low that the crystals which do form are very small even if the freezing is slow. Perhaps more important is the slow growth of these crystals during storage as a result of the transfer of water in the vapor phase. The relatively large crystals tend to grow at the expense of the small crystals, leading to the possible occurrence of soggy spots and dehydrated spots when the product is thawed. One way to prevent this is by very rapid freezing to establish a load of uniform crystals with no large ones present. Freezing of 1 hr versus 4 hr makes very little difference in crystal size. Freezing in a matter of minutes makes a considerable difference and this is the reason liquid nitrogen freezing has some definite advantages, especially significant with foods of relatively high moisture content.

Ice crystal size is particularly important in high-moisture products such as fruit fillings, custards, cheesecake, etc. Large ice crystals tend to cause a greater breakdown of the structure of the fruit and the gels. When the product is thawed, pie fillings will be less viscous, the fruit will be mushy instead of firm, and cheesecakes may have a granular texture.

Trucks can be fitted with liquid nitrogen systems to hold low tempera-

TABLE 25.4
FREEZING RATE FOR TYPICAL FOODS

Food	Conventional (−30°F Air Blast) (Min)	Liquid Nitrogen
Fish sticks	13	40 sec
Pizzas	24	1½ Min.
Entrées	130	5 Min.
Coffee cakes	46	1 Min.
Chicken pot pies	90	5 Min.
Beef patties	16	1½ Min.

Source: Liquid Carbonic Co.

tures while transporting frozen foods. The essential parts of the system are a tank of liquid nitrogen, a line of tubing to carry the liquid, and spray heads within the truck. The expanding nitrogen inside the cylinder creates enough pressure to force the liquid through the line and out the spray nozzles. To make the system practical, it is necessary to add valves with either thermostatic or manual controls, and safety devices to close the valves when the doors are opened. If the controls are manually operated, there will be a remote-indicating thermometer scale mounted where the driver can see it, so that he can adjust the temperature by means of control switches in the cab.

Another design of nitrogen-cooled truck, cold wall trailer, does not use spray heads inside the storage compartment. Instead, the refrigerant gas circulates between the double walls of the truck. The entire inside wall of the compartment then becomes the cooling surface.

Packaging

Much of the decline in quality of products during frozen storage can be traced to moisture loss. Drying has adverse effects on color, texture, and flavor. The interior tends to become harsh and tough or crumbly and the crust becomes dull and sometimes color changes occur. Cream fillings may develop gumminess or crack, icings craze and become dull, and whipped toppings lose volume. Moisture-vapor transfer can be largely prevented by proper packaging. Texture changes of a more complex sort, as well as a decline in yeast viability in unbaked products, also affect quality but there is not much that packaging can do to prevent these changes.

Moisture loss from the product is largely attributable to the low content of moisture in the chilled air as it flows from the evaporator coils. Although the relative humidity at that point is high, even approaching saturation, the absolute moisture content is low, and any appreciable warming of the air, as is bound to occur in a storage area, will bring the relative humidity to a low level. This relatively dry air expedites water-vapor loss from the product unless it is sealed in a substantially impervious package. The long times that some frozen bakery foods remain in the storage and distribution systems also predispose to drying.

If moisture loss is excessive, underweight packages may be delivered to the customer. For an item weighing 1 lb, loss of 2% moisture means a reduction of about ⅓ oz in the net weight. Mass-produced products often do not have this large a safety margin in their total weight, at least on an average. Loss of 2% moisture during frozen storage is well within the range of possibilities.

Paperboard itself offers very little protection against moisture-vapor transfer. Aluminum foil is excellent in this regard and is also an excellent heat transfer material—a good characteristic when the product is being frozen and a negative one while it is being shipped and displayed (when some insulation value is desirable).

If possible, the packaging material should also provide a barrier against loss (or absorption) of odors. Vanillin and many other aromatic flavors dissipate fairly rapidly, even at freezer temperatures, unless some barrier is interposed. Once again, foil is at the top of the list in protection. Plastic films are not particularly effective, although the flavor retention varies depending on the chemical properties of the aromatic substances. The package itself can contribute off-odors to the product. Some of the more frequent causes of off-odors from cartons and films are use of recycled paper, insufficient removal of ink solvents, and rancidity development by the fat that soaks into the board.

Claims are sometimes made that packaging can delay the development of rancidity by inhibiting the entry of oxygen. Unless the package is hermetically sealed in a material having a very low oxygen transmission rate, however, the practical effect is very slight. Even under these circumstances, the package should be nitrogen-flushed or vacuumized if substantial benefits are to be obtained.

Unbaked products, such as bread doughs, are often packed in printed bags of 5 mil polyethylene, after freezing. This is the sale package. Multiples are packed for shipping in A-fluted special construction corrugated cases with moisture-resistant adhesive and they are date coded.

It is obvious that the total package must have enough mechanical strength to protect the contents against crushing during normal handling. Films are of very little help in this regard, but they can protect the basic structural material against puncture, tears, and abrasion so that the package remains intact after encountering these kinds of damage. Plastic films which are pliable and tough at freezer temperatures, such as certain kinds of polyethylene and polypropylene, and foil are of particular value. Most board materials stiffen as the temperature decreases, and their strength is reduced by moisture penetration. Carton strength can be increased by increasing board thickness, reinforcing the corners, peripheral gluing of the end panel, and the use of double walls.

The carton should be of a size to minimize head space. Excessive free space within the carton not only acts as insulation slowing down the freezing rate, but allows faster dehydration.

If transparent panels are part of the package, they must be of film treated to prevent fogging. Polyvinylidene-coated Cellophane or styrene, or polyvinylidene-coated polyesters are used most often.

HEAT-TREATMENT IN HERMETICALLY SEALED CONTAINERS

Bakery products can be preserved by enclosing them in hermetically sealed containers and giving them a heat treatment. Although some flexible pouches have been used, especially for military rations, the usual container is a metal can. The initial impetus for mass production of canned items came from the Armed Forces, since the container and method are relatively expensive compared to conventional means of processing. There are some commercial applications, however, especially for gourmet cakes, campers' rations, and other uses where a long storage life is needed.

Canning also offers a method by which special dietary breads and sweet goods can be distributed to persons requiring these special foods. Low-sodium bread, gluten-free bakery foods, and diabetic goods are seldom available at the local grocery because of the limited demand, and purchasers are faced with the prospect of making long trips to obtain them. The frequency of these trips can be greatly reduced by purchasing a large quantity at one time, but this is feasible only if the products have a long shelf-life. Canning provides the needed stability. These products can also be distributed through the mail, a route which is not practical for conventionally packaged goods.

It is impossible to bake doughs and batters inside sealed cans because of the gas evolution which occurs.[4] Baking in open cans, followed by sealing, leads to the possibility of contaminants entering the container subsequent to heat treatment and prior to closing. Baking in open cans, then sealing, and finally subjecting to a sterilizing heat treatment leads to severe damage in almost all bakery products.

A system which was found to be practical for large-scale production using a minimum of specially-designed equipment involves the following steps: (1) The dough piece is proofed in an unsealed can until it reaches a volume known to yield a baked product that completely fills the container. (2) A lid is loosely clinched on the can, leaving a passage-way for egress of gases but effectively confining the dough completely within the can as it continues to expand. (3) The can and its contents are baked in a conventional oven for a predetermined time. (4) Immediately upon removal from the oven the sealing is completed, so as to minimize the entrance of contaminants and ensure the development of a high vacuum as the contents cool to room temperature. (5) The can is quickly cooled to prevent heat damage in the product.

---

[4] Recent work at Natick laboratories has resulted in the development of practical techniques of baking (processing) in sealed cans. By careful control of the amount of leavening and moisture, reduced from the normal, and sealing the unbaked dough or batter under vacuum, a good product can be achieved. The technique has not been tried on a commercial scale as yet.

Canning is by no means a perfect preservation method, but it does confer some protection to bakery products. For example, it prevents moisture loss, mechanical damage, and contamination by microorganisms and other particles. It also protects against absorption of odors from the environment. If the contents are under a partial vacuum or in an atmosphere of carbon dioxide, oxidative changes can be minimized. Texture changes due to starch retrogradation, and flavor changes (due to non-enzymatic browning, for example), as well as some other deteriorative reactions can be expected to proceed at the normal rate. A negative feature is the necessity for the product to conform to the contours of the can which results in a nontypical appearance that may antagonize the consumer.

Temperatures reached inside masses of dough or batter during conventional baking procedures are not adequate for destroying the spores of some food poisoning organisms. In ordinary canning, as of corn and meats, much longer times and much higher temperatures are applied to give practical sterility, while acidic products, such as tomatoes and most fruits, can be safely processed at lower temperatures and for shorter periods of time. The potential hazard to consumers arising from the mild treatments which could be applied to canned bakery products was recognized by personnel at the Quartermaster Food and Container Institute for the Armed Forces and many studies were conducted to define conditions under which these products should be packed and stored.

In canned cakes and other products with high sugar contents, the relatively low water activity of the crumb normally prevents growth of bacteria or germination of their spores. Most authorities regard soluble solids contents above 72% to be completely inhibitory. In canned bread, this safe level is not reached.

One particular heat-resistant species of bacteria, *Clostridium botulinum*, is potentially extremely toxic in canned bread, as in many other foods. These bacteria are frequently found in soil and airborne dust and, therefore, may be present in several of the ingredients used in the manufacture of canned bread. The bacteria or spore, in itself, is harmless; however, when conditions are favorable for the germination of this spore, a highly poisonous toxin is produced by the growing bacteria. Consumption of a food containing this lethal toxin by a human or other warm-blooded animal produces the illness botulism, which can, and usually does, result in death.

Two solutions to this toxicity problem are potentially feasible: (1) process the canned bread with sufficient heat to destroy the bacteria and its spores, as is standard practice in most canned foods (canned meats, for example), or (2) modify the formula and conditions within the canned bread so that the bacteria or spore, if present, cannot germinate and produce toxin (modify the pH, for example).

While canned bread is baked in a 400°–450°F oven, the temperature within the loaf never exceeds 210°F during baking. Since a temperature of 250°F for approximately 3 min is required to destroy the botulinum spores, baking cannot accomplish sterilization. Research demonstrated that heat processing of canned bread in a retort (under high pressure, high temperature steam) to sterilize the baked bread produced objectionable discoloration and off-flavors rendering the product unacceptable.

The second alternative proved more promising. Bacteriological research sponsored by the Quartermaster Corps demonstrated that *Cl. botulinum* spores in canned bread of moisture contents of 35.0% or less, regardless of pH, would not germinate and produce toxin. In addition, this research demonstrated that *Cl. botulinum* spores in canned bread of pH 4.8 or less, regardless of moisture content, would not germinate and produce toxin. Consequently, the military canned bread product is manufactured in such a manner as to yield a finished product containing less than 35.0% moisture and a pH value of 4.8 or less, thereby providing bacteriological safety.

To ensure bacteriological safety during storage it is necessary that the bacteriological inhibiting properties of the finished product (sugar solids contents in canned poundcake, fruitcake, and pecan roll and the moisture content and pH value in canned bread) do not change. Imperfectly sealed tin cans would afford opportunity for change in these critical factors. To preclude this hazard all canned baked products are subjected to the "flip-testing" operation to screen out imperfectly sealed tin cans.

The preservation of canned bakery foods thus is dependent upon four factors: (1) Adequate heat treatment during a baking step. (2) Proper timing of the final sealing operation so as to establish a vacuum within the can. (3) Formulating to maintain a suitable water activity in the finished product. (4) Maintaining the pH of the crumb at a suitable level.

Of course, an initial low load of food poisoning organisms must be assured by proper sanitary procedures, as in all preservation methods.

Procedures and Equipment for Canned Bakery Products[5]

The principal modification in manufacturing canned baked products is that these products are baked in tin cans rather than in the customary baking pans. Canned baked products utilize standard bakery ingre-

---

[5] Adapted from an article by McWilliams (1960).

FREEZING AND OTHER SPECIAL PRESERVATION METHODS 523

Courtesy of Kroger Baking Co.
FIG. 25.14. CAN LIDS BEING LOOSELY CLINCHED ON CANS OF BAKED PRODUCTS PRIOR TO PLACING THE CANS IN THE OVEN.

dients and conventional mixing and processing machinery. The resulting dough or batter is deposited into the tin cans and the can lid is then loosely clinched into place by a can-sealing machine (Fig. 25.14). The loosely-clinched lid permits escape of leavening gases and steam evolved during baking in the standard baking oven (Fig. 25.15). Canned baked products may be baked in either a tunnel or tray oven; if baked in a tray oven, the use of wire baskets to keep cans evenly spaced during baking is advisable.

Immediately upon removal from the oven, the tin cans, with loosely-clinched lids, are hermetically sealed by an automatic can-sealing machine (Fig. 25.16). As the sealed can and its contents cool, the steam atmosphere within the can condenses, creating a natural, high vacuum. A high internal vacuum of not less than 25 in. of mercury is

524 BAKERY TECHNOLOGY AND ENGINEERING

FIG. 25.15. CANNED DOUGH PRODUCTS BEING LOADED INTO THE OVEN.

Courtesy of Kroger Baking Co.
FIG. 25.16. SEALING THE LIDS ON CANS OF BAKED PRODUCTS IMMEDIATELY AFTER REMOVING THEM FROM THE OVEN.

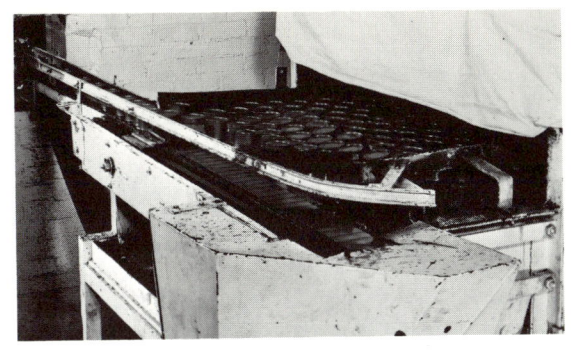

FREEZING AND OTHER SPECIAL PRESERVATION METHODS 525

Courtesy of Kroger Baking Co.
FIG. 25.17. CANNED BAKED PRODUCTS ENTERING WATER SPRAY COOLER IMMEDIATELY FOLLOWING CAN SEALING.

TABLE 25.5
SPECIFIC HEAT OF BAKERY PRODUCTS

Product	Moisture (%)	Latent Heat of Fusion (Btu/Lb)	Specific Heat above 32°F (Btu/Lb/°F)	Specific Heat below 32°F (Btu/Lb/°F)
Bread	36	52	0.60	0.28
Coffee cake	27	39	0.54	0.25
Layer cake	28	40.5	0.545	0.255
Cake doughnuts	22	32	0.51	0.235
Cheesecake	61	88	0.755	0.37
Pound Cake	22	32	0.51	0.235
Yeast-raised doughnuts	34	49	0.584	0.275
Danish pastry	24	35	0.52	0.245
Devil's food cake	29	42	0.55	0.26
Chiffon cake	34	49	0.584	0.275

Source: Liquid Carbonic Co.

necessary to preserve natural flavors and to prevent can corrosion during storage. In order to achieve this high internal vacuum, can sealing must be accomplished within 60 sec after removal of the can from the oven. Thus, removal of cans from the oven must be carefully coordinated with can sealing.

Following this sealing operation, the canned baked products are rapidly cooled. Unless cooling is accomplished quickly, the color and flavor of the product in the can is impaired by "auto-baking." Rapid cooling may be accomplished in several ways, namely: (1) exposure (on rack) to fan-driven, rapidly moving air streams, (2) passage through a water spray tunnel, as shown in Fig. 25.17, or (3) immersion in running cold water.

To make certain that the can is perfectly sealed and possesses a high internal vacuum, the cooled can is run through an additional automatic machine known as a "flip-tester" (Fig. 25.18) which determines the

526   BAKERY TECHNOLOGY AND ENGINEERING

Courtesy of Kroger Baking Co.

FIG. 25.18. CANNED BAKED PRODUCTS BEING PASSED THROUGH "FLIP-TESTER" PRIOR TO BEING PACKED INTO CARTONS.

presence or absence of vacuum within the can in the following manner. One end of the can (usually the top end) is placed under a close-fitting, rubber-seated bell. A 27- or 28-in. vacuum is applied within the bell above the can end by means of a vacuum pump. When the vacuum within the bell exceeds the vacuum within the can by 5–6 in., the can lid bulges outward like the head of a drum producing an audible "flip." This outward bulging of the can lid activates a mechanism which rejects this can from the moving line. Cans possessing little or no vacuum are rejected as "mis-seals" or "leakers." The lids on cans having internal vacuums in excess of 20 in., of course, will not bulge outward and will, therefore, pass through the machine as acceptable. After flip-testing the clean dry cans are packed into containers for shipment.

Tin cans used for manufacturing canned baked products may be purchased from any of several can manufacturers. The tin cans should be enamelled internally with a lacquer known among can manufacturers as "C" enamel to eliminate can corrosion after baking. Tin cans may also be enamelled or lithographed externally. The darker the color of the can exterior the better will be its baking characteristics because dark colors absorb heat while light colors reflect heat.

Can clinching, can sealing and flip-testing equipment is fully automatic and operates at production rates of from 60 to 180 cans per minute. Even greater production rates can be obtained by installing supplementary canning machinery. These can-processing machines are obtainable from can manufacturers on a rental basis or by purchase.

Possible formulations and processing steps for individual canned baked products are exemplified by bakery foods included in military rations: (1) canned white bread, (2) canned poundcake, (3) canned fruitcake, and (4) canned pecan roll described as follows:

The military canned white bread in four can sizes, is defined in the current revision of Military Specification MIL-B-1070, "Bread, Canned." Manufacture of the military canned white bread utilizes a bleached and matured, enriched hard winter wheat flour, compressed yeast (or equivalent of active dry yeast), salt, and sugar (cane, beet, or corn). Less common bakery ingredients in the formulation are D-sorbitol and edible lactic acid (to increase acidity and improve keeping properties of canned bread), inactive dry yeast (for added vitamin fortification), and a special rancidity-resistant shortening known as "100-hr shortening." A large percentage of shortening is employed in the formulation to provide a high calorie content in the canned bread and to soften the crumb so that the effects of texture staling are less obvious.

Absorption in the dough is held at 50% or less to facilitate achieving a finished baked bread moisture content of 35% or less to assure adequate keeping properties. The formula utilized in the military canned bread is listed as follows:

Ingredients	Parts by Weight
Hard wheat flour enriched	100.00
Water, not more than	50.00
Compressed yeast	2.00
Salt	1.75
Sugar (cane, beet, or corn)	0.50
Shortening	20.00
D-sorbitol	7.00
Edible lactic acid (80%)	0.30
Inactive dry yeast	1.50

Military canned bread is made by the 100% sponge process. All of the sifted flour, water, and yeast are combined into a sponge using a moderate amount of mixing in the customary manner. Temperature of the sponge at completion of mixing is held between 78° and 82°F. The sponge is fermented for not less than 3 hr in an air-conditioned fermentation room or in a cabinet fermentation box. Prior to combining with the sponge, the balance of the canned bread ingredients (sugar, shortening, D-sorbitol, salt, and lactic acid) are mixed into a creamed mass to achieve even distribution of the ingredients in the dough. The fermented sponge is then placed in the mixer, combined with the creamed mass, and mixed at high speed until the gluten is fully developed. Temperature of the resulting dough is controlled by use of ice water or brine in the cooling jacket of the mixer so that the dough, when dumped from the mixer, does not exceed 86°F.

Without floor time, the canned bread dough is then divided into dough pieces of the proper weight. The standard commercial dough divider capable of scaling uniform 10-oz dough pieces is satisfactory for the 401 × 441 can size. For the smaller can sizes, an automatic bun divider is required. Alternatively, 2 5-oz pieces, scaled on the bun divider, may be used for the 401 × 411 can size. Can size, scaling weight, and yield of baked bread are summarized in Table 25.6.

After dividing, the dough pieces may be rounded in the standard rounder; however, this operation is not required. Prior to placing in the tin can, the dough pieces are covered by a film of shortening (instead of greasing the cans). This may be accomplished by rotating the dough pieces over a short moving belt coated with melted shortening, under a wide, flexible drag-chain. The dough pieces then are deposited by hand into clean, dry, empty tin cans and the lids are attached in a clinching machine. In this operation the lids are loosely attached by a single or "first-roll" operation. By code markings imprinted on the can lid, the batch number and date of baking are marked on each can.

The cans of bread then are proofed. In order to determine the proper proof, the lids of several control cans for each dough batch are not clinched but merely placed on the cans so that they may be removed for observation. When the proofed dough occupies approximately 50–60% of the total can volume, the cans are loaded into the oven for baking. Proofing must be carefully controlled since underproofing will yield a loaf of bread which does not fill the can completely and overproofing results in a compression streak in the baked loaf. When properly proofed, the canned bread is loaded into the oven for baking. The cans are evenly spaced in the oven (minimum distance between cans approximately 1½ in.). The canned bread is baked at 425°F for 15–35 min, depending upon can size. Procedures on can sealing, cooling, flip-testing and packing have been described.

TABLE 25.6
CAN SIZE, SCALING WEIGHT, AND NET WEIGHT OF CANNED BREAD

Can Size	Scaling Weight (Oz)	Minimum Baked Contents (Oz)
401 x 411	10.0	9.50
300 x 407	5.0	4.50
300 x 308	4.0	3.75
300 x 200	2.0	1.75

FIG. 25.19. CANNED POUND CAKE.

Canned Pound Cake.—The military canned pound cake (see Fig. 25.19), in four can sizes, is defined in the current revision of Military Specification MIL-P-3234, "Pound Cake, Canned."

Ingredients employed in the manufacture of canned pound cake are all common to cake manufacture and include a bleached soft wheat flour, granulated sugar, shortening (rancidity resistant 100-hr type), whole eggs, egg yolks, salt and vanilla flavoring. The formula utilized in the military canned pound cake is listed as follows:

Ingredients	Parts by Weight
Soft wheat flour	25.00
Shortening	25.00
Whole eggs	12.50
Egg yolks	12.50
Granulated sugar	25.00
Salt	(as required)
Vanilla flavoring	(as required)

The pound cake batter is prepared in the normal manner by creaming the shortening with the sugar or flour and then gradually adding the balance of the other ingredients until a smooth homogeneous mixture is obtained.

Prior to filling with batter, the cans are lined with vegetable parchment paper utilizing a die-cut paper disc for the can bottom and a die-cut strip for the can walls. For the 300 x 200 can, a fluted paper cup made from vegetable parchment paper may be used. Cake batter is then deposited into the cans utilizing a can filler or a cake depositer modified to feed tin cans automatically. Can size scaling weight and yield of baked cake are summarized in Table 25.7.

After filling, the lids are loosely attached to the cans in a clinching machine by a single or "first-roll" operation. By code markings im-

530 BAKERY TECHNOLOGY AND ENGINEERING

TABLE 25.7
CAN SIZE, SCALING WEIGHT, AND NET WEIGHT OF CANNED POUND CAKE

Can Size	Scaling Weight (Oz)	Minimum Baked Contents (Oz)
401 x 411	12.5	11.50
307 x 409	8.5	7.75
300 x 308	5.0	4.50
300 x 200	2.5	2.20

FIG. 25.20. CANNED BAKED FRUITCAKE.

printed on the can lid, the batch number and date of baking are marked on each can. The cans are then loaded into the oven for baking at 350°F for 15–40 min, depending upon can size. The cans are evenly spaced in the oven (minimum distance between cans approximately 1½ in.). Procedures on can sealing, cooling, flip-testing and packing are those previously described.

Canned Fruitcake.—The military canned fruitcake (see Fig. 25.20), in four can sizes, is defined by the current revision of Military Specification MIL-F-3232, "Fruitcake, Fresh and Fruitcake, Canned."

Ingredients employed in the manufacture of canned fruitcake are all common to fruitcake manufacture and include bleached hard wheat flour, shortening (rancidity resistant 100-hr type), whole eggs, granulated sugar, salt, vanilla flavoring, water, bleached seedless raisins, diced glacé cherries, diced glacé pineapple, diced glacé citron, diced glacé orange peel, diced glacé lemon peel, and pecan pieces. The formulas used for the cake batter and fruit blend are listed as follows:

Cake Batter

Ingredients	Parts by Weight
Bleached hard wheat flour	24.00
Shortening	18.00

Whole eggs	20.00
Granulated sugar	27.00
Salt	0.75
Vanilla flavoring (approx.)	0.25
Water (approx.)	10.00
Total	100.00

Fruit Blend

Ingredients	Parts by Weight
Raisins, seedless, bleached	25.00
Cherries, diced	25.00
Pineapple, diced	15.00
Citron, diced	7.00
Orange peel, diced	6.00
Lemon peel, diced	2.00
Pecan pieces	20.00
Total	100.00

TABLE 25.8
CAN SIZE, SCALING WEIGHT, AND NET WEIGHT OF FRUITCAKE

Can Size	Scaling Weight (Oz)	Minimum Baked Contents (Oz)
401 x 411	24.50	24.0
300 x 407	12.50	12.0
300 x 308	9.50	9.0
300 x 200	5.25	5.0

The batter for the fruitcake is prepared by creaming the shortening with the sugar or flour and then gradually adding the balance of the other ingredients during mixing until a smooth homogeneous mixture is obtained.

Before blending with the cake batter, the blanched raisins and drained glacé fruits are blended thoroughly with the balance of the fruit-and-nut blend. Cake batter (35 parts) and the fruit-and-nut blend (65 parts) are then mixed thoroughly to yield the finished fruitcake mix.

Prior to filling with fruitcake mix, the cans are lined with vegetable parchment paper utilizing a die-cut paper disc for the can bottom and a die-cut strip for the can walls. For the 200 x 300 can, a fluted paper cup made from vegetable parchment paper may be used. The fruitcake mix is then deposited into the cans utilizing a can filler or a cake depositer modified to feed tin cans automatically. Can size, scaling weights, and yield of baked cake are summarized in Table 25.8.

After filling, the lids are attached loosely to the cans in a clinching machine by a single or "first-roll" operation. By code markings imprinted on the can lid, the batch number and date of baking are marked on each can. The cans are then loaded into the oven for baking at 300°–325°F for 30 min to 2 hr, depending upon can size. During baking, the canned fruitcake should be spaced evenly in the oven (minimum distance between cans approximately 1½ in.). Procedures on can sealing, cooling, flip-testing, and packing are those previously described.

Canned Pecan Roll.—The military canned pecan roll in four can sizes is defined in explicit detail in the current revision of Military Specification MIL-P-35000, "Pecan Roll, Canned."

Ingredients employed in the manufacture of canned pecan roll are all common to yeast-leavened pastry baking and include bleached and matured hard wheat flour, nonfat milk solids, shortening (rancidity resistant 100-hr type), water, compressed yeast (or active dry yeast), granulated sugar, egg yolks, salt, whole eggs, cake crumbs, ground cinnamon, pure vanilla extract and midget pecan pieces. The pecan roll is composed of two distinct portions, i.e., the dough and the filling. The formulas for each are listed as follows:

Dough Formula

Ingredients	Parts by Weight
Hard wheat flour	46.00
Nonfat milk solids	2.00
Water	15.50
Shortening	16.00
Compressed yeast	2.00
Granulated sugar	10.00
Egg yolks	8.00
Salt	0.50
Total	100.00

Filling Formula

Ingredients	Parts by Weight
Granulated sugar	23.00
Whole eggs, frozen	20.00
Shortening	14.00
Ground cinnamon	4.00
Salt	1.00
Pure vanilla extract	1.00
Cake crumbs	25.00
Midget pecan pieces	12.00
Total	100.00

FREEZING AND OTHER SPECIAL PRESERVATION METHODS 533

The pecan roll rough is prepared by a straight dough method. The temperature of the dough is controlled so that it does not exceed 82°F. The dough is given only sufficient fermentation time to relax the flour gluten and achieve optimum machinability.

The pecan roll filling is prepared by blending all ingredients on slow speed in a mixer until a uniform creamed mass is obtained.

The pecan roll dough is continuously sheeted on a mechanical bench (Fig. 25.21) so that the dough sheet is not less than 10 in. wide and a 9 sq in. piece does not weigh more than 1 oz. The filling then is continuously sheeted onto the pecan roll dough and is synchronized so as to yield equal weights of dough and filling over any given surface area. The resulting sheeted dough and filling then is rolled mechanically and continuously in a spiral (as in a cinnamon bun) so that the roll has 6 distinct layers of dough and 5 layers of filling when cut at a right angle to the length of the roll. Cutting to the proper size and weight is accomplished mechanically utilizing a "guillotine" cutter.

Prior to filling, the tin cans are lined with silicone-treated vegetable parchment paper utilizing a die-cut disc for the can bottom and a die-cut strip for the can walls. The raw pecan roll is then placed in the tin can so that the dough strip is parallel to the can wall. Can size, scaling weight, and yield of baked pecan roll are summarized in Table 25.9.

After filling, the lids are attached loosely to the cans in a clinching machine by a single or "first-roll" operation. By code marking imprinted on the can lid, the batch number and the date of baking are marked on each can. The cans are then loaded into the oven for baking at 400°F for 20–60 min, depending upon can size. During baking the cans should be spaced evenly in the oven (minimum distance approxi-

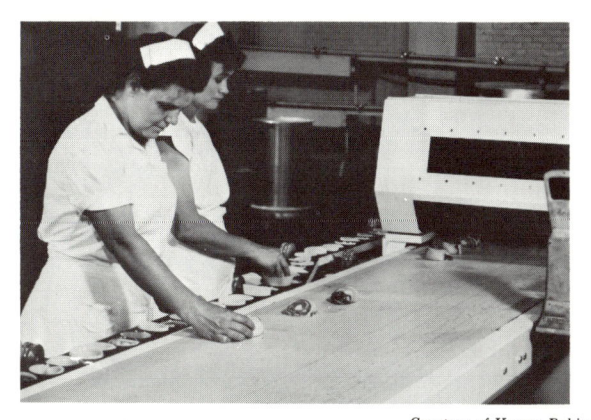

Courtesy of Kroger Baking Co.

FIG. 25.21. PECAN DOUGH CUT INTO PIECES BEFORE BEING PLACED IN PAPER-LINED CANS.

TABLE 25.9
CAN SIZE, SCALING WEIGHT, AND NET WEIGHT OF PECAN ROLL

Can Size	Scaling Weight (Oz)	Minimum baked contents (Oz)
401 x 411	20.50	19.50
300 x 407	10.50	10.00
300 x 308	8.25	8.00
300 x 200	4.50	4.25

mately 1½ in.). Procedures for sealing, cooling, flip-testing, and packing are those previously described.

Packaging in Flexible Pouches

The armed forces conducted the initial and most important experimentation in the packaging of bakery products in hermetically-sealed flexible pouches, just as they did in cans. Flexible pouches have the advantage of better configuration for carrying in pockets and they do not have hard sharp edges to cause injury when the soldier falls on the container.

In a typical preparation method, from 3.5 to 3.75 oz of cake batter are deposited in flexible pouches made of 0.5 mil polyester film, 0.35 mil aluminum foil, and 3.0 mil polyolefin. The polyolefin is U.S. FDA approved material for thermal processing in contact with foods up to 260°F. The pouch is hermetically sealed and processed at 250°F in a retort to both cook and sterilize the product.

Pouches are held vertically in racks which control the thickness of the product. Channels are provided at the sides for circulation of cooking steam and cooling water. Pressure must be closely controlled to allow rising and texture development but prevent bursting of the pouch. Excessive pressure at the end of the cycle would cause compression of the product. Control is accomplished by sensing the deflection of a monitor pouch and relaying the signal to air and steam pressure servomechanisms.

A fully satisfactory bread has apparently not been baked in hermetically-sealed pouches. Thermal reaction of fermentation products which are normally evaporated during baking but retained in the pouch, lead to a dark brown crumb and off-flavors. Westcott (1969) described a chemically-leavened bread which is reasonably well accepted. Other formulation changes to minimize deterioration of flavor and texture during long storage included use of high protein flour and as much sugar and shortening as possible, while reducing or eliminating milk solids. Density of the bread is about twice as great as that of conventional bread.

Compressed and dehydrated bread packed in flexible pouches was also described by Westcott. Compression saves space—a valuable consideration in many military situations—and dehydration not only assists in preservation but also maintains the product in its compressed form. The procedure for making dehydrated compressed bread includes the following steps: (1) Thermal conditioning slices of conventional sponge and dough white bread (without crusts) by steam treating at 10 psig for 10 min. (2) Tempering and equilibrating at 25°F for 18 hr. (3) Compressing and freezing concurrently between platens refrigerated at 0°F. (4) Vacuum freeze-drying to 8–10% moisture. (5) Packaging in a hermetically-sealed pouch made of material substantially impervious to moisture and oxygen. Thickness is reduced by about ⅔ in the compression step.

The slice can be brought to an acceptable condition approximating its original condition by dipping it into a cup of water for 6 sec, then removing the slice and draining away the excess water, and finally allowing the slice to expand and absorb the moisture for about 5–10 min. Some cakes and waffles have been processed in a similar manner.

RADIATION PRESERVATION

The preservation of bakery foods by treating them with ionizing radiation has been the subject of many studies conducted or financed by the armed forces' research facilities. There is no commercial application at this time and U.S. FDA clearance has not been granted.

The goal of irradiation is to destroy food spoilage organisms. Enzymic changes cannot be prevented at practical levels of treatment. Effects on appearance, flavor, and texture are generally unfavorable with browning reactions and stale flavor development often observed. Proper formulation of the baked product and irradiation at low temperatures can minimize these undesirable changes.

To be effective in increasing storage life, the irradiated material must be enclosed in hermetically sealed containers. Both cans and pouches have been used. Glass containers could also be used but appear to have no possible practical advantages.

Treatment has been accomplished by exposing to Cobalt-90 and electron beam irradiation.

BIBLIOGRAPHY

ANON. 1956. How a continuous food freezer handles a variety of bakery items at high speeds. Bakers Weekly *169*, No. 9, 32–35.
ANON. 1962. Freezing unbaked fruit pies. Am. Inst. Baking Bull. *101*.
ANON. 1964. The freezing of commercial bakery products. U.S. Dept. Agr. Marketing Res. Rept. *674*.
BAKER, J. S., and LINDEMAN, C. G. 1967. Packaged preleavened dough containing sodium acid pyrophosphate, and sodium and potassium bicarbonate. U.S. Patent 3,297,449. Jan. 10.

BAEUERLEIN, R. J. 1964. Latest developments in freezing. Proc. Am. Soc. Bakery Engrs. *1964*, 81-86.
BECHTEL, W. G. 1963. Fundamentals of freezing bakery foods, their storage and defrosting. Bakers Weekly *197*, No. 13, 23-24, 33.
CATHCART, W. H. 1941. Further studies on the retardation of the staling of bread by freezing. Cereal Chem. *18*, 771-777.
CATHCART, W. H., and LUBER, S. V. 1939. Freezing as a means of retarding bread staling. Ind. Eng. Chem. *31*, 362-368.
CONROY, J. P. 1971. Personal communication. July 22. Liquid Carbonic Corp., S. 135 LaSalle St., Chicago.
DRAKE, E. 1970. Up-to-date review of freezing. Proc. Am. Soc. Bakery Engrs. *1970*, 60-66.
KATZ, J. R. 1928. Gelatinization and retrogradation of starch in relation to the problem of bread staling. *In* A Comprehensive Survey of Starch Chemistry, Vol. 1, R. P. Walton (Editor). Chemical Catalog Co., New York.
KATZ, J. R. 1934. The staling of bread. Bakers Weekly *81*, No. 3, 43.
KLINE, L., and SUGIHARA, T. F. 1968. Frozen bread doughs. Baker's Dig. *42*, No. 5, 44-47, 49-53, 56-69.
MCINTYRE, D. L. 1965. Liquid nitrogen freezing—comparative economics and practices with other freezing methods. Proc. Am. Soc. Bakery Engrs. *1965*, 131-138.
MCWILLIAMS, C. S. 1960. Canned bakery products. *In* Bakery Technology and Engineering, S. A. Matz (Editor). Avi Publishing Co., Westport, Conn.
PENCE, J. W., and HANAMOTO, M. 1959. Studies on the freezing and defrosting of cakes. Food Technol. *13*, 99-106.
PENCE, J. W., LUBISICH, T. M., MECHAM, D. K., and SMITH, G. S. 1955A. Effects of temperature and air velocity on rate of freezing of commercial bread. Food Technol. *9*, 342-346.
PENCE, J. W., LUBISICH, T. M., STANDRIDGE, N. N., and MECHAM, D. K. 1955B. A progress report on freezing, storage, and defrosting of bread. U.S. Dept. Agr. Mimeo Circ. *ARS-74-4*.
PENCE, J. W. et al. 1955C. Studies on the preservation of bread by freezing. Food Technol. *9*, 495-499.
RYAN, J. P. 1968. Some practical applications of liquid nitrogen freezing. Proc. Am. Soc. Bakery Engrs. *1968*, 131-142.
SMITH, L. 1966. Late developments in freezing methods. Proc. Am. Soc. Bakery Engrs. *1966*, 153-156.
TRESSLER, D. K. 1960. Freezing bakery products. *In* Bakery Technology and Engineering, S. A. Matz (Editor). Avi Publishing Co., Westport, Conn.
WESTCOTT, D. E. 1969. New bakery products for military feeding. Proc. Am. Soc. Bakery Engrs. *1969*, 202-209.
WISEBLATT, L. 1967. Reduction of the microbial populations in flours incorporated into refrigerated doughs. Cereal Chem. *44*, 269-280.

SECTION IV

Technical Functions in Bakery Operations

CHAPTER 26

RESEARCH AND DEVELOPMENT

INTRODUCTION

The distinction between research and development is important, because they have very different orientations and justifications. There are several possible definitions for these two functions, but the ones published by the National Science Foundation (Anon 1963A) are probably the most useful.

"Basic research is research in which the primary aim of the investigator is a fuller knowledge or understanding of the subject under study, rather than a practical application thereof.

"Applied research is directed toward practical application of knowledge and covers research projects which represent investigations directed toward discovery of new scientific knowledge and which have specific commercial objectives with respect to either products or processes.

"Development is the systematic use of scientific knowledge directed toward the production of useful materials, devices, systems or methods, including design and development of prototypes and processes."

There is very little true research being conducted by the baking industry. Technical efforts are directed primarily to the development of specific new products. In the absence of a store of fundamental knowledge constantly supplemented by the results of pioneering investigations, such development work must be based on published research in some related field or on combinations of features and methods already known to be satisfactory. The results of bypassing the research stage are thought to be a reduction in risks and in development costs. Unfortunately, major progress is severely restricted at the same time.

New developments embodying concepts radically different from those which have been used previously are rare in all food industries. There are many possible reasons for the infrequency of appearance of innovation. The idea for a distinctly new product or process is very difficult to come by. Most people do not get even one such flash of genius in their lifetime. The raw material then, is scarce, and, once the idea has been verbalized sufficiently to allow it to be put on paper in an understandable form, few managers have the insight needed to recognize its commercial value. The investment in time and money required to implement a fundamental departure from past practice is likely to be relatively great and the apparent risk correspondingly large. Since no one has done anything like it before, the chances for a good payout look small and, indeed, they usually are. It appears superficially to be much safer to find out what the competitor has produced, then make it red instead of green, cut the price, and advertise it on television.

The potential rewards of a well-directed research program are great, however, and the executive who is far-sighted enough to provide adequate funding for well thought-out projects which may not mature for 5 yr or more is making the best possible investment for his company's future. Research must not be regarded as a miracle drug capable of revivifying an already moribund company. It will not be effective under these desperate conditions. Its most important effects are cumulative and long term. Substantial breakthroughs leading to a unique competitive position can occur only after several years of concentrated, well-directed effort.

Research differs from most other company activities in that there may be no significant achievements for long periods of time and there is great difficulty in assigning a monetary value to the discoveries after they have been made and communicated. The rewards of applied research and product development are easier to visualize and the time span between funding and fruition is generally less. It is not too difficult to justify expenditures which will probably result in the designing of a new item suitable for marketing.

According to Heid (1963), the objectives of applied research and development in the food industry are: (1) To produce, maintain, and increase sales by (a) improving processes, products, and packages, (b) developing new uses for products, and (c) developing new products, processes, and packages, plus testing acceptability of these products. (2) To eliminate losses and hazards of losses (by troubleshooting and by developing profitable utilization of surpluses, residues, and wastes, and by avoiding nuisances, damage suits, etc.) (3) To minimize dependence on raw material in inadequate or undependable supply (as the development of synthetics, improvement in tin-plating procedures, etc.)

(4) To act as technical consultants to top management in evaluating proposed new equipment and processes, keeping management informed of developments of potential interest and importance (in nuclear energy, etc.). (5) To increase the profit on invested capital and on unit sales volume (by ensuring better, more uniform products at lowest possible cost). (6) To deal with governmental agencies in relation to technical matters including labeling, standards of identity and quality, waste disposal, etc.

Other authors regard some of these functions as more appropriate for a quality control or technical service department.

Stability in staffing of the R&D department and the existence of a detailed plan in which the long-term goals of the company are described are among the factors necessary for maximizing the usefulness of R&D. Only a few of the factors contributing to the successful operation of an R&D department can be discussed in this brief chapter. More thorough treatments can be found in the books by Walters (1965) and Stanley and White (1965).

ESTABLISHING A PRODUCT DEVELOPMENT POLICY

To evaluate the effect new products could have in your company's future, existing and expected conditions must be analyzed. The following steps, slightly modified from Rives (1964), can be helpful in this evaluation. (1) Prepare a long-range (5–10 yr) forecast of sales of existing product lines. (2) Prepare a long-range profit plan for the company based on existing product lines. (3) Prepare an inventory of the company's capabilities and resources, including but not restricted to (a) means of distribution, (b) geographical limitations, (c) financial limitations, (d) technical staffing limitations, (e) legal limitations, such as antitrust requirements, and (f) existing equipment. (4) Determine the most favorable market opportunities for new products based on company's capabilities and resources. (5) Prepare a modified long-range profit plan, incorporating the probable effect of new products. (6) Prepare a statement of the new company objectives including the intent of expanding sales and profits through the introduction of new products. (7) Assign new product responsibility and formulate procedures for establishing projects. (8) Provide for evaluation of new product performance.

ADMINISTRATION OF THE RESEARCH AND DEVELOPMENT DEPARTMENT

Relationship of R&D to Other Departments

Because the success of the R&D department is essential to the health of the company and because its goals and methods of operation are unlike those of other departments, it should report directly to the president. In this way its influence can be felt throughout the company and support at the highest level will be continually evident. The filtering of information through a nonscientific channel, such as will occur if R&D is given a more subordinate position, will inevitably result in much slippage and distortion. By making the director of R&D a member of the executive committee, the president and other members can be expected to derive some benefit from the advice and example of a scientist.

There must be a single administrator responsible for all R&D functions. Fragmentation of the individual activities among other departments such as engineering or marketing is extremely inefficient and inappropriate. Process development, process engineering, and package design (with the exception of graphics), as well as product development, must be directed by one administrator in order that the close coordination essential to success in these activities will be possible.

The use of terms such as "research" or "product development" in other than their scientific connotation, as, for example, the use of "research" to denote consumer survey studies conducted by marketing, or "product development" to mean the sales program involved in the introduction of new or modified products, is inexact and may tend to confuse top management. Unless the R&D director is both positive and persistent in making clear to the chief executive the difference between scientific activities and other activities similarly named, confusion will inevitably develop as to the proper role of marketing and R&D in new product development.

It is usually found desirable to restrict the official contacts of the personnel of other departments with R&D personnel to formal channels of communication. Direct contacts at lower echelons can lead to dissemination of erroneous and sometimes harmful information. Many breaches of security in new product development can be traced directly to informal discussions in the laboratory (Wade 1965). Free food also has an overwhelming attraction for many people, and its availability in the R&D area can lead to a stream of distracting visitors unless access to the area is rigidly controlled.

Interior Organization

It is customary to separate the R&D department into a research section, dealing with fundamental problems not directly connected with a marketable product, a development section responsible for product and process development, and an engineering section responsible for implementing on a commercial scale the laboratory or pilot plant processes of the development group. Lines of demarcation are not always clear and there should be no attempt to emphasize the difference between research, development, and engineering lest valuable contributions be ignored because of their unorthodox origin. In smaller companies it may be best to eliminate administrative separation of these functions.

Line organization within the development staff can be formed in at least two distinct ways. Personnel can be divided into administrative groups on the basis of the products or processes dealt with or on the basis of the disciplines involved. By the former method, all persons working with vegetables would be supervised by one person while those concerned with fruits would be in a different group. The latter method would place chemists in one section and bacteriologists in another. There are refinements of these systems which need not concern us at this time. Each method has its advantages and disadvantages, but, in general, the product-oriented scheme is best suited for relatively small companies interested in short-range development projects while the discipline-directed system is better for larger companies with a wide range of interests and a long-term development policy.

Some companies may find that a completely different type of organization is better for them. The system should at least be consistent and it should be predetermined. Allowing groups to form and break up on the basis of short-term projects is a very poor policy.

Budgeting

The establishment of a realistic budget and then holding expenditures within this budget are essential parts of the procedure by which top management is assured that the R&D department is being operated in an efficient and predictable manner. The amount to be allocated to R&D, either in toto or by project, should be settled by conferences in which the desired output is related to company goals and resources.

In practice, allocations for R&D have often been based on a percentage of the previous year's sales, or whatever the competition is spending multiplied by some arbitrary factor. Research differs from many other company activities in that there may be no significant achievements for long periods of time and there is great difficulty in assigning a monetary value to the discoveries which have been made and described. A few science administrators have been extraordinarily successful in creating a kind of mystique which led to such things as the publication of numerous articles recommending a "hands off" style of management and a science-centered administration as the ideals. Tolerance of top management and stockholders of this situation has caused some research directors to reach the mistaken conclusion that no measure of the contribution of research to their company's financial welfare was necessary or even desirable. When hard times come and cost-cutting is required in order to survive, as it was for many companies in 1970 and 1971, such departments were the first to be decimated. Very few companies can afford to support a group of dilettantes, scientific or otherwise, in the current economic climate. Furthermore, the mystique has now been largely taken over by marketing.

Development has been in a somewhat better position. The personnel concerned with development have been expected to produce because their results are highly visible. Development projects are funded with the idea that a payoff will occur within some finite time period. Even here, however, much stricter budgetary controls can be expected in the future with more accurate attribution of development costs to specific products. However unpleasant and unscientific it may seem, the science administrator is going to find that a knowledge of budgeting strategy is essential to the proper performance of his job.

Continuity of the research effort over a period of years is necessary if it is to be efficient. Research expenditures cannot be alternately expanded and contracted without destroying a large part of the department's effectiveness. Shifting goals make for budget uncertainty, and major changes in management objectives during the year should always be accompanied by an immediate R&D assessment (distributed to top management) of the effect the changes will have on expenditures. It is probably better strategy to accept minor changes without attempting to modify the budget.

The budgetary controls involved in R&D can be regarded as being of two basic kinds. Policy controls are concerned with the nature, scope, and direction of the total effort, while operational controls are concerned with planning and evaluating specific projects during their life cycles. Policy, or company strategy, will dictate how much money is to be allowed for the overall R&D activity including administration, depreciation, etc. Out of this total will be allocated amounts for individual projects. It seems that R&D efforts tend to diverge from the predicted path more often than nonresearch activities; and a decision must be made whether to demand a strict accounting in the frame of project goals for money grants, or to allow considerable freedom in fund dispersal as long as progress is being made in the general direction of company goals. There is no single answer which will apply to all firms, but experience seems to indicate the desirability of moderately rigid guidelines, always understanding that technological breakthrough may suddenly establish new requirements which cannot be anticipated.

There are several details which experience has shown to be important. Production time and materials used for experimental runs in the plant should be charged to an R&D account. Allocations should be made in the budget for these runs. Generally, it will be found that some or all of the experimental product can either be recycled or packed off as saleable product, in which case R&D should be credited with the equivalent yield. Indirect costs which are difficult to associate with specific projects include library, telephone, secretarial and clerical salaries, administration, utilities, building depreciation, etc. If charges are to be made for occupancy or similar overhead items, the exact amount should be agreed upon at the beginning of the budgeting period.

To be effective, project controls must alert the manager to any deviation from the plan in achievement, cost, or time. Budget variance provides a comparison between the work which has actually been accomplished and the amount which was planned. A monthly report of expenditures by account is essential to the planning of the department's activities. A budgeting system is inadequate if it does not deliver such reports promptly. The R&D manager should insist upon receiving timely, accurate reports from the accounting department. He should promptly verify all charges by consulting vouchers, payrolls, orders, etc. Any unexplained items should be resolved by consulting with the comptroller.

SYSTEMATIZING NEW PRODUCT DEVELOPMENT

Before development projects can be intelligently assigned, it is necessary that a company plan be set up describing the areas of interest for the present and future. These should be made as narrow as possible to avoid wasted effort. A statement such as "the company is interested in any product that will make a profit" is evidence of an abdication of top management's responsibility to provide necessary guidance. Top management should know the limitations of marketing capabilities, available finance, legal restrictions, plant capacity, and other factors determining the type of product which the company can successfully make and distribute. The more clearly these limitations are set forth, the less is the chance that abortive projects will be initiated.

Within the fields of interest, market research should be asked to identify rather broad areas of marketing opportunities. Generally speaking, it is of doubtful value to ask market research to specify a definite product which is wanted. Desires of the consumer are likely to be amorphous and poorly defined until crystallized by the offer of a finished product. Furthermore, specifications arrived at by consumer research may be impossible of achievement in practice. The better approach is to design a product on the basis of broad guidelines developed by market research. When a superior or different product becomes available because of advances in technology, it is perfectly reasonable for R&D to develop a prototype and then request marketing to determine consumer acceptability of that specific item.

In some cases, it is necessary to reproduce a known item in order to meet competition. Market research will probably have little part in this decision. The originator of the demand will be sales who reports that a competitive product is steadily encroaching on the volume of an existing company item. Sometimes, a strikingly novel and apt idea is suddenly brought forth and management immediately realizes that it represents a substantial opportunity. In other cases, R&D will realize that a new development in technology makes possible the production of an article devoid of some of the objectionable features of existing counterparts. Each of these new product ideas must be fully coordinated with all other departments before a research project is initiated.

There are nearly always more projects recommended than can be adequately funded. Souder (1970) lists four kinds of techniques which have been used, or suggested, for selecting from the list of proposed projects those which should be supported. These are capital budgeting formulas, cost prediction formulas, scoring and ranking methods, and resource allocation methods.

The capital budgeting approaches are standard return on investment and discounted rate of return calculations modified by the inclusion of risk parameters such as the probability of commercial and technical success. A computed value for each project is discounted for the risk. Projects are ranked in order of the resulting values, and successively less promising projects are selected until the total allocation of funds is exhausted. Uncertainties result from the evolutionary nature of a development project which provides constantly changing prospects of success or failure, as well as the effect of competitive R&D activities which may suddenly make the whole project obsolete.

Cost prediction formulas are based on the premise that historical relations exist between the cost of a project and the sales of the resulting product. This is at best a vague relationship suitable for use only when more accurate means are not available.

Scoring and ranking criteria are often used for selecting projects. Numerical values are assigned to several factors, such as product life, patentability, market size, competition, project cost and duration, etc. The raw values or values weighted by some previously chosen factor are summed, and the projects ranked in order of their total scores. The obvious difficulty in these methods is the uncertainty in the assigned values.

Resource allocation techniques are intended to provide bases on which to decide how much to spend for a given project out of a series of projects taking into consideration the total company situation, now and as projected. Data collected from all levels of the organization are submitted to computer analysis to determine the relative value of competing projects funded at various levels.

Sources of Ideas

In a survey of over 150 American companies, Booz, Allen, and Hamilton found that 88% of new product ideas came from within the companies. Marketing together with research and development personnel contributed 60%. Sources of ideas, according to Kill (1965) might be (A) Internal: (1) Sales, advertising, and merchandising staff. (2) R&D personnel. (3) Production and engineering staff. (4) Employee suggestions. (B) External: (1) Consumers' suggestions. (2) Trade suggestions (wholesalers, retailers). (3) Suppliers' suggestions. (4) Competitive products (domestic and foreign). (5) Technical and trade publications. (6) Patents.

Some companies like to distribute suggestion forms among all employees, in the hope that a startling new idea will be elicited. There should be a requirement that the submitter give the reasons why he believes the product or process would be worthwhile.

Ammerman (1963) lists the following possible sources of new product ideas: (1) Company suggestion plans. (2) Request new product ideas from the sales staff and provide a place for them on sales reports. (3) Contests both within and outside the company. (4) Government publications such as the *Product List Circular*, published by the Small Business Administration. (5) Permanent product scouts who travel abroad as well as in the United States looking for new product ideas. (6) Industrial research firms. (7) Market research firm reports. (8) Advertising agencies. (9) Journals and other publications. (10) Consultation with suppliers. (11) Trade fairs. (12) Plant tours.

Brainstorming or group-think sessions with deferred evaluation has had a certain vogue. The validity of such approaches to idea generation has been questioned in a number of experimental research studies. Results seem to indicate that individuals working alone are more effective than groups in producing truly novel but practical ideas. Tauber (1971) described an idea-generating method suitable for use by individuals. He assumed that creativity is a special form of problem-solving in which combinations of words represent product ideas. A list of words representing some important characteristics or concepts associated with existing products is set up in grid or matrix form and all cross-classifications evaluated for desirability or practicality.

The compensation, if any, for a successful idea should be clearly spelled out on the suggestion form. An idea does not become company property merely because the originator has described it to a company representative, even though the submitter may be an employee. Unless the employee has been hired specifically to invent, his inventions do not automatically become company property. If he has used company time and company property to reduce the invention to practice, his employer may acquire a royalty-free license or some other equity. Situations have occurred where a suggestion is made in an apparently off-hand manner by an employee or outsider, and then a claim for compensation presented when the idea is put into practice. For this reason, a clear understanding of the relative rights of each party should be reached at an early stage.

The least productive and most dangerous source of ideas is the outsider who submits an unsolicited suggestion. These are best returned without a review of any kind. It has been suggested that incoming correspondence which might include such suggestions should be screened by a person without technical training who will immediately seal up and return any communication as soon as he becomes aware it contains suggestions for a new product. The reason for these precautions is that a legal liability to the submitter could result from apparent utilization of a suggestion even though a similar idea had earlier occurred to a company agent. Often these suggestions will describe products which are already under development and this creates a very sticky situation indeed. Experience has shown that rarely, if ever, is a useful product developed from an idea originating outside the company. Further discussions of this point can be found in the article by Auber (1965).

Controlling Product Development Projects

When a new product idea has been approved for development, a series of events is initiated which must be carefully planned, closely controlled, and efficiently managed to maximize the probability of technical and marketing success.

Outlines of two different plans for controlling new product development step by step will be presented in this section. Each plan has different advantages and disadvantages depending on company size and organization, and other factors.

The key operating element in plan No. 1 is a Product Planning Committee (PPC) composed of the president of the company, the director of research and development, the head of marketing, the chief finance officer, the manager of production, and such other executives as are thought to have an immediate interest in and responsibility for new product development. The committee appoints a secretary, who issues agenda, takes notes of the transactions and issues minutes, and maintains records of the individual projects.

In the first plan for controlling new product development, entry of an idea into the system occurs as a result of the submittal to the secretary of the Product Planning Committee of a new product idea. A standard form which is made available to all employees can be used. Normally, the initiator will fill out the designated blanks himself, but in some cases the secretary will make these initial entries. The secretary assigns a number to each idea received. His function is strictly clerical, i.e., he performs no screening operation. If necessary, additional information is solicited from the submitter in order to clarify vague or inadequate terminology. The proposal, with such additional information as he has been able to accumulate, is read by the secretary to the PPC at the next meeting.

Experience has shown that most of the suggestions entering the system either will be close matches to others which have been considered earlier, will fall outside the company objectives, or will be clearly nonfeasible for some other reason. If the proposal has any merit, a followup representative such as the secretary is assigned to extract from the submitter and other sources as much information as is necessary to allow a reasonably accurate evaluation of the proposal. The PPC, on the basis of the completed information, either abandons the idea or assigns an analysis team, usually consisting of one person from marketing and another from R&D to further process the suggestion.

The function of the analysis team is to make a study of the marketing and technical aspects of the problem sufficiently extensive in scope to allow the PPC to determine if (1) a marketing opportunity exists, (2) the company is in a position to take advantage of the marketing opportunity, (3) development of the product is feasible, and (4) capital costs of getting into production can be afforded. The data at this stage will necessarily be crude and embody a considerable degree of uncertainty.

After the analysis team has completed its study, a brief but comprehensive report is submitted to each member of the PPC. At the next meeting, the committee decides to (1) request additional work, (2) abandon the idea, or (3) advance the proposed product to the level of a priority project.

In the latter case, the analysis team is disbanded, the project is given a name and assigned a place on the priority list (all priorities are temporary and can be changed at any meeting of the PPC), and a product team assigned. Unless there are very cogent reasons for a different composition, the product team will include representatives from marketing, R&D, and production (engineering may be included in place of production if it is a separate department).

The product teams are delegates of the PPC and thus of the president, and operate with his authority to gain action on necessary development problems and to coordinate the activities of the several departments. Team members will not ordinarily be department heads. If their efforts are successful, their final act will be the submitting to the PPC of a "Proposal to Manufacture and Market," a document which will recommend that the committee authorize expenditure of the funds required to produce and sell the new product. More will be said about this document later. Alternatively, the team may at any time recommend that the project be abandoned because of technical nonfeasibility or new marketing information.

In the interim between the assignment of a product team and their issuance of a "Proposal to Manufacture and Market," the necessary research, development, engineering, and marketing studies will have been completed. Occasional reports (not necessarily on any fixed schedule) are made to the PPC, and informal minutes are kept of the team meetings. Each project has an account to which expenditures for time, materials, and services are charged.

Each member of the team is responsible for the successful participation of his department in the development work necessary to produce the new item. When necessary, he enlists the aid and authority of his department head. Problems in securing cooperation of other departments, plans for future work, estimates of phase completion dates, fund requirements, and chances for success are discussed at team meetings.

From time to time, the composition of the team may be changed by the PPC as need changes for the participation of different departments. Prototypes of the new product (including package designs) plus market research data are presented to the PPC as they become available. Based on these exhibits and the reports of the product teams (presented orally or in written form), the PPC decides at each meeting whether to abandon the project, continue it as planned, or to alter direction. In the normal course of events, at each meeting some of the teams will present additional data of importance and the project will ordinarily be continued in such cases. If work is to continue, a priority is assigned or continued.

During the development process, if it is successful, equipment designs will be completed, product costs will be finalized, ingredient sources will be determined, and all arrangements brought to the point where successful production can be assured. The results of these studies will be set forth in the "Plan to Manufacture."

As stated previously, the "Plan to Manufacture" is essentially a proposal to top management that expenditures necessary to production and marketing of a new product be authorized. An important feature of the plan is a complete specification for the new product which gives firm, unequivocal requirements for each important characteristic of the product and of the manufacturing process. None of these requirements is to be changed without the prior concurrence of all interested parties, and production is charged with the responsibility of seeing that the quality assurance provisions are met. In case of disputes over the provisions of the plan, e.g., when production expresses doubt about its ability to consistently meet the quality standards deemed necessary by marketing, arbitration is performed by the PPC. Acceptance of the details of the plan by each responsible department head results in the transformation of this document into a specification which is used for the commercial product.

The second plan for controlling development projects for new products is better suited for small companies. Consideration of a new product is initiated by the submittal to the president of the company (or his representative) of a brief description of a proposed new item together with a statement of its supposed advantages over other available foods of the same type. The proposal can originate from any of the division heads within the company, from an employee suggestion plan, or from a source outside of the company. Unless the president finds that the suggestion appears to have no merit, he forwards the proposal to marketing, together with a directive to ascertain the marketing potential of the proposed item. If marketing concludes that the proposed new product has inadequate sales potential, their recommendation for abandonment of the project is sent to the president for final disposition. This recommendation is accompanied by a detailed justification for the adverse decision. The president bases his further actions on marketing's memorandum plus other advice and information.

Should marketing, on the basis of their tests and surveys, deem the proposed new product to have a reasonable chance of success, they establish certain broad and tentative specifications of a preliminary nature including: (1) Maximum acceptable unit sales price and minimum permissible margins. (2) Product (package) size. (3) Minimum storage life at some definite temperature with the method for determining the end point clearly specified. (4) Production capacity to be targeted. (5) General characteristics of the product in terms of appearance, flavor, and texture. (6) Limitations of the home preparation requirements (equipment, time).

These preliminary specifications, for which marketing assumes the responsibility, are incorporated into a memorandum. The original is forwarded to R&D and is accompanied by both the initial proposal and the directive received from the president. A copy of the memorandum is forwarded to the president. After an analysis of marketing's recommendation, the R&D staff submits to marketing either (1) a proposed schedule in which probable success of the proposed development is stated percentagewise, within the framework of total man-hours required, total research costs (including labor) and duration of the project,[1] or (2) indicates to marketing that the product as specified is nonfeasible due to technological problems or to some unrealistic limitations established by marketing and suggests changes, if appropriate. If the nonfeasibility is due to the establishment of limitations which seem to be impossible to meet, marketing and R&D confer in an attempt to reconcile their differences of opinion. If agreement is not reached in this conference, the file on the matter is submitted to the office of the president for final action.

After having studied the plan of R&D, marketing submits a memorandum to the president in which it is recommended either (1) that the schedule of time and costs for development be accepted, or (2) that consideration of the project be terminated because of excessive research costs and the limited probability of success. In either case, written concurrence of the president is required before the project can be considered terminated.

If the president concurs with marketing that R&D should perform the work they have outlined, a formal research project is initiated and appropriate funds to support it are allocated. Simultaneously, a committee consisting of one representative each from marketing, R&D, and production is set up to coordinate and expedite all activities directed toward getting the new product on the market. This committee has primary responsibility for the achievement of successful production. The members of the committee are appointed by the various divisions, with due notice to and concurrence by the president, and will ordinarily include persons having close and continuing contact with the actual work being performed. For example, R&D might appoint the technologist responsible for work on the project as its representative.

Each member of the committee is responsible for coordinating the activities of his department with the work being done by the other departments. Each member receives copies of the R&D progress reports on their project, and the representatives of marketing and production are responsible for informing the other members of the committee of all pertinent actions taken by their respective department. This information must be relayed to the other members within the shortest practicable time after the action is taken. Written concurrence of all committee members must be obtained before major actions, such as the purchase of production equipment, are undertaken. Information can

---

[1] An example of such a schedule statement is: "The project you have described would require approximately 2 man-years of labor, and $25,000 in total costs. It would be completed in 1 calendar year with a 75% probability of success."

be exchanged and concurrence obtained during committee meetings if desired, and in this case, the transactions are entered in the minutes of the meeting.

All decisions made in committee meetings are set down in the minutes, copies of which are circulated to all interested parties, including the president. The original of the minutes is retained in the file held by R&D. The representative of R&D on the committee acts as the secretary and is responsible for transcribing and reproducing the records of the meeting and for circulating them to the other members as soon as possible after each meeting. If either of the other committee members objects to the accuracy or completeness of the minutes or wishes to make additions or corrections for other reasons, he files in the record a memorandum setting forth his opinions. Copies of this memorandum are also sent to the president.

The final aim of the committee is production and marketing of the new product and its work does not stop prior to that stage unless the project is terminated by the authority of the president. When the product is being successfully produced, the committee will disband upon mutual agreement that their work has been completed. In this type of system, the final goal of the committee is an operating production line and distribution system rather than the plan described for the preceding system.

CONDUCTING DEVELOPMENT WORK

The initial step in any development project is a thorough literature search to determine the existing state of the art. The search should encompass not only scientific and technological periodicals and reference books, but also the patent literature, technical bulletins of ingredient and equipment suppliers, and the company files which may contain reports of previous work along similar lines.

Results of the initial literature should be incorporated in a formal report. This important step in the development project is frequently neglected, with the result that changes in personnel or other interruptions in continuity lead to the necessity for doing the work all over again. If time and funds are available, the literature search should be supplemented by discussions with workers in the field and visits to equipment installations.

The techniques of experimental design, conducting the experiment, and statistical evaluation of results are presumably known to the reader and will not be discussed here. In the following sections will be described some special approaches which might fit particular situations and yet be overlooked by the investigator.

Use of Consultants

The use of consultants and contract research institutions to provide specialized assistance during a development project which seems to be beyond the available capacity of a company's internal staff is often economically justifiable. Countless hours of literature search and much fruitless experimentation can frequently be saved by resorting to the consultant's expertise. Such assistance is particularly valuable when a company is considering entry into new fields. At the start of a project a consultant who is an expert in the particular technology can be called in to advise on possible approaches. If competent, he will often be able to point out deficiencies in some of the initial proposals drawn up by R&D. He may have specific knowledge of how similar problems were solved in other companies. Since the consultant presumably is acquainted with the history of litigation on the type of product being considered, legal considerations, and especially the patent situation, can be analyzed.

In some cases, a consultant may be hired to work alongside the R&D staff on a particularly difficult problem. The wisdom of this approach is questionable; if the staff is adequate in number and skills it should be able to handle the details of development work. If not, the preferred solution is to hire more and better permanent staff, not to rely indefinitely on consultants. The consultant's time is generally considerably more expensive than that of the salaried technologist. Consultation during the course of an investigation, and particularly if a stalemate seems to have been reached, is often worthwhile, in order to resolve internal disputes.

Contract research organizations can be used for projects requiring special talent or equipment and particularly in areas outside the client company's usual fields of interest. Contract research is performed by profit-making corporations, nonprofit institutes, and universities. By contracting for outside development work, new investments in staff and facilities are reduced. Some of the values which have been attributed to outside research are: provides new viewpoints, resolves internal conflicts, relieves heavy in-house work loads, gains services of specialists, and saves time. Multiclient studies in which several companies jointly sponsor a program on some major problem of mutual interest are becoming popular.

The cost of a contract research project may be some negotiated firm figure, but is more often set as a maximum figure with periodic billings of overhead (usually a fixed percentage of salaries), direct salaries, rebilled charges (for travel, chemicals, etc.), and profit. Administration of the project is best allocated to a single individual in the client company who will make periodic audits of progress and expenditures. Conclusions of value are then transmitted by this project officer to interested parties in his organization.

In setting up an outside contract for research it is very important to specify the goals as clearly as possible. Much wasted effort can result from failure to give adequate direction to the investigators. Frequent detailed reports should be insisted upon and these should be supplemented by visits to the research facility for informal discussions with the technologists doing the work.

Operations Research

Operations research is a formal means of analyzing business problems. The traditional instrument of the technique is a team made up of scientists from various disciplines with an operations research specialist as the leader. Each member contributes the specialized knowledge of his field as well as any experience he has had with theories and models that might help solve the problem. Operations research has been used in planning the development and introduction of new products, although evidently not to a great extent in the food industry.

One widely-used operations research tool is "critical path analysis," or "network analysis," which can be used in project planning and control to determine which activities must be done in series and which can be done in parallel. Characteristic of these systems is a diagram or chart showing the temporal relationship of all the different tasks. These may be called PERT (Program Evaluation and Review Techniques) diagrams, Gantt charts, etc. The information contained in the charts can also be compiled in tabular form for computer analysis. Using these charts, or computer models, the analyst can find the shortest time through the network. This path determines the time expected to be required for completion of the project when all parts are scheduled in the proper sequence, and it is called the critical path. An example of the use of charting methods for controlling new product development is Raytheon's "Product Planning Monitor Schedule" which is essentially a Gantt chart giving target and performance dates for all the steps involved. The chart is revised on a monthly basis using the most recent inputs of information.

Although some dramatic successes have been claimed for this procedure, it does have certain defects. For example, all steps are considered as indispensable, or of equal weight, when, in fact, it is well recognized that some stages or components can be eliminated or condensed if management is willing to take certain risks or accept an inferior product, i.e., critical path analysis does not necessarily identify critical operations. Furthermore, all time estimates will be in error by an amount related to the predictive ability of the estimator, and these errors tend to be cumulative. Technical projections cannot be accurately made until some preliminary work has been done, in many instances.

As long as its faults are recognized, critical path analysis can be a worthwhile tool in the planning of development projects. The research administrator should have at least a superficial knowledge of these techniques not only because they may be helpful in guiding research projects and integrating them into the overall company activities, but also because they may be suddenly introduced by management with some disruptive effects on R&D customs. A review book of considerable value is Critical Path Analysis (Lang 1970).

Recording Data

In addition to the usual reasons for keeping notes on the experiments performed during a development project, the necessity for establishing priority and reduction to practice for patent purposes dictates use of a formal recording system. A haphazard collection of loose data sheets is of little or no legal value.

The research notebook should be permanently bound, not loose-leaf. Pages should be numbered and a record kept of the individual to whom it is issued. When the book is completed or its use terminated for other reasons, a brief index of its contents should be made and filed. The index can be prepared by photocopying the table of contents prepared by the experimenter during his use of the book. The book itself should then be stored in a safe or some other secure place.

Entries should be made in ink or indelible pencil. The date the experiment was performed should be placed on each page. A witness who understands the substance of the experiment but who has not participated in it should affix his signature and the date of signing to each page. No marks, including corrections, should be made on the page after the witness has signed.

The following outline for the description of the experiment has been recommended (Anon. 1963B): (1) Reference number of the experiment and subject or title of project. (2) Object of the experiment—what is intended to be accomplished by it. (3) Apparatus and procedures—references can be made to published descriptions or procedures, or to those described in other notebooks. Anything new should be fully described. (4) Starting materials—source and grade of ingredients; any special treatment that has been applied to them before the experiment; age and storage conditions. (5) Results: (a) products—details of all essential characteristics, (b) processes—refer to engineering drawings or photographs where possible, and (c) samples—identify any samples retained or set out for analysis. The number assigned may be the conbined research book number, page number, and a sample designation mentioned on that page.

Alternate procedures will no doubt suggest themselves to the reader.

Evolutionary Operations

The technique of evolutionary operations (EVOP) is of special value for product improvement, cost reduction studies, and other investigations where radical changes are not anticipated. The advantage of this approach is that regular production lines are used. The difficulty in translating laboratory findings to production practice, which seems to be especially great in bakery formulations can be reduced.

The basic principle of EVOP is the making of changes during ordinary production which do not alter the finished product sufficiently to make it unmarketable. The changes are made in a systematic and predetermined way, and the results are carefully recorded and analyzed statistically, thus differentiating this method of investigation from the more-or-less intuitive changes made by line personnel to improve machining characteristics or product quality.

EVOP can be applied readily to a two-variable situation although the statistical procedure on which it is based, mapping of response surfaces, can be applied to situations of any degree of complexity. However, at any given time or place, EVOP should limited to optimizing 1 or 2 variables.

EVOP procedure facilitates a constant probing in all directions to find a set of operating conditions or combination of ingredients that will result in an improved product, less scrap, greater production, etc. If the time and temperature of processing are factors under consideration, a continuous study can be undertaken with the present time and temperature as the central point and variations made in all directions. This naturally leads to a design where the number of time-temperature variations tried are five: (1) current procedure, (2) higher temperature and shorter time, (3) lower temperature and shorter time, (4) lower temperature and longer time, and (5) higher temperature and longer time. Formula changes can be made in a similar pattern, and such studies are particularly useful in finding the lowest possible raw materials cost for a product of given acceptability characteristics. Of course, all changes in finished products offered for sale must be within the constraints imposed by label statements and other product claims.

A word of caution is appropriate at this point. It is possible to progress from an article with a high level of acceptability to an article of very poor acceptability by a series of steps each of which causes a change that is imperceptible by any known or practicable means of acceptance testing. Each of a series of changes can be selected so as to yield a product which the expert or consumer panel cannot differentiate at a significant level from the preceding modification, but the total effect of several of the changes will often result in a final version which is not well received by the consumer. Formula alterations for the sake of cost reductions can result in loss of market by this sequence of events, if the results of each successive change are compared with the previous slightly modified product. For this reason, it is very important to use the original product as the standard rather than to compare a new version with the immediately preceding modification.

The EVOP technique has been described in considerable detail by Kramer (1965). He implies that EVOP studies are best conducted by the quality control section while other authorities incline to the view that the product development group is more suitable for this work.

EXAMPLES OF PRODUCT DEVELOPMENT SYSTEMS

Actual examples of product development procedures are rather infrequently described because of security reasons, but it may be instructive to read what has been published about the procedures at some of the larger food companies.

Kill (1965) described a system which can be assumed to resemble the sequence of events at Nabisco.

(1) The idea is submitted on a form addressed to the R&D laboratory. It includes, besides administrative and control data, a project title or description, the ultimate objectives of the project, potential company benefits, and estimated cost of implementation.

(2) Industrial intelligence, such as availability of competitive items, potential demand, etc., is collected.

(3) A profit study with projected sales volume is made.

(4) The research department will calculate cost of man power, materials, and equipment needed to develop a prototype acceptable to the sales and merchandising departments.

(5) The production manager lists requirements for his department as he sees them.

(6) The product development committee considers a wide variety of aspects of the contemplated product as it affects the company's future before it passes on the desirability of the project. The committee may be composed of some or all of the following: members of the Board of Directors, owners, general executives, president, vice president, secretary, treasurer, or comptroller.

(7) If approved, the project is assigned a priority and time limit.

(8) Assignment to a product development group is followed by the production of prototypes. Progress is communicated to and discussed with the production manager, who can commence preliminary design work or express opinions as to the feasibility of the process. Liaison with marketing is maintained in a similar manner. Sometimes these liaison functions are performed by the product manager, usually assigned to the marketing department. Packaging development must continue simultaneously.

(9) A detailed description of all production costs are given to the finance department for a profitability study. If, as is often the case, adequate profits cannot be projected using the costs and prices at this stage, the various departments are asked to modify their requirements and adjust their calculations.

Hormel uses a client-for-hire system by which research costs are charged to marketing for specific projects. New product ideas are first evaluated by marketing. Those deemed desirable are discussed with the director of R&D to ascertain their technical feasibility before a project is set up. If it is decided to proceed, the following sequential steps are taken in what can be called Phase I: (1) The objective is defined. What is the project expected to accomplish? (2) A justification is provided. How will the company benefit? (3) Preliminary specifications are written. The product or process is described as accurately as possible, including the physical, chemical, and organoleptic properties, package design, cost limitations, etc. (4) Priority, timing, work required, and other administrative aspects of the project are established. (5) Supporting data are supplied to facilitate the determination of scientific feasibility and the design of experiments.

When the above steps have been completed, a project leader is selected. He searches the literature, decides upon an approach, outlines the method of attack, and estimates requirements of time, money, and skills. Marketing decides whether or not to continue, based on this information.

The project is readied for final review in Phase III. After presentations by all responsible functions, the project receives final approval or rejection from a group vice-president, the R&D director, and either the corporate vice president or a divisional manager.

In Phase IV, R&D personnel take over the responsibility for the project, and a team is selected to work for the leader. The team outlines the experimental approach and issues weekly reports covering money and time expended as well as monthly reports on technical progress.

According to Alleman (1967) the key points in Kroger's bakery product development program are: (1) Have a definite goal or objective for each project. (2) Follow a set plan. (3) Keep eyes and ears open for new ideas. (4) Be flexible and adjust to changing times. (5) Be aggressive, don't be afraid to try new ideas. (6) See that all work is done carefully and accurately. (7) Be sure you know the cost of new products. (8) Get best possible consumer evaluations before going too far. (9) Accept help from any source. Don't be too proud. (10) Make every project justify itself. Don't do useless work. (11) Have enthusiasm for all new developments. If you are not impressed with your own work don't expect enthusiasm from others. (12) Have a positive attitude at all times and drive the projects to the goal of goals—more profits.

S. C. Johnson Co. has sponsor groups for new product development. These groups include (1) the man who had the idea, (2) the R&D man who is going to supervise the lab work, (3) the man who has to sell the product when it is completed, (4) financial and production personnel, and (5) a member of the new products department.

Wolf (1959) described the product development system established at Arnold Bakeries: (1) Ideas are obtained from employees, executives, and outside sources. (2) Market Research evaluates the idea on the basis of concept tests with consumer panels. (3) Management selects those ideas which can be manufactured profitably and assigns priority. (4) Development work is started. (5) Final product characteristics are specified by management and market research after examining the initial prototypes. (6) Experimental plans are set up by the laboratory. (7) Test bakes are made and evaluated by R&D personnel on the basis of the specifications established by management. (8) Prototypes which appear to meet the requirements are evaluated for acceptability by the market research department using a consumer panel. (9) Acceptable items are coordinated with production to develop suitable processing methods. Time studies enable predictions to be made of labor costs.

BIBLIOGRAPHY

ALLEMAN, H. J. 1967. The practical development of new products. Proc. Am. Soc. Bakery Engrs. *1967*, 287–292.

AMMERMAN, G. R. 1963. New product development. Presented at the September 27, 1963 meeting of the Wisconsin Section, IFT.

ANON. 1963A. Reviews of data on research and development. Nat. Sci. Found. Bull. *41*.

ANON. 1963B. Will your notebook stand up in court? Chem. Eng. Progr. *59*, No. 7, 12–15.

ANON. 1968. How much should your company spend on R&D? Business Management *34*, No. 2, 57–60, 62.

AUBER, R. P. 1965. Outside ideas—dynamite! Res. Management *8*, 183–190.

BALDERSTON, J. 1969. Successful administration of a research laboratory. Res. Develop. *20*, No. 6, 24–25, 27–28, 30.

CARLSON, A. W. 1961. Planning a laboratory. Cereal Sci. Today 6, 236–238.
GUILL, J. H., Jr. 1965. What the bakery production man should know about food and drug labeling and regulations. Proc. Am. Soc. Bakery Engrs. *1965*, 214–219.
HAYDEN, A. J. 1968. New product development as viewed by the production head—a major challenge in coordination. Mfg. Confectioner 48, No. 8, 25–27, 33.
HEID, J. L. 1963. Research and development. *In* Food Processing Operations, M. A. Joslyn and J. L. Heid (Editors). Avi Publishing Co., Westport, Conn.
HEID, J. L. 1971. New products from smaller companies. Food Prod. Develop. 5, No. 5, 47–49.
HILTON, P. 1971. Exploit new product technology. Food Prod. Develop. 5, No. 5, 38, 40.
HOLAHAN, J. L. 1963. Bringing new products and processes into the plant. Food Technol. 17, 395–396, 398.
HOLLANDER, M. B. 1970. Get the most out of R and D. Res. Develop. 21, No. 12, 18, 20, 22.
KILBORN, R. H., and AITKEN, T. R. 1961. Baking laboratory layout and procedures. Cereal Sci. Today 6, 253–254, 257–259.
KILL, J. F. 1965. New product development in cakes, sweet yeast raised products, and cookies. Proc. Am. Soc. Bakery Engrs. *1965*, 244–248.
KRAMER, A. 1965. The effective use of operations research and EVOP in quality control. Food Technol. 19, 37–39.
LANG, D. W. 1970. Critical Path Analysis. Dover Publications, New York.
LOWE, W. C. 1961. Identifying and evaluating the barrier problems in technology. *In* Technological Planning on the Corporate Level, J. R. Bright (Editor). Harvard Business School, Boston.
MARTING, E. 1964. New Products—New Profits. American Management Assoc., New York.
MATTSON, P., and LOTT, D. 1971. What do users and prospective users think of external product development services? Food Prod. Develop. 5, No. 5, 50, 52.
RIVES, R. C. 1964. What is your new product policy? *In* New Products—New Profits, E. Marting (Editor). American Management Assoc., New York.
ROBERTS, E. A. 1968. The myths of research management. Sci. Technol. No. 80, 40–46.
SCHWARTZ, D. A. 1971. Conducting meaningful preference research for less than $1,000. Food Prod. Develop. 5, No. 5, 26, 29, 42.
SEILER, R. E. 1965. Improving the Effectiveness of Research and Development. McGraw-Hill Book Co., New York.
SOUDER, W. E. 1970. Pitfalls in R&D. Business Horizons 1970 (June) 54–56.
STANLEY, A. O., and WHITE, K. K. 1965. Organizing the R&D Function. American Management Association, New York.
TABER, A. P. 1968. Evaluation of R&D. Res. Develop. 19, No. 10, 22–27.
TAUBER, E. M. 1971. Systematic generation of ideas for new foods. Food Prod. Develop. 5, No. 2, 58–59, 62.
WADE, W. 1965. Industrial Espionage and Mis-use of Trade Secrets, 2nd Edition. Advance House Publishers, Ardmore, Penn.
WALTERS, J. E. 1965. Research Management: Principles and Practice. Spartan Books, New York.
WILLIAMSON, M. A. 1965. How to manage R&D innovation. Res. Develop. 16, No. 8, 26–27.
WILLIAMSON, M. A. 1968. R&D management tomorrow. Res. Develop. 19, No. 8, 69–70, 72.
WOLF, A. 1959. From an idea to a finished product. Baking Ind. No. 23–28.
ZIEMBA, J. W. 1966. R&D guides Green Giant. Food Eng. 37, No. 1, 98–100.

CHAPTER 27

QUALITY CONTROL

INTRODUCTION

Although quality control is a relatively old concept, with a well-recognized value to manufacturing companies, its goals and the scope of its function are still not clearly understood by many chief executives. The necessity for making decisions as to the staffing, specific activities, responsibilities, and authority of this department can create a great deal of anxiety, especially for those managers who do not have technical backgrounds. The purpose of this chapter is to review the opinions of specialists in the field as to the proper role of quality control and then to add some general observations on the relationship of quality control to other departments in the bakery. Some of the administrative and procedural principles involved in the management of a quality control department are also discussed, but there will be no details of sampling or testing procedures.

MISSION OF QUALITY CONTROL

Kramer and Twigg (1962) defined quality control as the maintenance of quality at levels and tolerances acceptable to the buyer while minimizing costs to the vendor. Amerine *et al.* (1965) defined quality control as the "application of sensory, physical, and chemical tests in industrial production to prevent undue variation in quality attributes, such as color, viscosity, flavor, etc." These and most other authors, have not given sufficient emphasis to the third parties in all transactions involving food—the Federal, State, and local regulatory bodies.

In addition to satisfying the consumer, the product must meet the requirements of governmental regulatory agencies. A food which does not meet the minimum acceptability requirements of all customers may result only in a few complaints but a product which does not meet all of the applicable legal requirements may be confiscated and the manufacturers subjected to punitive fines and other penalties. This situation must be emphasized because it is becoming more critical every day; yet many food producers are not aware of the changing climate. A product may look good, taste good, have good texture, and perform well in its intended application, and still be unfit for distribution. To be suitable for sale, it must also be wholesome, conform to all applicable labeling and packaging requirements, and be prepared and stored under conditions tending to prevent contamination by noxious or esthetically undesirable materials (actual contamination need not be shown). Quality control and all other departments of food handling companies must remain aware of these restrictions at all times.

POSITION OF QUALITY CONTROL IN THE TABLE OF ORGANIZATION

It is agreed by all authorities that the quality control function must be completely separated, administratively, from the production and purchasing departments because of conflicting goals of these functions. Production properly aims for maximum output with minimum rejections, and purchasing attempts to procure raw materials at the lowest possible price, while quality control must be relied upon to maintain some fixed level of quality regardless of the effect on production rate or ingredient costs. Although the aims of marketing and quality control are somewhat alike, the general administrative principle that scientific personnel should not be managed by persons who are not scientists dictates that quality control must remain separate from marketing.

Most companies have found that the best administrative arrangement is to have the chief of quality control report directly to the president or executive vice president. Alternatively, there can be a vice president of technical services who administers quality control operations as well as research, development, and similar activities.

FUNCTIONS OF A QUALITY CONTROL DEPARTMENT

The basic definitions quoted previously can be supplemented by a statement of the functions encompassed by statistical quality control (slightly paraphrased from Allan 1959): (1) Acceptance component (the traditional quality control function and based on fixed standards)—approves good product and sets aside defective product for rework or scrap. (2) Prevention component—uses data generated by inspection to indicate areas where an out-of-control situation is starting to develop. (3) Assurance component—uses data from customer complaints and quality audits or reviews to assure that the extent of conformance is maintained at a satisfactory level.

The implementation process undertaken in order to see that the functions are properly carried out would include: (1) Preparing specifications for raw materials, including ingredients and packaging materials. (2) Preparing specifications for finished products, including the package. (3) Preparing outline procedures, in which the essential conditions for manufacture are listed. (4) Performing or supervising sampling of raw materials and finished products. (5) Performing tests necessary to determine compliance with specifications and applicable Federal, State, and local regulations, including sanitation inspections. (6) Determining compliance of finished products and production and storage areas with all applicable Federal, State, and local regulations. This includes determining the compliance of label statements with packaging laws. (7) Conducting a continuous program of devising new and improved tests. (8) Assisting production and engineering in trouble-shooting when an out-of-control situation exists. (9) Performing supervisory and administrative functions applicable to personnel engaging in the above activities.

It does not include: (1) Performing sanitation procedures (e.g., fumigations, etc.). (2) Performing maintenance procedures. (3) Performing technical service functions for marketing, production, or procurement.

Certainly the quality control department should never be regarded as being responsible for production and engineering functions such as checking the accuracy of meters, instruments, thermometers, timers, etc., except in conjunction with production and engineering during trouble-shooting operations triggered by an out-of-control situation.

Wolf (1970) describes how quality control functions in a large organization, starting with the development of a new product. The quality control manager directs the chemical and the bacteriological testing of all new ingredients that are used in the product. Specifications are written for each ingredient that has been selected for the new product. These specifications are used by the purchasing department in selecting suppliers for the ingredients. Before a supplier is approved, the quality control sanitation inspector checks the facilities of the supplier to assure that the facility meets the sanitation and microbiological standards.

The quality control department actively assists the process engineering group in setting and evaluating process standards. The optimum processing temperatures are specified by the pathogenic laboratory manager to eliminate the danger of bacterial contamination and growth. All processes are checked to assure compliance with all Federal and State regulations.

If new equipment has to be built for the process, the quality control department is consulted to assure that the new equipment meets all U.S. FDA and Good Manufacturing Practice directives. After the equipment is built and tested, and the quality control department takes samples of products at different processing stages to determine whether or not there is bacterial growth during processing.

All incoming ingredients for the products are checked for bacterial, chemical, and physical properties before use.

While the new product is placed into production, the plant quality control manager works with the new product and process engineering managers to become familiar with all phases of production. Check-sheets are prepared listing all critical processing specifications that have to be monitored by the quality control process inspector during mass production. The quality control process inspector's job is to notify the production foreman if a standard is not followed.

Before a new product is authorized for sale, the executive committee approves the quality standards for the product. The standards for color, volume, texture, symmetry, flavor, and weight are established. The quality control line inspectors guide the production people to assure that all substandard products are rejected.

The shipping quality control inspector checks the temperature of the products and the condition of the shipping cases before shipment. The shipping inspector must also check the truck or rail car, to assure that the product is shipped at the correct temperature in a sanitized vehicle.

The sanitation inspector conducts daily plant inspections and notifies the production foreman if a sanitation deficiency exists. Once a month the plant is thoroughly inspected and graded. Twice a year an independent outside agency inspects the facilities and grades the plant sanitation level. Immaculate sanitary conditions in a food manufacturing plant are essential to produce quality products.

Specifying ingredients, processing, finished products, and sanitation standards are meaningless unless these standards are observed.

Some of the standards, such as texture or flavor of a product, are subject to interpretation. For example, if a quality control line inspector rejects a product, he places a "hold tag" on it. The "hold tag" cannot be removed from the product without quality control authorization. In addition, no product with a "hold tag" on it can be shipped. The production foreman, whose product has been rejected by a quality control line inspector, can appeal the decision if he disagrees with the decision of the quality control line inspector. The production foreman then notifies the production manager. If the production manager agrees with the production foreman, he will try to convince the quality control manager that the product in question is up to standard. If the quality control manager disagrees, the vice president of production and vice president of R&D decide the fate of the product. If no agreement is reached, the president of the company makes the final decision. This system of checks and balances minimizes the chance of accepting a substandard product or rejecting an acceptable product.

Allen (1968) lists the following "Ten Commandments" of quality control, particularly applicable to biscuit factories: (1) Make up complete formulas showing all the ingredients and any allowable tolerances in sugar, water, leavening, etc. (2) Clearly show on the formulas the complete mixing conditions, including temperature, times, etc. (3) Have mixer personnel record observed mixing conditions for each batch. Insist that it be filled out as the batch is mixed, not before nor long after. (4) Post the correct dough weight for each variety by the machine and have the machine man record weights periodically—every 15 min. (5) Post the heat pattern, time of bake, size, and count for each variety at the delivery end of the oven, and have the baker record these measurements periodically. Be sure the light is good at the oven inspection doors and the delivery end of the oven. Before each run, give the baker a sample to duplicate in color. (6) Have the laboratory run the moisture and pH on each batch and report the results to the foreman or baker immediately. (7) Establish and post the standard weight and tolerance for each package. (8) Package weights should be taken at least every 15 min and recorded. The records are invaluable, not only for quality control, but in any underweight controversy with a government inspector. (9) Be sure that size and count specifications are accurately made on new varieties before the packing material is ordered. (10) Have random samples of product picked off the line by a disinterested party for inspection. It is often amazing how different a product looks in the package than you thought it looked coming out of the oven or on the packing table.

Technical Services

From time to time, members of the quality control staff may be called upon to provide advice and assistance to other departments of the company. They may be asked to assist in solving urgent processing problems or to act as expert witnesses in legal proceedings, for example. In well-run companies, these extramural tasks should be relatively infrequent and it will not be necessary to have a separate group to handle them, but in companies which sell ingredients such as flour, many man-hours may be needed for handling customer complaints, advising on the best conditions for use of product, evaluating specifications, etc. In these companies, it may be desirable to have a separate technical service branch, to which all of the customer inquiries can be directed, thus eliminating the need for frequent interruptions of the experiments and analytical work constituting the principle duties of research and quality control personnel.

Persons selected for such a technical service group should have familiarity with the methods and equipment of the customer industry. It is not essential that they have an extensive background in their own manufacturing techniques. Field work is often required, and a willingness and ability to work with the customer's production personnel is essential.

The technical service group will usually not have extensive laboratory or pilot plant facilities of their own, and they should be able to call upon quality control or research personnel for specific short-term work to solve those few problems which cannot be solved by verbal consultations or field studies.

Records

It should be obvious that accurate, permanent records must be kept showing all significant actions taken by the quality control department, since legal or administrative questions may arise concerning products shipped many months before.

Detailed record keeping is assuming increasing importance in preventing liability losses due to presumably defective products. Recent emphasis in the courts of the legal doctrine of "strict liability," which holds that a plaintiff need not prove negligence in manufacture but simply that a defect existed at the time of use or consumption, has created added hazards for companies not maintaining adequate quality control records. The records should show that all defective products are destroyed or reworked, and any evidence that the recommendations of a quality control manager have been overridden is likely to have very unfortunate effects if the product in some way causes injury or disease. Any company that feels that destruction of product is too costly should consider the effect on their finances of a few losses in the courts, where awards of $100,000 and up are commonplace. Judgments assigning criminal liability for defective products are also becoming more frequent.

Courts no longer allow the manufacturer to hold confidential the company files and records. Disclosure and interrogatory procedures are now intended for the benefit of the plaintiff and permit almost total examination at any time.

All records relating to quality control should thus be in condition for review of the company's files. The claims representative of the company's insurance carrier and its corporate legal counsel can provide advice on the establishment of the records system.

Two important documents that belong in a company's quality control file are a "Certificate of Insurance" (issued by a responsible carrier) and a "Hold Harmless Agreement" provided by each vendor who supplies ingredients, packaging materials, equipment that contacts foods, etc. The validity and scope of these certificates should be approved by the company's insurance representative and its legal counsel.

Documentation through all steps in handling consumer complaints is highly important in protecting against broad liability. Admission of fault where there is some doubt, merely in order to calm down an angry customer, is very dangerous. Examination of the supposedly defective product, questioning the offended customer, and entering the results in the records are minimum steps.

There should be a well-developed plan for tracing the distribution or sale of a company's product in case a faulty or dangerous condition is discovered.

ESTABLISHING STANDARDS AND WRITING SPECIFICATIONS

It is the finished product quality which is of prime importance. All other requirements must be directed toward this goal.

When a new product is being developed, marketing or an executive committee must decide upon the minimum essential limits of product quality. Quality control and manufacturing then set the quantitative in-process and finished product specifications which will ensure that the product as offered for sale meets these requirements. The product development group acts in an advisory capacity both for raw materials and processing descriptions. A similar division of responsibilities is desirable when it is necessary to write specifications for existing products.

If the finished product quality which marketing regards as essential cannot be met within the existing technological limitations, either concessions must be made by them or the project must be abandoned as being nonfeasible. It is important to obtain the written concurrence of all interested parties to the finished specification. If there are demands for changes which cannot be met, the conflict must be resolved by top management.

The philosophies or motivations behind the establishment of specifications for raw materials (including packaging materials) and for finished products are quite different. The ultimate criterion of the quality of the finished product is its acceptability to the consumer, and this may include its performance in equipment of the user when that requirement is applicable. Determining these limitations is properly a function of market research and, once they are determined, the requirements are embodied in a finished product specification (as modified by considerations of cost and available facilities).

The essential limitations for raw materials (ingredients) must be set by R&D on the basis of their knowledge of what is necessary in order to allow the finished product to meet its specifications. Raw materials specifications should be made as broad as possible so that purchasing may procure the lowest-priced ingredients which will function satisfactorily. Redundant limitations should be scrupulously avoided. All raw materials should be covered by some sort of specification and testing procedure. Frequently, a supplier will submit a specification which covers an ingredient known to be satisfactory. Such specifications should be carefully screened to remove any limitations which would restrict the source of supply unnecessarily.

In addition to the specifications for raw materials and finished product, limitations may be applied at various stages in the manufacturing process. The establishment and enforcement of in-process standards is justified by the need for preventing excess scrap and must be based on technological considerations alone.

Finished Product Standards

Ideally, measurement of the acceptability of a product should be based on evaluations of it, in the way it is usually consumed, and by panels of testers representative of potential buyers in the marketing area. When appropriate, home preparation trials should be used. For institutional and manufacturing materials, the tests might include an evaluation of the performance of the product in the types of equipment used by potential customers. As a practical matter, such consumer and user tests are clearly impossible for routine quality control purposes, and the buyers' requirements must be expressed by a workable specification arrived at through the development or selection of tests which translate the targeted consumers' desires into chemical, physical, or organoleptic terms.

The relationship of the results of these tests to the fundamental factor of consumer acceptability depends upon the wise choice of the conditions of the test as well as on some uncontrollable circumstances. In no case, however, can a physical or chemical test be expected to give a perfect correlation with consumer ratings of a food.

Tests made after the sample has been stored for some time may be more meaningful than tests conducted on fresh product, although the two sets of results should be capable of being related by some constant factor. Nonetheless, retaining a product in stock until long-term storage tests have been completed is impractical. To prevent unnecessary increases in inventory, the finished product should be tested as expeditiously as possible. Tests which require several days for completion should be avoided.

Specifications should be subject to change if improved evidence becomes available. Case histories of consumer complaints on existing items are useful guides in revising the standards. A system of tabulating these complaints together with a periodic review is very worthwhile. The availability of new equipment (plant or laboratory) or improved ingredients may make it possible to institute more rigorous standards, leading to a better product at equal or lower cost.

Ingredient Specifications

Ingredient requirements are initially established by R&D, and they are based on information accumulated during new product development or process improvement studies. These requirements may be modified as experience is gained in the manufacture of the product and should be reviewed frequently during the early history of its commercial production.

There are many functional qualities of ingredients which are not subject to evaluation except by performance tests conducted under conditions resembling as closely as possible those existing in the plant. It is generally agreed that it is preferable to substitute tests of specific characteristics for performance tests when the former become available with the advance of technology.

Quality control must assure itself that the tests proposed by R&D can be performed in a timely and reproducible manner with the available facilities. The manner and frequency of sampling should be left to the decision of quality control unless there are clear-cut reasons why they must be prescribed by R&D.

TEST METHODS

The limits given for a quality factor listed in a specification must list the reference source of the test procedure which can be conducted under standard conditions. These tests may be developed in the laboratory to meet a particular need, but it is more common to adapt methods described in reference works devoted to analytical procedures or to refer directly to these published techniques. Many thoroughly verified test methods for foods are given in the latest edition of AOAC Methods (Anon. 1971). Other societies concerned with special types of food have published collections of analytical procedures appropriate to their special field of interest. See, for example, Cereal Laboratory Methods (Anon. 1970). Individual tests are described in scientific journals, but these are not likely to be as well-seasoned as those reviewed and investigated by the committees of the various societies.

The ways in which new analytical methods are developed, verified, and standardized are generally known to scientists and technologists and will not be discussed here. Special tests should be described in complete detail in the specifications themselves, or in a handbook of laboratory procedures maintained by the quality control administration.

The tendency in modern quality control testing is to rely more and more on instrumental methods, as on gas chromatography for testing for off-odors, spectrophotometry for color standardization, etc. Organoleptic tests cannot be entirely replaced by instrumental methods at the present state of our knowledge, however, because of insufficient understanding of the fundamental factors affecting acceptability and uniformity of foods. Consumer panels for quality control are expensive, slow, and unwieldy; while expert panels are not entirely satisfactory because of the difficulty in relating their scores to consumer evaluation and in assembling the panel on short notice. Expert panels can be of great value in detecting deviations from a standard. As a practical matter, individual judgments of flavor, texture, and appearance made by the quality control technologist must often be relied upon both for finished products and many raw materials.

SAMPLING

It is an old axiom that a test can only be as good as the sample. The development of a statistically valid sampling procedure is sometimes more difficult and complex than developing a new analytical technique, and it is quite frequently much harder to administer and police. Statistical quality control textbooks should be relied upon for guidance. Two of the publications relating to the application of statistically valid sampling methods are MIL-STD-105D and ASTME-122-S6T (Anon. 1964).

SANITATION INSPECTIONS

Inspections of the plant designed to detect unsanitary processing conditions which could lead to product contamination or a citation by one of the government regulatory bodies are operations justifiably assignable to quality control. Sanitation procedures are never a proper function of quality control personnel except in those emergency situations when all hands must cooperate in an effort to correct an out-of-control condition. The sanitarian and the cleanup crew, not quality control, must be held responsible for sanitation. In plants large enough to maintain a full-time sanitarian and assistants, these personnel should be placed under the jurisdiction of production. Quality control should have an opportunity to pass on the acceptable nature of sprays, powders, poisons, etc., used in disinfestation procedures.

When an official inspection is made by a representative of one of the government regulatory bodies, he should be accompanied in his rounds by the quality control chief or his assistant. A member of the production staff should also participate in this inspection. Comments of the official inspector should be recorded and forwarded by the quality control representative to the appropriate department for action. Performance of the corrections directed by the inspector should be policed by the quality control department, and further contacts (if they are necessary), should be handled by the chief.

ROLE IN PROMOTING A QUALITY-CONSCIOUS ATTITUDE IN OTHER DEPARTMENTS

The quality control department can be an effective agency in promoting a positive attitude toward quality improvement. The attitude of employees engaged in producing the goods offered for sale is a factor affecting quality, although the relative contribution of employee attitude versus machine limitations is probably heavily weighted in favor of the latter. Nonetheless, sloppy or haphazard work can result when employees are not aware of the importance of quality to the maintenance of the company's financial strength, and, therefore, to their jobs. If it is known that quality control will consistently detect departures from the norm, an alert attitude is fostered in production people. Customer complaints which are received by quality control can be brought to the attention of the responsible operator and his foreman.

One approach to securing emotional involvement of personnel in quality improvement is the use of such flamboyant and ephemeral programs as "Zero Defects" with variants POP, POW, PRIDE, etc. The net value of these programs in general, and the Zero Defects program in particular, is likely to be very small. The usual experience is that the average production worker tends to be very cynical about these programs and lets superficial acquiescence cover a complete lack of interest. Even those workers who can be motivated initially suffer a letdown after the high-pressure campaign terminates and may lose what real enthusiasm they originally had.

Zero Defects is especially bad, in the opinion of some, because it sets an impossible goal. No one likes to shoot at a target he knows he can't hit. Furthermore, the strong pressure to reduce defects may very well lead to concealment of errors with the results that quality control cannot perform its function properly.

EXTENT OF THE CONCERN OF QUALITY CONTROL

As a technological matter, the concern of quality control must start with raw materials. Quality of finished product is inseparable from quality of components. Seldom are there processing variations which will compensate for raw material inadequacies. Conversely, use of top quality ingredients is of no avail if the processing conditions are not adequately controlled.

The question of where the concern of quality control ends is partly a matter of policy. In most cases there is no effective control over some stages in the distribution cycle, and none over the conditions in the store or in the consumer's pantry. The easy answer is to say that product quality is a quality control concern until the material is consumed, but, realistically, if there is no control over conditions encountered by the product, an attempted evaluation of these conditions or of the product after it encounters them, is of only academic interest, or at best, the concern of R&D who might find in the data guidance for designing products to be stable under some presumed average set of conditions. It is an elementary scientific principle that testing when one or more important conditions are unknown is a waste of time. That is why the practice of securing samples from many different outlets and examining them for guidance in quality control is fundamentally unsound.

Where a limited number of controlled storage outlets are in question, the problem is slightly more clear-cut. Then, each storage area must be sampled and it must be sampled on a routine basis. The results of the evaluation are applicable only to that storage area and only to the set of conditions existing during the history of the sample. If enough personnel are available to do the necessary sampling, the testing, and the evaluation of results, some information subject to analysis and/or extrapolation can often be obtained.

If a program of sampling product in retail outlets is to be undertaken, it is very important to set down at the beginning exactly what is to be determined. The goals must be defined in precise terms. When this is attempted, it is often found that the desired answer cannot be obtained using the contemplated procedure or, in fact, any conceivable procedure. If whoever designs the project is allowed to use generalities and nonscientific nomenclature in setting the goals, then a program which has a built-in failure potential may be put into effect.

In the author's opinion, it is far better to have a policy of testing product after storage in the laboratory under conditions of controlled temperature and humidity than it is to waste funds in accumulating data which cannot be extrapolated to new situations. The conducting of such tests on existing products is a proper function of quality control.

CONSTRUCTION OF CONTROL CHARTS

The following discussion is adapted from a paper by Stewart (1964).

Statistical quality control can be applied to the two types of quality factors, variables and attributes. It is important to understand the difference between these two types of data. When a record is made of actual measured quality characteristic, such as the weight, diameter, length, width, or thickness of a cookie or cracker, the quality is said to be expressed by variables. When a record shows the number of articles conforming and the number of articles failing to conform to any specified requirement, it is said to be a record by attributes. Examples of attributes are: packages with good seal or no seal; broken or unbroken cookies; and packages with code date or no code date.

The Shewhart Control Charts that are widely used in statistical quality control are either measurement charts or attribute charts. The advantages of Shewhart Charts over some other methods of graphing data are that they show the measurements in chronological sequence and facilitate visualizing the relationship of data to quality limits.

The most widely-used measurement charts are the average and range charts, commonly called X-Bar and R charts. The average and range charts are used when the quality characteristic of interest is actually measured each time a sample is inspected. For each characteristic studied, separate X-Bar and R charts must be made. Only one kind of measurement at a time can be recorded on these charts.

A useful quality control chart cannot be made without reliable data. Before any charts are made, study the line from which the samples will be taken and make some preliminary decisions based on equipment limitations.

Control charts can be applied to finished products or to any phase of the baking operation. Control charts can be applied to scaling operations, dough weights, temperatures, oven times, oven temperatures, etc. They are wonderful tools for spot-checking the weaknesses of the three M's—Materials, Manpower, and Machinery.

BIBLIOGRAPHY

ALLAN, D. H. W. 1959. Statistical Quality Control. Van Nostrand Reinhold Co., New York.

ALLEN, M. C. 1968. The most important thing we have to sell. Snack Food 57 No. 12, 33–35.

ALLGAUER, A. J. 1970. Quality assurance:methods. Proc. Am. Soc. Bakery Engrs. 1970, 191–200.

AMERINE, M. A., PANGBORN, R. M., and ROESSLER, E. B. 1965. Principles of Sensory Evaluation of Food. Academic Press, New York.

ANON. 1971. Methods of Analysis, 9th Edition. Association of Official Agricultural Chemists, Washington, D.C.

ANON. 1970. Cereal Laboratory Methods, 7th Edition. American Association of Cereal Chemists, St. Paul.

ANON. 1964. ASTM Standards. American Society for Testing and Materials, Philadelphia.

DALBY, G., and HILL, G. 1960. Quality testing of bakery products. In Bakery Technology and Engineering, S. A. Matz (Editor). Avi Publishing Co., Westport, Conn.

DUNTLEY, J. M. 1961. QC laboratory operations. Cereal Sci. Today 6, 286–287.

FEIGENBAUM, A. V. 1961. Total Quality Control—Engineering and Management. McGraw-Hill Book Co., New York.

HOWER, R. K. 1964. Some reflections on flour control. Cereal Sci. Today 9, 314.

KILBORN, R. H., and AITKEN, T. R. 1961. Baking laboratory layout and procedures. Cereal Sci. Today 6, 253-254, 257-259.

KRAMER, A., and TWIGG, B. A. 1962. Fundamentals of Quality Control for the Food Industry. Avi Publishing Co., Westport, Conn.

LANNUIER, G. L. 1970. The future of quality control in pie production. Proc. Am. Soc. Bakery Engrs. *1970*, 123-126.

MARKEL, M. F. 1969. The impact of food laws on the function of bakery engineers. Proc. Am. Soc. Bakery Engrs. *1969*, 53-59.

MEEK, D. C. 1969. A total quality system. Cereal Sci. Today *14*, 189-192.

PRATT, D. B. JR. 1960. Management looks at quality control—a communications problem. Cereal Sci. Today *5*, 90-92, 99.

STEWART, T. J. 1964. Practical Quality Control. Schulze-Burch Biscuit Co., Chicago.

STRAUSS, A. 1964. Specifications for ingredients. Proc. Am. Soc. Bakery Engrs. *1964*, 96-102.

TENGQUIST, H. N. 1968. A relationship between laboratory and production. Proc. Am. Soc. Bakery Engrs. *1968*, 181-185.

WOLF, A. 1970. Quality assurance: principles and organization. Proc. Am. Soc. Bakery Engrs. *1970*, 183-188.

CHAPTER 28

NUTRITIONAL CONSIDERATIONS IN FORMULATING BAKERY PRODUCTS

During the past several years, there has been an increase of public interest in the nutritional composition of bakery foods. Much of this recent emphasis has come from so-called consumer groups and consumerists, but various government agencies have also started to examine the effect of bakery goods on the dietary intake of individuals and segments of the population. The primary thrust seems to be directed toward the addition of nutrient factors which are either absent or present in less than optimal amounts, the latter being determined on the basis of some arbitrary standard. Formerly, it was not considered desirable to do more than replace those vitamins, minerals, and amino acids which were removed or destroyed by processing.

The consumer, as distinguished from consumerists, appears to be reasonably well satisfied with the wholesomeness and nutritional adequacy of foods available in the supermarket, and to be somewhat distrustful of supplemented foods. There are, however, certain persons who are unusually alert to claims of special nutritional value. This group is probably large enough to constitute a worthwhile market for specialty items.

MARKET OPPORTUNITIES

Approaches to dietary modification for nutritional improvement are of two different kinds. One relies on changing the quantity or combination of conventional foods consumed by the targeted population. As a preliminary step, the dietary effect of existing conventional foods, as presently consumed, are studied. These studies result in tabulations of the composition of foods, distribution of these foods in normal or average diets of some delimited segment of the population (defined by geography, social status, age, race, income, etc.), and the effect of these factors on the health and well-being of individual members of the group. Finally, steps for improving the nutritional status are recommended or implemented.

The second approach to nutritional modification relies on the supplementation of existing foods with natural or synthetic additives, to provide what is regarded as a superior diet. The discussions in this chapter will be primarily concerned with supplementation of bakery foods.

It is important to recognize that there are two distinct markets for nutrient-supplemented foods: (1) knowledgeable and relatively affluent consumers who can buy specialty foods at relatively high prices, and (2) persons who are undernourished because of poverty or ignorance and require commodity-type foods distributed in large quantities at very low prices (or free of charge under government subsidy). The specialty market is generally capable of interpreting nutritional claims according to their own standards, and they may accept products that deviate considerably from the norm in appearance, texture, and flavor. Complicated preparation techniques (e.g., involving blenders, etc.) are not necessarily negative features. On the other hand, the mass markets usually require products which closely resemble a familiar item of diet in all organoleptic properties and which can be prepared for consumption with very simple techniques and available utensils.

Markets for specialty products in the bakery field have been explored by many manufacturers. Low-salt, low-sugar (diabetic), and nonallergenic (gluten-free) breads are offered in limited quantity nearly everywhere, but these are not supplemented products in the sense in which that term is used here. High-protein and vitamin-enriched breads are, of course, well-known. Use of vitamin and mineral enrichment in bakery products other than bread seems to be increasing. In many cases, supplementation is used as a means of increasing marketability, and prices are not advanced over other premium loaves.

Schemes for improving the diets of impoverished groups in emerging countries have seldom relied upon bakery products as vehicles for introducing nutrients. There are at least three reasons for avoiding such foods: (1) the targeted population generally exists at a low technological level and are not accustomed to bakery products as a staple of diet, relying more on gruels, porridges, and other simpler foods; (2) bakery foods usually have limited storage stability and cannot be satisfactorily distributed over long distances and by primitive transportation methods; and, (3) the sophisticated production techniques required for many bakery foods dictate the use of skilled personnel and expensive equipment which are not often available. The most common forms of dietary adjuncts have been beverages, gruels, and unleavened breads (chapatties, tortillas, etc). But leavened bread modified with vitamins, minerals, and lysine has had a limited success in India, where government subsidies and educational programs have overcome some of the drawbacks.

KINDS OF SUPPLEMENTATION

The principal emphasis in the popular press and by most technical and semitechnical groups working in this field seems to be on protein, vitamin, and mineral supplementation. Addition of specific fatty acids or increasing the caloric content has not received much attention, although some manufacturers used to claim that their products gave quick energy, or more energy, which probably meant that these foods contained more calories than did competitive products or some vaguely identified standard. Such claims in the present climate of opinion are likely to give rise to suspicions that the products contain "empty" calories, whatever they are.

Claims based on other special ingredients, such as the traditional and perhaps mystical benefits of milk, honey, whole wheat, and the like, are no longer common. These ingredients impart an aura of wholesomeness to a product. Bizarre and outlandish claims are often made for "organic," "pure," or "natural" materials such as raw sugar, sea salt, and vegetables grown without the use of chemical fertilizers. One of the unsolved mysteries in the regulatory field is the apparent immunity of producers and publicizers of "organic" and "natural" foods to prosecution for the therapeutic claims made for these products.

CONTROLS AND GUIDELINES FOR SUPPLEMENTATION

Vitamins and minerals (certain salts) are GRAS (generally recognized as safe) and can be added to nonstandardized bakery foods as desired. An excess of some of the vitamins can apparently have harmful effects on the consumer, and different people vary in their susceptibility depending upon their age, health, etc. It is highly unlikely that a harmful excess of any vitamin or mineral could be ingested in the form of bakery products, even though they were supplemented at fairly high levels.

There are definitions and standards of identity for certain bakery products, among them white bread, enriched bread, milk bread, raisin bread, and whole wheat bread (and the corresponding rolls). All bakery technologists should be acquainted with these standards. They limit the kinds and amounts of ingredients which can be used in products offered for sale under the names listed. Vitamins, minerals, and protein enrichments cannot be indiscriminately added to standard products. Enriched bread must contain, in each pound, not less than 1.1 mg and not more than 1.8 mg of thiamine, not less than 0.7 mg and not more than 1.6 mg of riboflavin, not less than 10.0 mg and not more than 15.0 mg of niacin or niacinamide, and not less than 8.0 mg and not more than 12.5 mg of iron. Optional ingredients are not less than 150 USP units and not more than 750 USP units of vitamin D, and calcium salts in such quantity that each pound of the finished food contains not less than 300 mg and not more than 800 mg of calcium. There are no clear-cut limitations on protein supplementation.

Some bakery associations have recommended that the U.S. FDA amend the enriched bread standards to increase minimum levels of thiamine to 1.8 mg per lb of bread, riboflavin to 1.1 mg, niacin to 15 mg, and iron to 25 mg. Calcium, an optional enriching ingredient, is expected to have a minimum set at 600 mg per lb.

There are two important sets of official standards for nutrient intake required for health. These are the Minimum Daily Requirements (MDR), which is accepted by the U.S. FDA as a basis for nutritional claims, and the more extensive Recommended Daily Allowances (RDA), which was compiled by the National Research Council. Tables 28.1 and 28.2 summarize these guidelines. The MDR covers 6 vitamins and 4 minerals, while there are RDA's for 10 vitamins, 5 minerals, protein, and total calories.

The MDR's are generally lower than the corresponding RDA's. As of the moment, either of these sets of standards can be used as a basis of nutritional claims on labels, etc. Since use of the MDR's allows a lower level of supplementation, it is the standard frequently chosen. It is customary to express the nutritional claim as, e.g., "One-third of the Minimum Daily Requirement of Vitamin C for adults."

MATERIALS USED FOR SUPPLEMENTATION

Vitamins

There are several sources for most of the individual vitamins, but only 2 or 3 large firms maintain stocks of all of them. The latter companies will supply premixes of any specified composition and will guarantee potency. These premixes can also be preweighed into batch-

TABLE 28.1
MINIMUM DAILY REQUIREMENTS OF SPECIFIC NUTRIENTS

Nutrient	Infants	Children 1–5 Yr Inclusive	Children 6 Yr and Over	Adults	Pregnancy or Lactation
A (USP units)	1500	3000	3000	4000	4000
B_1 (mg)	0.25	0.50	0.75	1.00	1.50
B_2 (mg)	0.60	0.90	0.90	1.20	1.20
Niacin (mg)	...	5	7.5	10	10
C (mg)	10	20	20	30	30
D (USP units)	400	400	400	400	400
Calcium (gm)	...	0.75	0.75	0.75	1.50
Phosphorus (gm)	...	0.75	0.75	0.75	1.50
Iron (mg)	...	7.5	10	10	15
Iodine (mg)	...	0.1	0.1	0.1	0.1

TABLE 28.2
RECOMMENDED DAILY ALLOWANCES[1]

	Age[2] Years From–Up to	Weight (Kg)	Weight (Lbs)	Height (Cm)	Height (In.)	Kcalories	Protein (Gm)	Vitamin A Activity IU	Vitamin D IU	Vitamin E Activity IU	Ascorbic Acid (Mg)	Folacin[4] (Mg)	Niacin (Mg) equiv.[5]	Riboflavin (Mg)	Thiamine (Mg)	Vitamin B₆ (Mg)	Vitamin B₁₂ (μg)	Calcium (Gm)	Phosphorus (Gm)	Iodine (μg)	Iron (Mg)	Magnesium (Mg)
Infants	0 – ⅙	4	9	55	22	kg × 120	kg × 2.2[3]	1500	400	5	35	0.05	5	0.4	0.2	0.2	1.0	0.4	0.2	25	6	40
	⅙ – ½	7	15	63	25	kg × 110	kg × 2.0[3]	1500	400	5	35	0.05	7	0.5	0.4	0.3	1.5	0.5	0.4	40	10	60
	½ – 1	9	20	72	28	kg × 100	kg × 1.8[3]	1500	400	5	35	0.1	8	0.6	0.5	0.4	2.0	0.6	0.5	45	15	70
Children	1 – 2	12	26	81	32	1100	25	2000	400	10	40	0.1	8	0.6	0.6	0.5	2.0	0.7	0.7	55	15	100
	2 – 3	14	31	91	36	1250	25	2000	400	10	40	0.2	8	0.7	0.6	0.6	2.5	0.8	0.8	60	15	150
	3 – 4	16	35	100	39	1400	30	2500	400	10	40	0.2	9	0.8	0.7	0.7	3	0.8	0.8	70	10	200
	4 – 6	19	42	110	43	1600	30	2500	400	10	40	0.2	11	0.9	0.8	0.9	4	0.8	0.8	80	10	200
	6 – 8	23	51	121	48	2000	35	3500	400	15	40	0.2	13	1.1	1.0	1.0	4	0.9	0.9	100	10	250
	8 – 10	28	62	131	52	2200	40	3500	400	15	40	0.3	15	1.2	1.1	1.2	5	1.0	1.0	110	10	250
Males	10 – 12	35	77	140	55	2500	45	4500	400	20	40	0.4	17	1.3	1.3	1.4	5	1.2	1.2	125	10	300
	12 – 14	43	95	151	59	2700	50	5000	400	20	45	0.4	18	1.4	1.4	1.6	5	1.4	1.4	135	18	350
	14 – 18	59	130	170	67	3000	60	5000	400	25	55	0.4	20	1.5	1.5	1.8	5	1.4	1.4	150	18	400
	18 – 22	67	147	175	69	2800	60	5000	400	30	60	0.4	18	1.6	1.4	2.0	5	0.8	0.8	140	10	400
	22 – 35	70	154	175	69	2800	65	5000	—	30	60	0.4	18	1.7	1.4	2.0	5	0.8	0.8	140	10	350
	35 – 55	70	154	173	68	2600	65	5000	—	30	60	0.4	17	1.7	1.3	2.0	5	0.8	0.8	125	10	350
	55 – 75+	70	154	171	67	2400	65	5000	—	30	60	0.4	14	1.7	1.2	2.0	6	0.8	0.8	110	10	350
Females	10 – 12	35	77	142	56	2250	50	4500	400	20	40	0.4	15	1.3	1.1	1.4	5	1.2	1.2	110	18	300
	12 – 14	44	97	154	61	2300	50	5000	400	20	45	0.4	15	1.4	1.2	1.6	5	1.3	1.3	115	18	350
	14 – 16	52	114	157	62	2400	55	5000	400	25	50	0.4	16	1.4	1.2	1.8	5	1.3	1.3	120	18	350
	16 – 18	54	119	160	63	2300	55	5000	400	25	50	0.4	15	1.5	1.2	2.0	5	1.3	1.3	115	18	350
	18 – 22	58	128	163	64	2000	55	5000	400	25	55	0.4	13	1.5	1.0	2.0	5	0.8	0.8	100	18	350
	22 – 35	58	128	163	64	2000	55	5000	—	25	55	0.4	13	1.5	1.0	2.0	5	0.8	0.8	100	18	300
	35 – 55	58	128	160	63	1850	55	5000	—	25	55	0.4	13	1.5	1.0	2.0	5	0.8	0.8	90	18	300
	55 – 75+	58	128	157	62	1700	55	5000	—	25	55	0.4	13	1.5	1.0	2.0	6	0.8	0.8	80	10	300
Pregnancy						+200[6]	65	6000	400	30	60	0.8	15	1.8	+0.1	2.5	8	+0.4	+0.4	125	18	450
Lactation						+1000[6]	75	8000	400	30	60	0.5	20	2.0	+0.5	2.5	6	+0.5	+0.5	150	18	450

1. The allowance levels are intended to cover individual variations among most normal persons as they live in the United States under usual environmental stresses. The recommended allowances can be attained with a variety of common foods, providing other nutrients for which human requirements have been less well defined.
2. Entries on lines for age range 22–35 yr represent the reference man and woman at age 22. All other entries represent allowances for the midpoint of the specified age range.
3. Assumes protein equivalent to human milk. For proteins not 100% utilized factors should be increased proportionately.
4. The folacin allowances refer to dietary sources as determined by *Lactobacillus casei* assay. Pure forms of folacin may be effective in doses less than ¼ of the RDA.
5. Niacin equivalents include dietary sources of the vitamin itself plus 1 mg equivalent for each 60 mg of dietary tryptophan.
6. Add these amounts to appropriate age allowances.

sized containers, or formed into tablets such as are used in bread enrichment.

Vitamins can be obtained either as the pure substances or in encapsulated form, which reduces the odor and flavor problem in highly enriched dry mixes. Encapsulation is of little value if the vitamins go through a wet processing step, especially if heat is applied. The fat-soluble vitamins are often supplied as oil solutions, in which case it is advisable to specify an antioxidant since the corn oil vehicle can contribute a rancid flavor to the finished product.

Vitamins are very expensive on a per-pound basis, but the cost of supplementing with vitamins is relatively low due to the small amounts required, so that about 20 MDR's of 6 vitamins, or 5 RDA's of 10 vitamins can be supplied for about 1¢ ingredient cost.

Vitamin claims should be effective at the point of consumption, not at the point of production, so it is important to conduct stability tests which will give an indication of the amounts of vitamins lost during normal distribution and storage. Overages are then added to compensate for the expected loss.

Minerals

The mineral nutrients most commonly added to bakery products are calcium, phosphorus, and iron. Calcium and phosphorus are frequently added in the form of a relatively inert calcium phosphate, such as tricalcium phosphate. Since these salts must be added in fairly large amounts in order to achieve supplementation at a substantial percentage of the RDA per portion, undesirable effects on dough properties are sometimes observed. Calcium phosphates are good buffers and may cause a change in dough pH. The calcium ion can have a toughening or insolubilizing effect on the gluten, thus changing the machining behavior of the dough.

Iron can be added in several forms (Table 28.3). The different compounds vary widely in cost per pound of active ingredient, and also apparently vary in the extent to which they can be utilized or absorbed by the body. Undesirable color reactions sometimes occur if the iron is present in the ionic state, so insoluble compounds are preferred for supplementing bakery products.

In late 1969, the baking and milling industries petitioned the U.S. FDA to triple the levels of iron in enriched flour and bread. Final action on this petition has not been taken, but many large bakeries have instituted the practice of enriching nonstandardized products, which do not require special approval for modification of the formulas (provided, of course, that the ingredients themselves are approved).

TABLE 28.3
CODEX OR FOOD GRADE IRON SALTS AND THEIR COST

Name	Formula	Percentage of Iron in Formula	Cost ($/Lb)[1]	Iron Cost ($)/Lb
Ferric ammonium citrate	9% NH_3, 65% hydrated citric acid	17	1.34	7.88
Ferric ammonium sulfate	$FeNH_4(SO_4)_2 \cdot 12H_2O$	11.6	0.68	5.86
Ferric phosphate soluble	45% citric acid	13	1.13	8.69
Ferric orthophosphate	$FePO_4 \cdot XH_2O$	28.6	0.60	2.10
Sodium iron pyrophosphate	$Na_8Fe_4(P_2O_7)_5 \cdot XH_2O$	14.5	0.44	3.03
Ferric pyrophosphate soluble	40% citric acid complex	11	1.12	10.18
Ferrous fumarate	$FeC_4H_2O_4$	32.5	0.98	3.01
Ferrous gluconate	$C_{12}H_{22}FeO_{14} \cdot 2H_2O$	11.3	0.96	8.50
Ferrous sulfate	$FeSO_4 \cdot 7H_2O$	20.1	0.235	1.17
Ferrous sulfate dried	$FeSO_4$ (86%)	31.7	0.255	0.80
Ferrous reductum (iron reduced)	Fe	96	0.420	0.44

Source: Courtesy of Mallinckrodt Chemical Works.
[1] Prices as of April 30, 1970.

Iodine is usually added as iodized salt or potassium iodide. The amount required is so small that the cost is almost negligible, even for farily high levels of supplementation. Effects on color, flavor, texture, and functional properties should be undetectable.

It is probably not often necessary or desirable to add magnesium to bakery products. Where this is to be done, magnesium chloride is probably the compound of choice. The oxide, another cheap source of the element, may have some effect on pH of the dough.

Since mineral supplements are not volatile and do not undergo storage reactions which destroy the active ingredient, the percentage of the element placed in the food should be the same as that reaching the consumer. That is, storage losses need not be considered in calculating the amount of supplement to be added. Some questions have been raised about the possibility of the element reacting to form a compound which cannot be utilized by the body, or reacting with metals in the processing equipment or container and being left behind, but conclusive information on these points is not available. In dry mixes, it may happen that the supplements become unevenly distributed during transfer and filling operations, as a result of differences in density.

Fats

Special kinds of fatty materials, such as polyunsaturated fats, cannot be publicized as ingredients of a particular food because of current regulations, reflecting the existing uncertainties about their actual benefits to health. There is no clear-cut, statistically significant advantage of a diet high in polyunsaturated acids for preventing deterioration of the circulatory system, such as atherosclerosis. Large-scale, long-term studies which have been conducted up to this time seem to indicate that the consumption of polyunsaturated acids may be one of several factors associated with cholesterol deposits in the arteries, arteriosclerosis, and the incidence of heart attacks. The factor which has been emphasized was the content of polyunsaturated fatty acids. Single unsaturated bonds apparently have little or no effect. Fully saturated fatty acids are thought to be bad in large quantities and more or less neutral in effect when consumed in low or moderate quantities.

The natural fats and oils commonly used in foods range in unsaturated fat content from coconut oil at about 8% to safflower oil with about 75% polyunsaturates. The free fatty acids from spring wheat flours contain less palmitic and less linoleic acid than those from winter and biscuit flours (Morrison 1964). Adjustment of the polyunsaturates content of bakery products containing shortening can be made sometimes by using appropriate oils. The functional properties of the different oils cannot be made equivalent by any acceptable procedure, however. Hydrogenation destroys the polyunsaturated nature of the oils, of course.

Protein

Protein malnutrition is a problem affecting some groups whose diet consists mostly of cereals or other starchy foods. Because bread-like products are staples in many countries, it may be desirable to improve the protein intake by adding protein-rich materials to wheat flour or to the dough as a separate ingredient. Alternatively, specific amino acids can be added to improve the protein-efficiency ratio of the other available nitrogenous substances. Lysine is the limiting amino acid in many cereal derivatives.

Wheat mixes blended for the milling of bread flour tend to have a typical and constant amino acid distribution (Hepburn and Bradley 1964). The pattern of amino acids depends more upon the total nitrogen of the sample than upon the particular variety. When calculated on an equal-nitrogen basis, samples of wheat with high and low nitrogen contents differ in the amounts of certain amino acids.

Protein supplements must be added at the parts per hundred level in order to make a substantial contribution to nutrient intake, as compared to parts per million for some of the vitamins. Thus, cost becomes a very important factor, especially when the dietary improvement is intended for large numbers of impoverished persons. Effects on the physical properties of doughs and the organoleptic properties of the finished products are often limiting factors. Many potential supplements which would otherwise be excellent sources of protein have found limited application because of high cost, functional deficiencies, or poor organoleptic properties.

The ideal protein source for adding to bakery products should be a cheap, bland white powder with a high protein efficiency ratio (or, at least, contain relatively large percentages of the essential amino acids which are present in low amounts in wheat flour). It should have no unpleasant esthetic or ethical connotations. Since there is no natural animal or vegetable derivative which fulfills all of these requirements, some compromises must be made. The following sections will cover some of the protein sources which have been used, or suggested, for bakery product supplementation.

Single-cell Protein.—Much effort has been devoted to studying production of utilizable protein by single-cell cultures, that is, by cultures of algae, yeast, or molds. These organisms turn inorganic sources of nitrogen, such as ammonia or ammonium nitrate, into cell protein when grown under the proper conditions. In some processes, they are used to convert the nitrogenous materials in wastes, such as sewage, into cell proteins. The advantages of using these organisms is that they can be handled in suspension, like liquids, and processing is relatively simple. They can also be fairly efficient insofar as the amount of energy used is concerned in converting inorganic nitrogen into protein.

In the case of algae (or green plants), the energy used in converting inorganic nitrogen into protein comes mainly from sunlight. For yeasts and molds, an energy source in the form of carbohydrate or some other food must be added, which increases the cost of production. The energy source can be such nonfood materials as the waste liquid from paper mills.

In spite of all the effort and funds expended on development of single-cell processes, none of those studied has become commercially successful as a source of protein for general use. Some yeast is "primary grown" for special supplementation requirements, and yeast and mold by-products are available in moderate quantities. Brewers' yeast is used mainly for animal feeding. Many, if not all, of these materials have strong flavors which sharply limit their use in foods. Inactive dry yeast also has an adverse effect on dough properties, probably because of the free glutathione content.

There is some question as to the theoretical economic advantage of single-cell cultures. Although the increase in cellular material is rapid compared to green plants in the field, the necessity for elaborate tanks, piping, etc., and the relatively high labor requirement seem to be negative features.

Milk Derivatives.—Whole milk in any form is too expensive to be used primarily for its protein content. Nonfat dry milk (MSNF) is a fairly good source of protein, but it too is expensive and carries a large amount of carbohydrate (lactose) which makes it difficult to fit it into some formulations. Whey has even more carbohydrate than MSNF but it is relatively inexpensive and it avoids some of the functional properties of the latter, especially when it has been properly heat-treated.

Whey powder itself is of little value for protein supplementation. It is high in lactose and mineral salts, containing only 12–13% protein. Methods have been developed for separating the protein, however, and concentrates of up to about 90% protein are available in limited quantities. This protein has good PER (protein efficiency ratio) and is bland when prepared from raw materials that are of good quality. Acid wheys, containing products resulting from bacterial action, usually have off-flavors that are difficult to remove by ordinary processing methods.

Casein has been a widely-used protein supplement. It has a good PER and is easily digested by most people. When used in doughs or batters, it increases the absorption and viscosity considerably. Although it is more expensive than some other supplements, imported supplies and other factors make it less expensive than MSNF as a source of protein. Flavors vary widely between suppliers, and it is advisable to check each shipment carefully. Sodium or calcium caseinates provide different solubility characteristics.

Fish Protein Concentrate.—Fish meal, as produced by hot-air drying of mixed varieties of small fish which have not been cleaned, is used in animal feeds but is not suitable for human consumption. Solvent extraction of fresh whole or cleaned fish can be used to produce a relatively bland high-protein powder that might be used to increase the nutrient quality of bakery foods.

There has been intense political pressure behind fish protein concentrate in the United States, and this has obscured some unfavorable aspects of the material when used as a human dietary supplement. Fish protein concentrate, as now prepared, cannot compete on a cost basis with oilseed proteins. Even the most optimistic estimates do not place the cost of the material at less than 30¢ per lb of protein. This is several times the cost of protein from defatted soy flour and more than double the estimated cost of soy protein isolate. To justify the use of FPC (fish protein concentrate) in spite of the great discrepancy in cost, there should be some offsetting advantage in organoleptic properties, functionality, or nutrition. None has been pointed out up to this time.

Flavor is an important factor that tends to be glossed over by proponents of FPC. The intensity of the off-flavor depends upon the way the concentrate has been prepared and the grade and freshness of the raw material; but even the best powders appear to contribute detectable off-flavors at rather low addition rates. One recent report, describing a study conducted with Moroccan children fed on a weaning ration containing FPC, said "The 3% level of enrichment was probably the maximal practicable, as it caused a perceptible fishy taste to the food and there were some adverse reactions from the mothers" (Tavill and Gonik 1969). It is very difficult to conceal significant off-flavors by formulation changes, and generally not much can be done in this respect by processing.

Meat By-products.—Most of the protein-containing by-products of slaughter-house operation are not commonly used in food. Included are blood, bones, some trimmings and viscera, hide, hair, feathers, etc. These materials are usually converted for nonfood purposes, such as animal feed or fertilizer, but in some cases they are suitable for food use if properly processed. An example is gelatine derived from bones or hog hides.

Although such materials might be used for large-scale protein supplementation, they are by-products and the ultimate supply is limited by the number of animals slaughtered. Because they are perishable, they must be processed quickly or frozen, giving some consequent economic disadvantages. Changing them into bland protein concentrates for food supplementation may involve techniques not yet invented but probably expensive. If gelatine in regarded as representative, protein from these sources might cost 50¢ to $1.50 per dry pound.

Oilseed Proteins.—There are several plants grown primarily for their oil content. When the oil has been pressed or extracted from the seeds, there remains a solid residue which contains other nutrients such as carbohydrates and proteins, as well as considerable fiber. Some oil seeds of worldwide commercial significance are soybean, sunflower, rape, peanut, flax, and coconut. Cottonseed is a special example in which the seed is the by-product of another raw material not grown primarily for the oil content. The cakes left after oil extraction and solvent removal are valuable for animal feeding, and there have been many efforts to process these materials into human dietary products. These efforts have been the most successful in the case of soybeans, but some applications have also been found for cottonseed meal derivatives.

The American soybean contains approximately 38% protein. Based on an average yield, an acre of beans will produce over 700 lb of protein per year, in addition to valuable amounts of oil. This is over ten times the protein that livestock could produce grazing on the same land. It is also more protein than virtually any other staple food plant will yield. Thus, it is obvious that soy offers a plentiful and economical source of protein.

The soybean was originally grown mainly for the oil content, the defatted meal being regarded as a by-product of very limited utility. Recognition of the advantage of using high protein supplements, such as soybean meal, for animal feed led to an increasing demand so that the yield to the processor from the sale of oil is now only about ½ that received from the meal.

Soy protein has long been used for food in the orient. Some of the dishes are miso (a flavoring paste), tofu (a curd or cheese), soy sauce, and tempeh. A soy milk (suspension of ground beans) is used in some countries. Thus, the utility of the product is well-established and there is presumptive evidence of its safety and nutritional value when used over long periods of time. Large numbers of people have become acquainted with the idea and flavor of soy as a result of these uses.

Soy meal is relatively cheap. An average, calculated from prices over a period of several years, shows a cost for protein from this source of about 9¢ per lb. The supply is plentiful in most years, and could be substantially increased if an assured market existed for the additional material.

Proteins can be isolated from soybean meal by various extraction methods, and purified by dissolving and reprecipitating. The protein, as isolated, is reasonably versatile. If well purified, it is nearly tasteless. It does contribute some viscosity and moisture-absorbing powers, which are not always desirable. It coagulates at some pH levels and is moderately sensitive to heat.

All things considered, it appears that soybeans are the preferred source of protein for mass feeding of undernourished populations.

Use of protein-rich additives in bread doughs can cause the doughs to have unsatisfactory machining properties and the bread to have non-typical appearance, texture, and flavor. Numerous studies have been conducted to find practical methods of overcoming these adverse effects. Typical examples were described by Tsen *et al.* (1971). They found that satisfactory bread containing up to 16% soy flour could be made by conventional methods if the dough conditioners sodium stearoyl-2 lactylate and calcium stearoyl-2 lactylate were used. This is a practical and legally acceptable solution since both these substances are now being used commercially in the baking industry for their dough improving qualities, and have been approved by the U.S. FDA as safe food additives.

Other oilseed meals may have limited utility for the protein supplementation of bakery foods, but in each case, negatives are apparent. Coconuts contain much less protein that other oilseeds, the residue from oil extraction of copra being only about 20% protein. Furthermore, the harvesting and processing are not conducive to the production of food-grade products. The protein is damaged so that its nutritive value is reduced, and there is danger of aflatoxin from the molds, which grow on the drying copra. For these, and other reasons, coconuts cannot be considered a reliable source of protein.

Defatted peanut meal is produced in considerable quantities in other parts of the world, but not in the United States. Aflatoxin is also a problem with this material since it is often held and processed under conditions conducive to mold growth. Nonetheless, it does have some potential as a protein source, but it is likely to be considerably more expensive than other oilseed meal because the nut itself is more costly.

Cottonseed meal has a good protein content. It also contains a toxic substance called gossypol which can be removed by certain procedures. Gossypol-free strains of cotton are also being developed. Cottonseed meal processed to various particle sizes and degrees of browness are commercially available for specialty purposes, such as giving the visual effect of spices in cakes, biscuits, etc. Because it is tied in with the production of cotton, this is an unreliable raw material for large-scale protein supplementation.

Millfeeds.—The residues remaining from production of flour, semolina, farina, rye flour and meal, corn meal, and other granular or powdered cereal products, collectively called millfeeds and used as components of cattle rations, have fairly high protein contents. There might be some potential value for these materials as supplements for specialty food products, but the high percentage of fiber, the pronounced flavor, the limited storage stability, the dark color, and the physical properties create obstacles to such usage. Similar problems can be envisioned in trying to apply the high-protein fraction of the corn wet-milling operation to foods.

It might be possible to extract bland nitrogenous substances from these materials, with or without prior enzyme digestion, but not much has been done along this line.

BIBLIOGRAPHY

ANON. 1968. Improvement of the nutritive quality of foods. J. Am. Med. Assoc. 205, No. 12, 50–51.
ANON. 1970. Whys and ways of adding nutrition. Snack Food 59, No. 9, 50–51.
BABAYAN, V. K. 1971. Bakery fats. Bakery Dig. 45, No. 2, 20–23, 26, 74.
CZERNIEJEWSKI, C. P., SHANK, C. W., BECHTEL, W. G., and BRADLEY, W. B. 1964. The minerals of wheat, flour, and bread. Cereal Chem. 41, 65–72.
ELVEHJEM, C. A. 1956. Studies on amino acid supplementation of cereals. Cereal Sci. Today 1, 162–164.
GATES, J. C., and KENNEDY, B. M. 1964. Protein quality of bread and bread ingredients. J. Am. Dietetic Assoc. 44, 374–377.

GOTTHOLD, M. L. M., and KENNEDY, B. M. 1964. Biological evaluation of protein in steamed and baked breads and in bread ingredients. J. Food Sci. 29, 227-232.

LACHANCE, P. A. 1971. Protein quality and PER: concepts important to future foods. Food Prod. Develop. 5, No. 3, 39, 42, 66.

MORRISON, W. R. 1964. The free fatty acid content of some wheat flours. J. Sci. Food Agr. 14, 870-873.

NELSON, J. H., GLASS, R. L., and GEDDES, W. F. 1963. The triglycerides and fatty acids of wheat. Cereal Chem. 40, 343-351.

TAVILL, F., and GONIK, A. 1969. Weaning ration containing 3% fish protein concentrate. Am. J. Clin. Nutr. 22, 1571-1578.

TSEN, C. C., HOOVER, W. J., and PHILLIPS, D. 1971. High-protein breads. Bakers Dig. 45, No. 2, 20-23, 26, 74.

Index

Absolute humidity, 388
Absorption test, for shortenings, 74
Acceletron, 429
Acetic acid, 167
Acetone dicarboxylic acid, 35
Acid-enzyme process, 54
Active dry yeast, 42
Active oxygen method, 69
Aflatoxin, 125, 586
Agitators, 274, 318-319, 321-322
Air classification, 5-7, 19
Air conditioning units, 395, 397, 401-402
Air injection units, 264
Air washer, 400
Airslide cars, 264
Alberger process salt, 162
Albumen, *See* Egg whites
Algae, 28
Alkylbenzene sulfonate, 26
Allspice, 138-139
Almond paste, 130
Almonds, 127-130
Aluminum pans, 479-480, 519
Aluminum salts, 31
Alveograph, 16-17
AmFlow Incorporator, 370
AmFlow Process, 361, 363-364, 366, 368-374
Amino acids, 12, 21, 94, 111, 150
Ammonium bicarbonate, 35, 186, 202, 259
Ammonium chloride, 157
Amylases, 149-151, 153, 234
Amylopectin, 8
Amylose, 7, 76
Analog controllers, 286
Analysis
  spices, 135
  water, 27-28
Angel food cakes, 39, 165-171
Anise, 140
Annatto, 146
Antioxidants, 61, 79-80
Apples, 118-119, 137, 251-252
Applesauce, 193
Arkady, 157
Army bread, 212
Arsenic, 26-27
Ascorbic acid, 10, 159, 312
Ash
  bakery product, 29
  corn syrups, 56
  flour, 8, 10, 17
Aspergillus oryzae, 153
Auto-baking, 525
Automatic batch scales, 281
Automatic batching systems, 294-296
Automatic feeders, 282

Avidin, 111
Azodicarbonamide, 159

Babassu, 63
Babcock test, 95
Bacillus mesentericus, 156
Bacteria, 42-43, 97-98
Bacteriological tests, 27-28
Bag loaders, 469
Bagels, 359
Bagging equipment, 468-470
Baker Do-Maker, 361, 366-368, 373-374
Baker's cheese, 92
Baker's chocolate, 142
Baking chamber construction, 420-421
Baking conditions,
  angle-food cakes, 169
Baking powder, 40-41
Bananas, 193, 253
Band guides, 422-423
Band ovens, 418-423
Band tension, 444-445
Bands, oven, 421-422
  slicer, 438-446, 456-457
Barium, 27
Barley, 1, 149
Batavia cinnamon, 136-137
Baumé determination, 56
Beaten biscuits, 182
Beef tallow, 63, 65-66, 73
Beet powder, 146
Beet sugar, 49, 53
Bench balances, 278
Benzoyl peroxide, 5, 19
Beta-carotene, 146
Bing cherries, 122
Bins, storage, 262, 264-266
Biological oxygen demand, 28
Black Mission figs, 120
Blackstrap molasses, 53
Blast freezers, 507-511
Bleached sulphite paper, 476
Bleaches, flour, 5
Bloom-strength, 161-162
Blueberries, 118, 138
Bottoming pan, 494
Botulism, 521
Bowl-type rounders, 330-331
Bran, 3
Bread, 1, 14, 41, 78, 460, 499-500, 525, 527-528, 534
Bread wrappers, 460-468
Break rolls, 3
Breakfast tarts, 255-256
Brews, 361-366
Brookfield viscosity test, 103
Broths, 366-369

INDEX

Brown sugar, 53-54
Browning, nonenzymatic, 85, 111
Budgeting, 541-543
Buffers, 161
Buhr mills, 3
Bulk-handling, of eggs, 113-114
Bun, dividers, 296, 528
   formula, 212
   packers, 471, 473
   rounders, 352
Burners, 418-419, 426-429
Butter, 61, 64, 71, 83
Butterfat, 61, 64, 73, 82, 95
Buttermilk, 40, 83, 88-89
Butylated hydroxyanisole (BHA), 80
Butylated hydroxytoluene (BHT), 80

C-enamel, 526
Cacao products, 142-145
Cadmium, 27, 33
Cakes, 2, 14, 73-74, 118, 138, 189-190, 507, 525
   continuous processing, 378
   faults, 197-198
Calcium, 94, 161
   iodate, 364
   lactate, 40
   peroxide, 155, 157, 159, 365
   salts, 31
   stearoyl lactylate, 79
Calimyrna figs, 120
Can enamels, 526
Candied (glacé) fruits, 123
Cane sugar, 49, 53
Canned bakery foods, 480, 520-534
Canthaxanthin, 146
Capillary melting point, 68
Caramel color, 146-147
Caraway, 139-140
Carbohydrates,
   flour, 7-8
   milk, 93
Carbon black, 146
Carbon chloroform extract, 26
Carbon dioxide, 35, 41-42, 371, 400-401, 512
Cardamom, 139
Carmine, 146
Carotenoids, 93, 154
Carrot oil, 146
Caseinates, 83
Cashews, 130-131
Cassava flour, 244
Cassia, 136-137
Cellophane, 460, 472, 474-475, 519
Cellulose, microcrystalline, 59
Cephalin, 110
Charcoal caraway, 139-140
Check weighers, 303
Cheese, 83, 91-93
   bread, 212
   cake, 91, 525
   fillings, 257
Cherries, 122-123

Chiffon cakes, 173-174, 195-196, 525
Chilled water systems, 317
Chlorides, 26-27, 33
Chlorination, 29
Chlorine, 19, 33
   dioxide, 5
Chocolate, 142, 144, 241
   bitter, 142
   bittersweet, 142
   cakes, 194
   crumb, 91
   liquor, 142, 143
   products, 77, 86, 249, 492-493
Cholesterol, 94, 110
Chopin graph, 16-17
Chorleywood bread process, 225-226, 377
Chromium, 27
Chuck wagon bread, 213
Chute-end trough, 408
Cinnamon, 136, 237
Citrates, 94
Citric acid, 80, 94, 167
Cleanup stage, 310
Clips, for bags, 469
Clostridium botulinum, 521
Cloves, 137
Coagulation, 29
Coatings, 61, 247-250
Cobalt-90, 535
Cochineal extract, 146
Cocoa, 142-144
   analysis, 144-145
   pigments, 144
Cocoa butter, 63, 66, 73, 142
Coconut, 132-134, 249
   depositers, 483, 485
   oil, 63, 71, 73
Coders, 464, 532-533
Coffee, 137
Coffee cakes, 517, 525
Cold wall trailer, 518
Coliform count, 27, 98
Collagen, 161
Color, water, 28
Colors, for food, 145-146
Compressor, 508
Compression streaks, 528
Computers, 296
Conalbumin, 111
Condensed milk, 83
Condenser, 508
Conditioners, for chocolate, 492-493
Conditioning, 2
Conduction, 413
Congealing point, 69
Consultants, 552-553
Consumer research, 540, 543
Contaminants, of water, 26-27
Continuous belt freezer, 509
Continuous processing
   cake batters, 378-380
   equipment and procedures, 366-375
   formulations and ingredients, 361-366
Contract research, 552-553

INDEX

Control charts, 571-572
Controlled flow trough, 408
Convection, 412-413
Cookie mixes, 39
Cookie-forming equipment, 353-355
Cookies, 2, 15, 20, 53, 59, 138, 199-201, 326, 489-490
  formulations and procedures, 184-187
  ovens for, 419-420
Coolers, 433-435
Cooling tunnels, for enrobed goods, 495
Copper, 26, 31
Corn, flour and meal, 19-20, 155
  oil, 63, 73
  sugar, 55, 57
  syrup, 40, 54-58, 172, 242, 259, 270-272
Cottage cheese, 85, 92
Cottonseed, flour, 146
  oil, 63, 66, 73
Coupon inserters, 464
Crackers, 29, 31, 37, 41, 230-235, 314, 322-323
Cream, 83, 91
  fillings, 252, 518
  puffs, 139, 183-184
Cream of tartar, 38, 166
Creamers, 319
Creaming, 165, 196-197, 307, 313
  test, 72, 74
Creme filling depositors, 488-489, 492
Critical path analysis, 553
Cross grinding, 443-444
Cross-grain molders, 342
Crumpets, 352-353
Cryogenic freezing, 511-518
Cryotransfer process, 513-515
Curd, 92
Curling rollers, 348-349
Currants, 119-120
Custard, 137, 252
  pies, 251-252
Cutting angle, 442
Cyanide, 26-27

Danish pastry, 67, 91, 118, 180, 222-224, 347-348, 525
Deck ovens, 414
Dehumidification, 399-400
Dehydrated bread, 534-535
Dehydrofrozen fruit, 251
Delivery, bulk, 263-264
Dendritic salt, 162
Depanners, 432-433
Deposit cookies, 204, 353
Depositers, 483, 486-487
Depositing machines, 204
Design temperature, 395
Detailer, 494
Developers, continuous, 371-374
Development, 307-309
Devil's food cakes, 194-195, 525
Dew point, 388, 393, 398, 402
Dewar flasks, 512
Dextrins, 20, 42, 151

Dextrose, 57-58, 201
  equivalent, 54-55
Diacetyl, 92
Diastase, 151. *See also* Amylases
Diastatic malt, 150-151
Diatoms, 28
Dicalcium phosphate, 38-39
Dietary modification, 574-575
Dietetic foods, 153, 520
  sodium-free, 35
Digital controllers, 286
Dilatometry, 70
Direct fired ovens, 418
Disc slicers, 458-459
Displacement meters, 290
Disposable containers, 259
Divider oil, 299-300
Dividers, dough, 296-305, 329, 351-352, 528
Dockers, 353
Dough, brakes, 182, 346-347
  extruders, 346
  hook, 321
  improvers, 157-158
  oilers, 484
  pump, 371
  specific heat, 394
  temperatures, calculation, 226-227
Doughnuts, 118, 239-240, 348, 356-359, 407, 525
Dried eggs, conversion factors, 109
Dried whole milk, 86
Drop- side trough, 408
Drum-type rounders, 331
Dry corn milling, 21
Dusting flour, 265
  applicators, 485-486
"Dutched" chocolate products, 143-144

Eclairs, 139, 183-184
Egg bread, 212
Egg whites, 108, 110, 167
Eggs, bacteriology, 112
  composition, 109-112
  conveying, 259
  in cakes, 190-191
    cookies, 200
    pie fillings, 251
Electrical hygrometer, 392-393
Electronic ovens, 423-424
Emulsifiers, 61, 76-79
End labels, 464
End-seal applicators, 464
English muffins, 352-353
Enocianina, 146
Enriched bread, 576-577
Enrober, 493-494
Enzymes, 22, 85-86, 112, 153-155
Equal-arm balances, 278
Ethanol, 35, 41, 309
Ethyl vanillin, 141-142
Evaporated milk, 83
Evaporator, 508, 518
EVOP, 555-556

592 INDEX

Extensograph, 16-17

Farinograph, 15-16
Fats, 61-75, 150
Fatty acids, 61
   distribution in food fats, 63
Fermaloid, 157
Fermentation, 31, 33, 111, 153, 160, 233, 387, 527
   loss, 235
   rooms, 387, 393-394
      construction details, 394-402
Ferrous gluconate, 146
Fig bars, 353
Figs, 120-122
Filberts, 124
Fillings, 237, 518
   for, pies, 251, 517
      sweet yeast-leavened products, 253-257
Filter receivers, 262
Filtration, 29
Final proofers, 403-407
Fire point, 72
Fish protein concentrate, 583-584
Flash point, 72
Flat breads, 19
Flat icing, 239
Flavoprotein, 111
Flavoring substances, 112
   in bread, 155
Flexible pouches, 534-535
Flexographic printing, 477
Flexure-plate Leverage System, 278-279
Flip tester, 525-526
Floors, for proof boxes, 398-399
Flour, aging, 261
   bread, 1, 209
   brushes, 485
   cookie, 119-200, 205
   cracker, 230-231
   grades, 5, 7-8
   pastry, 1
   streusel, 237
Flowrator, 290
Fluid shortenings, 275
Fluidizing, 262
Fluorides, 33, 46
FMC Bread Weight Controller, 303-305
Foam drying, 114
Foil, 519
Foil laminated films, 478-479, 519
Fondant, 240
Fondant sugar, 50
Free fatty acid content, 69-70, 75, 95
Freeze-drying, 115
Freezers, mechanical, 507-511
Freezing, 496-518
   eggs, 113-114
Freezing point depression, 497, 507
French bread, 211
Fried pies, 178-180
Frost point hygrometers, 393
Frostings, 237, 507

Frozen storage, 496-507, 518-519
Fructose, 8, 42, 52, 58
Fruit filling depositer, 489
Fruit juices, 40
Fruitcake, 138, 172, 522, 530-532
Fruits, 118-124. *See also* specific fruits
Frying fats, 75
Fuels, 425-426
Fungicides, 156

Gantt charts, 553
Gate-end trough, 408
Gauges, 274
   band tension, 444-445
Gelatin, 33, 161-162, 242, 246
Gelometer, 161
Genoise, 172
Germ, 3
Ginger, 138
Gingerbread, 138, 194
Glacé fruits, 530
Glassine, 472, 475-476
Glazes, 239
Gliadin, 12
Glucono-delta-lactone, 38
Glucose, 8, 42, 46, 52, 55, 111
Glutathione, 43
Gluten, 12, 14, 31, 79. 189, 308-309
Gluten-free bakery foods, 520, 575
Glutenin, 12
Glycerol, 132, 172, 243, 248
Golden Delicious apples, 119
Good Manufacturing Practices, 562
Gossypol, 586
Graham bread and flour, 3, 157
Graham crackers, 53, 78, 248, 320
Grain Standards, 13
Grape, 139
Grape skin extract, 146
Gravimetric, feeders, 284-286
   hygrometers, 390
Greaseproof papers, 475-476
Greasing machines, 491
Green-dough method, 225-226
Guides, band, 439-440
Guillotine cutters, 349, 484
Gum arabic, 244
Gums, 244, 506
Gunther D-100, 242-243

Hair hygrometers, 392
Hard sweets, 78, 353-354
Head meters, 288
Hearth bread, 2, 5
Heat exchangers, 275
Heat transfer mechanisms, 410-413
Hemicelluloses, 20
Hemoglobin units, 154
High ratio cakes, 191
HLB system, 76
Hoffman-Dalby Farinograph test, 101
Home-style bread, 212
Hones, 455-456
Honey, 40, 58

INDEX 593

Horizontal dough mixers, 315–320
Humidification, 399
Humidistats, 393–394
Humidity, control, 394
  lockout, 398
  measurement, 388
Hydration, 308, 310
Hydrogen, bonding, 308
  peroxide, 35
Hydrogenation, 66–67
Hydrol, 57
Hyfoama, 242–243
Hygrometers. *See* type of hygrometer

Ice cream cones, 184
Ice crystals, 497–498, 507
Icing depositers, 486–487
Icings, 24, 33, 49, 237, 239–241, 320, 507
Ideas, sources, 545–546
Impact milling, 5
Importata, 92
Impulse sealers, 463
Indirect fired ovens, 418
Inferential meters, 288
Infestation, 5
Infrared moisture meters, 97
Ingredient function
  cakes, 189–190
  cookies, 199–201
  yeast-leavened baked goods, 207–210
Insulation, 397
Interesterification, 67
Intermediate proofer, 328, 334–339, 389
Invert syrup, 49, 52, 201, 259
Invertase, 189
Iodine value, 72
IQF berries, 124
Iron, 26–27, 31, 33
  nutritional supplements, 580
Italian bread, 211

Jacketed mixers, 317–318, 325
Jams, 254
Jelly, 24, 59, 237, 254, 492
  depositers, 487
Jelly roll equipment, 490–492
Jonathan apples, 119

Kadota figs, 120
Kernel paste, 130
Kjeldahl procedure, 12, 18
Konpetua, 375–376
Korintje cinnamon, 136

Label printers, 464
Lactalbumin, 93
Lactic acid, 42, 90, 92, 387, 527
Lactoglobulin, 93
Lactometer, 96
Lactose, 58–59, 61, 82, 90
Lakes, 146–147
Lambert cherries, 122
Lard, 63, 64–65, 67, 71, 73, 175, 274
Latent heat of fusion, 496–497
Lead, 27

Leaf fats, 64
Leaveners, chemical, 29, 35–41
Leavening acids, 37–40, 189
Lecithin, 8, 76–77, 110, 200–201, 248
Lemon, 238
Level plane unloader, 432
Lintner value, 152
Lipids, eggs, 110–111
  flour, 8–9
  milk, 93–94
Lipoxidases, 154–156
Liquid shortenings, 67–68
Liquid sponge. *See* Broths
Literature searches, 551
Load cells, 266, 279
Loss-in-weight feeders, 282–284
Lowerator, 405
Lye dipping, 218
Lysine, 21, 581
Lysozyme, 111

Macadamia nuts, 124
Macaroons, 1, 133
Mace, 137
Magnesium, 31, 94, 160
Maintenance
  dough dividers, 301–302
  intermediate proofers, 337
  molders, 345
  rounders, 333
  wrappers, 465–467
Malic acid, 167
Malt, 149–153
Malted milk, 83, 91
Maltose, 8, 42, 54, 153, 387
  value, 152
Maltotriose, 55
Manganese, 26–27, 33
Mannitol, 59
Maple syrup, 58
Maraschino cherries, 122, 147
Margarine, 67, 163
Marketing, 506
Marshmallow, 24, 33, 110, 237, 241–247, 483
Marzipan cakes, 172
Maturing agents, flour, 5
  rye, 19
Matzos, 181–182
Meat by-products, 584
Mechanical benches, 348–349
Mechanical conveying, flour, 261
  sugar, 266–267
Mechanical development processes, 309, 311–312
Melba toast, 496
Melibiose, 8
Meringues, 1, 110, 166
Metering, 287–293
Meters, 271, 288
Methyl silicone, 75
Microscopic clump counts, 97
Microwave ovens, 423–424
Microwave proofing, 358, 407

INDEX

Milk, 21, 29, 82–91, 201, 366
  concentrated products, 84
  quality tests, 95–106
Milk chocolate, 142
Millfeeds, 586
Milling, 2–7, 152, 160
  rye, 19
Mineral supplementation, 579–580
Minerals, flour, 9–10, 18
  malt, 150
  water, 161
Minimum Daily Requirements, 577
Miso, 585
Mixatron, 325
Mixers, 314–323
Mixing techniques
  bread and rolls, 309–312
  cakes, 196–197
  crackers and cookies, 313–314
Mixing tolerance, 155, 310
Mixograph, 16
Moisture, tests, 17, 96–97
  translocation, 389–390, 498, 518
Molasses, 40, 52–53
Molasses raisin bread, 213
Molders, 339–346
Molecular distillation, 78
Monocalcium phosphates, 38–39, 157
Monoglycerides, 77–78
Montmorency cherries, 122
Morton whisks, 315
Most Probable Number, 27
Multiplate freezers, 508
Multiple beam scales, 278
Multitier proofers, 405–406
Muscat raisins, 119
Mutton tallow, 63

Napoleon cherries, 122
Negative pressure systems, 262
NEPA yolk color test, 116
Niacin, 10
Nitrates, 26–27
Nitrogen, blanketing, 274–275
  liquid, 511–513
  peroxide, 19
Nondiastatic malt, 152–153
Nonfat dry milk, 82, 84, 88
No-punch processes, 309
No-time processes, 309
Nucleotides, 44
Nutating meters, 291–292
Nutmeg, 137
Nutritional improvement, 574–575
Nuts, 124–134, 314

Oakes continuous dough machine, 376–378
Oakes mixer, 242
Oats, 1
Oil, processing, 62
  sprayers, 484–485, 488
Oils, 61–75
Oilseed proteins, 584–586

Oleo oil, 65–66, 71
Oleoresin, paprika, 146
  vanilla, 141
Oleostearin, 65
Olive oil, 63
Open inspirator burner system, 426–427
Open-tube melting point, 68
Operations research, 553–554
Orifice plate, 283, 288
Osmophilic yeast, 243
Ovalbumin, 111
Oven loaders, 431
Ovens, auxiliary equipment, 431–436
  fuels, 425–426
  pretzel, 219–220
  types, 414–418
Overwrapping machine, 472
Ovoinhibitor, 111
Ovomucin, 111
Ovomucoid, 111
Oxidizing agents, 158–160, 309, 312
Oxygen, 511–512

Packaging, cookies, 201
  frozen foods, 518–519
Palm kernel oil, 63, 73
Palm oil, 63, 73
Pan-drying, eggs, 114–115
Pancake mixes, 39
Paniplus, 157
Pans, 435–436, 479–480
Paperboard, 518–519
Paprika, 146
Parallel ground blades, 444
Pasteurization, 84–85, 112–113
Pastries, 139
Pâte à chou, 183
Peaches, 118, 137
Peanut, meal, 127, 249
  oil, 63, 73
Peanut butter, 126–127, 163, 238
  and cracker sandwiches, 490–491
Peanuts, 125–126
Pears, 137–138
Pecan roll, 527, 532–534
Pecans, 131–132, 530
Pectin, 251, 254
Peel oven, 414
Pentosans, 20
Peroxide value, 69
Perpetua, 375
PERT, 553
Phenols, 26–27
Phosphates, 94, 160
Phosphatides, 77, 93
Phosphoric acid, 80
Physical dough testing, 15–17
Pickup stage, 310
Pie, crust formers, 349–351
  crusts, 165, 174
  fillings, 251, 517
  unloaders, 432
Pies, 2, 251–253, 506, 515
Pigments, egg yolk, 111

INDEX

Pineapple upside down cake, 239
Piping, 271
Pistachios, 124
Piston meter, 291
Pizzas, 39, 517
Planetary mixers, 320-321
Plansifters, 3
Plastic coconut, 133
Plastic range, 68
Plasticity, fats, 70-71
Platform scales, 278
Pneumatic conveying, flour, 260-266
  sugar, 267-269
Polyester films, 534
Polyethylene, 472, 476-477, 519
Polyglycerol emulsifiers, 79, 245
Polyoxethylene sorbitan monostearate, 78
Polypropylene, 477-478, 519
Polystyrene, 480
Polyunsaturated fats, 580-581
Popovers, 183
Poppy seed, 139
Portion packaging, 470-471
Positive displacement meters, 288, 292
Positive pressure systems, 262-263
Potassium, 33
  acid tartrate, See Cream of tartar
  bicarbonate, 35
  bromate, 157-158, 312, 364
  iodate, 157, 159, 364
Potato bread, 216-217
Pound cakes, 171-172, 522, 525, 529-530
Power requirements for dough mixing, 323-325
Preferments, 362-365, 366
Premixed gas system, 428
Premixing, 312-313
Preservatives, 156-157
Preserves, 254
Pretzels, 41, 163, 218-220, 355
Primary bevels, 442
Processing methods
  breads and rolls, 210-218
  cakes, 196-197
  canned bakery foods, 522-534
  doughnuts, 356-359
  streusels, 238-239
Product development, 537-539, 541, 551-556
  examples, 556-558
Product planning committees, 546-549
Proofing, 387-388
  conditions, 388, 528
  enclosures, 387, 393-394
    construction details, 394-402
    heating and humidification prerequisites, 402-403
  systems, 357-358
Propionates, 43, 156
Proportional feeders, 286
Propyl gallate, 80
Proteases, 153-154, 158, 309
Protein, enriched bread, 213
  tests, 18
  supplementation, 581-586
Proteins, eggs, 111
  flour, 8, 12-13, 18-20
  malt, 150
  milk, 93
Psychrometers, 390-391
Psychrometric chart, 391
Public Health Service Drinking Water Standards, 25-27
Pudding, 253
Puff pastry, 180-181
  shortenings, 67
Pulverizing, sugar, 51
Pumpernickel, 19, 215
Pumpkin, 138, 193, 253
Pumps, 271, 275
Purifiers, 3, 19
PVC, 519

Quality control, 560
  functions, 561-564
  mission, 560-561
  position in organization, 561
  records, 565-566

Rack proofers, 404
Radiation, 410-412
  preservation, 535
Raffinose, 8
Raisin bread, 212
Raisins, 119, 314
Rancidity, 69, 79-80, 519
Rapeseed oil, 63, 73
Recommended Daily Allowances, 577-578
Reciprocating slicers, 447-451
Reducing substances, 14, 43, 309
Reduction test, bacterial, 97
Reel oven, 415-416
Refinery syrup, 51
Refining, oils, 62, 66
Refrigeration, 325, 507-509
Rennin, 92
Research, 537-538, 541
  allocation techniques, 544-545
  notebooks, 554-555
Reverse osmosis, 29
Reverse sheeting molder, 342-343
Reversible sheeters, 347-348
Ribbon, blenders, 315
  burners, 426
Riboflavin, 10, 146
Rice bran oil, 63, 73
Ricotta cheese, 92
Rigid packages, 479-480
Roll depanner, automatic, 433
Roll dividers, 296
Roll-forming equipment, 351-352
Roller, dryers, 85-86
  mills, 3, 19
Rolls, 1, 41, 352
  continuous processing, 374-376
Rotameters, 288-289
Rotary, airlock feeders, 268
  cutters, 204

596 INDEX

molders, 204, 354-355
ovens, 415-416
Rotogravure, 477
Rounders, 329-334
Runner peanuts, 125
Rye, 1, 18-21
  bread,146, 153, 214-215

Saccharin, 59
Safety codes, 338-339, 345-346
Safflower oil, 63-73
Saffron, 146
Saigon cinnamon, 136
Salmonella, 112
Salt, 31, 146, 149, 162-163, 309, 324
  effect on proteinases, 154
  in cookies, 201
  in crackers, 232-233
Salt-rising bread, 215-216
Salters, 483-484, 486
Sampling 569
  procedures, 260
Sandwiching machines, 488-490
Sanitary surveys, 25
Sanitation, 243, 259, 338-339, 345, 380-385, 569-570
Sauces, 237
Scale hoppers, 262
Schaal test, 69
Scorched particles, 98
Sedimentation test, 18
Selenium, 27
Service bins, 262
Sesame oil, 63
Shadowing effect, 411
Shortbread, 187, 314
Shortening values of common fats, 175
Shortenings, bulk handling, 259, 273-275
  for continuous processed doughs, 365-366
    cookies, 200
    crackers, 232
    puff pastry, 181
  function in cake batters, 190
Sifters, 262
Sifting, 165
Silicones, 436
Silver, 27
Single-cell proteins, 582
Sitosterol, 9
Skim milk, 83
Slicer guides, 439-440
Slicers, 447-459
Slicing theory, 438-446
Slide plate unloader, 432
Slide-end trough, 408
Slip point, 68
Sloping bottom trough, 408
Smoke point, 72, 75
Soda crackers. *See* Crackers
Sodium, 33
  acid pyrophosphate, 38-39, 40
  aluminum phosphate, 38, 40
  aluminum sulfate, 38
  bicarbonate, 31, 35-37, 40, 189
    specifications, 36
  desoxycholate, 168
  diacetate, 156
  ferrocyanide, 162
  lauryl sulfate, 115, 245
  silicoaluminate, 108
  stearoyl fumarate, 79, 366
Sodium-reduced bread, 520, 575
Solids fraction index, 70-71
Solubility index, 98
Sorbic acid, 243
Sorbitan monostearate, 78
Sorbitol, 59, 243, 527
Sorghum, 1
Sorghum oil, 63, 73
Sour cream, dried, 91
Sourdough French bread, 217-218
Sours, 214
Soy flour, 1, 21-22
  enzymatically active, 154-155
Soybean oil, 63, 66, 73
Soybean protein, 584-585
Soybeans, 125
Spanish peanuts, 125
Specific heats, 525
Specific humidity, 389
Specifications, 566-568
Spice cakes, 193
Spices, 135-140
Spindle mixers, 322-323
Sponge batter depositers, 491
Sponge cakes, 171-173
Sponge-and-dough procedure, 223-225, 309-311, 387, 527
Spongeflow, 364
Spray drying, 85-88
  eggs, 114-115
Spread, 201-204
Stability tests, fats, 69
Stabilizers, 506-507
Staling, 498-499, 507, 517, 521
Stamping machines, 204
Standard plate counts, 97
Standards, 566-568
Starch, 7-9, 20, 42, 49, 151-152, 251
  duster, 486
Static electricity, 260, 263
Stayman Winesap apples, 119
Steam, as oven heat source, 429
  in baking, 430-431
  leavening effects, 166
Stencil machines, 490
Sticky buns, 239
Strahmann continuous developer, 377-378
Straight dough method, 224
Strain gauges, 279
Strawberries, 123-124, 254-255
Strength, flour, 14
Streusels, 125, 237-239
Sucrose, 8, 42, 49-52, 137, 167
  in cookies, 201
Sugar, glaze, 239
  granular, bulk handling, 260, 266-270

particle size, 50
liquid, bulk handling, 269–270
powdered, 247
snaps, 203
syrups, 51–52
wafers, 184–187
Sulfates, 26–27, 160
Sulfhydryl groups, 158
Sulfur dioxide, 53
Sunflower seed oil, 63, 73
Superheating, milk, 85
Suspended hopper scales, 278–280
Sweet chocolate, 142
Sweet doughs, 41, 220–222, 240, 346–347
Sweetness, relative, corn syrups, 54
  sugar, 52
Swiss rolls, 247, 490–492
Syntron feeders, 483
Systematizing product development, 543–551

Tanks, 271, 273
Technical services, 564–565
Teflon, 340, 352–353, 436, 457, 464
Tempeh, 585
Tempering, 2
Tempering chocolate products, 495
Tempilsticks, 464
Test methods, 568–569
Thawing, 500, 505
Theobroma, 142
Thermoformed containers, 480
Thermophilic spore counts, 98
Thiamine, 10, 160
Thompson raisins, 119
Titanium dioxide, 146
Toast, 82
Tocopherols, 9
Tofu, 585
Toluol distillation, 97
Tooth forms, 440–443
Topping, applicators, 483
  extruders, 487
  salt, 163
Toppings, 237
Torsion balances, 278
Totalizing flow meters, 288
Traveling tray ovens, 416–417
  design features, 418
Trehalose, 44, 46
Triacetin, 168
Triethyl citrate, 168
Trouble-shooting guide
  angel food cakes, 170
  bread and rolls, 227–230
  bread wrapping machines, 467–468
  icings, 241
  layer cakes, 197–198
  pie crusts, 180
  sweet doughs, 222
Trough elevators, 297, 324
Troughs, 296–297, 323, 403, 407–409
Tube pans, 168
Tunnel ovens, 417–418

Turbidity, 26, 27, 28
Turbine meters, 289
Turbo-mills, 5
Turmeric, 146
Twin-cone blenders, 315
Twist bread molders, 342, 344

Ultramarine blue, 146
Ultraviolet lights, 270
Umbrella-type rounder, 331
Universal cake mix, 192
Unloaders, 431–432
Unloading, bulk, 263–264

Vacuum bread conditioners, 434
Vacuum depanners, 432–433
Valencia peanuts, 125
Valves, 274
Vanadium, 33
Vanilla, 140, 191, 237
Vanillin, 141–142, 519
Venturi tube, 283, 288
Vertical mixers, 320–323
Vienna bread, 211
Virginia peanuts, 125
Viscometers, 70
Vitamin E, 9
Vitamin supplementation, 577–579
Vitamins, 10–11, 94–96
  malt, 150
Volumetric feeders, 292–294

Wafer ovens, 424–425
Walking finger unloader, 432
Walnuts, 134
Wash applicators, 484
Washes, 178
Water, in crackers, 232
  quality, 24–26, 161
Water icing, 239
Water meters, 288
Water treatment, 25, 28–29
Wattmeters, 324–325
Waxed paper, 472, 477
Weighing, 278–287
Wet bulb thermometers, 390–391
Wheat and flour constituents, 7–10
Wheat varieties, 1–2, 7
Whey, 83, 89–90
Whey protein denaturation test, 99–100
Whipping, 165, 307
  proteins, 242–243
  test, 116
Whisk, 490
White Adriatic figs, 120
White layer cakes, 191–193
Whizzolater, 246
Whole wheat, bread, 153, 212–213
  flour, 3
Wickets, 468–469
Wiley melting point, 68
Winterizing, oils, 66
Wire whip, 321–322
Wire-cut cookies, 204

Wrapping, effect on temperature changes, 502-503
  equipment, 460-468

Xanthophyll, 93

Yeast, 31, 35, 41-47, 160, 207-208, 270, 309
  compressed, 42-43
  foods, 29, 157-158, 160, 232
Yellow layer cakes, 193-194

Yellow prussiate of soda. *See* Sodium ferrocyanide
Yield, flour, 3
Yolks, 108-109
  pigments, 111
York Imperial apples, 118-119

Zero defects, 570
Zinc, 26-27
Zone control, 429-430
Zwiebach, 496